OXFORD

THE CHRISTIAN CHURCH

Edited by
Henry and Owen Chadwick

OXFORD HISTORY OF THE CHRISTIAN CHURCH series is intended to provide a full survey of the Christian churches and their part in the religious heritage of humanity. Particular attention will be paid to the place of the churches in surrounding society, the institutions of church life and the manifestations of popular religion, the link with the forms of national culture, and the intellectual tradition within and beyond Europe.

Titles in the series include:

England, Ireland, Scotland, Wales
The Christian Church 1900–2000
Keith Robbins (2008)

Christianity in India
From Beginnings to the Present
Robert Eric Frykenberg (2008)

East and West: The Making of a Rift in the Church
From Apostolic Times Until the Council of Florence
Henry Chadwick (2003)

Reformation in Britain and Ireland
Felicity Heal (2003)

A History of the Churches in Australasia
Ian Breward (2001)

The Church in Ancient Society
From Galilee to Gregory the Great
Henry Chadwick (2001)

The Early Reformation on the Continent
Owen Chadwick (2001)

The Papacy in the Age of Totalitarianism, 1914–1958

JOHN POLLARD

Great Clarendon Street, Oxford, OX2 6DP,
United Kingdom

Oxford University Press is a department of the University of Oxford.
It furthers the University's objective of excellence in research, scholarship,
and education by publishing worldwide. Oxford is a registered trade mark of
Oxford University Press in the UK and in certain other countries

First published 2014
First published in paperback 2016

Published in the United States of America by Oxford University Press
198 Madison Avenue, New York, NY 10016, United States of America

British Library Cataloguing in Publication Data
Data available

Library of Congress Cataloging in Publication Data
Data available

ISBN 978–0–19–920856–2 (Hbk.)
ISBN 978–0–19–876615–5 (Pbk.)

For John Ainscough

Acknowledgements

As always I owe a huge great debt of gratitude to friends, colleagues, and students: to Professor Owen Chadwick for persuading me to write the book in the first place; to Meredith Carew for giving me information about the background to Mussolini's introduction of the Racial Laws; to Lucia Faltin, who advised on some aspects of relations between Czechoslovakia and the Vatican and also between the Vatican and the first Slovak Republic; to Pat Goldrick for providing me with a access to a digitized copy of the *Actes et Documents*; to Casey Hammond for advising me about Padre Gemelli's early career; to Nick Hands, who checked the footnotes of the early chapters; to Edmund Kunji, who translated the correspondence between Visser t' Hooft and Jan Willebrands; to John Nurser for showing me documents from the World Council of Churches Archives; to the late Peter James for giving me much advice on some scientific questions; to Paolo Valvo for making some unpublished work available to me; and to Stewart Stehlin, Jonathan Steinberg, and Michael Walsh for reading various drafts, making useful suggestions and drawing attentions to errors—Michael also translated into English the unpublished draft encyclicals *De Divini Divinis Humanisque Iuribus In Russiarum Regionibus Impiisime Violatis* and *Vera Ecclesia*.

I am grateful to the British Academy Small Research Grants' Scheme, Cambridge University Travel Fund, Trinity Hall Vice-Master's Fund for financial assistance with research trips, and to the British School at Rome for awarding me the Balsdon Fellowship for 2013–14.

Similarly, I am in the debt of the staff of the British Library, Cambridge University Library, the library of the Gregorian University in Rome, the library of the Fondazione Giovanni XXIII in Bologna, the staff of the Vatican Secret Archives, the archive of the Congregation for the Doctrine of the Faith, the Archivio Centrale dello Stato, the Filmoteca Vaticana, the Archivio Arcivescovile of Bologna, the Marchesi Della Chiesa for access to the papers of Benedict XV, Professor Michele Abbate of the Archives of the Italian Ministry of Foreign Affairs, the archivists at the Scottish Catholic Historical Archives in Edinburgh, the dioceses of Brentwood, Glasgow, and Westminster, and the staff of the Public Records Office (The National Archives), Kew.

I am also grateful to the late James Walston and Nora Galli De' Paratesi for their hospitality, encouragement, and intellectual stimulation in Rome, and to John Ainscough for all his support.

Finally, I should like to thank Lizzie Robottom and Karen Raith of Oxford University Press and to Elizabeth Stone at Bourchier for all their support and patience during the final stages of the book, and Maureen MacGlashan for compiling the index.

Cambridge
April 2014

Contents

Pope Benedict XV, 1915

Mary Evans / SZ Photo / Scherl

Cardinal Pietro Gasparri, Secretary of State to Benedict XV and Pius XI, 1914–1929
Mary Evans / SZ Photo / Scherl

Pope Pius XI, 1927

Mary Evans / SZ Photo / Scherl

Pope Pius XII, during ceremony of consistory in the Vatican, 15 January 1953
Mary Evans/Epic/Tallandier

Abbreviations

ARCHIVAL SOURCES

AAB	Archivio Arcivescovile di Bologna (Bologna Archiepiscopal Archives)
ACDF	Archivio della Congregazione per la Dottrina della Fede (formerly Congregation of the Holy Office and Index)
ACS	Archivio Centrale dello Stato (Italian National Archives)
AdRP	Archivi delle Rappresentanze Diplomatiche (Archives of Apostolic Delegations and Nunciatures)
AES	Affari Ecclesiastici Straordinari (Congregation for Extraordinary Ecclesiastical Affairs); Sessioni refers to meetings or sessions of this congregation
AFDC	Archivio della Famiglia Della Chiesa (Archive of the Della Chiesa Family, Benedict XV)
AHP	*Archivum Historiae Pontificiae* (Rome)
ASMAE	Archivio Storico del Ministero degli Affari Esteri (Historical Archive of the Italian Ministry of Foreign Affairs)
ASV	Archivio Segreto Vaticano (Vatican Secret Archives)
b.	busta
BDA	Brentwood Diocesan Archives, UK
c	or cart. Carteggio
C&S	*Church and State*
CHR	*Catholic Historical Review* (Washington, DC)
DAUS	Delegazione Apostolica negli Stati Uniti (Apostolic Delegation in the United States)
DBI	*Dizionario Biografico degli Italiani*
DDI	Documenti Diplomatici Italiani
EHJ	*English Historical Journal* (Oxford)
fasc.	fascicolo
FCO	Foreign and Commonwealth Office
HJ	*Historical Journal* (Cambridge)
JCH	*Journal of Contemporary History* (Cambridge)
JEH	*Journal of Ecclesistical History* (Cambridge)
LaCC	*La Civiltà Cattolica* (Rome)
L'OR	*L'Osservatore Romano* (Rome; Vatican City after 1932)
NARA	National Archives and Records Administration
OFM	Order of Friars Minor
RSC	*Rivista di Storia della Chiesa in Italia* (Milan)

rub	rubricca
SCHA	Scottish Catholic Historical Archives, ED, Archdiocese of St Andrews and Edinburgh
sf.	sotto-fascicolo
SS	or SdS Segreteria di Stato (Secretariat of State)
TMPR	*Totalitarian Movements and Political Religions* (Abingdon, England)
TNA/PRO	Public Records Office, Kew, London (UK National Archives)
WDA	Westminster Archdiocesan Archives, UK

1

Introduction

With the outbreak of the First World War, which preceded the election of Benedict XV in September 1914 by almost exactly one month, the world entered a new, 'totalitarian' age. The period of the three subsequent pontificates saw two 'total' wars, the First World War and the Second, and the first stages of another war that was nearly completely global in its spread—the Cold War. The period also saw the rise of four major totalitarian regimes—the Soviet Union after 1917, Fascist Italy after 1922, Nazi Germany after 1933, and Communist China after 1949—plus various minor, attendant totalitarian or authoritarian regimes such as the Soviet satellites in Eastern Europe, Communist North Korea, and North Vietnam, Franco's Spain. The papacy in this period was thus forced to confront and contend with not only the horrors of total war, and the strains which they imposed upon a worldwide religion, millions of whose adherents were fighting each other on behalf of their national rulers, but also the horrors inflicted by regimes pursuing totalitarian ideologies in effective conflict with the principles of Christianity and Catholicism and, in some cases, committed to their extirpation. It thus faced challenges far greater than anything that had arisen since the Reformation of the sixteenth century or the French Revolution and its aftermath in the late eighteenth and early nineteenth centuries: arguably, National Socialism and Communism posed a more serious threat to the survival of Roman Catholicism than any of those previous challenges.

On the other hand, the election of Pope John XXIII in October 1958 marked the beginning of dramatic changes in the development of the papacy, and the Roman Catholic Church more generally, as a result of the reforms of the Second Council of the Vatican, which John called together in 1959. Significant for the history of the papacy and Catholicism, it also meant the beginning of a change in the policy which Vatican diplomacy pursued towards the Communist world, or at least the Soviet Union and its East European 'satellites', the previously intransigent defence of the 'Church of Silence' being replaced by a softer *Ostpolitik*, as a means of saving what was left of Catholic institutions in the countries behind the Iron Curtain. Thus began a new and different era in the history of the papacy.

The papacy faced other kinds of challenges in the period 1914–58, especially developments in methods of warfare, science, and technology. The impact of the former was first felt by Benedict XV during the First World War, but worse, much worse, was to come during the Second, when, apart from much more lethal weapons of mass destruction, Europe was ravaged by wars of racial extermination. And after Hiroshima, Pius XII was confronted with the moral dilemma posed by the use of thermonuclear weapons. Other developments were, potentially at least, more benign, such as the emergence of the mass electronic media: radio, cinema, and television. Less benign from the point of view of the papacy were advances in medical and psychological sciences which would pose a serious challenge to the Church's teaching, not least on the ethics of reproduction and sexuality, which had been reiterated by Pius XI as recently as 1930 in *Casti Connubii*. In broader terms, the popes in this period were forced to grapple with the broader theological and ethical issues raised by the discoveries of modern science.

SCOPE AND STRUCTURE

The papacy is the supreme governing organ of a worldwide religion, the Roman Catholic Church. The papacy is, therefore, an essentially *cultural* institution, with universalistic claims founded upon scriptural authority: 'Go forth and teach all nations, baptising in the name of the father, the Son and the Holy Ghost',[1] and 'Thou art Peter and upon this rock I will build my church and until thee I will give the Keys of the Kingdom: the gates of hell shall not prevail against it.'[2] This very specific mandate given to Peter, 'the Prince of the Apostles', and the fact that, in traditional Catholic historiography, he was regarded as the first bishop of Rome, was martyred and buried there, and is the figure from whom all the subsequent bishops of Rome have descended by 'apostolic succession',[3] forms the basis of the papal claims to primacy of authority over all Christian bishops and churches and Christian people. It also provides the scriptural warranty for the doctrine of Papal Infallibility that, in teaching *ex cathedra* on matters of faith and morals, the popes cannot err.[4] The sui generis nature of

[1] *The New Testament of Our Lord and Saviour Jesus Christ According to the Rheims Version Revised by Bishop Challoner* (London, n.d.), Matthew, XXVII, 19–20.

[2] *The New Testament of Our Lord and Saviour Jesus Christ*, Matthew, XVI, 18–19.

[3] For a discussion of the problems around the historical origins of the papacy, see Eamon Duffy, *Saints and Sinners: A History of the Popes*, New Haven, CT, 1997, 1–5.

[4] For an explanation of the development of the dogma of Infallibility, see *New Catholic Encyclopedia*, 2nd edn., Washington, DC, 2003, 7, 448–452 (henceforth NCE), citing the definition of the decree of the First Vatican Council, *Pastor Aeternus*, of 1970:

> The Roman Pontiff, when he speaks *ex cathedra*, that is, when discharging his office of pastor and teacher of all Christians, and defines with his supreme apostolic authority a doctrine concerning faith or morals that is to be held by the universal Church, through the divine assistance promised him in St Peter, exercises infallibility with which the divine Redeemer wished to endow his Church . . . such definitions of the Roman Pontiff are not, of themselves, by the consent of the Church, reformable.

the papacy as an international *ecclesiastical* institution should always be borne in mind, given the tendency of some recent historians and political scientists to attempt to assimilate the *modus operandi* of the papacy to that of secular political institutions, national and international.[5] The papacy is an ecclesiastical entity, run by a celibate priesthood who also have an eye for their *own* personal sanctification and salvation, hence attempts to impose political science/international relations theory and paradigms upon it and Vatican diplomacy have only limited utility. Of course, in pursuit of its objectives, the papacy is involved in politics, in the *realpolitik* of international diplomacy and politics.

The purpose of this volume of the *Oxford History of the Christian Church* is to present the history of the papacy in the reigns of three popes, Benedict XV (1914–22), Pius XI (1922–39), and Pius XII (1939–58). While it will inevitably touch upon many matters affecting the worldwide Church, its objective is not to provide a history of individual 'national' churches. It is essentially a history of the governing organ of the Catholic Church, the papacy, rather than the Catholic Church as a whole, unlike in a preceding volume of the *Oxford History of the Christian Church* by Owen Chadwick, where he effectively gives us a history of Catholicism in that period.[6]

This work is, therefore, focused on the policies and priorities of the Holy See between 1914 and 1958, that is, chiefly maintaining intact the deposit of the faith and morals against the dangerous doctrinal and scientific novelties of the modern world, and preserving the internal unity of the Catholic Church against heresy and schism. The papacy was also deeply concerned about promoting and expanding its missionary outreach, and about the reunion of the other Christian churches, especially the Orthodox, with Rome. Through Vatican diplomacy, concordats, and the mass mobilization of the laity in such organizations as Catholic Action, it sought to protect the legal, institutional, and property interests of the Church in many different countries, combat what it considered its most dangerous foes—Freemasons, Protestants, secularists and anti-clericals, Communists, and Nazis—and promote its mission, the evangelization of the world.

Given the long time period covered by this work, it will be important to evaluate the balance between the most basic elements in the history of the papacy, continuity and change, and to consider what were the longer-term trends in that history between 1914 and 1958, and whether and when there were major turning points and 'ruptures' in that development: there already is some controversy in the existing historiography about the latter.

This volume will be structured on a mixed chronological and thematic basis, in more or less the same way in which the themes are treated in the

[5] See, for example, M. Richards, *Vicars of Christ: Popes, Power and Politics in the Modern World*, New York, 1998.

[6] O. Chadwick, *A History of the Popes, 1830–1914*, Oxford, 1998.

second part of this chapter—'The Legacy of Pius X'. But it will not always be possible to stick to this framework. For example, churches in China, Korea, and Vietnam were essentially *missionary* ones, so their fate after the Second World War could well have been dealt with in Chapter 11, but because they were the victims of Communist expansion in Asia, a facet of the Cold War, they have been dealt with in Chapter 10.

'All history is provisional' is something of a cliché, but a useful one. There is still plenty more work to be done on the papers from the pontificate of Pius XI now available in the Vatican Archives, and until the papers of Pius XII are made available, any history of his pontificate must very definitely be provisional, patchy, and, often times, speculative. This work aims to provide a starting point, a framework for further study of this period in the history of the papacy by offering a panorama which is as comprehensive as possible of the multiple aspects of the three pontificates. Many of the judgements arrived at here will, no doubt, be challenged, modified, and even, in some cases, overturned in the fullness of time and in the light of further research.

HISTORIOGRAPHY

There are few, if any, historiographical disputes focused on the reign of Benedict XV. On the other hand, the relatively recent (2006) opening of the papers in the Vatican Archives for the pontificate of Pius XI, which has resulted in a spate of publications in the last few years, has opened up a debate about the relationship between Pius XI and his Secretary of State, Eugenio Pacelli, especially in the last months of his life: the differences in their approach to the fascist dictators, and whether or not it can be argued that there was a fundamental rupture in Vatican policy with the death of Pius XI and the election of Pacelli as his successor in 1939.[7] Otherwise, the works of such authors as Kent,[8] Pollard,[9] Rhodes,[10] and Stehlin[11] have stood the test of time and the opening up of the files in the Vatican Archives for 1922–39 remarkably well.

The pontificate of Pius XII has fared rather differently. There has been controversy surrounding his policies, especially those during the Second

[7] See E. Fattorini, *Hitler, Mussolini and the Vatican: Pope Pius XI and the Speech that was Never Made*, Cambridge, 2011; and the review of the same by Johannes Ickx, 'Gli omissis di Emma Fattorini', *Archivium Historiae Pontificae*, 46 (2008), 425–437.

[8] Peter C. Kent, *The Pope and the Duce: The International Impact of the Lateran Agreements*, London, 1981.

[9] John F. Pollard, *The Vatican and Italian Fascism 1929–1932: A Study in Conflict*, Cambridge, 1985.

[10] A. Rhodes, *The Vatican in the Age of the Dictators, 1922–1945*, London, 1973.

[11] S.A. Stehlin, *Weimar and the Vatican, 1919–1933: German–Vatican Relations in the Interwar Years*, Princeton, NJ, 1983.

World War, since the late 1950s.[12] With the publication and staging of Rolf Hochhuth's play, *The Deputy*, in 1963, Pius XII's wartime actions became the centre of major public controversy. [13] Hochhuth castigated Pius XII's response to the Holocaust, which prompted a first round of articles and books in defence of Papa Pacelli.[14] In 1999, the argument was reignited by the publication of John Cornwell's *Hitler's Pope*,[15] which has provoked a stream of polemical works, sometimes sickeningly hagiographical, sometimes hysterically hostile, for and against the wartime pope. Among the supporters of Pius XII, Pierre Blet,[16] Sister Margherita Marchione,[17] and Richard Rychlak stand out.[18] Against Papa Pacelli are, most notably, Daniel Goldhagen, with his vigorous condemnation of Catholic anti-Semitism,[19] Michael Phayer,[20] and Susan Zuccotti.[21] The latter specifically deals with the response of Pius XII to the Holocaust in Italy. More balanced and nuanced accounts of these difficult issues are to be found, by José Sanchez,[22] Giovanni Miccoli,[23] Frank Coppa,[24] and, recently, Robert Ventresca, who has given us a serious full-length biography.[25] Michael Phayer's second book takes his study of Pius XII into the post-war, Cold War, period, and in particular focuses on the allegations concerning the Vatican's role in the 'Ratlines', through which Nazi and other war criminals were able to escape to freedom in Spain and Latin America.[26]

Such is the nature of the dispute over Pius XII's response to the Holocaust that one seriously doubts whether it is a genuine historiographical controversy.

[12] See, for example, Edmond Paris, *Le Vatican contre l'Europe*, Paris, 1959.

[13] R. Hochhuth, *The Deputy*, trans. Richard and Clara Winston, preface Dr Albert Schweitzer, Baltimore, MD, 1997; originally published and staged in Germany as *Der Stellvertreter* in 1963.

[14] See, for example, the article of Cardinal G.-B. Montini (later Pope Paul VI), 'Pius XII and the Jews', *The Table*, 29 June 1963; and Pinchas Lapide, *Three Popes and the Jews*, New York, 1967.

[15] John Cornwell, *Hitler's Pope: The Secret History of Pius XII*, London, 1999.

[16] P. Blet, SJ, *Pius XII and the Second World War: According to the Archives of the Vatican*, trans. Lawrence J. Johnson, Herefordshire, 1999.

[17] Margherita Marchione, *Pope Pius XII: Architect of Peace*, Mahwah, NJ, 2000.

[18] Ronald J. Rychlak, *Hitler, the War and the Pope*, Huntington, IN, 2000.

[19] Daniel J. Goldhagen, *A Moral Reckoning: The Role of the Catholic Church in the Holocaust and its Unfulfilled Duty of Repair*, New York, 2003.

[20] Michael Phayer, *The Catholic Church and the Holocaust, 1930–1965*, Bloomington, IN, 2008.

[21] S. Zuccotti, *Under his Very Windows: The Vatican and the Holocaust in Italy*, New Haven, CT, 2000.

[22] José M. Sanchez, *Pius XII and the Holocaust: Understanding the Controversy*, Washington, DC, 2002.

[23] Giovanni Miccoli, *I dilemma e I silenzi di Pio XII*, Milan, 2000.

[24] Frank J. Coppa, *The Policies and Politics of Pope Pius XII: Between Diplomacy and Morality*, New York and Oxford, 2011.

[25] Robert A. Ventresca, *Soldier of Christ: The Life of Pope Pius XII*, Cambridge, MA, and London, 2012.

[26] Michael Phayer, *Pius XII, the Holocaust and the Cold War*, Bloomington and Indianapolis, IN, 2008; on the Vatican and 'Ratlines', see Mark Aarons and John Loftus, *Ratlines: How the Vatican's Nazi Networks Betrayed Western Intelligence to the Soviets*, London, 1991.

There is by now a consensus among most historians of the papacy about what the pope did or did not know about the Holocaust, when he knew, what he did and did not say, and what he did and did not do. The discussion of John Cornwell's views on American chat shows, and the literally thousands of, in many cases, tendentious and sensationalist, and often inaccurate, newspaper articles in the early 2000s suggest that this is a highly *political* dispute, between Jews and Catholics in the USA and between liberal and more conservative Catholics, those favourable or hostile to Pope John Paul II and, latterly, Pope Benedict XVI. John Cornwell has made it clear that his book has a political purpose, to prevent the canonization of Pius XII,[27] it also serves as a protest against the 'reactionary policies' of the Polish pope.

SOURCES

The opening of the papers from the pontificates of Benedict XV and Pius XI in the Vatican Archives—Archivio Segreto Vaticano—has made the work of scholars of this period immensely easier than previously. But there is a relative lack of archival sources for the pontificate of Pius XII because, at the time of writing, the Vatican had still not opened up papers for 1939–58 to scholars, though a *selection* of diplomatic papers for the period of the Second World War has been published in the form of the *Actes et documents du Saint-Siége relatifs a la seconde guerre mondial.*[28] These are supplemented by the diplomatic papers of the powers, like the *Foreign Relations of the United States*, the *Documenti Diplomatici Italiani* of Italy, the *Documents Diplomatiques Français*, the *Documents of British Foreign Policy*, and documents from Germany.[29] There are also the speeches and radio messages, encyclicals and other official statements of Pius XII, rather more, in fact, than for the previous two pontificates. In this regard, Claudia Carlen's multivolume edition of the papal encyclicals in English has been invaluable,[30] as has Ugo Bellocchi's edited collection of the principal papal documents for the whole period under consideration.[31]

[27] Cornwell, *Hitler's Pope*, 382–384.

[28] ADSS, *Actes et Documents du Saint-Siège relatifs à la Seconde Guerre mondiale*, vols 1–11, ed. Pierre Blet SJ, Robert Graham SJ, Angelo Martini SJ, and Burkhart Schneider SJ, Vatican City, 1965–81.

[29] FRUS, *Foreign Relations of the United States: Diplomatic Papers*, Washington, DC; *I Documenti Diplomatici Italiani*, Ministero degli affari esteri, Rome; *Documents on British Foreign Policy, 1919–1939*, London; *Documents on German Foreign Policy, 1918–1945*, London, 1949–57.

[30] Claudia Carlen, I.H.M. (ed.), *The Papal Encyclicals*, vol. II (1903–39) and vol. IV (1939–58), Raleigh, NC, 1981.

[31] U. Bellocchi (ed.), *Tutte le Encicliche e Principali Documenti Pontifici*, vols VIII–X, Vatican City, 2000–3.

There are yet other useful sources for the pontificate of Pius XII. Given the geographical location of the Vatican in the Italian capital, the fact that probably 95 per cent of the Vatican bureaucrats and diplomats in this period were Italians, and the close and frequent contact between them and high-ranking Italian politicians, officials, and businessmen, much is to be gleaned from a variety of diaries and memoirs about attitudes prevailing in the Secretariat of State. Two diaries in particular are worth citing, that of a key Italian man of business, Senator Alberto Pirelli,[32] is a precious source of information for the first four years of the pontificate of Pius XII, as are the diaries of Galeazzo Ciano, Mussolini's son-in-law, and his foreign minister between 1937 and 1943.[33] There are also volumes such as that written by Sir Owen Chadwick, *Britain and the Vatican during the Second World War*, based on the diaries of Sir D'Arcy Osborne, Britain's minister to the Holy See, 1939–46,[34] and the memoirs of Harold Tittman, American chargé d'affaires in the Vatican in the same period.[35]

The secondary literature on the whole of the period under examination is quite simply enormous, especially for the pontificate of Pius XII, as has been seen. Where key specialist studies already exist, I have not tried to 'reinvent the wheel'. Equally, those readers familiar with my 1999 biography of Benedict XV will become aware that I have practised a little 'recycling', since no major biography of Papa Della Chiesa has been published since then.

THE ORIGINS OF THE MODERN PAPACY, 1846–1903

The papacy underwent a transformative process of institutional development in the period 1914–58. Some of the elements in that process had their roots in previous pontificates so it can be said that the three pontificates of this period witnessed but a stage in the ongoing process of the emergence of the modern papacy. As Mazzonis has observed, 'It would be no exaggeration to say that the Church of the twentieth century, that which we ourselves have known, saw its foundations solidly laid and its characteristic institutional structures emerge in the difficult years between 1850 and 1870.'[36] In addition, events in the pontificates of Pio Nono's successors, Leo

[32] A. Pirelli, *Taccuini, 1922–1943*, ed. Donato Barbone with intro. by Egidio Ortona, Bologna, 1984.

[33] *Ciano's Diary, 1939–1943*, ed. with intro. by M. Muggeridge, London, 1947.

[34] O. Chadwick, *Britain and the Vatican during the Second World War*, Cambridge, 1986.

[35] Harold H. Tittman, Jr, *Il Vaticano di Pio XII: Uno sguardo dall'interno*, trans. Marco Sartori, Milan, 2004.

[36] F. Mazzonis, 'Pio IX, il tramonto del potere temporale e la riorganizzazione della chiesa', in B. Angloni et al. (eds), *Storia della Societá Italiana*, vol. XVIII: *Lo stato unitario e il suo difficile debutto*, Milan, 1981, 266.

XIII and St Pius X, are key to understanding the institutional development of the papacy between 1914 and 1958.

Pio Nono's greatest contribution to the evolution of the modern papacy was undoubtedly his proclamation of the doctrine of Papal Infallibility during the First Council of the Vatican in 1870. While extremely controversial at the time, even within the Church, and even though it was to be formally invoked only once by a pope in the future, Infallibility gave the Roman pontiffs an enormous moral and spiritual authority over the worldwide Church and created the basis for the practice of increasingly frequent papal pronouncements on a wide variety of subjects of significance to the laity. Leo XIII, for example, used the encyclical to pronounce on Biblical scholarship (*Providentissimus Deus*, 1893), the Eucharist (*Mirae Caritatis*, 1902), marriage (*Arcanum*, 1880, *Quam religiosa*, 1898, and *Dum multa*, 1902), on Thomism as the basis of Christian philosophy and theology (*Aeterni Patris*, 1879), the education of the clergy (*Depuis le jour*, 1999), and Catholic missions (*Sancta Dei Civitas*, 1880).

Secular matters also attracted his attention, thus he made three public pronouncements on the dangers of socialism (*Inscrutabili Dei Consilio* and *Quod Apostolici Muneris*, both in the first year of his pontificate and, to a lesser extent, in *Rerum Novarum*, 1891), four on 'the Christian constitution of states' (*Diuturnum*, 1891; *Immortale Dei*, 1885; *Libertas*, 1888; and *Graves De Communi Re*, 1901), as well as two each on slavery (*In Plurimus*, 1988; and *Catholicae Ecclesiam*, 1890), and two on Freemasonry (*Humanum Gens*, 1884; and *Dall'alto Dell'apostolico seggio*, 1890). When these are taken together with *Rerum Novarum*, of 1891, which was the Catholic Church's first attempt to address the problems created by industrialization and urbanization in Europe, and the encyclical on duelling (*Pastoralis Officii*, 1891), it can truly be said that Leo had comprehensively addressed most of the burning questions of the spiritual and secular worlds of his time and thus established the practice of popes pronouncing authoritatively on all economic, political, and social matters.

THE LEGACY OF PIUS X

The Reform of the Roman Curia

When Cardinal Giuseppe Sarto, the Patriarch of Venice, was elected to the papal throne in July 1903 he had had no experience of the Roman curia, its men, and their ways.[37] He kept on most of his predecessor's chief men,

[37] For a biographical sketch of Pope Pius X, see Carlo Falconi, *The Popes in the Twentieth Century*, trans. Muriel Grindrod, London, 1967.

though he did not retain the Secretary of State, Cardinal Mariano Rampolla del Tindaro, who had been the leading contender in the 1903 Conclave until Cardinal Puszyna attempted to exercise a veto against him on behalf of the Emperor Franz Josef.[38] In Rampolla's place the new pope appointed the very young, and relatively inexperienced, Mgr Rafael Merry del Val, rather than either of Rampolla's assistants, Mgr Pietro Gasparri, Secretary of the Congregation for Extraordinary Ecclesiastical Affairs (AES), or Mgr Giacomo Della Chiesa, the *Sostituto* (Substitute Secretary of State). Merry del Val's appointment was to have serious consequences for the direction of policy in Pius X's reign.

Though there was no general reshuffle of the top personnel in the Vatican, Pius X did later attempt to carry out a fundamental structural reform of the Roman curia. Neither Pius IX nor Leo XIII had done much in the way of institutional reform, even though the structure and size of the Roman curia were still essentially that of the governing body not only of the worldwide Church, but of the former Papal States, or rather what had been left of them prior to the occupation of Rome by Italian troops in September 1870. As a result, the central government of the Church was a chaotic welter of congregations, offices, and tribunals, some rendered quite redundant by the fact that the pope no longer exercised territorial sovereignty and a few that duplicated the functions of others. In addition there was much financial waste, nepotism, and what, at best, could only be described as old-fashioned working practices and perks, and, at worst, systematic plunder of the Church's meagre resources.[39] A further scandal was the presence in Rome of thousands of 'nomadic' priests, especially from the south of Italy, who had left voluntarily from their dioceses and gone to the Eternal City in search of more lucrative employment, and who subsisted on Mass offerings and charities. As far as the financial organization of the Roman curia was concerned, there were far too many congregations with autonomous powers to raise and spend money and too little control over their operations.

Pius X charged Monsignor (later Cardinal) Gaetano De Lai with the responsibility for the plan of curial reform, which resulted in the *motu proprio Sapienti Consiglio* of June 1908, by which a total of twelve curial congregations were suppressed, their functions being absorbed by others; however, this still left some further work of rationalization to be completed in the field by Benedict XV between 1914 and 1922. A major change was that the formerly separate Secretariat of Briefs was merged with the Secretariat of State and this was joined to the Congregation of Extraordinary Ecclesiastical Affairs,

[38] For an account of the 1903 conclave, see G. Zizola, *Il Conclave: storia e segreti. L'elezione papale da San Pietro a Giovanni Paolo II*, Rome, 1993, 177–185.

[39] A. Majoloni, *Il Giornale D'Italia*, 19 June 1925.

of which the Secretary of State now became prefect.[40] The goal of separating the administrative and judicial functions was not entirely achieved, but the curia was rationalized into eleven congregations, three tribunals (Rota, Segnatura, and Penitentiary), and five offices.[41] Pius also introduced fixed salary scales for employees of the Roman curia instead of the fee-farming system which had previously prevailed, and even considered trimming the staffing of the papal court, with the radical idea of reducing the papal armed corps to one, but resistance from the members of the 'black' aristocracy thwarted this plan. It was not until Paul VI came to the papal throne in 1963 that the plan would be taken out of the drawer and implemented, and even then it took Papa Montini five years to push it through.[42]

Papa Sarto was also almost equally as unsuccessful in his efforts to rationalize the financial affairs of the curia. The various congregations were tenacious in their determination to retain control of their finances, especially Propaganda and the Congregation of the Council (of Trent), thus the pope's aim of consolidating all accounts into a single, central fund, under the aegis of the Amministrazione per I Beni della Santa Sede (henceforth ABSS) was frustrated. The ABSS was responsible for administration of 'Peter's Pence' collections from the faithful of the world on which, together with the fairly modest income from Rome rental property, bank interest, and dividends, the Holy See's finances depended.[43] Similarly, the Opera per pias causas, which would later develop into the so-called 'Vatican Bank', also remained autonomous. Pius did manage to separate the administration of the Apostolic Palace from the ABSS, and place it under the control of the Cardinal Secretary of State.[44] But he failed to disengage the finances of the Vatican from the clutches of the Banco di Roma and its all-powerful director, Ernesto Pacelli, or free the Holy See from its commitments to various Italian Catholic organizations and newspapers.[45] This would make an unfortunate legacy for his successor, Benedict XV.

Pius X's reforms rendered the Roman curia much more efficient and effective. Power had now been concentrated into four dicasteries—Secretariat of State-Congregation for Extraordinary Ecclesiastical Affairs, the Holy Office, the Consistory, and, increasingly, Propaganda Fide (which at this time was still also responsible for the Eastern churches in communion with Rome).

[40] H. Jedin (ed.), *History of the Church*, vol. IX: *The Church in the Industrial Age*, trans. Margaret Resch, London, 1981, 398.

[41] Jedin, *History of the Church*, IX, 397; see also Falconi, *The Popes*, 27.

[42] Thomas J. Rees SJ, *Inside the Vatican*, Cambridge, MA, 1996, 18.

[43] John F. Pollard, *Money and the Rise of the Modern Papacy: Financing the Vatican, 1850–1950*, Cambridge, 2005, 83–86.

[44] Benny Lai, *Finanze e finanzieri del Vaticano tra l'Ottocento e il Novecento da Pio IX a Benedetto XV*, Milan, 1979, 222.

[45] See Pollard, *Money*, 100–107.

The Secretary of State would henceforth normally take the lead, though much would depend upon the personalities of the pontiff and the heads of the other dicasteries. While the Dominicans exercised much influence in the papal court by virtue of their occupation of the office of Master of the Sacred Palace—that is, official theologian to the pope—by the beginning of Papa Sarto's reign, the Jesuits possessed a stronger power base in the Vatican since the direction of the important periodical, *La Civiltà Cattolica*, the Vatican astronomical observatory, and the chief of all pontifical universities, the Gregoriana, were all in their hands. After the appointment of Wlodimir Ledóchowski as father general in 1915, the influence of the Jesuits would expand even further.

The Codification of Canon Law

Perhaps Papa Sarto's greatest positive legacy, greater even than the reform of the Roman curia, was his launching of the great project for the codification of Canon Law in 1904, even though it did not come to fruition in his lifetime. Until then, the various laws which regulated every aspect of the Church's life and functioning were scattered over a variety of different kinds of texts, dating from different epochs, many glossed and over-glossed, and some in contradiction with each other.[46] Proposals to rationalize and homogenize them had been discussed for literally centuries, but Pius was determined to do something about it, to equip the Catholic Church with a unified set of legislation which could be called upon to provide the answers to the many questions that confronted the hierarchy at every level. He thus appointed Mgr (later Cardinal) Pietro Gasparri, a noted canonist, assisted by Mgr Eugenio Pacelli, to carry through the task, with a commission of cardinals and prelates and through consultation with bishops all over the world.[47] The task took over twelve years and the Code was promulgated by Pope Benedict XV in 1917 (see Chapter 2).

Despite the failure of some of his reform attempts, Pius X left the machinery of the Roman curia much more fit for its purpose as the central government of the Catholic Church than he had found it. And, as Giuseppe Croce explains, the social and cultural milieux of the Roman curia also changed during the pontificate of Pius X; it was now less aristocratic and dilettantish, more widely recruited and professional.[48]

[46] See the preface by Cardinal Pietro Gasparri in Edward N. Peters (ed.), *The 1917 or Pio-Benedictine Code of Canon Law in English Translation*, San Francisco, CA, 2001, 1–19.

[47] See preface by Gasparri in Peters, *The 1917*, 1–19; P. Gasparri, 'Storia della codificazione del diritto canonico per la chiesa Latina', in ASV, Codex Juris Canonici, Scatola 1–97; and F. Jankowiak, *La Curie romaine de Pie IX à Pie XI: le gouvernement centrale de l'église et la fin des états pontificaux, 1846–1914*, Rome, 2007, 587–667.

[48] Giuseppe M. Croce, 'Regards sur la Curie romaine de 1895 à 1932', in Vefie Poels, Theo Salemink, and Hans de Valk (eds), *Life with a Mission: Cardinal Willem Marinus van Rossum (1854–1932)*, Nijmegen, 2010–11, 59–65.

Pius X and Liturgical Change

Papa Sarto left some other positive legacies. In 1911, he introduced liturgical changes, the most important of which was an exhortation to the laity to take frequent communion. He embarked on a campaign to encourage this from the beginning of his pontificate, culminating in the decree of the Congregation of the Council 'De quotidiana SS. Eucharitiae sumptione'.[49] The faithful were urged to communicate 'frequently and daily'. These measures were followed up with exhortations and the use of Eucharistic congresses to spread the word: as a further incentive to frequent communion, the sick were dispensed from the rigours of the Eucharistic fasts. In the decree 'Quam Singulari', of October 1910, it was declared sufficient for children to be able to recognize the difference between the Eucharistic bread and ordinary bread in order to take communion.[50] Pius also issued a decree forbidding the use of 'profane' music in the Liturgy and strongly encouraging the singing of Gregorian chant. He further established a commission for the revision of both the Breviary and the Roman Missal.[51]

Taking all of these initiatives together with the fact that he inspired Dom Beauduin to found the monastery of Mont-Cesar near Leuven in Belgium precisely for the study of Liturgy, it could be argued that Pius X was the first pope to give a serious impetus towards the development of the Liturgical Movement in the Catholic Church. Even if he had not done that, he would still be remembered for changing the practice of the Catholic Church in regard to the reception of communion by the faithful.[52] As Duffy says, 'The admission of children to communion was one of those minor-seeming changes which profoundly transformed the religious and social experience of millions of Christians.'[53]

The Priesthood and the Laity

As the twentieth-century pope with the greatest pastoral experience, as parish priest, cathedral canon, seminary administrator, and then bishop, Pius rightly deserves his title of the 'parish-priest pope'. Consequently, he had a real concern for the effectiveness of the pastoral ministry at all levels of the

[49] AAS, 1910, Anno 11, II, 577–583, De aetate admittendorum ad primam communionem eucharisticam

[50] AAS, 1910, II, 577–583.

[51] Jedin, *History of the Church*, IX, 410–411.

[52] According to Jedin, *History of the Church*, IX, 405, fn 7, in the Belgian diocese of Malines-Mechelen the average number of communicants per inhabitant per year fluctuated around 2.7 between 1870 and 1900, and reached around 5.1 in 1911, and even 7.6 in 1912. See also Margaret M. McGuiness, 'Let Us Go to the Altar', in James O'Toole (ed.), *Catholic Religious Practice in Twentieth Century America*, Ithaca, NY, and London, 2004, 191–198, for the impact which Pius X's exhortations to frequent communion had in the United States.

[53] Duffy, *Saints and Sinners*, 247.

ecclesiastical hierarchy. Pius personally scrutinized the files of all candidates for Episcopal nomination and insisted that all bishops make the five-yearly *ad limina* visit to the pope to report on the discharge of their responsibilities.[54]

Even the modernist crisis had a positive spin-off. It prompted Pius to review the question of priestly formation, including the organization of seminaries. He sought to reform the curriculum followed in seminaries, even if, under the impact of the crisis, this resulted in a further isolation of seminarians from the secular world. In Italy he endeavoured to remedy the problem of dioceses that were so small that they possessed inadequate facilities for the training of priests or no seminary at all, by creating larger, regional seminaries. He also had a profound commitment to catechetical training: after his election as pope, he continued to teach the catechism to his larger flock.[55] He urged upon bishops and clergy the need for sound, effective catechesis, and in Italy he instituted diocesan and regional congresses for this purpose.[56] And the parish catechetical teams which he promoted always included a lay element.[57] In 1910, he ordered the publication of a standard catechism for the whole of Italy, in the hope that its use would later be extended to the universal Church. He thus set a clear agenda for his successors.

Finally, there is a very real sense in which Pius was the founder of Catholic Action, the organization which. in the three successive pontificates. was to play such a key role in the papal strategy for grappling with the challenges and threats presented by secularism, anti-clericalism, and totalitarian ideologies. With his fiercely hierarchical ecclesiology, he was the first pope to conceive of Catholic Action as the 'participation of the laity in the apostolate of the Hierarchy'. His reorganization of the Italian Catholic movement in the encyclical *Fermo proposito*, 1905,[58] created an Italian Catholic Action organization that was essentially the precursor of the model which Pius XI would seek to 'export' to the whole Church in the 1920s and 1930s (see Chapter 6).[59]

The Missions

Catholic missionary endeavour faced serious problems during the pontificate of Pius X. While the so-called 'Scramble for Africa' in the nineteenth century had opened up virtually a whole new continent for missionary

[54] Chadwick, *History of the Popes*, 374.

[55] Jedin, *History of the Church*, IX, 414–415.

[56] See, for example, John F. Pollard, *The Unknown Pope: Benedict XV and the Pursuit of Peace, 1914–1922*, London, 1991, 36–37.

[57] See the encyclical *Acerbo Nimis*, in Carlen, *Papal Encyclicals*, III, 2935, where he set out the role and duties of 'Confraternities of Christian Doctrine' in each parish.

[58] *Fermo proposito*, in Carlen, *Papal Encyclicals*, III, 37–41.

[59] John F. Pollard, 'Pius XI's Promotion of the Italian Model of Catholic Action in the World-Wide Church', *Journal of Ecclesiastical History*, 64(4) (October 2012), 758–784.

activity, there and elsewhere missionaries had to contend with the very difficult demands of whoever was the colonial power. The Catholic Church responded to the new challenges in the African continent, as well as Asia, by founding twenty-eight new missionary congregations in the latter half of the nineteenth century.[60] It was also in this period that Leo XIII initiated the training of indigenous clergy. The Church–State conflicts of the early 1900s affected the missions in French and Portuguese territories, the largest African colonial empires after that of Britain.[61] But the situation in French colonies was tempered by the shrewd, pragmatic response of colonial administrators, who continued to use missionary religious orders to bolster colonial rule even though the same religious orders were banned in metropolitan France. Thus the French government continued to support French (largely Catholic) schools in the Near East where it was always seeking to extend its influence.[62]

Another major area of Catholic missionary activity was French Indo-China: in what are now Cambodia, Laos, and Vietnam, plus British-ruled Burma, there were one million Christian in 1914.[63] Elsewhere in Asia, the situation was less promising. Though an ecclesiastical hierarchy had been established in Japan in 1891, it did not produce great fruit, largely because of xenophobic resistance to the importation of a foreign religion.[64] Efforts to establish diplomatic relations between the Holy See and the Empire of Japan would encounter similar opposition from the Buddhist 'clergy' until 1941 (see Chapter 6). While Dutch religious orders and congregations had established missions in the Dutch East Indies, now Indonesia, their work was hampered by intolerant, overwhelmingly Protestant, Dutch colonial administrators.[65]

Even the Philippines, whose population, as a result of Spanish colonization, was largely Catholic, gave the Holy See major headaches before the First World War. The Spanish–American War had led to the occupation and annexation of the archipelago by the United States in 1898. It thus became, in effect, 'mission territory'.[66] The legacy of Spanish domination was not, in any case, an entirely positive one. The indigenous clergy were largely disregarded by the (Spanish) religious orders, and when most of the latter were expelled there was a desperate shortage of Catholic clergy to minister to the

[60] *Annuario Pontificio*, 1948, 703–715.

[61] Jedin, *History of the Church*, IX, 554, suggests that the impact of the 1910 Revolution on Portuguese missionary effort in Africa was negative, claiming that there were only 5,000 Catholic Africans in Mozambique in 1914.

[62] Jedin, *History of the Church*, IX, 415.

[63] Jedin, *History of the Church*, IX, 539.

[64] Jedin, *History of the Church*, IX, 539.

[65] Jedin, *History of the Church*, IX, 539.

[66] John F. Pollard, 'Leo XIII and the United States of America, 1898–1903', in Vincent Viaene (ed.), *The Papacy and the New World Order: Vatican Diplomacy, Catholic Opinion and International Politics at the Time of Leo XIII, 1878–1903/La papauté et le nouvel ordre*

population.[67] On the other hand, American occupation was followed by an influx of hundreds of Protestant missionaries. Even worse, with separation of Church and State, according to the American constitutional tradition, education was secularized and religious instruction in schools was abolished.[68] To add to the Philippine Church's woes, in 1912 a schismatic Church, the Iglesia Catolica Filipina Independiente, was established by Gregorio Aglipay, taking 1 million Catholics and 50 of the 825 clergy with it.[69]

Leo XIII had responded to the calamitous Philippine situation with the apostolic letter *Quae mare sinico* in 1902, as a result of which new bishops were appointed and consecrated and the seminaries reopened.[70] The vexed question of the friars' lands, whose exactions on tenant farmers had been partly responsible for support for Aglipay, was eventually resolved by negotiations between the apostolic delegate in Manila, Mgr Guidi, and the local American administration: the Catholic Church received 8 million dollars in compensation for their expropriation.[71] Nevertheless, it would take the whole of Pius X's reign and more to rebuild the Church in the Philippines.

There were also scattered Catholic missions in the various British, French, and German territories of Oceania, and an apostolic delegation for Australia, New Zealand, and Oceania was established for them in April 1914. Missionaries tended 'to follow the flag'. As a result, colonial powers tended to prefer missionaries of their own nationality who would better serve their patriotic interests. Thus, in the Belgian Congo, Leopold II used the Scheut Fathers. By 1910 there were 50,000 Catholics in Belgium's largest African colony.[72] In turn, this inevitably meant that many missionaries were nationalist and racist in their outlook. In this context, Aubert's statement that 'Missions were infected with the spirit of nationalism' seems an understatement.[73]

On the other hand, Leo XIII had demonstrated a certain 'post-colonialist' outlook towards the missions in his encyclical, and even before the end of his reign there had been an attempt to establish a nunciature in China, prompted by Fr Lebbe.[74] This initiative, like all future ones, was opposed by the French, who exercised a general 'protectorate' over all Catholic missions in China. This identification of the Catholic Church with a European colonial power proved disastrous during the Boxer Rebellion of 1900, when hundreds of missionaries, including a bishop, were slain by the Chinese.

mondial: Diplomatie vaticane, opinion Catholique et politique internationale au temps de Léon XIII, Leuven (Belgium), 2005, 465–477.

[67] Pollard, 'Leo XIII and the USA', 472.
[68] Pollard, 'Leo XIII and the USA', 473.
[69] NCE, 11, 258.
[70] NCE, 11, 258.
[71] Pollard, 'Leo XIII and the USA', 475.
[72] Jedin, *History of the Church*, IX, 549.
[73] Jedin, *History of the Church*, IX, 557.
[74] Jedin, *History of the Church*, IX, 557; for the work of this indefatigable and far-sighted missionary, see D. Bays, 'From Mission to Chinese Church', *Church History and Biography*, 98 (Spring 2008), 9–10.

Pius X does not appear to have been very proactive in missionary matters. Apart from the creation of the odd apostolic vicariate and prefecture, his reign witnessed few initiatives in this field. Perhaps the most important was a result of the 1907 reform of the Roman curia: dioceses in North America and north-western Europe were taken out of the hands of the Congregation De Propaganda Fide and its attention was turned henceforth principally towards Africa and Asia by 1908. Aubert claims that 'Reviewing the missionary activities under the pontificates of Leo XIII and Pius X, one must describe this period as epoch-making and highly important for Africa as well as the Pacific.'[75]

The Anti-Modernist Crusade

But of all his various policies, the pontificate of Pius X is probably remembered most for the anti-modernist crusade.[76] As Jedin points out, 'Modernism' had been developing since the reign of Leo XIII: in September 1899, Leo XII sent a warning to the bishops of France against 'alarming tendencies attempting to invade the exegesis of the Bible'.[77] It was partly this concern which prompted the establishment of the official Pontifical Biblical Commission in1902. The attack on theologians, biblical scholars, and ecclesiastical historians—mainly French, like Alfred Loisy, but also British, German, and Italian, including Antonio Fogazzaro, whose novel, *Il Santo*, was put on the Index of 'Prohibited Books'—who sought to use modern scientific method in their work had become an obsession with Pius by 1907, when he issued two major documents, the decree *Lamentabili* and the encyclical *Pascendi Dominici Gregis*, against them and their ideas.[78] *Pascendi*, whose subtitle is 'On the Doctrines of the Modernists', is a summation of all the heretical errors which Pius X believed threatened the Church in his time, most of which the so-called 'modernists' would not have owned to. The encyclical established a veritable system of surveillance and control over the thought of the clergy at all levels, culminating in the 'anti-modernist' oath to be taken by them all. Very soon, a purge of seminaries, theological faculties, and of the priesthood itself got under way. The headquarters of the anti-modernist 'secret police' was the Sodalitium Pianum (also known as La Sapinière) of Mgr Umberto Benigni, inside the Secretariat of State; he operated through his agents in Italy, France, and parts of other parts of Catholic

[75] Jedin, *History of the Church*, IX, 555–557.

[76] See Falconi, *The Popes*, 32–42; and Chadwick, *History of the Popes*, 346–366.

[77] Carlen, *The Papal Encyclicals*, II, *Depuis le jour*, 8 September 1899, 458–459.

[78] For the text of *Lamentabili*, see AAS, XL, 8, 3 July 1907 and for that of the encyclical, see Carlen, *Papal Encyclicals*, III, 371–398.

Europe.[79] There can be no doubt that Pius was thoroughly behind Benigni in his efforts to identify and root out 'modernists'. The chief anti-modernist zealots in the Roman curia in addition to the pope himself were cardinals Merry del Val, Gaetano De Lai, Prefect of the Consistorial Congregation, and the Spanish Capuchin friar José Vives y Tuto (Vives fa Tutto, 'Vives does everything' as he was known in the Vatican), Secretary to the Holy Office of the Inquisition. Others who belonged to the Sodalitium Pianum were a rising prelate, Mgr (in 1911, cardinal) Willem Marinus van Rossum, who was a consultor of the Holy Office and a member of the Commission for the Codification of Canon Law; Mgr Eugenio Pacelli, also a member of that Commission and a rising star in the Secretariat of State; and Cardinal Teodoro Gotti.[80] Ironically, when Vives went mad in 1908 and had to be confined, Rampolla, who had been cast out in 1903, was appointed in his place and remained there until his own death in December 1913.[81]

No one, not even bishops, cardinals, and high-ranking prelates were spared the denunciations of Benigni's agents or the suspicions of Pius X. Cardinal Andrea Ferrari, archbishop of Milan, Cardinal Pietro Maffi, archbishop of Pisa, Cardinal Léon-Adolphe Amette, archbishop of Paris, and Cardinal Anton Fischer, archbishop of Cologne, were all subjected to humiliating harassment for their 'softness' on modernism.[82] Even Pius X's eventual successor, Benedict XV, Mgr Giacomo Della Chiesa, archbishop of Bologna as he then was, fell under the suspicion of modernism.[83] As is clear from his pastoral activities as archbishop of that city, Della Chiesa disliked the excesses of the anti-modernist crusade and even found himself occasionally a target of them, but he was emphatically not himself a modernist.[84] Aubert provides an impressive list of those cardinals and prelates who had reacted against the witch hunt: Gustav Piffl of Vienna, Léon-Adolphe Amette of Paris, most of the German bishops, Desiré-Joseph Mercier of Malines-Mechelen, Pietro Maffi of Pisa, Speculator, a curial cardinal, Agostino Richelmy of Turin, Francesco di Paolo Cassetta, prefect of Studies, Andreas Steinhuber, prefect of the Index.[85] Towards the end of his reign, the Jesuits in particular had turned against the anti-Modernist campaign. So much so that Pius 'even contemplated relieving Fr Wernz of the direction of the Society . . .' but both the pope and the 'black pope' suddenly died.[86]

Pius X's obsession with 'modernism' had serious short to medium-term consequences for the Church; despite the efforts of his successor to put a

[79] E. Poulat, *Catholicisme démocratique et socialisme: le mouvement catholique et Mgr Benigni e la naissance du socialisme à la victoire du fascisme*, Paris, 1977.

[80] O. Weiss, 'Glaubenswechter van Rossum', in Poels et al. (eds), *Life with a Mission*, 67–82.

[81] Falconi, *The Popes*, 50.

[82] Chadwick, *History of the Popes*, 356.

[83] Peter Hebblethwaite, *John XXIII: Pope of the Council*, London, 1984, 62.

[84] See Pollard, *The Unknown Pope*, 40–45.

[85] Jedin, *History of the Church*, IX, 479.

[86] Jedin, *History of the Church*, IX, 479, fn 7.

stop to the excesses of Benigni and his friends, the three Scotton brothers, all priests, in the Veneto,[87] a climate of suspicion and fear lingered for some years afterwards, discouraging intellectual exploration and debate.

Church–State Relations

Pius X's eleven-year reign saw a serious deterioration in the Church's relations with several key states: only in Italy was there a slight improvement in the relationship between its ruling class and the papacy, with benefits for the Italian Church. Church–State conflicts in Europe were partly due to unwelcome developments in the politics of the states concerned. They were also, in large part, due to the intransigent, and sometimes, insensitive diplomatic policy of the pope and his Secretary of State, Cardinal Merry del Val.

Italy

When Pius became pope in 1903, Italy was still in the throes of its first major period of industrial development, admittedly almost entirely restricted to the north-western regions.[88] Industrialization and urbanization presented the Italian Church with significant pastoral problems,[89] and it also threw up a serious political challenge, the emergence of a Marxist, revolutionary working-class movement, the Italian Socialist Party (PSI), and its collateral trade union and peasant organizations.[90] The presence of the PSI had been a major factor which panicked the Italian ruling class during the tumults, convulsions, and violence of the so-called 'End of Century crisis'.[91] Leo XIII's social encyclical, *Rerum Novarum* of 1891, provided the basis for the development of Catholic counterparts to the various organizations of the working-class movement, and a sort of 'ideology' with which to combat Marxist socialism.[92] Pius X was innovatory, introducing more widely into Italian local politics the clerico-moderate alliances—electoral coalitions of Catholics and conservative liberals—which he had first employed in Venice.[93] Furthermore, after 1904, he repeatedly relaxed the *Non expedit*, the Vatican ban on Catholic participation in Italian politics, permitting Catholics to vote for liberal-conservative parliamentary candidates

[87] Falconi, *The Popes*, 41–42.

[88] C. Seton-Watson, *Italy from Liberalism to Fascism, 1870–1925*, London, 1967, 284–297.

[89] John F. Pollard, *Catholicism in Modern Italy: Religion, Society and Politics since 1861*, London, 2008, 51–68.

[90] See M. Clark, *Modern Italy, 1871–1995*, London, 1996, 140–145.

[91] Clark, *Modern Italy*, 140–145.

[92] For the text, see Carlen, *Papal Encyclicals*, II, *Rerum Novarum*, 15 May 1891, 241–261.

[93] Pollard, *Catholicism*, 67–68.

who promised to protect the Church's interests (most importantly, not to support the introduction of a divorce law): in some cases, even allowing Catholics to be candidates.[94] This was a realistic policy, a further retreat from temporalistic intransigence. And despite the ritual reiteration of the protest over the Italian 'usurpation' of Rome, Papa Sarto's attitude towards the Savoyard Royal family was much less inflexible than that of his predecessor. This practical political collaboration against the Socialists and other radical elements, helped by the pragmatism of the dominant Italian liberal-conservative politician of the period, Giovanni Giolitti, contributed towards a lessening of the tensions between Church and State. Though Giolitti's motto was that Church and State were 'two parallels that should never meet', his governments and those of other leading politicians were happy to do 'under-the-counter' deals to relieve the restrictions of the ecclesiastical legislation, and even that notorious 'priest-eater', Ernesto Nathan mayor of Rome, was willing to make behind-the-scenes concessions to the Holy See.[95] By 1914, the relations between the Vatican and the Quirinale were not warm, but they certainly were not chilly and Catholic support for Giolitti's colonial venture, the Libyan War of 1911–12, consolidated the process of interpenetration between the Catholic political and financial elites and their liberal-conservative counterparts.[96]

France

The situation in France was not so encouraging. In the wake of the Dreyfus affair, relations between the Third Republic and the Vatican were severely strained, but at least they continued to exist on a diplomatic level.[97] All this changed shortly after Pius X's election. The visit of President Loubet of France to the Quirinale in April 1904 provoked a rupture. Whereas the Vatican tolerated non-Catholic sovereigns, princes, and heads of state calling upon the King of Italy, provided they visited the Vatican first and that they followed Vatican protocol to the letter, Catholic heads of state were effectively barred from setting foot in Rome. Thus Emperor Franz Josef of Austria met his Italian ally, King Victor Emmanuel III, in Venice out of deference to the pope's wishes. Though relatively mild,[98] the papal protest to other powers about Loubet's visit leaked out and, splashed all over the French press, was taken as a deliberate insult in the Élysée and Quai d'Orsay.[99] France then withdrew its envoy to the Vatican, claiming that Vatican was only keeping a nuncio in Paris in order to influence the elections.[100] Loubet's

[94] Pollard, *Catholicism*, 67–68. [95] Pollard, *Money*, 92–93.

[96] Richard A. Webster, *The Cross and the Fasces: Christian Democracy and Fascism in Italy*, Stanford, CA, 1960, 31–37.

[97] M. Larkin, *L'Église et L'État en France, 1905: la crise de la Séparation*, Toulouse, 2004, ch. 3.

[98] See ASV, AES, Sessioni, 1029a. 20 Marzo 1904. Francia. Loubet a Roma.

[99] Larkin, *L'Église*, 141–145. [100] Larkin, *L'Église*, 141–145.

visit to the Quirinale was almost certainly a deliberate provocation on the part of a militantly anti-clerical French government. The subsequent attitude of the Vatican was high-minded but counterproductive.

In 1905, the French parliament passed the Law on the Separation of Church and State, decreeing the strict secularization of all public institutions and life.[101] The Concordat of 1801 was unilaterally abrogated and the government measures went beyond merely formal, legal separation, expropriating *all* the property of the French Church, including places of worship, which in some cases provoked a violent reaction on the part of the faithful.[102] In addition, the law laicized Catholic educational, medical, and charitable institutions, religious orders and congregations were dissolved and dispersed—a veritable diaspora of French religious, male and female, ended up in various other European countries—and marriage was declared an entirely civil institution.[103] The only legal means for Catholics to ensure the continuation of worship was through newly constituted *associations cultuelles*, which provided a legal framework for the holding of all Church property in a secular state.[104] But Pius X forbade French bishops and priests to have anything to do with them in his encyclical *Gravissimo Officii Munere* of August 1906, even though the bishops had decided, by a clear majority, to the contrary.[105] In an earlier encyclical, *Vehementer Nos*, of February 1906,[106] Pius had set out the principled reasons for his denunciation of the policies of the French government. Like his predecessor of the same name, in the *Syllabus of Errors*, and like Leo XIII in his encyclical *Immortale Dei* of November 1895,[107] he declared that the very idea of the separation of Church and State was a 'pernicious error', for God is owed not only private but public worship too.[108] Above all, he asserted the absolute, sole authority over the Church of the Hierarchy, and in particular the Roman Pontiff, which no civil government could infringe.[109]

Relations between the Church and the Third Republic progressively deteriorated thereafter, not helped by the pope's refusal to allow the writings of Charles Maurras, monarchist, nationalist, and anti-Semitic, to be placed on the Index, while the Christian Democratic ideas of Marc Sangnier and his organization Le Sillon were.[110] According to Cobban, '. . . Action Française

[101] Larkin, *L'Église*, 147–160.

[102] ASV, AES, Sessioni, 1069. 6 Febbraio 1906. Francia. Legge della separazione dello Stato dalla Chiesa. All present at the meeting agreed that they should not encourage and approve of active and violent resistance to the taking of inventories of Church property but should not say so publicly in case this upsets the faithful, who might not obey the bishops. The minutes of this and other sessions held to discuss France suggest that Merry del Val was not really much more intransigent than Rampolla . . .

[103] Larkin, *L'Église*.

[104] Larkin, *L'Église*.

[105] For the text, see Carlen, *Papal Encyclicals*, III, 63–65.

[106] Carlen, *Papal Encyclicals*, III, 45–51.

[107] Carlen, *Papal Encyclicals*, II, 114.

[108] Carlen, *Papal Encyclicals*, III, 46–47.

[109] Carlen, *Papal Encyclicals*, III, 47.

[110] Falconi, *The Popes*, 176.

was treated as an ally by Pius X, which could only have inflamed French anti-clerical feeling'.[111] Even if Leo XIII and Rampolla had still been in office, it is hard to see how they could have avoided the rupture with France given the anti-clerical mood in that country. But Larkin is undoubtedly right when he says that, 'Certainly, the consequences of the Separation in France would have been less crippling if Rampolla had been materially in charge.'[112] However, Rampolla was not in charge any more and did not approve of the new policies. Rampolla's pupil, Mgr Giacomo Della Chiesa, was Sostituto until 1907, and according to Sforza, he tried to avoid the worst:

> As long as he remained, as Under-Secretary of State, until his exile to Bologna, della [sic] Chiesa tried, respectfully and prudently to prevent the relations of France and the Vatican from degenerating to the point of disastrous rupture, the obvious termination according to him, of Pius X's and Merry del Val's policy. He gained nothing by his efforts except to be no longer received by the Pope.[113]

The methods of Pius X and his Secretary of State, Merry del Val, were undoubtedly '. . . needlessly gladiatorial'.[114] They were scarcely less so in the disputes which developed with Portugal and Spain during the course of the pontificate.

Portugal

The Republic 'secular and indivisible' of France became the model for anti-clerical regimes elsewhere in Europe and in Latin America from the early 1900s onwards, Portugal being the first country to move in this direction. Portuguese politics had been fairly unstable from the middle of the nineteenth century. A strong republican element among the liberal political groupings also held strongly anti-clerical convictions so that already, in 1901, Leo XIII had been obliged to publicly condemn a decree against religious orders and congregations.[115] In February 1908, the reigning king, Carlos I, and his son, Crown Prince Luis, were assassinated. Two years later, their successor, the young Manoel II was deposed by a military insurrection, driven into exile, and a republic was proclaimed. The 1910 Revolution was quickly followed by a campaign of secularization and anti-clerical legislation. The Jesuits were expelled, ecclesiastical property was expropriated, divorce was

[111] A. Cobban, *A History of Modern France*, vol. 3: *1871–1962*, London, 1962, 89–90.

[112] M. Larkin, *Church and State after the Dreyfus Affair: The Separation Issue in France*, London and Basingstoke, 1974.

[113] C. Sforza, *Contemporary Italy*, New York, 1944, 185.

[114] Falconi, *The Popes*, 76.

[115] Carlen, *The Papal Encyclicals*, II, *Gravissisimas*, 16 May 1901, 487–488.

introduced, and marriage was made 'exclusively civil'.[116] Pius X and Merry del Val agonized over the response to be made to events in Portugal, holding several plenary meetings of the Congregation for Extraordinary Ecclesiastical Affairs.[117] In 1911, Pius eventually published the encyclical *Iamdudum* (on the Law of Separation in Portugal),[118] which denounced to the bishops of the world the various anti-clerical measures enacted in Portugal. In many ways, they were *worse* than the Separation Laws in France. They made the life of the Portuguese Church extremely difficult through strict regulation of all religious ceremonies outside of churches, the banning of the reading of papal and Episcopal pastoral letter, and the expulsion of all but one of the Portuguese bishops from their dioceses.[119] Inasmuch as it was sometimes accompanied by violence against the clergy, the persecution in Portugal resembled more closely the persecution of the Church which was enacted in Mexico following the promulgation of the Constitution of Queretaro in 1917 (see Chapter 3) because it was clearly aimed at squeezing the lifeblood out of Portuguese Catholicism.

Church–State relations remained one of the focal points of Portuguese politics until 1918, when a definite improvement began to make itself felt.

Spain

The situation in Spain was different again from that in both France and Portugal. Here, relations between Church and State were ostensibly good, on a formal level. The real problem was the developing conflict between the Church and sections of Spanish society. Below the surface, among many of the industrial working class and the landless peasantry, there rumbled a veritable anti-clerical volcano which spewed forth during the 'Tragic Week' in Barcelona in 1909 and resulted in the burning of twenty-one churches and forty religious houses in Barcelona alone.[120] It was a horrible rehearsal for what would happen after the establishment of the Republic in 1931 and, even worse, after General Francisco Franco's *pronunciamento* in July 1936 (see Chapter 6). While the Spanish Church was legally and institutionally strong, its hold on the Spanish people was becoming more tenuous: fundamentally, Catholicism

[116] A. Rhodes, *The Power of Rome in the Twentieth Century: The Vatican in the Age of the Liberal Democracies*, London, 1983, 214–217.

[117] ASV, AES, Sessioni, 1148. 13 novembre 1910. Portogallo, 1150. 18 dic. 1910. Portogallo. Rampolla (it is clear from the minutes of these sessions that the Portuguese government was ferociously hostile to the Church), 1163. 7 gennaio 1912. Portogallo. Confraternita' di culto e Pensioni del Clero and 1169. 28 novembre 1912. Portogallo. Bolla della Crociata.

[118] Carlen, *Papal Encyclicals*, III, 127–130.

[119] ASV, AES, Sessioni, 1150. 18 dic. 1910. Portogallo (largely devoted to problem of government's demand that bishop of Beja resign).

[120] Raymond Carr, *Modern Spain 1875–1980*, Oxford, 1980, 76.

had become the religion of the peasantry (though not all of them), the landed aristocracy, and sections of the urban middle class.[121] Following the 'Tragic Week', the parliamentary ministries of José Canalejas between 1910 and 1912 sought to trim the Church's power, and in particular that of hated religious orders, by the 'Law of the Lock'.[122] Though the law had only limited and temporary effects, it produced a violent Catholic reaction.[123] 'Reaction' is the key word here. Spanish Catholicism at the levels of the hierarchy, the religious orders and congregations, and even of much of the devout laity was *reactionary*, demanding power and privileges and public recognition which were anomalous, out of date, and unheard of in other Catholic countries. On the other hand, despite the best efforts of a handful of socially minded priests, the Spanish Church produced little in the way of the practical social Catholicism that was emerging strongly in Belgium, France, the Netherlands, parts of Germany, and even Italy at this time.[124] Even less was it capable of producing a Catholic party capable of defending the Church's interests in parliament: but to so many Spanish Catholics no such defence was necessary. The illusion was to be brutally shattered by events from 1931 onwards.

Latin America

The only encyclical which Pius X published on matters relating to Latin America was *Lacrimabilu Statu*, of June 1912, to the bishops of the continent, decrying the continuing mistreatment of the Indians of South America, despite the abolition of slavery, 'Christian charity, which holds all men, without distinction of colour, as brethren . . .' and urging them to seek to alleviate the lot of the Indios.[125] But the treatment of the Indians was not the only major problem facing the bishops of Latin America. Parts of the continent had already been a battleground between clerical and anti-clerical forces in the nineteenth century. The 'export' of European liberalism to Latin America brought in its wake the emergence there of political forces, usually backed by Masonic lodges, which sought to reduce the economic, social, and political influence of the Church, through laws decreeing the separation of Church and State, expropriation of ecclesiastical property, the introduction of civil

[121] Carr, *Modern Spain*, 40–43.

[122] ASV, AES, Sessioni, 1919.1141, 17. Luglio 1910. Spagna. Merry del Val had been talking tough with the Spanish government over latter's right to control the opening of religious houses. See his letter to Spanish Ambassador, 20 June 1910. The problem of Spain occupied another seven sessions, 1136, 1138, 1139, 1140, 1141, 1142, and 1145.

[123] Carr, *Modern Spain*, 42.

[124] P. Misner, *Social Catholicism in Europe: From the Onset of Industrialisation to the First World War*, New York, 1991, especially chs 11–15.

[125] Carlen, *Papal Encyclicals*, III, *Lacrimabili Statu*, 7 June 1912, 131–133.

marriage and divorce, and the secularization of education. The constitution of the first Brazilian Republic of 1889 was a case in point.[126] More extreme measures were sometimes invoked, such as the expulsion of the Jesuits and foreign (usually Portuguese or Spanish) clergy, and the dissolution of religious orders and congregations more generally. The early twentieth century was witness to even more serious threats to the status and interests of the Church in several Latin American states: for example, Ecuador broke off diplomatic relations with the Holy See in 1901. But the most serious horrors were those unleashed against the Mexican Church during and after the revolution of 1910–17.

The Oriental Churches

The signing of the concordat with Serbia in 1914 illustrates the concern of the Vatican for the future of the Latin and Greek Catholic minorities scattered throughout Eastern and southern Europe and the Ottoman Empire. In 1914 the Roman Catholic Church counted roughly 300 million adherents worldwide: of these the non-Latin rite Catholics amounted to six and a half million.[127] There were non-Latin rite Catholic minorities in the Russian Empire, in the eastern borderlands of the Austro-Hungarian Empire, in the territories of the Ottoman Empire (Anatolia and the Middle East), and in the emerging nation states in the Balkans which had liberated themselves from Ottoman rule—Albania, Bulgaria, Greece, Rumania, and Serbia.[128] Vatican hopes for the conversion of the other Oriental churches, the 'schismatic' Orthodox ones, principally in Russia but also in the Balkans—were encapsulated in the 'Prayers for the Conversion of Russia', which Leo XIII had added to the end of the Mass.[129] The Orthodox Russian Empire, with its designs on Constantinople, consequently remained the great obstacle to these Vatican ambitions.

The Vatican's Diplomatic Standing in Pius X's Reign

At the end of Pius X's pontificate in 1914, the Holy See had diplomatic relations with only fourteen states. In Europe it had relations with Austria-Hungary, Bavaria, Belgium, Prussia, Russia, Serbia, and Spain; relations with the Netherlands, which had been broken following the refusal to allow the Holy

[126] E. Dussel, *The History of the Church in Latin America: Colonialism to Liberalism*, trans. and rev. Alan Neeley, Grand Rapids, MI, 1981, 101.

[127] ASV, AES, IV Periodo, Stati Eccl., 602, 42, Statistiche delle religioni nell'Est-Europa.

[128] Chadwick, *History of the Popes*, 543–549.

[129] For the text of the prayer, see *The Small Roman Missal*, Leeds, 1944, 82–83.

See to participate in the Hague peace conference of 1899,[130] had still not been patched up by the end of Pius X's reign.[131] In Latin America seven republics continued to maintain links with the Vatican. In effect, the pope had full diplomatic relations with the ruler of only one great power—the Emperor Franz Josef of Austria-Hungary. Habsburg–papal links were a sort of 'special relationship' because the Austro-Hungarian Empire, as the last great Catholic power, played a pivotal role in the Holy See's diplomatic strategy as a bulwark against the Orthodoxy of the 'Russian steamroller', especially in the Balkans. It was also seen by the men in the Vatican as, in some way, serving to counterbalance the Protestantism of the Second Reich: whether it really did so is open to debate.

While there was a Prussian ambassador in the Vatican, this was not reciprocated by the presence of a nuncio in Berlin. Similarly, though there was a Russian envoy to the Vatican, there was no papal envoy in St Petersburg. In both cases, the problem was religious differences. The latter two powers maintained tenuous relations with the Holy See because both the Protestant Kingdom of Prussia and the Orthodox Russian Empire contained substantial Catholic minorities. In the former they were to be found in the Rhineland, Westphalia, and Silesia, and in the latter, in Russian Poland, the Ukraine, and Lithuania. Vatican–German relations had now more or less recovered from the effects of the *Kulturkampf* of the previous century,[132] and had been sealed by the visits of Kaiser Wilhelm in the 1890s.[133] But comments describing the Lutheran reformers as 'enemies of the cross of Christ, . . . they mind the things of earth, . . . whose God is the belly', made by Pius X in his 1910 encyclical *Editae aepe* on the great Counter-Reformation saint Charles Borromeo seriously upset German Protestants and the governments of Prussia, Bavaria, and Saxony.[134] In the case of the Orthodox Russian Empire, the treatment of the Polish Catholics and the Ruthenian Catholic minority in the Ukraine by successive tsars in the nineteenth century, plus continuing restrictions on the Catholic Church in Russia itself, still caused problems with Rome.[135]

The Holy See had no relations at all with the United States of America or the British Empire. In the case of America, the envoy was withdrawn as early as 1867 by Congressional fiat. In the aftermath of the Spanish–American

[130] See J.P. Hans de Valk, 'A Diplomatic Disaster: The Exclusion of the Holy See from the 1899 Hague Peace Conference', in Viaene (ed.), *The Papacy and the New Order*, 435–452.

[131] ASV, AES, Sessioni, 1156. 16 Febbraio 1911. Olanda. Rappresentanza pontificia in Olanda.

[132] For an overview of the *Kulturkampf*, see Chadwick, *History of the Popes*, 254–265; and Jedin, *History of the Church*, IX, 26–45 and 55–76.

[133] See John Pollard, 'A Court in Exile: The Vatican, 1870–1929', *The Court Historian*, 12(1) (June 2007), 45.

[134] Carlen, *Papal Encyclicals*, III, *Editae Saepe*, 26 May 1910, 117.

[135] For papal protests against governmental policy towards Catholics in the Russian Empire, see Chadwick, *History of the Popes*, 409–433. See also, ASV, AES, 1154. 5 Febbraio 1911. Russia.

War of 1898, Leo XIII tried to exploit the Taft mission sent to the Vatican to sort out the difficult problems relating to the Church in the Philippines, now a US colony, as means of restoring relations with the USA, but failed.[136] For Britain, the end of relations with the Vatican came in 1874—'when the status of the Vatican, following the Italian occupation of Rome, could not be clarified by British lawyers'.[137] This was unfortunate for the Holy See. Apart from the growing Catholic minority in the USA—the result of migratory flows from France, Germany, Ireland, and so on, following the Spanish–American War of 1898, the USA acquired four ex-Spanish colonies: Cuba, Guam, the Philippines, and Puerto Rico, with majority Catholic populations, roughly 10 million. Similarly, the British Empire contained substantial Catholic minorities in Canada, Australia, New Zealand, South Africa, and so on, plus a Catholic majority in Ireland. In addition, there were many Catholic missions in British colonies and protectorates in Africa, Asia, the Caribbean, and Oceania.

By 1911, the situation in the Balkans was not only a matter of concern in the chancelleries of Europe, it was also viewed with apprehension in the Vatican. The Holy See's principal worry was growing Russian influence. This, and concern about future of the Latin and Greek Catholic minorities in the Ottoman Empire, prompted the Vatican to appoint apostolic delegates to the emerging nation states in the peninsula. In general, the Vatican relied upon the weight of Habsburg influence in the Balkans to protect Catholic interests there, influence which was increasingly challenged by Serbia and Russia during the successive Balkan Wars of 1911–12 and 1912–13.

The turbulent, unstable situation in the Balkans and, in particular, the rise of Serbia, eventually induced the Vatican to instruct the nuncio in Vienna to make contact with the Serbian minister to Austria for the purpose of negotiating a concordat in 1909. Serbia was willing to do so, but various circumstances, including fear of the Orthodox Church, slowed things down. In 1913, Mgr Scapinelli di Leguigno, nuncio in Vienna, stressed the need for the Holy See to establish relations with Serbia because it was expanding and with it the number of Roman Catholics in the kingdom, thanks to its role in the Balkan Wars.[138] But the Serbs were afraid that the Holy See would make demands that would upset the Orthodox Church. On the other hand, the Serbs wanted

Communicazione dei decreti della S. Sede all'Episcopato russo, Stampa 992, p. 9. The Vatican's chief complaint against the Russians was that all communications with bishops and clergy had to go via Russian embassy and Ministry of the Interior.

[136] Pollard, 'Leo XII and the USA', 476.

[137] Pollard, 'Anglo-Vatican Relations', in Frank J. Coppa (ed.), *Encyclopedia of the Vatican and the Papacy*, Westport, CT, 1999, 30.

[138] Rita Tolomei, 'Le relazioni serbo-vaticane dal congresso di Berlino alla prima guerra mondiale', in G. De Rosa and Giorgio Cracco (eds), *Il Papato e l'Europa*, Soveria Mannelli, 2001, 361–378.

to remove the Austrian 'protectorate' of Catholics: this was their most important aim. In 1913, during the Second Balkan War, the Serbs acquired Macedonia and thus yet more Roman Catholics. At this stage, the Serbian government demanded the use of the Old Slavonic liturgies for their Catholic subjects, while, on the sidelines, the Austrians objected that they were forbidden to Slav Roman Catholics in their territories.[139] After tortuous negotiations, which would be par for the course with predominantly Orthodox states, the Concordat was signed in Rome on 2 June 1914 and ratified by parliament on 26 July—just two days before the outbreak of war.[140]

The Approach of the First World War

Pius X died on 21 August 1914. Pious contemporaries and some historians until recently have claimed that it was of a broken heart—broken by the outbreak of a terrible 'big' war which he had repeatedly predicted—*il guerrone* ('the big war').[141] There has been some debate about the role which Vatican diplomacy played in the July crisis which led to the outbreak of the war. Some have claimed the Holy See helped precipitate the war by advising Franz Josef that Austria was in the right and should humble Serbia.[142] Merry del Val did express such sentiments, but so did other European diplomats: they all did so on the assumption that Austro-Hungarian action would, at most, precipitate a limited conflict localized in the Balkans, not the European-wide war which ensued.[143] Though the Vatican did little to restrain Austria-Hungary, it did offer to arbitrate the dispute with Serbia.[144] Others have argued that, by concluding the concordat with Serbia, which Austria-Hungary fiercely opposed, the Holy See helped consolidate the authority of the Serbian government over its newly acquired Catholic subjects, increased the Balkan State's prestige, and correspondingly stiffened its resistance to Austrian demands.[145] This is to exaggerate the significance of Vatican diplomatic influence at that time. The Vatican contribution to the outbreak of the First World War was a more general one. As Jedin has stated, 'The Catholic Church did little to dampen the increasing chauvinism of Catholics on all sides . . . The Holy See's benevolent attitude towards the *Action Française* of Maurras and Daudet, pioneers of the [sic] integral nationalism, supports the interpretation that Vatican did little

[139] Tolomei, 'Le relazioni serbo-vaticane, 364.

[140] Tolomei, 'Le relazioni serbo-vaticane, 378.

[141] J.D. Gregory, *On the Edge of Diplomacy: Rambles and Reflections, 1902–1928*, London, n.d., 88; and Falconi, *The Popes*, 52.

[142] Falconi, *The Popes*, 86.

[143] ASV, SdS, Guerra, 1914–1918, Rubricella 244, fasc. 29, 'Tanto per la verità' (n.d.).

[144] F. Engel-Janosi, *Il Vaticano tra Fascismo e Nazismo*, Florence, 1973, 150–151.

[145] Cornwell, *Hitler's Pope*, 57–58; Duffy, *Saints and Sinners*, 250, says that the concordat with Serbia helped increase the tensions in the Balkans but does not say how.

[to] restrain growing nationalistic and militaristic tendencies of European Catholics.'[146]

In the face of the July crisis, Vatican diplomacy was passive, impotent, and irrelevant. It is no accident that, in the most recent and authoritative analysis of the causes of the First World War, *The Sleepwalkers*, by Cambridge historian Christopher Clark, there is no mention of Pius X, Merry del Val, the papacy, the Holy See, the Vatican, or even the Catholic Church.[147] Following the rupture of relations with France, the Holy See had little diplomatic influence in Europe, particularly among the great powers. Consequently, its ability to arbitrate between the great powers was virtually nil. Indeed, not since the death of Pius IX in 1878 had the Catholic Church possessed so little influence on the international scene as in the summer of 1914.

[146] Jedin, *History of the Church*, IX, 520.

[147] Christopher Clark, *The Sleepwalkers: How Europe Went to War in 1914*, London, 2013.

2

'Useless Slaughter': Benedict XV and the First World War

GIACOMO DELLA CHIESA (1854–1914)

Giacomo Giambattista Della Chiesa was born prematurely on 21 November 1854, the sixth child of the Marchesi Giuseppe and Giovanna Della Chiesa. The family formed part of the Genoese patriciate, their name and coat of arms inscribed in the Golden Book of the former Republic.[1] Giacomo's mother's family, the Migliorati of Naples, was also aristocratic and had already provided a pope—Innocent VII. However, by the 1850s the Della Chiesa family was no longer wealthy and Giacomo would not have been able to continue his education without the support of wealthier relatives.[2]

The smallness and physical frailty consequent upon Giacomo's premature birth meant that much of his early education was at home. In 1866 he entered the Istituto Danovaro e Giusso, one of the best academies in Genoa, where he was a successful, though not exceptional, student.[3] His vocation for the priesthood emerged early on,[4] but his was an obviously Catholic home, so it felt the conflict between the loyalty of a Genoese aristocrat in the service of the Savoyard king, Victor Emmanuel II, who came to the throne of the Kingdom of Italy in 1861, and the papacy, whose 'temporal power' Victor Emmanuel progressively 'despoiled' during the process of Italian unification between 1859 and 1870.[5]

After graduating from high school, Giacomo wanted to proceed immediately to the diocesan seminar, but his father insisted that he do so only after successfully completing his university studies. Giacomo accepted reluctantly, but was allowed to study scholastic philosophy and apologetics as a lay student at the

[1] For biographies of Benedict XV, see K. Jankowiak, 'Benoit XV', in P. Levillain (ed.), *Dictionnaire de la papauté*, Paris, 1997; W.H. Peters, *The Life of Benedict XV*, Milwaukee, 1959; Pollard, *The Unknown Pope*; and F. Vistalli, *Benedetto XV*, Rome, 1929.

[2] C. Sforza, *Contemporary Italy*, New York, 1944, 165.

[3] Archivio Famiglia Della Chiesa (henceforth AFDC), white 10.

[4] Peters, *Life of Benedict*, 5–7.

[5] Falconi, *The Popes*, 96.

diocesan seminary while at university. University was a challenge for Giacomo, not intellectually but because of its strongly anti-clerical atmosphere. Giacomo quickly showed where his loyalties lay by joining the Society for the Promotion of Catholic Interests.[6] When Giacomo graduated from the Royal University of Genoa in 1875 with a doctorate in law, his father agreed to an ecclesiastical career, but insisted he go to Rome, to the Collegio Capranica and the Gregorian University, which, the Marchese believed, would permit a more rapid career development than staying at home. Giacomo was a diligent student, who attended lectures assiduously, especially those of Cardinal J.B. Franzelin (official theologian to the First Council of the Vatican) and Fr Antonio Ballerini, the famous moralist. His first pastoral experience was as catechist to the children of the parish church of S. Maria in Aquiro near the Pantheon, and he was ordained on 21 December 1878, in the presence of his family, by Cardinal Monaco La Valletta, the pope's vicar for the Rome diocese in St John Lateran (the cathedral of Rome). He celebrated his first Mass, not at the tomb of the Prince of the Apostles as most newly ordained priests in Rome aspired to do but, prophetically, at the Altar of the *Cathedra*, in the apse of St Peter.

He graduated doctor of theology, cum laude, in 1879, and in 1880 he received a doctorate in canon law and entered the Academy of Noble Ecclesiastics, the training ground of Vatican diplomats: Cardinal Consalvi, who had successfully negotiated the restoration of the Papal States at the Vienna Congress in 1815, Pope Leo XIII (1878–1903), Cardinal Rampolla del Tindaro, and Cardinal Merry del Val were all alumni.[7] Giacomo very quickly shone in this elite group. It was here that, in 1884, he met Monsignor (as he then was) Rampolla. Rampolla was impressed by Giacomo's intelligence and industry and had him appointed Professor of Diplomatic Style at the Academy and *apprendista*, apprentice, in the Congregation of Extraordinary Affairs, of which Rampolla was secretary.

Giacomo's career took a further bound the same year when Rampolla was appointed to the Madrid nunciature, the second most important posting in the Vatican diplomatic corps after Vienna, and took Giacomo with him as secretary to the nunciature. Thus began Giacomo's experience of Vatican diplomacy in action and his close relationship with the man who became both his mentor and friend. In June 1887, Rampolla was appointed Secretary of State to Pope Leo XIII and cardinal, and Giacomo returned with him to Rome. In 1888 and 1889 Giacomo was sent to Vienna on confidential business, to sort out the troubled affairs of the Austrian Christian Social Party, whose leader was vocally anti-Semitic.[8] Very quickly, Giacomo developed a

[6] Pollard, *The Unknown Pope*, 4.

[7] For some brief sketches of the history of the Academy, see *Pontifica Accademia Ecclesiastica: Terzo centenario (1701–2001)*, Rome, 2003.

[8] J. Schmidlin, *Papstgeschichte der neuesten Zeit*, vol. III, Munich, 1953, 182.

mastery of the Vatican's peculiar ways, and in 1902 Leo XIII considered him as a possible archbishop of his native city, although Rampolla dissuaded the pope from this appointment in order to keep Giacomo by his side. Francis McNutt, an American papal chamberlain at Leo's court, made these observations about Giacomo's role in the Vatican:

> He was usually esteemed a great diplomat. Frankly, I must say that he impressed me as a meticulous, accomplished bureaucrat; a conscientious, painstaking understudy of Cardinal Rampolla . . . He possessed a vast store of carefully sorted information upon which to draw; he was accurate and very precise, acquainted with all the rules and traditions of his chancellery and not ignorant of those of other governments. In matters of protocol—etiquette, precedence etc.—he was infallible as a man could possibly be. Of brilliancy or originality, I never perceived a trace, but since an exhibition of such traits was not required during his years of subordinate service, it was proof of the greatest wisdom and tact on his part to dissemble any such he may have possessed.[9]

Nevertheless, Giacomo Della Chiesa was a power and influence in the Vatican after his appointment in 1902 as *Sostituto* (substitute Secretary of State). Along with the Secretary for Extraordinary Ecclesiastical Affairs, Mgr Pietro Gasparri, who was appointed at the same time, the *Sostituto* was the most important person in the Vatican after the pope and the Secretary of State. Their offices were the clearing houses for all essential matters in the government of the Church, to which came many other Vatican officials and bishops from all over the world, giving them a remarkable knowledge of the universal Church. Frequently, in the absence of the Secretary of State, the *Sostituto* dealt directly with the pope himself. It is clear that, by 1900, Giacomo had established for himself a unique reputation as a cautious, discreet, and diplomatic powerbroker.

Giacomo's power was not to last for long, because his world was turned upside down by Leo's death in 1903. The failure of Rampolla to get elected pope was of crucial importance to Giacomo's future. The strongest candidate until the sixth ballot, Rampolla was knocked out of the contest by Cardinal Puszyna, archbishop of Cracow (then in the Austrian Empire), who pronounced a 'veto' on behalf of Franz Josef.[10] Thereafter, despite Rampolla's very dignified reaction, his vote declined and Cardinal Giuseppe Sarto, Patriarch of Venice, was elected in his stead. By tradition, a new pope meant a new Secretary of State—a tradition not to be broken until 1922. Rampolla was accordingly retired to the insignificant post of Archpriest of St Peter's and Prefect of the congregation which supervised its fabric. Della Chiesa and Gasparri were both eligible candidates for the Secretariat of State, yet they

[9] F.A. McNutt, *A Papal Chamberlain*, London, 1936, 321.
[10] Falconi, *The Popes*, 8.

were passed over and the man whom Pius X did choose, Mgr Merry del Val, was relatively inexperienced. Relations between Merry del Val and Della Chiesa were not good and were worsened by differences of opinion over relations with France, and also the 'modernists' (see Chapter 1). In 1907 Merry del Val rid himself of his awkward subordinate by having him appointed archbishop of Bologna. So Della Chiesa's transfer to Bologna was a defeat and banishment from the Vatican, and he clearly saw it in those terms. In a letter to a friend in 1912, following renewed speculation that he was to be sent to Madrid, Della Chiesa remarked: 'But I must not get involved in matters of diplomacy: I was thrown out of it and I really do not wish to return.'[11]

Bologna provided Della Chiesa with a substantial experience of episcopal ministry because the diocese was full of problems. The city of Bologna was an essentially an agrarian, administrative, and university one, whose the politics had drifted left-wards since 1900. Its university was also strongly anti-clerical in tone, and on the Emilian plain around the city the Socialist labour movement had established a strong following among the farm workers.[12] Della Chiesa carried out a complete pastoral visitation of his diocese, an enormous task since Bologna was the fourth largest diocese in Italy, roughly 670,000 souls. From the visitations, he quickly became acquainted with the problems, mainly of political origin, facing Italian bishops at that time.[13] One was that the teaching of the catechism had been virtually eradicated from Bologna's schools.[14] Another was civil marriage: Archbishop Della Chiesa was obliged to tell the parochial clergy to urge upon the faithful the unfortunate necessity of contracting both kinds, civil and religious, for their own benefit, especially in order to preserve their legal rights of inheritance.[15] The Bologna experience brought home to Della Chiesa the unsatisfactory nature of Church–State relations in general in liberal Italy. The Church lived with the threat of further anti-Church legislation: on the other hand, as an 'established' Church, it suffered the interference of the local state authorities in its financial affairs.

Carrying out instructions from Rome was another problem for Italian bishop in this period, in particular the directives about 'Modernists' and the Christian Democrats. Della Chiesa inherited a very difficult situation in Bologna and it seems that he was sent to 'cleanse the Augean stables of modernism at Bologna'. The new archbishop was reluctant to carry out the

[11] AFDC, Lettere e Scritti Varie, 3 January 1912.

[12] See Pollard, *The Unknown Pope*, 30–2.

[13] For the records of the visitation, see Archivio Arcivescovile di Bologna (henceforth AAB), 'Diario delle Visite Pastorali di S.E.R. Mons. Giacomo della Chiesa, Arcivescovo'.

[14] AFDC, Lettere e Scritti Varie, 'Atti del Congresso Eucaristico Diocesano', 16–18 November 1910, 30.

[15] *Bollettino della Diocesi di Bologna* (henceforth BDB), Anno 1, no. 3, December 1910, 97–98.

suppression of modernism, in particular to dismiss people, which brought him into conflict with Cardinal De Lai. He was even suspected of being a 'Modernist' himself, but, as Webster writes:

> they (the integristes) made the one serious mistake of attacking a cardinal who was eminently *papabile*. When Pius X died suddenly in 1914 Cardinal Giacomo Della Chiesa of Bologna, a constant target of integriste enmity, was elected to succeed him as Benedict XV; the integristes never recovered.[16]

Democratic political tendencies were the other great bugbear of the Roman curia under Pius X and were seen as going hand in hand with modernism. Della Chiesa's attitude towards the Christian Democrats prior to the First World War is difficult to ascertain. He may well have regarded the social reformism of the movement as too radical; according to Molinari, Della Chiesa was appointed to Bologna to 'hammer the newly-born Democrazia Cristiana' movement.[17] This is entirely plausible, but other evidence suggests that he was not hostile towards the movement and its leader Romolo Murri. Gabriele De Rosa wrote that Della Chiesa 'had strong sympathies for Murri, the orthodox Murri, that is . . .'.[18]

It was also difficult for Italian bishops in the early 1900s to avoid being involved in politics, and Della Chiesa was no exception. He had to follow Pius X's policy of clerico-moderate alliances (see Chapter 1) and his own laity pushed him in that direction.[19] The target of the clerico-moderate alliances was socialism, because the Italian Socialist Party, and the allied network of trade unions, peasant leagues, and cooperatives, was extending its influence in Emilia-Romagna, as elsewhere in Italy.[20] The record of Della Chiesa's pastoral visitations confirms that the Bologna diocese was facing process of 'dechristianization' in those parishes where agrarian socialism had taken strongest root. Della Chiesa also used his *Bollettino diocesano* to condemn the theory and practice of class struggle, a coded way of attacking socialism, but perhaps also the more militant Christian Democrats.[21] Della Chiesa thus experienced a baptism of fire in Emilia-Romagna: it was here, according to Veneruso, that 'he learnt to recognise and evaluate the power and nature of socialism'.[22]

[16] R.A. Webster, *Christian Democracy and Fascism in Italy, 1860–1960*, London, 1961, 21.

[17] F. Molinari, 'Il carteggio di Benedetto XV con Mons. Ersilio Menzani', in *Rivista di Storia della Chiesa in Italia*, 20(2) (July–December 1966), 433.

[18] G. De Rosa, *Luigi Sturzo*, Turin, 1977, 435.

[19] R. Zangheri, *Storia delle città: Bologna*, Bari, 1986, 98.

[20] N. Sauro Onofri, *La Grande Guerra nella città rossa: socialismo e reazione a Bologna dal 1914–1918*, Milan, 1966, 131.

[21] BDB, Anno 1, no. 3, December 1910, 109.

[22] D. Veneruso, 'Benedetto XV', in F. Traniello and G. Campanini (eds), *Dizionario Storico del Movimento Cattolico in Italia, II, I Protagonisti*, Casale Monferrato, 1982, 129–156.

With the archbishoprics of Turin, Florence, Rome (the pope's vicar), Palermo, Naples, Venice, and Milan, Bologna was traditionally a 'cardinalatial' see, but it was seven years before Archbishop Della Chiesa received his red hat. This is only explicable in terms of a powerful blocking lobby in the Roman curia. Not until May 1914 did Pius X announce the name of Della Chiesa among a list of new cardinals, and there is evidence that, even then, Pius X inserted his name against the advice of his Cardinal Secretary of State.[23]

Della Chiesa's banishment to Bologna was comparable to the exile of Msgr Giovanni Battista Montini (later Pope Paul VI) to Milan in 1954 as Falconi argues,[24] and it provided him with the experience of the diverse demands of the pastoral office of a bishop which made his election to the papacy in 1914 possible.

CONCLAVE

As Albert Monticone has pointed out, the First World War was a battle between two 'opposing cultures, economies, political-social models on the basis of which the decisive armed confrontation had been prepared for years'.[25] This conflict inevitably manifested itself in the conclave of 1914. A leading contemporary Italian Catholic journalist described the meeting of the Belgian Cardinal Mercier and Cardinal Hartmann of Cologne: 'I hope', said Hartmann, 'that we shall not speak of war.' 'And I hope that we shall not speak of peace,' came back the tart reply.[26] More seriously than this anecdotal evidence is the fact that, as the conclave opened, German Catholics presented a declaration to the cardinals, justifying their government's decision to go to war, and a reply by French and Belgian Catholics was also received.[27] The war inevitably weighed heavily upon the minds of the cardinal electors. The international situation made the election of a non-Italian pope unlikely because thirty-five out of the sixty-six cardinals eligible to vote were Italians, and eighteen of the thirty-one non-Italian cardinals belonged to one or other of the belligerents,[28] whereas at this stage of the war Italy was still neutral. It also ruled out the election of any Italian who had served as nuncio to any of the warring powers in the previous decades, like Domenico Ferrata (Paris) or Antonio Agliardi (Vienna and Munich). But as important, if not more, than

[23] S. Leslie, *Cardinal Gasquet: A Memoir*, London, 1953, 94.
[24] Falconi, *The Popes*, 108.
[25] A. Monticone, *Nitti e la Grande Guerra, 1914–1918*, Milan, 1961, 155.
[26] E. Vercesi, *Il Vaticano, l'Italia e la guerra*, Rome, 1925, 65.
[27] M. Liebman, 'Journal secret d'un conclave', *La Revue Nouvelle*, 19(38) (1963), 37.
[28] For an account of the 1914 conclave, see Zizola, *Il Conclave*, 190–196.

the international situation was the question of Pius X's legacy, whether the new pope would carry on his anti-modernist crusade and his policies towards France, or whether he would make a clean break with the past.

Until recently, the outcome of the 1914 conclave was seen as being uncertain until the end, or a surprise, with Della Chiesa emerging as a kind of compromise candidate or transitional pope, like John XXIII.[29] It is now clear, however, that Della Chiesa was a major front-runner from the start and, moreover, that he was the only candidate who consistently increased his vote (apart from the fifth round).[30] Indeed, there were attempts during the conclave to prevent the election of the archbishop of Bologna, according to Cardinal Piffl, Archbishop of Vienna, whose diary, written in strict violation of Pius X's rules about secrecy, provides an accurate account of the battles. Attempts were first made by the supporters of Cardinal Maffi, archbishop of Pisa, to deny votes to Della Chiesa by claiming that he was '*un mediocris homo*', 'a mere bureaucrat'.[31] Cardinal Hartman also tried to persuade his German and Austro-Hungarian colleagues not to vote for Della Chiesa because he was 'anti-German' and so his election would be an insult to the memory of Pius X.[32] When Della Chiesa was elected, Cardinal De Lai, the leader of the intégriste faction, demanded an examination of the ballots to ensure that Della Chiesa had not voted for himself. If this was meant as a shot across the new pope's bows to remind him of the power of the curial block, it did not work.

The election of Della Chiesa can be explained by a variety of reasons. Firstly, Maffi was too 'modern' and Italian for many Italians and non-Italians alike. Like Maffi, Della Chiesa was clearly a candidate opposed to the policies of Pius X and Merry del Val but was moderate in his anti-integralism. In international affairs, he was seen by some to be anti-Austrian whereas Piffl's diary says that the five Austrian cardinals present consistently voted for him. We do not know the French voted, but it is unlikely that they voted in a united fashion or that they were prejudiced against him. This ensured a sympathetic reception from both the Entente and Central Powers.

And though Della Chiesa was not as demonstrably pro-Italian as Maffi, there was no reason for the Italian government to have had reservations about his election, and this was important. The trouble to which the Italian government had gone to in order to be seen to apply the Law of Guarantees during the conclave demonstrates the importance to both sides of good Italo-Vatican relations at this time.

[29] Schmidlin, *Papstgeschichte*, III, 189, fn 123; Sforza, *Contemporary Italy*, 163–164; and G. Seldes, *The Vatican: Yesterday, Today, Tomorrow*, New York, 1934, 111–112.

[30] Zizola, *Il Conclave*, 195.

[31] Liebman, 'Journal secret', 45.

[32] Liebman, 'Journal secret', 45.

Ultimately, the election of Della Chiesa was a very rational choice because of all the 'serious' candidates—Maffi, Basilio Pompilii, Merry del Val, Domenico Serafini, Ferrari, and himself—he had easily the best mix of curial, diplomatic, and pastoral experience required of a pope facing the horrors and uncertainties of the First World War: in this sense, his was a model *curriculum vita* for a twentieth-century pope, certainly much more so than that of either his two immediate successors. His election also represented a clear break with the past and with the pontificate of his predecessor, especially as regards the question of modernism, which is why he eschewed the name 'Pius' and chose 'Benedict', which was, among other things, the name of the last archbishop of Bologna to be elected pope, Prospero Lambertini. Della Chiesa acted decisively after his election, banishing Merry del Val to the insignificant curial office of prefect of the congregation responsible for the fabric of St Peter's, while two more 'troublemakers', Monsignori Benigni and Canali, were also demoted. As Secretary of State in place of Merry del Val he chose Cardinal Ferrata, and when the latter died within a few weeks, his long-time colleague Pietro Gasparri. He declined a grand coronation in St Peter's and insisted on a ceremony in minor key in the Sistine Chapel in deference to the terrible suffering which had already engulfed the people of Europe.

THE VATICAN DURING THE FIRST WORLD WAR

Over four out of the seven and a half years of Benedict's pontificate lay under the shadow of the First World War. It is inevitable, therefore, that much of the most recent literature on the pontificate is concerned with Benedict and the war, and with the controversies surrounding his diplomacy during the course of it, in particular the most well-known of all his acts, the 'peace note' of August 1917. Initially, at least, the diplomatic policy of Benedict and Gasparri did not differ very much from that of Pius X and Merry del Val. Almost immediately after his election, the new pope made his first pronouncement on the War. On the 8 September 1914, he repeated his predecessor's call for prayers to end the war, and included an appeal to the powers for peace. Though the statement lacked neither force nor urgency, there was still a feeling in the Vatican, as elsewhere, that the war would be over by Christmas. But by 1 November, when Benedict published his first encyclical, *Ad Beatissimi*, no such illusion could be maintained. The Battle of the Marne in early to mid-September brought the stalemate of trench warfare to the West; the Western Front was effectively established by the end of that month and the battle of Ypres a month later confirmed it. The military situation on the Eastern Front, between Germany and Austria-Hungary on the one hand and Russia on the other, while more fluid, was no less undecided. Turkey's junction with the

Central Powers and declaration of war on its Slav neighbour at the beginning of October made victory on the part of the 'Russian steamroller' less likely.

In his encyclical *Ad Beatissimi*, Benedict addressed himself to the causes of the war, as well as to its consequences. According to his analysis, the causes had their origins in the ills afflicting the whole of human society. He castigated the current 'contempt for authority, the injustice in the relations between classes and the attainment of material goods made into the sole object of human activity and the unrestrained striving after independence', which can be interpreted as a broad attack on liberal individualism in general. In a paragraph with the interesting title of 'The Classes and the Masses', he condemned 'class hatred', and, in particular, frequent strikes, without, however, reiterating Leo XIII's criticisms of the capitalist system against which the strikes were directed.[33] In his analysis of the specific causes of the war, he drew attention to the 'absence in relations between men of mutual love with their fellow men'.[34] Once again condemning the horrors of the war in no uncertain terms, he urged its solution by declaring, 'Surely there are other ways and means whereby violated rights can be rectified?', but as yet, he offered no clear, practical answer to his own rhetorical question.[35]

Ad Beatissimi was to be the first of many attempts on Benedict's part to bring about an end to the war. In allocutions and encyclicals, in other public statements, and, above all, in careful, patient, secret negotiations, he and Gasparri repeatedly sought first to prevent the war from spreading, as in the months leading up to both the entry of Italy into the conflict in May 1915 and that of the USA in April 1917, and then to bring the two sides to the negotiating table. It is the sheer, dogged persistence of their efforts that is so impressive, as is their work to provide humanitarian aid to both military and civilian victims of the conflict on both sides. As the Vicar of 'the Prince of Peace', Benedict genuinely believed it to be his duty to do no less, and in pursuit of those aims he and Gasparri sought to preserve a stance of impartiality for the Vatican which the latter justified on the grounds of the 'paternal-universal character of the pope and the supreme interest of the Church'.[36]

While virtually no biographer or historian doubts the underlying benevolence, pacifism, and humanitarianism of Benedict's motives, some historians and contemporary observers have challenged the impartiality of Vatican diplomacy during the course of the conflict, and its disinterestedness. Dragan Zivojinovic, for example, has argued that, 'Although the Vatican pretended to be impartial and neutral, there is now evidence that its sympathies lay

[33] Carlen, *Papal Encyclicals*, III, 146.
[34] Carlen, *Papal Encyclicals*, III, 146.
[35] Carlen, *Papal Encyclicals*, III, 145.
[36] ASV, AES, Italia, 1427, fasc. 569, Imparzialità della S. Sede, memorandum by Gasparri (n.d.).

with the Central Powers, particularly Austria-Hungary.'[37] These are serious allegations, echoing contemporary claims from the beginning of the conflict that the Vatican was sympathetic towards the Central Powers, Germany and Austria-Hungary, to the point that Benedict was regularly described as the 'Pape boche' in the French press. This sort of criticism came not only from hostile, anti-clerical quarters. Cardinal Aidan Gasquet, Britain's only curial cardinal in 1914, was appalled by the pro-German atmosphere which he found in the Roman curia, and among the Italian Catholic clergy and laity in general. In November 1914, in a letter to British Foreign Secretary, Lord Grey, about the imminent arrival of a British mission to the Vatican, in whose genesis he himself had played an important part, he wrote:

> The Pope and his Secretary have been quite correct in their attitude, but the mentality of the clergy generally is astounding . . . Germany and Austria and Bavaria have been at work for the past two years and more and when the War started they had the ground well-prepared. Prussia does not leave things to chance and had a good deal of wisdom of the serpent.[38]

Even allowing for Gasquet's patriotic passion, his interpretation of the situation is broadly supported by others. Matthias Erzberger, an influential German Catholic politician, confirmed the strength of the German lobby in the Vatican in a report on his visit to Rome in the spring of 1915, when he sought to dissuade Italian politicians from going to war against Austria.[39] Monticone provides a very clear and plausible explanation of the situation which Gasquet so strongly deplored, and which led to repeated accusations of partiality for the Central Powers on the Vatican's behalf. He argues that, on the one hand, there were strong German influences, political and cultural, in the Vatican due to 'the gamut of German research projects, publications and conferences in Rome on theological, ecclesiological and spiritual topics', whereas, 'there was on the other hand a crisis in the relationship with French culture', due, no doubt, to the 'Modernist' leanings of so many French Catholic intellectuals: he also points to the influence of the Germans and Austro-Hungarians in the Jesuit headquarters in Rome, especially Wlodimir Ledóchowski, who was elected father general of the Society in 1915. The predominance of German and Austro-Hungarian influences in the Vatican merely reflected the broader hegemony of those influences in Italy, as a result of that country's thirty-year adherence to the Triple Alliance.

[37] D.R. Zivojinovic, *The United States and the Vatican Policies, 1914–1918*, Boulder, CO, 1978, 4.

[38] As quoted in Leslie, *Cardinal Gasquet*, 214: this book chronicles the indefatigable efforts of Gasquet and his colleagues to offset German and Austro-Hungarian influences in the Vatican, especially in the period before Italy's entry into the war in May 1915.

[39] K. Epstein, *Matthias Erzberger and the Dilemma of German Democracy*, Princeton, NJ, 1959, 121.

This situation was not helped by the poor relations between the Entente Powers and the Vatican. The Central Powers had three diplomatic representatives at the papal court: in addition to the Austro-Hungarian ambassador there were envoys for Prussia and for Bavaria, the two major states of the German Empire. The Entente had only two, the Russian and Belgian envoys. The former had little influence due to the tensions in the Holy See's relations with Orthodox Russia, as a result of which no nuncio was permitted in St Petersburg,[40] and the Belgian ambassador had little clout either. Indeed, contemporary commentators were unanimous in describing the lack of sympathy with which the plight of Belgium (and Serbia) was greeted in the conclave of 1914.[41] Even Gasparri had little time for Belgian claims of victimization, declaring that the little kingdom should have given way to the German invasion.[42] In part, the Entente powers were to blame for this situation: as has been seen, Britain had not had a representative visit the Holy See since the 1870s and France had ruptured relations with the Holy See in 1905. Zivojinovic argues that Benedict was partial to the Central Powers because 'he was elected with Austrian influence' and because he was dependent on Erzberger, the German Centre Party leader, on account of his fund-raising activities on the pope's behalf: 'This relieved the pope's situation but made him, and the curia, dependent upon Germany and on occasion ready to voice views that reflected Germany's desires and needs.'[43] Zivojinovic's allegations are based on evidence in the Erzberger papers, which claim that the Vatican was almost bankrupt at the death of Pius X, and that his successor could hardly pay his staff.[44] In fact, Benedict inherited a relatively strong financial position at his election.[45] In any case, as Pfiffl's diary demonstrates, Benedict was fortunate to have obtained the support of the Austro-Hungarian cardinals, though it also shows that their government was less than enthusiastic about him, and that Cardinal Hartmann's voting reflected the German government's distinct hostility to his candidature (Chapter 2). Again, though the inflow of monies from Peter's Pence was disrupted by the war, at a time when the Vatican was spending big sums on relief work, Benedict received increasingly large sums from the United States,[46] but no one has suggested that he was in any way influenced in his policy towards that country as a result. Perhaps the last word should be left

[40] See E. Hachey (ed.), *Anglo-Vatican Relations*, Boston, MA, 1972, 34, where the British minister wrote that so bad were relations with Russia that its envoy to the Vatican, Nelidorf, was virtually *persona non grata*.

[41] Hachey, *Anglo-Vatican Relations*, 213–214.

[42] Hachey, *Anglo-Vatican Relations*, 213–214.

[43] Zivojinovic, *The United States*, 12–13.

[44] See Epstein, *Matthias Erzberger*, 408–409.

[45] Pollard, *Money*, 111–12.

[46] A. Scottà (ed.), *La Conciliazione ufficiosa. Diario del barone Carlo Monti 'incaricato d'affari' del governo italiano presso la Santa Sede (1914–1922)*, 2 vols, Vatican City, 1997, II, January 1917 (henceforth *Diario*), where Monti says that Benedict told him the bulk of Peter's Pence came from first the United States and then Germany.

to J.D. Gregory, a member of the British Legation to the Holy See, who on other matters was highly critical of Benedict, but who said of him: 'I am convinced that he is not either temperamentally or politically pro-German.'[47]

What is much more convincing about Zivojinovic's interpretation of the general thrust of Vatican policies and sympathies during the First World War is his claim that Benedict and Gasparri were essentially committed to the preservation or restoration of the status quo: there is even a lot to be said for his argument that it was this obsession, in a rapidly changing international situation, which rendered nugatory many of Benedict's peace efforts.[48] Benedict's instincts were conservative, especially in foreign relations. It was essentially in the interests of the Holy See that the international status quo be preserved. Benedict and Gasparri were also very aware of the threat which the disruptive forces of socialism and anarchism posed to the social and political order. In particular, they could not be indifferent to the fate of Austria-Hungary, the last Catholic great power and a bulwark against Russian Orthodoxy and Pan-Slavism.[49] The collapse of the Central Powers was no more desirable than the westward and southward march of a victorious Russia, which might end in the seizure of Istanbul/Constantinople and the erection of Santa Sofia into a sort of Orthodox St Peter's. The commitments which Britain and France had given to Russia on the eventual partition of the Ottoman Empire were a constant source of anxiety in the Vatican. Gregory claimed that Benedict was obsessed with Russia.[50] Sir Henry Howard, British minister to the Vatican, explained why in a report to London:

> The Vatican is filled with alarm and foreboding by the agreement made between H.M.'s Government and Russia, giving Russia possession of Santa Sophia, with an extraterritorial zone to which the (Russian) Holy Synod may be transferred—the erection of a rival establishment, as it were, to the Vatican on the shores of the Bosphorus. This can later lead, the Vatican believes, to the Orthodox Church extending its sway to the shore of the Adriatic.[51]

Gasparri confirmed these fears to Carlo Monti: 'the installation of the Russians in Constantinople would be a grave blow to the interests of Catholicism', and for Monti's benefit he added that it would undermine Italian influence in the East as well.[52]

[47] Gregory, *On the Edge of Diplomacy*, 17.

[48] Zivojinovic, *The United States*, 12.

[49] A. Monticone, 'Benedetto XV e la Germania', in G. Rumi (ed.), *Benedetto XV e la Pace—1918*, Brescia, 1990, 22, also makes the point that there was traditionally a close personal relationship between the popes and the Habsburg family in the nineteenth century: 'The archdukes of the various branches of the Habsburgs grew up in comparative familiarity with the pope: from Vienna came ingenuous poetry and hand-knitted goods and Rome replied with medals and objects of personal devotion.'

[50] A. Randall, *Vatican Assignment*, London, 1956, 13.

[51] Quoted in Hachey, *Anglo-Vatican Relations*, xx.

[52] *Diario*, I, 416, 9 August 1916.

The Vatican was not entirely neutral in its attitudes towards France and Britain either, because the former, or at least its government, was strongly Masonic and anti-clerical, and the latter was Protestant. Though, as Vistalli has argued, the French and Belgians were both fundamentally Catholic peoples and the British Empire contained significant Catholic minorities,[53] the Vatican had feared their victory, but it also had a lot to fear from that of a Protestant, Prussian-dominated Germany dragging the Catholic Habsburg Empire in its wake. Even allowing for the unhappy plight of Catholics in Russia, the maintenance of the *status quo ante* suited the Vatican best. Though their views were to change as time passed and circumstances changed, at the beginning of the conflict Benedict and Gasparri sought an alteration of the international status quo as they understood it in only one respect; they obviously desired a revision of what they saw as the very unsatisfactory relationship between the Holy See and Italy. This, and the broader aim of seeking to restore the Holy See's international influence and prestige, were powerful influences on the Vatican's diplomatic activities between 1914 and 1920. While it is undeniably true that the underlying motive for the Vatican's attempts to mediate between the belligerents was the desire to end what Benedict described in his peace note of August 1917 as the 'useless slaughter' of the war as quickly as possible, such efforts would and did lead to what the Italian historian Italo Garzia describes as 'a greater international presence' for the Holy See.[54] Under Benedict and Gasparri the Vatican was not, therefore, a totally disinterested observer during the First World War.

The outbreak of the First World War certainly led to a change in the international standing of the Holy See. Governments quickly grasped the potential moral importance of the pope as a neutral, given the large numbers of Catholics on all sides. President Poincaré of France sent a carefully neutral but cordial reply to Benedict's letter informing him of his election,[55] and both Germany and Austria put aside initial reservations to woo the new pontiff.[56] As has been seen, even the usually sceptical and suspicious Italian government recognized the potentially enhanced international position of the Holy See by quickly establishing a permanent channel of communication with the newly elected pontiff through Monti.[57] Within five months of the outbreak of the war, the British government also recognized the pope's new position, as well as the pernicious effects of the palpably strong influence of the Central Powers at the papal court, by sending a diplomatic envoy to the Vatican. The French at first opposed this initiative, and then confirmed its wisdom by

[53] Vistalli, *Benedetto XV*, 39.

[54] I. Garzia, *La Questione Romana durante la I guerra mondiale*, Naples, 1981, 68.

[55] R. Poincaré, *Au Service de la France*, vol. V, Paris, 1928, 305–306.

[56] Garzia, *La Questione Romana*, 14.

[57] For an account of the circumstances in which Monti began his role as go-between, see *Diario*, I, 171–174.

stationing an unofficial envoy to the Vatican, M. Loiseau, in Rome.[58] At the end of 1915, the Kingdom of the Netherlands also re-established relations with the Vatican, sending an envoy to the pope in order to foster its plans for a peace conference to be held in The Hague.[59] In 1915, a special, non-diplomatic, papal delegation in Berne, the first since Switzerland had broken off relations in 1873, was established to supervise joint Swiss–Vatican humanitarian efforts. It was also useful in the Vatican's attempts to bring about peace, since the Swiss capital was to be the scene of various peace initiatives (as well as being a spy centre) throughout the war.[60] The British legation at the Holy See quickly grasped the significance of these developments; it realized that, in collaboration with other members of the 'league of neutrals'—the Netherlands, Spain, Switzerland, and perhaps even the United States—the Holy See was building the potential for a serious peace effort.[61] The reaction of the Italian government was rather different and offers the strongest evidence that these developments constituted an enormous increase in the international standing of the Holy See, with the potential to upset the balance of power between the Vatican and Rome. Despite her own improved, albeit unofficial, relations with the pope, Italy sought to dissuade all three powers from establishing relations with him for fear that they would strengthen Benedict in demands for a satisfactory settlement of the Roman Question.[62]

Recognition of its importance as a moral authority also had drawbacks for the Vatican; belligerents on both sides sought to appeal to its authority in pursuit of their own agendas. The Entente powers were especially anxious to elicit the moral condemnation of the pope for the German violation of Belgian neutrality and also German atrocities in Belgium, most notably the sack of Louvain and the burning of its university library. Another major cause of complaint was the enforced labour and, even worse, deportations of civilian populations from northern France. The representatives of the Allied governments at the Vatican, not to mention the press in Britain, France, and Belgium, repeatedly demanded that Benedict condemn these, and other, manifestations of German 'frightfulness'.[63] The Vatican's response to these demands was to point out that it was receiving complaints about the other's behaviour from both sides, not just from the Entente. Thus in 1916, Russia was accused by the Germans of sending 1,500 Jewish families into the front

[58] C. Loiseau, 'Ma mission auprès du Vatican (1914–1918)', *Revue d'histoire diplomatique*, 64 (1966), 100; and 'Une mission près le Saint-Siège, 1914–1919', *Revue des Deux Mondes* (May 1956), 54.

[59] Garzia, *La Questione Romana*, 61.

[60] F. Panzera, 'Benedetto XV e la Svizzera negli anni della Grande Guerra', *Rivista Storica Svizzera*, 43 (1993), 323.

[61] Gregory, *On the Edge of Diplomacy*, 87.

[62] Report of Count De Salis, British minister to the Vatican, on his mission, in Hachey, *Anglo-Vatican Relations*, 7.

[63] Hachey, *Anglo-Vatican Relations*, 7.

line as human shields on the Eastern Front, and in 1917 Germany also complained about the mistreatment of civilian populations by black British and French troops.[64] Indeed, by the end of the war, the Vatican Archives were bulging with 'white', 'grey', 'green', and 'orange books' produced by belligerents on both sides containing accounts of alleged atrocities perpetrated by the enemy, along with carefully argued and documented ripostes to them.[65]

The Vatican argued, and quite reasonably, that before it could pass judgement it would need to examine all allegations, thus turning itself into a veritable court of justice, a kind of international war crimes commission for which, of course, it was not equipped: in any case, the nature of the conflict would have made it almost always impossible to carry out proper investigations of the facts.[66] Even in the apparently open-and-shut case of the violation of Belgian neutrality, the Germans produced a weighty tome of evidence in support of their contention that the Belgians had already violated their own neutrality by conversations with the French high command before the outbreak of the war, and that Belgian civilians had repeatedly broken the rules of war by firing on German soldiers.[67] Gasparri's other argument was that condemnations would have impeded the pope's humanitarian work, of which the Entente countries were the chief beneficiary, but 'the Holy See preferred the good of suffering humanity'.[68] And when the question of responding to demands for the condemnation of atrocities by various powers came up in the Sacred Congregation for Extraordinary Ecclesiastical Affairs, the consultative body of the Secretariat of State, the very pertinent point was made by more than one cardinal member that such condemnations could seriously damage the Holy See's peace efforts.[69]

In the end, the Vatican limited itself to private protests and generic public statements, a condemnation of all atrocities by all sides, as on 22 January 1915, when Benedict declared, in a consistorial allocution, 'And We do proclaim it

[64] ASV, AES, Stati Eccl., 1316, fasc. 455, Libri diplomatici pubblicati da vari Stati belligeranti, Libro bianco tedesco sulle crudeltà delle truppe russe contro i civili e i prigionieri di guerra tedeschi.

[65] ASV, AES, Stati Eccl., 1316, fasc. 455, Libri diplomatici pubblicati da vari Stati belligeranti, Libro bianco tedesco sulle crudeltà delle truppe russe contro i civili e i prigionieri di guerra tedeschi. This file contains fifteen such complaints from the various belligerents, plus from one neutral—Holland.

[66] The Holy See did possess at this time two major tribunals, the Segnatura and the Sacra Rota, but both were, of course, competent only in canon law, and not civil/public law of any kind.

[67] ASV, AES, Stati Eccl., 1316, fasc. 455, Germania-Inghilterra-Austria-Francia-Belgio-Olanda, 1914–1918, Libro tedesco sulla neutralità violata dal Belgio.

[68] ASV, AES, Stati Eccl., 1316, 1427, fasc. 569, Imparzialità della S. Sede, 9.

[69] ASV, AES, Stati Eccl., 1369/1372, fasc. 517, Sessioni, minutes of meeting of 16 August 1916; the Italian historian Luigi Salvatorelli, *La Politica della Santa Sede dopo la guerra*, Milan, 1937, 9–10, was of the same opinion: 'It was difficult for the Vatican to try to act as a moral arbiter in the conflict. The Vatican was liable to find itself utterly cut off from one side or another.'

without modification, condemning openly every injustice by whatever side it has been committed.'[70] When the Vatican did, very occasionally, single out an individual target, as in the condemnation of the German violation of Belgian neutrality in a note to the Belgian government in January 1915, it immediately brought down upon itself the fury of the other side. The German press waxed wrathful for several weeks and attacked Benedict as 'Der französische papst'.[71] There was another reason why Benedict was so unwilling to morally condemn the actions of either side—this was Gasparri's concern for 'the supreme interest of the Church'. War has always been a problem for a universalistic, worldwide religion like Roman Catholicism. War, and especially the First World War, which was strongly inspired by national rivalries and hatreds, cut across the loyalty and solidarity of Catholics in a damaging way for the Church. To have systematically condemned the atrocities of each side would have risked alienating the loyalty to the papacy of countless numbers of Catholics. This was exactly the same dilemma which Pius XII would face in the Second World War, albeit, given the Holocaust and other Nazi atrocities, in an even more serious form. In following his policy of impartiality, however wisely, Benedict was running grave risks. There was a great deal of hostility towards it, even among Catholics, in the countries of the Entente. Benedict's own position was in strong contrast with that of the ultra-patriotic stance of Cardinal Mercier, Primate of Belgium, who was constantly getting into serious trouble with the German occupying authorities, which caused much annoyance in the Vatican: Benedict went so far as to say, wearily, that Mercier wanted to be a 'martyr'.[72] Benedict and Gasparri tried to restrain Mercier, and at the same time protect him from the Germans.[73] Inevitably, Mercier's heroic stance was much preferred in the Entente countries, so much so that their press presented the Belgian prelate as a kind of 'anti-pope' to Benedict.[74]

ITALIAN INTERVENTION

During the first eight months of the First World War, the diplomatic policy of Benedict and Gasparri was made easier by the fact that the Vatican was the 'guest' of another neutral power, the Kingdom of Italy. All that changed

[70] As quoted in Peters, *Life of Benedict*, 121.

[71] As quoted in Peters, *Life of Benedict*, 121.

[72] *Diario*, I, 189, 19 January 1915; and R. Morozzo Della Rocca, 'Benedetto XV e nazionalismo', *Cristianesimo nella Storia*, 17 (1996), 563.

[73] Morozzo Della Rocca, 'Benedetto XV e nazionalismo', 564.

[74] Morozzo Della Rocca, 'Benedetto XV e nazionalismo', 564.

on 24 May 1915, when Italy entered the war on the side of the Entente. Italian intervention in the First World War was to cause the Vatican huge problems, conditioning the whole development of its diplomatic activity. It therefore opposed that intervention quite vigorously and actively until the last moment.

At the outbreak of the First World War in August 1914 the Italian government had remained neutral which, in the circumstances, was really the only sensible course of action. Though it was the third partner in the Triple Alliance with Germany and Austria-Hungary, Italy had nothing to gain by going to war on the side of her allies. The attempt by the government of Prime Minister Salandra and Foreign Minister Sonnino to persuade Vienna to sacrifice the 'unredeemed lands' of Trieste and Trento, two Italian-speaking territories still under Habsburg control, as the price of Italian military support, or even continuing neutrality, failed. Vienna believed that a cession of territory on the principle of nationality would undermine the whole basis of the empire. The presence of the British and French navies in the Mediterranean was a further disincentive to hostilities with the Entente. In any case, there was little support from Italian public opinion for entering the war on the side of Germany and Austria-Hungary: only the Nationalist extremists were in favour of this option.[75] But, eight months later, the Italians had abandoned neutrality and, in the secret Treaty of London, agreed to enter the war on the side of Britain, France, and Russia.

The primary motivation for intervening in the war was to complete the process of Italian unification by acquiring the 'unredeemed lands' and secure a more defensible north-eastern frontier. Italy was also made some vague promises in relation to future colonial gains in Africa and the Middle East. Another factor influencing Salandra and Sonnino in their decision to go to war was the belief that participation in a successful war would solve Italy's domestic problems by generating national unity and restoring the authority of the political class, seriously damaged, so they believed, by the compromises made by their arch-enemy, the Italian elder statesman Giovanni Giolitti, with socialism and political Catholicism in the preceding fourteen years.

As soon as they became aware of Salandra and Sonnino's intention to abandon Italian neutrality, Benedict and Gasparri opposed it. Their reasons for doing so were numerous and obvious. In the first place, they were extremely anxious to prevent an extension of the bloodletting. They also feared that an extension of the war, especially between Austro-Hungary and Italy, would prolong the conflict. Another powerful consideration was the direct threat which Italian involvement in the war posed to the survival of the Austro-Hungarian Empire: the Vatican believed the survival of that empire was central to the protection of its wider geopolitical and spiritual interests.

[75] For a detailed account of the Intervention crisis in Italy, see Seton-Watson, *Italy*, 413–450.

In this regard, in January 1915, Gasparri sent this letter to the papal nuncio in Vienna:

> At this moment, the Holy Father, who has the greatest of concern for the existence of the Austro-Hungarian Monarchy due to a particular affection towards it and its August and Venerable Sovereign, as well as for the highest interest of the Church itself, notably the survival of the only Catholic great power, not to mention peace in Italy, wishes to open his heart to the Emperor, through your good offices, advising him in the strongest possible terms to avoid war with Italy at all costs.[76]

Benedict and Gasparri were also concerned about the possible domestic consequences of Italian intervention in the conflict. After the experience of Red Week in June 1914, when there had been rioting in various parts of Italy, they seriously doubted the capacity of the Italian state to survive a major armed conflict: like many other observers, they feared that such an experience, especially if Italy were to be defeated, would precipitate social and political revolution. In this they shared the concern of Giolitti. But, of course, another serious worry was how Italian involvement in the conflict would affect the Holy See and its diplomacy, in particular, how it would affect the Law of Guarantees and the arrangements therein for the Vatican's relations with other powers: there was no provision in the Law for the eventuality in which Italy went to war against powers with whom the Holy See continued to have amicable relations. In that case, it would be difficult for the Vatican to preserve its neutrality, maintaining the distinction between its policies and those of a belligerent Italian government. Finally, according to Garzia, Benedict was afraid that if Italy entered the war she would inevitably be present at a peace conference but that the Holy See would not and would thus fail to make any improvement in its position vis-à-vis Italy.[77]

The Vatican's efforts, up to the last moment before Italian intervention, to mediate between Italy and Austro-Hungary and thus avert Italian entry into the war are thoroughly documented in the Vatican Archives. They consisted of attempts to persuade the government in Vienna to make significant territorial concessions to the Italians. In January 1915, for example, Gasparri addressed an appeal to the Emperor Franz Josef through the papal nuncio in Vienna: 'The salvation of the Empire requires the Emperor to make this painful sacrifice and to make it immediately.'[78] The Vatican also transmitted conciliatory missives between the German and Austro-Hungarian governments and Italy in the negotiations over the cession of territory in the 'unredeemed

[76] ASV, SS-Guerra, 1914–1918, rub. 244, fasc. 29, Gasparri to Scapinelli di Leguigno, 12 January 1915.

[77] Garzia, *La Questione Romana*, 20: according to Hachey, *Anglo-Vatican Relations*, xvii, the Vatican also feared for the effects of Italian intervention on the flow of Peter's Pence.

[78] ASV, SS-Guerra, 1914–1918, fasc. 258, Gasparri to Scapinelli, 17 January 1915.

lands', and over a putative German loan to Italy.[79] When it became clear that the Catholic Party in Austria was hostile to the idea of territorial concessions, the Vatican tried to use the good offices of Matthias Erzberger to dissuade them from their opposition.[80] It also sought to persuade the Italian government to accept Austrian concessions, which was difficult given the slowness and reluctance of the emperor and his foreign minister, Burián.[81] As late as 18 May, Benedict was still trying to persuade Salandra that the Austrians would make satisfactory concessions.[82]

The serious consequences for the Vatican of Italy's entry into the war very quickly became apparent. The position of the embassies of Austria-Hungary and the German states was crucial. The Law of Guarantees did not recognize the Vatican as an independent, sovereign state; indeed, the Holy See was not even the legal owner of the Vatican and Lateran palaces, and such like, because the Law only said that the pope 'enjoyed' their use.[83] When the Italian government asked the Vatican to take moral responsibility for the good behaviour of the embassies if they remained on Italian soil, so that they would not constitute a threat to Italian security, Benedict and Gasparri refused, preferring them to withdraw to Switzerland for the duration of hostilities. Taking responsibility for their good behaviour would have involved supervising their telegram traffic with Berlin and Vienna. While there is some evidence that the Central Powers rather relished the 'banishment' of their embassies to the Vatican, since it made it possible for their propaganda to paint the intentions of the Italian government in a bad light,[84] with the departure of their embassies the balance swung against the influence of Germans and Austrians in the Vatican. The Germans in particular feared the obstruction of communication with the Vatican would impede their influence there, which was one reason why they proposed various territorial solutions of the Roman Question: the other was to embarrass the Italians.[85] Benedict and Gasparri seriously considered asking the embassies of the Entente powers to withdraw as well in order to preserve the appearance of Vatican neutrality, but abandoned the idea as unnecessary and counterproductive: it would have intensified the Vatican's difficulties in communicating with powers.[86]

The seizure of Palazzo Venezia, the former embassy of Austria to the Holy See, by the Italian government in August 1916, following one of the

[79] ASV, SS-Guerra, 1914–1918, fasc. 258, Gasparri to Scapinelli, 17 January 1915.

[80] ASV, SS-Guerra, 1914–1918, fasc. 29, Erzberger to Benedict, 8 March 1915.

[81] ASV, SS-Guerra, 1914–1918, fasc. 29, Salandra to Gasparri, 8 March 1915.

[82] Seton-Watson, *Italy*, 448.

[83] For the text, see Pollard, *The Vatican and Italian Fascism*, 195–196.

[84] *Diario*, I, 219, 24 January 1915.

[85] S.A. Stehlin, 'Germany and a Proposed Vatican State, 1915–1917', *The Catholic Historical Review*, 60(3) (October 1974), 402–406.

[86] Garzia, *La Questione Romana*, 61.

first Austrian air raids on Italian cities with resulting civilian casualties, in this case Venice, caused alarm in the Vatican and tense relations with Italy. Benedict claimed that the incident once more demonstrated the inadequacies of the Law of Guarantees, fearing that the Vatican itself might suffer the same fate as Palazzo Venezia at the hands of an Italian government of a more strongly anti-clerical colour.[87] His worst fears appeared to have been realized when the Italian government laid claim to the Collegio Teutonico, the German college which lay on the very edge of the Vatican, even though the attempt failed.[88] The exigencies of the war also produced practical inconveniences for the Vatican, such as the call-up of its staff, lay and ecclesiastical, members of the papal court, and even high-ranking prelates: thus Monti spent much time seeking exemptions for members of the various 'armed forces' of the Vatican, especially the Noble Guard, and leading ecclesiastics, including Monsignori Pacelli and Tedeschini.[89]

The withdrawal of the Austrian and German embassies to Switzerland caused precisely the problems of communication for the Vatican which had been predicted, but the problem went further than that. Telegram and mail traffic to and from the Vatican was frequently subject to Italian censorship, causing enormous delays, much to Benedict's fury. Through Monti, and other go-betweens, Benedict and Gasparri repeatedly protested against these abuses.[90] The use of Vatican diplomatic bags (or those of other neutral powers) was no solution either, as Italy and other belligerent powers on both sides were not averse to intercepting them and, according to Alvarez, Italy had cracked all the Vatican's codes and cyphers and was reading all its telegraph traffic.[91] Another consequence of Italy's entry into the war was that *L'Osservatore Romano* and the Jesuit journal, *La Civiltà Cattolica*, were censored like any other Italian newspapers. Benedict felt, and not without reason, that the military censors were rather more lenient towards the anti-clerical rather than the Catholic press, with serious consequences for him during moments of tension between the Vatican and Italy. He repeatedly complained that his enemies were allowed to slander and insult him at will, but *L'Osservatore Romano*, and other Catholic newspapers, were frequently muzzled when they tried to defend him, the most notable example being when the anti-clerical journal *Il Travaso* produced a scurrilous poem against the pope.[92] Though the Italians

[87] *Diario*, I, 437, 30 August 1916.

[88] ASV, AES, 953, 343–344, Roma, 1918–1920, Ospizio di S. Maria del Anima e Campo Santo confisca.

[89] There are numerous references in the *Diario* to the exemptions which Monti was asked to obtain; see, for example, volume I, 212–213, 20 March 1915.

[90] G. Felice, *Il Cardinale Pietro Gasparri*, Milan, n.d., 169–177.

[91] D. Alvarez, *Spies in the Vatican: Espionage and Intrigue from Napoleon to the Holocaust*, Lawrence, KS, 2002, 108–110.

[92] *Diario*, I, 241, 4 July 1915.

did not impede the visits of ecclesiastics of enemy powers, like Cardinal Hartmann for example, they subjected them to intolerable surveillance.[93] The German Emperor even complained that, due to Italian pressure, the Vatican was failing to appoint the numbers of German and Austrian cardinals which the size of the Catholic populations of the Central Powers merited.[94] The precariousness of the pope's position in an Italy at war was revealed in an even more acute way in November 1916 when the Emperor Franz Josef died. Before the solemn requiem Mass for the deceased Catholic head of state in the semi-private Chapel of the Countess Matilda in the Vatican Palace, Benedict was obliged to seek assurances from the Italian government, via Monti, that it would maintain law and order during the proceedings.[95]

In these circumstances, as Garzia demonstrates, though direct, informal relations between Italy and the Holy See usually remained satisfactory, the Roman Question had once again become a real issue in their relationship, after years of merely ritual protests, and had returned to the international agenda.[96] The Spaniards, hoping to exploit their former links with Benedict in an attempt to play a major role in international affairs by once more by hosting a peace conference in Madrid, also offered the pope 'sanctuary' in the Escorial in May 1915.[97] Benedict turned down the offer: in fact, he never intended to leave Rome, and certainly the situation in Rome at that time did not warrant it, though there is evidence of plans being drawn up for such a contingency.[98] A more significant initiative was that of the Central Powers, who sought to exploit the revival of the Roman Question as a weapon against Italy. In October 1915, Mathias Erzberger, on behalf of the German Centre Party, proposed that the Law of Guarantees be amended to provide the papacy with territorial sovereignty over the Vatican and adjacent areas down to the Tiber, commutation of the financial obligations of Italy to the papacy, and international guarantees of the new order.[99] This found no favour in the Vatican. Indeed, Gasparri felt compelled to distance the Vatican from this partisan initiative. In an interview with *Il Corriere della Sera* on 28 June 1915 he insisted that the Holy See was not interested in foreign schemes but rather that it expected, 'an appropriate resolution of its situation not from foreign arms but from the triumph of those sentiments of justice which it is hoped will become stronger in the Italian people in accordance with their real interests'.[100]

[93] *Diario*, I, 293, 1 December 1915.

[94] Stehlin, 'Germany and a Proposed Vatican State', 420.

[95] ASV, AES, Italia, 879, fasc. 316, 1916, Cappella papale per i funerali dell'Imperatore d'Austria.

[96] Garzia, *La Questione Romana*, 105.

[97] Garzia, *La Questione Romana*, 105.

[98] ASV, AES, Italia e Principato di Monaco, 1369/1372, 517, pro-memoria of 10 August 1917.

[99] Epstein, *Matthias Erzberger*, 144–145.

[100] As quoted in G. Dalla Torre, *Memorie*, Verona, 1965, 1292.

This declaration would later make a negotiated solution of the Roman Question possible, but it was too late to prevent the Italian government from striking a decisive diplomatic blow against the Vatican. In the autumn of 1914, Sonnino became alarmed by evidence that the Vatican was determined to get to the peace conference, by further evidence that the victorious Central Powers would use that conference to impose a solution of the Roman Question upon Italy, and by an earlier, ingenious plan of Erzberger's for resolving the Roman Question and avoiding Italian intervention.[101] In response, he insisted upon inserting into the Treaty of London, signed with the Entente powers, a clause ruling out the possibility of a papal representative participating in an eventual conference:

> France, Great Britain and Russia shall support any such opposition as Italy shall make to any proposal in the direction of introducing a representative of the Holy See in any peace negotiations or negotiations for the settlement of questions raised by the war.[102]

News of this clause reached the ears of the Benedict and Gasparri in January 1916, but was not confirmed until the Bolsheviks published the texts of all the secret treaties they had found in the foreign office archives in Petrograd in December 1917.[103] Until the last, however, various members of the Italian government, including Salandra, Sonnino, and Orlando, persistently denied the existence of the clause, which did nothing to strengthen Benedict's trust in them.[104]

While Italy had remained neutral, the bulk of Italian Catholics had also preserved a neutralist stance. That stance can be explained by a number of factors. There was a vein of stubborn Catholic intransigence whose sympathies inevitably lay with Catholic Austria rather than with the 'Masonic', democratic, and Protestant or Orthodox powers of the Entente.[105] Although Benedict himself never used the 'Just War' theory, a key argument of Catholic supporters of neutrality was that Italian intervention against Austria could not be justified on the grounds of defence.[106] But this feeling was restricted to a small part of the Catholic clergy and intelligentsia: the main source of opposition ultimately came from the grass roots of the Catholic movement, and in particular from the Catholic peasantry who, like their Socialist counterparts, knew only too well that, in the event of war, they would provide the 'trench fodder'. The neutral stance of the papacy itself was a very powerful influence on Italian Catholics, but when the Italian parliament voted for intervention in May 1915, Catholics were deeply split, with some leaders of

[101] Epstein, *Matthias Erzberger*, 144–145.

[102] As quoted in J.A.S. Grenville, *The Major International Treaties, 1914–1945: A History and Guide with Texts*, London, n.d., 24–27.

[103] Seton-Watson, *Italy*, 449.

[104] *Diario*, I, 339, 28 January 1916.

[105] Dalla Torre, *Memorie*, 1294.

[106] Dalla Torre, *Memorie*, 1294.

the Catholic movement, like Father Luigi Sturzo and Filippo Meda, opting for war and Guido Miglioli, the leader of Catholic peasants, remaining neutralist to the end.[107] In response to this situation, Giuseppe Dalla Torre, by now the national president of the Catholic Unione Popolare, the precursor of the future organization Catholic Action, followed his instructions from the Vatican and laid down an official Catholic line: 'All support for the war, but no responsibility for it.'[108] This did not make the Church popular with the interventionists, who included the vociferous, violently anti-clerical Futurists and former extreme left elements, most notably Benito Mussolini. Equally, Benedict XV was not happy with the more markedly pro-war, patriotic tone of some Catholic associations and clergy.[109] It was a difficult, confused situation. Italian intervention had undermined Benedict's peace hopes and efforts, but the patriotic enthusiasm of Italian Catholics could also very easily compromise the Vatican's neutrality in the eyes of the Central Powers: *L'Osservatore Romano*, prompted by the pope, displayed a predictable coolness to the announcement of the entry of Catholic parliamentarian Filippo Meda into the Boselli government in 1916.[110] Meda's appointment was meant to signify the inclusion of even the Catholics in a government of 'national solidarity', but Benedict insisted that 'Meda only represents Meda', a rather unrealistic attitude in the circumstances.[111] On the other hand, he complied when asked by the Italian government to mobilize the support of bishops and clergy for the war effort, and in particular for government loans.[112] Ironically, the contribution of Italian Catholics to the patriotic cause was never enough to satisfy most interventionists, and particularly their press.

THE GERLACH AFFAIR

In January 1917 Benedict was faced by a scandal, 'the Gerlach affair', which threatened to seriously damage Italo-Vatican relations and thoroughly undermine the credibility of the pope's neutralist stance. Italian police investigations, following the blowing up of two Italian battleships, eventually led

[107] For an account of the behaviour of Italian Catholics during the Intervention crisis, see the essay by P. Scoppola, 'Cattolici neutralist ed interventisti alla vigilia del conflitto', in G. Rossini (ed.), *Benedetto XV, i cattolici e la prima Guerra Mondiale. Atti del convegno di studio tenuto a Spoleto nei giorni 7–8–9 settembre 1962*, Rome, 1963.

[108] As quoted in G. De Rosa, *Storia politica dell'Azione Cattolica in Italia*, vol. II, Bari, 1954, 423.

[109] F. Molinari, 'Il carteggio di Benedetto XV', 429.

[110] See Benedict's annotations of *L'Osservatore Romano* article of 14 September 1915, in ASV, SS, 1916, rub. 165, 19784, 13.

[111] F. Meda, *I cattolici e la Guerra*, Milan, 1928, 56.

[112] *Diario*, I, 315, 1 January 1916.

to Mgr Rudolph Gerlach, papal secret chamberlain, who was accused of being the leading light in an Italian espionage ring, with the role of financier and link to German and Austrian intelligence. It was bad enough that someone so close to the pope should be accused of such activities, but it was also alleged that he had maintained contact with his intelligence bosses via the Vatican diplomatic courier and brought the funds for the spies into Italy by that same means.

There does not appear to have been very much truth in the formal charges against Gerlach, even though he was convicted when the case against him and his fellow defendants came to trial, and was sentenced to life imprisonment with hard labour.[113] Much of the case rested on the testimony of renegade priest Mario Tedeschi, who claimed to have had close relations with Gerlach, but whose credibility as a witness was badly damaged by the fact that he was unable to recognize his photograph: his evidence was later cancelled from the court records and he was subsequently prosecuted for perjury.[114] One of the other accused, Valente, withdrew the charges he made against Gerlach, but the court ignored this development.[115] Papers in the Vatican Archives confirm Gasparri's claims that Gerlach's correspondence with Muhlberg, the Prussian minister to the Vatican, Ritter, the Bavarian minister, and Erzberger, was, as he and the Vatican always maintained, innocent, being part of Benedict's diplomatic and humanitarian efforts, but that does not rule out the possibility that he was also using the correspondence for other, illicit purposes.[116] Solid evidence that he was involved in the plot to blow up the battleships or that he was truly a spy was totally lacking, though Erzberger's biographer claims that he was in the German pay.[117] At most, it would seem likely that Gerlach acted as a paymaster for two anti-interventionist Italian newspapers, *Il Bastone* and *La Vittoria*. There is no evidence that he had used the Vatican for espionage purposes, indeed, the military tribunal made a point of saying that the Vatican was not involved in his spying activities. The fact that Gerlach was allowed to leave Italy before the trial opened suggests that the Italian authorities were anxious not to embarrass the Vatican, but also that they suspected he would have been able to make a very creditable defence had he been present at his trial.[118] On the other hand, his conviction and sentence satisfied both Allied governments and Italian anti-clericals.

The Gerlach affair attracted a lot of criticism of Benedict, both from outside and within the Vatican, casting doubt upon the soundness of his judgement.

[113] The best, most succinct, and up-to-date account of the Gerlach affair is in D. Alvarez, 'A German at the Vatican: The Gerlach Affair', *Intelligence and National Security*, 2(2) (April 1996), 443–453; for contemporary accounts, see De Salis, 'Report on My Mission', in Hachey (ed.), *Anglo-Vatican Relations*, 18–19, and *The Times*, 'The Italian Spy Trial', 8 August 1917, 16.

[114] Hachey, *Anglo-Vatican Relations*.

[115] Hachey, *Anglo-Vatican Relations*, 18.

[116] Hachey, *Anglo-Vatican* Relations.

[117] Epstein, *Matthias Erzberg*, 163.

[118] De Salis report in Hachey, *Anglo-Vatican Relations*, 19.

De Salis claimed that a number of leading Vatican personalities, including Cardinal Merry del Val, had warned him against appointing Gerlach to his service, or keeping him on after the Italian entry into war, claims which are confirmed by Carlo Monti.[119] In Benedict's defence it should be said that, hitherto, Gerlach had given no cause for concern to his superiors. The pope was also criticized for standing by Gerlach. He believed firmly and unshakeably in Gerlach's innocence; in one of his letters to Gerlach in April 1917, just before his trial opened in Rome, he wrote, 'I send you my blessing with my old and unchanged affection',[120] and as late as 1919, Benedict reaffirmed his belief in Gerlach's innocence by making him a domestic prelate.[121] Benedict's instincts were not entirely incorrect. For example, his suspicion that Gerlach had been convicted by a 'Masonic sanhedrin' were shared by both Orlando and Boselli, Italian prime minister at the time of the affair: the latter actually admitted to Monti that there were too many Masons on the military tribunal which tried Gerlach.[122]

The Gerlach affair illustrates very graphically all of the difficulties of Benedict's relationship with Italy during the war; indeed, the period from January to July 1917 was the one in which that relationship reached its lowest ebb. The affair brought out the worst in Benedict, his obstinacy, his notorious irascibility, and not a little paranoia. At its height, in early June, Monti recorded that he found the pope 'very excited, he told me that he had decided not to receive me again as the representative of the government, with which he resolved to have no further relations'.[123] It is also indicative of the tension at that time, that Monti felt obliged to warn the Italian prime minister that if there were any attacks on the Vatican in the wake of the Gerlach trial the Catholic associations would rise en masse against the government, though there was remarkably little criticism of the Vatican in the Italian press, as it turned out.[124] On the other hand, despite the brave and untiring efforts of Monti, Italo-Vatican relations remained volatile throughout the period of hostilities between Italy and Austria-Hungary, periodically erupting into tension over such matters as the departure of the ambassadors of the Central Powers, Palazzo Venezia, Article 15 of the Treaty of London, and the speeches of government ministers, especially the blatantly anti-clerical one of Bissolati. Benedict dug his heels in over the Gerlach affair: he tended to see it as a part of a Masonic, anti-clerical plot and refused to be bullied. There was always a little anti-Masonic paranoia on the part of both Benedict and his Secretary of State, but it was not entirely unjustified by events. Nor was their hostility

[119] ASV, AES, Italia, 1917, 893–894, fasc. 323, contains assorted papers relating to his curriculum vitae.

[120] ASV, AES, Italia, 1917, 893–894, fasc. 326, 4 July 1917.

[121] ASV, AES, Italia, 1917, 893–894, fasc. 326, 12 March 1919.

[122] *Diario*, II, 105, 2 June 1917.

[123] *Diario*, II, 92, 11 May 1917.

[124] ASV, AES, Italia, 1917, 893–894, 326, letter of 17 April 1917.

to Sonnino, the half-Jewish Anglican and completely irremovable Italian foreign minister, unjustified either. According to Orlando, 'Sonnino is the systematic opponent of any proposal made in the Council of Ministers in favour of the Holy See'.[125] Orlando also admitted that though many would have liked to remove Sonnino from his post, it was impossible.

BENEDICT'S HUMANITARIAN RELIEF EFFORTS DURING THE FIRST WORLD WAR

Christmas 1914 marked the point at which Benedict first sought to make a humanitarian intervention in the war, by appealing to the belligerent powers to accept a twenty-four-hour ceasefire in celebration of the birthday of the 'Prince of Peace'. He was not successful: though he received a sympathetic hearing from the British, German, and Austro-Hungarian governments, the French and Russians said no.[126] It was his first major rebuff, but he was to experience many more of them in the future, and they were to be increasingly bitter. Notwithstanding this, on 10 January, he published his 'Prayer for Peace', which he urged the bishops to commend to their clergy and faithful. The reception of this prayer by Catholics demonstrated the extreme difficulty of the Vatican's position during the war. In both Belgium and France, clergy, and even bishops, insisted on interpreting the purpose of the prayer in a manner tailor-made to fit the patriotic intents of their countries.[127] And one bishop actually went so far as to change the text of the prayer, adding the words 'on conditions honourable to our Fatherland'.[128] In these circumstances there was no chance of developing mutual comprehension among Catholics of the two warring camps.

The Papal initiative which was to bear most practical fruit was the decree, published in *L'Osservatore Romano*, of 23 December 1914, providing for 'spiritual and material assistance to prisoners'.[129] Even though the Vatican had already begun some relief operations earlier, out of this decree developed an array of Papal humanitarian relief measures throughout the course of the war and afterwards, which were comparable in extent to the work of the International Red Cross. The main thrust of these was the welfare of prisoners of war. By the spring of 1915, an organization called the Opera dei prigionieri (Service for Prisoners), had been set up in the Vatican, located in the offices

[125] *Diario*, II, 363–365, 13 August 1918.

[126] Garzia, *La Questione Romana*, 106–107.

[127] A copy of the prayer is to be found in AFDC, Libretto usato dal S. Padre Benedetto PP XV nella Basilica Vaticana per la preghiera della pace.

[128] Peters, *Life of Benedict*, 124.

[129] *L'Osservatore Romano*, 23 December 1914.

of the Secretariat of State, and by the end of the war it had dealt with 600,000 items of correspondence, including 170,000 enquiries about missing persons, 40,000 appeals for help in the repatriation of sick POWs, and the forwarding of 50,000 letters to and from prisoners and their families.[130]

As the conflict developed, Benedict's first priority was to alleviate the condition of sick, wounded, and invalid POWs in the camps, and to provide them with chaplains (of all faiths) and other services; in this regard, the visits of local bishops and clergy, and of the papal nuncios in Brussels, Munich, and Vienna, to the POW camps was very important.[131] The latter also inevitably involved the Vatican in negotiations over the condition of prison camps and the facilities provided there, as well as delicate questions about the maltreatment of prisoners.[132] Particular attention was devoted to young soldiers who had been wounded and captured in their first battle—in September 1916, Benedict received an especially heart-rending letter on this subject from a Mme Dumas, a widowed mother in the town of Nevers in France.[133] Benedict also pleaded the special case of the fathers of large families.[134] Another small, but nevertheless important, group were civilian internees, especially French and Belgians: the problems of humanitarian relief and moral condemnations of the actions of the military authorities became hopelessly intertwined when it was a case of civilian populations deported en masse, such as in Belgium in 1915.[135] Nevertheless, the Germans agreed to halt Belgian deportations thanks to the intervention of Benedict and the nuncio in Munich, Mgr Aversa.[136]

Switzerland rapidly became a major centre of the Vatican's relief humanitarian operations. The government of that neutral country was very anxious to assist in the pope's various projects for assistance to POWs, and a succession of Vatican special envoys, first Mgr Francesco Marchetti-Selvaggiani and then Mgr Luigi Maglione (later Cardinal Secretary of State to Pius XII) took up residence in Fribourg and Berne to coordinate these joint efforts; they were assisted by Count Carlo Santucci, a leading member of the 'black' aristocracy and president of the Banco di Roma.[137] The presence of the Prussian, Bavarian, and Austro-Hungarian legations in Lugano, following

[130] Dalla Torre, *Memorie*, 1289–1290; Jankowiak, 'Benoit XV', 221; according to Peters, *Life of Benedict*, branches of the Opera were established in Germany, Switzerland, and Austria.

[131] ASV, AES, Stati Eccl., 1401, fasc. 535–536, Visite di Msgr Valfré di Bonzo ai prigionieri italiani nei campi di Mathausen e Katzehan. The nuncio at Munich was responsible for visits to German prisoner-of-war camps.

[132] ASV, AES, Stati Eccl., 1401, fasc. 535–536, Visite di Msgr Valfré di Bonzo ai prigionieri italiani nei campi di Mathausen e Katzehan.

[133] ASV, SS, Guerra 1914–1918, rub. 244, fasc. 8, 22452, letter to the pope, 26 September 1916.

[134] ASV, SS, Guerra 1914–1918, rub. 244, fasc. 8, 24154, letter to the pope, December 1916.

[135] See ASV, AES, Italia, 1369/1372, fasc. 517, and AES, Stati Eccl., 1340, 492, Belgio-Germania, Per la liberazione dei civili belgi detenuti in Germania; Cardinal Hartman was asked by the Vatican to mediate with German authorities on their behalf.

[136] *The Tablet*, 4 April 1917.

[137] Panzera, 'Benedetto XV', 321–322.

their departure from Rome, also made this papal 'presence' especially useful. By January 1917, 26,000 POWs and 3.800 civilian detainees had been given the opportunity to convalesce in hospitals or sanatoria in Switzerland. The negotiations for these relatively modest operations were not easy, but those for the exchange of prisoners between the two sides were extremely difficult and drawn-out, frequently breaking down due to mutual suspicion.[138] The most difficult of all exchanges to arrange seem to have been those between Italy and Austria-Hungary—the Vatican never succeeded in bringing Italian or Austro-Hungarian POWs to Switzerland, and in February 1918 Maglione was still negotiating to obtain the release of sick Italian prisoners captured at the Battle of Caporetto five months before: he did not succeed.[139] The Vatican had almost as much difficulty brokering a truce to permit the burial of the dead on the Italo-Austrian front line in December 1915.[140] The Italians' record of looking after the interests of their captured soldiers during the First World War was not a good one.[141] A major motive for opposing repatriation of POWs on both sides was the fear that such a measure would breed defeatism among soldiers at the front: Sonnino was particularly obdurate about this.[142]

Both during and after the war one of Benedict's major concerns was the fate of children (see Chapter 3). In October 1916 he addressed an appeal to the clergy and laity of the United States for money to help feed the children of Belgium.[143] Feeding the famished was not restricted to children: the Vatican was involved in a number of operations aimed at providing foodstuffs for populations in or behind the war zones: to quote a few examples, Lithuania, Montenegro in both 1916 and 1917, Poland in 1916, Russian refugees in 1916, and Syria and Lebanon from 1916 through to 1922.[144] In the latter case, Benedict's efforts were once again obstructed by Sonnino.[145] According to Count Giuseppe Dalla Torre, ' the Christians of Syria and the East, subject to diseases, famine and oppressive maltreatment, recognised in him [Benedict] their most effective protector'.[146] The very specific reference to 'Christians' in that quotation was not accidental: the Vatican's relations with the Sublime Porte, the Ottoman government in Istanbul, had not been good for a long time, but they deteriorated further during the course of the war, due to the

138 Panzera, 'Benedetto XV', 321–322.

139 Panzera, 'Benedetto XV', 323.

140 *Diario*, I, 308–309, 17 December 1915.

141 G. Procacci, *Soldati e prigionieri italiani nella Grande Guerra*, Rome, 1993, 156.

142 *Diario*, II, 324–326, 21 and 24 May 1918.

143 *The Tablet*, 11 November 1916, 646.

144 ASV, AES, Stati Eccl., 1329, fasc. 484, Lithuania, 1915–16, Soccorsi della S. Sede in favore dei Lituani provati dalla guerra, sussidi; 1415, fasc. 561–562, Montenegro, 1916–17, Vettovagliamento della popolazione; and 1418, fasc. 562–566, Siria-Libano, 1916–1922, Vettovagliamento della Siria e del Libano. From the correspondence in these files it is clear that, as always, hostility between belligerent powers made negotiations for humanitarian work very difficult.

145 *Diario*, II, 363–364, 13 September 1918.

146 Dalla Torre, *Memorie*, 1290.

Turks' treatment of Christian populations in their empire and, most particularly, the massacres of the Armenians, who were considered disloyal. In April and May 1915 a campaign of what would now be called 'ethnic cleansing' or genocide was launched against the Christian, mainly Armenian, populations of Anatolia.[147] In July, the Apostolic Delegate in Constantinople, Mgr Dolci, was instructed to protest against the massacres; the governments of Germany and Austria-Hungary were also asked to bring pressure to bear on their ally to stop the killings, and Benedict himself sent an autograph letter on 10 September to the Sultan who, in his role as Caliph of Islam, was, like the pope, a worldwide religious leader.[148] The pope's intervention had only limited success; by the end of the war it was estimated that over a million Armenians had died, either killed outright by the Turks or as a result of maltreatment or from starvation.[149]

In a comment on the role of Benedict XV during the First World War, the leader of the future Italian Catholic Party, Father Luigi Sturzo, made the point that moral theology took a long time to catch up with the horrors unleashed by the new technology of warfare.[150] But it was not merely theology which had to catch up—men's imaginations took some time to come to terms with the appalling human effects of mines, submarines, and aerial bombardment. Benedict was particularly revolted by the effects of the latter on civilian populations, which were very evident in and around the battle zones of north-eastern Italy, especially Venice, Treviso, Padua, Trieste, and Pola. From early 1916 onwards, Vatican diplomacy accordingly devoted much attention to pleading with the military authorities to desist from these 'barbarous' practices.[151] It had only limited success, despite the support of Orlando who suggested a 30-kilometre 'air raid free zone': there continued to be bombardments of even 'open cities' right until the end of the war.[152] Benedict was truly prodigal in his efforts to relive suffering on all sides during the war. But he got little in the way of reward during the course of the conflict: on the contrary, as we have already seen, he was attacked from all sides. Ironically, the only lasting monument to his humanitarian efforts came not in any European state, but in Turkey: in Istanbul a statue was erected in his honour, even before the end of the war.

[147] For an account of the Armenian massacres, see Raymond H. Kevorkian, *The Armenian Genocide: A Complete History*, London, 2011.

[148] ASV, SS 1914–18, rub. 244, fasc. 64, 1915–16, Correspondence between Benedict XV and Sultan Mohamed V; and A. Riccardi, 'Benedetto XV e la crisi della convivenza multireligiosa nell'Impero Turco', in Rumi (ed.), *Benedetto XV*, 83–128.

[149] Riccardi, 'Benedetto XV', 89.

[150] De Rosa, *Luigi Sturzo*, 183.

[151] See the correspondence with the Austrian and German governments in AES, Italia, 843, fasc. 308–310, Bombardamenti di città indifese; and *Diario*, I, 242–244, 7 July 1915 and 339, 28 January 1916.

[152] *Diario*, I, 242–244, 7 July 1915 and 339, 28 January 1916.

PAPAL PEACE DIPLOMACY

After the failure of Benedict and Gasparri's attempt to keep the peace between Austria-Hungary and Italy in the months leading up to Italian intervention in May 1915, some prompting to resume their efforts and extend their scope must have come from the awareness that the pope was increasingly being seen by a variety of groups as a major force for peace. In May 1915 the pope received a delegation from the Dutch Roman Catholic State Party to discuss the possibility of a peace conference at The Hague.[153] A month later came the visit of the American women peace activists, Jane Addams and Alice Hamilton Balch, who, fresh from their own 'peace' conference at The Hague, set out to visit the European heads of state, including the pope: they recorded with some surprise the enthusiasm, informality, and cordiality of the reception which they received from Benedict.[154] In this same period began the succession of approaches from Jewish groups and individuals in both France and America, pleading for the pope to intervene in defence of Jews being maltreated in Russia or territories under Russian occupation.[155] Shortly before the publication of the apostolic exhortation to the belligerents, the Vatican had been involved in an attempt to assist in bringing about a separate peace between Germany and Belgium and France. It conveyed an offer, on behalf of Germany, to restore Belgian independence and sovereignty, and to negotiate the future of Alsace-Lorraine with France.[156] Cardinal Mercier's reply to the suggestion that he should pass the offer on to his government was a decisive 'no', and Mgr Baudrillart, the head of the prestigious Catholic Institut de France, and also the author of the French reply to the declaration of the German Catholics of 1914, made it clear that such a proposal was wholly inopportune.[157] Benedict blamed the failure of this démarche on the intransigence of the British.[158]

The publication of the apostolic exhortation, 'To the Belligerent Peoples, and their Rulers', of 28 July 1915 marks a turning point in the development of Vatican policy during the war; it was at this stage that Benedict and Gasparri recommitted themselves to active diplomacy in the cause of peace: a peace offensive that would culminate in the 'peace note' of August 1917.[159] Their decision to do so in July 1915 was determined by the fact that it was clear the belligerent powers were unable or unwilling to initiate peace moves themselves. The exhortation, written to commemorate the first anniversary of the

[153] Zivojinovic, *The United States*, 48.

[154] J. Adams, *Peace and Bread in Time of War*, New York, 1945, 12–19.

[155] P. Korzec, 'Les relations entre le Vatican et les organisations juives pendant la première guerre mondiale: la mission Deloncle-Perquel (1915–1916)', *Revue d'Histoire Moderne et Contemporaine*, 29 (1970), 340.

[156] *Diario*, I, 250–251, 17 July 1915.

[157] Garzia, *La Questione Romana*, 111.

[158] *Diario*, I, 250–251, 17 July 1915.

[159] For the text, see LaCC, 17 July 1915, 66, 3.

outbreak of the war, contained an apocalyptic warning of the dangers of not seeking a negotiated peace:

> Abandon the mutual threat of destruction. Remember, Nations do not die; humiliated and oppressed, they bear the weight of the yoke imposed upon them, preparing themselves for their comeback and transmitting from one generation to the next a sad legacy of hatred and vendetta.[160]

The phrase 'Nations do not die' was one of Benedict's most evocative and memorable, and was followed by a very explicit invitation to the belligerents to go to the negotiating table:

> It is not true that this conflict cannot be resolved without the violence of arms... Why not from this moment consider with a serene conscience the rights and just aspirations of peoples? Why not commence in good will an exchange, direct or indirect, of views with the purpose of keeping in mind as far as possible those rights and those aspirations and thus put an end to this conflict, as has happened in other circumstances? Blessed be he who first raises the olive branch of peace and extends his right hand to the enemy offering reasonable conditions for peace. The equilibrium of the world and prosperous and secure tranquillity of nations rests on mutual benevolence and the respect of the rights and dignity of others, rather than on a multitude of armies and a formidable ring of fortresses.[161]

The reference to an indirect as well as direct exchange of views was clearly a hint that the Holy See would be willing to assist in the making of secret contacts. After the exhortation fell on stony ground, Benedict desisted from major peace efforts until the autumn of the following year. In the meantime, he intensified his efforts to relieve suffering and to denounce the war, as the impassioned plea of his consistorial allocution of the 15 December 1915 against ' the fatal war on land and sea' shows.[162]

THE PEACE INITIATIVE OF THE CENTRAL POWERS

December 1916 marked a watershed in the First World War, a moment when the increasing futility of the military stalemate induced the Central Powers to seriously consider a negotiated peace. The German peace initiative came, as was nearly always to be the case during the First World War, at a time of their relative strength—the Central Powers had knocked Rumania out of

[160] LaCC, 17 July 1915, 66, 3. [161] LaCC, 17 July 1915, 66, 3.

[162] Bellocchi, 'É purtroppo vero', in *Tutte le Encicliche*, vol. VIII: *Benedetto XV (1914–1922)*, 88–90.

the war at the end of November and captured Bucharest at the beginning of December. On the other hand, during the Brusilov Offensive in June 1916, the Russians had driven the Austro-Hungarian armies back to the Carpathian mountains, threatening the collapse of the Habsburg Empire; indeed, it would have collapsed but for repeated German intervention.[163] In consequence, the government in Vienna was even more dependent than ever upon its German ally, and subservient to it; in effect, its satellite. The death of the Emperor Franz Josef of Austria and the accession of his nephew Karl I to the Habsburg throne that same November, represented a substantial change in the Austrian position. Henceforth, though young and inexperienced, the new emperor would become increasingly anxious to negotiate his way out of the war in order to escape what seemed to be the war's inevitable consequence—the collapse of the empire. This latent division between the policies of the two central empires would provide both the Vatican and the Entente powers with opportunities for peace diplomacy in 1917 and 1918.

Meanwhile, Germany took the peace initiative. On the 12 December, separate and different notes were handed to the United States Charge' d'Affaires in Berlin, and to Cardinal Gasparri in the Vatican.[164] The letter was conspicuous for the deliberate echoes of the language which the pope himself had used in all of his pronouncements on peace but most notably in the apostolic exhortation of July 1915, and concluded by saying, 'The Imperial Government is firmly confident that the initiative of the four Powers (Germany, Austria-Hungary, Bulgaria and Turkey) will find a friendly welcome on the part of His Holiness, and that the work of peace can count upon the precious support of the Holy See.'[165] The work of peace could, of course, always count upon the support of the Holy See. Nevertheless, the German peace note received a rather qualified welcome in the Vatican. The problem was that it contained nothing concrete at all in the way of suggestions for heads of discussion, or, even less, possible concessions. Benedict and Gasparri were by no means convinced of the usefulness of the initiative, and it is clear that they were made to understand by De Salis that Britain and France would not welcome any support that they gave it.[166] Peters concludes that, 'Benedict realised that if he offended the Entente Powers now, any future efforts would be met with antagonism.'[167] Because of the palpable lack of enthusiasm in the Vatican's eventual response to the note, and its unhappiness at the declaration of unrestricted submarine warfare, following the Allies' rejection of the German peace note, there was

[163] P. Kennedy, *The Rise and Fall of the Great Powers: Economic Change and Military Conflict from 1500 to 2000*, London, 1987, 337 and 339.

[164] H.C. O'Neill, *A History of the War*, London and Edinburgh, 1920, 689–690.

[165] O'Neill, *History of the War*, 691.

[166] O'Neill, *History of the War*, 696.

[167] Peters, *Life of Benedict*, 141.

a decided cooling in the relations between the Vatican and Berlin, which was not to change until Benedict issued his own peace note in August 1917.[168]

THE ENTRY OF THE UNITED STATES INTO THE WAR

Shortly after the German note was published, on 20 December 1916, US President Woodrow Wilson made his own appeal for peace. The key sentence in the note was:

> The President is not proposing peace; he is not even offering mediation. He is merely proposing that soundings be taken in order that we may learn, the neutral nations with the belligerents, how near the haven of peace may be for which all mankind longs with an intense and increasing longing.[169]

This was strongly reminiscent of Benedict's own appeal of July 1915, but had no more success in achieving its goal, coming too soon after the rejected German peace initiative. On the 24 December, *L'Osservatore Romano* came out in support of Wilson's initiative, but privately Gasparri was less enthusiastic.[170] Four months after his note, Wilson broke off relations with Germany. In the meantime, as indeed it had been doing for some previous time, the Vatican strove to avert the breach.

The cause of tensions between Germany and the United States was the former's adoption of submarine warfare, against both enemies and neutrals alike. As J.A. Salter points out, the First World War ' was as much a war of competing blockades, the surface and submarine, as of competing armies. Behind these two blockades the economic systems of the two opposing countries were engaged in a deadly struggle for existence.'[171] To the British and French naval blockade of their coasts, the Central Powers, chiefly Germany, replied with submarine warfare, and the Germans eventually decided upon the introduction of unrestricted submarine warfare, sinking without warning. As the sinkings took their toll and anger stirred in America, Benedict had tried to intervene. He regarded both the blockades and submarine warfare as essentially immoral, and both as probably violations of international law. He was almost certainly right. Hardach argues:

[168] Monticone, *Nitti e la Grande Guerra*, 13.

[169] As quoted in O'Neill, *History of the War*, 694.

[170] *Diario*, I, 525, 16 December 1916.

[171] J. A. Salter, *Allied Shipping Control: An Experiment in International Administration*, Oxford, 1921, 1.

> Such procedure [sinking without warning] was clearly contrary to established international law, but so, too was the unrestricted blockade of the Central Powers by the Allies from March 1915 onwards. Hence during and after the war, the Germans tended to regard the one as offsetting the other under international law. But to all save the Germans there was a marked distinction between the confiscation of goods and the sinking without warning of ships, together with their helpless crews and passengers.[172]

In the autumn of 1915 Gasparri had denounced 'the appalling and immoral submarine warfare' and condemned Germany's U-boat campaign to Canadian bishop, Mgr MacNally.[173] On the other hand, there was a feeling in the Vatican that the USA was not an impartial neutral, that it was helping one side—the Allies—against the Central Powers, and for largely selfish reasons. The United States was effectively committed to the Allies because of economic ties. Benedict particularly deplored the United States' arms trade with Britain and France, especially when it was carried on using passenger vessels, thus providing an excuse for their sinking by the Germans. As early as April 1915, in an interview published in a pro-German New York newspaper, Benedict had called upon the United States to enforce an arms embargo against both sides.[174] In 1916, he even claimed that the arms trade was 'contrary to the law of nations': though he was a lawyer by training, strictly speaking his judgement was wrong.[175] Even so, there is no evidence to support Zivojinovic's claim that the Vatican believed the sinking of passenger ships which carried arms was justified.[176]

The Vatican's hope that, despite the increasing tensions with Germany, the United States would remain neutral were based on the plausible assumption that the German and Irish Catholic groups in America would continue to influence public opinion in a neutralist direction. It also had reason to believe that United States Jewish opinion, which was hostile to Russia, could also be mobilized in support.[177] Thus, Benedict regarded Wilson's proposal for a 'League for Peace' on 28 May 1916 as a sop to Irish and German voters.[178] The Vatican urged restraint after the sinking of the SS *Arabic* in 1915, and Zivojinovic grudgingly admits that when, on 1 September 1916, German Ambassador Bernstorff told United States Secretary of State Lansing that passenger liners would not be attacked, 'The pope was credited by some for this concession on Germany's part.'[179] As late as February 1917, Benedict was

[172] H. Hardach, *The First World War, 1914–1918*, London, 1977, 37.
[173] As quoted in G. Spadolini, *Giolitti e I cattolici*, Florence, 1977, 178.
[174] Wiegand interview cited in Zivojinovic, *The United States*, 46.
[175] Quoted in Leslie, *Cardinal Gasquet*, 242.
[176] See L. Bruti Liberati, 'La Santa Sede e gli Stati Uniti negli anni della Grande Guerra', in Rumi (ed.), *Benedetto XV*, 132.
[177] Korzec, 'Les relations entre le Vatican', 341.
[178] *Diario*, I, 379, 29 May 1916.
[179] Zivojinovic, *The United States*, 50 and 70.

prepared to be a go-between in securing both the end of the blockade and of submarine warfare.[180] The United States declaration of war in April 1917 was greeted with dismay and perplexity in the Vatican. Commenting on the sour response of *L'Osservatore Romano, The Tablet* declared rather patronizingly, 'These are not easy matters for the Roman mind to grasp', but it admitted that 'Had not the President as short a time a go as last Christmas sent out the great peace message?'[181] He had indeed, and A.J.P. Taylor, speaking of Wilson's decision, says, 'It was ironical that he abandoned neutrality just when his mediation might have achieved some purpose at last.'[182] Gasparri was rather more cynical about Wilson's decision, claiming that it had been prompted by an overweening desire to be present at the peace conference.[183] For Benedict, the American decision was another tragedy, threatening to prolong the war even further.

THE PAPAL PEACE NOTE OF AUGUST 1917

Though the United States' entry into the war seemed to make the prospect of peace even more remote, by the summer of 1917 there were factors in the general situation which suggested that some peace initiative at this point might have success. Since the beginning of the year there had been tentative approaches on both sides. The brother-in-law of the Austrian Emperor, Prince Sixtus of Bourbon-Parma, had sought to open a channel of communication on his behalf with the French.[184] By February 1917 there were rumours of developing talks between representatives of Britain and France, and Austria-Hungary in Switzerland. Carlo Monti repeatedly asked both Benedict and Gasparri about the truth of these rumours and about alleged Vatican involvement in them: both denied the rumours, but some evidence suggests that they might have been thrifty with the truth in their answers to Monti.[185] It seems unlikely, however, that the Vatican was actively involved in these talks because Cardinal Bourne, archbishop of Westminster, told Benedict that any peace initiative on the pope's part would displease Britain.[186] The contacts which did take place were indicative of increasing war weariness in both camps. The Russian Revolution of February was an instructive example of what could happen under the strain of war—economic, social, and political breakdown. These were just the sorts of evils which Benedict and Gasparri, and others like Erzberger and Karl I, had been warning about. The mutinies

[180] Epstein, *Matthias Erzberger*, 127.

[181] *The Tablet*, 21 April 1917.

[182] A. J. P. Taylor, *From Sarajevo to Potsdam*, London, 1966, 42.

[183] *Diario*, II, 65, 7 April 1917.

[184] Poincaré, *Au Service de la France*, 68.

[185] *Diario*, 35–37, 1 February 1917.

[186] *Diario*, II, 33–34, 13 February 1917.

among French troops following the failure of the Nivelle Offensive in the spring of 1917 brought home to the Allies the grave risks they now faced. Again, by the summer of 1917, various international congresses were putting on the pressure for peace negotiations: in February, Catholic members of parliament from various countries had met to discuss peace in Switzerland;[187] in Stockholm, representatives of Europe's Socialist parties met to talk peace and there were rumours of a secret Masonic congress dedicated to that end.[188] All these developments must have weighed on Benedict's mind. As Taylor says, 'The Summer of 1917 saw the only real gropings in Europe towards peace by negotiation.'[189]

The most promising and interesting of the situations in the summer of 1917, and the one which undoubtedly influenced Benedict most in his decision to publish a 'peace note' in August, was that which had developed in Germany. Though militarily Germany was in a strong position, at home the war effort was potentially threatened by unprecedented parliamentary dissent. Led by Matthias Erzberger, a majority emerged in the Reichstag which passed a 'peace resolution' in July. Erzberger was in a uniquely powerful position for a civilian politician in wartime Germany. A major exponent of the Catholic Centre Party, he had run the country's propaganda and intelligence-gathering operations abroad, including Italy.[190] In early 1915 he had been sent on two missions to Italy to dissuade her from entering the war, and in the course of them had established contact with the Vatican, meeting Benedict twice, and had been instrumental in securing the consent of the German high command to Benedict's request that a truce on the Nieuw Chapelle battlefield be implemented in order to bury the dead.[191] By the summer of 1917, Erzberger had been converted from an annexationist viewpoint and was the Vatican's white hope in Germany: the man it believed would work as its agent of peace within the Empire. Aside from his parliamentary influence, Erzberger had already demonstrated the influence which he could exercise within the imperial government by his success in securing prisoner exchanges at Benedict's request.[192]

Monticone talks about the 'German origins' of Benedict's peace note.[193] In one sense he is right: Benedict believed that Germany was the key to a successful peace process: unlike the Allied Powers, Germany and Austria-Hungary were in control of large areas of occupied territory, most especially Belgium, whose restitution was, for the Allied Powers, the *sine qua none* of any

[187] Panzera, 'Benedetto XV', 333.

[188] E. Serra, 'La Nota del primo Agosto 1917 e il Governo Italiano: Qualche Osservazione', in Rumi (ed.), *Benedetto XV*, 50.

[189] Taylor, *From Sarajevo to Potsdam*, 42.

[190] Epstein, *Matthias Erzberger*, 163.

[191] Epstein, *Matthias Erzberger*, 119–120 and 126–127.

[192] Epstein, *Matthias Erzberger*, 126.

[193] Monticone, *Nitti e la Grande Guerra*, 14.

settlement.[194] Benedict therefore assumed that only the indication of a willingness on Germany's part to evacuate occupied territory would persuade the Allied Powers to come to the negotiating table. He and Gasparri made careful preparations for what was to become their major peace initiative. In May, in anticipation of this, Benedict was in contact with Karl and the Empress Zita of Austria-Hungary,[195] and he sent Mgr Eugenio Pacelli as nuncio to Bavaria, and therefore effectively papal representative to Germany, in place of Aversa who had died the previous month.[196] During the course of several conversations with Chancellor Theobald Bethmann-Hollweg and the Kaiser himself, Pacelli hammered out heads of discussion on which Germany would be prepared to negotiate peace, which included a general limitation of armaments, the establishment of international courts, restoration of the independence of Belgium, while the territorial question of Alsace-Lorraine and other such issues were to be settled by agreements between the countries concerned. It was on this that Benedict based his own 'peace note'. The problem was that, by August, Bethmann-Hollweg had been ousted by Generals Paul Hindenburg and Eric Ludendorff and replaced by Michaelis, a colourless bureaucrat who more or less did their bidding.

In content, Benedict's note of 1 August (actually sent to governments on 15 August) was a considerable improvement upon both his own previous pronouncements, and the German and American notes of the previous December. It did not content itself with vague references to 'exchanges of views' or 'the rights and just aspirations of peoples'. It set out systematic proposals for bringing the war to an end and securing a just and enduring peace:

1) A simultaneous and reciprocal decrease of armaments
2) International arbitration
3) True freedom and community of the seas
4) Reciprocal renunciation of war indemnities
5) Evacuation and restoration of all occupied territories
6) An examination in a conciliatory spirit of rival territorial claims.

Belgium, northern France, and the German colonies were explicitly mentioned by name under no. 6, and no. 7 talked equally explicitly of 'territorial questions . . . pending between Italy and Austria, and between Germany and France'.[197] In addition, Benedict went beyond the *status quo ante bellum* by insisting on the need to examine 'the remaining territorial and political questions, and particularly those which concern Armenia, the Balkan states, and

[194] Monticone, *Nitti e la Grande Guerra*, 14.
[195] Monticone, 'Benedetto XV e la Germania', 40.
[196] *Diario*, II, 73–75, 17 April 1917.
[197] As quoted in O'Neill, *History of the War*, 822–823.

the territories which form part of the former kingdom of Poland'.[198] This was the first time during the course of the war that any person or power had formulated a detailed and practical scheme for a peace negotiation.

The responses to the peace note were disappointing. The initial Allied response was summed up by an article in *The Times* of London. Headed 'German Peace Move', the article declared that, 'More peace proposals' have been put forth. This time they emanate from the Vatican.[199] The British government was slow to respond, sending only a letter of acknowledgment. The French never replied at all, combining their resentment at Britain's unilateral action with their usual suspicion of the papacy: Clémenceau dubbed Benedict's plan as ' a peace against France'.[200] Of all the Allied powers, Italy was the most overtly and publicly hostile. Its reply came from Sonnino in a debate on foreign policy in October in the Italian Senate, where he dismissed the pope's proposals as inadequate.[201] Sonnino's hostility was motivated by a number of factors. In the first place, his intelligence sources had convinced him that the German high command were not really serious about giving up Belgium, which eventually proved to be the case.[202] He was also concerned that, in any detailed negotiations over territorial questions, Italy's irredentist claims would be brushed aside because of its lack of military progress. The double-dealing of Britain and France earlier in the year make this a plausible scenario. Finally, Sonnino was tenaciously opposed to any increase in international prestige and profile which a successful peace initiative would bring the pope, fearing that Article 15 would be set aside by his allies, and that Benedict would be allowed a representative at the talks, if not the presidency of them.

The reaction of the Central Powers was equally disappointing. Despite the Emperor Karl's genuine support for Benedict's initiative, given the hopeless dependence of the Habsburg Empire upon German military support he was obliged to follow the lead given in Berlin. What was most striking was that the replies of the Central Powers omitted all mention of territorial questions.[203] The problem was that real bargaining power lay with the German high command, Hindenburg and Ludendorff, the Kaiser, and the Prussian military caste. They were not inclined to budge: as Kennedy points out, in the summer of 1917, especially after the success of the German U-boat offensive

[198] O'Neill, *History of the War*, 822–823; for the text of the 'peace note', see Bellocchi, *Tutte le Encicliche*, Des Le Début, 1 agosto 1917. Esortazione, 182–184 and <http//:www.firstworldwar.com/source/papalpeacenote.htm> (accessed 15 January 2014).

[199] *The Times*, 15 August 1917.

[200] As quoted in J.D. Holmes, *The Papacy in the Modern World*, London and New York, 1981, 12.

[201] Garzia, *La Questione Romana*, 163.

[202] For the replies of the Central Powers see ASV, SdS, Guerra, 1914–1918, rub. 244, fasc. 79, protocol, 5482.

[203] Garzia, *La Questione Romana*, 163–164.

in the Atlantic and the failure of the Russian offensive on the Eastern Front, 'Germany seemed on the point of victory'.[204] Benedict had overestimated the power of civilian politicians like Erzberger, and underestimated that of the military. Erzberger was actually prosecuted for treason after his conciliatory Ulm speech in 1917.[205]

It was precisely the need to crush the power of German militarism which Woodrow Wilson gave as his reason for rejecting the practicability of Benedict's proposals in the letter he sent, which effectively served as the official reply on the part of the Allied governments. Wilson argued that Germany simply could not be trusted: 'We cannot take the word of the present rulers of Germany as a guarantee of any thing that is to endure', and he implied that only a change of regime in Germany in a democratic direction would provide the necessary preconditions for peace.[206] As O'Neill says, 'the [President's] note very clearly closed the door to the initiation of peace in the near future . . . the other replies to the pope's note cease to have interest in the face of Mr. Wilson's answer. They came as an anti-climax.'[207]

By the spring of 1917 Wilson had already emerged as the dominant figure on the Allied side, and therefore as the future leader of the world, and this was confirmed by his reply to the papal peace note of August. As such, he would brook no rivals. This Calvinist idealist, who was 'convinced of his own moral and intellectual superiority', was also notoriously anti-Catholic (except at election time) and tended to see all Europeans as parochial and unenlightened, including Benedict.[208] According to Zivojinovic, Wilson's 'Peace without Victory' speech of January 1922 swept Benedict and his peace efforts aside.[209] The only 'victory' which the pope could claim over the president was a moral one: the famous 'Fourteen Points' speech made by Wilson in January 1918 was so close in content and formulation to Benedict's note that the only conclusion to be drawn is that it was heavily inspired by it.[210]

The pope and his Secretary of State were inevitably bitterly disappointed by the responses to the note and the ultimate failure of their initiative: Benedict told one of his friends that it was the bitterest moment of his life when he heard of the rejection of the note by Wilson.[211] Though there were many positive responses from bishops, clergy, and laity throughout the world, there were equally many hostile ones. A preacher in Notre Dame Cathedral exclaimed, 'Holy Father, we do not want your peace.'[212] The hardest of all to swallow were the responses which the note elicited in Benedict's homeland: in Naples

[204] For the replies of the Central Powers see ASV, SdS, Guerra, 1914–1918, rub. 244, fasc. 79, protocol, 5482.

[205] Epstein, *Matthias Erzberger*, 281.

[206] Epstein, *Matthias Erzberger*, 281.

[207] O'Neill, *History of the War*, 825.

[208] Zivojinovic, *The United States*, 52.

[209] Taylor, *From Sarajevo to Potsdam*, 43.

[210] Serra, 'La Nota del primo Agosto', 61.

[211] Zivojinovic, *The United States*, 39.

[212] As quoted in Morozzo Della Rocca, 'Benedetto XV e nazionalismo', 550.

he was denounced as 'the German pope'.[213] Posterity has been kinder to the papal peace initiative of August 1917. Enrico Serra has argued:

> it seems legitimate to conclude, on the basis of the tragic military events which followed, that the note was anything but premature. So much so that France and Britain decided to make contact with Vienna, while the new Italian prime minister, V.E. Orlando, proposed to establish direct (diplomatic) relations with the Holy See.[214]

CAPORETTO

The failure of the peace note was soon overshadowed by events in Italy: in late October and early November 1917 Italy suffered a catastrophic defeat at the hands of the Austro-Hungarians, backed by German forces. Within less than three weeks, the Italians were driven back from their positions on the Isonzo, on the other side of the Austro-Hungarian frontier, over 120 miles to the Piave, and only succeeded in stabilizing the exposed northern end of that line with great difficulty. In the rout, they lost nearly 300,000 men, not to mention precious stores and guns.[215] In this great national crisis, the Church, and especially the rural clergy of the Veneto region, were called upon to play a vital role to restore morale. On 12 November, Italian Prime Minister Vittorio Emanuele Orlando asked Benedict to order the bishops to tell the people of the front-line areas to stay put, in order to diminish the stream of panic-stricken civilian refugees who were hampering the efforts of the Italian armies to regroup.[216] In fact, information reached the Vatican that, in areas on the line of retreat of the Italian forces, both Italy's military and civil authorities behaved badly, often abandoning their posts: in the resulting chaos, and amidst widespread looting by Italian troops, the local bishops and clergy were often the only focus of authority.[217] Behind the lines, bishops and clergy were often also the main providers for those same refugees, church property being used for these as well as military purposes.[218] Benedict showed great patriotic concern, and his feelings were inspired in part no doubt, by the fact that the estate of his sister, Giulia Persico, lay only 8 kilometres behind the Piave. And, as Carlo Monti noted in his diary, the pope was also afraid for his only nephew Pino, who was fighting at the front: unknown to Benedict, Monti had tried several times, unsuccessfully,

[213] ASV, SdS, Guerra, 1914–18, rub. 244, fasc. 82, letter from archbishop of Naples, 28 August 1917.

[214] Serra, 'La Nota del primo Agosto', 59–60.

[215] Seton-Watson, *Italy*, 477–497.

[216] *Diario*, II, 206, 12 November 1917.

[217] *Diario*, 215–218, 25 and 26 November 1917.

[218] *Diario*, 215, 25 November 1917.

to persuade the authorities to send him to the rear.[219] As Benedict noted with a certain irony, the same Italian ministers and officials who had often obstructed his humanitarian efforts for prisoners and others, now besieged the Vatican with requests for information about their own sons or nephews taken prisoner by the enemy: 'You would not believe how many people are turning to us to have news.'[220]

Sonnino's hostility to the peace note, and indeed all papal peace initiatives, did not prevent the Italian Ministry of Foreign Affairs from seeking to use Vatican diplomacy to extricate Italy from her perilous predicament after Caporetto. On 14 November, the Secretary General of the Ministry, urged on Sonnino the necessity 'to take advantage of the Vatican, whose close links with Germany at the time of the papal note of last August we know about. The Vatican could be able to guarantee the word of the enemy sovereigns.'[221] When Gasparri was asked his opinion on this proposal he replied that Italy could not expect as much as the *parecchio* of Giolitti (i.e. that which Giolitti believed Italy could have obtained from Austria-Hungary in 1915 simply by remaining neutral, which was a lot—*parecchio*), because things had changed since then.[222] By the end of the month the situation at the front had stabilized, and the Italian government abandoned its initiative. But Vatican diplomacy was still needed to help Italy: Benedict sought to persuade Germany and Austria-Hungary not to permanently annexe the Italian territory which they had conquered in October and November.[223] Nevertheless, by the New Year, despite the reinforcements from her allies, Italy's plight was such that the Italian Finance Minister, Francesco Nitti, was again seeking the Vatican's good offices to negotiate a separate peace with Austria-Hungary.[224]

There is, about the Italian defeat at Caporetto, a certain element of hubris. Just at the moment that the offensive of the Central Powers was getting under way on the Isonzo front, Gasparri, on the Italians' behalf, had been taking soundings with the Emperor Karl about a peace based on the cession of Trento in exchange for an Italian colony.[225] Later that month Orlando asked Benedict to tell Germany not to wage war upon Italy, as she was doing with such effect at that time: Gasparri in reply pointed out that Italy should not have declared war on Germany and Victor Emmanuel III should not have visited Alsace-Lorraine.[226] In fact, Benedict and Gasparri showed considerable sympathy towards Italy throughout the conflict, and it could even be said that the Vatican's policy of impartiality towards the belligerents was temporarily

[219] *Diario*, 197, 4 November 1917; and 203, 23 November 1917.
[220] *Diario*, 205, 10 November 1917.
[221] DDI, Quinta Serie, vol. IX, doc. 438, 14 November 1917.
[222] DDI, Quinta Serie, vol. IX, doc. 233, Gasparri a Nitti, 14 December 1917.
[223] PRO, FO, 371/231892, De Salis to Balfour, 25 December 1917.
[224] *Diario*, II, 187–188, 21 October 1917.
[225] *Diario*, 186, 26 October 1917.
[226] *Diario*, 1914, 31 October 1917.

abandoned for the sake of Italy when Gasparri gave warnings to Nitti about an imminent Austro-Hungarian offensive in 1918.[227]

Though, in the long term, the rallying of Catholic clergy and laity to the patriotic cause helped improve Church–State relations in Italy, at the time some Italian authorities and newspapers showed scant gratitude or even recognition. In early 1918, both Orlando and the Vatican were contacted by a number of bishops in the front-line areas protesting numerous cases of their clergy being prosecuted for defeatism, spying, and contact with the enemy.[228] Another victim of Italian suspicion and paranoia in the wake of the Caporetto defeat was Giuseppe Dalla Torre, head of Italian Catholic Action, who was later investigated by the Commission of Inquiry into Caporetto for 'encouraging defeatism'.[229] More seriously, the interventionist and anti-clerical press, returning to their long-standing accusation that Benedict was a pawn of the Central Powers and in search of a scapegoat for Caporetto, cited the peace note as having spread defeatism among the Italian troops at Caporetto. Even some historians have supported this view: Clark, for example, has argued that the peace note, 'probably did have a devastating effect on Italian morale'.[230] The more malicious, like Mussolini's interventionist newspaper *Il Popolo D'Italia*, changed the pope's regnal name from Benedetto XV (meaning blessed) to Maledetto XV (meaning 'accursed'). And British newspapers took up the cry, the *Morning Post* and *The Times* blamed the lack of resistance at Caporetto on Benedict.[231] Of course, Benedict's famous condemnation of the 'useless slaughter' in the peace note could just as easily have affected the morale of the armies of the Central Powers as well as those of Italy, France, or Belgium.

THE DISINTEGRATION OF THE HABSBURG EMPIRE

By the beginning of 1918, Benedict's worst fears about the wider consequences of the war were being realized. The Bolsheviks had carried out their revolution and civil war was spreading throughout Russia.[232] Unrest was also spreading in the belligerent states, especially the Central Powers. In February 1918,

[227] F. Margiotta-Broglio, *L'Italia e Santa Sede dalla prima Guerra Mondiale alla Conciliazione*, Bari, 1966, 40.

[228] See, for example, ASV, SdS, Guerra, 1914–1918, rub. 244, fasc. 101, Bishop of Padua to Orlando, 18 February 1918.

[229] ASV, AES, Stati Eccl., 216, 49301, vol. vi, 93–100.

[230] Clark, *Modern Italy*, 197.

[231] *Diario*, II, 306, n. 98.

[232] See Benedict's condemnation of 'atheism erected into purported system of civilisation' in Bellocchi, *Tutte le Encicliche*, VIII, 68. A Lei Signor Cardinale. 24 December, 1917, 190–192, Allocuzione.

Benedict warned the Emperor Karl about the increasing influence of subversive elements in all the countries at war.[233] Karl hardly needed to be told, widespread strikes, a naval mutiny in Dalmatia, and open agitation among the various minority nationalities for 'self-determination' were beginning to tear his empire apart.[234] But even at this stage all was not lost: the Entente powers, for example, remained convinced that the survival of Austria-Hungary would still be essential to the maintenance of the post-war balance of power. In the same letter to Karl, Benedict therefore urged upon him the view that the only way out of the desperate situation in which the Habsburg Empire found itself was to seek peace at once, by appealing to President Wilson:

> In the present international situation, it is not England nor France but the President of the great American Republic alone: only he can bring about peace or the continuation of the war, and he wishes to dictate the peace in the time that remains of his presidential term.[235]

The Vatican's peace diplomacy continued into April when Gasparri reiterated to Nitti the need for peace negotiations between Italy and Austria-Hungary, but without success.[236] In August, Benedict had resolved not to engage in any further initiatives,[237] but the autumn brought a different situation: the impending collapse of Austria-Hungary. As late as October 1918, Benedict was still seeking to persuade Orlando of the continuing validity of the original Entente view, now somewhat eroded by events, that it was necessary to preserve Austria-Hungary.[238] Yet it is also clear that both Benedict and Gasparri were pragmatists: when they saw that it was impossible to save the Habsburg Empire they turned their attentions to Poland, arguing that this overwhelmingly Catholic state would provide a more than adequate substitute as a bulwark against both Germany and Russia.[239]

CONCLUSION

It can be argued that the failure of Benedict's peace diplomacy was due principally to three powers, Britain, the USA, and Germany. Britain repeatedly made it clear via its envoys to the Vatican that it did not welcome the pope's peace efforts. As De Salis explained to Gasparri, the British were not only fighting for Belgium, but for sterling as well.[240] In other words, they were

[233] ASV, AES, Stati Eccl., 216, vol. XIII, Benedict to the Emperor Karl, 28 February 1918.

[234] M. Cornwall (ed.), *The Last Years of Austria-Hungary*, Exeter, 1990, 118; and R. Okey, *The Habsburg Monarchy c. 1765–1918*, Basingstoke, 2001, 384–401.

[235] ASV, AES, Stati Eccl., 216, vol. XIII, Benedict to the Emperor Karl, 28 February 1918.

[236] *Diario*, II, 388, 25 October 1918.

[237] *Diario*, 362, 7 August 1918.

[238] *Diario*, 388, 25 October 1918.

[239] *Diario*, 390, 27 October 1918.

[240] *Diario*, 39, 22 February 1917.

engaged in a struggle for economic supremacy with Germany, not to mention naval mastery. They might consider a negotiated peace with Austria-Hungary, but a 'draw' with Germany was out of the question, whatever the cost. France and, even more so, Italy, were effectively clients of Britain. However much they might resent that status, they were obliged, out of economic weakness, to follow the British line; and Sonnino had his own good reasons for not wanting Benedict's impartial mediation.

The USA, or at least Wilson, was determined to play the role of arbiter in the conflict, whether it was at peace or war. Crusading, anti-European idealism and Wilson's international ambitions were the driving forces behind American policy towards the war, and her attitude towards Benedict's peace efforts. It was, therefore, pretty clear from the beginning of 1917 that unless a papal peace initiative elicited strong and practical support from the European powers at war, Wilson would oppose it. Britain, after the American entry into the war, was not prepared to gainsay Wilson's policy because of its dependence on the USA for any hope of winning the conflict.

In the case of Germany, the calculation by her military commanders after the failed Brusilov Offensive was that Russia could be pushed into capitulation, thus opening up vistas of territorial acquisitions in Poland, the Baltic States, and western Russia that were in fact largely realized by the Treaty of Brest-Litovsk of March 1918. This powerful temptation to return to the policy of the *Drang Nach Osten*, the imperialistic and colonizing drive to the East, coupled with the very correct perception that the survival of the Prussian military monarchy in an age of mass politics would require more than a negotiated, 'stalemate' peace, ruled out accepting papal mediation in August 1917. The fact that 1917 was the 400th anniversary of the start of the Lutheran Reformation did not augur well for the success of papal efforts in Protestant Germany anyway. And, of course, Austria-Hungary was capable of no independent response at all, utterly tied as she was to Germany.

Faced by these brutal realities, Benedict's patient, gentlemanly diplomatic efforts were to no avail. Zivojinovic has argued that Benedict was old-fashioned, out of touch and irrelevant, and J.D. Gregory has claimed, that the Vatican was 'a fifth-rate diplomacy'.[241] Both claims are highly contentious. Benedict's advice to the Emperor Karl certainly does not suggest that he was old-fashioned, out of touch, and blind to the importance of the United States. These were not the reasons for the failure of Benedict's effort. The turbine of modern, mass, total warfare produced forces that were not susceptible to a diplomacy based essentially on morality, on Catholic social doctrine, however much that doctrine might be in tune with the aspirations of other peoples, and even the principles of Wilsonianism. What Benedict was ultimately

[241] Zivojinovic, *The United States*, 13; and Gregory, *On the Edge of Diplomacy*, 89.

fighting against was nationalism (and militarism) in a variety of forms, and his failure to save Austria-Hungary was finally due to that as well.

Perhaps the cause of the failure of Benedict's peace diplomacy was more fundamental than all the explanations advanced so far. His was a fragile, high-risk strategy which depended absolutely upon the Vatican's ability to convince its diplomatic interlocutors of its impartiality and neutrality. In the end, the Vatican under Benedict was not entirely impartial and neutral. Certainly, many politicians and journalists, and consequently sections of the population, in the warring countries had serious doubts about the impartiality and neutrality of the Vatican during the First World War. In the Entente countries that scepticism was widespread and, in the case of France, it was deliberately fostered by anti-clerical propaganda hostile to the Vatican. The machinations of French representatives and journalists in Rome did much to put the Vatican in a bad light in the eyes of Frenchmen.[242] In this regard, the interview which Benedict gave to the French journalist Latapie in June 1915 was particularly damaging.[243] There was rather less hostility towards the Vatican in the Central Powers, but even Germany was prone to periodic waves of anti-Vatican feeling, the most notable example being when the Te Deum was sung in all Roman churches (except St Peter's) to celebrate the British liberation of Jerusalem from the infidel Turks in December 1917.[244] How justified these doubts about the impartiality and neutrality of the Vatican were during the war hardly matters: they were the unfortunate reality in which Benedict had to conduct his diplomacy. But it also has to be said that some attitudes and actions of the Vatican during the war did justify these doubts, like its sympathy towards Austria-Hungary and its preference for a peace based on the *status quo ante bellum*, which was increasingly at odds with the war aims of the Entente powers. There were even moments when the Vatican very clearly abandoned its self-imposed neutrality. One was the episode in which Gasparri gave a warning to Italy about an impending Austro-Hungarian military offensive, and another was even more serious than that. In April 1916, Gasparri, presumably with Benedict's blessing, sought to persuade the German high command to make special efforts to halt the Russian advance on Constantinople.[245] Though the initiative was aborted halfway through, as Morozzo Della Rocca, an Italian historian very sympathetic to Benedict, asks, 'Was this true neutrality?'[246] Of course it was not.

The lesson of Benedict's peace efforts is clear. Though entirely sincere in their aims, that is, to relieve suffering and stop the war, they were undermined

[242] Hachey, *Anglo-Vatican Relations*, 18.
[243] *Diario*, I, 236–237, 26 June 1915.
[244] *Diario*, II, 223, 15 December 1917.
[245] R. Morozzo Della Rocca, 'Benedetto XV e Costantinopoli: fu vera neutralità?' *Cristianesimo nella Storia*, 14 (1993), 550.
[246] Morozzo Della Rocca, 'Benedetto XV e Costantinopoli', 550.

by the hard reality that the Vatican had its own agenda and its own interests, its own 'war aims', so to speak. The papacy is a moral and religious power, not a secular and territorial one, but it still has its own temporal interests which can be at odds with those of other powers and thus ultimately make it impossible for it to be entirely impartial. In Benedict's case this was the urgent need to resolve the Roman Question and, consequently, a desire to be present at the eventual peace congress. But what alternative was there to Benedict's high-risk policy? He could, perhaps, have pursued his humanitarian relief efforts, made moral condemnations of the horrors and atrocities of war, and scrupulously abstained from any diplomatic involvement. This was the alternative which Merry del Val, who opposed Benedict's strategy throughout the war, would undoubtedly have followed. But such an approach would never have been acceptable to Benedict because he was temperamentally incapable of being so passive in the face of events. His charity and courage and, above all, his sense that duty obliged him to act, forced him to follow the policy which he did, with all its risks and dangers, its contradictions and its limited chances of success.

Though it failed to stop the war, Benedict's peace diplomacy eventually bore fruit. In the short term, it gave an immense boost to the diplomatic standing and influence of papal diplomacy, which was to be of great importance in the post-war period. In fact, Benedict's legacy has lasted nearly one hundred years.

3

Benedict XV: The Post-War World and the Church

THE VERSAILLES PEACE SETTLEMENT

On 1 December 1918, Benedict published the encyclical *Quod Iam Diu* in which he welcomed the respite brought by the Armistice of the previous month, and called upon Catholics to pray that the coming peace conference would bring 'a just and lasting peace'.[1] This was a tall order in a Europe ravaged by more than four years of war, where starvation persisted partly because of the continued Allied blockade, which Benedict condemned,[2] and which would experience economic, social, and political breakdown. In the spring and summer of 1919, the statesmen at the Versailles peace conference laboured to resolve the momentous and intractable issues with which they were confronted to reach a territorial settlement in the wake of the collapse of the Ottoman, Hohenzollern, Habsburg, and Russian Empires. Meanwhile, Europe's problems got worse. Influenza began to sweep through Central Europe, killing more civilians worldwide than the war itself, rapid demobilization fuelled political violence, and Bolshevism threatened more and more states.

Benedict and Gasparri were sharply critical of the peace which eventually emerged from Versailles and were afraid that its inadequacies exposed Europe and the Middle East to the continuing threat of war. They were not entirely wrong. The fundamental defect of the Versailles Peace Settlement, in their eyes, was that it was not based on Christian principles. It was easy to criticize the handiwork of the statesmen at Versailles, especially in retrospect, and many did, but as King Albert of the Belgians said, 'What would you have? They did what they could.'[3] Nevertheless, the peace settlement left Benedict

[1] Carlen, *Papal Encyclicals*, III, *Quam Diu*, 1 December 1920, 161–162.

[2] Bellocchi, *Tutte le Encicliche*, VIII, 274–275, *Nobis quidem*, Allocuzione.

[3] As quoted in S. Marks, *The Illusion of Peace: International Relations in Europe, 1918–1933*, London and Basingstoke, 1976, 23.

and the Roman Catholic Church with many problems, as well as a number of unanticipated opportunities.

BENEDICT AND THE PEACE CONFERENCE

The greatest defect of the peace conference in Benedict's eyes was quite simply the fact that his representatives were excluded from it, as Sonnino had intended. Though both Benedict and Gasparri had persistently denied that they wanted a place at the conference table for the Holy See,[4] those denials were as false as the denials of Sonnino that Article 15 of the Treaty of London excluded that presence. In 1916, an article was published in the prestigious Italian journal, *Nuova Antologia*, written by Umberto Benigni, regarding the eventual peace conference and the participants in it. Benedict saw the draft of the article and suggested modifications. He observed that the article gave the game away, 'it makes it too obvious that its [the article's] principal objective is to encourage the idea of the participation of the Holy See', and suggested that, as a start, the article should argue that 'all powers not interested in dividing the spoils should, nevertheless have a right to participate. Then to introduce the question of the admission of the neutral powers, as a matter of principle,' and not even to mention the papacy.[5] Curiously, when the article was eventually published, it ignored all of his suggestions and followed a different, more direct tack, arguing that if the Kings of England and Prussia, the Czar, all heads of their own churches, and the Sultan, Caliph of Islam, were entitled to attend the peace conference, then so was the pope.[6] Benedict's subtle modifications would not have had much effect anyway, and in 1917 and 1918 the Vatican waged a concerted diplomatic campaign to induce the Allies to abandon Article 15. Strong representations were made to the British government to persuade it of the injustice and inappropriateness of Article 15, an attempt which initially had some chance of success since Balfour had shown sympathy for the Vatican's claims. An attempt was also made to persuade American cardinal, James Gibbons, to lead a Catholic press campaign against papal exclusion from the peace conference, but he declined on the grounds that the position of Catholics in the United States was too delicate.[7] Gasparri also sought to mobilize the neutral powers, most especially faithful Spain,[8] and as a last desperate throw an attempt was made to get Cardinal

[4] Garzia, *La Questione Romana*, 139.

[5] ASV, AES, 1369/1372, memo, undated; comments in Benedict's hand.

[6] *Nuova Antologia*, 'Il Papa e il congresso di Pace', 1 March 1916.

[7] Zivojinovic, *The United States*, 140.

[8] ASV, SdS, Guerra, 1914–18, fasc. 70, 14480, Gasparri to nuncio in Madrid, 15 December 1918.

Mercier invited to the conference in the hope that the outstanding international eminence of the Belgian prelate could be used to raise matters of interest to the Holy See.[9] A plan was conceived whereby Cardinal Mercier would be either invited in his own right or be included in the Belgian delegation to the Versailles Conference. The Vatican was prepared to give Cardinal Mercier *carte blanche* in terms of what he might or might not say if admitted to the Conference, backed up by carefully orchestrated petitions for a restoration in some form of the temporal power signed by the cardinals of the world's leading residential sees.[10] However, Mercier was not, in fact, invited to the peace conference. All these efforts failed, but it is indicative of just how seriously the Italian government took them that Sonnino waged an equally vigorous diplomatic counteroffensive.[11]

Benedict's comments on the original draft of the *Nuova Antologia* article demonstrate that he feared that exclusion from the peace conference would damage the prestige and authority of the Holy See.[12] The papacy had been represented at the Vienna Peace Congress of 1814–15 where Cardinal Consalvi, the Secretary of State, had obtained entry to the inner circle of powers and had negotiated the restoration of the Papal States for his master, Pope Pius VII.[13] Benedict could not seriously expect Gasparri to do the same at Versailles, but the exclusion of the papacy from the Hague Conferences of 1899, due to Italian intervention,[14] still rankled, and the Vatican's participation in the peace conference, in any capacity, would have been a tremendous boost to its international prestige. Benedict did at least have a hand in bringing about the behind-the-scenes meeting between Mgr Bonaventura Cerretti, the Vatican Under-Secretary of State, and the Italian prime minister, Vittorio Emanuele Orlando.

In the event, exclusion was no great diplomatic defeat because none of the neutral powers were admitted to the conference, thus saving the Holy See a major loss of face. When matters that really touched upon the Vatican's interests came up at the conference, like the future of the German missions, Cerretti ensured that behind-the-scenes diplomacy obtained for the Holy See what it desired.[15] Indeed, Cerretti's success in protecting the German missions

[9] R. Aubert, 'Le Cardinal Mercier et la Question Romaine en 1918–1919', in Jean-Pierre Hendrickx, Jean Pirotte, and Luc Courtois (eds), *Le Cardinal Mercier (1851–1926), Un prélat d'avant-garde. Publications du professeur Roger Aubert rassemblées à l'occasion de ses 80 ans*, Louvain-la-Neuve, 1994, 281–282.

[10] Aubert, 'Le Cardinal Mercier', 257–260.

[11] DDI, Quinta Serie, vol. X, doc. 547, Sonnino to ambassadors in Paris and London.

[12] ASV, AES, Italia, 1917–18, 1369/1372, Benedict's memorandum on the draft of the *Nuova Antologia* article.

[13] E.E.Y. Hales, *Revolution and the Papacy, 1769–1846*, London, 1960, 230–236.

[14] De Valk, 'A Diplomatic Disaster', 435–463.

[15] V. De Marco, 'L'intervento della Santa Sede a Versailles, in favore delle missioni tedesche', in Rumi (ed.), *Benedetto XV*, 65–82.

demonstrated that the Holy See was recognized as the sovereign, international Catholic authority by the Great Powers. As for the Roman Question, Cerretti made far more progress in his clandestine talks with Orlando than could have been secured in open conference; indeed, even to have raised the issue in such circumstances would have set progress back for years by alienating Italy.

Exclusion from the conference almost certainly spared Benedict and Gasparri a lot of other problems. It is hard to see how the Vatican could have maintained its position of impartiality between the powers if it had taken part in the conference as controversial matters of war guilt, disarmament, reparations, and, particularly, territorial changes were being discussed and decided. It would have been even more difficult if it had actually signed the peace treaties, as Gasparri recognized. As we shall see, much of the Vatican's post-war diplomatic prestige and room for manoeuvre was built precisely upon its distance from the peace settlement. One of the most difficult issues facing the conference was that of Italian claims to parts of the Adriatic coast of the former Habsburg dominions, most especially Fiume (Rijeka), an issue on which Orlando felt compelled to abandon the conference in the summer of 1919. Gasparri was extremely unsympathetic towards the Italian claims. He argued forcefully to Carlo Monti that the Italians were unrealistic and that it was better that they 'give up their claims to a few shoals in the Adriatic and seek ample compensation in Asia Minor, where we could have in abundance those raw materials which we lack and for which we depend on foreign imports'; he also argued that the acquisition of Bolzano, with its German-speaking majority, was a mistake.[16] The merest hint of such feelings in public would have had a disastrous effect upon Italo-Vatican relations.

But there were far bigger issues on which the views of Benedict and Gasparri diverged radically from those not only of Italy but of the other Allied powers. The matter of most important concern was the 'German question'. In April 1918, Gasparri had expressed his and Benedict's view that one of the most dangerous consequences of the likely dissolution of the Habsburg Empire was that it would leave Germany more powerful than ever; furthermore, with the gains made in the Treaty of Brest-Litovsk with the Russian Bolshevik regime, to the already 63 million Reich Germans would probably be added 30 million Germans in the Baltic States, Austria, and the Sudeten Lands.[17] This perception was very much in line with the traditional policy of Rampolla, of whom Benedict and Gasparri had both been pupils. In November 1918, Gasparri reiterated his fear that Italy and France would be unable to contain the new German 'colossus' and that the 'successor states' to the Austro-Hungarian and Russian Empires would not be able to oppose it either.[18] In fact, as a result of Germany's defeat, in the short term the pendulum swung in favour of

[16] *Diario*, I, 467, 24 April 1919.
[17] *Diario*, I, 299, 20 April 1919.
[18] *Diario*, I, 395–396, 9 November 1918.

French hegemony over Europe, an adjustment to the European balance of power which was equally unacceptable to the Vatican. *L'Osservatore Romano* and *La Civiltà Cattolica* repeatedly stated their objections to the Allied treatment of Germany: according to the Jesuit journal, the Treaty of Versailles 'humiliated Germany'.[19] The Vatican objected in particular to the 'War Guilt' clause, the size of reparations and Allied attempts to bring the Kaiser to trial as a 'war criminal'. Gasparri made strenuous efforts to prevent the latter, using Cerretti to lobby the statesmen at Versailles, with some success.[20] He also argued that the size of the reparations bill imposed upon Germany was too harsh and threatened a quick return to European economic stability.[21]

THE VATICAN AND THE LEAGUE OF NATIONS

The most characteristically 'Wilsonian' feature of the Versailles Peace Settlement was the creation of the League of Nations, whose Covenant the American president had insisted be inserted at the beginning of the Treaty of Versailles. Italy was very anxious about the possibility that the Vatican would seek to join the League, and in May 1919 Orlando sent Monti to find out: Benedict gave a very non-committal answer.[22] The Holy See was not, however, invited to join nor did it seek admission. If their attitude in 1929, when the question of the Holy See joining the League was raised after the establishment of the sovereign, independent State of the Vatican City, is anything to go by, then Britain and France would have opposed its admission in 1920. The USA would surely not have supported the idea either: in June 1919, a certain Senator Sherman made a speech claiming that, 'twenty-four of the forty Christian nations are spiritually dominated by the Vatican, thus the pope wishes to rule the world through the League': the speech was dismissed by other senators, but President Wilson would have been too wary of the strong Protestant lobby in the United States to have ever countenanced Vatican involvement in the League.[23]

The Holy See's effective exclusion from the League was one reason for the hostility of the Vatican organs towards it. In June 1920, commenting on Benedict's encyclical *Pacem Dei Munus*, the Jesuit fortnightly strongly attacked the League, claiming that the themes of the encyclical:

[19] LaCC, 71, 2 (1929), 506.

[20] S. A. Stehlin, 'The Emergence of a New Vatican Diplomacy during the Great War and its Aftermath', in P. C. Kent and J. Pollard (eds), *Papal Diplomacy in the Modern Age*, Westport, CN, and London, 1994, 6.

[21] Stehlin, 'The Emergence of a New Vatican Diplomacy', 3.

[22] Stehlin, 'The Emergence of a New Vatican Diplomacy', 3.

[23] ASV, DAUS, V, 97, telegram of 21 June 1919 from Bonzano to Gasparri.

> have got nothing in common with that mockery, the so-called 'League of Nations' . . . which is the expression of an atheistic and utilitarian policy, with its harsh exclusions and odious presuppositions, where the Holy Name of God has no place and where the rights of Christ and his Church receive no recognition.[24]

The article also condemned 'the primacy of *egoistic and nationalistic* [original italics] considerations' in international politics, and concluded by declaring that, 'No, the pope does not approve of either exclusivisms or imperialisms, or of the other excesses of nationalism and patriotism.'[25] It was a comprehensive condemnation of the policies followed by the Allied powers since the end of the war. Though Benedict's encyclical was rather less forceful in its language than this article—it called for nations to 'unite in one league, or rather a family of peoples', as if the League did not already exist—it is likely that the Jesuit journal was expressing the pope's deeper feelings.[26]

In the encyclical Benedict once more appealed for worldwide disarmament and implicitly endorsed the idea of European integration. According to Mizzi, 'the first, hesitant mention of the possibility of European unification in a pontifical document is to be found in the encyclical *Pacem Dei Munus*, 1920'.[27] But the core of the encyclical was Benedict's lament that the peace settlement was not built on the Christian principles of justice and, above all, charity.[28] Benedict argued that because of the absence of charity—Christian love—latent hostilities between peoples continued and there could be no real reconciliation and therefore no lasting peace. His major concern was undoubtedly the relationship between France and Germany, which was to deteriorate badly in 1923 with the Ruhr crisis. Benedict's reference to charity was more than just an appeal for Christian love among nations, it also encompassed the practical application of that love, that is, charitable works: 'stretch the bonds of charity', he declared, and he went on to remind his readers that: 'we see immense areas utterly desolate, uncultivated and abandoned; multitudes reduced to want of food, clothing and shelter; innumerable widows and orphans bereft of everything. . . .'[29] Benedict was as active in seeking to relieve this suffering as he had been during the war. He himself gave donations on several occasions, and the Vatican raised 5 million lire alone to relieve the Russian famine 1921.[30] Benedict had a particular concern for children, and issued two separate encyclicals, *Paterno Iam Diu* in 1919 and *Annus Iam Plenus* in 1920, in which he appealed for funds to relieve their distress.[31] Perhaps the most enduring monument to his charity is the Save

[24] LaCC, 2 (1920), 567. [25] LaCC, 2 (1920), 567.
[26] Carlen, *Papal Encyclicals*, III: *Pacem Dei Munus Pulcherrimum*, 23 May 1920, 174.
[27] P. Mizzi, *L'Unione Europea nei documenti pontifici*, Malta, 1979, vi.
[28] Carlen, *Papal Encyclicals*, III, 171–175. [29] Carlen, *Papal Encyclicals*, III, 174.
[30] *Diario*, II, 567, 26 December 1920.
[31] Carlen, *Papal Encyclicals*, III, 169–170 and 203–205.

the Children Fund, to which he gave strong public support after it was established in 1919.[32] It was thanks to this support that collections for the children of Eastern Europe were taken up in Catholic, Anglican, and other churches on 28 December 1921, the feast of the Holy Innocents.[33] On the pope's death in 1922, the Save the Children Fund founder, Eglantyne Jebb, paid tribute to Benedict's work: 'Pope Benedict XV has died before the world has recognised the magnitude of the debt which it owes to him for his championship of the world's children.'[34]

THE VATICAN AND THE 'SUCCESSOR STATES'

Another problem for Benedict in the post-war peace settlement was the application of Wilson's principle of 'national self-determination'. In his various appeals for peace during the war, Benedict had demonstrated his unease with the phenomenon of emerging nationalist forces, indeed, on a copy of the peace note of August 1917, he wrote:

> The principle of nationality is a good thing when it is free; bad when it is imposed. On the basis of the principle understood in this sense, which means the principle of the aspirations of the peoples, so-called territorial questions should be regulated.[35]

The Jesuit journal took this thinking a stage further when, in 1919, it entitled an important article on national self-determination 'On the Just Aspirations of Peoples'.[36] In other words, no national ethnic group had an automatic right to self-determination and the nation state was not necessarily preferable to a multi-ethnic, dynastic state like the Habsburg Empire. The papacy had also shown wary concern over the linguistic struggles in Belgium—Flemish separatism[37]—and the grievances of French-speaking inhabitants of Ontario province in Canada.[38] At the same time, in private, Gasparri expressed an opinion that was not popular in the Allied countries, that is, that the creation

[32] R. Norton, 'Benedict XV and the Save the Children Fund', *The Month*, 28 July 1995, 281–283.

[33] Norton, 'Benedict XV and the Save the Children Fund', 281.

[34] As quoted in Norton, 'Benedict XV and the Save the Children Fund', 281.

[35] Cited in Morozzo Della Rocca, 'Benedetto XV e il nazionalismo', 552.

[36] LaCC, 71, 1 (1919), 451.

[37] Bellocchi, *Tutte le Encicliche*, VII, 139, *Cum simper, ut ips*, 10 February 1921, Epistola; the Vatican took the Flemish question so seriously that it was discussed by meetings of cardinals twice during Benedict's pontificate. See ASV, AES, Sessioni, 1920, 1236, 30 April, Belgio, Questione fiamminga, and 1921, 1238, 30 January, Belgio, Questione fiamminga.

[38] See the letters to Canadian bishops in Bellocchi, *Tutte le Encicliche*, VIII, 46; *Commisso divinitus*, 8 September 1916, Epistola; and 82, *Animus tuus*, 16 October 1918, Epistola.

of the successor states was not a good thing because they could not be self-sufficient, they would be vulnerable to the Bolshevik menace (a fear that had also prompted worries about too harsh a treatment of Germany), and that they would tend to fight among themselves, which history proved only too painfully to be correct.[39]

Ultimately, the Vatican's attitude towards emerging nationalities would be determined by essentially pragmatic considerations. Thus, when faced with the force of events—the declarations of independence by the Poles, Czechs, and other subject nationalities of the Habsburg Empire—in a public letter to Gasparri in November 1918 Benedict announced that he had told the nuncio in Vienna to establish friendly relations with all 'the various nationalities of the Austro-Hungarian Empire who constituted themselves into independent states'.[40] The same principle was adopted in face of the secession of Finland and the Baltic States—Estonia, Latvia, and Lithuania—from the Russian Empire. But there were bitter disputes over the rights and treatment of minorities in the successor states, and over boundaries between them, for example the most Catholic of the new states, Lithuania and Poland, engaged in repeated armed clashes over the Vilnius question in 1919 and 1920.

In October 1917, the members of Regency Council constituted in Warsaw, in anticipation of the restoration of the Kingdom of Poland under the tutelage of the Central Powers (Germany and Austria-Hungary), sent a letter to Benedict requesting recognition of their emerging state, and during a visit of Regency Council to Vienna, Mgr Kakowski, archbishop of Warsaw, spoke with the nuncio, Valfre' di Bonzo, to explain the needs of Church in Poland. A similar visit was made to Pacelli in Berlin. The result of this démarche was the surprise appointment of Mgr Achille Ratti, the Librarian of the Vatican, as 'apostolic visitator', in order for him to assess the situation.[41] But since Ratti's brief was to cover both Poland and Lithuania, Benedict was implicitly recognizing Lithuanian independence as well.[42] Benedict exhibited a particular solicitude for Catholic Poland so that in a letter to the Polish bishops he pointed out that only papacy had protested against the partitions of Poland—especially Clement XIV. Gregory XVI and Pius IX also did the same, and he reminded them that he himself had repeated his support for their aspirations in the 'peace note' of August 1917.[43] The Holy See formally recognized Poland on 30 March 1919 and Ratti became nuncio. Vacancies in the Polish episcopate created by the Russians were filled and Archbishops Kakowski and Dalbor were created cardinals in December 1919. As Gasparri would declare

[39] *Diario*, II, 391–392, 5 November 1918.

[40] *Diario*, II, 390, 27 October 1918.

[41] *Diario*, II, 390, 27 October 1918.

[42] *Diario*, II, 390, 27 October 1918. For an account of Ratti's experience of Poland and the Baltic States, see N. Pease, *Rome's Most Faithful Daughter: The Catholic Church and Independent Poland, 1914–1939*, Athens, OH, 2009, chs 1–4.

[43] Bellocchi, *Tutte le Encicliche*, VIII, 81, *Nel grave pericolo*, 15 October 1918, Epistola.

in his memoirs, 'With all of these nominations being made at the same time, the Holy See solemnly confirmed its recognition of Polish independence.'[44] But his Polish assignment quickly turned out to be a bed of nails for Ratti. As nuncio, he had to carefully avoid being drawn into domestic political disputes, cultivating good relations with all politicians of whatever party. Furthermore, he was faced by a situation in Poland which would influence his later policy as pope: the involvement of the clergy in politics. Indeed, when he succeeded Benedict in 1922 Ratti insisted that Mgr Teodorowiz, Armenian rite bishop of Leopoli, and Mgr Sapieha, prince-bishop of Cracow, resign the parliamentary seats to which they had been elected.[45] He faced further problems over the plebiscites in Silesia, the area disputed between Germany and Poland, where Cardinal Bartram of Breslau, against the instructions of the Vatican, openly favoured the Germans in Silesian plebiscites but did not tell Ratti, who had also been appointed supervisory commissioner. This seriously damaged Ratti's standing with the Polish episcopate.

Polish foreign policy, in particular its claim to large areas of the territory of its neighbours in order to recreate 'Greater Poland', also caused problems for Ratti and the Holy See. In April 1919, Polish troops entered Wilno (Vilnius), the capital of newly independent Lithuania, but which had a substantial Polish population. Poland also invaded the Ukraine, taking its capital, Kiev. Then her neighbours turned against her with the result that the Red Army appeared before Warsaw in the summer of 1920, provoking alarm in Central and Western Europe. Despite the fact that he had supported Polish claims to nationhood in his peace note of August 1917 and had also made the point to Monti in October 1918 that a resurrected Poland would serve as a strong bulwark both against the Bolsheviks and Germany,[46] Benedict felt obliged to urge moderation in Polish demands after the end of the war.[47]

The new state of Czechoslovakia, where Catholics were the overwhelming majority but whose political leadership, especially Thomas Masaryk and Edvard Beneš, was tainted by Freemasonry and anti-clericalism, presented problems almost immediately after its foundation. Initially, the problems emerged from inside the Czech (as opposed to Slovak) Catholic Church. The Jednota movement of priests demanding both services in the vernacular and the abolition of clerical celibacy was condemned by Benedict in letters to the bishops of Bohemia on two occasions in January 1920,[48] and the movement was eventually dissolved by them. But some of the more obstinate members

[44] G. Spadolini (ed.), *Il Cardinale Gasparri e la Questione Romana: con brani delle memorie inedite*, Florence, 1972, 91–92.

[45] Gasparri, *Il Cardinale Gasparri e la Questione Romana*, 93.

[46] *Diario*, II, 390, 27 October 1918.

[47] Morozzo Della Rocca, 'Benedetto XV e il nazionalismo', 559.

[48] Bellocchi, *Tutte le Encicliche*, VIII, 109; *Quandoquidem non*, 3 January 1920, Epistola; and 112, *Cum in catholiae*, 29 January 1920, Epistola.

formed a dissident, schismatic Church, which was, in its turn, condemned by the Holy Office.[49] Czechoslovakia would continue to cause many headaches for the men in the Vatican in the years to come.

Benedict and Gasparri had particular reservations about the emergence of Yugoslavia (the Kingdom of the Serbs, Croats, and Slovenes, as it was originally called). If they did not support extravagant Italian claims in the Adriatic, they were equally unhappy about the domination of two Catholic peoples—the Croats and the Slovenes—by the Orthodox Serbs. In January 1919, Gasparri actually despatched an emissary to Zagreb with the task of impeding this union, but it was too late.[50] Benedict went so far as to express the opinion that the Slavs in general were less intelligent but more numerous than other races.[51] In fact, notwithstanding the deep ethnic tensions in the new state, the treatment of Croatian and Slovene Catholics by the Belgrade government gave few grounds for complaint on the Vatican's part.[52] Despite all these problems, by the end of Benedict's reign the Holy See had established relations with all the successor states, including Austria and Hungary, and had begun moves towards negotiating concordats with several of them.

BENEDICT, BRITAIN, AND IRELAND

Ireland was arguably a 'successor state', born as it was out of a revolt against one of the powers at war, Great Britain, in the Dublin Easter Rising of 1916. A year later, in a conversation with Carlo Monti, Gasparri made a very revealing statement about Britain: 'The Holy See absolutely cannot afford to get on the wrong side of England which gives the broadest freedom to Catholics: it would be the end of Catholicism in England.'[53] He was exaggerating the dangers of such a rupture to British Catholics, but the Vatican could certainly not afford poor relations with the British Empire, in whose various dominions, protectorates, and colonial territories there were very substantial numbers of Catholics. Moreover, following the United State's withdrawal from world affairs in 1920, Britain became the world superpower by default, extending its influence through colonial gains at Versailles. The continuation of the British

[49] ASV, AES, Sessioni, 1257, 8, 1922, Cecoslovakia, Chiesa Nazionale. The government wanted the shared use of Catholic churches with the Orthodox. SU (the Holy Office) condemned schismatic churches (vernacular, clerical marriage, and democracy) on 15 February 1920. Schismatics still had a lot of influence in the clergy association, Jednota, so it was dissolved by bishops. The Prague government proposed a law to regulate mixed use of Catholic churches. The meeting unanimously decided to treat the Czech government firmly on this issue.

[50] *Diario*, II, 432, 28 January 1919.

[51] *Diario*, II, 438, 13 February 1919.

[52] S. Alexander, *Church and State in Yugoslavia since 1945*, Cambridge, 1979, 2–6.

[53] *Diario*, II, 474, 30 May 1918.

mission to the Holy See, which was in some doubt after the end of the war, was therefore enormously valuable to Benedict and Gasparri. But preserving good relations with Britain was one reason why Benedict and Gasparri found the Irish question to be one of the most troublesome they faced, and why they handled it with the greatest care.

Given the especially close historical ties between the papacy and Irish Catholicism—as La Bella points out, there was never any major schism or heresy in the history of the Irish Church[54]—one would have expected a strong degree of support for Irish nationalism in the Vatican. Certainly, there was no lack of supporters of Irish nationalism in the Irish ecclesiastical community in Rome, with Mgr Hagan of the Irish College at their head.[55] In addition, the Irish diaspora in Australia, New Zealand, Canada, and the United States, and especially some of its leaders, like Archbishop Mannix of Melbourne, also showed strong support for the Irish cause, and lobbied the Vatican accordingly.[56] But the position within the Vatican was rather different. *L'Osservatore Romano* was initially quite hostile, which is not surprising. Benedict was not enamoured of the idea of national self-determination per se so the Irish were not treated differently from, say, the Czechs before 1918, nor the United Kingdom of Great Britain and Ireland differently from the Habsburg Empire. The attitude of the Vatican organ was also swayed by suspicions that Sinn Féin had Bolshevik leanings.[57] But though Benedict never seems to have treated Catholic Ireland with the same solicitous concern as Catholic Poland, he and Gasparri were clearly sympathetic to the plight of the Irish,[58] and this came out in the pages of *La Civilità Cattolica*: in December 1920, it expressed support for proposals for peace, but urged that the link with the British Crown and the defence of the British Empire had to be guaranteed.[59] But other forces were at work to counter the influence of Benedict and Gasparri. Within the curia, their influence was balanced by that of their old enemies, Merry del Val and De Lai, on whose side that English super-patriot, Cardinal Gasquet, played a supporting role. Cardinal Bourne of Westminster also lobbied the Vatican on Britain's behalf.[60] And then there was the British envoy, who was continually being urged by the Foreign Office to press the British case, sometimes with scarcely veiled threats that Britain would break off relations if the Vatican did not comply with its wishes.[61]

The Vatican's policy towards Ireland seems to have followed that of the Irish episcopate: it was less than enthusiastic about either the Easter Rising of

[54] F. La Bella, *La Questione irlandese e il vaticano*, Turin, 1996, 5a.

[55] D. Keogh, *The Vatican, the Bishops and Irish Politics*, Cambridge, 1986, 34 and 39.

[56] See ASV, DAUS, V, 82/3 for the file of letters about Ireland received by the Apostolic Delegate in Washington, DC, Mgr Bonzano.

[57] Keogh, *The Vatican*, 40.

[58] Keogh, *The Vatican*, 83.

[59] LaCC, 71, 3 (1920), 97.

[60] Keogh, *The Vatican*, 40.

[61] La Bella, *La questione irlandese*, 62–63.

1916 or the hunger strike of Lord Mayor MacSwiney of Cork, which resulted in his death in 1920.[62] The Irish bishops were initially divided, but conscription, the summary execution of Irish Nationalists after the Rising, and the activities of the Black and Tans during the Anglo-Irish War won increasing sympathy among them for the nationalist cause. The Vatican was aware of the deep divisions between older and younger clergy in Ireland, thanks to a report by Mgr Cerretti in December 1918.[63] The Vatican was encouraged by the British to condemn the Irish nationalist movement, but refrained from doing so: it is unlikely that Benedict and Gasparri seriously contemplated such a step.[64] Instead, in April 1921, Benedict published a letter to the Irish bishops, appealing for peace. The genesis of the letter was a complex one. There was an inconclusive debate on Vatican policy towards Ireland in the Congregation for Extraordinary Ecclesiastical Affairs, in which Merry del Val had asked for a moral condemnation of the violent, terroristic methods of Sinn Féin, without calling for the same for the equally violent methods of the British auxiliaries, the Black and Tans. Benedict and Gasparri, further, commissioned a secret report on the Irish situation which recommended a pacific approach by the pope.[65] Archbishop Mannix also appears to have influenced the Vatican in this direction, though the content of Benedict's letter to the primate of Ireland, Cardinal Logue, could not have satisfied his partisan instincts.[66]

In his letter, Benedict followed the policy which he had maintained throughout the First World War, benevolent impartiality, coupled with practical suggestions for a peace process, and a call for Catholics to engage in charitable work in relief of the devastation and suffering in Ireland, setting an example himself by donating 200,000 lire.[67] He was motivated by a genuine horror of war and desire for peace, an unwillingness to divide the various Catholic communities of the British Empire by taking sides, and a concern not to stir up anti-Catholicism in Britain. The British Empire was the world in microcosm; the Irish conflict a miniscule version of the Great War. The core of his message was his heart-felt statement: 'we hope, and we implore the parties in conflict to bring to an end the fury of this war as soon as possible so that a stable peace and a sincere determination of the spirits will conquer the great flame of envy'.[68] The appeal had a mixed reception in Britain and Ireland: it

[62] La Bella, *La questione irlandese*, 128–129.

[63] ASV, AES, Stati Eccl., 1350, Italia, 1915–1924, vol. III, Missione di Msgr Cerretti a Parigi, Londra, Washington e scambio di corrispondenza, Cerretti to Gasparri, 9 December 1918.

[64] La Bella, *La questione irlandese*, 174–175.

[65] ASV, AES, Sessioni, 1921, 1238, 13 January, Irlanda, Situazione politica.

[66] Keogh, *The Vatican*, 75.

[67] For the text of the letter, see Bellocchi, *Tutte le Encicliche*, VIII, 143, *Ubi primum*, 27 April 1921, Epistola.

[68] Bellocchi, *Tutte le Encicliche*, VIII, 143, *Ubi primum*, 27 April 1921, Epistola.

heartened the majority, without satisfying the extremists on either side, or even the Irish 'lobby' in Rome.[69] The letter came at a critical moment; opinion in Britain and the British Empire was shifting against government policy because of the atrocities of the Black and Tans. Peace negotiations between representatives of the British government and the Irish Dáil suddenly and unexpectedly led to agreement in December 1921, and one of the last acts of Benedict's pontificate was the despatch of congratulatory telegrams to both sides on the signing of the Treaty.[70] Benedict was lucky to be spared the further horrors of the civil war between the supporters and opponents of the Treaty, which broke out shortly after his death.

PALESTINE, ZIONISM, AND THE VATICAN

With the exception of Russia, which the Allied Powers never managed to settle—its fate being decided in the civil war between the Bolsheviks and the various 'White' forces—the most difficult problem which faced them was the fate of the former Ottoman Empire. Their endeavours to settle its future, in the Treaty of Sèvres, failed because of the emergence of Turkish nationalism led by Kemal Atatürk, who successfully resisted the attempts of both the Greeks and the Italians to seize substantial parts of Asia Minor. What Versailles did settle, however, was the future of the Turkish Middle East where League of Nations mandates to govern were accorded to France for Lebanon and Syria and to Britain for Palestine, Transjordan, and Iraq. But the French were far from satisfied with this division of the spoils, and it was into the cauldron of Franco-British rivalries, and the resulting intrigues around the final settlement of Palestine in particular, that Benedict and Gasparri were drawn in the immediate post-war period. And it has to be said that the Vatican was not averse to stirring the pot, indeed it added another ingredient by encouraging the Italians to get involved. In 1919 and 1920, three cardinals, one British, one French, and one Italian, visited Palestine in turn, each being used to serve the interests of their home country. What was at stake was influence. The French sought to preserve the liturgical honours accorded their representatives in services of the various churches, in virtue of the 'protectorate' which they had exercised over the Christians under the Turkish regime: with the latter's fall, the protectorate, and the honours, lapsed but French governments refused to abandon them, and so the Vatican was dragged in to make a decision in favour of the French, which annoyed the Italians who had hoped to acquire some of the former French influence.

[69] La Bella, *La questione irlandese*, 175. [70] Keogh, *The Vatican*, 69.

Above and beyond striving to avoid being entangled in great power rivalries, the Vatican had two major concerns in Palestine: the administration of the Holy Places and the future of the Christian, especially Catholic, minority. The factor which seemed to threaten the Vatican's interests in both cases was the Balfour Declaration of 1917 which, preceding the British liberation of Jerusalem from the Turks, committed the British government to setting up a 'Jewish Homeland' in Palestine.[71] Benedict and Gasparri became convinced that an augmentation of the Jewish presence in Palestine posed a threat to Catholics' interests there. A particular fear was that the advent of British rule signified a takeover by the Jews of the administration in Palestine. There is no evidence that the proportion of Jews in the administration outstripped their presence in the population at large,[72] but this fear was not allayed by the appointment of a Jew, Sir Herbert Samuel, to be High Commissioner (governor) of Palestine. In the circumstances, it seems to have been a singularly tactless move on the part of the British, certainly not one likely to inspire confidence in the impartiality of their administration towards the various ethnic and religious groups in the country. Samuel tried to pre-empt Vatican hostility by making a visit to the pope in July 1920, but the attempt clearly failed. Benedict was not convinced by Samuel's protestations of impartiality.[73] The Vatican had hoped that an international body would be set up to deal specifically with the Holy Places, but the British rejected this idea in favour of continuing the set-up under the Turkish administration, whereby representatives of the various religious groups acted in a consultative capacity.[74] This was not a satisfactory solution for Benedict. In his allocution of June 1920, he had warned that 'it would be a terrible grief to Us and for all Christian faithful if infidels were placed in a more prominent position: much more if those most holy sanctuaries of the Christian religion were given into the charge of non-Christians': the reference to 'infidels' was clearly aimed at Jews and Muslims.[75] Eventually, the Vatican accepted the British proposal, with a proviso that all disputes over rights in the Holy Places would ultimately be settled by British courts.[76]

One of major international issues in which Cardinal Mercier became involved after the war was Palestine. He first proposed that Belgium assume responsibility for the international administration of Palestine and the Holy Places following the fall of the Ottoman Empire.[77]

[71] S. Minerbi, *The Vatican, the Holy Land and Zionism, 1895–1925*, Oxford, 1986, 117–120.

[72] Minerbi, *The Vatican*, 150.

[73] *Diario*, II, 563, 29 July 1920.

[74] Minerbi, *The Vatican*, 89–90.

[75] Bellocchi, *Tutte le Encicliche*, VIII, 145, *Causa Nobis*, 13 June 1921, Allocution.

[76] Minerbi, *The Vatican*, 89.

[77] R. Aubert, 'Les Démarches du Cardinal Mercier en vue de l'octroi à la Belgique d'un mandate sur le Palestine', in Hendrickx et al. (eds), *Le Cardinal Mercier*, 281–327.

The Vatican was very circumspect in its support for Mercier's plan, never allowing this to become public knowledge lest it offend the very powerful British Empire delegation. In fact, there was never really any serious likelihood that the British pass up the chance of extending their influence in the Middle East in favour of Belgium, though there was some talk of the Belgians exercising a 'moral protectorate' over the Holy Places in Jerusalem, Bethlehem, and Nazareth.[78]

The wave of Jewish immigration that followed British rule intensified Vatican fears for the future of Palestine as a whole. One fear was that many of the Jewish immigrants from Europe would have Bolshevik tendencies; many of the leading Bolsheviks—Leon Trotsky in Russia, Kurt Eisner in Bavaria, and Béla Kun in Hungary were Jews. In the latter case, the Church had been persecuted under the short-lived Soviet regime.[79] The influx of Jews also seemed to threaten an unwelcome modernization in broader terms: in March 1921 Benedict protested against the plans of Jewish businessmen to build what would now be called 'leisure complexes' near sacred sites, such as Mount Carmel and the Church of the Holy Sepulchre.[80] There were already fears that wealthy Jews, or Jews backed by American finance, would buy out Christian and Muslim landowners.[81] It was not only the Jews, however, whom Benedict feared. In his March 1919 allocution, he warned that 'non-Catholic foreigners, furnished with abundant means . . . are there spreading their errors'.[82] He was worried about British and American Protestant groups who appeared to be 'buying' converts by offering free education to Catholic and Orthodox Christians. By 1919, the Vatican must have begun to regret the passing of the Turkish administration which had been celebrated by the ringing of church bells in Rome in December 1917.

The arguments over Palestine demonstrated the strong vein of anti-Semitism in the Italian Church, and especially in the Jesuit order, which came out in the comments of *La Civiltà Cattolica* on events in the Holy Land, and on the pope's pronouncements on them, like the claim in March 1919 that Palestine was 'falling into the hands of the enemies of Christian civilisation'.[83] A year later it was even more blatantly anti-Semitic:

> the Jews are distributing their money inside the closed circle of the tents of Israel, using it to dominate Christians . . . The Jews are seeking to accumulate their money by taking it from Christians, regarding it as their legitimate right as chosen people to take possession of the spoils of Egypt.[84]

[78] Aubert, 'Les Démarches du Cardinal Mercier'. [79] LaCC, 72, 2 (1921), 519.
[80] LaCC, 72, 2 (1921), 87. [81] Minerbi, *The Vatican*, 153.
[82] LaCC, 70, 2 (1919), 4. [83] LaCC, 70, 2 (1919), 12.
[84] LaCC, 71, 3 (1920), 42–43.

The Jesuits' anti-Semitic campaign was starkly at odds with Benedict's policy during the war: in 1915 and 1916 the Vatican appears to have given its backing to the Deloncle plan for a Jewish 'homeland' in Poland, a proposal which received some support among Jews in France and the United States, though not in Britain.[85] Though there is no evidence that Benedict attempted to restrain the crude anti-Semitism of *La Civiltà Cattolica*, the overall thrust of Vatican policy on Palestine was anti-Zionist rather than anti-Semitic.

Benedict's concern, uttered in his allocution of March 1921, was that the Jews would 'obtain a position of preponderance and privilege in Palestine', and he complained that 'the situation of Christians in Palestine has not only not improved but has even become worse'.[86] As Sergio Minerbi has recognized, Benedict's policy boiled down to this: 'The Great Powers must guarantee the rights of Catholics, without impairing the rights of Jews and also without giving Jews any privileges.'[87] Gasparri's position was sharper and clearer than this, presumably because he felt able to speak with more freedom than the pope. Even before the end of the war, he told the Belgian ambassador that what he feared was the establishment of a Jewish state, with consequent damage to the rights of other, especially Christian, religious groups.[88] The policy which Benedict and Gasparri accordingly adopted towards Zionism more or less remained the one the Vatican followed until it decided, in 1992, that, in the aftermath of the Gulf War, recognition of the State of Israel was the only way to defend those rights.

GERMANY

On 28 June 1919, the German Reich established diplomatic relations with the Vatican. This abandonment of the old system whereby the individual states of Prussia and Bavaria, rather than the federal government of the Reich, were represented in Rome, and the Vatican in Munich, was one of the clearest signals of the new standing of the Holy See in the post-war world. With the fall of the Protestant, Prussian monarchy, objections to the presence of a nuncio in Berlin evaporated. The fledgling German democracy, the Weimar Republic, needed the support of the Vatican if it was to mitigate, or at least delay, the effects of the territorial losses in West Prussia, Upper Silesia, and on the Belgian border, decreed by the Versailles Treaty, and prevent the temporary transfer of the Saar, under the same Treaty, from being made permanent. According to Stewart Stehlin, the Vatican wished to avoid precipitate action in the realignment of diocesan boundaries and its concern for the rights of

[85] Minerbi, *The Vatican*, 149.
[86] As quoted in Minerbi, *The Vatican*, 44.
[87] Minerbi, *The Vatican*, 149.
[88] Minerbi, *The Vatican*, 59

minorities were crucial to the limited success of German policies.[89] Weimar Germany might be said to have enjoyed a 'special relationship', the latter's benevolent attitude being determined by the pro-German sentiments of Mgr Pacelli, the nuncio first in Bavaria and then in Berlin, and by Benedict's sense of justice, by his desire to see the balance of power re-established in Europe, and by his anxiety that Germany should function as a bulwark against communism. The Vatican even tolerated a governmental alliance between the German Catholic Centre Party and the Social Democratic Party: such an alliance would have been unthinkable and impossible between their Italian counterparts, but was essential in order for Weimar democracy to survive. But Pacelli drove a hard bargain: 'nothing for nothing' might have been his motto. The Vatican's recognition of the Weimar Republic was bought at a cost that would not finally become apparent until after Benedict's death: that is, a new concordat with Bavaria, which was intended to be the model for the rest of the German Reich, and which extracted maximum advantage for the Church.[89]

BENEDICT AND ITALY

The First World War transformed the relationship between Italy and the papacy. In part, this was the result of the steady, quiet diplomacy of Carlo Monti, who managed to smooth things over, despite the bitter arguments between the two sides (Chapter 2). He ensured that a much warmer, more relaxed, and cooperative spirit prevailed between the governing bodies of the two powers at the end of the war than had been the case at the beginning. The war accelerated processes of change that were wider and more radical than those on the strictly diplomatic/political level. As Pietro Scoppola has observed, the war radically altered the position of Catholics in Italian society and politics.[90] The support of at least some Catholic politicians for intervention, and the participation of the Italian Catholic masses, especially the peasantry, in the war, combined with the patriotic mobilization of both the Catholic clergy and lay organizations in the war effort, removed once and for all the anti-patriotic, anti-Italian stigma which had been attached to Italian Catholics since the Risorgimento. Some diehard anti-clericals, especially revolutionary interventionists, continued to inveigh against the Church, but with less conviction because their fellow interventionists, the Nationalists, had been moving in a Catholic direction since before the war, anxious to enlist Church support for their vision of a strong, authoritarian Italian state

[89] Stehlin, 'The Emergence of a New Vatican Diplomacy', 9.

[90] P. Scoppola, *La Chiesa e il fascismo: Documenti e interpretazioni*, Bari, 1971, xlii–xliv.

with imperial ambitions. There was still much anti-clericalism among the revolutionary left which, however, was discredited in the eyes of many by its militant neutralism and pacifism during the war. There was also an obstinate residue of Masonic anti-clericalism in the old Italian political class, especially among Republicans and Democratic Liberals. Nevertheless, on 9 November Church and State in Italy came together in a unprecedentedly official way when the Cardinal Vicar of Rome celebrated a solemn Te Deum for the Italian victory over Austria in the Church of Aracoeli, in the presence of the mayor of Rome, government ministers, and of HRH the Duke of Genoa, Lieutenant General of the Kingdom, in the absence of the King, who was still at the front.

There remained major outstanding problems in relations between the Vatican and Italy, including a new one: the resistance to the policy of 'Italianization' by the German, Slovene, and Croat clergy in the areas of Trentino-Alto Adige, the Istrian peninsula, and some islands in the Adriatic which Italy annexed in 1919.[91] But there were new areas of cooperation in the international sphere, like tacit Vatican support for Italian claims in Anatolia. A major benefit of improved relations with Italy was an amelioration of the working conditions of the offices of the Roman curia. Vatican officials were now treated with more respect and consideration than in the past, and cardinals, leading ecclesiastics, and lay members of the papal court were given diplomatic number plates for their vehicles in December 1918.[92] The 'guarantees' and 'immunities' of the Law of Guarantees were now being transformed into real 'extraterritorial' privileges for the Holy See. In 1919, Gasparri succeeded obtaining exemption from the Italian government's tax of all the Holy See's earnings from interest and dividends, thanks to his close relations with the first post-war Prime Minister, Nitti.[93] A not dissimilar measure was proposed by Prime Minister Giolitti in 1920, to have all stocks, bonds, and shares registered in the name of individuals, which would have caused difficulties for the religious houses. Once again, Gasparri persuaded the government to exempt the Church's holdings.[94]

The most important aspect of the changed relationship between the Holy See and Italy was the fact that a first serious attempt was made to resolve the Roman Question. In May 1917, a meeting of the Congregation for Extraordinary Ecclesiastical Affairs had advised that the best solution to Roman Question would be 'the creation of a small pontifical state based on the Città Leonina, with the addition of certain parts of Rome and access to the sea', plus extraterritorial guarantees in Italian territory for ambassadors accredited to the pope, and financial compensation of 200 million lire in

[91] *Diario*, II, 403–404, 3–8 February 1919.

[92] *Diario*, I, 447–448, 8 August 1916.

[93] Margiotto-Broglio, *L'Italia e la Santa Sede*, 379, doc. 60, Nitti a Gasparri, 26 November 1919.

[94] *Diario*, II, 555, 19 June 1920.

gold.[95] By the end of 1918, there were strong expectations in Italy and outside that a comprehensive agreement between the pope and the Italian state was not far off, and a growing belief in more restricted Italian governmental circles that the unofficial relationship with the Vatican carried on by Carlo Monti would be transformed into an official, diplomatic one at any moment.[96] Monti sounded out the prospects for talks with Orlando on Gasparri's behalf as early as December 1918,[97] and Gasparri had made his own private soundings with Nitti. But real progress came in May 1919 when, as a result of an almost chance conversation in Paris between Mgr Kelley (later Bishop of Oklahoma City) and Italian Prime Minister Orlando negotiations were opened for a settlement.[98] Kelley managed to persuade Orlando that Italy's hopes of succeeding to the position of leading Catholic power, following the demise of the Habsburg Empire, depended upon a settlement with the Holy See.[99] With Orlando's approval, Kelley travelled to Rome where he presented himself to Gasparri. The Cardinal Secretary of State and Benedict responded rapidly and favourably to Orlando by despatching Mgr Cerretti, the Under-Secretary of State for Extraordinary Ecclesiastical Affairs, to Paris with an outline plan for an agreement: the ostensible reason for Cerretti's visit to the peace conference was the question of the future of German missions.[100] Cerretti's bargaining position consisted of precisely the proposal made by the cardinals' commission of 1916, in addition to international guarantees. Success in the talks was prevented by the fall of Orlando's government in June. Orlando claimed that he could probably have squared the King, who was a notorious anti-clerical, but this is doubtful. It is even more doubtful whether Orlando could have carried his cabinet with him on any agreed package, given the opposition of Sonnino, and it is even less likely that could have got such a package through parliament.

Benedict did not give up his efforts to improve relations with Italy after this setback, and the re-establishment of relations with France in 1920 resurrected hopes of a similar development for Italy.[101] That same year he took the détente a stage further in his encyclical *Pacem dei Munus Pulcherrimum* ('On Peace and Reconciliation') of May 1920, by scrapping the ban on Catholic sovereigns and heads of state visiting the King of Italy.[102]

[95] ASV, AES, Sessioni, 1917, 1206. 29 May, Italia, Circa la situazione della Santa Sede in Italia. In the Appendice, Al capitolo III, Lettera c), 105–107, Trattato tra la Santa Sede e il Regno d'Italia.

[96] *Diario*, II, 403, 7 December 1918; 408, 14 December 1918; and 410, 19 December 1918.

[97] *Diario*, II, 410–411, 19 December 1918.

[98] D.A. Binchy, *Church and State in Fascist Italy*, Oxford, 1970, 235–237.

[99] Binchy, *Church and State*, 235.

[100] Binchy, *Church and State*, 236.

[101] Spadolini (ed.), *Il Cardinale Gasparri*, 233–234 and 267.

[102] Carlen, *Papal Encyclicals*, III, 171–175.

Italian politics increasingly preoccupied the Vatican during the remainder of Benedict's reign. In 1918, after seeking advice from the leading Belgian Catholic social activist, Mgr Denis Pottier, and the bishops of the Veneto region of northern Italy, he permitted the final abolition of the *Non expedit* and the formation of a Catholic Party, the Partito Popolare Italiano.[103] Gasparri later claimed that, 'The P.P.I. emerged as a result of a process of spontaneous generation without any political intervention on the part of the Holy See, neither for nor against.' This statement is, strictly speaking, true, it is also a trifle disingenuous. It is a well-known fact that no Italian Catholic at this time could engage in a major political act without the consent of the Vatican.

Benedict's agreement to the formation of the new party, a Catholic trade union confederation—the Confederazione Italian del Lavoro (CIL)—and his willingness even to countenance female suffrage, is a testimony to the fact that he had more advanced ideas about Catholic social and political activism than his predecessor Pius X and, as it turned out, his successor Pius XI. Much of his progressivism in all these respects was based on his personal trust in Fr Luigi Sturzo, whom he had appointed as head of the Unione Popolare, the precursor of Catholic Action, in 1915, and who became leader of the new party at its inception.[104]

But the Partito Popolare was to cause much difficulty to Benedict XV and his Secretary of State, as Italy moved into the period of working-class militancy that followed the end of the war and which was strongly inspired by the success of the Bolshevik Revolution in Russia. During the *biennio rosso* ('Red Two Years'), the Marxist revolutionary PSI established itself as the largest party in the Italian parliament, its industrial and agrarian unions mounted massive strikes and protests against rent and price rises, frequently accompanied by violence, and these culminated in the summer of 1920 in the Occupation of the Factories (in northern Italy) when it truly seemed as though Italy was on the brink of revolution.[105] What was happening in Italy was, of course, merely a reflection of the revolutionary unrest which plagued much of Europe, and especially the vanquished powers—Germany, Austria, and Hungary—and Russia in this period.

But the situation in Italy had a particular twist to it: there, much agitation on the part of, especially, the poor peasantry, was organized by Catholic unions led by Popolare MP, Guido Miglioli.[106] A particular incident of Catholic trade union militancy in Bergamo province elicited a public

[103] ASV, AES, 1918–1921, 953–955, 346, 'P.P.I., Pareri dell'Episcopato Veneto sul programma sociale dei cattolici nell'ora presente', letter of 27 January 1919; and 348, 'Mons. Pottier sulla questione del movimento democratico'.

[104] De Rosa, *Luigi Sturzo*, 182–183.

[105] Clark, *Modern Italy*, 206–213.

[106] J. Foot, '"White Bolsheviks"? The Catholic Left and the Socialists in Italy, 1919–1920', *Historical Journal*, 40(2) (1917), 415–433.

statement from Benedict in March 1920. Benedict issued no great encyclicals on Catholic social doctrine during the course of his pontificate, certainly nothing as coherent or complete as Leo XIII's *Rerum Novarum* (1891) or Pius XI's *Quadragesimo Anno* (1931). But his letter to the bishop of Bergamo constitutes a comprehensive restatement of his, and the Church's, established teaching on the Christian ethics of industrial relations. Underlying his teaching was the belief that, 'distinctions between social classes are of the natural order and in consequence are the will of God', and the resulting need of the poor to resign themselves to their lot.[107] He utterly rejected, therefore, the theory and practice of class war: on the other hand he reiterated the legitimacy of the right of workers to organize themselves in unions and to bring about an improvement in their material situation.[108] These principles were reiterated in a letter to all the bishops of the Veneto a few months later when he condemned 'class hatred' and told priests not to get involved in disputes between unions and employers.[109]

In face of mounting electoral success of the Socialists at both a parliamentary and local government level, it was assumed by the Italian hierarchy that the Partito Popolare would enter into 'clerico-moderate' alliances to stem the revolutionary tide. But the party refused to do this, arguing that go-it-alone intransigence was the only principled and effective strategy. After the local elections in the autumn of 1920, this policy left relations between Sturzo and his party on the one hand, and local bishops and the Vatican on the other, extremely strained. By the time Benedict died in January 1922, he and Sturzo had drifted further apart.

It was against this background that Fascism emerged in Italy. It arose in March 1919 as a radical, patriotic alternative to the neutralist Italian Socialist Party, the *fasci* were, from the beginning, characterized by a strong ex-servicemen's element and, consequently, the use of violence. Until 1920, Fascism remained a small, minority movement, restricted to the cities of northern Italy. Its programme also remained radical—anti-clerical, anti-capitalist, and anti-monarchical. Its opportunity came in the wake of the Occupation of the Factories, when Fascism extended its established strike-breaking activities into a wave of brutal, violent reaction against the working-class movement. The spectacular growth of Fascism in 1920 and 1921 took place in the small towns and countryside of northern and central Italy, in a rural and agrarian setting. Here the class war had not abated, with the continuation of bitter conflicts over labour contracts, tenancy, and share-cropping agreements. And the victories of the Socialists in the local election of 1920 created

[107] Bellocchi, *Tutte le Encicliche*, VIII, 329–331, *Soliti nos*, 11 March 1920, Epistola.
[108] Bellocchi, *Tutte le Encicliche*, VIII, 330, *Soliti nos*, 11 March 1920, Epistola.
[109] Bellocchi, *Tutte le Encicliche*, VIII, 368–369, *Intelleximus ex iis*, 14 June 1920, Epistola.

the impression that if the revolution had failed in the towns with the end of the Occupation of the Factories, it was about to triumph in the countryside.

The systematic violence of the Fascist squads was extended to Catholic institutions and persons, as the letters of bishops to the Vatican graphically explained. By the spring of 1921 a virtual civil war reigned in parts of northern and central Italy. Frequently the authorities, military, police, and judicial, turned a blind eye to Fascist activities,[110] and in some cases they helped them, on the grounds that Fascism was a patriotic reaction against the threat of Bolshevik revolution. This feeling was undoubtedly shared by some Catholics, clerical and lay, but the Catholic press, and in particular *L'Osservatore Romano*, consistently deplored the spread of Fascist violence: on the eve of the May 1921 elections, its attitude to the Socialists and Fascists was effectively 'a plague on both your houses'.[111] Mussolini and thirty-five Fascists entered parliament, an event which did not lead to an abatement of Fascist violence, so that, in July, Benedict was moved to publicly urge prayers for 'civil peace' in Italy.[112] By the time he was on his deathbed, the impact of Fascism had rendered Italy virtually ungovernable.

FRANCE

The position of Catholics and the Church in France had been enormously improved by the exigencies of the First World War, the unhesitating and unstinting Catholic support for the patriotic Union Sacreé of all Frenchmen and women. According to Larkin, Vatican's improving relations with Germany gave the final impetus to the French to re-establish the diplomatic links with the Holy See broken off in 1905.[113] Another was the consequence of the return of Alsace-Lorraine to France. Because these territories were legally still under the 1805 Napoleonic Concordat, relations with the Vatican became a pressing necessity.[114] In particular, Clémenceau demanded the replacement of the bishops of Alsace-Lorraine. As Gasparri pointed out, such demands were not legal: the incumbent bishops had not resigned and the territorial transfer had not been ratified by a peace treaty. He was under no illusions about the nature of the eventual agreement: 'a return to the concordatory regime with presentation of bishops has assuredly gone for ever'.[115] There

[110] See J.F. Pollard, *The Experience of Fascism in Italy*, London, 1998, 35.

[111] A.C. O'Brien, 'L'Osservatore Romano and Fascism: The Beginning of a New Era', *Church and State*, 13(3) (Autumn 1971), 445–463

[112] Bellocchi, *Tutte le Encicliche*, VIII, 495–496, *Oh Dio di bontà*, 25 July 1921, Chirograph.

[113] Larkin, *L'Église et L'État*, 240–241.

[114] M. Larkin, *Religion, Politics and Preferment in France since 1890*, Cambridge, 1995, 149–152.

[115] *Diario*, II, 337–338, 3 June 1918.

was much discussion about the desirability of a resumption of relations, in particular whether it should proceed or follow a resolution of the issue of the *associations cultuelles* (see Chapter 1).[116] The path to a normalization of relations was not easy: despite the conservative nature of the Horizon Bleu Chamber elected in 1918 there was a lot of resistance in France to normalization both from the anti-clerical left and the Catholic right.[117] There was also some ambiguity of attitude in the Vatican as well. As late as January 1920, Gasparri was warning Monti that a resumption of links with France could have its drawbacks: a French ambassador at the Vatican would continually be demanding things.[118] On the other hand, the prospects for an end to the separation of Church and State and for a solution of the vexed questions of the re-entry of the religious orders and of church property did not seem good at the end of Benedict's reign. Nevertheless, the exchange of envoys, with Mgr Cerretti, an experienced and senior member of the Vatican's diplomatic establishment, being sent as nuncio to Paris as proof of the importance in which the Vatican held the posting, and M. Jonnart as French ambassador, was accomplished in May 1920. The canonization of Joan of Arc in June 1920 provided a felicitous crown to these events, with French representatives being received in the Vatican. This was one of the greatest achievements of Benedict and Gasparri's diplomacy, its crowning triumph in the post-war period and a reversal of the mistakes of Pius X and Merry del Val. Thus, it seemed that there was a real chance that Leo XIII's policy of *Ralliement*, of Catholics accepting the Republic and working inside its institutions, would finally bear fruit under his pupils, Benedict and Gasparri. In broader terms, the resumption of relations with France, and also with Portugal in June 1918, suggested that at last the great wave of liberal anti-clericalism unleashed by the French Revolution was, perhaps, beginning to ebb. Perhaps, only perhaps, because in Mexico the persecution of the Church by the revolutionary regime seemed to be intensifying.

LATIN AMERICA

As during the reign of his predecessor (Chapter 1), parts of Latin America posed problems for the Holy See. In Peru, the coming to power of 'the radical

[116] ASV, AES, Sessioni, 1920, 1232, 11 March, 'Francia, tendenza alla ripresa delle relazioni diplomatiche'; and 1234, 10 April, Assoc. per il culto; for the background negotiations to the rapprochement, February–March 1920, see F. Charles-Roux, *Souvenirs diplomatiques. Une grande ambassade à Rome, 1919–1925*, Paris, 1961, 98–103.

[117] S. Marchese, *Francia e problema dei suoi rapporti con la Santa Sede (1914–1924)*, Naples, 1969, 319–321 and 351–355.

[118] *Diario*, II, 529, 30 January 1920.

party and other extremists' inevitably produced demands for legislation against the Church.[119] Already in 1913 the Constitution had been changed and the necessity for non-Catholics to seek permission for public worship had been removed, with the result that Protestantism had gained a foothold. Peru was thus breaking the agreement of 1875 whereby the Holy See gave the government *Giuspatronato*, that is, control over ecclesiastical appointments. In a report of 12 November1915, after the victory of the Liberal Party, the papal chargé d'affaires warned that they wanted to separate Church and State. Mgr Sanchez, archbishop of Lima, allegedly tore the new law from the hands of the vice-president and declared that there was a need for a Catholic Party.[120] Another familiar issue was the insistence by the liberals that civil marriage have precedence over the religious ceremony, with the danger that, in this most Catholic of Andean states, for the first time there would be two quite different forms of marriage, civil and religious.[121] On New Year's Day 1919, Benedict wrote to the bishops expressing concern about the developments in their country, especially the threat which Protestant sects posed to the faith of Peruvian Catholics.[122]

The situation in Bolivia was different, but equally serious. Here the government was proposing to dissolve all religious houses.[123] Gasparri's advice to the bishops was that they should, by every possible means, try to stop the passing of the law—the rich contemplative convents could provide financing of propaganda—that convents should seek to protect their property as much as possible and that, if the law were to pass, the bishops, especially that of La Paz, the capital, should negotiate with the government to retain the *principle* of the contemplative life and keep economic damage to a minimum.[124] Gasparri dismissed the idea of one convent in each diocese with the government paying subsidies as dangerous because one day 'they will say that they cannot afford it', nor did he think it possible to establish schools in the convents as a form of active monastic life 'given the lack of education of the religious who were quite unsuited for teaching'.[125]

There had also been attacks upon the Church in Mexico in the nineteenth century, but the great turning point in Church–State relations came with the revolution. Arguably, the Mexican Revolution of those years was the greatest upheaval in Latin America since the wars of independence against Spain in

[119] ASV, AES, Sessioni, 1916 1201, 13.1. Perú Giurispatronato e libertà dei culti Stampa, 1037, 6.

[120] ASV, AES, Sessioni, 1916 1201, 13.1. Perú Giurispatronato e libertà dei culti Stampa, 1037, 33.

[121] ASV, AES, Sessioni, 1203, 16 November 1916, Perù, Matrimonio Civile, citing 1039, 26, Mgr Vagni, chargé d'affaires of the nunciature to Gasparri, 10 June 1916.

[122] Bellocchi, *Tutte le Encicliche*, VIII, 234–236, *Inter egregias*, 1 January 1919, Epistola.

[123] ASV, AES, Sessioni, 1203, 16 November 1916, Bolivia.

[124] ASV, AES, Sessioni, 1203, 16 November 1916, Bolivia.

[125] ASV, AES, Sessioni, 1203, 16 November 1916, Bolivia.

the early years of the nineteenth century. The revolution was not only characterized by extreme violence and destruction, in effect a geographically widespread civil war, but involved radical cultural, economic, and social changes, one of whose chief 'victims' was the Roman Catholic Church. The new Mexican 'Constitution of Querétaro' of 1917, which was modelled on the separation laws in France, though in some ways more severe, included the expulsion of the Jesuits and Spanish priests, the nationalization of church property, the closing down of most religious houses, and a ban on religious 'acts' outside of churches.[126] The laws were ultimately aimed at cutting down to size an institution which, though it was Mexico's largest landowner, was seen as having done little for the poor, was closely associated with other great landowners and the rich elite generally, and had a clergy which was lacking in education. The Constitution was a root-and-branch attack upon the Catholic Church in Mexico. By the terms of article 130, the Mexican Church was disestablished and religious organizations and ministers of religion, and especially Catholic priests, had no legal status. According to article 3, no religious body or minister of religion could establish or direct primary schools; article 5 forbade the establishment of religious orders of whatever kind or purpose they might claim; article 27 deprived 'Religious associations', that is, the Church, of the right to acquire or manage real estate, and decreed that all churches and associated buildings were to be the property of the nation and that all new church buildings should become the property of the nation. All churches had to have a trustee who was responsible to the municipal authorities for the management of the building and the conduct of the services. Henceforth, public worship was to be entirely regulated by the various state governments, such that 'no place may be open for public worship without the permission of the Secretary of the Government, and prior permission of the Governments of the States . . . and the State legislatures shall decide, according to local need, the maximum number of ministers of religion'. Furthermore, all ministers of religion had to have been born in Mexico, thus the Mexican Church was especially badly hit by the expulsion of 2,500 Spanish clergy, with some Frenchmen also.[127] In order to prevent the Church from reacquiring some form of financial independence from the State in the future, ministers of religion were not allowed to inherit through themselves or another person the property of religious associations or associations of a charitable nature, nor could they be the testamentary heirs of other religious ministers or of any other persons to whom they were not related in the fourth degree, and all

[126] ASV, AES, Sessioni, 1220, 9 June 1917, 'Mexico, Situazione politico-religiosa Relazione', 5, no. 32, fasc. 108. Copy of *Constitución Política de los Estados Unidos Mexicanos* (firmada el 31 de Enero de 1917 y promulgada el 5 de Febrero del Mismo Ano), Mexico City, 1917.

[127] ASV, AES, Sessioni, 1220, 9 June 1917, 'Mexico, Situazione politico-religiosa Relazione', 5, no. 32, fasc. 108. Copy of *Constitución Política de los Estados Unidos Mexicanos*.

acquisitions of property by clergy and religious organizations had to be registered with the government.[128]

As a defence against Catholic opposition to the new religious status quo, ministers of religion were forbidden to criticize laws or government, they were deprived of the right of active or passive vote, and no 'confessional', Catholic parties might be established.[129] According to article 27 of the Constitution, the trials of violations of the laws were not to be tried by a jury.[130] Nevertheless, Catholic opinion, both national and international, was mobilized against the Querétaro Constitution. There were several protests of Mexican citizens against those articles of the Constitution attacking the Church, especially article 3 on education, which attracted 30,000 signatories in Mexico City, Puebla, Toluca, and Morelia.[131] In the United States, Archbishop John Ireland of Minneapolis/St Paul intervened with a long article 'Los Impostores Oficiales Mexicanos' ('Official Mexican Imposters') in *América Española*.[132] The Mexican bishops were deeply divided about how to respond to government policy. Thus the archbishop of Oaxaca would not sign the official protest of eighteen Mexican bishops in Cuba and USA because he feared more persecution in his diocese and insisted that the letter be shown to the Holy See first.[133] The archbishop of Mexico City similarly wanted the opinion of Mgr Giovanni Bonzano, Apostolic Delegate in Washington, in the absence of a papal envoy in Mexico.[134] Eventually, nearly all the bishops signed the protest except one. Initially, the Vatican was at a loss to know how to handle the Mexican situation.[135] Benedict wrote to the Mexican bishops in June 1917. Significantly,

[128] ASV, AES, Sessioni, 1220, 9 June 1917, 'Mexico, Situazione politico-religiosa Relazione', 5, no. 32, fasc. 108. Copy of *Constitución Política de los Estados Unidos Mexicanos.*

[129] ASV, AES, Sessioni, 1220, 9 June 1917, 'Mexico, Situazione politico-religiosa Relazione', 5, no. 32, fasc. 108. Copy of *Constitución Política de los Estados Unidos Mexicanos.*

[130] ASV, AES, Sessioni, 1220, 9 June 1917, 'Mexico, Situazione politico-religiosa Relazione', 5, no. 32, fasc. 108. Copy of *Constitución Política de los Estados Unidos Mexicanos.*

[131] ASV, AES, Sessioni, 1220, 9 June 1917, 'Mexico, Situazione politico-religiosa Relazione', 5, no. 32, fasc. 108. Copy of *Constitución Política de los Estados Unidos Mexicanos*, Ruiz, archbishop of Mexico, to Mgr Giovanni Bonzano, Apostolic Delegate in Washington, 2 April 1917.

[132] ASV, AES, Sessioni, 1220, 9 June 1917, 'Mexico, Situazione politico-religiosa Relazione', 5, no. 32, fasc. 108. Copy of *Constitución Política de los Estados Unidos Mexicanos*, offprint of Archbishop John Ireland's article, n.d.

[133] ASV, AES, Sessioni, 1220, 9 June 1917, 'Mexico, Situazione politico-religiosa Relazione', 5, no. 32, fasc. 108. Copy of *Constitución Política de los Estados Unidos Mexicanos*, Ruiz to Bonzano 17 May 1917.

[134] ASV, AES, Sessioni, 1220, 9 June 1917, 'Mexico, Situazione politico-religiosa Relazione', 5, no. 32, fasc. 108. Copy of *Constitución Política de los Estados Unidos Mexicanos*, Bonzano to Gasparri, 16 April 1917.

[135] ASV, AES, Sessioni, 1220, 9 June 1917, 'Mexico, Situazione politico-religiosa Relazione', 5, no. 32, fasc. 108. Copy of *Constitución Política de los Estados Unidos Mexicanos*, Carta de Nuestra Santo padre, el Papa Benedicto XV, a los Arzobispos y Bispos de los Estados Unidos Mejicanos, 15 June 1917.

the letter came *after* the bishops' protest. It stated that their protest was justified, it urged them to keep up the good work (more or less), and reassured them that both he and the Virgin of Guadalupe were with the bishops. But the letter contained no very clear guidance about to cope with the anti-clerical legislation. The letter reflected the fact that the Vatican, as well as the Mexican bishops, was divided about to react to the situation. At a meeting of the Congregation of Extraordinary Ecclesiastical Affairs in 1918 it was claimed that the Querétaro Constitution represented 'principles and criteria which are in every way intolerant, and a sort of "ultra-democratic statolatry"' but no decision was arrived as to whether the protest was licit or not.[136] Mexico would become a growing problem for the Vatican in the next two decades, but Pius XI, in both the 1920s and 1930s, would offer rather clearer instructions to the Mexican bishops about how to cope with persecution (see Chapters 6 and 7).

VATICAN DIPLOMACY AT THE END OF BENEDICT'S REIGN

At the death of Benedict, the diplomatic standing of the Holy See had been transformed. Whereas at his election in September 1914 the Vatican had relations with only seventeen states, in January 1922 that number had risen to twenty-seven.[137] Three of the world's major powers—Britain, France, and Germany—were now represented at the Vatican and a fourth, China, would also have been, but for the intrigues of the French (see Chapter 8). Three states which had established diplomatic relations in Benedict's reign had done so because of the war—Britain, Holland, and Switzerland. Most of the rest were creations of the peace—the so-called 'successor states'. The Holy See was thus the beneficiary of the rise of nationalism and collapse of multi-ethnic dynastic states, the Habsburg Empire in particular, which Benedict had deplored and sought to prevent. Yet Benedict and Gasparri adapted quickly and successfully to the post-war territorial settlement. By the end of Benedict's reign the Vatican had relations with all of the successor states to the Habsburg Empire.

[136] ASV, AES, Sessioni, 1220, 9 June 1917, 'Mexico, Situazione politico-religiosa Relazione', 5, no. 32, fasc. 108. Copy of *Constitución Política de los Estados Unidos Mexicanos*, Carta de Nuestra Santo padre, el Papa Benedicto XV, a los Arzobispos y Bispos de los Estados Unidos Mejicanos, 15 June 1917.

[137] The Russian envoy disappeared after the Bolshevik Revolution. The Austro-Hungarian envoy was replaced by envoys for the two separate states, and Yugoslavia replaced Serbia. Czechoslovakia, Romania, Britain, Switzerland, the Netherlands, Luxembourg, and France had all established relations by 1922; relations with Portugal had not been entirely severed in 1910. They were resumed in full in late 1918.

Other new states, even predominantly or overwhelmingly Protestant states like Estonia and Finland, hurried to obtain recognition from one of Europe's oldest powers. Even the embattled Bolshevik regime in Russia was anxious to win recognition from the Vatican in 1921.

In his allocution, *In hac quidem*, of 21 November 1921, Benedict effectively launched the policy of concordats that would be followed by both his successors.[138] The first fruit of that policy, the concordat with Latvia, only came after Benedict's death, in May 1922.[139] The policy of concordats was continued under Benedict's immediate successor, Pius XI, with the result that, by the death of the latter in 1939, the Vatican had succeeded in negotiating agreements (i.e. concordats, modus vivendi, and other conventions) with no less than fourteen states, and Pius XII concluded a further five during the course of his pontificate.[140]

This, and the fact that Pius XI retained Gasparri as Secretary of State until 1930, a decision unprecedented in the modern history of the papacy, raises an interesting question: how much of Benedict's diplomacy was really his own and how much was it inspired by Gasparri? It is always difficult to decide much how of a pope's policy is his own and how much that of his Secretary of State. The authors of the entry for Gasparri in the *Dizionario Biografico degli Italiani* clearly believe him responsible for many of the most important diplomatic initiatives between 1914 and 1922, in particular, they argue that Gasparri was the author of the policy of concordats:

> It is clear from the Vatican documents that it was Gasparri who pushed the Holy See along the path of a concordatory policy, and even though it is not always possible to establish a clear line of continuity, the beginning of the negotiations which led to the stipulation of all the succeeding concordats can be traced back to the period 1919 to 1921.[141]

This may be so, especially given that Gasparri was the chief editor of the Code of Canon promulgated by Benedict XV in 1917, which had set forth the rights and duties of the Church in relation to the secular powers, but it was also clear to everyone that formal agreements with the successor states were an objective necessity for the Holy See in post-war Europe. In any case, Giacomo Della Chiesa had always exhibited a clarity of mind and strength of will during his career: he was not the sort of ruler to bow to subordinates and have his policies largely determined by them. Gasparri sometimes intervened to curb the

[138] Bellocchi, *Tutte le encicliche, In hac Quidem*, 21 November 1921, Allocuzione, 510–512.

[139] Valerio Perna, *Relazioni tra Santa Sede e Repubbliche Baltiche (1918–1940): Monsignor Zecchini Diplomatico*, Udine, 2010, 71–73.

[140] P. Cipriotti and A. Talamanca (eds), *I Concordati di Pio XII*, Milan, 1976.

[141] *DBI*, Vol. 52, 'Gasparri, Pietro', 504–505.

effects on relations with Italy of Benedict's notorious irascibility, but then he also had to do the much same with Pius XI.

The success of Benedict's diplomacy should not be calculated solely by the numbers of states with which the Vatican had relations or the importance of those states. Largely as a result of war, the Vatican had become a new force in international affairs. Heads of state and government from the most variegated countries beat a path to Benedict's door in the years of peace. In 1919 the great President of the United States deigned to honour Benedict with his presence, as did the president-elect of Brazil and Emir Feysal of Hejaz.[142] The following year saw the visits of the chancellors of Austria and Germany, and 1921 those of the sovereigns of Denmark, and the crown prince of Japan; the visit of Belgian king and queen was prevented by Benedict's death. In March 1921, the Empress and the Regent of Ethiopia sent a delegation to greet Benedict and present him with gifts: an extraordinary act of recognition from a faraway land.[143]

Not everyone in the Vatican approved of the successes which Benedict had achieved in international affairs or of his efforts to ensure a lasting peace. Merry del Val was particularly critical. Writing to his friend Cardinal O'Connell, archbishop of Boston, in November 1921, Merry del Val lamented the

> prevalence of too much politics, worldly diplomacy and intrigue that are hardly in keeping with the lofty ideals of our mission, nor profitable to the best interests of God and his Church . . . We are drifting . . . Surely at a time when the world has lost its bearings and is anxiously seeking that which we alone are able to provide, we should not drift ourselves, or appear to juggle with principles, but hold up the lesson of light as God gave it to us and refrain from the tactics of human politics.[144]

No one could seriously claim that Benedict had failed to give a moral lead to the statesmen and peoples of the world, or that he had 'juggled with principles'. On the contrary, he had repeatedly set before the world the Christian principles on the basis of which alone, he believed, a just and lasting peace was possible. Under Benedict, the Vatican had escaped from the international isolation in which Pius X and Merry del Val had left it in 1914, and both during and after the war the Vatican had reasserted its moral and diplomatic influence, forcing powers, great and small, to take notice of it and obliging some to establish or re-establish relations with it in furtherance of their most essential national interests.

[142] LaCC, 71, 4 (1920), 265.

[143] LaCC, 72, 1 (1921), 175–176.

[144] As quoted in G. Fogarty, *The Vatican and the American Hierarchy from 1870 to 1965*, Collegeville, MN, 1982, 219.

BENEDICT AND DOCTRINAL ORTHODOXY

Though he had been suspected of modernism, Benedict was certainly not himself a modernist, however that is defined. After his election as pope, he declared to the cardinals who had elected him, 'And We assure you that the Holy Father is not a modernist!'[145] But he strongly objected to the fanaticism and spite of the anti-modernist purges. He had made his position clear as archbishop of Bologna:

> It is far from my intention to condemn every new form of doctrine, indeed I applaud scientific/scholarly progress wherever it is found . . . but I believe that it is increasingly necessary to test every new theory against the 'sense of the Church', in order to have a secure criterion of acceptability . . . .[146]

But on another occasion he declared, 'When the faithful hear new doctrines, not in conformity with those approved by the pope, they should not allow themselves to be deceived . . . the pope has spoken. That is enough.'[147] So when he became pope, he and Gasparri removed Umberto Benigni from the Secretariat of State and closed down the *intégriste* organization La Sapinière, or so they thought, because, as late as 1919, it was found to be still in existence.[148] In *Ad Beatissimi*, of November 1914, he stuck to the line he had adopted while bishop, adopting the motto, 'Old things but in a new way.'[149] He himself did not use the concept of infallibility to define or develop doctrine, remaining content with the 'deposit of the faith' as he had inherited it and understood it.

Doctrinal orthodoxy was particularly evident in his encyclical on biblical scholarship, *Spiritus Paraclitus*, of September 1920.[150] Ostensibly a celebration of the life of St Jerome, the father of the Church, who devoted so much of his life to the study of scripture, the encyclical was probably motivated by concern that his condemnation of anti-Modernist excesses should not send the wrong signal. Another explanation might also be found in the fact that the debate about Darwin's theories of human evolution had entered another, vigorous phase precisely in his reign. *La Civiltà Cattolica*, for example, devoted several articles to the question 'Evolution or Stability of the Species?' in 1919 and 1920, and, after presenting the scientific evidence both for sides, came out against evolution.[151] In all these circumstances, Benedict probably felt the

[145] As quoted in Peters, *Life of Benedict*, 81; according to Peters, Benedict actually found a denunciation of himself for Modernism among the papers of his predecessor, 70.

[146] AFDC, Lettere e Scritti Varie, Pastorale per la quaresima, 10 February 1910.

[147] BDB, Anno 1, no. 3, December 1910, 109.

[148] G. Penco, *Storia della Chiesa in Italia*, vol. II, Milan, 1977, 493.

[149] Carlen, *Papal Encyclicals*, III, 104.

[150] Carlen, *Papal Encyclicals*, III, 177–194; already in 1916, Benedict had issued new regulations for the three biblical institutes in Rome, see Bellocchi, *Tutte le Encicliche*, VIII, 117–119, *Cum Biblia Sacra*, 15 August 1916, Breve.

[151] LaCC, 71, 3 (1920), 136 and 338; and 4 (1920), 137.

need to reassert the divine authorship and inerrancy of Scripture as affirmed by his predecessors Pius X and Leo XIII.[152]

There was one novel feature about his encyclical on the Bible, the stress on the need to make the whole of the Scriptures available to the faithful, and not just the Gospels, which was the usual practice.[153] This was in response to the long-established Protestant accusation that the Catholic Church denied the Bible to its people.[154] This was the positive side of *Spiritus Paraclitus*; arguably the negative consequence of the encyclical was more significant for it effectively froze Roman Catholic biblical scholarship until Pius XII reopened the subject in his own encyclical on Scripture, *Divino fflante Spiritus*, 1943 (Chapter 11).

Benedict was not only content to leave the deposit of the faith as he found it, introducing no changes or developments in doctrine; he also introduced no liturgical changes. His only contribution to the development of Catholic devotions was the impulse he gave to the intensification of the cult of Sacred Heart of Jesus, which reached a high point during his pontificate. In May 1915, he consecrated all the nations involved in the war to the Sacred Heart.[155] There were other such public manifestations of the cult and, when the Catholic University of Milan was opened in 1921, it too was dedicated to the Sacred Heart. To crown all his efforts, in May 1920 Benedict canonized Mary Margaret Alacoque, the Visitandine nun who had done so much to spread the devotion to the Sacred Heart in the seventeenth century. Yet even here, in the realm of popular devotion, he had to be on his guard against attempts to exploit the cult for nationalistic ends before and after the war. In particular, he sought to prevent the ambitious and energetic Padre Agostino Gemelli from distorting popular devotion in this way.[156]

In 1912 Pius X had established a uniform Italian text of the catechism. A few years later, Benedict launched his project for a new, universal catechism, no doubt prompted by the problems he had encountered over the teaching of the catechism in his Bologna diocese. In his apostolic constitution *Etsi Minime* of 1919 he cited the words of his predecessor Benedict XIV: 'There is nothing more effective than catechetical instruction to spread the glory of God and to secure the salvation of souls.' Two years earlier, he had set up a commission for the 'Compilation of a definitive text for a Catechism for the universal Church'.[157] Like the commission for the codification of Canon Law, it

[152] In the latter case, in the encyclical *Providentissimus Deus*; text in Carlen, *Papal Encyclicals*, II, 325–329.

[153] Carlen, *Papal Encyclicals*, II, 186.

[154] LaCC, 71, 3 (1920), 427.

[155] Morozzo Della Rocca, 'Benedetto XV e il nazionalismo', 562.

[156] F. De Giorgi, 'Forme spirituali, forme simboliche, forme politiche. La devozione al Sacro Cuore', *Rivista di Storia della Chiesa in Italia*, 48(2) (July–December 1994), 365–459.

[157] ASV, AES, Stati Eccl., 1432, 574–581, 'Testo Unico del Catechismo per la Chiesa Universale'.

was composed of experts but also consulted the opinions of the bishops.[158] In his letter to the bishops, Gasparri argued that the decision to establish a universal catechism was also motivated by 'the horrible war still raging among the nations and the need to have clear, consistent teaching throughout the Catholic Church'.[159] This was consistent with Benedict's argument in *Ad Beatissimi* that the war was ultimately the consequence of men having turned away from God and his Church. Almost all the bishops welcomed Benedict's initiative and deplored the confusing welter of different texts.[160] A universal catechism would have been one of Benedict's greatest achievements but was not to be realized until the pontificate of John Paul II.[161]

THE CODE OF CANON LAW AND THE REFORM OF THE ROMAN CURIA

Though short, Benedict's pontificate constituted a crucial stage in the reorganization and modernization of the government of the Church. One of the major events in Benedict's reign, and a landmark in the history of the Church, was the promulgation of the Code of Canon Law on 27 May 1917 (the Code actually came into force a year later).[162] The effect of the Code was to reinforce the authority of the pope and the Roman curia over the Church. In particular, it further centralized decision-making in the Church, especially in relation to the appointment of bishops. Article 329 formalized a tendency which had developed in the Church since the mid-nineteenth century, declaring that:

> Bishops are the successors of the Apostles and by divine institution are placed over specific churches that they govern with ordinary power under the authority of the Roman Pontiff.

The Roman Pontiff freely appoints them.[163]

A series of concordats with states in both Europe and Latin America, in some cases the denunciation of a concordat by anti-clerical governments—like those of France and Portugal—meant that the power of Episcopal nomination had passed to the Holy See. The growth of the Church in North America,

[158] ASV, AES, Stati Eccl., 1432, 574–581, 'Testo Unico del Catechismo per la Chiesa Universale', circular 27805 to apostolic delegates and nuncios, 10 March 1917.

[159] ASV, AES, Stati Eccl., 1432, 574–581, 'Testo Unico del Catechismo per la Chiesa Universale', Latin text of the letter to diocesan ordinaries, 18 March 1917.

[160] ASV, AES, Stati Eccl., 1432, 574–581, 'Testo Unico del Catechismo per la Chiesa Universale', replies.

[161] Rino Fisichella (ed.), *Catechismo della Chiesa Cattolica: Testo integrale e commento teologico, Direzione e coordinamento del Commento teologico*, Vatican City and Casale Monferrato, 1993.

[162] *NCE*, 2nd edn, 2, 973.

[163] Peters, *The 1917 Code of Canon Law*, 132–133.

the re-establishment of the hierarchy in England and Wales, Holland and Scotland in the second half of the nineteenth century, and the growth of missions elsewhere, meant that large numbers of dioceses were created and their bishops were appointed by Rome from the start.

Along with Infallibility, the codification of Canon Law must be considered one of the twin pillars of modern papal supremacy. And it was in Benedict's reign that Gasparri and his pupil Pacelli began their campaign to use concordats as a means of enforcing the writ of Canon Law inside states. Benedict's major contribution towards the implementation of the Code was to set up a Commission for the Authentic Interpretation of the Code of Canon Law, and a school of Canon Law studies.[164] The application of the Code was restricted to the Latin Church, but it was also in Benedict's reign that the first steps were taken towards creating a code for the Oriental rite churches.

Benedict could also be said to have completed another of Pius X's great projects: his reform of the Roman curia. Until 1917, *three* dicasteries, or departments, of the Roman curia were responsible for the censorship of books: the Congregation of the Index, the powerful Congregation of the Holy Office, and the office of the Maestro dei Sacri Palazzi Apostolici.[165] On 25 March of that year, the first two were merged and some of the functions of Maestro, who was effectively the house theologian of the Secretariat of State, also passed to the Holy Office.[166] This may well have been inspired by Benedict's unhappy experiences with the Maestro dei Sacri Palazzi Apostolici when he was archbishop of Bologna.[167]

It was also due to Benedict that a congregation was set up to oversee both seminaries and Catholic universities. This entirely new dicastery was created by a *motu proprio* of 21 November 1915.[168] To some extent this was a continuation of the reforms of seminary teaching, especially in Italy, which had been initiated by his predecessor. The section on Catholic universities was a recognition of the growing importance of Catholic universities throughout the world—Belgium, Canada, France, Lebanon, the Philippines, and the United States of America—in the education of laypeople.[169] During Benedict's pontificate, a Catholic university was also established under the leadership of Padre Gemelli in Milan.

164 *NCE*, 2, 974.

165 *Guida dell'Archivio della Sacra Congregazione per la Dottrina della Fede*, Rome, 1998, 9.

166 Bellocchi, *Tutte le Encicliche*, VIII, 151–153, *Alloquentes proxime*, 25 March 1917, Motu proprio.

167 Pollard, *The Unknown Pope*, 43.

168 Bellocchi, *Tutte le Encicliche*, VIII, 77–79, *Seminaria clericorum*, 4 November 1915.

169 See *Annuario Pontificio*, 1948, 896–900.

Benedict has been indicted by a number of authors for his allegedly poor management of the Vatican's finances.[170] In fact, he was a very careful manager of money, both as archbishop of Bologna and pope.[171] In Rome, though he was indeed most generous to the victims of war, nevertheless he ran a tight ship. Thus, one of his reforms of the Roman curia was intensely practical, the setting up a school inside the Congregation of the Consistory for young priests who spent three years on courses dealing with the important financial business of the Congregation.[172]

But undoubtedly the most important of his curial reforms was the establishment on 1 May 1917 of the Sacred Congregation of the Oriental Church, separating it from Propaganda Fide of which, hitherto, it had been a semi-autonomous section.[173]

THE VATICAN'S RELATIONS WITH THE ORIENTAL CHURCHES

The new congregation was given jurisdiction over all matters affecting the Oriental churches except those traditionally reserved to other dicasteries of the Roman curia.[174] In order to underline his concern for the Oriental churches, both those in communion with Rome and those not, Benedict assumed the office of prefect of the new congregation; few congregations had the pope as their head. He also created the Pontifical Oriental Institute in 1917 for research and training of priests,[175] and established a prayer to be said for reunion with the Orthodox churches—Preghiera per l'Unione dei Cristiani dell'Oriente alla Chiesa Romana.[176]

By the middle of his successor's pontificate, the jurisdiction of the congregation extended to all Byzantine rite churches in Eastern Europe, southern Albania, Bulgaria, Greece, Cyprus, and the Dodecanese Islands (under Italian rule since 1912), as well as those in the successor states of the former Ottoman Empire, plus Iran, Egypt, Eritrea, and northern Ethiopia. There was a complicated mix of

[170] See, for example, Seldes, *The Vatican*, 246; J.N. Molony, *The Emergence of Political Catholicism in Italy: Partito Popolare, 1919–1926*, London, 1977, 59; and F.-C. Uginet, 'Les finances papales', in Levillain (ed.), *Dictionnaire de la papauté*, 600.

[171] Pollard, *Money*, ch. 5.

[172] C. Pallenberg, *Vatican Finances*, Harmondsworth, 1973, 98.

[173] Bellocchi, *Tutte le Encicliche*, VIII, 161–162, *Dei providentis*, 1 May 1917, Motu proprio.

[174] *Annuario Pontificio*, 1918, 459.

[175] Bellocchi, *Tutte le Encicliche*, VIII, 187–188, *Orienti catholici*, 15 October 1917.

[176] Bellocchi, *Tutte le Encicliche*, VIII, 187–188, *Cum Catholicae Ecclesiae*, 15 April 1916, Breve.

schismatic churches, churches in communion with Rome, and small communities of Latin Catholics in these areas.[177]

The condition of the Oriental churches in the Middle East in aftermath of the First World War was piteous. Aside from the appalling suffering of the Armenians (Chapter 2), the Christians of Lebanon, Syria, and Mesopotamia had suffered very badly during the last years of Ottoman rule. Schools and other ecclesiastical property had been destroyed, both clergy and laity had been persecuted, and in many cases imprisoned, and some had even been murdered.[178] This was the result of what Andrea Riccardi has described as the breakdown of multi-religious coexistence in the Ottoman Empire during the course of the First World War: another example of the unfortunate consequences of nationalism.[179] For the Vatican, the future of the churches in communion with Rome looked bleak.

Benedict's allocution of 1919, with its slightly hysterical worries about both Jewish and Protestant activities, against a background of continuing uncertainty about the future of that and other ex-Ottoman territories, has to be read in this context.[180] He made strenuous efforts to help Christian, mainly Catholic, communities both before the end of the war and afterwards, sending considerable financial aid.[181] His encyclical of October 1920, elevating St Ephraim the Syrian, deacon and anchorite, to the honour of Doctor of the Church, though produced in response to requests from Eastern patriarchs and bishops, was clearly intended as a means of heartening and encouraging those communities, and Eastern Catholics generally.[182] In addition, it was a less than subtle reaffirmation of the primacy of the pope over the whole Church, as even its title *Principi Apostolorum Petro* indicates. This was a moment when Rome needed to mobilize all its resources in defence of its Eastern brothers.

During the course of the war, the Roman Church had faced other threats from the East, the most serious being of which was the clear intention of Czarist Russia, once it had defeated the Ottoman Empire, to take over both the Straits of the Dardanelles and Constantinople itself.[183] What was proposed was the re-establishment of Ottoman capital as the true centre of Orthodox, Slav Christianity, with the church of Santa Sophia, 'cleansed' of several centuries of use as a mosque, restored as its ultimate symbol. Such an eventuality would undoubtedly have led to the revival of the great competition between Latin

[177] *Annuario Pontificio*, 1948, 733.

[178] See Bellocchi, *Tutte le Encicliche*, VIII, 274–276, *Nobis quidem*, 3 July 1919, Allocution.

[179] Riccardi, 'Benedetto XV e la crisi'.

[180] Bellocchi, *Tutte le Encicliche*, VIII, 249–251, *Antequam ordinem*, 10 March 1919, Allocution.

[181] Dalla Torre, *Memorie*, 1298.

[182] Carlen, *Papal Encyclicals*, III, 195–201, *Principi Apostolorum Petro*, 5 October 1920.

[183] *Diario*, I, 248–249, 16 July 1915; and 275–276, 2 October 1915.

and Orthodox Christianity, between the 'two Romes', and to Latin Rome's disadvantage once Russia had established its expected hegemony in Eastern and South-Eastern Europe after the defeat of the Central Powers. Gasparri had protested against the support of Entente Powers for Russia's ambitions on the Bosphorus (see Chapter 2). A related worry was the consequent extension of Orthodox influence and control over the Holy Places of Palestine. Gasparri rejoiced when the Russian threat to Constantinople had finally receded.[184]

But a new threat appeared at the end of the war. Greece, having finally been dragged into the hostilities on the side of the Entente, now believed that her moment had arrived, that the *Megali Idea* (literally, 'the great idea') of winning back Constantinople from the Turks, as well as much of Western Anatolia with its Greek-speaking communities, was about to become a reality.[185] In this way, the Byzantine Empire would be resurrected on the ruins of the Ottoman caliphate and sultanate which had destroyed it. Greek control of Constantinople would also have led to a resurgence of Orthodoxy, a revitalization of its resources in competition with Rome. The reconversion of Santa Sophia was as central to the *Megali Idea* as it was to the Russian designs on Constantinople and, furthermore, had much support in Britain. It would have been a slap in the face for the Vatican, as this Anglican enthusiast explained in 1919:

> The traditional diplomacy of the Vatican has certainly laboured for decades under the influence of what would happen if the Oecumenical Patriarch, a dangerous witness against Roman claims, even when half-buried in the slum of Phanar and paralysed by Turkish tyranny, should emerge and be the symbol of a great and progressive Communion which functioned with glorious St Sophia's as its mother church.[186]

The Vatican on the Tiber was spared the nightmare of a rival Orthodox 'Vatican' on the Bosphorus by the objections of the British Foreign Office, who feared the effects of the desecration of a mosque in the city of the Caliph on the Muslim populations of the British Empire, and by resurgent Turkish nationalism, with diplomatic support from Benedict and Gasparri.[187] The Treaty of Sèvres of August 1920, of which Gasparri thoroughly disapproved, gave Greece much of what it desired: the rest could be taken by force of arms. Was not the Greek king, though of Danish and German blood, himself called after the founder of the great Christian city of the east? But in 1922 the Greeks suffered a terrible defeat at the hands of Turkish armies led by Kemal Atatürk,

[184] *Diario*, II, 475, 31 May 1919.
[185] E. Goldstein, 'Holy Wisdom and British Foreign Policy 1918–1922: The St Sophia Redemption', *Byzantine and Modern Greek Studies*, 15 (1991), 36–65.
[186] As quoted in Goldstein, 'Holy Wisdom', 48.
[187] Goldstein, 'Holy Wisdom', 48.

and King Constantine went back into exile.[188] Once again, Rome had been spared.

In fact, even before the end of the war, Rome seemed to be about to win new victories over Orthodoxy. Benedict and Gasparri entertained high hopes that the schismatic churches of both Bulgaria and Romania would turn to Rome in the wake of Russian defeats in the Balkans, and that Russia too might be converted. In September 1917, Benedict confided to Monti that 'it is not improbable that Romania and Bulgaria will unite with Rome',[189] and again in July 1918 Gasparri told Monti that the 'union of the Bulgarian and Romanian churches with the Holy See was imminent'.[190] It is difficult to understand on what the Vatican had built its hopes: the kings of the two Balkan countries were Catholics, but both had also been excommunicated. Perhaps they thought that, as the heads of defeated allies of the Central Powers, they might now believe that adherence to Rome would help them curry favour with the Entente. That really was not a very realistic assessment of the situation. Benedict's creation of a seminary for Romanian students in 1920 at Santa Susanna in Rome suggest that, by then, the Vatican had given up hope for reunification with the Romanian Orthodox Church. Not even increased Italian influence in the Balkans after the war was likely to change the religious situation there: so all of these hopes came to nothing. But one big, bright hope remained for years to come—the conversion of Russia.

The conversion of Orthodox Russia, like that of Protestant England, had been one of the great hopes of the Catholic Church since the early nineteenth century when relations between the Holy See and the Russian Empire had deteriorated (see Chapter 1). The First World War made matters worse: the Russian conquest of Austrian Poland—Galicia—led to the persecution of the Greek Catholic Church there, its metropolitan being imprisoned and church buildings handed over to the Orthodox Church. The fall of Czarism in the February Revolution of 1917 brought a glimmer of light. The provisional government declared complete freedom of religion and, when Kerensky became prime minister, the Russian offer to establish reciprocal relations with the Vatican strengthened these hopes.[191]

Even the Bolshevik seizure of power in October 1917 did not dim the optimism in the Vatican. While it meant the beginning of an official campaign of militant atheism against all religions, the separation of the Orthodox Church from the State, which was decreed in January 1918, seemed to be positively advantageous to Catholicism given the

[188] C. M. Woodhouse, *Modern Greece: A Short History*, London and Boston, MA, 1986, 207–210.

[189] *Diario*, II, 151, 20 September 1917.

[190] *Diario*, II, 348, 3 July 1918.

[191] Hansajkob Stehle, *Eastern Politics of the Vatican: 1917–1979*, trans. Sandra Smith, Athens, OH, and London, 1981, 14–15.

centuries-long dependence, nay subservience, of the Church to the Russian State. With disestablishment, it seemed likely that Orthodoxy would wither and decline in Russia.[192] The reports of Baron Ropp, archbishop of Vilnius, who actually declared that 'the great masses of Russians were more and more inclined towards recognition of the Roman pope', undoubtedly fed the Vatican's unrealistic hopes about improving relations with the Bolsheviks. This much is clear from the articles about the religious situation in Russia which were appearing in *La Civiltà Cattolica* in 1919, yet it is surprising considering that, at roughly the same time, articles were also being published in that same journal about the persecution of the Church by the short-lived Soviet government of Bèla Kun in Hungary.

Aside from the unremitting ideological hostility of the Bolsheviks towards *all* religions, two obstacles stood in the way of Catholic advances in Russia. One was the fact that the bulk of the Catholics in the territories of the former Russian Empire belonged to minority ethnic groups—Poles, Ukrainians, and Lithuanians. The Vatican's relations with the new Catholic states of Lithuania and Poland were already difficult and complicated enough, as Mgr Ratti found to his cost, but in the eyes of the Russians Catholicism was associated with Poland, which quickly became a major enemy of the new Soviet state. The Vatican was also, inevitably, seen as a dangerous 'foreign power'. Nevertheless, 1920 brought renewed hope that something could be achieved in Russia. The 'miracle on the Vistula', when the Red Army was defeated at the gates of Warsaw, and the worsening economic conditions in Russia, which resulted in famine and new economic policy, forced a softening in Lenin's attitude towards various religious groups.[193] As a result, the last months of Benedict's reign saw the 'Voronski Affair', when the eponymous Soviet trade representative in Italy negotiated a deal with Mgr Pizzardo, the *Sostituto*, to allow Catholic clergy into Russian territory in order to administer famine relief and 'promote moral and religious education' in return for the Vatican's *de facto* recognition of the beleaguered Soviet regime.[194] Gasparri also seems to have believed that the Bolsheviks saw the agreement as a means of isolating and weakening the Russian Orthodox Church: 'and here one sees the hand of Providence'.[195] It is said that among the last words that Benedict uttered on his deathbed were these: 'Have the visas come yet from the Bolsheviks?'[196] The illusions which Benedict and Gasparri nurtured about the prospects for the conversion of Russia would live on into the next pontificate.

[192] *Diario*, II, 61, 27 March 1917.
[193] Stehle, *Eastern Politics*, 26.
[194] Stehle, *Eastern Politics*, 27–30.
[195] *Diario*, II, 570, 4 January 1922.
[196] As quoted in Stehle, *Eastern Politics*, 29.

BENEDICT AND THE MISSIONS

In his first encyclical, *Ad Beatissimi*, Benedict expressed 'a loving desire for the salvation of the whole world'.[197] This was more than just a ritual acknowledgment of the evangelizing mission of the Church: Benedict was deeply concerned about the work of the missions throughout his pontificate. While he had inherited a flourishing situation from his predecessor, by the end of the war things had changed. Because of the war, many missions had been abandoned by their sponsors in the war-torn European powers; in any case, the need for service chaplains and the deaths of many priests in action depleted the numbers of those who, in the normal course of events would have gone out to reinforce the missionary effort in Africa, Asia, and Oceania. A further problem was the fate of the missions in the former German colonies: the Belgian, British, and French administrations, who acquired these territories under the system of League of Nations mandates, were anxious to expel German missionaries in order to remove their influence and consolidate their own rule. Benedict and Gasparri sent Mgr Cerretti to the Versailles peace conference to lobby the 'Big Four' on the subject, with success.[198] The long-established practice of a colonial power seeking to exploit missionary work in their own interest survived for a long time after the war. European colonialism could be beneficial to missionary activity because colonial powers favoured those missionaries who inculcated a respect for white, European cultural superiority and authority in the indigenous peoples. It was for this reason that the French Foreign Ministry in early twentieth century was concerned about the effects which the anti-clerical policies enforced at home would have upon its colonies and in other French 'spheres of influence'.[199] On the other hand, European colonialism was frequently a hindrance to the effectiveness of the Catholic Church's missionary outreach. French policies in the Ottoman Empire and China were a particular bugbear for Propaganda Fide. As early as 1901 there had been attempts to establish diplomatic relations with the Sultan and a further, more serious, attempt was made in 1915, with negotiations dragging on until 1923.[200] All of these attempts foundered on the opposition of the French, who were determined to exercise their prestige and influence in the Middle East through the 'Capitulations', which gave them a sort of protectorate over Christians within the Ottoman Empire. In practice, the protectorate meant that the French Dragoman (official interpreter and representative of an embassy to the Sublime Porte) presented Vatican envoys to the Sultan,

[197] Carlen, *Papal Encyclicals*, III, 307–309.

[198] See De Marco, 'L'intervento della Santa Sede', 65–68.

[199] Rhodes, *The Power of Rome*, 210–213.

[200] R. Mamara, *Verso le relazioni diplomatiche tra la Santa Sede e la Turchia. Secondo I documenti dell'Archivio Segreto Vaticano*, Istanbul, 2012, 50, 84–85 and 93–94.

at least for the first time.[201] In 1915, the Sultan once more intimated that he desired a direct relationship with the Holy See, a move which demonstrates the Vatican's increasing diplomatic importance in a time of war.[202] This put the Vatican in a predicament: according to Mgr Dolci, the Apostolic Delegate in Istanbul, a refusal would offend the Sultan and gravely damage the prestige and interests of the Church in the Middle East, yet to agree would seriously upset the French who would feel that French institutions were under attack. Eventually the Secretariat of State followed Dolci's suggestion that they tell the Sublime Porte that the Holy See would enter into diplomatic relations after the end of the war.[203] The existing relationship with the Ottomans became increasingly difficult under the pressure of Turkish atrocities against Christians, and by 1920 the sultan had changed his mind about diplomatic relations with the Vatican as a result of renewed French pressure.[204]

The most outrageous assertion of national, colonial interests over those of the universal Church was the obstacle which the French, supported by other European imperial powers, placed in the path of the establishment of diplomatic relations between China and the Holy See. They feared that such a development would diminish the influence which they exerted in that country through their 'protectorate' over the missions there, and by association, the 'unequal' treaties.[205] The Vatican would obviously have preferred this protectorate to lapse, as the French protectorate over Christians in the Ottoman Empire did when the caliphate and sultanate finally collapsed in 1921. It wished to defend its missions and missionaries through the strength of its own diplomatic efforts, rather than rely upon colonial powers with conflicting interests. Cerretti's success in dealing with the missionary question at Versailles in 1919 suggests that the Holy See now had the international prestige and stature to make such a policy work.

Benedict's missionary strategy was more radical than simply seeking to escape the entanglements of nationalism and colonialism, it was designed to prepare them for nothing less than the post-colonial future of the Church in Africa, Asia, and Oceania. His apostolic letter on the missions, *Maximum Illud* ('On the Propagation of the Catholic Faith throughout the World') of November 1919 did indeed warn of the perils of nationalism and colonialism. It highlighted the dangers for the missionary of serving the interests of his own country: 'Without a doubt, the whole of his work will become suspect . . . the native will think that he must submit himself to that nation . . . We must never forget that the missionary is an envoy not of his own country but of

[201] Mamara, *Verso le relazioni diplomatiche*, 50.
[202] Mamara, *Verso le relazioni diplomatiche*, 80.
[203] Mamara, *Verso le relazioni diplomatiche*, 82.
[204] Mamara, *Verso le relazioni diplomatiche*, 100–101.
[205] S. Leung, *Sino-Vatican Relations: Problems in Conflicting Authority, 1976–1986*, Cambridge, 1992, 43.

God.'[206] But the whole thrust of *Maximum Illud* was the call to the missionary orders and institutes to cooperate in the formation of an indigenous priesthood and indigenous episcopate in as many countries as possible, so that they might one day assume the government of the local churches: 'Once the indigenous clergy have been formed, then the Church has been well-founded and the task of the missionaries has been accomplished.'[207] The date of *Maximum Illud* is no coincidence. It followed within a few months of the establishment by the Treaty of Versailles of the mandatory system, whereby the former German colonies were entrusted to existing colonial powers—Belgium, France, Britain, and the latter's self-governing 'dominions', Australia, New Zealand, and South Africa—by means of League of Nation 'mandates', under the supervision of a committee of the League.[208] Benedict and Gasparri must have realized that, thanks to 'Wilsonian' influences, this was the first crack in the façade of European colonialism.

Benedict was critical of the failure of Catholic missionaries in several countries to form an indigenous clergy 'despite long years of missionary activity, and the work of the seminaries in Rome'.[209] Having in mind, perhaps, the persecution of Christians during the Boxer Uprising in China, and the nineteenth-century Ugandan martyrs whom he beatified in 1920, Benedict argued that 'if persecution comes a native church will have a better chance of survival'.[210]

Under the influence of the Belgian missionary, Fr Frédéric Vincent Lebbe, who was one of the main advocates of the 'indigenization' policy, he and his vigorous new prefect of Propaganda, the Dutch cardinal, Willem Marinus van Rossum (appointed 12 March 1918), sent Mgr Celso Costantini to China as Apostolic delegate with the specific task of laying the foundations of an indigenous Chinese episcopate.[211] The resistance of the missionaries was strong, and it was not until the pontificate of his successor, Pius XI, that Benedict's plans for the consecration of Chinese bishops was brought to fruition (see Chapter 7). The advent of Benedict, van Rossum, and Costantini signalled a new turn in the Vatican's policy for the missions.[212] Benedict followed up *Maximum Illud* with practical measures. He reorganized studies at the

[206] Bellocchi, *Tutte le Encicliche*, VIII, *Maximum Illud*, 30 November 1919, Enciclica. N.B. *Maximum Illud* does not appear in Carlen, *Papal Encyclicals*, III, because the editor of the latter does not consider it to have been an encyclical.

[207] Bellocchi, *Tutte le Encicliche*, VIII, *Maximum Illud*, 30 November 1919, Enciclica.

[208] Bellocchi, *Tutte le Encicliche*, VIII, *Maximum Illud*, 30 November 1919, Enciclica.

[209] Bellocchi, *Tutte le Encicliche*, VIII, *Maximum Illud*, 30 November 1919, Enciclica.

[210] Bellocchi, *Tutte le Encicliche*, VIII, *Maximum Illud*, 30 November 1919, Enciclica.

[211] Leung, *Sino-Vatican Relations*, 45.

[212] For the influence of Van Rossum on the direction which policy took at Propaganda, see Claude Prudhomme, 'Le Cardinal Van Rossum et la politique missionnaire du Saint-Siège sous Benoit XV et Pie XI (1918–1932)', in V. Poels, T. Salemink, and H. de Valk (eds), *Life with a Mission: Cardinal Willem Marinus van Rossum (1854–1932)*, Nijmegen, 2010–11, 123–141.

college of Propaganda Fide to provide practical training for future missionaries, including the provision of language teaching; he founded the Ethiopian College in 1919 for the training of clergy for that country; and he encouraged the spread of missionary support societies, such as the Clergy Mission Association, throughout the Church, bringing Don Angelo Roncalli (the future Pope John XXIII) to Rome to organize fund-raising. *Maximum Illud* was the most significant papal pronouncement on the missions until Paul VI's encyclical *Evangelii Nuntiandi* in 1976. Taken together with Benedict's other measures, it constituted a revolution in the Church's missionary policy.

BENEDICT AND CHRISTIAN UNITY

Like most Italian priests of his generation, Benedict was notoriously anti-Protestant. According to Carlo Falconi, it was from his tutor Padre Ballerini that he acquired his 'strong distaste for Protestantism'.[213] The protests about Protestant propaganda and proselytism in Italy, and especially in Rome, grew more and more vociferous as Benedict's pontificate progressed. In November 1915, he castigated the activities of the 'evangelical sects', accused them of taking people away from faith with material rewards, and urged the consequent need to strengthen the work of the Opera per la Preservazione della Fede:

> these emissaries of Satan, in the heart of our holy city, erect temples in which they reject the true worship of God; they erect pestilential pulpits in order to brazenly spread error amongst the people and they circulate calumnies and lies against the Catholic religion and its ministers.[214]

In 1919, the Jesuit organ made the point that adherents to Protestantism in Italy had doubled since the war and that certain factors encouraged further growth—tourism, return migration from America, and the well-funded activities of highly organized British and American groups.[215] While admitting the good material works done by Protestant groups both during and after the war, through the opening of recreational facilities for soldiers, and schools, colleges, orphanages, nursing or convalescent homes, and youth and student hostels—the YMCA and the YWCA—*La Civiltà Cattolica* complained that sole purpose of all this was to draw away Italians from Catholicism.[216] Of course, the pope's relief work in Russia was also a mission of propaganda and

[213] Falconi, *The Popes*, 100.

[214] Bellocchi, *Tutte le Encicliche*, VIII, 79–82, *A Lei, Signor Cardinale*, 21 November 1915, Allocuzione.

[215] LaCC, 70, 2 (1919), 231–233.

[216] LaCC, 70, 2 (1919), 231–233.

proselytism, an aggressive attack upon the Orthodox Church there. This was still an age in which the Roman Catholic hierarchy believed that 'error has no rights'.

Given Benedict's attitudes towards both Orthodox schismatics and Protestant heretics, it is ironical that the period of his pontificate witnessed an upsurge in ecumenical activity in other Christian churches. During the course of his pontificate, the Vatican was approached by Protestant leaders involved in initiatives aimed at bringing about closer relations between the churches, a movement to which the experience of the First World War lent an especial urgency. In the summer of 1914, the American Episcopal Church had made an approach for Vatican support for its project of a World Christian Conference: Gasparri's reply came to late to be of much value because the outbreak of the war dashed all hopes of a meeting, but established the pattern for all such exchanges. The Cardinal Secretary of State, on the pope's behalf, was politely vague but ended by reasserting that Benedict, as pope, was the 'one to whom all men have been given over to be fed, [is] the source and cause of all unity in the Church'.[217] In March 1918 it was the turn of the Scandinavian Lutheran 'metropolitans'—the bishops of Oslo and Zealand and the archbishop of Uppsala—to invite the Vatican to be represented at a conference in Uppsala to bring about peace. Though Archbishop Nathan Söderbolm was flattering in his letter, 'The pope speaks in the name of the whole Church when he champions peace', it elicited the same reply as previous invitations.[218] The leaders of the American Episcopal Church returned to the fray in 1919 when they sent another letter to Gasparri inviting the Catholic Church to participate in the founding of a World Conference on Faith and Order, which would be the precursor of the World Council of Churches. Gasparri passed on the letter to Merry del Val in his capacity as Secretary of the Holy Office, the guardian of the doctrine of the Church; not a very propitious choice in view of Merry del Val's hostility to Anglican orders. The answer (in Latin) was inevitably negative.

The episcopalians did not give up: further correspondence in April 1919 elicited the reply from Gasparri that:

> You may rest assured that the Holy Father will pray that the Holy Spirit will enlighten the minds and acts of all those who labour today for the reunion of Christendom—that they should acknowledge the centre of unity and rally around the same.[219]

[217] As quoted in R. Rouse and S.C. Neil (eds), *A History of the Ecumenical Movement*, London, 1954, 413.

[218] Rouse and Neil, *A History of the Ecumenical Movement*, 413.

[219] As quoted in R. Aubert, 'Cardinal Mercier's Visit to America in the Autumn of 1919', in J.-P. Hendrickx, J. Pirotte, and L. Courtois (eds), *Le Cardinal Mercier (1851–1926), Un prélat d'avant-garde/Publications du professeur Roger Aubert rassemblées à l'occasion de ses 80 ans*, Louvain-la-Neuve, 1994, 348.

In the Italian drafts written in Gasparri's own hand, and in the first English draft, the final words are 'rally around the Throne of Peter'. The Episcopalians were still undeterred and in May 1919 they sent a delegation to Rome led by the Bishop of Chicago. It was received in audience by the pope, who treated the delegates with great courtesy, but the answer was till the same, 'Everyone knows of the Catholic Church's position, and therefore it will not be possible for Us to take part in such a Congress or send a delegation.' He added in his kindly way that he did not want to disappoint them and prayed that they would 'see the light. . . .' In this episode, the Vatican's behaviour may be explained by the suspicion that the Anglicans and the Orthodox were growing closer.

All this was, of course, entirely predictable. The Roman Pontiff, fortified by Infallibility, was not at all likely to allow the character of the 'One, True Church' to be compromised by dealings with heretical bodies, however well intentioned. As with the individual cases of England and Russia, all that Catholics could do was to wait and pray that one day all non-Catholic Christians would be reconciled to Rome.

It is all the more extraordinary, therefore, that the 'Malines Conversations' of 1921–6, between Catholic representatives led by Cardinal Mercier, and Lord Halifax and other Anglicans, should have had their origin in Benedict's pontificate. The answer to the puzzle lies with Cardinal Mercier, whose heroic wartime role had established him as a figure of world stature in the Allied countries. In October 1919, for example, he received a standing ovation at the General Convention of the American Episcopal Church in Chicago where he made the most extraordinary statement for a Catholic prelate, 'I have greeted you as brethren in the worship of a common ideal, as brethren in the love of liberty and, let me add, as brethren in the Christian faith', and was delated to the Holy Office for it by Cardinal O'Connell of Boston.[220] Though, as has been seen, Benedict had not always approved of Cardinal Mercier's activities during the German occupation of Belgium, he had great respect and admiration for him. It was Mercier who proposed to Benedict in December 1920 that he host discreet discussions in his See city between theologians from the Roman Catholic and Anglican churches: in fact, he originally suggested inviting representatives of the Orthodox and other Protestant churches as well.[221] Ironically, under Mercier's influence, the Malines initiative was more readily accepted in the Vatican than at Lambeth. The archbishop of Canterbury was very cautious about giving his blessing for fear of offending the evangelical wing of his church.[222] Inasmuch as the first exploratory discussions were held

[220] As quoted in R. Aubert, 'Cardinal Mercier's Visit to America in the Autumn of 1919'.

[221] B. and M. Pawley, *Rome and Canterbury through Four Centuries*, London and Oxford, 1981, 262.

[222] Pawley, *Rome and Canterbury*, 263.

in Malines from 6 to 8 December 1921, it can be said that it was under the aegis of Benedict that the modern ecumenical movement was initiated in the Roman Catholic Church.

THE UNEXPECTED DEATH OF BENEDICT XV

The death of Benedict XV on 22 January 1922 was unexpected. Despite delicate health in childhood, he had been of a robust constitution throughout his adult life: he told Gasparri that in all his life he had only spent one and a half lire on medicine.[223] In old age his only infirmity was rheumatics. He died young, very young for a pope: he was only 67—the youngest reigning pope at his death—so he was spared the ailments of older men. His death appears to have been caused by catching a chill while waiting to say Mass for the nuns of the Vatican's Santa Marta hospice.[224] Rarely indisposed, Benedict did not pay much attention to the illness which developed, which eventually resulted in pneumonia. Without antibiotics there was very little his doctors could do for him.

According to Jemolo, there was unprecedented public mourning in Italy for Benedict.[225] Hebblethwaite says that 'For the first time since 1870, flags were flown at half mast on government buildings.'[226] This reaction may only have been an indirect tribute to the man, reflecting the extent to which Benedict's pontificate had improved the relationship with Italy. Italian obituaries for Benedict were decidedly mixed.[227] But he was mourned beyond Italy. Giuseppe Motta, Swiss president of the League of Nations, paid him a fulsome tribute, and Charles Schol, the president of the American Union of Jewish Congregations, wrote to the Apostolic Delegate in Washington, sending his condolences and calling Benedict 'a constant exponent of the finer spiritual values of life and a great standard-bearer of morality among men and of peace and concord among nations'.[228] However, because of the shortness of his pontificate, Benedict was quickly forgotten, becoming the 'unknown pope' of the twentieth century.

Benedict continued the policies of Pius X in regard to the reform of liturgical practice and of the Roman curia, and brought to fruition the great project of the codification of Canon Law. On the other hand, his pontificate marked a clean break with that of his predecessor in two important respects. Firstly, he abandoned the 'anti-Modernist crusade' and its fanatical persecution of clergy

[223] *Diario*, II, 398, 20 January 1922.

[224] Vistalli, *Benedetto XV*, 34.

[225] Arturo Carlo Jemolo, *Church and State in Italy, 1850–1950*, Oxford, 1960, 168.

[226] Hebblethwaite, *John XXIII*, 105.

[227] Pollard, *The Unknown Pope*, 211–212.

[228] ASV, DAUS, V, scatola 97, letter to Bonzano, 22 January 1922.

and laity alike, and sought a return to Catholic unity by demanding that 'the practice lately come into use, of using distinctive names by which Catholics are marked off from Catholics should cease'.[229] Nevertheless, Benedict did not entirely succeed in dispelling the unpleasant atmosphere of apprehension and suspicion engendered by the anti-modernist witch-hunts of Pius X's pontificate: it would hang like a pall over the intellectual life of the Catholic Church for several decades to come. Fear of the charge of 'modernism' and of being hauled up before the 'inquisitors' of the Holy Office in Rome would haunt theologians, biblical scholars, and ecclesiastical historians until the Second Vatican Council and beyond.[230] Secondly, Benedict, ably assisted by Gasparri, was responsible for revitalizing papal diplomacy, which had languished under his predecessor. Papal peace diplomacy during the war was a synthesis of Benedict's great moral passion and Gasparri's worldly pragmatism.

Benedict's pontificate marked a return to the policies of Leo XIII, and Benedict's mentor, Cardinal Rampolla del Tindaro. The concern and commitment which Benedict showed for both the Eastern churches and the missions were again positively Leonine. The emphasis on the autonomy and special needs of the Eastern churches and the reinvigoration of the missionary outreach of Rome's missionary outreach, through a renewal of the underlying ideology of that endeavour in a 'post-colonialist' direction were to bear great fruits. In this way, Benedict reinforced the foundations of the presence in Africa, Asia, and Oceania which the Roman Catholic Church enjoys today. Most important of all, under Benedict XV, the papacy had completely emerged from its pre-war isolation. Whereas, in 1914, the papacy seemed doomed to follow the Ottoman Caliphate, which by then was on its way out,[231] by the end of Benedict's reign the Holy See had assumed a high profile in international affairs, once again becoming a serious diplomatic actor in its own right, and thus was in a far better position to defend its worldwide interests.

Most important of all, Benedict committed the Holy See to using its growing diplomatic resources not only for the defence of the Church's own immediate interests but also to a permanent peace-making and humanitarian role. His immediate successor, Pius XI, and the Secretary of State he inherited from Benedict, actively supported the search for peace and security in Europe in the 1920s, and Pius XI followed the same policy, with Eugenio Pacelli as Secretary of State, from 1930 onwards. When Pacelli became pope himself in March 1933 he used Vatican diplomacy in various attempts to preserve the peace right up to the moment that Hitler declared war on Poland at the beginning of the following September (see Chapter 8). He also followed Benedict's example by setting up a Vatican Information Office to help trace missing

[229] Carlen, *Papal Encyclicals*, III, 144.
[230] But charges of 'social modernism' were not pursued after Pius X's death.
[231] Stehlin, 'The Emergence of a New Vatican Diplomacy', 75.

POWs and civilians and promoted broader humanitarian relief efforts during the course of the Second World War and after. Since 1945, successive popes have used their influence to assist in peace efforts—like John XXIII during the Cuban Missile Crisis of 1962,[232] Paul VI during the Vietnam War in the late 1960s,[233] and John Paul II during the Gulf and Iraq Wars.[234] Thus, Benedict's legacy has lasted nearly one hundred years. The Holy See's ongoing, active diplomatic role in world affairs in support of peace is the most valuable and lasting legacy of his brief reign. We can, therefore, conclude that, inspired by Leo XIII, and assisted by Gasparri, Benedict XV laid the foundations of modern, twentieth/twenty-first-century papal diplomacy.

[232] Hebblethwaite, *John XXIII*, 445–447.

[233] Hebblethwaite, *Paul VI*, ch. 29.

[234] Bernstein and Politi, *His Holiness*, 488–489.

4

Pius XI: Italian Fascism and the *Conciliazione*

INTRODUCTION

The pope who emerged from the 1922 conclave, Pius XI (Achille Ratti) faced many problems upon his election, and most were at home, in Italy. The biggest was the question of what attitude the Vatican should adopt towards the threat which the rise of the Fascist movement posed to the survival of the existing constitutional regime. But the arrival of Fascism in power, which initially seemed to pose a serious threat to the Church in Italy, also offered new, positive opportunities which would eventually bear fruit in the *Conciliazione*, in a satisfactory settlement of all the outstanding disputes between the papacy and the Italian state. It also finally resolved the long-standing financial difficulties of the Holy See.

The Italian situation would also affect the development of the papacy and the policies which it followed throughout the worldwide Church in other ways. In particular, in the process of coming terms with the new, authoritarian Fascist dictatorship, Pius XI concentrated all Catholic lay activities in Italian Catholic Action, as the Church's instrument for exerting beneficent moral influences in Italian society, and hopefully influencing the policies of government. The Italian model of Catholic Action would then be 'exported' to the whole of the Catholic world as a template for Catholic lay activism in all countries, whatever their political systems.

ACHILLE RATTI, 1857–1922

Pope Pius XI was born Achille Ratti into a lower-middle-class family, his father being a silk factory manager, in the town of Desio in the Brianza district of Milan province, on 31 May 1857. His French biographer, Chiron, says of him that he 'did not scorn the recognition and honours that came his way during his lifetime', thus Papa Ratti agreed to the erection of a massive statue in his honour in the main square of his birthplace.[1] He was educated, first by his mother, then in local elementary schools for two years, and this is when he first came into contact with some of his great passions—Italian literature and the Bible.[2] Papa Ratti's extraordinary familiarity with the Bible, both the Old and New Testaments, would become legendary during the course of his pontificate. In 1867 he entered the Milan diocesan junior seminary at Seveso, a step which could not have been a very radical change considering that, apart from his mother, all his previous teachers/mentors had been priests. His school career henceforth was quite simply brilliant.[3] When he entered the Milan Major Seminary in 1875 he was already a member of the Franciscan Third Order. He had also achieved outstanding marks in his secondary school leaving certificate.

Throughout his childhood, adolescence, and youth, Ratti was surrounded by the intellectual, theological, and political controversies of the Lombard capital, the battles between Catholic intransigents and conciliatorists (towards the liberal state, that is), between supporters of Don Davide Albertario's *Osservatore Cattolico* and those of the *Carroccio*.[4] Yet we do not know where Ratti, who was ordained priest in December 1879, stood in these disputes. Ordination coincided with his transfer to Rome where he studied for degrees in theology, philosophy, and Canon Law at the Gregorian University and the Pontifical Academy of Noble Ecclesiastics, and achieved the highest marks in all three.[5] Rome was very different from Milan, it was on the 'front line' between Italian Liberalism and Catholicism, and between the papacy and the 'usurping' Italian state. Perhaps it was a useful experience, a necessary prequel to his return to Milan where the liberal Calabiana was succeeded as archbishop by an intransigent, Andrea Ferrari, in 1894. After a brief spell in 1882 as curate at Barni, under the authority of his uncle, the rector Don Damiano Ratti, the young priest returned to Milan. Barni was one of his very few and short experiences of pastoral work, excepting his role as chaplain to the convent of the Cenacle in Milan and as a confessor to nuns in Rome: his six-month stint as archbishop of the Lombard capital in 1921 was the other.

From the end of 1882, Ratti dedicated himself to a career as a teacher and scholar, first in the diocesan Major Seminary and later in the very prestigious Ambrosian Library of Milan, where the librarians were expected to carry out scholarly research. It is claimed that in these years Ratti established a strong relationship with Rabbi Da Fano of the main Milanese synagogue and that he actually took some of his seminary students there, which seems unlikely given

[1] Y. Chiron, *Pio XI. Il papa dei Patti Lateranensi e del'opposizione ai totalitarismi*, Cinisello Balsamo, Milan, 2004, 15.

[2] Chiron, *Pio XI*, 18–19.

[3] Chiron, *Pio XI*, 25.

[4] Falconi, *The Popes*, 158–159.

[5] Chiron, *Pio XI*, 36–37.

the Church's extreme diffidence towards the Judaic religion.[6] While Milan provided the ideal milieu for this talented scholar of the natural sciences and letters, theology, and Liturgy, it also meant that Ratti found himself in the midst of the intellectual currents and controversies of the 1880s and 1890s. Falconi says that, yet again, he seems to have kept his distance from controversy, preferring instead to cultivate friendships among the great and good of Milan: like Duke Gallarati Scotti and his family, the Count Melzi D'Eril, the Marchese Ludovico Trotti, a great fan of Cavour, General Thaon di Revel, and other Milanese aristocratic families such as the Borromeo, the Caccia-Dominioni, and the Jacini.[7] Ratti would later make Carlo Caccia-Dominioni first his Maestro di Camera, effectively head of his Vatican household, and then a cardinal. So his experience was very much of Milanese 'high society', what Italians call *Il buon salotto*, rather than that of middle or lower-class society. It was also in Milan that he made the acquaintance of Fr Agostino Gemelli, a Franciscan friar and psychologist, who would later play an important role during his pontificate. But these mundane pleasures did not distract him from more spiritual things—in 1894, Don Ratti became an oblate of St Charles Borromeo, that is, a secular priest taking a special vow of obedience to serve his bishop in missionary and evangelistic enterprises and carry out the Spiritual Exercises of St Ignatius Loyala.[8] As the 'modernist' crisis unfolded in the Catholic Church in the last years of Leo XIII's pontificate and then during that of Pius X, who succeeded him in 1903, Ratti kept his head down. Hebblethwaite says this of the future pope:

> The truth was that no one knew where Ratti stood on important questions. He had successfully avoided showing his hand in all the disputes which had raged with such passionate intensity over the last thirty years. In the 'night battle' he had proved himself invisible.[9]

As his career at the Ambrosian developed, so did Ratti's other major pursuits and passions such as travelling—he visited most of the major libraries of Central Europe in search of books and manuscripts—and mountain-climbing—he became a skilled and intrepid practitioner.[10] He certainly scaled the heights of scholarship in Catholic Milan, becoming first Deputy Librarian and then, in 1907, Librarian of the Ambrosiana, the city's flagship cultural institution until the inauguration of the Catholic University in 1921. By the time he left, Milan had accumulated a long and prestigious publications record. Three years later, his reputation had reached Rome and he was nominated Vice-Prefect of an even more prestigious institution, the Vatican Library, by Pius X, and within a further four, he was made prefect by

[6] Chiron, *Pio XI*, 78. [7] Falconi, *The Popes*, 160–161.
[8] Chiron, *Pio XI*, 60–61. [9] Hebblethwaite, *John XXIII*, 106.
[10] Hebblethwaite, *John XXIII*, 45.

Papa Sarto's successor. At this point, he could have expected to stay among the Vatican's books and manuscripts for the rest of his life, with perhaps the hope of receiving a cardinal's hat as reward for his labours. But it was not to be. His career took a quite extraordinary, unexpected turn: he was given a papal diplomatic posting.

As has been seen in Chapter 2, Ratti's posting as, first, apostolic visitator and then nuncio in Poland was a demanding and difficult one, but it was also a tremendous learning curve for someone who had had only limited previous experience of administration and none at all of diplomacy. The first thing which Mgr Ratti learned quickly was that rank and status were terribly important in the Church. According to Mgr Angelo Roncalli (later Pope John XXIII), Pius XI made Roncalli an archbishop when he sent him to Bulgaria as apostolic visitor because, he said:

> I don't want a repeat performance of what happened to me in Poland. I was embarrassed at Episcopal meetings when I had to take my place as representative of the Holy Father, I had to take precedence over the Polish archbishops.[11]

He also experienced at first hand the problems created by clergy, especially higher clergy, who insisted on meddling in politics: in Poland, the bulk of the bishops supported the National Democratic Party of Roman Dmowski.[12] The 'Miracle on the Vistula', when the Red Army stood poised to seize the Polish capital in the summer of 1920, which Mgr Ratti witnessed from within the city because he refused to leave it along with the rest of the diplomatic corps, and the information which he was able to gather about the persecution of the Church in the Soviet Union, and the appalling conditions there more generally, left him with a deep horror and fear of Communism that would shape the policies of his pontificate. On the other hand, he 'drew on experiences of his nunciature to undergird his relatively enlightened view on the Jewish question'.[13] Above all, Ratti was disgusted by the interminable struggles between the various peoples of Poland and the Baltic states and shocked by the way in which these disputes, and the struggle between Poles and Germans during the Silesian plebiscites of 1920, deeply divided Catholics: the Polish/Baltic States experience made him forever suspicious of excessive nationalism. And, of course, his nunciature to Poland was one of the chief casualties of that struggle (see Chapter 3).

It was probably in part, at least, in order to extricate him from the very difficult position that he found himself in after the Silesian plebiscite, that Benedict removed him, sent him to succeed the saintly Andrea Ferrari as archbishop of Milan in May 1921, and made him a cardinal. But Papa Della

[11] Hebblethwaite, *John XXIII*, 114.

[12] Pease, *Rome's Most Faithful Daughter*, 33–34.

[13] Pease, *Rome's Most Faithful Daughter*, 33.

Chiesa had probably also decided that the Polish nunciature had sufficiently tempered Ratti for a major pastoral role, for the headship of Italy's largest and most important diocese outside of Rome. Ratti handled Milan with his usual business-like efficiency. But he was not to be there for long, not even long enough to conduct a visitation of the diocese's 1,000 parishes, though he did observe at first hand the rise of Mussolini and the Fascists, whose headquarters was in the city, and whose banners he permitted to be borne in procession into the Duomo.[14] In December 1921 he also inaugurated the new Catholic University of the Sacred Heart as papal legate on Benedict's behalf and renewed his acquaintance with its rector, Fr Agostino Gemelli, who would become such a powerful figure during Ratti's future pontificate. His last major act was to preside over the Lombard council of bishops on 10 January 1922 and pen a joint pastoral letter on the education of youth and civic peace. Soon thereafter, Benedict died and Cardinal Ratti was summoned to Rome for the conclave. Despite his brief episcopate in Milan, he had already gained a reputation throughout Italy as a bishop who tended to be conciliatory and extremely effective in the pastoral domain. Without putting him forward too much, the newspapers included him among the *papabili*.[15]

CONCLAVE AND ELECTION, 1922

Gasparri was the Camerlengo of the Holy Roman Church in 1922 and thus the man deputed to preside over the Holy See during the *sede vacante* and make arrangements for the conclave that would elect Benedict's successor. Since Papa Della Chiesa's death had been unexpected, Gasparri was faced with money difficulties in his role as Camerlengo. Finding little money in the papal treasury, he was forced to turn to the apostolic delegate in Washington, Mgr Giovanni Bonzano, to provide him with the necessary funds to defray the expenses of the conclave and coronation out of the monies accumulated from the Peter's Pence offerings of American Catholics.[16] Ironically, two of the American cardinals, O'Connell of Boston and Dougherty of Philadelphia, arrived at the doors of the conclave just in time to hear the news of Ratti's election (Farley of New York was in Switzerland when Benedict died and so made it to the conclave). In consequence, in deference to American Catholicism's growing demographic and financial power, the new pope would shortly change the rules for the conclave, extending to eighteen days the intermission between the death of a pope and the opening of the conclave to elect his successor.

[14] Chiron, *Pio XI*, 130.
[15] Pease, *Rome's Most Faithful Daughter*, 49–50.
[16] See Pollard, *Money*, 124–125.

That the conclave lasted four days before a pope was elected can be ascribed to the fact that the Sacred College 'remained structurally and politically almost identical to that under Pius X' because Benedict had not had time to make many more creations and the balance between *intégristes* and progressives remained more or less the same as in 1914.[17]

Though Ratti was *papabile*, he was clearly a compromise candidate. He was only elected after fourteen counts. Cardinal Maffi of Pisa was a leading contender, with ten votes at the beginning, but his candidacy exhausted itself after the first day. The front-runners were originally Cardinal Merry del Val for the curial, 'revanchist' party and Gasparri for the 'progressives', who wanted a continuation of Benedict's policies.[18] The candidacy of Cardinal Merry del Val never really took off, his votes stalling at seventeen in the fourth count. He was replaced as candidate of the curialists by Cardinal La Fontaine (Patriarch of Venice), but he too peaked at twenty-three on the eleventh count. According to Cardinal Pfiffl of Vienna there was a history of mental instability in La Fontaine's family.[19] By then, the supporters of Gasparri, who stalled at a peak of twenty-four votes in the sixth to ninth counts, had thrown in the towel and started to switch votes to Ratti. Gasparri was disliked by some electors, either as the close collaborator of Benedict by the integralists or, more generally, as a man tarred with cronyism: 'Gasparri was above all reproached for his nepotism . . . [it was claimed] that if he became pope he would be a plaything in the hands of his relatives.'[20] It was in this conclave that both Cardinals Merry del Val and De Lai were allegedly automatically excommunicated for trying to 'sell' votes to Ratti on condition that Gasparri was not reappointed as Secretary of State.[21] Pfiffl thought that Gasparri and Ratti had also come to some sort of agreement which, if true, would have incurred excommunication too.[22]

Ratti's final majority, forty-two over fifty-three, was very solid and clear. While Ratti's election was unexpected—he had been a cardinal for less than a year (though Benedict XV had been one for even less time)—he was eminently *papabile* with a combination of necessary qualities: a holy life; scholarship, particularly in the history of the Church; a stint in Vatican diplomacy and a short but intense pastoral experience in Italy's largest, and arguably most problematic, diocese; and good relations with the Italian state—a must for a new pope. There is no evidence that he was Benedict's creature, nor that he was his designated heir.

According to Zizola, Ratti did not accept at once, but made an elegant, poised speech of acceptance in Latin, which suggests that he knew which way

17 Zizola, *Conclave*, 201.
18 Zizola, *Conclave*, 202.
19 Zizola, *Conclave*, 200.
20 Zizola, *Conclave*, 201.
21 Spadolini, *Cardinale Gasparri e la Questione Romana*.
22 Zizola, *Conclave*, 202.

the wind was blowing from early on during the conclave. Reactions to his election were uniformly positive and Hebblethwaite says:

> At least one person was overjoyed at Ratti's election. Duchesne, the venerable church historian, was now 79 and in the last year of his life. He had known Ratti as librarian in Milan and Rome. He felt his whole life's work was vindicated. With his Breton faith undimmed he had survived being put on the Index of Forbidden Books and he now looked forward to a life of flourishing scholarship. . . .[23]

This can only mean that Ratti was not a fanatical anti-modernist, which is why Gasparri and his supporters could vote for him.

Popes are inevitably judged by their behaviour immediately after their election. Papa Ratti's behaviour was extremely revealing. He gave his first benediction, *Urbi et orbi* ('To the City and the World') following his election from the *external* loggia of St Peter's Basilica to the crowd in the square below, something which none of his predecessors since Pius IX had done to signify their role as 'prisoner of the Vatican'. Clearly, the new pope was sending a signal, a sign of benevolence and openness, towards the land of his birth. To those in the papal entourage his strong personality also shone forth from the beginning, 'He behaved as if he had always been pope', has probably been said about many of those elected to the throne of St Peter, but it was a more accurate description of Pius XI than most. What became quickly apparent was his business-like approach to the management of affairs and an authoritarian temperament, which brooked no disobedience. And, in a curious twist, he demonstrated a firm refusal to bow to Roman custom and practice. He insisted on bringing into the papal private apartment his housekeeper, 'Signora Linda' (Banfi), who had followed him from Milan. The Romans were scandalized by this move and naturally objected that no pope had ever allowed a lay woman to take up such a post in the Vatican, to which the new pope allegedly replied, 'Then I shall be the first.'[24]

GOVERNING THE UNIVERSAL CHURCH

One of the first major issues confronting a pope is always how to regulate his relationship with the Roman curia, the central governing organism of the Roman Catholic Church. A pope cannot, in the long term, govern *against* the Roman curia, he must govern *with* it, but depending upon his former relationship with the curia, and the forcefulness of his personality, he can impose his authority by introducing *changes to* the curia, both in terms of its staffing, especially at the key level of heads of the Roman dicasteries or congregations,

[23] Hebblethwaite, *John XXIII*, 106.

[24] L. Lazzarini, *Pio XI*, Milan, 1937, 312.

and even its institutional organization, that is, rearranging the functions allotted to each congregation. By comparison with Benedict XV, who made changes of both kinds in order to assert his authority (see Chapter 2), Pius XI made virtually no institutional innovations. However, the appointment of Mgr (later Cardinal) Giuseppe Pizzardo as the head of the Ufficio Centrale dell'Azione Cattolica (Central Office of Catholic Action) in 1937, with its seat in the Palazzo delle Congregazioni in Trastevere *was* an innovation, the first time in the history of the Church that provision had been made for an office directing Catholic lay activity throughout the world.[25] In this sense, it anticipated Paul VI's establishment of a pontifical Council for the Laity by nearly thirty years.[26] Pius XI's creation of the Special Administration was the only other institutional change.

Indeed, his reappointment of Cardinal Gasparri as Secretary of State, for which there was no precedent in the modern history of papacy, seems to indicate that he was happy with the composition of the Church's governing elite which he had inherited from his predecessor. Three factors may account for this: Benedict had already 'purged' the Roman curia of the most intransigently anti-modernists elements or cut them down to size (see Chapter 3). In any case, the modernist/anti-modernist dispute was no longer a serious issue, largely because Benedict had defused it; Pius XI had no major 'enemies' in the Roman curia (unlike Benedict); his period in the Vatican from 1911 to 1918 had been spent in the essentially 'unpolitical' Vatican Library, and though he had had experience as a papal diplomat in Poland and the Baltic States, he had had none in the Secretariat of State itself; hence he was happy to leave that in the capable hands of his former boss, Gasparri.

As Papa Ratti grew into the job, he increasingly asserted his absolute control over the Roman curia, issuing instructions and commands. According to his personal private secretary of eighteen years, Mgr (later Cardinal) Carlo Confalonieri, 'only he, the pope, gave the orders. He did not allow anyone tell him what to do. He considered the dicasteries and officials of the curia as executors of his superior dispositions.'[27] And he checked that everything he had ordered had been carried out properly.[28] He was always intensely jealous of his prerogatives, as against the claims of the individual congregations. Thus, in an audience, in 1938, with Domenico Tardini, by then Under-Secretary of State, Pius told him in no uncertain terms that he should not have referred a request from the bishop of Sankt Gallen (Switzerland) for an apostolic mandate to the Consistorial Congregation: 'What has the Consistorial

[25] ASV, AES, IV, 529, 597, Ufficio dell'Azione Cattolica, pro-memoria of 25 March, 1938.

[26] *Annuario Pontificio*, 1968, 1432.

[27] C. Confalonieiri, *Pio XI*, Cinisello Balsamo, 1993, 112.

[28] Confalonieiri, *Pio XI*, 123.

Congregation got to do with it? I am *l'Apostolico!*'[29] Pius was notoriously imperious, authoritarian, and sometimes even bad-tempered in his relations with his subordinates. Chiron relates an incident which occurred after the condemnation of Action Française in 1926: Pius insisted that Cardinal Billot renounce his cardinal's hat for opposing the papal condemnation, and when the bishop of Montauban, who had also supported Action Française, refused to resign, Pius started a canonical process to remove him.[30]

Francesco Borgoncini-Duca, nuncio to Italy, told Galeazzo Ciano, Italy's foreign minister, in August 1938 that Pius had 'a thoroughly bad character, authoritarian and almost insolent. Everybody is terrified of him in the Vatican.'[31]

Yet Papa Ratti had a distinctly human side: he knew how to temper his commands with humour. Thus, on being asked by the Father General of the Dominicans if he might attend the ceremonial opening by Mussolini of a garden on the Aventine, Pius replied that he could do so, as long as he didn't get involved in a football game with the Duce![32] Throughout his pontificate, Pius XI relied on three key elements of the curia. The first was the Secretariat of State which, as well as being a sort of clearing-house for all kinds of matters, was the 'foreign office' of the Vatican. What it was not, at least during the tenure of Cardinal Eugenio Pacelli, was the Vatican's 'prime minister's office', which it certainly is today. The next key dicastery was the Supreme Congregation of the Holy Office and Index, which played a crucial role, as shall be seen, not only in handling major issues of orthodoxy, like the threat seen to be posed by the ecumenical efforts of Protestant figures and movements in this period, but also the heresies emanating from the totalitarian ideologies of Communism, Fascism, and National Socialism. Finally, Propaganda Fide, the missionary congregation, also played an increasingly important role as Catholic missions throughout the world expanded and as Pius XI devoted more and more time to them. Other congregations were, of course, important, like the Supreme Tribunal of the Segnatura, which was responsible for deciding on offences against the moral law, and on the licitiness or otherwise of the political actions of the faithful; the Consistorial Congregation, which played a key role in the appointment and supervision of bishops; the Congregation of the Council (of Trent), which was responsible for enforcing the reforms of that sixteenth-century Counter-Reformation council of the Church; and the Oriental Congregation and its various offshoots, given Pius XI's concern about both the Oriental churches in communion and the

[29] ASV, AES, IV Periodo, Stati Eccl., Diario di S.E. Mons. Tardini dal 27 settembre al 29 ottobre 1938, entry for 7 October.

[30] Chiron, *Pio XI*, 317.

[31] G. Ciano, *Ciano's Diary, 1937–1938*, trans. with notes Andreas Mayor, intro. Malcolm Muggeridge, London, 1952, 147.

[32] ASV, AES, IV Periodo, Stati Eccl., Taccuini, audience of 15 April 1932.

Schismatic ones and the congregation for universities and seminaries, particularly since the number of Catholic universities increased throughout the world in this period: the apostolic constitution, *Deus Scientiarum* of 1930, which reviewed the seminary training of priests, imposed more work on this congregation. Another agency of the Vatican, the Amministrazione Speciale della Santa Sede (Special Administration of the Holy See or ASSS), headed by Bernardino Nogara was also very important. Pius XI clearly did not trust the existing Vatican financial agencies—the ABSS (Administration of the Assets of the Holy See) and the Opera Pias Causas, which handled various bank accounts—with the financial compensation paid by Italy in 1929. He was anxious about the efficient investment of this money and the fact that Nogara had an audience of the pope on average once every ten days demonstrates the importance which Pius XI placed on this matter.[33]

He made no radical changes in the personnel of the curia during the course of his pontificate, except for the replacement of Cardinal Gasparri as Secretary of State by Mgr Eugenio Pacelli, nuncio in Berlin, in 1930 (see Chapter 6). The death of Cardinal Merry del Val in 1930 removed one of the last great anti-modernist partisans from the curia, though he and De Lai were as isolated under Pius XI as they had been under Benedict XV.[34] In fact, the real innovation which Pius XI brought to the Vatican after his election was an 'entourage' of Milanese. Apart from his secretaries, Carlo Confalonieri and Diego Venini, he brought his housekeeper Linda Banfi, the leaders of Milanese Catholic Action, Luigi Colombo, Armida Barelli, and Adelaide Coari, the architect and sculptor, Luca Beltrami, the architect Giuseppe Momo, and the architect and builder Leo Castelli. Castelli became a controversial figure in the Vatican, monopolizing virtually all of the engineering and building contracts such that it was said by wags in the curia that the Vatican number plate, 'SCV' signified 'solo Castelli vive', 'only Castelli lives'! Domenico Tardini was not alone in resenting Pius's power and wealth.[35] Two other figures who played a key role during Papa Ratti's pontificate came from the Lombard capital: Bernardino Nogara who ran the Vatican's investments and other financial activities between 1929 and 1934 and Padre Agostino Gemelli, a scientist and convert to Catholicism who eventually became a Franciscan friar and the first rector of Milan's Catholic University.[36] Gemelli would play a major part in the work of the Congregation of the Holy Office and Index, and he became president of the Pontifical Academy of Sciences in 1935.

[33] Pollard, *Money*, 148.

[34] G. Azzolini, *Gaetano De Lai 'L'uomo forte': Cultura e fede nel Novecento nell'esperienza del cardinale vicentino*, Vicenza, 2003, 198.

[35] C.-F. Casula, *Domenico Tardini (1888–1961) e l'Azione della Santa Sede nella crisi fra le due guerre*, Rome, 1988, 294.

[36] G. Comacini, *Gemelli*, Milan, 1985.

During the course of the pontificate, several prelates rose to key positions of power: Mgr Giuseppe Pizzardo who, in reward for his diligent, assiduous, if unspectacular service in the Secretariat of State, but also his key role in the campaign to spread the Italian organizational model of Catholic Action to the rest of the Catholic world (see Chapter 6), became a cardinal in 1937 and head of the Central Office of Catholic Action and would become prefect of the Congregation for Universities and Seminaries during the pontificate of Pius XI's successor; Mgr Domenico Tardini,[37] who followed in Pizzardo's footsteps but did not become Cardinal Secretary of State until the election in 1958 of John XXIII, who, as Mgr Angelo Giuseppe Roncalli, had been Tardini's subordinate in the papal diplomatic service; and Nicola Canali, also made cardinal in 1937 and head of the Sacred Penitentiary. In addition, Mgr Alfredo Ottaviani was rising through the ranks of the Roman curia in the 1930s. As the Vatican Archives testify, these men played an especially key role in the decision-making level of Vatican power in the 1930s, having a finger in many pies, including the drafting of some of Pius XI's more significant encyclicals. In any case, by now the practice had been established of curial cardinals and other high-ranking prelates—like Tardini—serving on more than one congregation, thus better utilizing the pool of talent, expertise, and experience in the Vatican.[38] Consequently, most congregations included most of the curial cardinals, so the other congregations were represented *indirectly* on that of the Affari Ecclesiastici Straordinari, and also, to a lesser extent, on that of the Holy Office. In the absence of a 'cabinet'—the papacy was and is an absolute monarchy, after all—there was sort of rough and ready 'coordination' of policy, beyond the work of the Secretary of State.

By the end of Pius XI's reign, a new 'power centre' in the curia, led by the Secretary of State and comprising cardinals Pizzardo and Canali, and Monsignori Tardini and Ottaviani, with Mgr Giambattista Montini (the future Paul VI) as a somewhat detached subordinate, had emerged, and would consolidate and extend its influence under Pius XII.

CONSISTORIES AND THE SACRED COLLEGE

Pius XI was a fairly prolific creator of cardinals. He held nine consistories for that purpose, in 1923, 1925, 1926, 1927, 1929, 1930, 1933, 1935, and the last one in 1937. He does not seem to have had a particular strategy in doing so, merely responding to circumstances, that is, the deaths or retirement of cardinals

[37] See Casula, *Domenico Tardini*, passim, for his career.

[38] See, for example, *Annuario Pontificio*, 1935, 41–65, where it is very clear that most of the curial cardinals served on at least six or seven congregations other than their own.

in both the curia and the world's major residential sees. The result was that he did not change the overall balance in the Sacred College between Italians and non-Italians—62 per cent of the cardinals he created were Italian.[39] Nor did he change the balance between the numbers of curial cardinals and the holders of residential sees—in the 1935 consistory, for example, he created ten cardinals holding curial or diplomatic offices.[40] His very few innovations were geographical: he created two cardinals of the Eastern churches—Ignatius Tappouni, patriarch of Antioch of the Syrians, and Gregory Peter XV Agagianian, patriarch of the Armenians in 1937.

THE ROLE OF FR LEDÓCHOWSKI AND THE JESUITS

The Jesuit Order, whose headquarters lay, appropriately enough, just outside the Vatican in the Borgo Spirito Santo, undoubtedly constituted a 'semi-detached' centre of power and influence during Pius XI's pontificate. Jesuits headed a number of key Vatican-controlled institutions or institutions related to it, like the Gregorian University, the premier Catholic university and the chief academic institution for priests and trainee priests in Rome, the Vatican Astronomical Observatory, Vatican Radio (after 1931), and the authoritative fortnightly journal of comment and opinion, *La Civiltà Cattolica*. In addition, Jesuits carried out some key ad hoc missions for the pope, such as Bishop Michel d'Herbigny who acted as the leader of the Vatican's undercover operation in Russia (see Chapter 6); Fr James Walsh as head of the relief mission to Russia (see Chapter 6); and Fr Pietro Tacchi-Venturi, who played an absolutely crucial role as the pope's go-between with Mussolini and as a member of various Roman Congregations.[41]

But the most important by far among the Jesuit power-brokers in the Vatican, indeed the one who performed the role of a veritable *éminence grise*, was Wlodimir Ledóchowski, the 'black pope', the head of the Jesuit order itself. Ledóchowski (1866–1942), was General of the Jesuits from 1915 to 1942. A subject of the Habsburg Empire from a noble Polish family, he had one sister, Maria Teresa, who was a *beata* and another, Ursula, who was a saint.[42]

[39] M. Graziano, *Il secolo cattolico. La strategia geopolitica della Chiesa*, preface by Lucio Caracciolo, Roma and Bari, 2010, 61.

[40] Graziano, *Il secolo cattolico*, 61.

[41] G. Sale, SJ, *Le Leggi Razziali in Italia e il Vaticano*, Milan, 2009, 183–185, and Robert Aleksander Maryks, *'Pouring Jewish Water into Fascist Wine': Untold Stories of (Catholic) Jews from the Archives of Mussolini's Jesuit Father Pietro Tacchi Venturi*, Leiden and Boston, MA, 2012, 1–41.

[42] M. Walsh, *A New Dictionary of Saints East and West*, London, 2007, 411 and 609.

He was a major counsellor of Pius XI, advising on all sorts of matters and, most significantly, helping in the drafting or redrafting of several important encyclicals—*Divinum Mandatum, De sacerdotio Catholicae, Mit brennender Sorge, Divini Redemptoris,* and *Humani Generis Unitas*: there is clear evidence that he substantially modified the latter (see Chapter 7). His persistent anti-Semitism, which he tried, and sometimes succeeded, in intruding into these great papal documents, comes out most clearly in *Humani Generis Unitas.*[43] It is also clear in his comments on an early draft of *Divini Redemptoris*:

> Here one should allude to the part which the Jews have had in this whole movement (Communism). It would seem necessary that in such an Encyclical one should make, in passing and indirectly, at least an allusion to Jewish influences because it is certainly the case that not only the intellectual authors of Communism (Marx, Lassalle etc.) were all Jews, but that the Communist movement in Russia was orchestrated by Jews, and now also, although not always openly, in all regions if one gets to the root of things, the Jews are the chief makers and promoters of Communist propaganda.[44]

For this virulent anti-Semitism, he might almost be called the Vatican's evil genius.

UBI ARCANO DEI CONSILIO AND THE CHRISTIAN RESTORATION OF SOCIETY

Most new popes in the recent history of the papacy have produced a key encyclical as a sort of 'mission statement' early in their pontificates. Pius XI was no exception. In December 1922 he published *Ubi arcano Dei*, setting out the key themes and goals of his pontificate. In the encyclical, he began by ascribing the lateness of its publication to the busy first months of his reign, including the first celebration of an International Eucharistic Congress in Rome and the celebration of the third centenary of the foundation of the Congregation of Propaganda Fide, which he had inherited from his predecessor.[45] He continued by reciting the usual litany of complaints and lamentations about the failure of the world's statesmen to establish an enduring peace in the wake of the First World War, pointing in particular to the continuing conflicts in the Near East. To these woes, he added the internal strife between classes and the threat of revolution, especially that of Communism. He also lamented the increasing signs of the breakdown of the family, of human immorality

[43] See Georges Passalecq and Bernard Suchecky, *The Hidden Encyclical of Pius XI*, with an introduction by Gary Wills, New York, San Diego, CA, and London, 1997, 246–253.

[44] ASV, AES, IV Periodo, 548 571 Enciclica sul Communismo, Alcune Note Esplicative Sullo Schema dell'Enciclica sul Communismo, 2. Pag. 11b.

[45] For the text of *Ubi arcano De consilioi*, see Carlen, *Papal Encyclicals*, III, 226–239.

more generally, and, in particular, 'the inordinate desire for pleasure, concupiscence of the flesh'.[46] This he saw as being all part of a 'species of moral, legal and social modernism which We condemn no less decidedly than We condemn theological modernism'.[47] Though, like his predecessor, Pius XI was no fanatical anti-Modernist, it was necessary to publicly demonstrate orthodoxy.

He was further argued that the sad state of humanity had come about, 'Because men have forsaken God and Jesus Christ', and went on to enunciate the answer to this sad state of affairs: 'The peace of Christ in the Kingdom of Christ.'[48] In these words, and the phrase *Restaurare omnia in Christi* ('restore everything in Christ'), we see that hope for Christian 'palingenesis', rebirth, which would be the *leitmotif* and ultimate aim of his pontificate.

In *Ubi arcano Dei* he made his first reference to Catholic Action, 'the participation of the laity in the apostolate of the hierarchy', as a means of bringing about the restoration of Christ's kingdom in the world, particularly in the work of bringing non-Catholic Christians back to the true fold.[49] The spread of Catholic Action would also be one of the main concerns of his pontificate. He concluded the encyclical with what might at first glance appear to be the usual papal protest against the despoliation by the Italian state of the rights of the Holy See, but which, in the light of his first blessing after election from the external loggia of St Peter's, suggests a strong commitment to resolving the 'Roman Question'.

PIUS XI AND ITALIAN POLITICS, 1922–6

As has been seen, the Italian political situation on the death of Benedict XV was serious and it would degenerate even more in the coming months. Against the background of a virtual civil war in many of the provinces of northern and central Italy, provoked by waves of Fascist, squadrist violence against their political opponents and their economic and social organizations, Italian politics became ever more turbulent.[50] Though at times Mussolini seemed to be swept along by this violence, he was able to use it in his battles for power in the Italian capital. Here, parliamentary government

[46] Carlen, *Papal Encyclicals*, III, 230.
[47] Carlen, *Papal Encyclicals*, III, 237.
[48] Carlen, *Papal Encyclicals*, III, 230.
[49] Carlen, *Papal Encyclicals*, III, 235.
[50] As this book was being written, Albert Guasco's monograph, *Cattolici e Fascisti: La Santa Sede e la Politica Italiana All'Alba del Regime (1919–1925)*, Bologna, 2013, was published. This is the fullest and most up-to-date analysis of the developing relationship between the papacy and Fascism in this period, using the files in the Vatican Archives from the pontificate of Pius XI.

was slowly breaking down, partly under the impact of the effects of Fascist violence. It was becoming more and more difficult to establish and sustain effective governmental majorities. The increasing divisions emerging in the Partito Popolare as a result of Sturzo's intransigent parliamentary tactics during the long political crisis of the summer and early autumn of 1922, which led to the collapse of the first Facta government in June and the stillbirth of another Giolittian coalition in October, alienated increasing numbers of conservative Catholics. In June a short-lived secession of disaffected conservatives in the Unione Costituzionale failed to get off the ground, but in July the Roman aristocrat Prince Francesco Boncompagni-Ludovisi abandoned the *Popolare* whip in the Chamber of Deputies and joined the Nationalists, and, in September, eight *Popolare* Senators signed a letter to Sturzo protesting against the party's flirtations with the Reformist Socialists.[51] The direction in which all of these elements were moving was that of *Popolare* participation in a government of 'National Order' presided over by Orlando, Salandra, or Giolitti, and including right-wing forces—the Fascists not excepted. In these circumstances, Gasparri and Pius XI increasingly distanced themselves from the Catholic party, seeking instead to lift the Catholic movement above the fray and to subject it firmly to ecclesiastical control at every level, from the national to the parochial.[52]

On the other hand, Mussolini's policy towards the Church was now winning favour, as was demonstrated by *L'Osservatore Romano* and *La Civiltà Cattolica*, which, in a very short period of time, moved from blanket condemnation of the rising Fascist movement to more specific criticisms of the movement's undesirable elements and its violent activities, coupled with a cautious recognition of the movement's merits as a patriotic force fighting Bolshevism.[53] Throughout 1922 the Vatican endlessly reiterated the message that Catholic Action was non-political and that the clergy should abstain from politics. Since the only party the clergy were likely to support was the Partito Popolare, it was clear that the Vatican was, in every way, seeking to dissociate itself from that party. All of these statements were repeated at the beginning of October as Italy's political crisis deepened.

Following more Fascist successes in the provinces, including the 'defenestration' of the Socialists from Milan city council in July and a failed anti-Fascist general protest strike in August, Mussolini increased the pressure and the Fascists announced a 'March on Rome' to demand power from the king. In reality, the king bowed to the pressure and appointed the leader

[51] John Pollard, 'Conservative Catholics and Italian Fascism: The Clerico-Fascists', in M. Blinkhorn (ed.), *Fascists and Conservatives: The Radical Right and the Establishment in Twentieth Century Europe*, London, 1990, 33–35.

[52] Guasco, *Cattolici e Fascisti*, 147–154 and 213–215.

[53] Guasco, *Cattolici e Fascisti*, 147–154 and 213–215.

of Fascism prime minister on 31 October, before the Fascist squads converged on Rome. When it came, the Vatican greeted the outcome of the March on Rome with relief and satisfaction: the Italian political crisis seemed at last to have been resolved.[54] Mussolini's appointment brought immediate benefits to the Church in the form of a series of measures which he announced to parliament in early November, including a rise in the stipends of priest paid by the State and the reintroduction of religious education into primary schools, which was possibly part of a deal to secure the parliamentary support of the Partito Popolare for his government.[55] Mussolini's measures were a purely opportunistic device to win further support in the Catholic world and, by stealing some of its policies, isolate the PPI and make it appear redundant in the eyes of Catholics. In January 1923, the first (secret) meeting took place between Mussolini and Cardinal Gasparri. The Secretary of State was clearly impressed by the Duce, seeing in him a man 'with whom one could do business'.[56] The major outcome was a commitment on the part of Mussolini's government to rescue the failing Banco di Roma, in which the Vatican had considerable deposits and a substantial shareholding, in return for which the bank would cut its ties with the Catholic party.[57] In the summer of 1923, as the Acerbo Law, legislation to change Italy's electoral system, was debated in Parliament, the Vatican ordered Luigi Sturzo to resign from his position in the Partito Popolare, thus depriving the party of his leadership at a most critical juncture. When the time came for elections under the new system, in March 1924, the Italian Catholic world was deeply divided politically. Fifteen Catholics, former *Popolare* MPs and senators, stood in Mussolini's National Bloc of candidates along with other liberal-conservative camp followers of Fascism.[58] The Partito Popolare, on the other hand, followed its usual policy of independence and emerged as the second largest opposition party.

The last chance for Italian democracy came in the summer and autumn of 1924, following the murder by Fascist thugs of Giacomo Matteotti, leader of the Reformist Socialists (PSU). This provoked a wave of revulsion against Fascism throughout Italy, and Mussolini's government tottered on the brink of collapse as many of his newly elected parliamentary supporters deserted him. In common with other opposition parties, the Partito Popolare withdrew from Parliament in protest against the crime and constituted the so-called 'Aventine Secession'. In September, attempts were made to form an anti-Fascist government of opposition parties around the *popolari* and Reformist Socialists, but at this point Pius XI uttered a public denunciation

[54] See *L'Osservatore Romano*, editorial, 1 November 1922.

[55] Guasco, *Cattolici e Fascisti*, documents 60, 61, and 62, 406–411.

[56] ASV, AES, IV Periodo, 1934, 515, f. 529 Spoglio delle Carte del Card. Gasparri *Memorie*, vol. II. In these memoirs, Gasparri made a curious mistake: he claimed that his first meeting with Mussolini was in the summer of 1921.

[57] Pollard, *Money*, 115–118.

[58] Pollard, 'Conservative Catholics', 35–36.

of Catholic political collaboration with a Marxist party, despite the fact that such alliances had been made in Germany, Poland, and Czechoslovakia.[59] The pontiff had made his choice: he had chosen a still authoritarian Fascist regime, which seemed to him to offer the best defence against the threat of Bolshevik revolution and the best chance of resolving the 'Roman Question'. Italian Fascism was playing a counter-revolutionary role similar to that of the 'white' forces in Hungary or General Miguel Primo de Rivera's dictatorship in Spain. Another, not insignificant, consideration in the pope's mind might have been the fear of violence, disorder, and instability in Italy during the coming Holy Year of 1925 had Fascism lost power.[60]

The rise of Fcascism and its consolidation of power were paralleled by the declining presence of the Catholic movement in Italian civil society and politics. Within less than a decade of the Catholic movement's establishment of itself as a major presence in Italian society, the situation had dramatically changed. CIL and the Partito Popolare were gone, dissolved, along with other non-Fascist trade unions and political parties, in 1925 and 1926. Many of the Catholic peasant cooperatives had fallen victim to the squadrist violence of agrarian fascism between 1920 and 1924. In 1925, the Istituto Cattolica di Attività Sociali (ICAS) was created to replace the semi-moribund Unione Economica e Sociale. According to Brunori di Siervo, 'by founding I.C.A.S., it was hoped to save the "saveable", to prevent the fruits of the fifty years of Catholic activity in the economic and social fields from being lost to Fascism'.[61] ICAS almost certainly did prevent more losses to the new Fascist Ente Nazionale per la Cooperazione.

Another major sector of the Catholic movement, the Catholic banks, were the casualties of the banking crisis which ravaged Italy in the late 1920s, thanks in part to Mussolini's monetary policy: between 1926 and 1929 it is estimated that seventy-four Catholic banks and *casse di risparmio*—1,021 branches with a total loss of 1 million lire—either closed their doors or were taken over by more resilient institutions.[62] Only the presence of clerico-fascists on the boards of management of other Catholic banks saved them from the same fate. The establishment of an Istituto Centrale di Credito to supervise and provide liquidity to Catholic banks, underwritten in part by a Vatican commitment of 50 million lire and with a leading clerico-fascist senator, Stefano Cavazzoni, as governor, and Luigi Colombo of Catholic Action as his deputy, to assure the future of the Catholic banking sector, was one of the behind-the-scenes deals agreed

[59] Molony, *The Emergence of Political Catholicism*, 181–188.

[60] Molony, *The Emergence of Political Catholicism*, 180, and Guasco, *Cattolici e Fascisti*, 290.

[61] M.T. Brunori di Siervo, '"L'Istituto Cattolico di attivita" Sociale dalla nascita all seconda Guerra mondiale', *Storia Contemporanea*, 12(4–5) (October 1981), 746.

[62] A. Caroleo, *Le Banche cattoliche*, Milan, 1976, 80.

during the negotiations for a solution of the Roman Question.[63] The crisis of the Catholic banks could not have come at a worse moment for that branch of the Catholic movement which was so heavily dependent upon them—the press. Whereas in 1923 the Catholic movement could boast twenty-one daily newspapers, 90 per cent of which were to be found, as we would expect, in northern and central Italy, by 1929 that figure had been more than halved. The central problem of the Catholic press had always been financial and the largest combination of Catholic newspapers, Grosoli's Trust, had lurched from one crisis to another from the beginning of Benedict's reign.[64] The political divisions within the Catholic movement created by the defections of the clerico-fascists from the Partito Popolare also caused problems, and Fascist pressure to conform to the new press laws did the rest.[65] On the eve of the signing of the Lateran Pacts in February 1929, the Italian Catholic movement was much smaller in nearly all of its various forms and activities than it had been when Mussolini came to power in 1922, and the Catholic presence in Italian society was consequently diminished in size and effectiveness.

Pius XI observed the overall shrinking of the Italian Catholic movement with relative equanimity, because at least what remained, with the exception of the clerico-fascist Centro Nazionale Italiano, could be brought firmly and securely under the control of the church hierarchy via Italian Catholic Action (henceforth ACI). The essential characteristics of the Italian model of Catholic Action as it had developed by the end of the 1920s can be summarized as follows: virtually all lay Catholic organizations and activities in Italy were under its jurisdiction, youth, students, adult, male and female organizations, and what remained of Catholic economic/social activities and institutions after the 'demolitions' by Fascism; the organization was highly structured at every level, parochial, diocesan, and national, and all appointments of key lay officers were made by the clergy: at the national level they were made by the pope himself; lay officers at every level were shadowed by an 'ecclesiastical assistant', a priest, high-ranking prelate, or even a bishop. At the national level, Mgr Giuseppe Pizzardo, an official in the Secretariat of State, as 'general ecclesiastical assistant' and the pope's representative, was effectively the head of Italian Catholic Action. In the absence of a national Italian conference of bishop, ACI was directly answerable to the Vatican, and finally, by the terms of article 43 of the Concordat of 1929, ACI was enjoined to be strictly non-political. ACI was thus, in the context of the rigid, hierarchical, and clerical ecclesiology of Pius XI, truly 'The participation of the laity in the Apostolate of the Hierarchy.'[66]

What was left of the Catholic movement, male and female adult, youth, and student associations, economic and social organizations (ICAS), press,

[63] Pollard, *The Vatican*, 35–36.
[64] Pollard, *Money*, 118–121.
[65] Pollard, *Money*, 36–37.
[66] See Pollard, 'Pius XI's Promotion', 758–784.

publishing, and study groups were now firmly regimented under Vatican control. Pius XI actually brought trusted Catholic lay leaders from the Milan diocese, Luigi Colombo, Armida Barelli, and Adelaide Coara to head national Catholic Action sections in Rome. Whatever damage the rise of Fascism had done to the Catholic presence in Italian society in the early to mid-1920s, it had made it possible for the pope and his Secretary of State to achieve what was for them the ideal situation: a direct interlocutory relationship with the Italian state without the complicating presence of a strong Catholic party in politics. In consequence, in 1926 secret negotiations got under way for a settlement of the 'Roman Question' and other related issues between Church and State, which would culminate in the signing of the Lateran Pacts between Italy and the Holy See in February 1929.

THE NEGOTIATIONS FOR THE LATERAN PACTS, 1926–29

The negotiations of 1926–29 cannot be properly understood except within the broader context of Mussolini's process of consolidating power by reaching accommodations with Italy's various elite institutions and groups in what Alberto Aquarone has described as the 'block of consensus', the basic support structure of the Fascist Regime.[67] Having won the support of much of the northern landowning class for Fascism in the early 1920s, Mussolini went on to achieve the support of the industrial, commercial, and financial interests groups, and then the monarchy, the armed forces, and finally the Church for the construction of his regime during the late 1920s. But, as Adrian Lyttelton has pointed out, part and parcel of the process of consolidating power was the elimination of resistance to his compromises with the establishment from within his own party.[68] Though he cleverly used Roberto Farinacci to bring the more dangerous loose cannons of Fascism to heel between 1925 and 1926, the eventual dismissal of Farinacci, himself one of the most anti-clerical, independent, and violent of the local Fascist bosses, as party secretary signalled the subjugation of the party. Similarly, the removal of anti-clerical philosopher Giovanni Gentile from the post of Minister of Education, and the replacement of Aldo Oviglio as Minister of Justice by Alfredo Rocco, a former Nationalist, were absolute prerequisites for a settlement with the Vatican.

Yet, in 1926, Mussolini was far too preoccupied with the crisis of the lira to be serious about negotiations, and at this stage Pius XI does not appear to have been very optimistic about the prospects of success either, with the result

[67] A. Aquarone, *L'Organizzazione dello Stato Totalitario*, Turin, 1965, 15.

[68] A. Lyttelton, *The Seizure of Power: Fascism in Italy, 1919–1929*, London, 1987, 286.

that both were content with the progress being made by the Ecclesiastical Law Reform Commission set up by Rocco.[69]

Suddenly everything changed when Fascism turned from its demolition or absorption of Catholic economic and social organizations and started to lay hands Catholic youth groups, using as an excuse the new law on the Balilla (Fascist youth organization) early in 1926. This seems to have persuaded the pope and Gasparri that only by offering Fascism the glittering prize of a settlement of the 'Roman Question' as a bargaining counter could they protect the Catholic youth organizations. While, hitherto, the Vatican might had believed that some good could come from the efforts of Mattei-Gentili's Commission on Ecclesiastical Law Reform, and had tacitly approved of its work by allowing three canons of patriarchal basilicas in Rome to sit on it, the stakes had risen by the spring of 1926 and there was the feeling that to allow the Italian state to proceed unilaterally in this matter would set a dangerous precedent.[70] It is significant that, in the same period, Gasparri approved of Eugenio Pacelli's protest, as nuncio in Germany, against the initiative of the government of the State of Hesse to establish a mixed commission of civil servants and ecclesiastics to revise ecclesiastical legislation in that state.[71]

After the talks began, some Fascists, aided and abetted by Mgr Benigni, wanted to get Gasparri out of the way. He was regarded as too 'tough': without him, it was thought, it would have been easier to negotiate with Papa Ratti; consequently, there was a campaign of defamation against the Secretary of State.[72] This is one of the reasons why Gasparri was not involved *in prima persona* in the negotiations. But there is also evidence of serious differences of opinion between the pope and Gasparri. Gasparri did not originally believe that negotiating a concordat *and* a treaty was realistic—he resisted this for several days before inserting it into the *istruzioni* for the Holy See's negotiator on the pope's orders.[73] Presumably, his belief was that mutual diplomatic recognition between the Holy See and Italy, a settlement of the outstanding financial matters between them, and the recreation in some form of papal territorial sovereignty would have been sufficient to put the Holy See on a strong enough footing to negotiate a concordat with Italy at a later date, whereas Pius XI wanted everything now. On the other hand, it was Gasparri who persuaded the pope not to publish his letter of protest to Mussolini about violence against Catholic youth organizations and new restrictions on their liberty in December 1926. He believed that, given the situation in Italy at this time, it would have made things very difficult for Mussolini, and thus have

[69] Pollard, *The Vatican*, 38–39. [70] Pollard, *The Vatican*, 38–39.

[71] Sergio Pagano, Marcel Chappin, and Giovanni Coco, *I 'Fogli di Udienza' Del Cardinale Eugenio Pacelli Segretario Di Stato*, vol. I: *1930*, Vatican City, 2010, 89.

[72] Pagano, Chappin, and Coco, *I 'Fogli di Udienza'*, 59–62.

[73] Pagano, Chappin, and Coco, *I 'Fogli di Udienza'*, 62–63.

alienated him, if the letter had been published.[74] As Giovanni Coco claims, though Gasparri was not the leading negotiator, he thus had a crucial role in negotiations, advising the pope and at times moderating his responses to the vexations of Fascist harassment of Catholic organizations.[75]

The secret negotiations, which had gone through unofficial, preliminary stages before they formally began in December 1926, were actually conducted by the ecclesiastical lawyer Francesco Pacelli (brother of Eugenio Pacelli) for the Vatican and Domenico Barone, a high-ranking civil servant for the Regime, aided by the 'back channel' set up through Fr Tacchi-Venturi, SJ.[76] After Barone unexpectedly died at a delicate stage of the negotiations in January 1929, Mussolini took over direct responsibility on the Italian side. According to Gasparri, Mgr Borgoncini-Duca, Under-Secretary of State, prepared the draft of the Concordat because, 'he had taken an active part in the drafting of the other concordats concluded during the present pontificate . . . and took a great many of the articles of the [Italian] Concordat from them', saying that this only took three days.[77] But the requirement to agree on not only a concordat, but a treaty and financial settlement as well, ensured that the actual negotiations would be protracted (nearly three years) and difficult, though three years was not unusual—negotiating the Prussian concordat took nearly ten years. The length of the negotiations can also be put down to the many difficult issues encountered—about religious marriage, the extent of the new 'papal state' (the State of the Vatican City) and its exact status in international law, financial compensation for the loss of revenue from the Papal States, and last, but not least, the future of the remaining Catholic youth organizations.[78] The Fascist Regime's unilateral acts dissolving first the Catholic Boy Scouts and then the federation of Catholic Sports Clubs also caused huge difficulties; indeed, they prompted the pope to suspend the negotiations between June 1927 and January 1928. When, in March 1928, a new decree was published dissolving *all* non-Fascist youth groups, the Vatican stood its ground and broke off the negotiations entirely. Mussolini was forced to back down. Only in this way was the pope able to ensure the survival of the male and female youth organizations, GIAC and GFCI, as an integral part of ACI, although not prevent a further restriction of their activities in the sporting and cultural fields.

[74] Pagano, Chappin, and Coco, *I 'Fogli di Udienza'*, 65–66.

[75] Pagano, Chappin, and Coco, *I 'Fogli di Udienza'*, 50–51.

[76] Maryks, *Pouring Jewish Water*, 8–9.

[77] ASV, AES, IV Periodo, 1934, 515, f. 529, Spoglio delle Carte del Card. Gasparri *Memorie*, vol. II.

[78] For an account of the negotiations, see ASV, AES, IV Periodo, 1934, 515, f. 529, Spoglio delle Carte del Card. Gasparri *Memorie*, vol. II, 42–47.; Binchy, *Church and State in Fascist Italy*, chs 5 and 6; and F. Pacelli, *Diario della Conciliazione*, ed. M. Maccarone, Vatican City, 1959.

THE *CONCILIAZIONE* OF 1929

The reconciliation, or *Conciliazione* as it was known in Italian, between the Holy See and the Italian State, achieved by the Lateran Pacts which Gasparri and Mussolini signed on 11 February 1929, brought the Church considerable benefits.[79] The Lateran Treaty provided for the establishment of Vatican City as a sovereign, independent, and neutral state, and recognized the extraterritorial rights of other major churches, palaces, college seminaries, and office buildings belonging to the Holy See in Rome, thus realizing what all popes since Pius IX had aspired to, a restoration, albeit in miniscule form, of the former temporal power.[80] The Financial Convention gave substantial compensation for previous losses, ensuring the Vatican's future financial independence.[81] The third agreement, the Concordat, established the framework for a new relationship between Church and State in Italy, one that would be, in the long term, largely advantageous to the Church, ultimately providing for the rebuilding of the Catholic presence in Italian society. Religious marriage could now precede civil marriage, annulments in the Vatican's Sacra Rota tribunal were now recognized in state courts, and the terms of the Concordat implicitly excluded the possibility of divorce.[82] The Holy See was now free to fill all ecclesiastical offices in Italy, from parish priest to archbishops, but though the State had the right to raise objections to the choice in advance, all rights to the exercise by the State of the *exequatur* and *placet* (governmental assent to ecclesiastical acts), plus the royal power of patronage to ecclesiastical benefices in the former Kingdom of the Two Sicilies, were abolished.[83] The chaplaincies to the armed forces and hospitals were set on an official footing.[84] Though the State continued to administer former Church property and, in consequence, pay clergy salaries and expenses, religious orders and congregations and other religious institutions could once again freely acquire property. The personal legal privileges and immunities of the clergy were reasserted.[85] In the field of education, private (Catholic) schools now had parity with those of the State and the degrees conferred by the Catholic University of Milan also received recognition.[86] Finally, and very importantly, by the terms of article 43 the Italian State recognized the autonomous existence of ACI and its dependent youth organizations while prohibiting any involvement of the clergy in politics.[87]

[79] For the English text of the Lateran Treaty, the Financial Convention, and the Concordat, see Pollard, *The Vatican*, 197–215.

[80] Pollard, *The Vatican*, 197–202, articles 3–4, 9–11, and 13–17.

[81] Pollard, *The Vatican*, 215.

[82] Pollard, *The Vatican*, 212–213, article 34.

[83] Pollard, *The Vatican*, 208–209.

[84] Pollard, *The Vatican*, 208–209, articles 13–16.

[85] Pollard, *The Vatican*, 209–212, articles 29–31.

[86] Pollard, *The Vatican*, 213.

[87] Pollard, *The Vatican*, 214.

The Italian concordat of 1929 did not differ all that markedly from other concordats. Above all, it conformed to them inasmuch as, like those with Bavaria, Poland, and Prussia, it contained clear commitments on the part of the Holy See to ensure that diocesan boundaries followed state frontiers and that the clergy were, as far as humanly possible, to be nationals of those states.[88] However, both the Bavarian and Italian concordats have been contrasted unfavourably with that of Prussia.[89] This is puzzling since, whereas the Italian concordat extended religious instruction from primary to secondary schools, the Prussian government even refused to discuss questions of education,[90] and as far as the selection of bishops was concerned, the Italian concordat gave an absolute power of appointment to the Holy See, allowing for objections from the government, while the nuncio in Berlin had to go through a fivefold process involving inputs from the existing Prussian episcopate, cathedral chapters, and the government.[91] Nevertheless, while the *Conciliazione* did not mean a return to the *ancien régime* status of the Church, in several key respects it did represent a virtual turning back of the clock to the period before the 'Liberal Revolution' in mid-nineteenth-century Italy.[92]

THE 1931 CRISIS BETWEEN THE VATICAN AND REGIME

The honeymoon atmosphere generated by the signing of the Pacts in February 1929 did not last long. It was largely dissipated by Mussolini's need to 'talk tough' in the debates on the ratification of the Pacts in both houses of the Italian Parliament as a way of appeasing the more anti-clerical of his Fascist supporters, once the 'Plebiscite' of March had safely gathered in Catholic consensus for his regime.[93] Adding fuel to the flames were the difficulties which arose in the joint Implementation Commission over such matters as marriage, and Mussolini's insistence on tabling legislation to regulate the *culti ammessi* ('permitted cults', i.e. the Protestant churches) and Italy's Jewish community.[94] These pieces of legislation were arguably as much about extending 'totalitarian' control to another sector of Italian civil society, but they were also intended by Mussolini to assert the independence of the Fascist state from clerical pretensions. While there were moments during the parliamentary debates when Mussolini almost conceded the scale of the concessions he

[88] Pollard, *The Vatican*, 207, article 16.
[89] Pagano, Chappin, and Coco, *'I Taccuini'*, 50–51.
[90] Stehlin, *Weimar*, 424–425.
[91] Stehlin, *Weimar*, 425–426.
[92] See Pollard, *Catholicism in Modern Italy*, ch. 2.
[93] For a survey of Fascist reactions to the *Conciliazione*, see Pollard, *The Vatican*, 61–64.
[94] Pollard, *The Vatican*, 73–74 and 108–110.

had had to make to the Holy See, especially in the matters of marriage and the Financial Agreement, he generally adopted a confident, arrogant, and blustering tone. In particular, three of his statements to the Chamber of Deputies delighted his anti-clerical supporters while at the same time infuriated the men in the Vatican. In response to Arrigo Solmi's re-evocation of Cavour's famous axiom, 'A free church in a free state', Mussolini declared:

> Inside the State the Church is not only not sovereign it is not even free. It is not sovereign because that would be a contradiction of the concept of the State, and it is not free because it is subject to the institutions and laws of the State, and, indeed, to the terms of the Concordat.[95]

Even worse, in another passage, he expressed the obviously heretical opinion that:

> We should be proud of the fact that Italy is the only European nation which contains the headquarters of a world religion. This religion was born in Palestine but became Catholic in Rome. If it had stayed in Palestine, then in all probability it would have shared the fate of the many sects, like the Essenes, or the Therapeutae which vanished without trace.[96]

Pius XI was, inevitably, outraged by Mussolini's statements and expressed his feelings in an open letter to Gasparri which was published in the Vatican newspaper on 6 June. He carefully rebutted not only these statements but also Mussolini's interpretations of the meaning of the Pacts, like reaffirming the prior rights of the Church and the family over the education of youth, denying that the Italian State had a right of veto over ecclesiastical appointments, and attacking the new status of the Protestant churches.[97] He ended on an almost apocalyptic note, declaring the Lateran Pacts '. . . stand and fall together: if one goes, then so does the other, and with it goes the Vatican City and its State'.[98]

It was powerful rhetoric, but Gasparri dissuaded the pope from postponing ratification of the Pacts in response to Mussolini's speech in May and mobilized seven other cardinals in his support.[99] This was probably the high-water mark of Gasparri's influence. He later said that he left the Secretariat of State because 'he was not in accord with the pope as regards the implementation of the Concordat with the Italian government': in August 1929, with continuing disputes between the Holy See and Italy, the pope suggested that Gasparri retire and he indicated that he wanted to go.[100]

[95] *Atti Parlamentari del Regno d'Italia. Camera dei Deputati. Discussioni*, Rome, 1929, vol. 1, 152.
[96] *Atti Parlamentari del Regno d'Italia*, vol. 1, 152,
[97] *L'Osservatore Romano*, front page, 6 June 1929.
[98] *L'Osservatore Romano*, front page, 6 June 1929.
[99] Pagano, Chappin, and Coco, *'I Taccuini'*, 70–71.
[100] Pagano, Chappin, and Coco, *'I Taccuini'*, 74.

Shortly after the ratification of the Pacts, the Swiss Guards and other papal troops took formal possession of all the various parts of the pope's new domain, and on 25 July, Pius XI left the Vatican to lead a Corpus Christi procession in St Peter's Square, the first pope to do so for a little more than sixty-nine years. (When he later took possession of the cathedral of Rome, the Basilica of St John Lateran, in December 1929, he was also the first to do so since Pius IX in 1846.) Gasparri's description of the Corpus Christi procession is heavily coloured by a certain understandable emotion:

> The Pope comes out. This brief gesture, so simple, had in itself an historic, religious and social value that was profound . . . Now the mystical rite has been completed. The Lateran Pacts have been sealed by the Benediction of God. Long live Christ! Long live the Pope . . . It is the triumph of Christ with his Vicar.[101]

What added to this moment of public, papal triumph was the fact that all the Italian civil and military authorities were present, including the prefect of the Roman province and the governor (mayor) of Rome, as well as various Italian Catholic associations.[102]

An event of probably even greater symbolical significance was the state visit paid to the Vatican by King Victor Emmanuel III and Queen Elena of Italy, on 5 December 1929. Despite what Gasparri says about the Corpus Christi procession, it was this visit which really sealed the 'peace' between Italy and the papacy. In particular, the visit gave formal recognition to the independence of the State of the Vatican City from Italy, in the sense that the royal visitors had to stop at the edge of St Peter's Square and be received by Vatican officials, in particular the governor of the new State, the Marquess Serafini. Serafini's greeting to the king and queen is noteworthy:

> Your Majesties! in my capacity as Governor of the State of the Vatican City I have the honour to bid welcome to Your Majesties in the name of my August Sovereign, His Holiness of Our Lord, Pius XI, at the boundary of the new state and to salute in your arrival the culmination of many happy events and the auspices of a better future.[103]

It is also noteworthy that this most anti-clerical of Italian kings followed Vatican protocol and paid a visit to both the Blessed Sacrament Chapel in St Peter's Basilica and the tomb of the Apostle in its crypt, a formal, official recognition on the part of the highest authority of the Italian state of the key elements of the legitimizing ideology of the papacy.[104]

[101] ASV, AES, IV Periodo, 1934, 515, f. 529 Spoglio delle Carte del Card. Gasparri, *Memorie*, vol. II, 74, Corpus Domini.

[102] ASV, AES, IV Periodo, 1934, 515, f. 529 Spoglio delle Carte del Card. Gasparri, *Memorie*, vol. II, 74, Corpus Domini.

[103] ASV, AES, IV Periodo, 1934, 515, f. 529 Spoglio delle Carte del Card. Gasparri, *Memorie*, vol. II, 74, Corpus Domini, 88.

[104] ASV, AES, IV Periodo, 1934, 515, f. 529 Spoglio delle Carte del Card. Gasparri, *Memorie*, vol. II, 74, Corpus Domini.

These happy events did not entirely dissipate the tensions between the papacy and Italy. The disputes between them rumbled on through 1929 and 1930, largely about the functioning of Catholic Action and its youth organizations, which were still looked upon with a jaundiced eye by the Fascist authorities; the latter were inflamed by the publication of the encyclical *Rappresentanti in Terra*, which, as will be seen in Chapter 5, was actually addressed to all Catholics but was, nevertheless, interpreted by the Fascist regime as an attack upon its totalitarian policy with regard to educational and youth matters.[105]

Another source of attrition between the Vatican and the regime was the 20 September public holiday. The anniversary of the storming of Porta Pia by Italian troops had been established as a national holiday by the rulers of the liberal state to commemorate making Rome the capital of Italy, but in the eyes of the Vatican, and still at least some Italian Catholics, this national celebration was a day of sorrow not rejoicing. Consequently, in a diplomatic note of September 1929, Mgr Borgoncini-Duca, the first apostolic nuncio to Italy, argued that the abolition of this national holiday and its transfer to 11 February was the natural and logical outcome of the felicitous resolution of the Roman Question, even if Italy had made no commitment to abolition during the course of the negotiations.[106] The exchange of notes and ideas between the nuncio and Dino Grandi, the Italian Foreign Minister, but also Mussolini, and later between the new Secretary of State, Cardinal Pacelli, and Count Giorgio de Vecchi di Val Cismon, the first Italian ambassador to the Holy See, continued for a whole year.[107] Mussolini tried to parry Pius XI's insistent demands that the holiday be abolished by arguing that the holiday would 'wither away' by itself: obviously, he feared for the reactions in Fascist and nationalist quarters if he abolished it.[108] Eventually, he gave way and 'rearranged' the list of national holidays, omitting 20 September, albeit not without considerable mutterings among Fascist anti-clericals.[109] The abolition of the holiday marked the limit of the concessions extracted from

[105] See Pollard, *The Vatican*, 129–132.

[106] ASV, AES, IV Periodo, Italia 738–739, 251 Soppressione della festa del 20 settembre Sostituzione con l'11 febbraio, Borgoncini-Duca to Grandi (Italian Foreign Minister), 2 September 1929.

[107] ASV, AES, IV Periodo, Italia 738–739, 251 Soppressione della festa del 20 settembre Sostituzione con l'11 febbraio, Borgoncini-Duca to Grandi (Italian Foreign Minister), 2 September 1929, the rest of the *fascicolo*.

[108] ASV, AES, IV Periodo, Italia 738–739, 251 Soppressione della festa del 20 settembre Sostituzione con l'11 febbraio, Borgoncini-Duca to Grandi (Italian Foreign Minister), 2 September 1929, the rest of the *fascicolo*, Mussolini to Borgoncini-Duca.

[109] ASV, AES, IV Periodo, Italia 738–739, 251 Soppressione della festa del 20 settembre Sostituzione con l'11 febbraio, Borgoncini-Duca to Grandi (Italian Foreign Minister), 2 September 1929, the rest of the *fascicolo*, press cutting from *Il Popolo di Roma*, 'Il primo Consiglio dei Ministri', 12 September 1930.

Italy by the Vatican. More 'hawkish' elements had taken over in the National Fascist Party, Giovanni Giuriati as Secretary and Carlo Scorza as head of the Balilla.[110] Partly as a result of their pressure, tensions between the Church and the regime, and especially between Catholic Action and the Party, would mount during the rest of 1930 and early 1931 until they exploded into a serious crisis in the spring of 1931.

During the first four months of 1931, Fascist fears about the extent of Catholic Action activities, and in particular those of the youth groups and its *sezioni professionali* ('vocational sections'), that is, groups of Catholic workers and employers, grew in intensity and manifested themselves in various party organs. [111] They came to a head in May with the Vatican's celebrations of the fortieth anniversary of *Rerum Novarum*, Leo XIII's encyclical on economic and social matters. Thousands of Catholic workers, including delegations from Germany, France, and Britain, descended on Rome to greet the pope. On 15th of the month he published his own, commemorative, social encyclical, *Quadragesimo Anno*.[112] While the encyclical was strongly supportive of corporatist responses to the great capitalist crisis created by the Wall Street Crash, it reaffirmed the right of Catholics to organize freely in the trade union field. Of the Italian Fascist Corporative State it said little but what it did say was not exactly flattering:

> We are compelled to say . . . the State, instead of confining itself, as it ought, to the furnishing of adequate and necessary assistance, is substituting itself for free activity; that the corporative and syndical order savours too much of an involved and political system of administration; and that it rather serves particular political ends than leads to the reconstruction and promotion of a better social order.[113]

These words were very much those of Pius XI himself, rather than the main author of the encyclical, the German Jesuit Oswald von Nell-Breuning.

The publication of the encyclical was followed by a storm of criticism in the Fascist press, especially in its corporative mouthpiece, *Il Lavoro Fascista*.[114] More seriously, by now Catholic Action and its youth and vocational organizations, which had been under police surveillance for at least two months, came under physical attack which, though in part orchestrated by local Fascist party bosses, was also in some measure a reflection of general Fascist hostility towards the organizations, which had been whipped up by the press campaigns.[115] Then, on 30 May, Mussolini dissolved the youth organizations of Catholic Action. There is evidence that, in part, this was prompted by insecurity, by the fact that the Italian Fascist regime, faced by the social and

[110] Pollard, *The Vatican*, 134–137.
[111] Pollard, *The Vatican*, 139–147.
[112] For the text, see Carlen, *The Papal Encyclicals*, III, 415–443.
[113] Carlen, *Papal Encyclicals*, III, 430.
[114] Pollard, *The Vatican*, 138–139.
[115] Pollard, *The Vatican*, 146–147.

political consequences of the Great Depression which were hitting Italy at that time, felt threatened by a resurgence of anti-Fascist opposition, including that of Catholics.[116]

Mussolini was also influenced in all probability by a feeling of disappointment with the results of the concessions he had made in the *Conciliazione*: his attempts to turn the Church into an *instrumentum regni* had failed and, as he admitted bitterly to his brother, Arnaldo, 'We intended that the Church should become a pillar of the Regime. We never intended for a moment that the Regime should become the servant of the Church!'[117] What had also become clear by the spring of 1931 was that Vatican diplomacy had eluded Fascist efforts to harness it to the foreign policy being pursued by the Regime, in particular in relation to the north-eastern border areas acquired by Italy in 1919, where the Vatican insisted on the right of the minorities, German, Croat, and Slovene, to use their own languages for vernacular services of the Church, yet another example of the problems which the Versailles Peace Settlement created for the Church in Europe. Similarly, the Italian Foreign Ministry's attempts to persuade the Vatican to back up its protests against Yugoslav involvement in terrorism in the new territories failed miserably.[118] It was in this same period that Mussolini was also forced to recognize the ruthless pragmatism of the Vatican's attitudes to governments and forms of government. The Vatican's response to the fall of the King Alfonso XIII in Spain seems to have been an eye-opener for the Duce who commented thus:

> His Majesty the Catholic King of Spain has received no support from the Catholics. This is a fact. What are the reasons? . . . the Church does not have a clear policy on the question of political institutions, except in a very theoretical way; in the final analysis it judges all institutions by their behaviour towards the Church.[119]

Pius XI's response to the dissolution was bitter and angry; he denounced it in a series of speeches throughout June. Diplomatic efforts, including the 'subterranean' soundings of the Jesuit father Tacchi-Venturi, who had already served as an intermediary between the pope and Mussolini during the final stages of the negotiations for the Lateran Pacts, were useless as by now both sides had taken up intransigent positions. While Eugenio Pacelli, now Secretary of State, was inclined to a more conciliatory attitude to the Regime, the pope was outraged by the dissolution and uncompromising in his attitude. When the Fascist newspaper *Il Popolo di Roma* published a report claiming that Gasparri and three other cardinals thought that there was a difference of

[116] Pollard, *The Vatican*, 148–154.

[117] As quoted in U. Guspini, *L'Orecchio del Regime*, Milan, 1973, 108.

[118] See Pollard, *The Vatican*, 90–102.

[119] As quoted in R. De Felice, *Mussolini il Duce*, vol. I: *Gli anni del consenso, 1929–1936*, Turin, 1974, 824–825.

opinion between the two men, the pope ordered Mgr Tardini to visit the said cardinals and order them to pen a denial.[120] There is evidence that he even contemplated a denunciation of the Fascist Party and its doctrines on lines similar to those issued by the German bishops against the Nazi Party.[121] In the meantime, he was preparing a counter-blast to Mussolini, the encyclical *Non Abbiamo Bisogno* ('We have no need').[122]

Published in Italy on 7 August but previously distributed throughout the world, the encyclical systematically discredited the many claims made by the Fascist press and radio against Catholic Action and condemned the acts of violence against its members.[123] While there was no general condemnation of Fascist ideology like the bishops' condemnation Nazi ideology in Germany, in the encyclical Pius condemned Fascism for 'a real pagan worship of the State' and for educating Italian youth 'in hatred, violence and even irreverence towards the Pope himself'.[124] Moreover, he advised Italian Catholics to take such oaths allegiance to the Regime as it required, with the mental qualification, 'Saving the laws of God and the Church' or 'In accordance with the duties of a good Christian.'[125] This was by no means a condemnation of Fascism *tout court* but it did raise serious doubts about to the loyalty of Italian Catholics to the Regime.

The encyclical was inevitably greeted with howls of protest from most of the Fascist press, but some elements were more moderate in their analyses, clearly perceiving that a resolution of the crisis had to be found, and was indeed at hand.[126] The foreign reactions to the encyclical were usually critical of Mussolini,[127] another factor which made some Fascists realize that the prolongation of the dispute was not in the best interests of Fascism. But it took another month to negotiate a compromise, which was again largely the work of the indefatigable Padre Tacchi-Venturi.[128] The 'Accords for Catholic Action' of September 1931 were, inevitably, a compromise, largely a reiteration of the status of ACI as set out in article 43 of the Concordat of 1929, but in the preamble it was stated that the organization 'is essentially diocesan and is under the direct control of the bishops'.[129] This was a sop to those Fascists who feared that ACI was becoming a powerful *national* organization and were anxious to

[120] ASV, AES, IV Periodo, Stati Eccl., Taccuini di Cardinale Pacelli, 342, audience of 29 May 1931.

[121] ASV, AES, IV Periodo, Stati Eccl., Taccuini di Cardinale Pacelli, 343, audience of 6 July 1931.

[122] See ASV, AES, IV Periodo, Stati Eccl., Taccuini di Cardinale Pacelli, 343, audience of 2 July 1931, 'Osservazioni alla minuta dell'Enciclica', for the pope's discussions with Pacelli on the wording of the text

[123] For the text of the encyclical, see Carlen, *The Papal Encyclicals*, III, 445–458.

[124] Carlen, *Papal Encyclicals*, III, 453.

[125] Carlen, *Papal Encyclicals*, III, 455.

[126] Pollard, *The Vatican*, 159–161.

[127] Pollard, *The Vatican*, 160, fn 166.

[128] ASV, AES, IV Periodo, Stati Ecclesiastici, Taccuini, 343, see the audiences from 25 July to 31 August.

[129] For the wording of the Accords, see Pollard, *The Vatican*, 216.

restrict the influence of its head, Mgr Pizzardo. Normal diplomatic relations between the Holy See and Italy were resumed and in January 1932 Mussolini paid his first visit to the pope. But even this generally felicitous occasion was not without its difficulties: Pius XI was adamant that Mussolini should *not* come in Fascist, but official, ministerial uniform.[130] The audience which took place on 11 February, the second anniversary of the *Conciliazione*, went fairly well, all things considered, the pope smoothing things by telling the Duce that he had been praying for the soul of his brother Arnaldo, who had recently died.[131] But afterwards, Mussolini complained that his visit had not received sufficient attention in the Vatican press.[132]

THE INTERNATIONAL IMPACT OF THE *CONCILIAZIONE*

In the weeks following the signing of the *Conciliazione*, Mussolini was not the only protagonist who felt it necessary to defend his part in it. Pius and his newspaper, *L'Osservatore Romano*, spent a lot of time explaining and defending the concessions which the papal negotiators had made against the critics of the Lateran Pacts. In this case some of the criticism came from within Vatican circles. At the highest levels of the Roman curia there were cardinals like Merry del Val, Pompilji (Vicar of Rome), Pignatelli di Belmonte, Lauri, and even Cerretti, who believed that the Church had paid a very high price and had received too little in return.[133] And despite the undoubted benefits of the Concordat, there were even Italian bishops who were uneasy about a settlement with Fascism.[134] The leaders of the Italian Catholic movement in exile, ex-*popolari* like Fr Luigi Sturzo and Alcide de Gasperi ('in exile' in the Vatican) were also sceptical.[135] It was to answer these, but also foreign, critics that Pius devoted two major speeches to explaining the *raison d'être* of the Accords with Fascism, one to the College of Cardinals and another to the Diplomatic Corps accredited to the Holy See. Replying to congratulations of the Dean of the Sacred College, Pius said that the Pacts were meant to ensure the profound restoration of the conditions of religion in Italy, ' a restoration which the Concordat solemnly

[130] ASV, AES, IV Periodo, Stati Ecclesiastici, Taccuini, 344, audiences of 28 November.

[131] For an account of the visit, see A. Corsetti, 'Dalla preconciliazione ai Patti del Laterano: Note e Documenti', in *Annuario 1968 della Biblioteca Civica di Massa*, Lucca, 1969.

[132] C.M. De Vecchi di Val Cismon, *Memorie*, published posthumously in *Il Tempo*, January–March 1960, no. 17.

[133] De Vecchi di Val Cismon, *Memorie*, no. 15.

[134] Pollard, *The Vatican*, 50–51.

[135] Pollard, *The Vatican*, 55–57.

secures and which will be carried out loyally and coherently, of that there can be no doubt'.[136] This was the twin principle on which Papa Ratti's policy was based, the restoration of the temporal power *and* the restoration of the optimum legal conditions for a revival of Catholicism in Italy. The Doyen of the Diplomatic Corps accredited to the Vatican, the ambassador of Brazil, in a meeting especially requested by the Corps, read a eulogy of Pius XI's achievement running to six pages.[137] In his reply, Pius said that he had been receiving letters of congratulation from all over Italy, all over Europe, and all over the world—including Alaska and Africa: 'a real plebiscite, not only national but also international. Here is the most imposing guarantee [of papal independence] that can be imagined.'[138] Pius was well aware of the strong criticisms circulating in both Catholic and diplomatic circles about the exiguity of the territorial sovereignty granted to the State of the Vatican City and of the absence of international guarantees of the Lateran Pacts—the idea of registering them at the League of Nations had been rejected out of hand by Mussolini.[139]

France was the quarter from which much of this criticism came. It was clear to everyone that she was the chief 'casualty' of the *Conciliazione* for, with the final rapprochement between the papacy and Italy, the latter was now in a much stronger diplomatic position vis-à-vis France.[140] Though France had been a rather errant 'elder daughter of the Church' for some years, as long as there were no diplomatic relations between the Holy See and Italy, the latter's influence on the papacy had been limited. Some catastrophists in France described the *Conciliazione* as 'the alliance of the two Romes against France'.[141] Italians, for their part, were apt to exaggerate the consequences for Italy, Egilberto Martire, a clerico-fascist members of Parliament, claiming that with the demise of Habsburg Austria and the decline of Spain, Italy was now the leading Catholic power.[142] Non-Italians were also quick to detect a shift in the balance of power between France and Italy, which, of course, both had foreseen as a likely result of the *Conciliazione*, and to point to the increased prestige of Mussolini and Fascism. *The Times*, for instance, hailed the Duce 'as the greatest Italian statesman' since Cavour,[143] and a Hungarian government minister was reported as saying that he was 'the leading statesman of the

[136] ASV, AES, IV Periodo, 1934, 515, f. 529, Spoglio delle Carte del Card. Gasparri *Memorie*, 50.

[137] ASV, AES, IV Periodo, 1934, 515, f. 529, Spoglio delle Carte del Card. Gasparri *Memorie*, 50.

[138] ASV, AES, IV Periodo, 1934, 515, f. 529, Spoglio delle Carte del Card. Gasparri *Memorie*, 50.

[139] Pollard, *The Vatican*, 82–83.

[140] Pollard, *The Vatican*, 87.

[141] As quoted in Kent, *The Pope and the Duce*, 60.

[142] Pollard, *The Vatican*, 75.

[143] As quoted in Pollard, *The Vatican*, 75.

inter-war period'.[144] All this strengthened Mussolini's bargaining position in a number of ongoing tussles with foreign powers—France, Yugoslavia, and even Britain.

The *Conciliazione* undoubtedly raised the prestige of Italian Fascism abroad. Catholics in several countries now looked upon it with different eyes. For example, the late Peter D'Agostino, in his book *Rome in America*, gives a very full survey of the reactions of American Catholics, Jews, and Protestants to both the *Conciliazione* of 1929 and the crisis of 1931.[145] What his book also shows is that though the *Conciliazione* prompted very diverse reactions in America, as far as the Italian immigrant community there was concerned, it was almost a case of 'preaching Fascism': for many Italo-Americans, Italian Fascism was synonymous with Catholicism.[146]

But Italy was not the only diplomatic beneficiary of the *Conciliazione*. The success of Vatican diplomacy in negotiating the Pacts and winning the restoration of territorial sovereignty for the Holy See enormously increased its international standing and probably helped to bring the negotiations for a Prussian concordat to a successful close in June 1929 (see Chapter 6). In the longer term, Hitler would seek the 'blessing' of the Holy See for the new Nazi regime in Germany by means of a *Reichskonkordat* in 1933 (see Chapter 7: the ultimate recognition of the unprecedented prestige which the papacy enjoyed in international affairs.

THE *CONCILIAZIONE* AND THE FINANCES OF THE VATICAN

For the Holy See, the 'Financial Convention' was a crucially important part of the Lateran Pacts, which would eventually give it financial independence and stability. By the terms of the Convention, the Holy See was compensated for the loss of its territories in central Italy during the course of the unification process, and for its refusal to accept the annual payment stipulated in the Law of Guarantees, to the tune of 1,750 million lire, or 19 million pounds/90 million dollars at 1929 exchange rates.[147] Arriving at agreement on this figure had been one of the thornier questions facing those negotiating the Pacts and it had delayed the signing as a result.[148] As important as these large raw totals was the fact that their management and investment was placed in the hands of the

[144] Pollard, *The Vatican*, 75.

[145] Peter R. D'Agostino, *Rome in America: Transnational Catholic Ideology from the Risorgimento to Fascism*, Chapel Hill, NC, and London, 2004, ch. 7.

[146] D'Agostino, *Rome in America*, ch. 8.

[147] Pollard, *Money*, 142.

[148] Pollard, *Money*, 140–141.

most ingenious financier in the history of the papacy—Bernardino Nogara. A devout Catholic, Nogara was also a man with a 'Midas-touch', whose career had taken him to the board of directors of the Banca Commerciale Italiana which, in 1929, was Italy's largest and most successful private bank.[149] Above all, he was Milanese and thus, as far as Pius XI was concerned, a man to be trusted, and trust him he did. The 'windfall' the *Conciliazione* brought was not placed in the care of any of the existing Vatican financial agencies, but rather a new agency, the ASSS, under the direction of Nogara, who was answerable solely to the pope.

While 1,000 million lire of the compensation took the form of Italian government loan stock, the remaining 750 million lire was paid to the ASSS in instalments, given the delicate state of Italian finances at that time. Thus, from mid-1929 onwards Nogara set about investing the money in the loan stocks of various governments, shares in utility companies, gold and also 'baskets' of currencies which he was constantly changing through arbitrage operations.[150] When even Nogara's careful investments began to be affected by the whirlwind generated by the Wall Street Crash of October, he was forced to diversify, particularly into property transactions in Britain, France, Luxembourg, and Switzerland.[151] When the economic situation in Italy improved from 1932 onwards, he also began to invest in 'blue chip' companies there, arguably tying the Vatican's finances to the fortunes of the Regime, while massively expanding the 'Catholic' stake in the Italian economy overall.[152] As the skies of Europe darkened with the threatening clouds of war from 1936 onwards Nogara sought investments, and made deposits of currencies and gold, in the United States.[153] In moving the Vatican's investments into the marketplaces of the world, Nogara finally had inserted the papacy into the structures of international capitalism.

THE STATE OF THE VATICAN CITY

Pius XI was quick to spend the Vatican's newfound wealth. He had already embarked on a massive building spree in Rome before the *Conciliazione*,[154] and from 1929 onwards he poured vast amounts of money into providing suitable facilities—an electricity substation and workshops, shops, a telephone exchange, a prison, courts, a governor's palace, printing works for *L'Osservatore Romano*, a radio station, and so on—for the new State of the

[149] For a brief biographical sketch of Nogara, see Pollard, *Money*, 143–146.
[150] Pollard, *Money*, 47–48.
[151] Pollard, *Money*, 159–164.
[152] Pollard, *Money*, 171–177.
[153] Pollard, *Money*, 179–181.
[154] Pollard, *Money*, 179–181.

Vatican City, thus creating the Vatican that we know today.[155] It would be fair to say that he created Vatican City *ex novo* such was the scale of the demolitions of existing buildings, which included the removal of several dozen Vatican employees to housing elsewhere, and construction works in progress for many years all over the site.[156] If the restoration or building of churches, priests' residences, and seminaries in Italy are also taken into account, then Pius XI was truly a great 'building pope', on a par with Sixtus V.

Later in the 1930s, more money would be spent on cutting a grand 'triumphal way' through the medieval Borgo from the Tiber to St Peter's Square.[157] The result of all this was to attract media attention, with magazines like *The National Geographic* devoting huge amounts of space to the newest and smallest state in the world.[158]

CHURCH–STATE RELATIONS IN ITALY, 1931–8

The seriousness of the 1931 crisis in relations between the Vatican and Italy should not be underestimated: the basic elements were reminiscent of those episodes in 1927 and 1929 when the Fascists had tried to eliminate the Catholic youth organizations. Clearly, the more hard-line Fascists were trying exactly the same game in 1931, and would have succeeded but for the intransigence of Pius XI. The crisis is also notable for the fact that, in the encyclical *Non Abbiamo Bisogno*, the pope condemned elements of Fascist theory and practice for the first time. Crucially, the crisis had helped to clarify the relationship between 'the two Romes'. On the one hand, it was clear that the Fascist Regime was not going to be the *longa manus* of the Church, even less a pliant tool of the pope's policy for 'the Christian restoration of Italian society'. Moreover, Pius XI had managed to provide a protective shield for ACI, and in broader terms, the Catholic presence in Italian society: a Fascist state in which a capillary, non-Fascist organization, ACI, existed with a limited degree of autonomy hardly fitted Mussolini's description of the totalitarian regime—'everything inside the state'. There was no 'clericalization' or 'Catholicization' of Fascism but also no 'Fascistization' of Italian Catholicism

[155] The cost of such things as the demolition of dwelling houses within the confines of the new state and the rehousing of their inhabitants, the construction of a wall surrounding it, the railway 'spur' from the Italian state railway line, and the railway station were paid for by the Italian government. Pollard, *Money*, 150.

[156] See *Monumenti di un Pontificato. La cittá del Vaticano, le chiese, le case parrocchiali, i seminari*, Rome, n.d., which includes a complete list of buildings constructed or restored by Pius XI.

[157] *Monumenti di un Pontificato*, 151–153.

[158] *National Geographical Magazine*, February 1939.

and the restriction of the Church's activities to the sacristy. Even less was the pope going to be 'the chaplain of the King of Italy'. Indeed, *Non Abbiamo Bisogno* was intended as a clear declaration of Vatican independence from Fascist Italy to the world, and it was interpreted as such. Hence it can be argued that, despite the careful cultivation of appearances to the contrary, it was Pius and not Mussolini who was the victor in 1931.

Thereafter, the Church clearly did have a special relationship with Italian Fascism: the 'marriage of convenience' between the two as described by the Italian historian De Felice brought enormous benefits to the Church.[159] Fascism provided a protective framework for Catholic values, especially those enunciated in *Casti Connubi*, Pius XI's encyclical on the family, marriage, and women of 1930 (see Chapter 5). There was no divorce and, in principle, no abortion and no contraception in Fascist Italy.[160] In broader terms, Mussolini's policy of 'ruralization', which sought to prevent major, modernizing changes in the social structure of the countryside and consequently in the balance between town and country, benefited the Church, whose major strongholds lay mainly in the small towns and countryside of northern and central Italy.[161] This 'convergence' or parallel path between Italian Catholicism and Fascism was aptly symbolized by the participation of rural clergy and bishops in one of the Regime's economic campaigns, the 'Battle for Grain'.[162] Catholic complaints to Mussolini in these years were few and far between, and mostly about Italy's exiguous Protestant minorities whom Pius felt enjoyed a dangerous degree of toleration under the Regime. Needless to say, the minorities did not see it that way.[163] Under the umbrella of the September Accords of 1931, ACI flourished, expanding the membership of its organizations, and developing networks of parochial sports facilities, cinemas, and theatres,[164] so much so that, in 1935, the Fascists more once became anxious about their growth.[165] Eventually, out of the youth organizations of ACI would emerge the post-war, Italian Catholic ruling class, as Pius XI had always intended, the youthful cadres of the Christian Democratic Party.

All in all, Fascist Italy between 1931 and 1938 seemed to offer an ideal environment for the Catholic Church and therefore one that served as a model for the Holy See in its efforts to promote the Church's interests in other countries. In particular, ACI seemed to provide the perfect blueprint for the promotion of Catholic Action as a means of mobilizing Catholic laypeople in defence

159 R. De Felice, *Mussolini il Fascista. L'organizzazione dello stato totalitario, 1925–1929*, Turin, 1968, 178.

160 Pollard, *Catholicism in Modern Italy*, 98.

161 Pollard, *Catholicism in Modern Italy*, 98.

162 Pollard, *Catholicism in Modern Italy*, 98.

163 Pollard, *Catholicism in Modern Italy*, 96–97.

164 John Dunnage, *Twentieth Century Italy: A Social History*, London, 2002, 99.

165 Pollard, *The Vatican*, 183–184.

of the Church and its values, and would indeed be used as such by Pius XI and Mgr Pizzardo in their efforts to promote Catholic Action throughout the worldwide Church (see Chapter 5).

While the terms 'marriage of convenience' and 'years of convergence' as descriptions of Church–State relations in Italy between 1931 and 1938 are largely justified by events, there nevertheless remained an underlying tension, even an overt competitiveness, between the papacy and the Italian Fascist Regime in this period. The chief locus of this tension and this competitiveness was, inevitably, the city of Rome, the capital of both Roman Catholicism and Italian Fascism. Though the great international Catholic gatherings in Rome which characterized Pius XI's pontificate can be explained precisely as a function of the Eternal City's role as the capital of a worldwide religion, they were also part of a conscious strategy on the part of Pius XI to contest Mussolini's plans to 'Fascistize' Rome.[166] They provided an alternative to Mussolini's 'oceanic' gatherings outside his balcony in Piazza Venezia, 2 kilometres from St Peter's Square, as well as the great military parades on the Via dell'Impero, the wide avenue between Pizza Venezia and the Coliseum, which Mussolini had driven through medieval quarters of Rome lying atop the glorious ruins of the Roman forums which he wished to expose to public view.[167]

Richard Bosworth has recently drawn attention to one particular moment in this great competition between Pius XI and Mussolini in 1932–3, when the Regime commemorated the tenth anniversary of the March on Rome of October 1922. A grand exhibition was mounted in Rome's Palazzo delle Esposizioni on the Via Nazionale. Naturally, the Fascist authorities pulled out all the stops to attract millions of Romans, Italians, and even foreigners to this celebration of their achievements.[168] But, as Bosworth points out, the Regime's Exhibition of the Fascist Revolution 'was not the only show in town' at that time.[169] Pius had called an Extraordinary Holy Year in 1933–4 in commemoration of the 1,900th anniversary of the Crucifixion of Jesus Christ. While the exhibition drew large crowds, including not a few foreigners, in part thanks to generously subsidized rail travel, it could not rival the huge flocks of pilgrims who descended upon the Eternal City and participated in the many colourful and numinous celebrations in its various basilicas and squares.[170] However much Mussolini tried to make Rome a 'new', truly *Fascist*, city, it obstinately persisted in remaining the centre of world Catholicism as well.

[166] See Paul Baxa, *Roads and Ruins: The Symbolic Landscape of Fascist Rome*, Toronto, 2010, especially ch. 2.

[167] Baxa, *Roads and Ruins*, ch. 3.

[168] R.J.B. Bosworth, 'L'Anno Santo (Holy Year) in Fascist Italy 1933–34', *European History Quarterly*, 40 (2010), 439.

[169] Bosworth, 'L'Anno Santo', 439.

[170] R.J.B. Bosworth, *Whispering City: Rome and its Histories*, Yale, 2011, 179–182.

The 1933–4 'duel' between Mussolini and Pius XI in Rome reflected a broader battle between Italian Fascism and Catholicism in the 1930s. Fascism, like the other totalitarian dictatorships of Hitler and Stalin, had a strong tendency towards what Mosse and Gentile have described as 'the sacralisation of politics'.[171] Italian Fascism sought present a new kind of politics to the Italian people in a religious, as well as a militarized, guise, adopting not only uniforms and parades for all sections of the movement, but also ceremonies with elements obviously borrowed from Catholicism itself—altars, liturgies, litanies, credos, and so on.[172] But Mussolini's attempts to 'sacralize' politics were actually an admission of weakness, not strength. Whereas National Socialism successfully drew on non-Christian religions—paganism and the Norse gods—in the 'sacralized' ceremonies which it offered to rival those of the Christian churches,[173] Italian Fascism shamelessly plagiarized the whole repertoire of *Catholic* rituals and language. The debt to Catholicism was most apparent in the ceremonies which accompanied the solemn reinterment of Fascist 'martyrs'—squadristi fallen honourably or dishonourably in battle with their enemies in the period 1919–24—and in the late 1930s in Florence and Siena.[174] The sacralization of politics in Nazi Germany arguably filled a need in a country where secularization had already made inroads by the time that Hitler came to power. But there was no such spiritual 'void' in Fascist Italy where Catholicism remained the vibrant, and, after the *Conciliazione*, in some ways revivified, religion of the overwhelming mass of the Italian population.

CONCLUSION

The *Conciliazione* of 1929 was undoubtedly one of the high points of the pontificate of Pius XI and certainly his greatest achievement. Indeed, it must be regarded as one of the key turning points in the history of the modern papacy. Pius had succeeded in restoring a little of the temporal power of the papacy, something which his predecessors had dreamed of since 1870, and he had established the finances of the Vatican on a new and more secure basis. He

[171] G.L. Mosse, *The Nationalisation of the Masses: Political Symbolism and Mass Movements in Germany from the Napoleonic Wars through the Third Reich*, Ithaca, NY, and London, 1975; and E. Gentile, 'The Sacralisation of Politics: Definitions, Interpretations and Reflections on the Question of Secular Religion and Totalitarianism', *Totalitarian Movements and Political Religions*, 1(1) (2000), 18–55. For a further discussion of the phenomenon, see John Pollard, 'Fascism and Religion', in A. Costa Pinto (ed.), *Re-thinking the Nature of Fascism: Comparative Approaches*, London and Basingstoke, 2011, 147–151.

[172] Pollard, 'Fascism and Religion', 148–149.

[173] Pollard, 'Fascism and Religion', 150–151.

[174] Pollard, 'Fascism and Religion'.

had also, apparently, sorted out the difficult relations between the Church and the Italian State and thus placed the Church in a much stronger position within Italian society. But all this had been achieved at a cost, recognizing and effectively morally underwriting Mussolini's Fascist Regime. The 1931 crisis—and this is confirmed by the wording of *Non Abbiamo Bisogno*—revealed to Pius XI that the Italian Fascist Regime was rather less of an old-fashioned, authoritarian regime, like others in Europe at this time, than he had thought and more of a new political animal with definite totalitarian tendencies. Once the balance of power between the Holy See and the Regime had been re-established by the settlement of the crisis, Fascism's totalitarian policies were directed away from the Church. They would surface again in the late 1930s and culminate in a serious dispute over the Racial Laws in 1938–9. Another consequence of the accommodation with Italian Fascism was the eschewing of Catholic political independence—as in the abandonment of the Partito Popolare and the entrusting of Catholic 'political' activity to ACI. Moreover, ACI was taken as a model of the Catholic lay pressure group for use in 'all seasons' and within all political regimes, a notion which was thoroughly disproved by experiences elsewhere.[175]

The experience of negotiating with Fascist Italy would also provide a dangerously misleading model for how to deal with another fascist dictatorship, the Third Reich, after Hitler and the Nazis came to power in Germany in 1933.

[175] Pollard, 'Pius XI's Promotion', 780–784.

5

Pius XI: The Teacher and His Church

INTRODUCTION

Pius XI was a great teacher. In his exercise of the Church's *magisterium*, without explicitly making an *ex cathedra* pronouncement, unlike his successor Pius XII, he nevertheless exercised this on the understanding that his pronouncements had the authority of infallibility. In his seventeen-year pontificate, he set a record among twentieth-century popes for stating or restating the central truths of Catholic belief in encyclicals, or other significant public statements, on the following matters:

1. On the family and the Church's rights and responsibilities in the education of youth in *Divini illius Magistri* (otherwise known as *Rappresentanti in Terra*), 1930
2. On marriage, the family, and the role of women in *Casti Connubii*, 1930
3. On the absolute truth of Catholic doctrine and the dangers of Protestant ecumenical movements in *Mortalium Animos*, 1928
4. In that same encyclical, and others, he restated Catholic doctrine in relation to the Trinity, the Incarnation, the Redemption, and the Eucharist as a continuing/perpetual sacrifice for the sins of the world
5. The nature of the Catholic priesthood in *Sacerdotii Catholicae*
6. On the nature of the Church, especially in the unpublished encyclical *De Vera Ecclesia Christi*, setting out his own, very 'high church', ecclesiology
7. On Catholic social and economic ethics in *Quadragesimo Anno*, 1931, in which he elaborated on and developed the ideas set out in Leo XIII's encyclical, *Rerum Novarum* in the context of the greatest crisis that modern industrial capitalism had faced in its 200-year history.

In addition, he denounced, in the clearest terms, the great errors of his age: the materialist heresies of 'totalitarianism ('statolatry') in *Non Abbiamo Bisogno*, of 1931, Communism in *Divini Redemptoris*, 1937, and biological racialism in both *Mit brennender Sorge* and the unpublished encyclical, *Humani Generis Unitas* of 1938, while always ascribing the root and ultimate cause of these great evils to liberalism.

And whether he was the sole or only co-author of these documents, all of which he in any case scrutinized and revised with great care, in them he demonstrated his remarkable knowledge of sacred scripture, of both the Old and New Testaments.

His pontificate also left its mark on the Roman Catholic Church in other ways, in its system of government, in its relations with other, non-Catholic churches, by his tentative use of the media (radio), and by the introduction of new ways of mobilizing Catholics worldwide. There were no great changes in doctrine, Liturgy, or devotions (except, in the latter case, the introduction of the cult of Christ the King) and Papa Ratti reaffirmed his essentially conservative, traditionalist position in the history of the Church by considering the recall of the First Vatican Council.[1]

THE ECCLESIOLOGY OF PAPA RATTI

One of the most marked characteristics of the pontificate of Pius XI was his vision of the Church. This was a very 'high church' ecclesiology, which informed all of his policies and utterances. It was not simply a very strong sense of the authority of the Holy See, that he exercised as the successor of St Peter—the Petrine Primacy—of the divine authority possessed by the Church as a result of that Primacy. In many of his encyclicals, most of which were not fundamentally concerned with ecclesiastical authority, he never missed an opportunity to stress the absolute moral authority of the Church in matters of faith and morals. A few examples will suffice to illustrate this almost pathological determination to remind the world of the claims of the Roman Catholic Church. In his first encyclical, *Ubi arcano Dei Consilio* of December 1922, speaking of the role of the Church he stated that 'She alone is adapted to this great work [of pacification], for she is not only divinely to lead mankind, but moreover because of her very make-up and the constitution which she possesses . . .',[2] and in *Quas Primas* of two years later, when explaining the threefold nature of the Kingship of Christ, legislative, executive, and judicial, he speaks of 'The right which the Church has from Christ himself . . . to teach mankind, to make laws, to govern peoples in all that pertains to their

[1] I am grateful to Professor Michael Walsh for pointing out that though this feast was promoted in the nineteenth century by French legitimists, Pius XI made it a universal feast at roughly the same time that he condemned Action Française.

[2] Carlen, *Papal Encyclicals*, III, 234.

eternal salvation. . . .'[3] The doctrines espoused in *Quas Primas* percolated down to the local level of the Church: as early as 1927 a Belgian Catholic Action pamphlet declared that, 'Christ has given to the Church the power of ruling men. From this power derives the right to make civil and spiritual laws and to ensure that they are carried out.'[4] The absolute moral authority of the Church/Holy See is reiterated in *Mortalium Animos*, the January 1928 encyclical which condemned the ecumenical initiatives and movements of various non-Catholic churches, in *Ad Salutem*, published in April 1930 commemorating St Augustine of Hippo, where he cites the famous dictum attributed to St Augustine, 'Rome has spoken, the cause is finished',[5] and again in *Casti Connubii*, the encyclical on Christian marriage of December 1930, which puts papal authority in the starkest terms:

> (Catholics) . . . must suffer themselves to be guided and led in all things that touch upon faith and morals by the Holy Church of God through its Supreme Pastor the Roman Pontiff, who is himself guided by Jesus Christ Our Lord.[6]

In *Lux Veritatis* of December 1931, in which he commemorated the 1,500th anniversary of the Council of Ephesus, he asserted Petrine supremacy again and again, claiming that Ephesus set three key dogmas: the divine nature of Jesus, the consequent fact that Mary was the Mother of God, and finally that 'in matters of faith and morals the Roman pontiff has a God-given authority, supreme and high and subject to none over all and several faithful Christians'.[7]

But the clearest and strongest enunciation of what could legitimately described as a form of Catholic 'totalitarianism' is to be found in the first draft of an unpublished encyclical, *De Vera Ecclesia Christi*, dated 25 October 1931.[8] It is far from clear why the encyclical was drafted in the first place. Was it intended as a further response to non-Catholic ecumenical activity? If that is the case, then why so soon after *Mortalium Animos*? Or was it drafted during the summer of 1931, at the height of the crisis in relations with Italian Fascism, as a means of reinforcing the position of the Holy See in the struggle? If this was what prompted the writing of the encyclical, it was never published, which would suggest that the September Accords (see Chapter 4) seemed to render it superfluous. Or was it a response to the persecution against the Church which had commenced under the Second Republic in Spain? In fact, its opening paragraphs suggest that it was conceived as a

[3] Carlen, *Papal Encyclicals*, III, 276.

[4] *Plans pour cercles d'études d'action catholique*, 'La Royauté de Christ dans la Société Humaine', 1, Bruges, 1927.

[5] See Carlen, *Papal Encyclicals*, III, 379.

[6] See Carlen, *Papal Encyclicals*, III, 379

[7] Carlen, *Papal Encyclicals*, III, 464.

[8] The text is in ASV, AES, IV Periodo, Stati Eccl., 1931–1939, fasc. 662, 'Due progetti di encicliche di Pio XI', 7282/79, *De Vera Ecclesia Christi*; the date is given at the end, on the last page. This has been translated into English by Professor Michael Walsh as 'On the True Church of Christ'.

defiant gesture against *all* the enemies of the Church as Pius perceived them at that time and as he describes them in the encyclical.[9]

The encyclical goes on to describe the Roman Catholic Church in thoroughly scriptural terms, and states 'For the Church is the Kingdom of God which Christ came to establish in the world and about which He himself said to Peter, "on this rock I will build my Church . . . and I will give you the keys of the Kingdom of Heaven" '(Matthew 16:18–19).[10] On this basis of scriptural authority, Pius XI reasserted all the claims made for the spiritual and moral authority of the Roman Catholic Church and, above all, the papacy by his predecessor Pius IX over sixty years before:

> This office of teaching by the Roman Pontiff as successor of Peter and Vicar of Christ on earth, and by the Bishops as successors of the Apostles, 'is exercised by her (the Church's) most solemn judgement or in her ordinary and universal magisterium' (the words in quotation marks are an approximate quotation from a text of the First Vatican Council, session 3, chapter 3).[11]

And in case any doubt still lingered about his own personal teaching authority, Pius XI spelt it out: 'This entire deposit of faith, both written and handed down by tradition, to be observed without anxiety, safeguarded from any error, is entrusted to Ourself to be disclosed to the minds of the faithful.'[12]

None of all this was, arguably, completely new: it had been said before but never before had it been brought together in such a comprehensive description and definition of the Roman Catholic Church and of the papacy and its ultimately divinely mandated authority. Unlike his successor, Pius XII, Papa Ratti may never have explicitly exercised infallible authority *ex cathedra*, yet this unpublished encyclical constituted a thunderous reassertion of the principle of infallibility and its bases in revelation and tradition.

CATHOLIC MISSIONS AND INDIGENIZATION

A major area in which Pius XI could be said to have followed firmly in the footsteps of his predecessors (Gregory XVI, Leo XIII, and Benedict XV) was that of the Catholic missions. During the course of his pontificate, the pope gave a great deal of impetus and support to Catholic missionary activity. Moreover, he continued the policy of Benedict in seeking to develop an indigenous clergy but improved on this by setting out to create indigenous

[9] M. Walsh (trans.) 'On the True Church of Christ'.
[10] M. Walsh (trans.) 'On the True Church of Christ'.
[11] M. Walsh (trans.) 'On the True Church of Christ'.
[12] M. Walsh (trans.) 'On the True Church of Christ'.

episcopates, often encountering the hostility of colonial–imperial powers, and sometimes even of some of the missionaries themselves.

Prompted by the impact of the Missionary Exhibition, which he had organized during the Holy Year of 1925 to demonstrate his commitment to the development of the Catholic missions, Pius XI established a permanent missionary museum in the Lateran Palace (later transferred to the Vatican). The British minister to the Holy See devoted a whole section of his annual report for 1925 to 'The Missionary Organisation of the Catholic Church', thus providing some interesting facts and figures about them, not least of which was the statement that 'It is easily the largest missionary organisation working under a unified direction and radiating its activity from a single centre. . . .'[13] Under the 'red pope', Cardinal Marinus Willem van Rossum, that is, the prefect of the Congregation of Propaganda Fide, the total number of Catholic missionaries employed in the world in 1925 was 14,702, of whom 8,196 were non-indigenous and 4,516 indigenous priests.[14] In addition Catholic missions were served by 732 indigenous lay brothers and 3,187 non-indigenous ones: there was a much closer balance between indigenous and non-indigenous nuns employed—11,158 and 12,944, respectively.[15] The priests were largely drawn from the religious orders and congregations, the Jesuits being in the lead with nearly 1,400 priests working in the mission fields, followed by the Franciscans and the Paris Society for Foreign Missions.[16]

The success of the Missionary Exhibition inspired Pius to publish an encyclical on the missions, *Rerum Ecclesiae* of February 1926, addressed to all the bishops.[17] The role of van Rossum in the drawing up of the encyclical is not entirely clear, certain documents do suggest it.[18] Pius was anxious to get all Catholics, bishops, clergy, and laity, involved in missionary work in some way, through prayers, fund-raising, and the release of diocesan clergy to work in the missions: in particular, he stressed the need for the development of missionary societies, both clerical and lay in each country.[19] He had already moved the headquarters of the major missionary organization, the Society for the Propagation of the Faith, from Lyons to Rome, where 'We have also re-organised it, conferred on it, as it were, Roman citizenship, and given it charge of meeting all the present needs of the missions, as well as those which will arise in the future.'[20] This may simply have been an another example of 'Romanization' but he was also responding to the concerns of

[13] Hachey, *Anglo-Vatican Relations*, 96–98; not surprisingly, the minister's concern was principally about the British Empire and the scarcity of British priests for the missions there.

[14] Hachey, *Anglo-Vatican Relations*, 98.

[15] Hachey, *Anglo-Vatican Relations*, 98

[16] Hachey, *Anglo-Vatican Relations*, 98.

[17] For the text, see Carlen, *Papal Encyclicals*, III, 281–291.

[18] See Prudhomme, 'Le Cardinal van Rossum', 136–138.

[19] Prudhomme, 'Le Cardinal van Rossum', 281–284.

[20] Prudhomme, 'Le Cardinal van Rossum', 284.

American Catholics, who by now were major contributors to the missionary fund-raising effort though their Board of Catholic Missions. It was also, undoubtedly, part of a strategy to reduce the influence of the French missionaries, and their government, in the Catholic mission field, and thus prepare for decolonization.[21]

The prime thrust of the encyclical was a plea about the urgent need for the development of an indigenous clergy. Pius XI thus had anticipated the process of decolonization which would take place in the decades following 1945. He concluded his encyclical by condemning those missionaries who practised racial discrimination against non-European clergy, 'Anyone who looks upon these natives [of the south or east] as members of an inferior race or as men of low mentality makes a grievous mistake.'[22]

There was some progress towards the formation of indigenous clergy: the British Minister in his 1925 report stated that, whereas in 1913 indigenous clergy had constituted just 22 per cent of all priests working in the missions, by 1918 this had risen to only 24 per cent, and by 1925 had reached 26 per cent of the total, claiming that the increase had been most marked in China.[23] Even so, an increase of 4 per cent in fourteen years was not great news. The 'indigenization' of the missionary churches encountered resistance on many levels, from the colonial authorities, from colonial settler communities, and even from missionaries themselves. A case in point was the Dutch East Indies, now Indonesia. Despite the fact that the head of Propaganda after 1915 was a Dutchman, van Rossum, most of the Dutch missionaries, as well as their 'mother houses' in Holland, opposed indigenization in the 1920s.[24] But by the early 1930s, under pressure from the Vatican, the situation had improved, 75 per cent of the priests working in Indo-China were indigenous, 57 per cent in India, 42 per cent in Japan, but only 22 per cent in China, and 9 per cent in Africa.[25] Nothing daunted, Pius XI ordained six Chinese bishops with his own hands in St Peter's in 1926, the first step towards an indigenous hierarchy, and several Indian and Japanese bishops during the course of his pontificate.[26]

A further strand in Pius XI's mission policy was the encouragement of the founding of congregations of women religious, especially nurses, to work in the mission fields, a boost to which was given by the Catholic Nursing Congress held in Rome in 1935: nuns were even allowed to be midwives for

[21] Hachey, *Anglo-Vatican Relations*, 88.

[22] Hachey, *Anglo-Vatican Relations*, 287.

[23] Hachey, *Anglo-Vatican Relations*, 98.

[24] See Hans de Valk, 'Hollandia docet? Cardinal van Rossum and the Catholic Missions in the Dutch East Indies (1918–1932)', in Poels et al. (eds), *Life with a Mission*, 143–157.

[25] As cited in James Hagerty, *Cardinal Hinsley: Priest and Patriot*, Oxford, 2008, 179.

[26] See his homily on the occasion of the consecration of the first Japanese bishop on 30 October 1927, *Anno vix elapso*, in Bellocchi, *Tutte le Encicliche*, IX, 226–227.

the first time.[27] A particular emphasis was placed on the creation of institutes of indigenous women religious, usually with simple vows, which began to appear in China, Indochina, and Africa.[28] In 1935, Propaganda set about devising a set of regulations for these indigenous institutes.[29]

While the expansion of the Church, with the erection of more bishoprics and other missionary sees (apostolic vicariates and prefectures)[30] was promoted in all mission territories during the course of his pontificate, China was a particular focus of Pius XI's concerns. He greatly encouraged the apostolic delegate there, Mgr Costantini, who achieved a great deal during his time in China, appointing the first Chinese apostolic prefects, Puchi and Lihsien in 1924, establishing an exclusively Chinese religious congregation in 1927, the Catholic University of Peking in the same year, and even a branch of Catholic Action in 1928–9.[31] His greatest achievement was the effective establishment of a 'Chinese Church', by holding a first council of its bishops and ordinaries, the Concilio Sinense, at Shanghai in 1924, which adopted 861 'canons' or regulations for the Chinese Church.[32]

Costantini encountered many obstacles in his work. First there were the missionaries themselves, especially those belonging to religious orders who tended to operate entirely independently of both each other and a higher authority, and to treat local Catholics in a rather high-handed manner. Costantini won a considerable victory over them at the Council of Shanghai, which abolished the prostrations of the Chinese before missionaries, and declared that the 'missions were no longer the little feudal possessions of religious orders'.[33] Another issue that Costantini set about tackling at the Council was the objections to the so-called 'Chinese Rites', that is the veneration which the Chinese had for centuries, if not millennia, paid at the shrines of their ancestors and which had been problematical for Chinese Christians who wished to pay their respects to their ancestors.[34] In January 1933, Mgr Edward Mooney, Apostolic Delegate in the Far East, allowed the same relaxation of the rules for Japanese Catholics as a strictly 'patriotic' act,[35] and in late 1939 these changes were confirmed by a papal instruction.[36] Pius XI intervened to

[27] E. Sastres Santos, 'La vita religiosa nella storia della Chiesa e della società', in De Rosa and Cracco (eds), *Il Papato*, 128–131.

[28] Sastres Santos, 'La vita religiosa', 152–153.

[29] Sastres Santos, 'La vita religiosa', 135.

[30] For figures of numbers of bishoprics and other ecclesiastical jurisdictions created by Pius XI, see entry on Pius XI in P. Levillain (ed.), *Encyclopedia of the Papacy*, vol. II, London, 1998, 1199–1209.

[31] B.F. Pighin (ed.), *Chiesa e Stato in Cina. Dalle Imprese di Costantini alle Svolte attuali*, Venice, 2010, 27.

[32] Pighin, *Chiesa e Stato*, 27.

[33] Pighin, *Chiesa e Stato*, 104; see also D.E. Munghello (ed.), *The Chinese Rites Controversy: Its History and Meaning*, Monumenta Serica, Monograph Series XXXIII, Nettetal, 1994.

[34] Pighin, *Chiesa e stato*, 104.

[35] *NCE*, 2nd edn, 3, 516.

[36] Bellocchi, *Tutte le Encicliche*, IX, *Plane Copertum est*, 8 December 1939, Instructio.

support Costantini in his battles with difficult (mainly French) missionaries by sending an apostolic letter on the subject.[37] With the appointment of Chinese bishops, even his endeavours to establish an indigenous clergy bore some fruit: when he left China in 1933, 23 out of 121 missions were ruled by Chinese clergy.[38]

The French authorities in China were another problem. The Vatican was deeply unhappy with the French 'protectorate' over indigenous Christians and the missions of religious orders, which, apart from anything else, were hypocritical inasmuch as most religious orders were banned in France. Costantini tried to avoid meeting French diplomats and indeed being associated with the representatives of any of the imperial powers in China, given Chinese resentment of 'the Unequal Treaties' which the European Powers had forced upon the Celestial Empire in the late nineteenth century.[39]

The protectorate hindered the Vatican from establishing direct relations with all missionaries. Costantini tried to ignore it and in 1929 urged on the Vatican the necessity of some sort of diplomatic agreement with China *before* the fall of the protectorate which would either be replaced by a treaty of friendship with China or die a natural death. But Gasparri told him to hold back because of the lack of a legitimate government, leaving Costantini disconsolate.[40] The Chinese would have been delighted to establish diplomatic relations with the Holy See but, as in the past, the French blocked the move because it would have meant a diminution of their influence.[41] Eight years later, the cardinals of the Congregation for Extraordinary Ecclesiastical Affairs debated another Chinese démarche for the establishment of diplomatic relations but without a successful outcome.[42]

Hanging over the work of Costantini and the Catholic missionaries were worries about the spread of Communism in China. The former Celestial Empire, in the 1920s and 1930s, was barely at peace, what with local warlords contesting the government in Peking, Japanese invaders along the coastal provinces, and the advance of the armed Communist Party in the interior. Foreign missions increasingly came under attack both from local warlords and the Communists, with death and destruction visited on them as a result.[43] It was an ominous portent of the chaos and civil war into which China would be plunged in the 1940s. Nevertheless, Costantini achieved much in China

[37] Bellocchi, *Ab Ipsis Pontificatu exordiis*, 15 June 1926, Epistola.

[38] Pighin, *Chiesa e Stato*, 29.

[39] See John K. Fairbanks and Kwang-Ching Liu (eds), *The Cambridge History of China: 1800–1911*, vol. 11, Part 2, Cambridge, 1976, ch. 2, 'Late Ching Foreign Relations, 1866–1911'.

[40] ASV, AES, IV Periodo, Relazione circa le Trattative per stabilire relazioni diplomatiche in Cina, Fondo Cina-Giappone, P.O. 45, fasc. 57, ff. 84–85.

[41] Pighin, *Chiesa e Stato*, 77.

[42] ASV, AES, Sessioni, 1380, 25 November 1937, Cina, Trattative per Relazioni Diplomatiche.

[43] Pius XI's allocution, *Amplissimum Conlegium*, in Bellocchi, *Tutte le Encicliche*, IX, 221–225.

between 1922 and 1933, moving it slowly and steadily along the path towards a more deeply rooted native Christianity and winning a progressive change in the atmosphere, in particular with regard to the attitude of French.[44]

Another mission field which greatly occupied Pius XI's attention was Africa. Until 1930, there had been apostolic delegates of the Propaganda congregation in the Union of South Africa, Egypt, and the Congo, all instituted by the reigning pontiff. The rest of Africa, divided between the British, French, Portuguese, and Spanish Empires, largely went its own way, unsupervised from Rome. This changed in 1928 when the Colonial Office in London embarked on a wide-ranging reform of the education of the indigenous populations in its African possessions. As a result, the Vatican sent Mgr Arthur Hinsley, the Rector of the English College (the Venerabile) in Rome as Apostolic Visitor to the missions in the British territory to assess the situation and advise the Propaganda on how best to protect Catholic missions during the inevitable shake-up. Hinsley reported back and then was sent to Africa as a more permanent Apostolic Delegate based in Mombasa, Kenya.[45] As well as having to deal with some colonial administrators of an essentially secularist outlook who were unwilling to subsidize Catholic mission schools, and were happy to close them if they did not feel that they came up to scratch, there was the hostility of some Protestant missionaries, the deleterious effects of the fall in funding collected for the worldwide missions from 66 million to 38 million lire as a result of the Great Depression, and the serious problem of the steady advance south of Muslim influence—at its worst in northern Nigeria, southern Sudan, and the coastal regions of East Africa.[46] But, as always, rivalries between missionary religious orders, often of a different nationalities, were a serious impediment to the successful application of Rome's centralizing policy of supervising and coordinating the work of Catholic missions. As an Irish missionary, Fr McCarthy, explained in 1937:

> in Tanganyika there are nine vicariates and six different missionary societies each with its own different ideas, codes of rules and regulations, its own system of education and finances and manner life, all of which are guarded, pursued and adhered to with grim missionary determination as being the one and only.[47]

Tanganyika was probably somewhat exceptional, being a former German colony that was now British mandated territory, but the situation was not much better elsewhere in British Africa thanks, principally, to a lack of British missionaries and hence the reliance on 'foreigners', chiefly French, German, and Dutch orders. By and large, in Belgian, French, Portuguese, and Spanish Africa, things were better, if only because, ironically, due to the nationalistic

[44] Pighin, *Chiesa e Stato*, 79.
[45] Hagerty, *Cardinal Hinsley*, chs 5–9.
[46] Hagerty, *Cardinal Hinsley*, 150–152 and 167.
[47] As quoted in Hagerty, *Cardinal Hinsley*, 181.

policy pursued by the colonial authorities, there was much greater homogeneity among the missionary clergy.

Yet nationalism clearly was a problem for the Vatican in its efforts to supervise and coordinate Catholic missionary activity—thus Hinsley ordered that the Italian Catholic Mission and the Austrian Catholic Mission in the Sudan change their names to simply 'Roman Catholic Mission'.[48] And, in December 1929, in an allocution to an audience of missionaries, Pius XI stated baldly:

> The missions must have nothing to do with nationalism. They must solely be concerned with Catholicism, with the apostolate . . . nationalism has always been a calamity for the missions, indeed, it would be no exaggeration to say that it is a curse.[49]

It was a *cri de coeur*. The governments of the European empires were always seeking to extract advantageous privileges from the Vatican with regard to their colonial territories. As well as the religious protectorate in China, the secular French Republic insisted on the retention of its 'liturgical honours' in the Middle East, a relic of its protectorate over Catholics in the territories of the former Ottoman Empire. The Italians were particularly resentful of the privileged status of the French in the Near and Middle East and protested about it on more than one occasion after the *Conciliazione* of 1929, feeling that event should have given them greater consideration from the Vatican.[50] They even supported the efforts of the Secretariat of State in 1928 and 1929 to establish diplomatic relations with the secular Turkish Republic that had succeeded the Ottoman Sultans, but these were frustrated, ironically, by opposition from Muslim clerics there.[51] The Italians also tried to mobilize the support of papal diplomacy in their efforts to wrest the Palestinian mandate from Britain but again to no avail.[52] Even Italy's attempts to utilize Catholic missionary effort to bolster its prestige within its own empire encountered resistance inside the Vatican, with the result that it refused to permit the extension of the provisions of the 1929 Concordat to the Italian colonies other than the Dodecanese Islands.[53]

Though the Vatican admitted that the British authorities were less demanding in their relationship with the Vatican than other colonial powers, British requests to be advised in advance of appointments of colonial bishops and apostolic delegates, plus a demand that more of these be made from among British subjects, caused irritation. At a plenary meeting of the Congregation for Extraordinary Ecclesiastical Affairs in 1927 some cardinals present at the session interpreted

[48] Hagerty, *Cardinal Hinsley*, 151.

[49] Bellocchi, U. (ed.), *Discorsi di Pio XI*, Rome, 1960, II, 214–215, 'Ai Religiosi Missionari'.

[50] Pollard, *The Vatican*, 85–87.

[51] See DDI, 7 Serie, vol. VII, 108, no. 119, note of 20 February 1928.

[52] Pollard, *The Vatican*, 89–90.

[53] Pollard, *The Vatican*, 89–90.

the request as virtually a demand for a governmental *nihil obstat* and were determined to resist such incursions into the privileges of the Holy See.[54]

If Pius XI's pontificate is taken as a whole, then it is clear that he brought a new direction to the missionary outreach of the Roman Catholic Church. In particular, he sought to bring as many missions as possible under the more direct supervision of Propaganda Fide *on the ground*: as well as the apostolic delegates whom he had appointed to supervise the missions in Africa and China, he chose others to supervise the missions in French Indo-China, Palestine, and the Netherlands Antilles. Taken together with the apostolic delegations in British India, the Dutch East Indies (now Indonesia), Japan, and in Sydney, which was effectively responsible for Australia, New Zealand, and the Pacific Islands, this meant that virtually no Catholic missions in Africa and Asia were now unsupervised. Pius even considered establishing an apostolic delegation in a newly independent Arab, and overwhelmingly, Muslim nation, Iraq, formerly a British mandated territory, but independent after 1927 and a member of the League of Nations in 1932.[55] This demonstrates that he was seeking to promote the survival and growth of the Church in any future circumstances. The transfer of Mgr Costantini from being apostolic delegate in China to Secretary of Propaganda Fide in 1933 would ensure that this strategy was carried forward into the pontificate of his successor.

THE PRIESTHOOD AND THE RELIGIOUS CLERGY

During the course of his pontificate, Pius XI published three major documents affecting the Catholic clergy—the apostolic letter *Unigenitus Dei* of March 1924 on the clergy of religious congregations and orders,[56] the apostolic letter *Deus Scientiarum Dominus* of March 1931 specifically on the education of the clergy, and the encyclical *Ad Catholici Sacerdotii* of May 1935 on priestly formation.[57] All three exalted the role and importance of the Catholic priest, Pius declaring in the encyclical that, above all, the priest was the human medium through which God dispensed the grace of the sacrament.[58]

In addition to these central functions of priesthood, Pius emphasized the priest's role as the 'Power for Good' in society, helping to promote the missions, social justice, and, of course, Catholic Action in the parishes.[59]

[54] ASV, AES, Sessioni, 1814–1938, 1297, 15 November 1926, Inghilterra. Dei maggiori dignità ecclesiastici.

[55] ASV, AES, IVO Periodo, Taccuini, audience of 3 April 1932.

[56] Bellocchi, *Discorsi di Pio XI*, I, 95–101.

[57] AAS, 24 May 1935.

[58] AAS, 24 May 1935, 500.

[59] AAS, 24 May 1935, 502 and 513.

The encyclical inevitably contained a section on clerical celibacy, the defining characteristic of Catholic priesthood and an issue which was discussed in the very wide consultations that preceded its preparation. The Congregation of the Council, along with the Congregation of the Oriental Churches, circulated apostolic delegates and nuncios:

> who had under their jurisdiction communities of the Oriental churches, or who have them living in their territory, to find out what impression a pontifical document which, in dealing with the holiness of the priesthood, alluded to the perfection and advantages of ecclesiastical celibacy.[60]

The reactions were, allegedly, overwhelmingly positive, even Oriental Church communities, and some 'schismatics' responding enthusiastically to the idea according to those who replied to the circular.[61] Indeed, some, like Mgr Fumasoni-Biondi, apostolic delegate in Washington, argued that the long-standing rationale for celibacy—that it is was necessary if priests were to give themselves wholly to the mission of saving souls—was borne out by the experience of the Ruthenian clergy in the United States. According to Fumasoni-Biondi, these priests were not very fruitful in their ministry and were particularly lacking in initiatives to set up Catholic schools, youth clubs, charitable works, and 'religious institutes', because of the time they had to devote to their families. He raised the not insignificant question of the financial problems which bishops faced maintaining the families of priests, and concluded his response to the Congregation of the Oriental Church by stating that the Church had only 'tolerated' married priests in the Oriental churches.[62]

Mgr Roncalli, apostolic delegate in the Bulgarian capital, urged more caution: in view of the likelihood of 'mass conversions' from Orthodoxy in that country, they should avoid anything that might be threatening to married clergy.[63] Mgr Drapier, the French apostolic delegate in Indochina, was of the same opinion.[64]

[60] ASV, AES, IV Periodo, Stati Eccl., 1931–1939, 663, 1939 (sic), Documenti, appunti, informazioni ecc. Che servirono per la preparazione dell'Enciclica di S.P. Pio XI De sacerdotio catholico (dicembre 1935), Roma, 27 July 1932, Considerare la Grandezza del Sacerdozio.

[61] ASV, AES, IV Periodo, Stati Eccl., 1931–1939, 663, 1939 (sic), Documenti, appunti, informazioni ecc. Che servirono per la preparazione dell'Enciclica di S.P. Pio XI De sacerdotio catholico (dicembre, 1935), Roma, 27 July 1932, Considerare la Grandezza del Sacerdozio., responses from papal envoys in Yugoslavia, Greece, Syria, Lebanon, and Poland.

[62] ASV, AES, IV Periodo, Stati Eccl., 1931–1939, 663, 1939 (sic), Documenti, appunti, informazioni ecc. Che servirono per la preparazione dell'Enciclica di S.P. Pio XI De sacerdotio catholico (dicembre, 1935), Roma, 27 July 1932, Considerare la Grandezza del Sacerdozio., Fumasoni-Biondi, Apostolic Delegate to Cardinal Sincero, Segretario del S.C. Orientale, 8 August 1932, sub Segreto Pontifico.

[63] ASV, AES, IV Periodo, Stati Eccl., 1931–1939, 663, 1939 (sic), Documenti, appunti, informazioni ecc. Che servirono per la preparazione dell'Enciclica di S.P. Pio XI De sacerdotio catholico (dicembre, 1935), Roma, 27 July 1932, Considerare la Grandezza del Sacerdozio., 27 July 1932, Considerare la Grandezza del Sacerdozio.

[64] ASV, AES, IV Periodo, Stati Eccl., 1931–1939, 663, 1939 (sic), Documenti, appunti, informazioni ecc. Che servirono per la preparazione dell'Enciclica di S.P. Pio XI De sacerdotio catholico (dicembre, 1935), Roma, 27 July 1932, Considerare la Grandezza del Sacerdozio.

In the end, the encyclical was indeed cautious on the issue of celibacy, stating that stating that the commendation of celibacy in the Latin Church did not mean disapproval of the different discipline prevailing in the oriental Church.[65]

Another keynote of *Ad Catholici Sacerdotii* was the emphasis on education. In the introduction to the encyclical, Pius referred to *Deus Scientiarum Dominus*, 'Our special purpose in this decree was to make even broader and higher the culture and learning of priests.'[66] *Deus Scientiarum Dominus* did rather more than that, according to Maurilio Guasco, it 'provoked a veritable earthquake in the history of the formation of the clergy . . . because the document contemplated the suppression of nearly all theology faculties, especially attached to seminaries'.[67] The Commission, established in 1929 under the chairmanship of Mgr Ernesto Ruffini of the Holy Office, and which included such luminaries as Gemelli, the Dominican Padre Cordovani, later in-house theologian of the Vatican, had carried out a searching enquiry into the education of priests worldwide.[68] The enquiry revealed serious inadequacies in priestly formation, especially in Italy, and sought to remedy this by detailed instructions in *Deus Scientiarum Dominus*, which covered all aspects of the functioning of seminaries.[69] The Commission remained in existence after the publication of the decree in order to supervise the application of seminary reform, especially in Italy where often poorly staffed diocesan seminaries were merged into larger regional ones, on the orders of the pope.[70]

Unigenitus Dei had also been largely concerned with the formation of the regular clergy, particularly those destined for the missions. It is significant that, during the course of Papa Ratti's reign, a further sixteen houses of priestly formation for male religious congregations and orders were added to the existing forty-four, though it is not clear how much this increase was due to the pope's encouragement and support.[71] *Unigenitus* also tackled an issue which was essentially a logical consequence of the implementation of the Code of Canon Law: the adequacy or otherwise of the statutes of religious orders and congregations. As a result, in the early 1920s, the Sacred Congregation of Religious demanded that all of the statutes be examined and revised in accordance with the relevant canons and in the spirit of their founders' intentions.[72] The subsequent process

[65] Carlen, *Papal Encyclicals*, III, 506.

[66] Carlen, *Papal Encyclicals*, III, 598.

[67] Maurilio Guasco, 'La formazione del clero al tempo di Pio XI', in De Rosa and Cracovo (eds), *Il Papato*, 96.

[68] Guasco, 'La formazione del clero', 99.

[69] Guasco, 'La formazione del clero', 103.

[70] See *Annuario Pontificio*, 1948, 915, for the list of fifteen regional seminaries in Italy, of which eight were created by Pius XI.

[71] *Annuario Pontificio*, 1948, 916–919.

[72] Sastres Santos, 'La vita religiosa', 121–123.

of revision, which continued throughout the rest of Pius XI's reign and into that of his successor, revealed an extraordinary diversity of rules and regulations, and in a very few cases actually led to the dissolution of the institutes concerned.[73]

THE PAPACY'S RELATIONS WITH NON-CATHOLIC CHURCHES

The fear in the Vatican of the Protestant 'peril' did not abate after Benedict's death. In the interwar period, countries with an overwhelming Catholic majority like Italy, Spain, and Portugal, and also the Latin American states, were regarded in the Vatican as being the target of major, carefully organized campaigns of Protestant proselytism. In Italy itself, the danger seemed to present itself in the form of return migrants from the United States of America, who brought with them the creeds of the Pentecostalists, the Baptists, and even the Jehovah's Witnesses. Such was the fear of Protestantism, that in 1931 the Vatican's congregations of the Council and the Concistory circulated very precise instructions to the Italian bishops on the methods to be adopted to deal with the threat.[74] Exaggerated fears about the efficacy of Protestant propaganda lay behind Pius XI's programme of church building in Rome and other Italian cities and the establishment of the Opera per la Preservazione della Fede. On the other hand, the Great War had both multiplied the peace/ecumenical initiatives emanating from the Protestant side and provoked similar Catholic concerns and pleas to the pope about the need for religious unity in an imperilled world from countries as disparate as Argentina, Britain, the Netherlands, and Poland.[75] Despite all this, the attitude of Pius XI towards the Malines Conversations seems to have been initially benign, even supportive at the beginning of his pontificate. When Mercier had an audience with the new pope in March 1922, he sought and was given assurances that the Vatican was happy for him to continue with the discussions. Gasparri reiterated this in a letter to Mercier:

> The Holy Father has fully approved of what your Eminence has done so far. Your task is to enlighten our brothers who are in error and moreover guide them towards the truth and unity. It is very good to carry out this work of

[73] Sastres Santos, 'La vita religiosa', 121; *Annuario Pontificio*, 1948, 674–724, lists religious orders and congregations and the date of the confirmation/revision of their statutes.

[74] ASV, AES, IV Periodo, Italia, 795, P.O., fasc. 392, f. 60.

[75] G. Caprile, SJ, 'Pio XI e la ripresa del Concilio Vaticano', LaCC, 117 anno, vol. III, 1966, 37–39.

the apostolate: indeed, it is extremely meritorious. The Apostles did not do anything else.[76]

Gasparri's apparently sanguine view of the Conversations may have been influenced by the extraordinary pronouncement of the Lambeth Conference of 1920, which set out in Latin what amounted to no less than an offer to accept conditional reordination of bishops and priests.[77] This must have made the Conversations look as if they were officially sponsored by Randall Davidson, then the archbishop of Canterbury, and that the Church of England was disposed to submit to Rome on key doctrinal issues. In reply to a letter from Archbishop Davidson, the Secretariat of State was careful not say anything which might be interpreted as recognition of Anglican orders, thus the letter was addressed to 'The very Reverend and dear Lord President'.[78] Presumably the wafer-thin justification of this extraordinary form of address was the fact that Randall had chaired the Lambeth Conference two years previously. At this stage, even Cardinal Bourne, the archbishop of Westminster and head of the English Roman Catholic hierarchy, does not appear to have been hostile to the talks.[79]

So the talks at Malines went ahead and during the second 'round', in March 1923, the original group of Frere, Armitage Robinson, Halifax, Mercier, van Roey, and Portal, was joined by Canon Hemmer and Fr Batiffol on the Catholic side, and Bishop Charles Gore and James Beresford Kidd for the Anglicans, while the archbishops of Canterbury and York gave their approval.[80] The talks went through further rounds in November 1923, May and October 1925, but by then strong opposition to them had developed within the Roman curia led by Cardinal Aidan Gasquet and, more seriously, by Cardinal Merry del Val, the Secretary of the Holy Office.[81]

Pius XI began to get cold feet, not least because of this opposition but also because of the growing disquiet of the English hierarchy. At the end of 1925, the Secretariat of State was given the very clearest indication of the attitude of the English Catholic bishops to the goings-on at Malines, in a letter from Cardinal Bourne, archbishop of Westminster. Bourne said that 'the hopes of the Anglicans are based on the false premise that, despite Infallibility and *Apostolicae Curae* of 1896, the Catholic Church will in

[76] ASV, AES, Stati Eccl., 1922–1927, P.O. 312, Chiesa Cattolica e Chiesa Anglicana, f. 66, letter of 11 April 1922.

[77] ASV, AES, Stati Eccl., 1922–1927, P.O. 312, Chiesa Cattolica e Chiesa Anglicana, f. 66, Mercier to Gasparri, 10 April 1922, 'Confidentiale. Annexe II'.

[78] ASV, AES, Stati Eccl., 1922–1927, P.O. 312, Chiesa Cattolica e Chiesa Anglicana, f. 66, letter of Gasparri.

[79] Aubert, 'Le Cardinal Mercier', 404.

[80] Aubert, 'Le Cardinal Mercier', 406–407.

[81] Aubert, 'Le Cardinal Mercier', 406–407.

some way change'.[82] Cardinal Bourne went to complain, rather bitterly, that the Conversations:

> were damaging to English Catholicism. Any attempt on the part of the Bishops and clergy to reassure their people and probable converts is discounted by the fact that they have no official information of what takes place at Malines, while the Archbishop of Canterbury and other Bishops and leaders of the Church of England are kept informed.[83]

He concluded by quite rightly pointing out that that the Anglican delegates to the talks were well aware of the divisions within their church and that they could not even be said to represent the small part of it to which they belonged.[84]

Rather cleverly, given the notoriously bad relations between Bourne and Amigo, Bishop of Southwark, Gasparri then asked the latter for his opinion. In his reply of 16 January 1926, Amigo repeated almost all of Bourne's of arguments and added that 'It is significant that the total number of conversions in England in 1924 was 441 less than in 1923. . . .'[85]

Meanwhile, other developments began to influence the Vatican: the recognition of Anglican orders by Old Catholics in the Netherlands, Germany, and Switzerland in 1925,[86] and the Church of England's growing contacts with the Orthodox world, not to mention the Anglican 'intrusion' into Palestine, which caused considerable anxiety in the Vatican (see Chapter 3). And, at the end of the year, to add to the clear sense of the growing disquiet of English Catholics towards the Conversation, the Secretariat of State learnt from the Brussels nuncio, Micara, that the French Catholic journal *Nouvelles Religieuses* had already revealed much of the substance of the Conversations. In January, Mercier died and the talks died with him. Gasparri instructed Micara:

> Your Excellency must visit the Archbishop of Malines [Van Roey, following Mercier's death] and tell him that the meetings held by the lamented Cardinal Mercier are now considered to be part of the movement of Protestant confessions seeking union with the Roman Church and that the Holy Father therefore considers that they have ceased to be opportune and desires that they should be terminated.[87]

[82] ASV, Stati Eccl., 1922–1927, P.O. 312, Chiesa Cattolica e Chiesa Anglicana, f. 66, Bourne's memorandum of 15 December 1925.

[83] ASV, Stati Eccl., 1922–1927, P.O. 312, Chiesa Cattolica e Chiesa Anglicana, f. 66, Bourne's memorandum of 15 December 1925.

[84] ASV, Stati Eccl., 1922–1927, P.O. 312, Chiesa Cattolica e Chiesa Anglicana, f. 66, Bourne's memorandum of 15 December 1925.

[85] ASV, Stati Eccl., 1922–1927, P.O. 312, Chiesa Cattolica e Chiesa Anglicana, f. 66, Bourne's memorandum of 15 December 1925, Amigo to Gasparri, 20 February 1926.

[86] Pawley, *Rome and Canterbury*, 279.

[87] ASV, Stati Eccl., 1922–1927, P.O. 312, Chiesa Cattolica e Chiesa Anglicana, f. 66 Gasparri to Micara, 15 December 1926; see also J. A. Dicks, *The Malines Conversations Re-visited*, Leuven, 1989.

The final word on ecumenical initiatives, from whatever quarter, and the death blow to all those efforts, came at the beginning of 1928 with the publication of the encyclical *Mortalium Animos*. By then, Merry del Val and his *intégriste* friends were firmly back in control of what would now be called 'ecumenical' relations, probably because, apart from anything else, Pius and Gasparri needed to have them on their side if they were to bring to a successful conclusion the ongoing negotiations with Mussolini's government to bring an end to the Roman Question (see Chapter 4) This much is clear from decisions of the Holy Office in 1927. One was the instruction sent out by that congregation on 8 July forbidding Catholics to attend the Lausanne Ecumenical Conference.[88] The other was the debates around decision of the Holy Office in March 1927 forbidding German Catholics from associating with the Chiesa Alta Ecumenica, literally 'the Ecumenical High Church', an initiative of elements within the Evangelical Lutheran Church.[89] Mgr Pacelli had reported in detail from Berlin on the organization and its links with Catholic clergy.[90] In his seven-page report to the cardinals of the congregation Merry del Val argued that the Alta Chiesa Ecumenica was merely a symptom of some very serious developments: 'we have to acknowledge the influence of many errors . . . of dogmatic liberalism and modernism in all its forms—today the question is assuming huge importance and we must recognise it as a most grievous threat'.[91] He drew particular attention to what he described as the 'unionist' movements in Germany, Britain, and America, and mentioned the 'Parliament of Religions' in Chicago 1893 at which Cardinal Gibbons, two Catholic bishops, Gladstone, 'and his friend the Abbot Tosti' had been present; the 'Faith and Order Congress of 1914; the Stockholm and Lausanne conferences after the war; and 'the solemn Lambeth Appeal of 1920 . . . by 250 pseudo-bishops'.[92] He did not mention Mercier's visit to the Episcopal Church Convention in 1919, but his friend in Boston, Cardinal O'Connell, had undoubtedly told him about this and other untoward incidents during the Belgian cardinal's stay in America (see Chapter 3). His report ended by requesting that 'the Holy Father, when he judges it opportune, should publish a doctrinal Encyclical on the Unity, indeed I would say, uniqueness, of the

[88] Oliver Tompkins, 'The Roman Catholic Church', in Rouse and Neill (eds), *History of the Ecumenical Movement*, ch. 15, 682.

[89] ACDF, RV 1927, 28 Alta Chiesa Ecumenica, Fascicolo, 'Pareri Degli Eminentissimi Cardinali', Feria IV, 9 March 1927, Relazione sull'Alta Chiesa Ecumenica (in Germania).

[90] ACDF, RV 1927, 28 Alta Chiesa Ecumenica, Fascicolo, 'Pareri Degli Eminentissimi Cardinali', Feria IV, 9 March 1927, Relazione sull'Alta Chiesa Ecumenica (in Germania)., despatch no. 36374, Berlin, 15 November 1926.

[91] ACDF, RV 1927, 28 Alta Chiesa Ecumenica, Fascicolo, 'Pareri Degli Eminentissimi Cardinali', Feria IV, 9 March 1927, Relazione sull'Alta Chiesa Ecumenica (in Germania), Feria IV, 9 Marzo 1927, Relazione sull'Alta Chiesa Ecumenica (in Germania), 1.

[92] ACDF, RV 1927, 28 Alta Chiesa Ecumenica, Fascicolo, 'Pareri Degli Eminentissimi Cardinali', Feria IV, 9 March 1927, Relazione sull'Alta Chiesa Ecumenica (in Germania), 3–4.

visible Church'.[93] In this he was joined by the voices of the other cardinals present, and this is what probably led to the penning of *Mortalium Animos*.

Certainly, *Mortalium Animos* dismissed all ecumenical initiatives and movements as essentially expressions of 'Pan-Christianity', that is, religious indifferentism or even simply atheism, without any attempt to differentiate between them, and in particular to give any especial value to the Malines Conversations.[94] The concept of 'the one true church' was repeated throughout the encyclical like a mantra, and the absolute teaching authority of the Roman pontiff was reiterated with a thunderous clarity approaching Boniface VIII's claim that it was necessary to be subject to the Holy See in order to be saved.[95] And that necessarily meant that Christian believers must accept 'the Conception of the Mother of God without stain of sin with the same faith as they believe that the mystery of the August Trinity, and the Incarnation of Our Lord just as they do the infallible teaching authority of the Roman Pontiff. . . .'[96] In these circumstances, all that was left for errant and separated brethren was 'to draw nigh to the Apostolic See.[97]

Mortalium Animos naturally resulted in much disappointment, even bitterness, in non-Catholic circles. Though the leaders of the ecumenical movement decided not to formulate an official reply to it, Archbishop Söderblom of Uppsala, perhaps the most important of them, did write a response not only criticizing the style of the encyclical and its content, but also contrasting the Roman Catholic response to the ecumenical movement unfavourably with that of the Orthodox churches, especially the Ecumenical patriarchate.[98] There was also disappointment among some Catholics, most notably those already engaged in ecumenical activities, like the abbey of Chevetogne in Belgium, which had a particular interest in the Oriental churches.[99]

Bourne was probably almost certainly right to conclude that the Malines Conversations were doomed because Halifax, Frere, and the other Anglicans were representative of only a small fraction of Anglicans and they were in no way officially authorized by Canterbury to treat on its behalf: it is also inconceivable that the evangelical wing of Anglicanism, that is, the more Reformed element in the Church which was probably in a majority, was ever going to accept some sort of submission to Rome: the archbishop of Canterbury's hesitations in 1925 were proof of this.[100] On the other hand, there was clearly ignorance, naiveté, and some self-delusion on the part of Mercier and the

[93] ACDF, RV 1927, 28 Alta Chiesa Ecumenica, Fascicolo, 'Pareri Degli Eminentissimi Cardinali', Feria IV, 9 March 1927, Relazione sull'Alta Chiesa Ecumenica (in Germania), 5.

[94] Carlen, *Papal Encyclicals*, III, 313–314.

[95] Carlen, *Papal Encyclicals*, III, 317.

[96] Carlen, *Papal Encyclicals*, III, 317.

[97] Carlen, *Papal Encyclicals*, III, 318.

[98] Tompkins, 'The Roman Catholic Church', 684.

[99] Tompkins, 'The Roman Catholic Church', 684.

[100] Aubert, 'Le Cardinal Mercier', 416.

other Catholic participants, and this meant that whatever agreement might have been arrived at would never have been acceptable in Rome. But the failure of Malines was also due in large part to the presence of Cardinal Merry del Val in the Holy Office. The man who had undoubtedly helped to produce the decree *Apostolicae Curae*,[101] which in 1896 condemned Anglican orders as 'utterly void and invalid', and issued uncompromising condemnations of 'modernism' in the reign of Pius X, was not going to permit any compromises with Anglicanism in the 1920s, or any other non-Catholic-inspired ecumenical initiatives.

Mortalium Animos also ruled out *any* form of cooperation with non-Catholic Christians, particularly over such burning questions of international relations and the pursuit of peace and social justice, throughout the 1930s. This precluded Catholic participation in the conferences of the 'Life and Work' movement, an ecumenical initiative the Vatican viewed with some suspicion, and the 'Faith and Order' conference in Lausanne, both in 1927. When the French theologian, Yves Congar, requested Vatican permission to attend the conference, at which William Temple, archbishop of Canterbury, the Swedish Bishop Aulén, the Swiss theologian Karl Barth, and the Orthodox theologian Bulgakov were going to be present, he was reminded that, according to the Decree of the Holy Office of 4 July 1919, 'De participatione catholicorum societatis *Ad procurandam christianitatis unitem*', Catholics could only take part in such meetings as private persons, simple observers, or as journalists.[102] He did go; Christopher Dawson, editor of *The Tablet*, attended and gave a paper at the Oxford Conference in 1937; and four Roman Catholic priests attended the Edinburgh Conference of 1937 as 'private observers'.[103] When, as a result of the two 1937 conferences, it was decided to form the World Council of Churches in 1939, Dr Temple, archbishop of York, wrote a courtesy letter to Pacelli as Secretary of State, informing him of the development and requesting continued communication. Pacelli's successor, Cardinal Maglione, instructed the Apostolic Delegate in Britain, Mgr Godfrey, to tell Temple that the Vatican would be happy for confidential relations to continue with English bishops.[104] So, by the end of Pius XI's pontificate, some ecumenical communication, albeit more with the periphery than the centre, had been established with the Roman Catholic Church.

[101] For *Apostolicae Curae*, see Pawley, *Rome and Canterbury*, ch. 2.

[102] ASV, AES, Stati Eccl., 1922–1927, P.O. 312, Chiesa cattolica e Chiesa Anglicana, f. 72, reply from Secretariat of State of 8 April 1937, to Fr. Congar, who had asked permission to attend a 'Faith and Order' conference in Lausanne.

[103] Tompkins, 'The Roman Catholic Church', 686.

[104] Tompkins, 'The Roman Catholic Church', 686.

THE AFFAIR OF 'AMICI D'ISRAELE' AND VATICAN ATTITUDES TO THE JEWS

It is undoubtedly in the light of the Vatican's negative reaction to Anglican and other ecumenical movements and initiatives in the first half of the 1920s that the curious affair of the Amici d'Israele should be interpreted. The Amici d'Israele was an international organization in good standing with the Vatican, which numbered priests, prelates, and even cardinals of the Holy Roman Church (including Rafael Merry del Val) among its members. The movement, as well praying for the conversion of the Jews, advocated greater understanding of the position of the Jews among Catholics.[105] In particular, the society proposed a change in the wording of Good Friday Liturgy, that of the eighth prayer, *Pro Conversione Judaeorum* ('For the Conversion of the Jews'), which speaks of the 'perfidious Jews'.[106] This, or a delation by an unsympathetic observer, prompted a thoroughgoing investigation of the society by the Holy Office.[107] The results were catastrophic for the Amici d'Israele, leading to a decree of dissolution being published against it in March 1928.[108]

The rejection of the plea for the removal of the offending prayer, and the decision to disband the organization, was prompted by what were seen as quasi-heretical elements in its publications. These tended to diminish or dismiss the differences between Jewish and Christian belief to the point where they claimed that Jews, like Christians, could share in the Kingdom of God, prompting the exasperated comment of one consultor of the Holy Office that, 'It is inconceivable that those who crucified Christ can belong to the kingdom of the Eternal Father.'[109] Bearing in mind all of Pius XI's claims, that the Roman Catholic Church was the New People of God, under a New Covenant, and so on, it was not surprising that he and the Holy Office of Merry del Val should have regarded the efforts of the Amici D'Israele to promote an 'ecumenical' understanding between Jews and Christians as being as dangerous as the ecumenical initiatives of non-Catholic Christians. It is no coincidence that the decree of dissolution should have been published within a few weeks of the publication of *Mortalium Animos*.

[105] See ACDF, Rerum Variorum, n. 2 (Prot. 125/28), Amici d'Israele.

[106] For the text of the prayer, see *Ordo Hebdomadae Sanctae Instauratus*, Vatican City, 1956, 91: this is the Good Friday Liturgy as revised by Pius XII, but the wording remained the same as in his predecessor's pontificate.

[107] ACDF, RV, S.O. 125/1928.

[108] ACDF, RV, S.O. 125/1928, Suprema Sacra Congregazione del Sant'Uffizio, Progetto di Decreto, Pro Feria IV, 14 March 1928.

[109] ACDF, RV, S.O. 125/1928, 13.

Hubert Wolf reads the Amici D'Israele Affair in an essentially anti-Semitic key.[110] Pius XI's anxiety to include a section to the decree condemning anti-Semitism suggests otherwise. They were, in any case, other factors at work. The Amici D'Israele condemnation was motivated by theological concerns, not very different in nature from the theological basis of Catholic prejudices against the Anglican, Lutheran, Reformed, and Orthodox churches. In all probability, the Vatican was also influenced by suspicions regarding the personal behaviour of leading figures in Amici D'Israele.[111]

RELATIONS WITH THE EASTERN CHURCHES ('UNIATE' AND SCHISMATIC)

Pius XI's policy towards the Eastern churches, both those in communion with Rome and the 'schismatics' did not differ markedly from that of Benedict. Like his predecessor, Pius XI carefully cultivated relations with those churches in communion with Rome, hence his elevation of two of the leaders of those churches to the cardinalatial purple (Chapter 4). In 1923 Pius took advantage of the 300th anniversary of the martyrdom of St Josaphat of Polotsk to laud the apostolic zeal of the bishops of churches in communion with Rome.[112] Five years later he followed this up with an encyclical, *Rerum Orientalium* of September 1928, in which he announced that the Institute of Oriental Studies was to be transferred to a location close to the Università Gregoriana and asked that all bishops send at least one priest to train at the Institute.[113] But caring for the non-Latin rite Catholics was not easy. Mgr Angelo Roncalli had a difficult task tending the small Greek, as well as Latin, Catholic communities in Bulgaria, Greece, and Turkey successively.[114] Eastern churches in communion with Rome were not popular in those countries with an Orthodox majority—like Bulgaria and Greece (see Chapter 6) but also Romania and Yugoslavia—hence the strenuous efforts made by the Holy See during this pontificate to provide them with the protection of a concordat (see Chapter 6). The problems created by the anti-Polish attitude of the Greek Catholics in western Ukraine also alarmed the Vatican, which clashed with the Polish government as a result (Chapter 6). And policies pursued by the Vatican under Pius XI

[110] Hubert Wolf, *Pope and Devil: The Vatican's Archives and the Third Reich*, trans. Kenneth Kronenberg, Cambridge, MA, and London, 2010, ch. 2.

[111] See Theo Salemink, 'Cardinal Willem van Rossum and Amici Israel (1926–28): The Conversion of Jews and the Debate on Zionism', in Poels et al. (eds), *Life with a Mission*, 172–186.

[112] Carlen, *Papal Encyclicals*, III, 259–291.

[113] Carlen, *Papal Encyclicals*, III, 329–334.

[114] See Hebblethwaite, *John XXIII*, chs 7, 8, and 9.

threatened to alienate some of the heads of the Oriental churches, in particular the decision to establish a single Code of Canon Law for those churches in parallel with that for the Latin Church. Some of the Eastern patriarchs, like the Maronite and Melkite, resisted codification seeing it as 'Latinization' and an encroachment upon their autonomy, which it was.[115] Nevertheless, though Pius XI wanted legal uniformity, he also genuinely wished to preserve 'diversity of rites'.[116] Despite all these difficulties, in 1929, following the *ad limina* visits of Armenian and Ruthenian bishops, in his encyclical *Quinquagesimo Ante*, he exclaimed that 'the Eastern Church draws nearer'.[117]

Pius also persisted in the policy of trying to bring the Orthodox masses, and clergy, back to Rome. *Rerum Orientalium* was much about the 'Schismatic' churches as those in communion with Rome, thus Pius talked enthusiastically about the unifying role of 'the Holy Eucharist and devotion to the Blessed Virgin', and declared, 'We invite most sincerely the Schismatics to join Us in this Unity of the Church.'[118] In the Balkans, he continued to hope for mass conversions or the possibility of corporate reunion with local autocephalous Orthodox churches, even when confronted by the implacable hostility of their leaders, and the scepticism of Mgr Roncalli.[119] His own intransigent attitude towards mixed marriages did not help. He thundered against King Boris of Bulgaria, who, having married Princess Giovanna of Italy in a Catholic ceremony, then had a splendid, second ceremony in Sofia's Orthodox cathedral for *raison d'état* in 1930, and then compounded his sin by having his firstborn baptized in the Orthodox Church.[120] The Vatican's long-drawn out tug-of-war with Catholic King Carol of Romania over his coronation in 1922 did not improve matters (see Chapter 6).

The big prize was, of course, Russia, but as the years passed the Russian Orthodox Church showed no more propensity to draw nearer to Rome than the Bolshevik regime a desire to desist from the persecution of Catholics. The Vatican's successful efforts to secure the freedom of Russian patriarch Tikhon and pardons from the Turkish authorities for various metropolitans earned it little credit in the world of Orthodoxy.[121] Part of the problem was the aggressive and polemical attitude towards the Russian Orthodox Church of Jesuit father Michel D'Herbigny, whom Pius put in charge of

[115] Giovanni Coco, 'Pio XI e l'Unità dei Cristiani. Le chiese d'Oriente', in De Rosa and Cracco (eds), *Il Papato*, 286–287.

[116] Coco, 'Pio XI e l'Unità dei cristiani', 286–287.

[117] Carlen, *Papal Encyclicals*, III, 347.

[118] Carlen, *Papal Encyclicals*, III, 262–263.

[119] See Angelo Giuseppe Roncalli (Pope John XXIII), *Edizione nazionale dei diari di Angelo Giuseppe Roncalli-Giovanni XXIII*, Bologna, 2004, which shows that Roncalli was frequently at odds with the Vatican over relations with Greek rite Catholics.

[120] ASV, ARdP, Archivio della Delegazione di Bulgaria, 1210, Busta 4, Titolo III, Segreteria di stato, fasc. 1 deals with Boris's marriage and the baptism of his child; see also Hebblethwaite, *John XXIII*, 137–140.

[121] Coco, 'Pio XI e l'Unità dei cristiani', 268 and 278–279.

the Russian mission in 1922: D'Herbigny had no respect for the Orthodox bishops or clergy and his activities in Russia inevitably brought the charge of proselytism upon the Catholic Church—(see Chapter 6).[122] D'Herbigny was also abrasive in his relations with Benedictine abbot Lambert Beaduin, one of the pioneers of the Liturgical Movement and an exponent of a more 'softly, softly' approach to improving relations with the Orthodox.[123] The fact that Beaudouin, who had originally been charged by Pius XI to found an 'ecumenical' monastery, first at Amay and then Chevotogne, and an ecumenical journal, *Irénikon*, fell out of favour in Rome in 1931 can largely be attributed to D'Herbigny.[124] In 1934, D'Herbigny, in his turn, fell out of favour. The Russicum was put into the hands of Mgr Tardini, and Eugène Tisserant, formerly Vatican Librarian, took over the Congregation for the Oriental churches, signalling a change of tack in attitudes towards the Orthodox.[125]

In all of his encyclicals, allocutions, and letters on the persecution of the Church in Russia, there were constant references to separated brethren and prayers for conversion. But by the end of his reign, Pius XI was hardly any nearer to a reconciliation with the schismatic Eastern churches than he had been at the beginning. His only crumb of comfort was that, in 1930, after five years of negotiations, a group of 10,000 Malabar (Indian) Christians entered into communion with Rome as the Malankarese Church.[126]

FAITH AND MORALS

The pontificate of Pius XI, unlike those of either Pius IX, who proclaimed the dogmas of the Immaculate Conception of Mary and Papal Infallibility, or Pius XII, who promulgated the dogma of the bodily assumption of the Blessed Virgin into heaven, made no new doctrinal definitions. But the proposals from his ecclesiastical consultors envisaged placing on the agenda of a recalled Vatican Council calls for a further definition of the role of Mary in the 'economy of salvation', in particular a declaration of her role as a universal mediator with her son, and the question of her assumption into heaven. But the recalled council did not, of course, take place.[127] Pius XI did make several allusions to Mary's role as universal mediator in his encyclical on the

[122] Coco, 'Pio XI e l'Unità dei cristiani', 273.

[123] *NCE*, 2, 199–200: Beaudouin, Lambert, 1873–1960.

[124] Coco, 'Pio XI e l'Unità dei Cristiani', 274.

[125] Coco, 'Pio XI e l'Unità dei cristiani', 275.

[126] E.A. Livingstone (ed.), *Oxford Dictionary of the Christian Church*, 3rd edn, Oxford, 1997, 1024; ODCC hereafter.

[127] Caprile, 'Pio XI', 31–33.

rosary, *Ingravescentibus Malis* of September 1937.[128] As well as being a homily on the 'excellencies' of the rosary, the encyclical is a thinly disguised attack upon both Soviet Communism and German National Socialism, against which he invokes the protection of the Virgin Mary, reminding his readers of the exaltation of her role as mediator with her son for all Christians by St Bernard, who said, 'Such is the will of God, who has wished that we should have all things through Mary',[129] and her invocation by Pope St Pius V for aid against the Turks before the Battle of Lepanto in 1571.[130] Speaking of his recovery from the grave illness which he suffered, Pius XI attributed it to St Teresa of Lisieux, but added, 'But We know that everything, though, that everything comes to us from Almighty God through the hands of Our Lady.'[131] *Ingravescentibus Malis* was Pius XI's last encyclical, which raises the question of whether, had he lived, he would eventually have made an important pronouncement about Marian dogma.

But it was in the area of morals that he did make a major intervention: his encyclical on Christian marriage and related matters, *Casti Connubii* of 1930.[132] Leo XIII's *Arcanum Divinae Sapientiae*, 1880, was the first papal encyclical on marriage, but neither of his successors had seen fit to make a major public declaration on this matter, so one is obliged to ask why Pius XI thought it necessary to do so. The answer would appear to lie in the social/cultural developments taking place in Europe in the decade following the end of the First World War. As a result of the exigencies of total war women had been called out of the private sphere of the home into many jobs—usually menial and labouring—to take the place of men called to the front. Following the war, many refused to give up the independence which paid work had given them and demanded political acknowledgement of their contribution to the war effort in the form of admission to the suffrage: they were successful in Britain, Germany, and the USA, but not in France or Italy. Under the Weimar Republic and also in Britain women also achieved some parity with men and restrictions on both divorce and contraception were relaxed in both countries. And in Russia, under the first wave of Bolshevik reform after 1917, there was a wholesale emancipation of women, a liberalization of divorce laws, and decriminalization of abortion and homosexuality. Even if, as Sheila Fitzgerald says,[133] the party was perhaps more conservative than young Bolsheviks in matters of sexual mores and the family, from the outside it looked as if Soviet Russia had embarked upon a systematic destruction of the 'bourgeois' family and essentially patriarchal relationship between men

128 Carlen, *Papal Encyclicals*, III, 563–566.
129 Carlen, *Papal Encyclicals*, III, 564.
130 Carlen, *Papal Encyclicals*, III, 563.
131 Carlen, *Papal Encyclicals*, III, 566.
132 For the text, see Carlen, *Papal Encyclicals*, III, 391–414.
133 S. Fitzgerald, *The Russian Revolution*, 2nd edn, Oxford, 1994, 86.

and women, thus eliciting a condemnation from Pius XI, in his encyclical, of the social policies of Soviet Communism.[134]

But a factor which must have influenced the timing of the publication of the encyclical was almost certainly the Lambeth Conference of bishops of the Anglican Communion in 1930. In its final report, Lambeth asserted that where there is 'a clearly felt obligation to limit or avoid parenthood, and where there is a morally compelling reason for avoiding complete abstinence . . . other methods may be used'.[135] Given Pius XI's concern about the ecumenical initiatives being pursued by Anglicans towards the Lutheran, Old Catholic, and Orthodox churches in the 1920s, he must have thought that the Lambeth declaration necessitated him making a solemn restatement of traditional Catholic teaching on contraception at this time. This much is clear from one of the key paragraphs of the encyclical, in which he condemned contraception as 'frustrating the marriage act' and declared:

> Since, therefore, openly departing from uninterrupted Christian tradition some recently have judged it possible solemnly to declare another doctrine regarding this question, the Catholic Church . . . through Our mouth proclaims anew: any use whatsoever of matrimony exercised in such a way that the act is deliberately frustrated . . . is an offence against the law of God. . . .[136]

Pius's only concessions to modern practices were an acceptance of the legitimacy of sexual intercourse during the woman's infertile period, and of the so-called 'rhythm method' of contraception.[137] Despite this nod towards a legitimate form of 'birth control', the Vatican during the pontificate of Pius XI remained deeply uneasy about the so-called 'rhythm method' and particularly concerned about the diffusion of information about the method, even in elements of the Catholic press in America where, given the impact of the Great Depression, family planning was a serious issue.[138] In 1936 the Holy Office conducted an enquiry into the phenomenon and decreed that Catholic publications should not publish information about the method and that it should only be resorted to in extreme circumstances.[139] The Apostolic Delegate in Washington conveyed the decision of the Holy Office to the head of the Administrative Committee of the US National Catholic Welfare Conference for diffusion among the hierarchy.[140]

[134] Carlen, *Papal Encyclicals*, III, 406.

[135] As cited in ODCC, 410.

[136] Carlen, *Papal Encyclicals*, III, 399–400.

[137] Carlen, *Papal Encyclicals*, III, 399–400.

[138] See Lucia Pozzi, 'The Problem of Birth Control in the United States under the Papacy of Pius XI', in C. R. Gallagher, D. I. Kreutzer, and A. Melloni (eds), *Pius XI and America: Proceedings of the Brown University Conference (Providence, October 2010)*, Zurich and Berlin, 2012, 227.

[139] ACDF, Rerum Variarum, 1936, 2 (407/1934).

[140] Pozzi, 'The Problem of Birth Control', 228.

Abortion was even more firmly condemned in the encyclical, along with sterilization and the prohibition of marriage on eugenic grounds.[141] Pius made clear his doubts about the theory and practice of eugenics in general.[142] The Vatican was especially alarmed by attempts to pass sterilization bills in Britain in 1935,[143] and in Uruguay in 1936.[144] In the latter country, there was a further attempt to introduce a law on euthanasia in 1937 and also one for a compulsory certificate giving a clear bill of health to couples based on prenuptial health tests in 1938: there was also a parliamentary discussion of voluntary euthanasia again in Britain in 1937.[145] In both cases, Catholic Action militants allegedly helped to scupper the legislation.[146] Even in most Catholic Italy, at the height of his racialist folly in 1939, Mussolini considered introducing similar legislation.[147] Nothing came of this, whether due to pressure from the Vatican or the eventual onset of war is not clear. Naturally, the pope reaffirmed the sacredness of Christian matrimony and consequently condemned divorce, civil marriage, and also 'mixed marriages', that is, those between Catholics and non-Catholics.[148]

Given its subject matter, the encyclical inevitably touched on the role and rights of women, an issue which was so topical in European and American society in the 1920s. While Pius stood by a fairly conservative view of women as exemplary wives and mothers, citing the famous dictum of St Paul, 'Let women be subject to their husbands', he added that, 'This subjection, however, does not deny or take away the liberty which fully belongs to the woman, both in view of her dignity as a human person and in view of her office as a wife and mother and companion. . . .'[149] One is led to the conclusion that the position of Pius XI on the 'woman question', like that of his predecessor, was a complex, nuanced one which emphasized her pre-eminent role as wife and mother, but conceded her rights as a member of society beyond the family, while condemning the 'exaggerated liberty' of female emancipation.[150] This would explain the presence of three women in the 'entourage' which he brought from Milan in 1922. Two of them were leaders of Italian Catholic Action, prompting Francesco Casella, historian of ACI, to comment that 'at

[141] Carlen, *Papal Encyclicals*, III, 396 and 401.

[142] Carlen, *Papal Encyclicals*, III, 401–402.

[143] ASV, AES, IV Periodo, Gran Bretagna, Progetto di Sterilizzazione, 1935; see also SCHA, St Andrews and Edinburgh, 29/91 Scottish Hierarchy Minute Book, 18 October 1934, Sterilisation.

[144] ASV, AdRP, Uruguay, 1236, Archivio di Mons. Filippo Cortesi, fasc. 22, 'Unione Civica contro progetto di legge per libero aborto e l'eutanasia (1931–36)'.

[145] ASV, AES, IV Periodo, Gran Bretagna, Progetto di Sterilizzazione etc.

[146] ASV, AdRP, Archivio di Mons. Giuseppe Fietta (1936–1939), fasc. 35, Situazione politica nell'Uruguay dal 1937 al 1939.

[147] This information was supplied to me by my Oxford DPhil student, Ms Meredith Carew.

[148] Carlen, *Papal Encyclicals*, III, 404.

[149] Carlen, *Papal Encyclicals*, III, 395.

[150] Carlen, *Papal Encyclicals*, III, 395.

his command, women acquired roles and functions which they had never had before'.[151] The third was his housekeeper.

THE CHRISTIAN EDUCATION OF YOUTH

Pius XI's concern about the preservation of the purity of Catholic doctrine extended to its teaching. Thus, in January 1935 he issued a decree on the matter. Surprisingly, he did not carry forward Benedict and Gasparri's initiative for a catechism for the universal Church. Five years earlier, he had already published a major encyclical on the Christian education of youth—*Divini Illustri Magistri*, otherwise known as *Rappresentanti in Terra*.[152] This encompassed much bigger issues than the teaching of the catechism, touching on the respective rights of the family, the Church, and the State in the education of young people and also the kinds of education to be imparted to them. Basing his argument upon notion of the superiority of the Church to the State and its role as a 'supernatural mother', Pius proclaimed the prior rights of the Church to the education of youth, a right shared, naturally, with the family.[153] In a passage that was clearly designed to contest the totalitarian pretensions of the Soviet, Italian Fascist, and Mexican regimes, he declared that:

> they would be in open contradiction with it [right reasoning] who dared maintain that the children belong to the State before they belong to the family and that the State has an absolute right over their education.[154]

Given the situation at this time in Mexico, where the anti-clerical state preached secularism in its schools, which Catholic children were obliged to attend, this statement should also be read as an attempt to bolster the resistance of Catholic parents there.[155] Pius went on to define quite precisely the rights and duties in the sphere of education, so that there be no doubt as to the prior claims of the Church and the family.[156]

Pius also took the opportunity to denounce various educational theories and practices that were spreading in both America and Europe in the post-war period such as 'pedagogic naturalism', which was becoming fashionable at this time, 'co-education', and sex education, against whose dangers he inveighed.[157] Consequently, he dwelt at length upon the benefits of Catholic schools, urging parents to make monetary sacrifices in support of them, and warning that not to send children to them where they were

[151] M. Casella, *Azione Cattolica nell'Italia contemporanea (1919–1969)*, Rome, 1992, 181.
[152] Carlen, *Papal Encyclicals*, III, 352–372.
[153] Carlen, *Papal Encyclicals*, III, 55–56.
[154] Carlen, *Papal Encyclicals*, III, 358.
[155] Carlen, *Papal Encyclicals*, III, 364.
[156] Carlen, *Papal Encyclicals*, III, 358–361.
[157] Carlen, *Papal Encyclicals*, III, 362–363.

available, especially in 'other countries of mixed creeds', meant running the risk of mortal sin.[158] 'Segregated' Catholic education was obviously a more and more attractive proposition to a Church faced by rampant secularism and anti-clericalism. For the same reason, the establishment of Catholic universities accelerated during Pius XI's pontificate, no less than five being canonically erected between 1922 and1939—Lublin (Poland), Bogota (Colombia), Montreal (Canada), Nijmegen (Netherlands), and Santiago (Chile)—to add to the thirteen existing ones.[159] Catholic universities provided all sorts of benefits to the Church—a 'safe' environment for Catholic undergraduates, a training ground for Catholic teachers, and, in the 'schools of Catholic Action' which were often attached to them, a nursery for a future Catholic political class.

LITURGY AND SACRED ART

Pius XI took no major initiatives in the realm of Liturgy. As has been seen, his handling of the Amici d'Israele demand for the alteration of the Good Friday Liturgy suggests that he was happy to leave well alone. His only public pronouncement on the Liturgy was the papal bull *Divini cultus* of December 1928, in which he sought to reinforce the instructions for the use of music in the Liturgy laid down by Pius X in 1906, banning 'profane' music from churches and restoring the Gregorian chant (see Chapter 1) Seminaries were to provide instruction for would-be priests in the use of Gregorian chant, sung offices were to be restored in major basilicas, cathedrals, and monastic churches, with a choirmaster and boys' choirs.[160] The emphasis was to be on the human voice rather than musical instruments and, when the latter were employed, the organ was to have pride of place.[161]

Pius had very strong views on another liturgical–aesthetic issue—sacred art. In an allocution of 27 October 1932, at the opening of the Vatican picture gallery created by Milanese architect Luca Beltrami, he took a very strong stand against 'modern' sacred art. He denounced, 'so-called works of sacred art, which certainly do not evoke the sacred if only/indeed they deform the object into a caricature and even into a profanation of itself... Our hope, Our ardent wish is that such art is not allowed into Our churches.'[162] It is not known what he thought of the presence in the Exhibition of Sacred Art, which was

[158] Carlen, *Papal Encyclicals*, III, 362–363.
[159] *Annuario Pontificio*, 1948, 896–899.
[160] Bellocchi, *Tutte le Encicliche*, XI, 257–260.
[161] Bellocchi, *Tutte le Encicliche*, XI, 261–262.
[162] Bellocchi, *Tutte le Encicliche*, XI, 185.

held in Rome the same year, of a section on 'Futurist Sacred Art'. Given the notorious anti-clericalism, if not atheism, of Filippo Marinetti, the leader of the Italian Futurists, it is not likely that he would have been impressed.[163] His horror of modern art was shared by his Secretary of State. Cardinal Pacelli made very clear in a letter to the nuncio in Brussels, Mgr Micara, that he did not approve of the Art Deco style employed in *De Jonge Werkman* (the Young Workman), one of the publications of Belgian Catholic youth organizations, they were 'too modern', 'too Nordic'.[164] Papa Ratti's taste in architecture was as conservative as in the other arts. He favoured a neo-classical style, not very different from that adopted by Fascism though sometimes heavier and more pompous, examples of which can be seen in and around the Vatican, on the Janiculum hill, and, worst of all, in the Palazzo di San Calisto in Trastevere, not to mention the rather podgy, diluted classicism of the church of San Roberto Bellarmine in the fashionable Parioli district of Rome built during his pontificate, which became the titular church of Pope Francis I when he was a cardinal. We can be sure that Pius would *not* have approved of the stark, pioneering modernism of the churches being built in the 1920s and 1930s by the German architect Rudolf Schwartz.[165]

DEVOTIONS, BEATIFICATIONS, AND CANONIZATIONS

If it can be concluded that Papa Ratti was fairly conservative in his liturgical and artistic tastes, then he was also such in regard to the extra-liturgical devotions practised in the Church. Apart from a fervent devotion to the Eucharist, which he would commend repeatedly to clergy and laity alike throughout his pontificate, his own spiritual life had been characterized from when he was a young priest in Milan by the use of the Spiritual Exercises of St Ignatius Loyola.[166] Two years after his election to the papal throne, he commended the Spiritual Exercises in his apostolic letter *Meditantibus Nobis*, of 3 December 1923, for use by both clergy and laity,[167] and again in his encyclical *Mens Nostra* of December 1929.[168]

[163] See C. Adams, 'Leap of Faith: Futurism, Fascism and the "Manifesto of Futurist Sacred Art"', *Piety and Pragmatism: Spiritualism in Futurist Art*, catalogue of the Exhibition at the Estorick Gallery, London, 2007, 44–45 and 106.

[164] ASV, AES, IV Periodo, Stati Eccl. (1931–1939), Olanda, 72, 31, 1936–1940, GOC—De Jonge Werkman.

[165] See P. Hammond (ed.), *Towards a Church Architecture*, London, 1962, 129–133.

[166] Chiron, *Pio XI*, 61.

[167] Bellocchi, *Tutte le Encicliche XII*, 33–40.

[168] Carlen, *Papal Encyclicals*, III, 333–343.

'Prayer, prayer, and prayer' should have been Papa Ratti's motto, and he devoted a whole encyclical, *Miserentissimus Redemptor* of May 1928, to the efficacy of prayers of reparation to the Sacred Heart of Jesus for the assaults upon the Church in different parts of the world by 'wicked men'.[169] In his last encyclical, *Ingravescentibus Malis*, he also urged upon the faithful, especially married couples, the efficacy of daily recital of the rosary as an antidote to the evils and perils of the world, especially those posed by atheistic Communism and pagan Nazism.[170] His only 'novelty' was the introduction of a new feast of Christ the King to be celebrated on the last Sunday of October.[171] As has been seen, the establishment of this feast had what may rightly be described as a 'political' purpose, that is, it was intended to rally and mobilize Catholics in defence of the rights of the Roman Catholic Church. But it also instituted a new devotion which took off not only among members of Catholic Action, especially the young, but Catholics generally.

Beatifications and canonizations often reveal much about a pope's priorities, particularly if his is a longish pontificate. During the course of Pius XI's pontificate there were nearly 500 beatifications and 34 canonizations, more than in any pontificate so far.[172] More important than the numbers was the fact that Pius reformed the regulations governing the processes, thus making it easier and quicker to create more *beati* and saints.[173] His clear strategy or strategies reveal, other than something about his own spirituality, his practical priorities—charitable and educational good works—and the need to fortify the faith of Catholics in 'mission' areas like North America and countries like Britain where the Church was seeking to re-establish itself. Probably the most important canonizations were those of St Thérèse of Lisieux, both because she was an especial spiritual favourite of Ratti, but also because her canonization in 1925 symbolized the Vatican's improving relationship with France, as did that of St Jean de Vianney, the 'parish priest saint'. A further 'child of France' canonized by Pius XI was Bernadette Soubirous, who had experienced the visions of the Virgin at Lourdes. Pius also canonized the first 'American' saint, St John de Brébeuf, a Jesuit missionary among the Huron, and his companions. Likewise, he canonized both Thomas More and John Fisher, martyrs of Henry VIII's Reformation, and other English martyrs of this period in 1935, which could be interpreted as a sign of his concern about the Protestant 'peril'.[174] The canonizations of Robert Bellarmine, another

[169] Carlen, *Papal Encyclicals*, III, 321–328.

[170] Carlen, *Papal Encyclicals*, III, 321–328.

[171] Carlen, *Papal Encyclicals*, III, *Quas Primas*, 277.

[172] V. Ciciliot, 'Alcuni riflessioni sui modelli di santitá nelle beatificazioni e nelle canonizzazioni di Pio XI (1922–1939)', 2, unpublished article; I am grateful to Dr Ciciliot for allowing me to read this.

[173] In the motu proprio *Giá da qualche tempo*, AAS, 22 (1930), 87–88; and *Norme servandae in costruendis processibus ordinariis in super causis historicis*, AAS, 31 (1939), 174–177.

[174] Ciciliot, 'Alcuni riflessioni', 21–22.

Jesuit, and Albert the Great, were a recognition of intellectual as well as spiritual gifts. Among the Italians who were raised to the altars were Joseph Cottolengo, who had been heavily committed to charitable and welfare work, and John Bosco, a noted educationalist, the latter canonized during the special Holy Year of 1933–4. In a rather clumsy way, the Fascists attempted to carry out a nationalistic 'appropriation' of the latter.[175]

As far as 'living saints' were concerned, unlike his successor Pius XII, Pius XI preserved a rather aloof attitude towards Padre Pio, the Franciscan friar who claimed to have the stigmata and whose cult attracted a huge following, especially in southern Italy.[176] According to Luzzatto, 'Pius XI was even more diffident (than Benedict XV) . . . In his pontificate the Vatican's severity towards padre Pio almost reached the point where he was deprived of his sacerdotal functions. In 1931 he came close to being suspended *a divinis*.'[177]

This lack of sympathy for a popular southern devotion was typical, perhaps, of the more 'intellectual', less 'emotional', religiosity of a northern Italian.

PIUS XI, THE MEDIA, AND THE MOBILIZATION OF CATHOLICS WORLDWIDE

Pius XI clearly saw the great benefits of a strong Catholic press, particularly in the battles against the Church's enemies, and for this reason he held an international conference of the Catholic Press in Rome in 1936. But there have long been suggestions that Pius XI was less comfortable with the electronic media, for example, that he never used the telephone, and these have been confirmed in part by one of his own speeches, the one which he never gave to the Italian bishops assembled in the Vatican on 11 February 1939 because of his death.[178] But that speech should be taken at its face value, as should Pius XI's unwillingness to use the telephone, which was likely to have been tactical, occasioned by his increasing, and justified, suspicions about the activities of Mussolini's secret police inside Vatican City.[179] In fact, Pius was usually quick to make use of modern inventions when the occasion presented itself; thus, he was the first among twentieth-century European monarchs to completely abandon travel by horse and carriage following an accident in 1926, and he soon found himself almost inundated with gifts from motorcar

[175] Bosworth, 'L'Anno Santo', 436.

[176] S. Luzzatto, *Padre Pio: miracoli e politica nell'Italia del novecento*, Turin, 2007, 384.

[177] Luzzatto, *Padre Pio*, 384.

[178] For the English text of the speech, see Fattorini, *Hitler, Mussolini and the Vatican*, 210–215.

[179] See Alvarez, *Spies in the Vatican*, 159–160.

manufactures, especially Italians and American.[180] Though he never set foot in one himself, he also urged missionaries to use the aeroplane.[181]

That said, though he did allow a team from Paramount News to film his inauguration of Vatican Radio, he did not use the medium of the film in the way that his successor was to do (see Chapter 8). He was very concerned about the impact of the cinema upon the morals of the faithful, especially the young. In *Divini Illustri Magistri* of 1930 he was already sounding the alarm about the dangers to youth of immoral plays and films,[182] and in 1936 he wrote a full-blown encyclical, *Vigilanti Cura*, to the American hierarchy on the movie industry.[183] In it, Pius praised the initiative taken by US Catholics in forming a 'League of Decency' to monitor and attempt to moderate the output of Hollywood, an initiative also supported by Protestants and Jews.[184] Interestingly, in his native Italy at this time the network of little parochial cinemas was screening films produced by several specifically Catholic film-making companies.[185] There would also be moves during his reign to establish a worldwide Catholic Cinema Centre on the lines of those already in existence in France and the Netherlands.[186]

Pius XI's great excursion into the world of the electronic media was reserved for the radio. On 12 February 1931, the pope inaugurated a small radio station inside Vatican City with a message in Latin.[187] Initially, however, Vatican Radio *broadcast* very little: it was largely reserved for communication with papal envoys and Catholics around the world.[188] As pleas from Catholics in various parts of the world mounted for Vatican Radio to be used to counter Communist, and later Nazi, propaganda, it was used for that, as well as, in the broadcasts in April 1937 in several languages, the text of *Mit brennender Sorge*.[189] In 1932 and 1936 the Vatican considered proposals to establish a Catholic world radio network, but nothing came of them.[190]

But Vatican Radio came into its own as a means of linking together Pius XI as Supreme Pastor with Catholics throughout the world. 'The 'pilgrim journeys' of Paul VI, John Paul II, and Benedict XVI were a long way in the future but what effectively took their place in the 1930s was the rapid development

[180] V. Moretti (ed.), *Le Auto dei Papi: Settant'anni di Automobilismo Vaticano*, Rome, 1981, 7.

[181] Sastres Santos, 'La vita religiosa', 135.

[182] Carlen, *Papal Encyclicals*, III, 167.

[183] Carlen, *Papal Encyclicals*, III, *Vigilanti Cura*, 517–523.

[184] See G. Black, *The Catholic Crusade against the Movies: 1940–1975*, Cambridge, 1997.

[185] Dunnage, *Twentieth Century Italy*, 99.

[186] ASV, AdRP, IV Periodo, Olanda, 1081A, b. 92/3, sf. Azione Cattolica, circular letter of Pizzardo nuncios, 25 March 1935, regarding proposed establishment of world Catholic cinema organization.

[187] See John F. Pollard, 'Electronic Pastors: Radio, Cinema and Television from Pius XI to John XXIII', in James Corkery and Thomas Worcester (eds), *The Papacy since 1500: From Italian Prince to Universal Pastor*, Cambridge, 2010, 182–203.

[188] Pollard, 'Electronic Pastors', 184.

[189] Pollard, 'Electronic Pastors', 187.

[190] Pollard, 'Electronic Pastors', 186.

and diffusion of the phenomenon of national or international Eucharistic Congresses—Dublin, 1932; Buenos Aires, September, and Melbourne, December 1934; Lourdes, April, Cleveland, Ohio, and Lima, September 1935; Manila, February, New Orleans, October, and Madras, December 1937; and Budapest, August 1938—as the primary means of bringing large numbers of Catholics together in different parts of the world. The advent of Vatican Radio now made it possible for Pius XI's speeches to be broadcast to the faithful present at these events during the course of his pontificate, giving them a stronger sense of belonging to the universal Church and of their closeness to the pope.

GREAT ROMAN GATHERINGS

While the great international gatherings at Eucharistic congresses were important in Pius XI's strategy of giving the world's Catholics a strong sense of identity and of allegiance to the papacy, he also sought to achieve that end through a series of gatherings held in the capital of Catholic Christianity, Rome:

1922 International Eucharistic Congress (actually planned by Benedict XV)

1. 1925 Holy Year and Missionary Exhibition;
2. 1926 International Catholic Athletic Competition (cancelled because of Fascist attacks on Catholic youth)[191]
3. 1927 Anniversary of St Francis;
4. 1929 Celebrations of the Pope's Sacerdotal Jubilee;
5. 1931 Fortieth Anniversary Celebrations of *Rerum Novarum*;
6. 1932 International Exhibition of Sacred Art;
7. 1933–4 Extraordinary Holy Year;
8. 1935 Exhibition of the Catholic Press;
9. 1936 International Congress of Catholic Nurses and Peace Congress of Catholic ex-Combatants;
10. 1937 International Congress of Catholic Doctors; and
11. 1939 International gatherings of Jeunesse Ouvriers Cretiens (Young Christian Workers) which was cancelled because of the outbreak of war and other smaller gatherings of specialist groups.

[191] ASV, AdRP, IV Periodo, Parigi, Cerretti, b. 390, press cutting, *Echo de Paris*, 5 September.

Bringing Catholics to him also offered an effective means of contesting Mussolini's attempts to 'fascistize' the Eternal City (see Chapter 4).

ROME AND THE CATHOLIC WORLD UNDER PIUS XI

Under Pius XI, and his successor, the processes of centralization and 'Romanization' in the Roman Catholic Church were accentuated. Early on his reign, the pope seems to have been concerned about any signs of 'independence' exhibited by national hierarchies, thus in 1924 Cardinal De Lai, the prefect of the Consistorial Congregation which deals with bishops, sent a letter to Mgr Pacelli, nuncio in Germany, in these terms:

> It is the intention of the Holy Father to regulate the general meetings of the Bishops so that they do not undermine the role of provincial councils and synods or become national (episcopal) councils.[192]

He added for good measure that national meetings of bishops had also been taking place in England (and Wales), of the archbishops in France, the Irish bishops at Maynooth, and American bishops in Washington.[193] In a further letter in December 1925, De Lai announced that the pope had reiterated that they must not take the place of the 'councils or conferences of bishops as established by Canon Law'.[194] It is hard to know whether these letters genuinely reflected the pope's views or whether they were coloured by De Lai's own integralist and ultramontane feelings. If the pope and De Lai were trying to emasculate embryonic national bishops' conferences then they failed. In fact, during the course of the pontificate they flourished and continued to resist encroachments on their independence, as in the case of the Irish bishops who were initially unhappy about the appointment of a papal nuncio to their country in 1929.[195] The appointment of an apostolic delegate to Britain in 1938 was similarly regarded with some misgivings on the part of the hierarchy of England and Wales, even though the *political* benefits to the Church of having some sort of Vatican representative in London were clear and, for the Scottish bishops, it ensured that the humiliation of receiving communications from the Secretariat of State via the archbishop of Westminster was

[192] ASV, AdRP, IV Periodo, Berlino-Bonn, 1196 (Nunziatura Pacelli), busta 38 Conferenze vescovili di Fulda, De Lai to Pacelli, 27 February 1924.

[193] ASV, AdRP, IV Periodo, Berlino-Bonn, 1196 (Nunziatura Pacelli), busta 38 Conferenze vescovili di Fulda, De Lai to Pacelli, 27 February 1924.

[194] ASV, AdRP, IV Periodo, Berlino-Bonn, 1196 (Nunziatura Pacelli), busta 38 Conferenze vescovili di Fulda, De Lai to Pacelli, 27 February 1924.

[195] See Keogh, *The Vatican*, 155.

ended.[196] Finally, it is hard to imagine how the German Church could have put up what limited resistance it did to the Nazi regime after 1933 without the national organization of the Fulda bishops' conference.

On the positive side, 'Romanization' was pursued by ensuring that more and more bishops had had some training in Rome and had therefore imbibed 'Roman ways'. To this end Papa Ratti established more national colleges or seminaries in Rome: the Ethiopian College (inside Vatican City) 1930, the Institute of Christian Archaeology 1925, a higher education institute for the Carmelites 1935, a training college for Dutch priests 1930, the Pio Brasiliano college 1934, the Pio Romeno 1930, a college for the special training of priests for the Russian mission (usually referred to as the Russicum) 1929, as well as rebuilding the College of Propaganda Fide on the Janiculum.

On the other hand, there is little evidence of a correspondingly greater *internationalization* of the highest echelons of the governing organs of the Church, of the better geographical representation in the Vatican. As has been seen, there was certainly no change in the composition of the College of Cardinals, Italians retaining a clear majority. Similarly, there was no increase in the numbers of non-Italians heading the congregations, offices, and tribunals of the Roman curia. Only three non-Italian cardinals held high office there in this period—Cardinal Rafael Merry del Val (British-Spanish), who was Secretary of the Holy Office between 1914 and 1930; Eugène Tisserant (French), who was responsible for the Oriental churches, and Van Rossum (Dutch) who was prefect of Propaganda from 1918 to his death in 1932.

There was, however, during Pius XI's pontificate a slow but perceptible trend towards the employment of non-Italians at lower levels of the Roman curia, especially in the Secretariat of State and the papal diplomatic corps. Several non-Italians served as papal envoys of some description: the Americans Edward Mooney, later cardinal archbishop of Detroit, as apostolic delegate in both British India and Japan in the late 1920s and early 1930s (where Joseph Hurley served with him), and John Collins, papal chargé d'affaires in Liberia in the late 1920s. Britons Arthur Hinsley and William Godfrey served as apostolic delegates in British Africa and Britain respectively, Maltese-born Caruana held the difficult job of apostolic delegate in Mexico in the 1920s, the Frenchmen Drapier and Ogè served in Indochina and Liberia respectively, the Dutchman Kierkels in British India, and the Irishman Pasquale Robinson as nuncio in Dublin. Francis Spellman, later archbishop of New York, and Joseph Hurley both worked in the Secretariat of State in the 1920s and 1930s respectively, and the latter also served as Pius XI's translator and interpreter.[197]

[196] SCHA, ED, 29/91 Scottish Hierarchy Minute Book, 29 December 1926; on the establishment of the Apostolic Delegation in Britain, see Thomas Moloney, *Westminster, Whitehall and the Vatican: The Role of Cardinal Hinsley, 1935–1943*, London, 1985, ch. 4.

[197] C. Gallagher, SJ, *Vatican Secret Diplomacy: Joseph P. Hurley and Pope Pius XII*, New Haven, CT, 2008, ch. 3.

In this way, at least, the Vatican was beginning to open up to non-Italian influences.

THE AMERICAN CHURCH AND THE VATICAN

Pius XI demonstrated a very lively interest in the life of the Church in all of the world's continents and at different moments during his reign he showed particular concern for the difficulties faced by it in countries such as France, Germany, Mexico, Poland, and Spain, but his fundamental attitude towards the national churches did not change except in one case, that of the United States of America. It is emblematic of the changing perceptions of the importance of American Catholicism that, in 1922, he modified the rules governing the conduct of future conclaves, extending the period of time that cardinals had to reach Rome from nine to eighteen days. Obviously this change benefited other cardinals resident in the Western hemisphere, but it was very much conditioned by the pleas of Cardinals Dougherty of Philadelphia and O'Connell of Boston, who had arrived too late to take part in the election of Benedict's successor. In the consistory two years later, he created three new American cardinals including, for the first time, the archbishop of Chicago, George Mundelein.

A possible explanation for this development was demographic—the Catholic population of the United States rose from 19 million in 1926 to 21 million in 1940, making it the fastest growing Catholic population outside Europe.[198] But it was not just demographics that attracted the attention of the Vatican to the American Church. A powerful consideration was monetary: from the end of the First World War American Catholics were making probably the biggest contribution to the financing of the Vatican and its worldwide projects through their diocesan collections for Peter's Pence and the American Board of Catholic Missions.[199] Cardinal George Mundelein of Chicago, the first American 'bricks and mortar' bishop, was especially generous towards the Vatican, even during the worst years of the Great Depression.[200] The Vatican came to rely heavily upon American Catholic munificence in Pius XI's reign and its expectations of American bishops are vividly illustrated by the discussions between the pope and his Under-Secretary of State, Mgr Tardini, in October 1938, about the most suitable

[198] *The Statesman's Yearbook, 1930*, London, 1930, 448; and *The Yearbook of American Religion*, New York, 1941, 136.

[199] John F. Pollard, 'American Catholics and the Financing of the Vatican in the Great Depression: Peter's Pence Payments (1935–8)', in Gallagher et al. (eds), *Pius XI and America*, 195–208.

[200] See Pollard, *Money*, 136–137 and 157–158.

candidate to fill the archbishopric of New York left vacant by the death of Cardinal Patrick Hayes.[201] During the course of the discussion, Tardini made it clear that he preferred Mgr Francis Spellman, auxiliary bishop of Boston, to the pope's favourite, Mgr John McNicholas, archbishop of Cincinnati, on the grounds that Spellman was good with money and especially at raising it whereas McNicholas had loaded his diocese with debts.[202] Cardinal Pacelli, Tardini's boss, was also for Spellman and so, after Pius XI's death and the former's election as pope, Spellman was appointed to New York and did not disappoint the expectations of the Vatican in the matter of fund-raising. Despite his doubts about Spellman, Pius XI was clearly very impressed by the generosity of Americans, thus in 1922 he publicly praised the US Senate for allocating 2.5 million lire to the relief of famine in Europe,[203] and he acknowledged the huge amounts of money which American Catholics had raised for the same effort in 1924.[204] Yet the American way of life worried the men in the Vatican. There was concern about the 'plague of divorce' in American society and the publication of *Vigilanti Cura* in 1936 showed that Pius XI believed it necessary to fortify American Catholics against the perils of the modern media. Nevertheless, by sending his Secretary of State, Cardinal Pacelli, on a visit to twelve out of the sixteen ecclesiastical provinces of the American Church in 1936, the pope manifested his recognition and blessing to American Catholics, to demonstrate that, in the eyes of the Holy See, American Catholicism had 'come of age'.

PIUS XI AND THE SCIENCES

Pius XI had a healthy respect for science and scientists—he corresponded with the astronomer Edwin Hubble and the astrophysicist Georges Lemaître, and when Professor Paul Vignon requested permission to examine the Shroud of Turin in 1936, Pius was happy to let him do so, remarking that 'faith, religion, piety (in which we are competent) are one thing, science is something else'.[205] His respect for scientists and science induced him to restart the process initiated by his predecessor of transforming the semi-moribund Pontificia

[201] See Gallagher, *Vatican Secret Diplomacy*, 111, on the matter of the Vatican and American bishops.

[202] ASV, AES, Quarto Periodo, 1922–1939, Diario di S. Ecc. Mons. Tardini dal 27 settembre al 29 ottobre, 4 October 1938.

[203] Bellocchi, *Tutte le Encicliche*, XI, *Annus Fere*, 10 July 1922, Epistola, 28.

[204] Bellocchi, *Tutte le Encicliche*, XI, *Amplissimum Conssessum*, 24 March 1924. Allocuzione, 125.

[205] As cited by Jean-Dominique Durand, 'Lo stile di governo di Pio XI', in De Rosa and Cracco (eds), *Il Papato*, 56.

Accademia dei Lincei, which had once counted Galileo amongst its members, into the Pontifical Academy of the Sciences in 1936, assigning a meeting place, the Casina, in the gardens of the Vatican City State. The Casina was a very appropriate meeting place for the new body since it had been built by Pius IV (1558–62) as a venue for academic discussions with philosophers and poets.[206]

Pius XI had already given signs of his determination to renovate the Lincei by appointing Fr Gemelli as its president following the death of Gianfranceschi in 1934.[207] The choice of Gemelli was an interesting one. A friend of Ratti's from his Milanese period, Gemelli shared the same very conservative political views and authoritarian temperament. But as rector of the Catholic University of Milan and a world-recognized scientific authority, Gemelli, who was a biologist, physician, and experimental psychologist, was a prestigious figure in Italian intellectual circles. Allegedly a 'clerico-fascist',[208] he nevertheless did not take the Fascist oath imposed on Italian University professors in 1931 and so had to resign from the Consiglio Superiore dell'Educazione Nazionale, the coordinating body for Italian higher education, nor would he allow the formation of a branch of the GUF, the Fascist student organization, at the Catholic University, while he welcomed some professors to the institution who had not taken the oath in state universities.[209]

Between them, Gemelli and the pope succeeded in recruiting scientists of worldwide renown, particularly in physics, Catholic and non-Catholic alike, into membership of the Academy, which by 1939 also included Max Planck, the 'Father' of Quantum Physics. Amongst the 1936 members were a number of great names including the Norwegian mathematician, meteorologist, and geologist Koren Bjkenes, the Danish atomic physicists Vilhelm Friman and Niels Bohr, the Dutch-American physical chemist Peter Joseph Wilhelm Debye, and the British physiologist Sir Charles Scott Sherrington.[210] Fr Georges Lemaître, SJ, professor of mathematical methodology at the University of Louvain, was also recruited in 1936.[211] He would play an important role in the pontificate of Pius XII as the latter's scientific adviser (see Chapter 11). Yet, despite his already established fame for the theory of relativity, not to mention the fact that he was a mentor of Lemaître, Albert Einstein was not elected to the Academy. Einstein was not considered for election, not because he was

[206] I am grateful for this information, which was kindly supplied by the late Mr Peter James.

[207] For an account of the circumstances in which the Academy was refounded, see R. Ladous, *Des Nobels du Vatican. La fondationdde l'académie pontificale des sciences*, Paris, 1994, 30–35.

[208] A. Pellicani, *Il Papa di Tutti: La Chiesa cattolica, il Fascismo e il Razzismo*, Milan, 1964, 81–82, and Webster, *Christian Democracy and Fascism in Italy*, 155–157.

[209] Ladous, *Des Nobels du Vatican*, 68–69.

[210] See *Annuario Pontificio*, 1948, 901–908, and the *Larousse Dictionary of Scientists*, London, 1994, 57–58, 181–182, and 469–470.

[211] *Annuario Pontificio*, 1948, 906.

a Jew, but *because of his pantheistic idea of religion as a 'mystical sentiment of the universe'*.[212] Another glaring omission was Enrico Fermi, an Italian physicist who received the Nobel Prize in 1938. Fermi was not offered membership but it could not have been because he was married to a Jew because another Jew, and friend of Fermi, the Italian scientist Tullio Levi-Civita, was made a member in 1936 and had helped Pius bring the Academy into existence.[213]

Indeed, it was Pius who took the radical step of overruling Gemelli's preference for a 'club' of the international, Catholic scientific elite and instead opened it up to the cream of the scientific world regardless of religion. In the foundation of the Pontifical Academy, Pius and Gemelli were assisted by others, including Mgr Giovanni Mercati, prefect of the Vatican Library. His influence was crucial in the decision to make a break with the past and relegate the mediocrities of the Nuovi Lincei, who constituted two thirds of the membership, to the status of emeriti.[214] Pius also cut the new organization free from the control of the Roman curia, making it solely answerable to himself. This made it a much more independent and international organization, rather than a sort of curial, in-house scientific 'think tank'.[215]

The academicians caused no embarrassing controversies, and did not rock any theological or philosophical boats, even on the major issue of Darwin's theories of evolution, but Darwin remained a difficult, dangerous issue for the Church. It has never publicly and authoritatively pronounced on Charles Darwin's theories, let alone condemned them as science, in the way that it did with the theories of Galileo, in all probability precisely because it did not wish for a repeat of that unfortunate episode.[216] Nevertheless, as has been seen (Chapter 3), Darwin's theories were the subject of considerable interest to the Jesuit fathers who edited *La Civiltà Cattolica* in the early 1920s, and the Holy Office was extremely wary of those Catholic authors, especially priests, who seemed to have an easy acceptance of Darwin's ideas. Indeed, it had condemned the theological works of at least three priests whose attitude towards Darwinian theory was deemed unacceptable back in the late nineteenth century, always making a distinction between scientific hypotheses and theological or philosophical truth.[217] During the pontificate of Pius XI, the Holy Office was again called upon to deal with other such works, like that of the French Jesuit, Fr Teilhard de Chardin, who was accused of *evoluzionismo*, but no action was taken against him.[218] On the other hand, when Teilhard

[212] Ladous, *Des Nobels du Vatican*, 87.

[213] Ladous, *Des Nobels du Vatican*, 81.

[214] Ladous, *Des Nobels du Vatican*, 81.

[215] Ladous, *Des Nobels du Vatican*, 81.

[216] Though it did condemn the theories of his grandfather, see *Index Librorum Prohibitorum (SSMI. D.N. PII PPXI)*, Vatican, 1938, entry 121: Darwin, Erasmus, *Zoonomia or the laws of organic life*, 22 December 1817.

[217] See ACDF, Sezione della Censura dei Libri, N. 904/1923, Henry de Dorlodot-*Le DARWINISME au point de vue de l'orthodoxie catholique, Premiere partie. L'origine des espèces*, Bruxelles-Paris, 1921.

[218] See ACDF, Sezione della Censura dei Libri, 1931, N.1528/1931.

de Chardin and another French priest and paleontologist, Henri Breuil, were proposed by Gemelli for membership of the Pontifical Academy of Sciences in 1936, they were blackballed by the Secretariat of State, on advice received from Cardinal Baudrillart in Paris, who accused them of 'Darwinian tendencies'.[219] Teilhard de Chardin's pamphlet, 'Sur quelques représentants possibles du Péché originel' ('On some possible interpretations of original sin'), had already got him into trouble with Cardinal Merry del Val, Secretary of the Holy Office, back in 1922.[220] Another book, by Belgian priest Fr Dorlodot, allegedly advocated that 'absolute evolution' was compatible with Church teaching.[221] Though the author was ordered to withdraw his book from circulation and the publisher, no less an institution than the Catholic University of Louvain, was censured, Dorlodot was not himself publicly condemned and nor was his work placed on the Index, thanks to the intervention of Fr Gemelli, one of the consultors employed by the Holy Office.[222]

The 1920s was the decade in which the works of Sigmund Freud began to arrive in Italy. One would, therefore, have expected some response from the Holy Office, but none was forthcoming. Fr Francesco Gaetani wrote critical articles about Freud in *La Civiltà Cattolica* in 1920s and published his very critical work *Psychoanalysis* in 1925.[223] Gaetani was appalled by the emphasis on sex and managed to write about Freud while effectively holding his nose. The fact that Freud was a Jew confirmed all the Jesuit father's worst prejudices: that fact would also turn Italian Fascism against psychoanalysis after the racial 'turn' in its policies in the mid-1930s. But the prestige of Gemelli overcame the suspicion and hostility towards experimental psychology among many Catholics, though less so among Fascists.[224]

As early as 1925, Gemelli was arguing that:

> one cannot deny that Freud and Adler, from the functional point of view, have done a great service, insofar as the study of this obscure life of the instincts . . . appears much more important in demonstrating how these functions project themselves in conscious life.[225]

Whereas, as Colombo points out, 'Psychiatry and psychology were almost entirely eliminated in favour of neurology under Fascism . . .',[226] Gemelli remained open-minded, and when, in 1938, the Jewish editor of the journal *General Archives of Neurology, Psychiatry and Psychoanalysis* was forced to

[219] Ladous, *Des Nobels du Vatican*, 60. [220] Ladous, *Des Nobels du Vatican*, 60.

[221] Ladous, *Des Nobels du Vatican*, 4–5.

[222] Ladous, *Des Nobels du Vatican*, 4–5, letter of Gemelli, 17 December 1925.

[223] Daria Colombo, 'Psychoanalysis and the Catholic Church in Italy: The Role of Father Agostino Gemelli, 1925–1953', *Journal of the History of the Behavioural Sciences*, 39 (4) (Fall 2003), 333–348.

[224] Colombo, 'Psychoanalysis and the Catholic Church', 333–348.

[225] A. Gemelli, OFM, 'Le strutture e funzioni pschichiche', 88–89.

[226] Colombo, 'Psychoanalysis and the Catholic Church', 340.

sell the journal, Gemelli bought it.[227] Gemelli would, however, be less supportive of Freud in later years (Chapter 11).

'UN CONCILIO MAI CELEBRATO': PIUS XI'S PLAN TO RECALL THE FIRST VATICAN COUNCIL

At the very beginning of his pontificate, in 1922, Pius XI was so impressed by the experience of two events in Rome, the 26th International Eucharistic Congress and the celebration of the 300th anniversary of the founding of the Propaganda Fide Congregation, which brought together large numbers of bishops from all over the world, that he began seriously to consider the recall of the Council of the Vatican suspended in 1870. Thus, in his encyclical *Ubi Arcano dei Consilio* of December 1922, referring to the two gatherings, he declared that:

> [they] carried our thoughts to the possibility of another similar meeting of the whole episcopate here in the centre of Catholic unity . . . we scarcely dare include in the programme of Our Pontificate the re-assembling of the Ecumenical Council which Pius IX, the Pontiff of our youth, had called . . . We as the leader of the chosen people must wait and pray for an unmistakeable sign from the God of mercy and love of His holy will in this regard (Judges, vi, 17).[228]

He considered that 'after the holocaust of the Great War, in which Catholics found themselves on opposing sides, a Council would display and reinforce Catholic unity'.[229]

That 'unmistakeable sign' does not seem to have appeared and Pius did not recall the Council, in all probability chiefly because long and difficult negotiations with Italy for a resolution of the Roman Question took up his attention following the very arduous Holy Year of 1925, and after their successful outcome in 1929 the world presented him with a succession of increasingly intractable problems.[230] Nevertheless, the planning and consultation which the pope set in motion in1923 threw up a series of major issues which would be largely addressed in other ways during the course of his pontificate. Drawing on the list of matters with which the Council had not been able to deal before its dispersal in September 1870, the Dominican friar Edouard Hugon and the Servite priest Alexis Lépicier elaborated a massive agenda for

[227] Colombo, 'Psychoanalysis and the Catholic Church', 342.

[228] Carlen, *Papal Encyclicals*, III, 235.

[229] Hebblethwaite, *John XXIII*, 310.

[230] Caprile, 'Pio XI', 34, says that Pius XI decided to suspend the project in January 1924: see also Silvio Negri, in *La Corriere della Sera*, 27 January 1959.

a recalled Council. Of the issues hanging over from the first Vatican Council, Lépicier identified the following:

1. *De fide*, a dogmatic declaration of Catholic faith, including the Trinity, of the nature and creation of man, of man's elevation and fall (original sin), of the mystery of the incarnation, of the divine grace of the Redeemer and of the universal mediatory role of the Blessed Virgin.
2. *De Ecclesia*, of the Church as a perfect society, supernatural, visible, universal, necessary and infallible; its doctrinal, sanctifying, legislative, judicial and coercive authority and its relationship with the civil powers.[231]

To these he added issues which had emerged since 1870, like the need for a small catechism and a Code of Canon Law for the Oriental churches, a code of international law to regulate relations between states and peoples and the problems of peace and war, and finally the problem of socialism, to which he added a definition of the bodily assumption of the Blessed Virgin Mary into heaven.[232] Father Hugon added to Lépicier's list the question 'De regno socialii Domini Nostri Iesu Christi'—the social kingdom of Our Lord Jesus Christ, 'De Actione Catholicae', defining the role, structure, and function of Catholic Action and in particular the place of workers' organizations (trade unions) within this; 'De Scholis (Puerorum)' on the education of youth, particularly the necessity for religious education, the problem of co-education, and the role of the State; and, finally, 'De Officiis ac Muneribus Mulierum in Societate' on the role of women in public life in relation to their natural function.[233]

This list of 'agenda items' is striking for several reasons: firstly, it would have meant a very lengthy and protracted second meeting of a resumed First Vatican Council; secondly, in the matters of the code of international law, socialism, Catholic Action, the education of youth, and the role of women in society it was extremely responsive to the great issues thrown up by the war and its aftermath; thirdly, in many significant ways it anticipated the agenda of the Second Vatican Council between 1961 and 1965, and finally—though of course Pius XI did not actually reconvene the Council—during the course of his pontificate he actually addressed all these issues, except the catechism and a code of Canon Law for the Oriental churches,[234] in major public statements of some sort or another, particularly encyclicals.

[231] Caprile, 'Pio XI', 31. [232] Caprile, 'Pio XI', 31. [233] Caprile, 'Pio XI', 32.
[234] This project was not to be realized until the reign of John Paul II.

6

The 'Foreign Policy' of Pius XI in the 1920s

INTRODUCTION

The diplomatic policy and practice of Pius XI did not substantially differ from that of his predecessor, the continuation as Secretary of State of Cardinal Gasparri ensured that, and even when Gasparri left office and was succeeded by Cardinal Eugenio Pacelli in 1930 there was still no fundamental change of direction. The papacy continued actively to encourage peace and international reconciliation between the powers in Europe, especially between France and Germany, and Gasparri and Pius XI continued Benedict's policy of benevolence towards Germany, believing that it had been harshly treated at Versailles and that this would have serious consequences. In Europe, beyond the great power rivalries and disputes, most problems were with governments of the 'successor states', and also Italy, which were part of the aftermath of Versailles, continuing disputes over territorial changes, and the treatment of minorities. Papal diplomacy was obviously also directed towards the protection of the Church's interests in all countries, whether in Europe or overseas. As the 1920s progressed, Papa Ratti would face increasing threats from the Church's enemies on a broad front—liberal, Masonic and socialist anti-clericalism, and Communism—the problems posed by German National Socialism and Italian Fascism would materialize in the 1930s. Throughout the pontificate, the underlying strategy of Pius and his two Secretaries of State, Pietro Gasparri (1922–30) and Eugenio Pacelli (1930–9), was to defend the Church's interests by a three-pronged strategy of establishing good diplomatic relations with states, negotiating concordats, and encouraging the growth of the laypeople's organization, Catholic Action, in the countries concerned, in order to defend the Church in the public arena.

THE PAPACY, THE LEAGUE OF NATIONS, AND THE POST-WAR INTERNATIONAL SITUATION

As has been seen (Chapter 3), the Vatican had taken up a rather diffident attitude towards the League of Nations from its inception. This continued into Pius XI's pontificate. Though called upon to participate or send an observer—in itself a recognition of the Holy See's international moral stature—the Vatican refused. After 1929, it could justify this stance on the grounds of its commitment in the Lateran Treaty to neutrality and impartiality in the international sphere, 'The Holy See . . . declares that it intends to remain and will remain outside the temporal rivalries between other States and outside the international congresses set up with that object. . . .'[1] But, before then, no such excuse existed. On the other hand, it was prudent for the Holy See not to get involved in international disputes. But that did not mean that it was not interested in the work of the organizations at Geneva, indeed both the bishop of Geneva, Fribourg, and Lausanne and the Apostolic Nuncio at Berne had a watching brief at the League of Nations. Moreover, the Holy See could not but be interested in the practical work of the League, like that of the International Labour Organization. For this purpose, Madame Florentine Steenberghe-Engeringh, the Dutch president of the International Union of Catholic Women's Leagues (IUCWL), which comprised nineteen leagues in forty countries, was deputed to represent Catholic interests. In December 1932, in response to a letter from Mgr Maglione, the Nuncio in Berne, Mgr Pizzardo wrote that the Union, and its head, should be treated as the official spokespersons, on certain issues affecting women and the family, of the Holy See at the League of Nations organization.[2]

Vatican diplomacy also took a keen interest in all the major international conferences of the 1920s. Thus, shortly after his election, in a letter to the archbishop of Genoa, Pius XI expressed his strong hope for a successful outcome of the conference on reparations then taking place at Genoa.[3] Unfortunately, the conference was largely a failure, no further consensus being reached on the main issue. But at the nearby resort of Rapallo, Germany and the Soviet delegation (which was officially excluded from the conference) reached an agreement establishing close economic ties and granting Russia the first measure of escape from isolation through the grant of German diplomatic recognition.[4] Though the Vatican deplored Rapallo at the time, Germany's

[1] Pollard, *The Vatican*, 82–85 and 203, text of the Lateran Treaty, Article 24.

[2] ASV, AES, IV Periodo, Stati Eccl., 437, 390–397 (1930–1947), Unione Internazionale Leghe Femminili, 391, pro-memoria to nuncio in Berne, 29 December 1932.

[3] Bellocchi, *Tutti le Encicliche*, IX, 'Con vivo piacere', 7 April 1922. Epistola.

[4] Marks, *The Illusion of Peace*, 44–45.

new *Ostpolitik* would later prove of benefit to its own negotiations with the Bolsheviks.

VATICAN POLICY FROM THE RUHR CRISIS TO THE LOCARNO 'HONEYMOON'

The Vatican's pursuit of peace and reconciliation in Europe faced a major challenge during the very serious crisis, which erupted over the Franco-Belgian invasion and occupation of the Ruhr in January 1923, following Germany's failure to keep up the reparations payments laid down by the Treaty of Versailles, and which lasted virtually a year.[5] The Vatican had several interrelated concerns during the crisis: a genuine fear that it could spark war, a fear that was shared by other powers; fears for the political stability and economic viability of Germany; a concern that the separatism in the Rhineland regions encouraged by the French and Belgians threatened the Reich's territorial integrity (and the stability of ecclesiastical jurisdictions); and fear that the crisis would encourage Communism in Germany and drive its government further into the arms of Soviet Russia.

Under continual pressure from both sides, the Holy See sought to play a moderating, mediatory role, avoiding condemnations of both the occupation itself and the German policy of resistance, both of which it disapproved.[6] It was even more disapproving when the 'passive' resistance degenerated into violence on both sides. Perhaps its most positive achievement was the despatch of Mgr Gustavo Testa on a mission of 'charity and pastoral care' in March 1923.[7] Through Testa, the Vatican was able to disburse practical and financial assistance to the inhabitants of the Ruhr, help in obtaining the release of German prisoners from the French, and provide itself with detailed, but dispassionate, knowledge of the ongoing situation. Given the very tense situation, Testa's mission could so easily have ended badly, like Mgr Ratti's mission during the Silesian dispute between Germany and Poland two years earlier.

Stehlin summarizes the outcome of the Vatican's role in the Ruhr crisis as follows:

> Despite France's refusal to alter course, the Vatican by virtue of its moral force and influence throughout Europe had helped to alter the thinking in some political circles and had caused Paris at least to be more cautious.[8]

[5] The best analysis of the Vatican's role during the Ruhr Crisis is to be found in Stehlin, *Weimar and the Vatican*, ch. V.

[6] For the difficulties of this balancing act, see Pius XI's allocution of 23 May 1923, *Gratum Nobis*, Bellocchi, *Tutte le Encicliche*, IX, 71–72.

[7] Stehlin, *Weimar and the Vatican*, 229–237.

[8] Stehlin, *Weimar and the Vatican*, 251.

The consequences for the Vatican's relations with France, however, were less positive than for those with the German Reich. With the latter, the Holy See had earned a great deal of credit which would translate partly into the agreement on the Bavarian concordat and partly into being able to use Germany's *Ostpolitik* as the 'umbrella' for talks with the Soviets. In France, on the other hand, despite the efforts of its nuncio, Mgr Cerretti, it created a lot of suspicion and resentment towards Vatican diplomacy, which was seen as pro-German, which, to a degree, it was: Gasparri had arguably underestimated both French fears for their security and their economic problems. The Vatican's role during the Ruhr Crisis would provide ammunition for Édouard Herriot (prime minister of France) in his attempt to eliminate the French embassy to the Vatican in 1924.

One of the most positive outcomes of the Ruhr Crisis was the Dawes Plan, which sought to tackle the underlying cause of the occupation, the dispute over reparations, and which had, in part, been foreseen by Gasparri.[9] Appropriately enough, the Vatican's main financial agency at the time, the ABSS, and several individuals in the Vatican hierarchy, subscribed to the private loans to Germany which were intended to 'refloat' the payment of reparations.[10] In the short term the Dawes Plan had a powerfully positive effect on international relations in Europe, creating so much more trust between statesmen, most notably Briand of France and Germany's Stresemann, that the way was opened to the Locarno Treaties of December 1925. Throughout the period of negotiations and after the Vatican supported Briand's policy, which came under fire from both the left and right of the French political spectrum.[11] The Locarno Treaties brought satisfaction to the Vatican on a number of counts. Firstly, they vindicated Gasparri's profound criticisms of the Versailles Settlement and the exclusion of Germany from the League. Secondly, a repeat of the Ruhr occupation was precluded by the Rhineland Pact, 1927, which involved Britain and Italy guaranteeing Germany's borders with France and Belgium, and the end of the military occupation of the Rhineland was brought forward to 1930. Stresemann was also successful in having German violations of the disarmament clauses of the 1919 Peace Treaty brushed under the carpet and Germany was admitted to the League.[12] Yet Stresemann's policy of fulfilment (of the Versailles Treaty) cannily avoided making commitments to Germany's eastern frontiers, that is, those with Poland and Czechoslovakia: Gasparri had always doubted the

[9] Stehlin, *Weimar and the Vatican*, 211.

[10] ASV, AES, IV Periodo, Stati Eccl., 511, fasc. 520 Città del Vaticano, Prestiti Dawes and Young, circular from Secretariat of State to Vatican financial agencies, 27 November 1934.

[11] Rhodes, *The Vatican in the Age of the Dictators*, 111

[12] Marks, *The Illusion of Peace*, ch. 3.

durability of those with Poland.[13] Though it is now fashionable to talk about 'the illusion of peace' after Locarno, and it certainly did not last very long, at the time it seemed as if a new era of peace was finally dawning, and the Vatican shared in the enthusiasm.

THE VATICAN'S RELATIONS WITH THE POWERS, 1922–30

The British Empire

One of the legacies which Pius XI inherited from his predecessor was the strength of the Vatican diplomatic position in 1922. The Holy See had good relations with most states, and relations with the British Empire were especially good. The Vatican recognized that, in the absence of the United States, which had returned to a policy of 'isolation' after 1920, Britain remained the pivotal international power and appreciated its moderating role in Europe and attempts to achieve a just and stable settlement there. The link with Britain was considered to be of such importance that the Vatican pulled out all the ceremonial stops when George V and Queen Mary came on a state visit in May 1923.[14] As well as signifying recognition of the Holy See's diplomatic importance by a global superpower, the visit suggested that Protestant prejudice against the international head of Catholicism was now somewhat lessened, inasmuch as the only previous visit by a British monarch, that of Edward VII in 1903, had been a purely private one.[15]

As a Protestant power with substantial Catholic communities in the dominions, protectorates, and colonial territories of its empire—especially in Australia, Canada, Ireland, and Britain itself—the British Empire sometimes posed problems for Vatican diplomacy.[16] Britain was as concerned as any other power about the *nationality* of leading Catholic officials in its colonial territories, thus it lobbied the Vatican about the appointment of British citizens as apostolic delegates and vicars apostolic

[13] Pease, *Rome's Most Faithful Daughter*, 40.

[14] Hachey, *Anglo-Vatican Relations*, 43; see also ASV, Sacri Palazzi Apostolici, Amministrazione, busta 146, XII, fasc. 8, Protocollo, Visita dei Sovrani della Gran Bretagna a SS Pio XI, 9 maggio 1923.

[15] Pollard, 'A Court in Exile', 45.

[16] Lord Curzon, British foreign secretary in the early 1920s, estimated that there were 14 million Catholics and 7,000 Catholic missionaries in the British Empire at that time; Hachey, *Anglo-Vatican Relations*, 1923, 42.

(bishops where there was no established local Catholic hierarchy) on several occasions.[17] The Vatican was sympathetic but had to point out that, in the absence of adequate numbers of clergy who were British subjects, it was almost inevitable that foreigners would have to be nominated to these posts.[18] A further concern for the Vatican was that though it was willing to inform the British legation in advance of the appointments it was proposing, it did not wish the Foreign Office to try to exercise some kind of veto.[19] This was exactly the concern which the Vatican had in relation to all colonial powers.

The Vatican followed developments in Ireland particularly closely. It was deeply concerned about the civil war that had developed between the supporters ('Treatyites') and opponents ('anti-Treatyites') of the 1921 treaty with Britain, which gave birth to the new dominion, the Irish Free State. According to the British Minister to the Holy See, 'the Holy See used its good offices in 1923 in an effort to persuade Éamon de Valera that he should help end the Irish Civil War'.[20] In fact, the Vatican burnt its fingers in Ireland in 1923. Mgr Salvatore Luzio, the apostolic visitor whom it sent to Ireland, in the hope bringing about peace, managed to alienate both the bishops and the ministers of the Free State government, and was forced into a humiliating and embarrassing exit.[21] Luzio's abortive mission probably delayed the establishment of diplomatic relations between the Irish Free State and the Holy See for several years. Though the Irish government kept an unofficial representative in Rome, the Marquis McSweeney,[22] in the absence of formal diplomatic links with the Irish Free State, the Vatican seems to have deferred to Britain on all matters affecting Ireland.[23]

Of course, like all new 'successor' states, the Irish Free State was anxious to achieve diplomatic recognition from the Vatican, if only to strengthen its position in relation to the former colonial power, Britain. Eventually, an Irish envoy, Charles Bewley, presented his credentials in the Vatican in June 1929, a propitious year con sidering it was the hundredth anniversary of Catholic Emancipation,[24] and a Irish Franciscan friar, Mgr Pascal Robinson, was accredited as first nuncio to the Irish government a few months later, not without some resistance from the Irish bishops who inevitably feared more direct Vatican interference in their affairs.[25] In the event, Robinson handled

[17] Hachey, *Anglo-Vatican Relations*, 1925, 99–100.

[18] See the discussion in the Congregation of Extraordinary Ecclesiastical Affairs, ASV, AES, Sessioni, 1297, 1926, Impero Britannico, nomine alle maggiori dignità ecclesiastiche nell'Impero Britannico.

[19] See the discussion in the Congregation of Extraordinary Ecclesiastical Affairs, ASV, AES, Sessioni, 1297, 1926, Impero Britannico, nomine alle maggiori dignità ecclesiastiche nell'Impero Britannico.

[20] As cited in Hachey, *Anglo-Vatican Relations*, xxvii.

[21] For an account of the episode, see Keogh, *The Vatican*, ch. V.

[22] Keogh, *The Vatican*, 121.

[23] Hachey, *Anglo-Vatican Relations*, xix.

[24] Keogh, *The Vatican*, 153.

[25] Keogh, *The Vatican*, 154–155.

the Irish episcopate with greater sensitivity than Luzio had done in 1923 and he also managed to handle the transition from Cosgrave to De Valera, from a pro-Treatyite to anti-Treatyite government with aplomb, despite some local difficulties, and the problem of British objections to De Valera's insistent, and entirely justified, requests for an audience with the pope.[26] Robinson's appointment brought with it an additional boon; it gave the Holy See an unofficial, 'back channel' to the London government until the appointment of an apostolic delegate in London in 1938.[27]

Communities of Irish Catholics seemed to pose a problem elsewhere in the British Empire, for example in Australia, where there were strong tensions between the Catholic population, who were mainly of Irish extraction, and those of Protestant origin.[28] Mgr Bernardini, secretary in the Apostolic Delegation, informed Rome that: 'In Australia it is frequently said that the Catholic religion is not Catholic but Irish.'[29] The presence of Archbishop Mannix of Melbourne was an added difficulty since, as a pro-Irish Republican, he not only ostentatiously boycotted the 'British' establishment, that is, the Governor of the State of Victoria, but caused divisions among fellow Catholics.[30]

There was a similarly difficult problem in Canada. In 1930, the British Minister to the Vatican complained that 'the Canadian Catholic community is torn into factions', that is, between the Irish and French-speaking Canadians.[31] Mgr Giuseppe Cassulo, appointed apostolic delegate to Canada, did not find it easy to cope with the warring factions, who even sponsored rival higher educational establishments in Ottawa, the federal capital.[32]

Vatican diplomacy faced more serious issues in the British mandated territory of Palestine, and in the British island colony and naval base of Malta. Palestine gave great concern to the Secretariat of State during Pius XI's pontificate, as it had done during that of his predecessor (see Chapter 3) because of the British administration of the Holy Places and the growing numbers of Jewish immigrants. As ethnic tensions between Jews and Arabs led to riots and other violence in 1936, the Vatican became seriously alarmed.[33] The role

[26] ASV, ARP, IV Periodo, Archivio della Nunziatura D'Irlanda (1929–39), Busta 4, Titolo I, fasc. 1, 1933, February, exchange of correspondence between Mgr Robinson and Pacelli.

[27] ASV, ARP, IV Periodo, Archivio della Nunziatura D'Irlanda (1929–39), Busta 4, Titolo I, 1935, 2 December, no. 45, correspondence over Ethiopian War; 1938, 7 July, Robinson says that HM government would prefer a British subject to be apostolic delegate in London, and 17 August, De Valera trying to act as an intermediary in the Spanish Civil War.

[28] See the press cutting from the Sydney *Daily Telegraph*, 22 March 1923, 'Manifesto of Protestant Workmen' (a long conspiracy theory diatribe) in ASV, AdRP, IV, Periodo, Australia, Box 45, Questioni Varie.

[29] ASV, AdRP, IV, Periodo, Australia, Box 45, Questioni Varie. Gran Bretagna, fasc. 88, Azione Cattolica, Mgr Bernardini to Secretary of State, 14 February 1934.

[30] ASV, AdRP, IV, Periodo, Australia, Box 45, Questioni Varie. Gran Bretagna, fasc. 88.

[31] Hachey, *Anglo-Vatican Relations*, 1930, 180.

[32] Hachey, *Anglo-Vatican Relations*, 1930, 180.

[33] A. Giovanelli, *La Santa Sede e la Palestina. La custodia della Terra Santa fra la fine dell'impero ottoman e la Guerra dei sei giorni*, Rome, 2000, 119.

of Mgr Barlassina, the Latin Patriarch of Jerusalem, who was of Italian nationality, exacerbated matters because of his hostility towards the British, and nearly brought Anglo-Vatican relations to breaking point.[34] Hanging over all the other issues like a cloud were Italian Fascist designs on the Mandate.[35]

Italian influence was also an issue in the troubled affairs of Malta and the eruption of a Church–State conflict there nearly led to a diplomatic rupture between Britain and the Vatican in 1930.[36] The spat seems to have begun with Gasparri's rather impertinent protest against the reception by the governor of three visiting Anglican bishops in the throne room of the palace in Valletta.[37] It was exacerbated by the fact that the Maltese premier, Lord Strickland, made insulting remarks about the Italian religious, the Maltese clergy, and even the pope himself. Pius XI's wounded *amour-propre* made things even worse. As a result of his intervention, the very full and balanced report of Mgr Pascal Robinson that the Apostolic Visitor sent in response to a British government request, which criticized both Strickland and the Maltese clergy, was only published in part, that is, the parts which were most damning of Strickland and his government.[38] The threat of excommunication of all those who voted for Strickland's party prompted energetic protests on the part of Britain, leading to the withdrawal of its minister to the Holy See and his replacement, for some months, by a chargée d'affaires.[39]

The most interesting aspect of the Maltese *imbroglio* is the way in which it reflected in microcosm so many of the problems which the Holy See faced in its relations with European states in the interwar period. There was an element of ethnic tension, as represented in Malta by the pro-British element, led by the Constitutional Party/Labour Party electoral compact, and the pro-Italian element, represented by large numbers of clergy, especially Italian heads of religious orders, and the Nationalist Party. For the British the pro-Italian element came under increasing suspicion because of Italian Fascist designs on the Maltese Islands. Then there were politicking clergy—especially those who supported the Nationalist Party—whom the lacklustre Maltese bishop, Caruana, failed to control. The presence of turbulent lay political personalities, especially Lord Strickland, the colonial premier and leader of the Constitutional Party, did not help matters. The Vatican also nursed fears about the spread of Protestantism, Masonry, and even Communism (within the Labour Party) in Malta. Finally, there was a certain amount of dissatisfaction with clerical indolence and with the fact that the Church allegedly owned

34 Giovanelli, *La Santa Sede e la Palestina*, 116–119.

35 Giovanelli, *La Santa Sede e la Palestina*, 126; and Pollard, *The Vatican*, 89–90.

36 For an up-to-date account of the dispute, see Aappo Laitinen, 'Early Signs of Discord: The Holy See, Britain and the Question of Malta', in Gallagher et al. (eds), *Pius XI and America*, 233–258.

37 Rhodes, *The Vatican*, 58.

38 Rhodes, *The Vatican*, 58–59.

39 Hachey, *Anglo-Vatican Relations*, 184.

half of all landed property in the islands. All these issues were brought to the fore by the introduction of parliamentary democracy to the Maltese Islands.[40]

In the end, a settlement of sorts was reached—Malta coming once more under direct colonial rule—but the tensions between conservative clergy and more radical lay politicians were only temporarily defused: they would resurface after the Second World War in the form of serious conflicts between the Maltese Church and the Labour Party leader, Dom Mintoff.[41]

France

Despite the concerns of both the French government and public opinion over the attitude taken by the Vatican during the Ruhr Crisis, their relations steadily improved thereafter. In particular, the key and vexed question of the *associations cultuelles*, the bodies intended to administer the property of the Church under the terms of the 1904 Law of Separation but rejected by Pius X, was finally resolved.[42] The Chapon–Renaud proposal to convert the organizations into *associations diocésaines*, that is, under the control of the bishop and diocesan clergy, was accepted by the French Council of State and led to an agreement with the Vatican.[43] In order to overcome the misgivings of the intransigent wing of post-Concordatory bishops, Pius XI published his encyclical *Maximam Gravissimamque* in January 1924, which argued strongly and convincingly the reasons why, while still refusing to accept the Law of Separation, the Holy See was satisfied with legal guarantees contained in the Chapon-Renaud plan.[44] As Larkin explains:

> With the a*ssociations diocésaines*, the French Church could now corporately own property instead of being reliant on private individuals; and with a legal roof over its head, it could at long last terminate its eighteen years of mentally living with bags packed, ready to go no one knew where.[45]

But the consolidation of relations with France was briefly interrupted by the emergence of the 'Cartel des Gauches' government of Édouard Herriot following elections in 1924, which led to brief flurry of anti-clerical rhetoric and lawmaking, and the temporary recall of the French ambassador at

[40] See Godfrey A. Pirotta, *Malta's Parliament: An Official History*, Malta, 2006, ch. 3.

[41] Pirotta, *Malta's Parliament*, 134.

[42] For the negotiations that led to the resolution of the issue, see E. Poulat, *Les Diocésains. République française, Église catholique. Loi de 1905 et associations cultuelles, le dossier d'un litige et de sa solution (1903–2003)*, Paris, 2007.

[43] Larkin, *Religion, Politics and Preferment*, 154, where he explained that this then replaced all the individual parochial *associations* which were intended to be under lay control, which was not acceptable to the Church.

[44] For the text of the encyclical, see Carlen, *Papal Encyclicals*, III, 265–269.

[45] Larkin, *Religion, Politics and Preferment*, 157.

the Vatican, Charles Jonnart, in June 1924. Gasparri was unperturbed, as he explained to the British Minister, it was one of the most important interests of France—especially colonial interests—that she maintain good relations with the Holy See.[46] And as the same minister, Sir Odo Russell, pointed out, a small French presence at the Vatican had to be maintained, if only because of Alsace-Lorraine and 'the question of the French mandate in Syria, where the Church has extensive property and large establishments, for the protection of which France becomes responsible'.[47] Herriot's government fell in April 1925, and Jonnart returned to Rome, with Gasparri announcing that 'The Holy See could not have had a better Easter egg.'[48] Catholic France's experience of dealing with the Herriot government had one longer-term consequence, the reorganization of Catholic political forces under General Edouard de Castelnau, who formed the Fédération National Catholique in February 1925 to rally Catholics to fight Herriot's anti-clerical proposals. The organization would prove extremely effective in mobilizing the Catholic vote in the 1928 elections.[49]

Other European States

The Vatican's relations with the two Iberian Catholic states were good, somewhat better, in fact, than they had been with the pre-war liberal regimes. In Portugal, after over a decade of both political instability and anti-clerical measures under the Republic, the military coup of 1926 brought a huge improvement in the position of the Catholic Church. Confiscated property was restored to it, religious education reintroduced, and religious orders readmitted to Portugal. Following the entry into the Portuguese cabinet in 1928 of António Salazar, who was a close friend of the Patriarch of Lisbon, Cardinal Emmanuel Goncalves Cerejeira, and, like him, an integralist and 'organicist', a Missionary Agreement was signed with the Vatican which defined the role of the Church in the Portuguese colonies.[50] By the mid-1930s, Salazar's peculiar, austere, effectively civilian, dictatorship had established itself in Portugal, and the Church and its political wing, the Centro Católico, acquiesced in it, especially since Salazar resisted the Fascist 'temptation'.

On the surface, the Church, in the dominions of the Most Catholic King of Spain, was in a much stronger position vis-à-vis the state than in probably any other European country. But though constitutionally strong, materially wealthy, and buttressed by the religious orders' position in secondary

[46] Rhodes, *The Vatican*, 86.
[47] Hachey, *Anglo-Vatican Relations*, 157.
[48] Rhodes, *The Vatican*, 88.
[49] Larkin, *Religion, Politics and Preferment*, 157.
[50] Cipriotti and Talamanca, *I Concordati di Pio XII*, 18–22.

education, the Church was rather less secure in popular sympathies. It had failed to establish the substantial networks of Catholic economic and social organizations common in the Benelux countries, France, Germany, and Italy,[51] and was strongly identified in the minds of many of the emerging working classes of the industrial cities and the poor peasants of the south of Spain, with the upper classes—the factory bosses and landowners.[52] On the other hand, the Church had the support of the king, the pious if rather morally errant Alfonso XIII, and his court.[53] But Alfonso was faced by an increasingly difficult political situation, already by the end of the First World War the system of parliamentary monarchy was breaking down in Spain. Alfonso, and the Church, were saved, temporarily, by General Miguel Primo de Rivera, whose military *pronunciamento* in 1923 led to a 'directory', or personal dictatorship, in Spain that lasted until 1930.

The Holy See also had excellent relations with Catholic Belgium which, in its relations with the Vatican in the post-war period, benefited from the, albeit fading, aura of Cardinal Mercier's international prestige. The small country also enjoyed much credit in the Vatican due to the prestige of the Catholic University of Louvain (Leuven) and the vigour and effectiveness of the various forms of Catholic social activism which had been developed there, especially the Catholic women's and youth organizations—in the latter case the Jeunesse Ouvrière Chrétienne ed by the charismatic Fr Joseph Cardijn.[54] The Holy See also had good relations with the Netherlands, where there was a large and well-organized Catholic minority, though in this case there was a temporary setback when the political machinations of the anti-papal Protestant Christian Historical and Anti-Revolutionary parties in the Second Chamber of the States General (the lower house of Parliament) led to the suppression of the Dutch embassy to the Vatican in 1926.[55] It is likely that this was the ultimate form of the Protestant backlash against the staging of an international Eucharistic Congress, albeit in the privacy of a football stadium, in Amsterdam in 1924.[56] Mgr Schioppa, the nuncio in The Hague, was scathing in his criticisms of the 'insipidness and weakness' of the Catholic party in the Dutch parliament during the battles over the embassy.[57] Schioppa remained

[51] See F. Lannon, *Privilege, Persecution and Prophecy: The Catholic Church in Spain, 1875–1975*, Oxford, 1987, ch. 6.

[52] Carr, *Modern Spain*, 41–44.

[53] See Vicente Carcel Orti, 'Pio XI e Alfonso XIII, Re di Spagna', in Jean-Pierre Delville and Marko Jacov (eds), *La Papauté Contemporaine/Il papato contemporaneo*, Leuven and Louvain-la-Neuve, 2009, 377–391.

[54] See Pollard, 'Pius XI's Promotion', 776–777.

[55] ASV, AES, IV Periodo, Olanda, 53, P.O., fasc. 10–12, Schioppa to Gasparri, 20 March 1926.

[56] M. Chappin, SJ, 'Cardinal Van Rossum and the international eucharistic congresses', in Poels et al. (eds), *Life with a Mission*, 106–107.

[57] ASV, AES, IV Periodo, Olanda, 53, P.O., fasc. 10–12, Schioppa to Gasparri, 13 April 1929.

as nuncio, but as a sign of papal disapproval was also accredited to Kaunas (Lithuania). The Netherlands did not re-establish full diplomatic relations with the Vatican until early in 1944.

The papacy's relations with Hungary were good in the post-war period. One of the 'rumps' of the former Austro-Hungarian Empire, interwar Hungary was a 'victim' of national self-determination. Consequently, it was an ardent advocate of the revision of the Versailles Peace Settlement. It now covered only a third of its former territory, having lost much land and population to neighbouring Austria, Czechoslovakia, Romania, and Yugoslavia, with the result that the nuncio in Budapest was kept busy dealing with complaints from Hungarian bishops over those parts of their flocks and property which now lay beyond the new national borders.[58] In addition to territorial dismemberment, Hungary had gone through the trauma of the short-lived soviet republic of Béla Kun and the subsequent white terror which had swept it away. In the aftermath, the Hungarian elites, with the tacit support of Church, had gerrymandered the parliamentary system to keep the left from power and set up Admiral Miklós Horthy as regent of a 'kingdom without a king', the Habsburgs being forbidden to return to their various thrones by France and its allies among the successor states to the Hungarian part of the former dual empire. Those who advocated a Habsburg restoration believed that they had the support of the Holy See since the Habsburgs were Catholics. But, as Rhodes explains,

> It is no doubt true that, on traditional grounds, the Papacy would have welcomed the restoration of what was until 1918 the principal Catholic dynasty in Europe . . . But Pius XI was not a traditionalist. With him, dynastic interests were nothing compared with the interests of the faith . . .[59]

So on pragmatic, *realpolitik* grounds, the Vatican carefully avoided being associated with the partisans of the Habsburg pretender, Archduke Otto, which would, of course, have wrecked its relations with Hungary's neighbours, who were always very carefully watching events in there.[60] Thus, in June 1931 the Czechoslovakian Minister to the Vatican, in an audience with Cardinal Pacelli, expressed concern about the visit of Empress Zita to the

[58] ASV, AES, IV Periodo, Cecoslovacchia, 61, P.O., fasc. 97, Esecuzione 'Modus vivendi' 1928, Commissione Applicazione dell (sic) 'Modus vivendi', letters from Gasparri of 28 January 1928 to bishops of Berlin, Prague, and Esztergom asking them to nominate representatives to the Commission for the 'division of the endowments of the parts of those dioceses in Czechoslovakia'.

[59] Rhodes, *The Vatican*, 142.

[60] See the report of Nuncio Schioppa to Gasparri on 5 October 1922, informing him that he had carefully abstained from attending a Mass to commemorate the birthday of Archduke Otto, the Habsburg heir, and also of Nuncio Rotta to Pacelli on 23 March 1933 on renewed upsurge of pro-Habsburg feeling, in ASV, AES, Ivo Periodo, 77, P.O. 57, Ungheria, 10, 17, Questione Monarchica.

Pope and attempts to restore the Habsburgs. He was especially concerned about the possibility of marriage between the Habsburg pretender, Otto, and Maria of Savoia (the royal family of Italy).[61] Ironically, the Hungarians were also interested in the affairs of Czechoslovakia, so that only a week after the latter audience, in another the Minister of Hungary asked for news about the negotiations of the *modus vivendi* between the Holy See and Czechoslovakia. Pacelli noted in his diary that 'I replied in vague terms, without mentioning the note which had just been delivered to the (Czech) Minister.'[62] Like all the other 'great powers', the Vatican had to tread carefully in the minefield that was international relations in Central and Eastern Europe between the wars.

Despite its small size, Switzerland played a very important role in Vatican diplomacy. It was a country with a large Roman Catholic minority (46% of the population), especially in the Chur, Fribourg, Sankt Gallen, and Sion dioceses, but there were still problems over the rights of cantonal governments to nominate clergy. There was a particular problem in Italian-speaking Canton Ticino, where Fascist Italy nursed irredentist claims, which is why there was only an Apostolic Administrator at Lugano instead of a permanent bishop.[63] But Switzerland was also enormously important on the international level, hence the Vatican's determination to win for the nuncio the status of doyen of the diplomatic corps in Berne.[64] Geneva was, of course, the headquarters of the League of Nations and part of the Berne nuncio's role was to observe the proceedings at Geneva and report back to the Secretariat of State.[65] Other international organizations had their HQs there, like the international Red Cross, about which the men in the Vatican were rather suspicious. In addition, it was an obvious place for the holding of international conferences—like the International Association of Workers, the Zionist Congress, and the Communist fellow-travelers in the International Youth Organization for Peace.[66] It was also the place where ecumenical (Protestant) international meetings increasingly took place—like the Lausanne conference in 1937—and where, in consequence, the World Council of Churches would eventually set up their HQ in 1937. Above all, the Swiss Confederation was a fellow

[61] ASV, AES, IV Periodo, Stati Eccl., 430B, 1933–1940, Udienze del Card. Pacelli al Corpo Diplomatico, 19 June 1931.

[62] ASV, AES, IV Periodo, Stati Eccl., 430B, 1933–1940, Udienze del Card. Pacelli al Corpo Diplomatico, 26 June 1931.

[63] ASV, AES, IV Periodo, Stati Eccl., see 236, 42 Lugano 1933–34 Attacchi fascisti contro il Vescovo e il Clero.

[64] ASV, AES, IV Periodo, Stati Eccl the nuncio was eventually given the role of doyen of the diplomatic corps, see 193, 4–5 Berna 1923–53 Precedenza.

[65] See, for example, Maglione's report on the League in ASV, AES, IV Periodo, Stati Eccl., 180 P.O., 1-2, 1922–1926.

[66] ASV, AES, IV Periodo, Stati Eccl pro lavoratori, 1922–1925, P.O., 192, 3 Berna, 1922–1925, Zionist congress; congressi mondiali di Gioventù per la Pace and JOC took place.

neutral country with which the Holy See had had close ties in time of war and during attempts at peace-making, and might have to have again.

RELATIONS WITH NON-EUROPEAN STATES

Japan

It is indicative of the growing international prestige of the Vatican in the mid-1920s that there was even strong support at the Imperial Japanese Court and in the government for the establishment of relations with the Holy See.[67] After their takeover of the formerly German-ruled Marshall Islands under a League of Nations mandate, the Japanese sent a mission to the Vatican to discuss the status of the German missionaries there, and in 1927 the Japanese Diet voted to use 114,000 yen for establishment of a mission to the Holy See. There were objections from Buddhists and Protestants alike and the project was abandoned but relations between the Vatican and Tokyo remained otherwise cordial and Holy See continued to hope that it would be possible to establish a link.[68]

The United States

As far as the Vatican's relations with the USA were concerned, there had been no major contacts on a diplomatic level, official or unofficial, since after the visit of Woodrow Wilson to the Vatican in 1920. In addition, the Holy See found America's withdrawal into isolation perplexing and disappointing. On the other hand, the generosity of American Catholics had become crucially important to the Vatican's finances during the course of the First World War and this had been recognized by the raising of *two* Americans, Archbishop John Hayes of New York and George Mundelein of Chicago (the first in a Midwestern see) to the Sacred College in 1923.[69] Commenting on this event, the British Minister declared that, 'The increasing strength of the Catholic Church in America means increasing influence in the Vatican; and so it would be no exaggeration to say that the US is now looked up to as if it were the leading Catholic nation.'[70] Vatican attitudes towards the United States were always affected by the strong manifestations of anti-Catholicism: there had been a major resurgence of the phenomenon, closely tied to Ku Klux Klan

[67] Hachey, *Anglo-Vatican Relations*, 89.
[68] Hachey, *Anglo-Vatican Relations*, 125.
[69] Pollard, *Money*, 137.
[70] Hachey, *Anglo-Vatican Relations*, 70.

activity, in the mid-1920s.[71] In this situation, the nomination of a Catholic, Al Smith, Governor of New York, as Democratic presidential candidate in 1928, placed both American Catholics and the Vatican in a quandary.[72] It raised among American non-Catholics all the usual fears about Roman Catholic interference in politics, so much so that a visit of Cardinal Luigi Sincero to various religious orders in the USA was curtailed on the orders of the Vatican 'lest his presence give rise to the impression that the Vatican was attempting to influence the elections in favour of Governor Smith'.[73] In the end, Smith was defeated by a mixture of anti-Catholic prejudice and opposition to his support for the repeal of prohibition.[74] While the anti-Catholic backlash was deplored in the Vatican, Herbert Hoover's victory was looked upon with equanimity, mixed with a 'certain apprehension lest Mr Hoover's victory may prove to be the triumph of a narrow and exaggerated nationalism. . . .'[75]

The Vatican may well have hoped that a Smith presidency would assist more vigorously in bringing the persecution in Mexico to an end. In fact, in 1928 it was already involved in such an effort. Considerable campaigning and lobbying from both the influential Knights of Columbus and the National Catholic Welfare Conference (NCWC) led to intervention by the US ambassador in Mexico, Dwight Morrow, who introduced Fr Burke, the representative of NCWC, to President Calles in April 1928, because he believed that 'an ending to the religious dispute was in the interests of the general pacification of the country'.[76] As a result of this and a further meeting between Calles and Archbishop Ruiz, an agreement was reached. Yet the Vatican does not seem to have fully appreciated the usefulness of US diplomacy on its behalf at this time: it would become more appreciative of US support in 1935 (see Chapter 7).

Soviet Russia

Cardinal Gasparri summed up the Vatican's policy towards the Soviets in the early 1920s with these words:

> The church has—theoretically speaking—no prejudice against a communist form of government . . . The church requires only that states, regardless of what kind, do not attempt to hinder or attack the free development of the religious and sacramental life that is the purpose and obligation of the church.[77]

71 Fogarty, *The Vatican*, 229.
72 Fogarty, *The Vatican*, 235; and Hachey, *Anglo-Vatican Relations*, 147.
73 Hachey, *Anglo-Vatican Relations*.
74 Fogarty, *The Vatican*, 235.
75 Hachey, *Anglo-Vatican Relations*, 1928, 148.
76 Hachey, *Anglo-Vatican Relations*, 1928, 144.
77 As quoted in Stehle, *Eastern Politics*, 36.

Despite Catholic concerns about any form of socialism, this was entirely in line with the Vatican praxis laid down by Leo XIII in *Graves De Communi* in 1901.[78] Thus, the Vatican continued trying to open fruitful contacts with the USSR after Benedict's death in 1922: after contact was established with Soviet Foreign Minister Chicherin at the Rapallo conference, it embarked on the papal relief mission to the Russian famine, headed by the American Jesuit, Fr Edmund Walsh.[79]

The purpose of Walsh's mission was, of course, more than just philanthropic. Though his instructions from the pope did not permit him to contact and assist Catholic clergy in Soviet territory, they did give him full powers to treat with the Bolsheviks on behalf of the Holy See.[80] But the papal relief mission was plagued by difficulties. Firstly, it did not have much relief to distribute—only 2 million dollars compared to the nearly 66 million dollars of the American Relief Administration—and this aroused the suspicion and annoyance of the Soviets.[81] Also, as Stehle explains, 'the foreign policy and the religious policy of the Soviets was not synchronised', and so while, on the one hand, some Catholic priests and Bishops Cieplak and Budkiewicz were put on trial, and, in the latter case, executed, the Soviet Foreign Office, as a goodwill gesture to the Vatican, had the body of the Polish Jesuit saint Andrzej Bobola sent to Rome.[82] Since this saint had directed his evangelizing efforts towards Orthodox Christians, the gesture could be construed as indicating a preference for Catholics. It was also a clear sign of Soviet political instability during Lenin's last illness. Walsh did not help matters: he upset the Soviet authorities with his 'Yankee manners', and in November 1923 he finally left Moscow.[83]

Yet the Soviets, particularly Chicherin, did desire *de jure* recognition of their regime by the Holy See with the establishment of formal diplomatic relations through the appointment of a nuncio in Moscow, which demonstrates that they were as ruthlessly pragmatic as Gasparri. But the Vatican played hard to get, desiring concessions on religious instruction to the young, Church property, and the release of imprisoned priests: in the end, it was unwilling to concede a nunciature for fear of giving away its trump card and offered only an apostolic delegation.[84] In this way it missed the bus. Early in 1924, Austria, Britain, Greece, Norway, and Switzerland all established relations with the Soviets, followed by France later in the year, prompting Chicherin's comment that '*De jure* recognition by the Vatican would have been much more valuable for the Soviet government two years ago than now', a judgement echoed

[78] See Carlen, *Papal Encyclicals*, II, 479–490.

[79] For an analysis of the mission, see Marisa Patulli Trythall, 'Pius XI and American Pragmatism', in Gallagher et al. (eds), *Pius XI and America*, 25–85; and Stehle, *Eastern Politics*, ch. II.

[80] Stehle, *Eastern Politics*.

[81] Stehle, *Eastern Politics*, 42–44.

[82] Stehle, *Eastern Politics*, 53–54.

[83] Stehle, *Eastern Politics*.

[84] Stehle, *Eastern Politics*, 58–61.

by the British minister to the Holy See.[85] Despite this setback, the Vatican persisted in its efforts to reach an agreement with the Soviets, continuing the secret talks between Mgr Pacelli and the Soviet ambassador in Berlin through 1924 and 1925—not without hope since Lenin's New Economic Policy was accompanied by some relaxation of the 'Godless' campaigns.[86] The sticking points in Pacelli's conversations with, first, Ambassador Kretinski and then Chicherin himself were twofold: Soviet control over the appointment of bishops and priests, a new one, and religious instruction of youth, an old chestnut.[87] Pacelli's conversations dragged on until 1927.

In the meantime, the Vatican had added a second string to its Russian bow, a clandestine mission to Russia in order to build a clandestine ecclesiastical hierarchy of secret bishops conducted by Mgr Michel d'Herbigny, SJ, who was consecrated bishop by Pacelli in the Berlin nunciature in March 1926. A few weeks later, d'Herbigny made an extensive trip around the western parts of the Soviet Union, in his turn consecrating as bishops a total of four rather surprised priests whose function was to act as apostolic administrators of existing dioceses with Bishop Neveu, based in Moscow as apostolic delegate.[88] D'Herbigny's mission was not only secret. He himself was not even informed of Pacelli's continuing negotiations. Moscow did know, of course, and it inevitably viewed D'Herbigny's mission as duplicity on the part of the Vatican.

The situation of the Catholic Church in Russia began to deteriorate shortly after the completion of D'Herbigny's mission, partly because of it and partly for other reasons. Over the next few years the bishops whom D'Herbigny had consecrated were rolled up by the Soviet secret police, one by one, along with other high-ranking clergy.[89] In the late 1920s, 'war scare' paranoia swept the Bolshevik Party as a result of Britain's ending of relations with Soviet Russia following the Arcos incident in May 1927.[90] The Vatican's success in negotiating concordats with Poland (1925), Lithuania, Romania (both in 1927), and Czechoslovakia (1928), all states within the so-called 'Cordon Sanitaire' along the Soviet's western frontiers, must also have aroused further paranoid fears of the Vatican orchestrating a conspiracy against them. The fact that Stalin, with his policy of 'Socialism in One Country' was more securely in power by the end of the 1920s and had begun to radicalize Soviet policy, particularly in relation to the countryside and peasantry through the inauguration of collectivization, would also help explain why the persecution of the Catholic Church intensified. The renewed 'Godless' campaigns effectively reduced Catholicism in Russia to a few churches in metropolitan areas protected by

[85] As quoted in Stehle, *Eastern Politics*, 61; see Hachey, *Anglo-Vatican Relations*, 1925, 107.

[86] Rhodes, *The Vatican*, 134.

[87] Stehle, *Eastern Politics*, 75–76.

[88] Stehle, *Eastern Politics*, 98–99.

[89] Stehle, *Eastern Politics*, 129–133.

[90] See A.J.P. Taylor, *English History, 1914–1945*, London, 1970, 323–324.

foreign embassies and consulates—like those of France, Germany, and Italy in Moscow.

The Vatican's response was a condemnation of Bolshevism which was publicized worldwide, yet even at this juncture it secretly informed the Soviets, via the German embassy in Moscow, that the pope's letter to Cardinal Pompily, Vicar for Rome, containing the condemnation was intended as a purely political and not religious statement.[91] This was having its cake and eating it, but it was clearly prompted by the fear that the pope's statement might cause further Soviet repression of Catholics. It only confirmed the Kremlin's paranoid belief that the Vatican was lining up with its capitalist enemies. Vatican policy towards the Soviets certainly hardened after 1929. It is difficult to know what exactly caused the renewal of persecution, the 'Deubner Affair', in which a priest was accused of spying for Russia in the Vatican,[92] or the change in Vatican policy occasioned by the handover of power between Gasparri and Pacelli in the Secretariat of State: a Pacelli embittered with the Soviets because of the failure of his Berlin negotiations.

Probably all of these factors had a role in the change of policy, but undoubtedly the hopelessness of the Church's situation in Russia, and the persecution of the Church in Mexico, and later Spain (see Chapter 8), behind which the Vatican saw the hand of the Bolsheviks, induced the pope to order the preparation of an encyclical on Russia, *Divinum Mandatum*, which was to be published on 25 October 1931, the feast of Christ the King; however, though it reached the stage of page proofs at the Vatican printing press, it was never actually published.[93] Why not is still unclear. *Divinum Mandatum* contains a condemnation of Bolshevism and a warning that the Communist 'contagion' was spreading, as well as a detailed account of the persecutions of religion within the Soviet Empire. There also a considerable section devoted to the Vatican's evangelizing efforts in Russia, including the efforts of Pius and his predecessor to provide for the training of priests for both the Latin and Slavic rites to work in Russia. The encyclical was clearly designed to kill two birds with one stone, because it was also intended as an appeal to members of the Russian Orthodox clergy and faithful to return to the fold of the one shepherd, as is crystal clear from its opening words:

> A divine mandate was entrusted to Us through these words which Christ the Lord spoke to the first of Our predecessors, 'feed my sheep' . . . We have care for the salvation of so many who are separated from the bosom of the Church. . . .[94]

[91] Taylor, *English History*, 134. [92] Alvarez, *Spies in the Vatican*, 147–151.

[93] For the text of the encyclical, see ASV, AES, IV Periodo, Stati Eccl., 1931–1939, Pos. 662, P.O., Due progetti di Encicliche di papa XI, 'De Vera Christi Ecclesiae' and 'Contro la Persecuzione in Russia'

[94] English translation of *Divinum mandatum*, copyright Professor Michael Walsh, 1.

So the Vatican remained committed to the double strategy which had been inaugurated under Benedict XV: of trying to defend the existing Catholic Church in the Soviet jurisdiction while at the same time seeking the conversion of the Orthodox by all means possible. But in the pursuit of these goals, Pius and his advisers had made three serious mistakes: they had employed Polish clergy whom the Russians hated and suspected; they had employed Jesuits, who were also traditionally regarded with suspicion in Russia; and they had adopted a duplicitous policy of clandestinity.

THE SUCCESSES AND FAILURES OF THE CONCORDATORY POLICY OF PAPA RATTI

The policy of seeking cast-iron legal guarantees for the Church's property and functioning from the governments of new, 'successor' states, was nothing new. The first major concordat, in an historical line of concordats in the modern period, was that with Napoleon I's new imperial regime in 1801. This served as a sort of prototype for future concordats since it covered all the major areas that would figure in later ones—the juridical status of the Church; the State's role in clerical appointments; the control of church property; marriage law; education; the status of religious orders and congregations; and the exemption of the clergy from military service.[95] The promulgation of the Code of Canon Law in 1917 (see Chapter 3) gave greater clarity to the Holy See's expectations in relation to the content of concordats, especially in the matter of the appointment of bishops, and the fact that Cardinal Gasparri and Mgr Pacelli had been the major architects of the Code meant that they would pursue them tenaciously. Concordats seemed, to the men of the Vatican, the ideal, if not only, way to deal with a Europe which had been drastically remodelled by the Versailles Settlement, whose fundamental principle, 'national self-determination', had caused the disappearance of old state authorities and the emergence of completely new ones, and had brought about massive changes in international boundaries, which disrupted the centuries-old pattern of ecclesiastical territorial jurisdictions.

During the pontificate of Benedict XV there were simply not the opportunities for the conclusion of concordats. Four out of the just over seven years of the pontificate were ones of war, and it is obviously not feasible to conclude concordats with warring powers for fear of offending their enemies. Only just over two years of the pontificate remained in which to conclude concordats with those countries most likely to be willing to do so, the successor states of

[95] See F. Coppa, *Controversial Concordat: The Vatican's Relations with Napoleon, Mussolini and Hitler*, Washington, DC, 1999, Part I.

Eastern and Central Europe. Some of the concordats which were signed in the early to mid-1920s were the fruits of negotiations already begun under Benedict.

GERMANY

Relations between the Holy See and the post-war democratic regime in Germany were probably more cordial than those with the government of Kaiser Wilhelm II. In the wake of the Ruhr crisis, relations with the Weimar Republic became increasingly close under Pacelli's tutelage, with the result that Germany became a veritable 'laboratory' for the policy of concordats. In 1924, Pacelli, still nuncio to both Bavaria and the Reich and still based in Munich, concluded a new concordat with the Bavarian government which guaranteed a place for the Church inside the educational system and, in particular, ensured the teaching of the Catholic religion in schools. After his move to the new nunciature in Berlin in July 1925, his efforts were rewarded by further concordats with Baden and Prussia. The most important was undoubtedly that with Prussia, since this state covered 63 per cent of the surface area of the post-war Reich and ruled 60 per cent of its population.[96] Given that the majority of the Prussian population was Protestant (63%) and that it was governed by a Socialist-dominated coalition, negotiations were inevitably more difficult than those with Bavaria, a largely Catholic state.[97] The concordat was, however, signed in June 1929, but Pacelli's demand that the Holy See appoint bishops without governmental approval was rejected and education received no mention: the only major papal victory was in the matter of the establishment of a Catholic bishopric in Berlin, something long resisted by the government of the Second Reich.[98] Overall, Prussia, and by extension the Reich, were the greatest beneficiaries of the Prussian Concordat: Prussia had conceded little, but the integrity of the German border dioceses of Trier and Speyer in the Saarland had been preserved. The Saar had been temporarily separated from Germany and placed under League of Nations administration in order to ensure the exploitation of its coal mines as part of reparations to France, and, in order to lay the foundations for the ultimate separation of the territory from Germany, the French had pressed for a separate ecclesiastical administration. The concordat with Baden, the other south German state with a Catholic majority, was largely negotiated by Pacelli, on the lines of those in Bavaria, but only concluded in 1932, after he had left Germany.[99]

[96] *Statesman's Yearbook, 1930*, 925 and 961.

[97] For the negotiations, see Stehlin, *Weimar and the Vatican*, 412–429.

[98] Stehlin, *Weimar and the Vatican*, 425–426.

[99] Stehlin, *Weimar and the Vatican*, 429–431.

But the conclusion of a concordat with the Weimar Republic (the German Reich) eluded Pacelli and would not be realized until the advent of the Nazis to power in 1933 (see Chapter 7).

CONCORDATS WITH SUCCESSOR AND OTHER STATES

Overall, under Pacelli's management, the concordatory policy of Gasparri and Pius XI had been a success in Germany. But though concordats multiplied in the 1920s and early 1930s (a total of fourteen were concluded during Pius XI's pontificate), the policy was to have rather more mixed results elsewhere in Europe. With or without concordats, the problems which had first presented themselves in the relations between the Holy See and the successor states in Benedict's reign continued through that of Pius XI. Very often, the problem was not just the domestic issue of Church–State relations, which was certainly difficult during the process of the political consolidation of the new states, but also the repercussions for the Holy See of boundary changes and bitter border disputes among the new states, and also between new states and old ones, like Yugoslavia and Italy.

THE BALTIC STATES

Even though all the Baltic States had been most anxious to obtain recognition of their independence—which, in the case of Lithuania, was postponed until 1922 because of French ambitions to recreate the old Polish–Lithuanian Commonwealth as a powerful buffer between Germany and Russia—the Vatican's relations with two of them were to be troubled throughout the interwar period. An apostolic delegate for the Baltic States was appointed in 1922 and a concordat was concluded with Latvia despite the fact that Catholics there were in a minority.[100] The apostolic delegation was extended to Estonia regardless of the fact that Catholics numbered less than 10,000 in a population of over 1.1 million.[101]

All three Baltic republics were naturally anxious that Catholic ecclesiastical jurisdictions should be modified to ensure that none of their national territory or citizens were left under the authority of a bishop based in a foreign country, as a means of consolidating national independence. The national

[100] Perna, *Relazioni*, 231.

[101] *Statesman's Yearbook, 1930*, 830.

question loomed large in Latvia when the government, political parties, and press accused the Holy See of favouring the Lithuanian ethnic minority in Latgalia.[102]

But this was nothing compared to the complications which papal diplomacy faced in Lithuania. First of all, the Lithuanians resented the fact that, as the largest Baltic state, they had to share an internuncio with their two smaller neighbours. Matters were made worse by Gasparri's decision in 1925 to accredit Mgr Schioppa, nuncio in The Hague, to Kaunas as well, as a reprisal against the Dutch Parliament's abolition of their embassy to the Vatican.[103] When this issue was resolved there remained the problem of Vilnius (in Polish Vilna), the historic capital of Lithuania, which had been seized by the Poles during the 1921 war against Lithuania. The question of the treatment of the resulting Lithuanian minority in the Vilnius region of Poland poisoned relations with the Holy See, which came close to being broken off in 1925 when the Vatican announced that it had signed a concordat with Poland: the apostolic delegate, Mgr Antonino Zecchini, decided to withdraw from the country and the nunciature was left in the hands of his assistant, Mgr Luigi Faidutti.[104] At this juncture even Catholic politicians were outraged and the bishops and clergy did little to defend the Holy See. Arguably, it was largely the latter's fault: Gasparri clearly saw that a concordat with Catholic Poland was a much bigger catch than good relations with Lithuania and was prepared to pay the price.

In both Latvia and Lithuania the attitude of the national political elite was also a problem. Not only was it highly nationalistic and thus sensitive on issues relating to Lithuanian sovereignty and integrity, it also contained an anti-clerical element which, in the case of Lithuania, despite the concordat of 1924, challenged the right of the Church to organize its laypeople in Catholic Action on the Italian pattern.[105] Only in the serious domestic political and international diplomatic crises provoked by Lithuania's being forced to cede the Memel (Klaipeda) territory to Nazi Germany in March 1939, were the Lithuanians prompted to re-establish proper diplomatic relations with the Holy See.[106]

Poland was clearly very much higher in the Vatican's post-war priorities than troublesome Lithuania. With a population of over 27 million, of whom 75 per cent (22 million), were Catholics, it was the fourth largest of the predominantly Catholic countries of Europe in the interwar period, after Italy, France, and Spain.[107] Then, of course, there was the personal link

102 Perna, *Relazioni*, 185–187.

103 Perna, *Relazioni*, 185–187.

104 Perna, *Relazioni*, 101–109.

105 ASV, AES, IV Periodo, Paesi baltici, Lituania, 99, Azione Cattolica, Pizzardo to archbishop of Kaunas, 30 June 1932

106 Perna, *Relazioni*, 215–216.

107 *Statesman's Yearbook, 1930*, 1192.

between Pius XI and Poland: Ratti's experience there between 1918 and 1921 has led one American historian to dub Ratti 'the first Polish pope'.[108] Ratti seems to have developed a strong liking for Marshal Józef Piłsudski, the charismatic hero of Poland's struggle for national independence, in particular.[109] That did not, however, entirely prevent friction between the restored Polish state and the Vatican. One problem was a 'politicking' clergy some of whom, like Archbishops Sapieha and Teodorowicz, stood for Parliament and supported the National Democratic Party of Dmowski, the long-time opponent of Piłsudski: in 1922 Pius felt obliged to send a strongly worded note to Polish bishops and clergy warning against interference in Poland's political arena.[110]

The turbulent politics of the Second Polish Republic not only slowed negotiations for a concordat but, when one was eventually hammered out in the Vatican in 1925, its passage through Parliament was made difficult thanks to the opposition of the usual anti-clerical elements, as well as dissent among Catholic clergy and bishops.[111] Inevitably, the concordat was a compromise which did not satisfy all the aspirations of both sides but met their minimum requirements. As usual for a newly independent successor state, Poland insisted that no part of its national territory should fall under foreign ecclesiastical jurisdiction and on the right of veto over episcopal appointments, though it failed to obtain its demand that the Free City of Danzig should be ecclesiastically part of Poland.[112] For its part, the Holy See ensured freedom for the operations of the Church, religious instruction in state schools for Catholics, and a clause that limited the amount of Church-owned property the State could include in its land redistribution campaign.[113]

Despite the concordat, Poland continued to give concern in the Secretariat of State. The key problem was the usual one in the successor states, an ethnically divided and contested border area, that of Western Ukraine, which contained a volatile mix of Poles, Ruthenians, Ukrainians, and White Russians, and three major religious groups apart from the Jews: Latin rite Catholics, Greek Catholics, and Orthodox Christians. Poles and Ukrainians had battled for control over Western Ukraine, formerly the Galician territory of Austria-Hungary, in 1918–19, and the resurrected Polish state had prevailed. A Ukrainian separatist movement using terroristic methods, the OUN, continued to exist and had considerable sympathy

[108] Pease, *Rome's Most Faithful Daughter*, 52.
[109] Pease, *Rome's Most Faithful Daughter*, 51.
[110] Hachey, *Anglo-Vatican Relations*, 51.
[111] Pease, *Rome's Most Faithful Daughter*, 70–72.
[112] Pease, *Rome's Most Faithful Daughter*, 69.
[113] Pease, *Rome's Most Faithful Daughter*, 69.

and support among the Ukrainian Greek Catholic clergy: in only 5 months in 1931, 30 priests were arrested by the Polish police for terrorism,[114] and in one year 130 churches and chapels were destroyed by the Polish Army as 'dens of Ukrianianism'.[115] The clerical–Fascist ideologues of Ukrainian nationalism saw Catholic Christianity as a central element in a nationalist movement defending the Ukraine from Russian Communist 'barbarism'.[116] The Polish government was very distrustful of the Greek Catholic Church because of its links with Ukrainian nationalist movements, and in particular of its head, Mgr Szeptyckyj, Archbishop of Leopoli (Lvov). In 1923 the Warsaw government had demanded that Szeptyckyj write a submission of loyalty to Poland before they would permit him to return to his See: in the end, the Vatican succeeded in reducing this to a verbal statement of loyalty.[117]

In this context, the 'neo-union' policy of Bishop D'Herbigny (see Chapter 5) was a further irritant to the Holy See's relations with Poland. 'Neo-union' meant the creation of an additional religious grouping—a Byzantine-Slavonic rite but with a celibate priesthood—to add the already complex and divisive ecclesiastical situation in Western Ukraine.[118] This infuriated the Polish government, which, like the Polish episcopate, saw direct conversion of Orthodox Christians to the Latin rite as the best means 'Polonizing' the Ukraine, and which claimed that a half a million had done so compared to the miserly 30,000 who had joined the Byzantine-Slavonic rite.[119] In 1932, the row between Warsaw and Rome came to a head. Pius XI was forced to back down a little and the influence of D'Herbigny in the Vatican was in decline. A year later, he was sent 'into exile' in Belgium, and in 1934 the Commissio pro Russia was brought under the control of the Secretariat of State with Tardini in charge.[120]

There was also the ever-present danger of Communism in Poland as it 'seeped' through the frontier in the border areas and was present among the country's industrial working class. This, the Polish nationalism of the majority Latin Catholic clergy, and the anti-clerical tendencies of some Socialist supporters of Marshal Piłsudski, the country's hero-president, meant that Vatican policy towards Poland was a difficult balancing act throughout the 1920s and most of the 1930s.

[114] See Anton Shekhovtsov, 'By Cross and Sword: "Clerical Fascism" in Interwar Western Ukraine', *Totalitarian Movements and Political Religions*, 8(2) (June 2007), 276.

[115] Pease, *Rome's Most Faithful Daughter*, 170.

[116] Shekhovtsov, 'By Cross and Sword', 279–280.

[117] Hachey, *Anglo-Vatican Relations*, 52.

[118] Pease, *Rome's Most Faithful Daughter*, 156.

[119] Pease, *Rome's Most Faithful Daughter*, 171.

[120] Pease, *Rome's Most Faithful Daughter*, 167, for a very carefully reasoned and plausible account of the reasons for D'Herbigny's fall.

CZECHOSLOVAKIA

Of all the successor states, Czechoslovakia presented perhaps the most complicated problems for Vatican diplomacy. It was probably the most multi-ethnic of all the multi-ethnic successor states, as it was composed of Czechs and Slovaks, who together constituted 60 per cent of the population, Germans 30 per cent, and smaller minorities of Hungarians, Ruthenians, 'ethnic Jews', and some Poles. There were fundamental divisions between the east—rural, agrarian, and mainly Catholic Slovakia—and the west, more industrialized, urban, and anti-clerical Bohemia and Moravia (what is now the Czech Republic).[121] Slovakia under Mons Andrej Hlinka's fiercely separatist Slovakian Catholic party became increasingly alienated from the Prague government from the mid-1920s onwards, and a growing embarrassment for the Vatican.

The boundaries of the new state were such that, whichever parties had been in power, the Vatican would have had problems, with dioceses split between Germany, Poland, Hungary, Romania, and Czechoslovakia, plus the division of their properties. The country was also deeply politically divided on party lines: because of ethnic differences there were *four* Catholic parties. The core of the new political class (Czech) nationalist, democratic, and even social democratic, was anti-clerical—especially President Tomáš Masaryk and Foreign Minister Edvard Beneš. The former dreamt of separating Church and state, and creating a secular state.[122] Other problems included the insistence by the ruling elite on an attempt to create a new national civic 'religion' centred around Jan Hus a heretic burnt at the stake by the Church in the fourteenth century: the celebration of a national day for Hus was the cause of the first major crisis in relations between the Czechoslovak state and the Vatican.[123] Even worse, in the early 1920s, in his attempts to generate national feeling, Masaryk supported the emergence of a schismatic national Czech Church whose priests had been demanding an end to clerical celibacy since 1918.[124]

The instability of the governing parliamentary coalition meant that Masaryk and Beneš had to appease various parties with particularly strong anti-clerical leanings, like the Socialists and the Agrarians, from time to time, while the Catholic parties were unwilling to sacrifice their role in government

[121] A. Innes, *Czechoslovakia: The Short Goodbye*, London and New Haven, CT, 2001, 2.

[122] J. Korbel, *Twentieth Century Czechoslovakia: The Meanings of its History*, New York, 1977, 49.

[123] See the voluminous files on this in ASV, AES, IV Periodo, Cecoslovacchia, 61, P.O., fasc. 57, 1925 Feste di Giovanni Hus.

[124] ASV, AdRP, IV Periodo, Cecoslovacchia, Indice Provvisorio, Mons. Clemente Micara (1920–1925), B. 15, fasc. 1, Jednota del Clero.

for defence of the Church from the opposition benches.[125] In these circumstances, a diplomatic spat with the Vatican could quickly become a crisis, with the result that two nuncios were forced to depart the country. Mgr Francesco Marmaggi left in 1926 because of the question of Hus, and his successor, Mgr Pietro Ciriaci, was declared *persona non grata* in 1933 for making an unfortunate reference to the *Gens Slovakorum*, literally the 'Slovak Nation', at a time when the Slovaks were already showing worryingly secessionist tendencies: he was then expelled for this gaffe.[126] Relations were eventually patched up and Mgr Francesco Ritter was appointed nuncio in 1935.

Given the anti-clerical attitudes of Masaryk and his followers, a concordat was out of the question even though Catholics in Czechoslovakia constituted 80 per cent of the population of the new state. Instead, for over eight long years the two sides first negotiated and then sought to implement a *modus vivendi*. Beneš was the chief proponent of this on the government side. It is hard to know, however, how sincere he was. He *claimed* that he respected the Church and wanted good relations with it, but he was a Freemason and supported the national holiday for Jan Hus. He seems to have been playing a diplomatic game of 'good guy' to Masaryk's 'bad guy'.[127]

The *modus vivendi* which was finally signed in 1927 consisted of six clauses:

1. Diocesan boundaries were to be aligned them with those of the new state
2. Religious orders and congregations were to be led by Czech superiors
3. Bishops had to be reliable Czech citizens and the Czech government was to have a preventive veto over the appointment of diocesan ordinaries, coadjutor bishops with rights of succession, and army chaplains
4. All bishops were to take an oath of allegiance to the Czech State
5. Church assets, chiefly land, were to remain under State administration, subject to further agreements
6. The Czech Parliament would legislate for the implementation of the *modus vivendi*.

Clause 5 proved extremely difficult to implement, the problem being exacerbated by the new state's early law on land reform, which meant the

[125] ASV, AES, IV, Periodo, Cecoslovacchia, 61, P.O., fasc. 57, 1925 Feste di Giovanni Hus e Conseguenze, minutes of the Session of the Congregation of Extraordinary Ecclesiastical Affairs.

[126] ASV, AES, IV, Periodo, Cecoslovacchia, 61, P.O., fasc. 57, 149, 1933, Incidente fra Governo e Mons. Ciriaci.

[127] See the account of the discussion between Mgr Francesco Borgoncini-Duca, Secretary of Extraordinary Ecclesiastical Affairs, and Beneš in the Czech embassy to the Holy See, on 13 December 1924, in ASV, AES, IV, Periodo, Cecoslovacchia, 61, P.O., fasc. 57, Num. V Colloquio di mons. Segretario delle S.C. AA.EE.SS col ministro Benes, 13 dicembre 1924.

expropriation of estates of over 150–200 hectares. In fact, this was used by the Czechs to delay the division of diocesan property. A further problem was the need to settle the division of the property between the old, pre-1919 dioceses and the new ones, especially in Slovakia. Thus, the German bishop of Breslau and the Hungarian archbishop of Esztergom were reluctant to accept any settlement: they went to the court at The Hague to enforce Peace Treaty clauses relating to property transferred from one territorial jurisdiction. In the short term this probably gave the Vatican a bargaining counter.[128]

There are clear hints from Ciriaci's reports to Pacelli that ultimately the Czech political elite was determined to change Church–State relations radically, that is, to achieve separation, but they failed.[129] The Vatican cannily appointed temporary Apostolic Administrators for those parts of dioceses in Czechoslovakia whose bishop lived outside the national boundaries (which also appeased the Germans and Hungarians) and refused to make a final settlement of the Slovakian dioceses, that is, the erection of an archbishopric and suffragan bishoprics, thus thwarting Prague's radical plans by holding the trump card in its hands until the end of the Second World War. In any case, after the Munich Agreement of 1938 led to a partial dismemberment of Czechoslovakian territory, with the lion's share going to Germany and smaller slices to Hungary and Poland, the Vatican was forced to make new arrangements for the pastoral care of Catholics inside the new frontiers.[130]

Part and parcel of Gasparri and the pope's 'European' policy were attempts to improve relations with all states, successor states or not, especially where, as in the cases of Bulgaria, Greece, Romania, Turkey, and Yugoslavia, these contained substantial Catholic minority communities, Latin or Greek, with a view to improving the legal, political, and social standing of those minorities (in the case of the new Kingdom of Yugoslavia, Catholics were close to being a majority of the population). In all these cases, though the political elites were not Catholic, they had good reason to seek sound relations with the Holy See. So the Vatican quickly recognized Yugoslavia, which could be regarded as a sort of 'greater Serbia', and sought good relations with

[128] ASV, AES, IV, Periodo, Cecoslovacchia, 61, P.O., fasc. 57, 97, Esecuzione 'Modus vivendi' 1928, Commissione Applicazione dell (sic) 'Modus vivendi', letters from Gasparri of 28 January 1928 to Bishops of Berlin, Prague, and Eszgertom asking them to nominate representatives to the Commission for the 'division of the endowments of the parts of those dioceses in Czechoslovakia'; see also the letter of Ciriaci to Mgr Alfredo Ottaviani, 29 June 1928, in which he says 'The issues relating to the Commission are so numerous and complicated as to make one lose one's head!'

[129] ASV, AES, IV Periodo, Cecoslovacchia, 149, 1933, Incidente fra Governo e Mons. Ciriaci, Ciriaci to Pacelli, 2 February 1934; this is confirmed by Korbel, *Twentieth Century Czechoslovakia*, 49.

[130] L. Faltin, 'Czechoslovakian–Vatican Relations between 1945 and 1948 with Particular Reference to the Beginning of the Cold War', MPhil thesis, Anglia Ruskin University, 2004, 9–10.

it, and with Romania. It also sought to conclude concordats with both states in order to secure the rights of the substantial Catholic minorities which the territorial change imposed by the Versailles Settlement brought them. But whereas the concordat of 1926 was able to guarantee reasonably cordial relations with Romania, and consequently a fairly tranquil life for that country's Greek and Latin Catholic minorities, the Vatican had far less success with Yugoslavia.

ROMANIA AND YUGOSLAVIA

Post-Versailles Romania acquired 2 million Catholics, which was sufficient to persuade the government that it was necessary to establish diplomatic relations with the Holy See in 1921 and eventually conclude a concordat. In the short term, however, there was the more pressing and delicate question of the King's coronation. As a member of the Sigmaringen branch of the Hohenzollern royal house, Ferdinand was a Catholic and so the Vatican was determined that he should not be crowned by the Metropolitan of the Orthodox Church, which was still the majority religion in Romania.[131] Ferdinand had enough problems over the coronation with his recalcitrant new subjects in Transylvania, who were ethnically mostly German or Hungarian, but honour was satisfied on all sides by an essentially secular ceremony, with the King crowning himself and his Queen.[132] A concordat was signed with Romania on 10 May 1927 but was kept secret until after the Romanian Parliament had passed a general law regulating religious organizations a year later because of fears of concerted opposition from the Orthodox Church.[133] The Vatican obtained almost everything it wanted in the Romanian Concordat, especially a settlement of the complicated financial affairs of the Transylvanian Church, but Romania also greatly benefited. By its reorganization of the hierarchies of the Latin and Greek churches in June 1930, the Holy See officially recognized the post-war boundaries of 'Greater Romania'. This was always the ultimate prize for the successor states in their negotiations with the Vatican.

[131] See the lengthy correspondence between Mgr Marmaggi, nuncio in Bucharest, and Cardinal Gasparri, in ASV, AES, Quarto Periodo, P.O. 37–38, fasc. 30, Incoronazione del Re di Romania.

[132] ASV, AES, Quarto Periodo, P.O. 37–38, fasc. 30, Incoronazione del Re di Romania, Marmaggi to Gasparri, 11 September 1922.

[133] AdRP, IV Periodo, Romania (1921–1936). Indice 1243A, III, and Mariuca Vadan, *Le Relazioni Diplomatiche tra la Santa Sede e la Romania (1920–1948)*, Vatican City, 2001, 238–292, for the text of the concordat, the appendices, and the text of the Romanian law regulating the activities of the various religions.

As far as Yugoslavia was concerned, the attempts to replace the concordat of 1914 with one which would cover the whole of what was officially the 'Kingdom of the Serbs, Croats and Slovenes', and thus guarantee the rights of the Catholic *majorities* in the two western constituent parts of the kingdom, Slovenia and Croatia, ended in failure, despite long, tortuous negotiations beginning in 1922 and then taken up again in 1931, and a document that was only finally agreed in 1935.[134] The draft concordat was accepted by the lower house of Parliament, the *Skupština*, but owing to the mobilization of anti-Catholic opinion by the Serbian Orthodox Church, the government dropped ratification by the Senate.[135] This failure to secure the legal standing of the Church in Croatia in particular would help poison relations between Croatian Catholics and the Serb-dominated government in Belgrade, and contribute to the triumph of the Fascist Ustasha regime in 1941 (see Chapter 8).[136]

ALBANIA, BULGARIA, AND GREECE

Apostolic delegates were stationed in those Balkan countries, Albania, Bulgaria, and Greece, with which the Holy See did not have diplomatic relations, in order to supervise Catholic minorities. In this regard, Mgr Angelo Roncalli, the future John XXIII, played a vital role as apostolic delegate successively in Bulgaria, Turkey, and Greece.[137] The Vatican tried to negotiate a concordat with Albania, where there was a small Catholic minority in the north of the country, without success, despite the good offices of Italy, in whose Adriatic 'sphere of influence' Albania lay, and despite the desire of King Zog to achieve Vatican recognition for his newfound status after 1929. Some of the members of the Congregation for Extraordinary Ecclesiastical Affairs regarded the Albanians as 'a barbarous nation', a description with which many other contemporary observers would have concurred, and believed that they could not be trusted to keep to a legally binding international agreement.[138] The situation was just as difficult with Greece, but for different reasons. Here, the Vatican tried on three separate occasions to negotiate a concordat: once with the declining monarchy in 1922, then with new Hellenic Republic in 1931–3, and finally, under the restored monarchy, with

[134] See ASV, AES, Sessioni, 1360, Yugoslavia Nuovo Progetto di Concordato, 24 June 1934, contains the latest draft of the concordat and the Yugoslavian government response, and the minutes of the meeting of the Congregation which discussed them.

[135] Alexander, *Church and State*, 5.

[136] Alexander, *Church and State*, 6.

[137] See Hebblethwaite, *John XXIII*, chs 7 and 8.

[138] ASV, AES, Sessioni, 1363, Albania, 17 December 1934, Stampa 1252 Albania Eventuali Trattative per un Concordato-Relazione, 11 and Sommario, 59.

the dictatorship of General John Metaxas in 1938.[139] Suspicion of the Latin bishops and clergy of Greece, who sometimes had Italian names even if they were actually of Greek birth and nationality was the major stumbling block: this suspicion increased in the late 1930s as Mussolini flexed his muscles in the Mediterranean and cast covetous eyes towards Greece. Another problem was the small congregations of Greek and Armenian Catholics who attracted the particular hostility of the Orthodox Church.[140]

The Catholic minority was even more exiguous in Bulgaria, just over 60,000 in a total population of five and half million.[141] There was, in reality, no hope of reunion between the Orthodox Church there and Rome, or of a concordat. The unfortunate episode of King Boris's marriage (see Chapter 5) rendered the situation even less propitious for an agreement with the Vatican.

PIUS XI, CATHOLIC POLITICAL PARTIES, AND CATHOLIC ACTION

It was rarely the case that concordats could stand alone as the guarantees of the Church's rights in a given country. The role of Catholic laypeople, whether in Catholic political parties and/or in non-political Catholic lay organizations, like Catholic Action, was also crucially important. But despite the vogue for 'Wilsonian' democracy in Europe after 1918, the upper echelons of the hierarchy of the Roman Catholic Church remained unconvinced of the virtues and benefits of parliamentary government. Indeed, from the point of view of the Vatican, democracy, especially in the successor states, often resulted in instability. Sure enough, by the early 1930s, most of those states had either reverted to the authoritarian form of government of the pre-war period or had become dictatorships of one political complexion or another, which was not necessarily viewed as a bad thing in the Vatican.[142] Even more significantly, Catholic political parties did not prove themselves to be very effective in defending the Church's most fundamental interests. In Italy, as has been seen, Benedict XV and Gasparri had reason to complain about the unsatisfactory attitude of the PPI to the 'Roman Question', not to mention its role in the 1921 general

[139] See ASV, AES, Sessioni, 1347, 9 February 1932, Grecia, Concordato, p. 6, the draft of Mgr Margotti, Apostolic Delegate, and Hebblethwaite, *John XXIII*, 150–152, on Roncalli's démarches during the Metaxas dictatorship.

[140] ASV, AES, Quarto Periodo, Grecia, 28, P.O. 25, 728/31, letter from Mgr Margotti of 16 March 1931 on the 'very sad conditions' of Catholics in Greece.

[141] Hebblethwaite, *John XXIII*, 119.

[142] Leaving aside the distinction between 'successor' and 'non-successor' states, in the first category lay Bulgaria and Hungary, in the second Austria, Poland, Lithuania, Estonia, Yugoslavia, Bulgaria and Romania, Portugal, Greece, and, by 1939, Spain.

elections (see Chapter 3). Gasparri and Pius XI, and his nuncio Schioppa, were less than satisfied by the role which the Dutch Roman Catholic State Party played in the parliamentary battles over the Dutch legation to the Holy See. In the many disputes between the papal nuncio and the Czech government, the nuncio complained that the role of the Catholic deputies in the Czech parliament was determined more by the exigencies of coalition politics than concern for the dignity and interests of the Holy See.[143] Similarly, Catholic politicians gave little support to the nuncio in his disputes with a succession of Lithuanian governments. And it has to be said that, throughout the history of the Weimar Republic, the Holy See was less than sympathetic to the strategy of the Centre Party in Germany, which included coalitions with the Social Democrat Party (SPD).

A factor which exacerbated the diffidence of Pius XI towards democratic Catholic parties was the role within them of the clergy. During the interwar period a remarkable number of priests was involved in European Catholic political parties, in most cases also as leaders: Archbishops Sapieha and Teodorowicz and other priests in Poland; Sturzo in Italy; Sramek, Hlinka, and Tiso in Czechoslovakia; Seipel in Austria; Nolens in the Netherlands; and Kaas in Germany. It was incomprehensible to Papa Ratti that a priest could serve two masters, the Church of God and a political party. When requests reached the Secretariat of State for priests to be allowed to stand for parliament, though the usual response was to reserve the decision to the local ordinary, it is clear that Pius XI thoroughly disapproved of such requests and sought to discourage them.

If not parliamentary democracy, then what was Pius XI's ideal Catholic state? Of course, the Holy See never publicly expressed a preference for a form of government, always arguing that any form of government was acceptable so long as it operated within the bounds of Catholic morality. But for Italian Catholic priests of Ratti and Gasparri's generation there was inevitably a nostalgic preference for governments of an authoritarian stamp, the semi-absolutist monarchies of the pre-1914 era, and a deep suspicion of parliamentary democracy because it seemed so often to act as a vehicle for the anti-clerical, secularizing policies of liberal democratic political forces, as most evidently demonstrated in France, Italy, Portugal, and Spain from middle of the nineteenth century onwards.

If, for Ratti, there was a 'platonic ideal' of a Catholic state then it was the Austria of Chancellors Seipel, Dollfuss, and Schuschnigg between 1919 and 1938. Despite his aversion to priest-politicians, Pius made an exception for Mgr Ignaz Seipel, who ruled Austria for most of the period between 1920 and his death in 1932.[144] His skilful political manoeuvring, which kept the left-leaning Socialists out of power, earned him much respect in the

[143] ASV, AES, Iv Periodo, Cecoslovakia, 61, P.O., fasc. 57, 1925, Feste di Giovanni Hus e Conseguenze, 11–23.

[144] Rhodes, *The Vatican*, 145, makes the point that, after Seipel's death, all other priests in the Austrian parliament were ordered to resign by their bishops.

Vatican.[145] According to one historian of Austria, 'Under Seipel, Austria was regarded as the second Stato Pontificio . . .'[146] The deep class tensions represented by a powerful and aggressive Socialist party, and the division between opponents and sympathizers with German National Socialism's aim of *Anschluss*, produced serious political instability bordering on civil war, which was only averted by violent action against the Socialist strongholds in Vienna. Longer-term stability was guaranteed through the installation of an authoritarian regime which claimed to be 'A Catholic, German and Corporative state.'[147] Dollfuss was Seipel's spiritual and political successor and thus claimed that his new regime was heavily influenced by the corporatist ideas set out in Pius XI's encyclical *Quadragesimo Anno* of 1931. Salazar's Portugal was also looked upon with a very benevolent eye in the Vatican of Papa Ratti.

CHARLES MAURRAS AND L'ACTION FRANÇAISE

But there was an alternative model in vogue among many Catholics, including Salazar, in the early 1920s and that was the authoritarian, monarchist, integral Catholic (and anti-Semitic) nationalism of Charles Maurras and his organization L'Action Française. Against the background of the Dreyfus Affair and Laws of Separation at the turn of the century, Maurras's organization and its eponymous journal became the focus of intransigent opposition to the French Republic and its predominantly anti-clerical ruling class among the Catholic clergy and laity.[148] Prepared to use violence not only against its enemies on the political left but also Catholics of a Christian democratic hue, like Marc Sangnier, L'Action Française was a powerful force among monarchists as well. Moreover, it increasingly drew admiration from Catholics outside of France, especially in Belgium. But Maurras was an atheist who cynically sought to use Catholicism as an instrument for his own political ends, chiefly the restoration of the monarchy in France.[149] Thus, the pacifist element in post-war papal diplomacy, which sought reconciliation between

[145] Rhodes, *The Vatican*, 146–146.

[146] Rupert Kleiber, 'Quadragesimo Anno e lo Staendestaat D'Austria Nuova (1934–1938)', in De Rosa and Cracco (eds), *Il Papato e l'Europa*, 350.

[147] On the foundation of this state, see Wolfgang Maderthaner, '12 February 1934: Social Democracy and the Civil War', in Rolf Steininger, Gunter Bischof, and Michael Gehler (eds), *Austria in the Twentieth Century*, New Brunswick, NJ, and London, 2002, 54–56.

[148] For a history of Action Française, see E. Weber, *Action Française: Royalism and Reaction in Twentieth Century France*, Stanford, CA, 1961 and E. Nolte, *Three Faces of Fascism: Action Française, Italian Fascism, National Socialism*, London, 1965, trans. L. Vennekitz.

[149] And created some sort of Fascist regime, as E. Nolte argues in *Three Faces of Fascism: Action Franciase, Italian Fascism, National Socialism*, trans. Leila Vennewitz, London, 1965, Part 2.

France and Germany, was at odds with his extreme brand of French chauvinism, hence the attack on the papal nuncio, Mgr Maglione, when he congratulated the President of the Republic for the success at Locarno in his New Year address as doyen of the diplomatic corps at New Year 1927.[150]

There had, for some time, been concern in the Vatican about Maurras's shameless *realpolitik*. Pius X had considered condemning Maurras's movement and, after the war, Benedict XV probably also held back for fear of disturbing the fragile process of improving relations with France. By 1926, Pius XI could be surer of his ground. France now enjoyed cordial diplomatic relations with the Vatican, despite the parenthesis under Herriot, and the issue of the *associations diocésaines* had finally been resolved. He chose an indirect means to publish his anathema, the diocesan newspaper of Cardinal Andrieu, archbishop of Bordeaux, but the message was clear, Catholics could not support Action Française because it preached 'atheism, agnosticism, anti-Catholicism and anti-Christianity, amoralism for the individual and society . . . the restoration of paganism with all its violence and injustice'.[151] According to Valentina Ciciliot, 'the decision to focus on a large number of French *beati* and saints during the Holy Year of 1925 . . . on the eve of the condemnation of Action Française was not an arbitrary one'.[152]

Whereas Leo XIII had failed in his attempt to impose the *Ralliement* to the Republic on French Catholics in the 1880s, which would probably have prevented both the Dreyfus Affair and the Law of Separation, his successor succeeded in imposing the ban on L'Action Française fifty years later, though not without some strong, lingering resistance on the part of elements of both the French clergy and laity, and a fanatical rearguard action on the part of Maurras and friends.[153] The British ambassador claimed that, in 1926, the ban on L'Action Française had, 'produced complete disunion among French Catholics and almost open defiance of the Vatican on the part of many priests, and something like desertion of their religion by a considerable body of the laity'.[154] This was certainly a bit of an exaggeration but it did cause temporary turbulence in the French Church, even though Pius XI's iron will triumphed over that of a dissident French cardinal, Louis Billot, who, when he continued to publicly oppose the ban on L'Action Française was forced to resign his cardinal's hat.[155]

Even though there were already some truly Catholic alternatives to L'Action Française like the Parti Démocratique Populaire,[156] the French experience

[150] Rhodes, *The Vatican*, 107. [151] Chiron, *Pio XI*, 312–313.

[152] Ciciliot, 'Alcuni riflessioni', 11. [153] Chiron, *Pio XI*.

[154] Hachey, *Anglo-Vatican Relations*, 104.

[155] S. Pagano, 'Dalla Porpora al chiostro. L'inflessibilità di Pio XI verso il cardinale Louis Billot', in Delville and Jacov (eds), *La Papauté contemporaine*, 295–411.

[156] See James F. MacMillan, 'France', in T. Buchanan and M. Conway (eds), *Political Catholicism in Europe, 1918–1965*, Oxford, 2002, 35, 43, etc.

certainly confirmed Ratti's prejudices against Catholic parties of any kind. Equally, his attitude to parliamentary politics as a whole was strongly conditioned by his Italian experience. Despite the difficulties with Fascism, and especially the conflict of 1931, this suggested that it was easier to win respect and concessions from authoritarian rather than democratic regimes, like the liberal democratic regime which had preceded Fascism.

INTERNATIONAL CATHOLIC ACTION

Pius XI's alternative to Catholic parties of whatever political hue was Catholic Action, indeed he has frequently been referred to as 'the pope of Catholic Action'. As has been seen, he devoted particular attention to the development of this form of Catholic lay mobilization and activism in Italy during 1920s, and from the mid-1920s onwards, the Vatican authorities made a sustained attempt to impose the Italian model of Catholic Action in as many countries as possible, as the 'template' for the organization of Catholic lay, especially social, activism in defence of the Church and the advancement of its mission.[157] The purpose of this new, worldwide organization was to provide cadres of Catholic laypeople trained to engage with secular society, and all its challenges and evils. They were expected to bring Catholic witness to bear on the key issues of public morality (divorce, artificial contraception, abortion, and eugenics) as well as matters of social justice, and to exercise a vigilant surveillance of the press, cinema, and radio. They were also to combat the perceived enemies of the Church—Protestantism, Freemasonry, and anti-clericalism, and by the end of the 1930s, the neo-pagan influences of German National Socialism as well. But the most dangerous enemy was perceived to be Communism, so one of Catholic Action's major tasks was to combat that menace wherever it reared its head.

Pius and Pizzardo proposed the Italian model of Catholic Action (ACI) as it had developed by the end of the 1920s (its essential characteristics have been set out in Chapter 4,). ACI was thus, in the context of the rigid, hierarchical, and clerical ecclesiology of Pius XI, the ideal organizational pattern for Catholic lay activism throughout the world.

The pope carried forward his campaign to 'export' the Italian model of Catholic Action by means of letters to national primates or the presidents of national Episcopal conferences, such as those to Cardinal van Roey, archbishop of Malines-Mechelen and primate of Belgium (August 1928), Cardinal Bertram, Prince-Bishop of Breslau and a leading figure in the German

[157] For a detailed account of this campaign, see Pollard, 'Pius XI's Promotion', 758–785.

Bishops Council (December 1928), and Cardinal Segura, Archbishop of Toledo and primate of Spain (November 1929). From his strategic position in the Secretariat of State, Mgr Pizzardo developed a growing correspondence with nuncios and apostolic delegates about Catholic Action. Sometimes he corresponded directly with local prelates and priests, and even laymen working in the field. But on the whole, he preferred to do his work via the Vatican's representatives, urging upon them the necessity for the national hierarchies to whom they were accredited to adopt the Italian model, as well as providing copies of publications produced by Italian Catholic Action to be translated into various languages, most commonly Mgr Luigi Civardi's *Manual of Catholic Action* (*Manuale di Azione Cattolica*), which set out in the clearest terms the organizational principles to be adopted.[158] Civardi's pamphlet was translated into English, French, German, and Spanish, and may have been rendered into other languages as well. The Belgian Catholic activist, Christine de Hemptinne, translated a Catholic Action manual into Spanish for Peruvian Acción Católica and into English for Australian and Indian Catholic Action, the latter then being translated into Tamil.[159]

The vitality and effectiveness of Catholic lay activity, in the social sphere especially, varied enormously from country to country at the beginning of Pius XI's reign. In France, Germany, and the Benelux states, Catholic lay activities were extremely diverse and highly developed, as they also were in Britain, Australia, Canada, and the USA; in the latter case they were directed from a strong national organization in Washington—the National Catholic Welfare Conference.[160] In other countries, however, the situation was very much less promising. While there was plenty of Catholic 'associationalism', it was largely devoted to para-liturgical or devotional activities, lay spiritual formation, and charity, divided into many specialist groups, and not coordinated at a diocesan or national level: social activism was less evident. Mgr Pascal Robinson O.F.M., papal nuncio to the Irish Free State, for example, reported on the depressing *inactivity* of Catholics there as late as 1935, despite the efforts of the bishops to establish a national Catholic Action organization.[161] Two other deeply Catholic countries, Portugal and Spain, presented a similar picture: the papal nuncio in Lisbon informed Pizzardo in 1930 that there was a virtual absence of Catholic social activism in that country,

[158] Luigi Civardi, *Manuale di azione cattolica*, 17th edn, Rome, 1934.

[159] Catholic Documentation Centre, University of Leuven, Belgium (henceforth KADOC), Archive of the de Hemptinne family, Papieren Christine de Hemptinne (henceforth AdCH), 30, Personalia, 9.5/1–2 Curriculum Vitae.

[160] See Douglas J. Slawson, *The Foundation and the First Decade of the National Catholic Welfare Conference*, Washington, DC, 1992, and E. Boyea, *The National Catholic Welfare Conference: An Experience in Episcopal Leadership, 1935–1945*, Washington, DC, 1987.

[161] ASV, AES, IV Periodo, Gran Bretagna, 252, P.O., 99 Azione Cattolica in Irlanda, report of the nuncio, Mgr Pascal Robinson OFM, of 10 April 1935.

where the Church had little influence among the working classes. Eventually, Acção Católica Portuguesa was developed to replace the political pressure group Centro Católico in 1933.[162] As far as Spain was concerned, according to Frances Lannon:

> Right up to the Civil War, Spanish Catholic Action often amounted to little more than a ritual lament that things were as they were, and an institutionalised aspiration that they should be different. Bishops loudly castigated lay complacency and inactivity, but offered no programme for action.[163]

In March 1938, Pizzardo, now a cardinal, was appointed to head a new Ufficio Centrale dell'Azione Cattolica (Central Office of Italian Catholic Action) in Rome to coordinate and support the work of national organizations. But in the field, the fruits of Pizzardo's efforts were limited. Many problems impeded progress: the unwillingness of individual bishops to surrender control of lay organizations to a national 'centre', especially where there were already rivalries in the episcopacy; the unwillingness of parochial clergy to shoulder further responsibilities; consequently, a scarcity of human and monetary resources and a natural unwillingness on the part of bishops and lay leaders in those countries where Catholic organizations were already successful and well developed to adopt a foreign model. While there were success stories for the Italian model in places like England and Wales and Australia, on the whole the most that was achieved was perhaps a keener and more general recognition of the need to organize and mobilize the laity in defence of the Church.[164]

THE VATICAN, LATIN AMERICA, AND THE MEXICAN TRAGEDY

While, as has been seen, there were clearly problems for the Roman Catholic Church deriving from the activities of anti-clerical political forces in several states of continental Europe, not to mention the Soviet Union, until the advent of the Second Spanish Republic in 1931 the real threats posed by these forces came from elsewhere, principally Latin America, and Mexico was the hot spot. For roughly nine years following the adoption of the Querétaro Constitution, the laws which it introduced were not very strictly enforced. During that time, however, the resumption of Catholic activities in the social field led to a

[162] A. Costa Pinto and M. Inácia Rezola, 'Political Catholicism, Crisis of Democracy and Salazar's New State', *Totalitarian Movements and Political Religions*, 8(2) (June 2007), 360.

[163] Lannon, *Privilege, Persecution and Prophecy*, 148–149: ch. 6 provides an excellent analysis of the Catholic movement in Spain.

[164] Pollard, 'Pius XI's Promotion', 773–780.

renewal of pressure on the Church, though it was an act of so-called religious 'aggression', the solemn and public dedication of Mexico to Christ the King in 1923, which ostensibly caused an enraged government to expel the apostolic delegate. The election as president of Plutarcho Calles, a committed socialist and fanatical anti-clerical, in 1926 worsened the situation further. Calles insisted on the rigid application of the laws and in particular the registration and restriction of the number of clergy who might administer the sacraments within a given area.[165] The result was patchy: in some states, governors hardly interfered with the clergy and their ministrations; in others, they sought to outbid Calles, and thus promote their chances of succeeding him, by enforcing severe restrictions. The intransigents among the Mexican bishops, aided by a group of equally intransigent Jesuits, responded by proposing the imposition of what amounted to an interdict, closing churches and suspending the administration of the sacraments. The Mexican intransigents were aided by Cardinal Pio Boggiani, formerly apostolic delegate in Mexico, who argued in a meeting of the Congregation for Extraordinary Ecclesiastical Affairs that the Holy See should confirm the 'interdict'.[166] The 'interdict' has to be counted as the major cause of the subsequent widespread popular protest against the government and eventually an organized, armed revolt of Catholics, the Cristiada, a movement that was especially strong in the western states of Mexico.[167] In turn, governmental repression of clergy and lay activists became more brutal and bloody, Mexico in this period yielding up twenty-five martyrs who were beatified by John Paul II and twenty-seven who were canonized.[168]

Pius was horrified by the atrocities committed by the *Cristeros*, which included violence and murder against schoolteachers who continued to work for the Republic. What most shocked the men in the Vatican was the support given to the armed revolt of priests and even bishops—like those of Huetulja and Durango.[169] In his apostolic letter *Paterna sane* of February 1926 to the Mexican episcopate Pius emphasized 'the willingness to persevere in passive resistance',[170] nothing else in the pronouncements could lead to the conclusion that this included the use of violence. Nor is there any evidence of the Vatican endorsing

[165] See Paolo Valvo, '"Una Turlupinatura stile messicano". La Santa Sede e la Sopensione del Culto Pubblico in Messico (Luglio 1926)', *Quaderni di storia*, 78 (July–December 2013), 198–199.

[166] ASV, AES, Sessioni, 1292. 18 July 1926. Messico. Stampa 1155; for an acute and detailed analysis of manoeuvring among the Mexican bishops, see Valvo, '"Una Turlupinatura"', 202–212.

[167] For a history of the Cristero rebellion, see J. Meyer, *La Cristiada: I. La Guerra de los cristeros*, Mexico City, 2005.

[168] V. Ciciliot, 'La Politica delle Canonizzazioni di Giovanni Paolo II', dissertation, Universitá degli Studi di Padova, Facoltá di Lettere e Filosofia, 235.

[169] Paolo Valvo, ' La Santa Sede e la Cristiada (1926–1929), *Revue d'histoire ecclésiastique*, 108(3.4) (2013), 840–875.

[170] Bellocchi, *Tutte le Encicliche*, XII, 2 February 1926. *Paterna sane*. Epistola apostolica.

the Cristiada in private communications with the Mexican bishops. Pius XI's constant, reiterated advice to the bishops was to ensure that their priests kept out of politics, that the laity should *not* form a Catholic political party, and that they should entrust the future to the careful and successful organization of Catholic Action as a public pressure group against hostile laws.[171]

In fact, the Pope and the Secretariat of State tried to moderate the fanatical zeal of some Mexican bishops, clergy, and laity. In July 1926, Gasparri advised the Mexican episcopate not to make an issue out of a recent government decree that the Mexican flag be raised on Church property on days of national significance. In October 1927, Pius ordered the intransigent bishops of Durango, León, and Tehuantepec to leave Rome in order to prevent the Holy See from being associated with and compromised by their intrigues.[172]

The Vatican's handling of the Mexican situation was not always very adroit or entirely effective. In 1928, President Hoover, concerned about the economic effects of the religious persecution and under pressure from the NCWC and some American bishops, decided upon the intervention of the American ambassador Dwight Morrow. This led to meetings between Fr Burke, representative of the NCWC, Archbishop Ruiz, and President Calles. These resulted in the *Arreglos*, a sort of *modus vivendi* whereby priests were to be reappointed to their cures, churches were to be reopened, and some church property restored, thus bringing the 'interdict' to an end in June 1929.[173] The *Arreglos* of June1929 could be seen as a sign of weakness on the part of the government, since the *Cristeros* were, at that time, having considerable military success against the regular troops, yet they failed to offer the one thing which Pius XI had stuck out for so long: reform of the laws against the Church. The assassination by a Catholic fanatic of president-elect Obregon in 1929 provided Calles with a pretext for largely ignoring the agreement, thus many Mexican bishops, clergy, and laity felt betrayed, particularly when many former *Cristeros* were killed in cold blood.[174]

CHANGING OF THE GUARD: THE DEPARTURE OF GASPARRI

The departure of Pietro Gasparri from the Secretariat of State conveniently coincides with the beginning of the new decade. This 'changing of the guard' in the Vatican can be regarded as an assertion of Pius XI's authority because

[171] Bellocchi, *Tutte le Encicliche*, XII, 2 February 1926. *Paterna sane*. Epistola apostolica.

[172] Valvo, 'Difendere la Fede in Messico. Ragiono dellem armi, ragioni della diplomazia (1926–1937)' forthcoming in M. Leonardis (ed.), *Fede e Diplomazia. Le relazioni internazionali della santa Sede nell'etá contemporanea*, Milan, 2014, 198–218.

[173] Valvo, 'La Santa Sede e la Cristiada', P. Valvo, 'Difendere la Fede in Messico.

[174] Fogarty, *The Vatican*, 235.

there is evidence that, though already 80, Gasparri didn't want to go.[175] Even though he had health problems and had to have time off, this still doesn't explain his going. After many years of a close relationship with his former superior (firstly as papal envoy in the Poland and the Baltic states), Pius wanted a change. Gasparri was probably too pragmatic and ruthless, and Papa Ratti 'more idealistic', as Giovanni Coco claims.[176] Perhaps the answer was simpler than that: Pius XI wanted more direct control over the Secretariat of State and this could only be achieved with a younger colleague, a real subordinate. It certainly was no longer possible with Gasparri, who enjoyed considerable prestige precisely on account of the achievements under his belt, not least the codification of Canon Law and the negotiation of the Lateran Treaties. One sign of the increasing distance between Gasparri and Pius XI is to be found in the fact that, during the discussions on the persecution of the Church in Mexican, back in 1926, the pope had accepted the Boggiani thesis against the advice of his own careful, cautious Secretary of State who had had his own diplomatic experience in Latin America.[177] Pius XI may also have felt that, with the signing of the Lateran Pacts in 1929, and thus the resolution of the greatest problem facing the Holy See, there was no further need for such a master of papal diplomacy as the venerable Gasparri.

With his departure, an era in Vatican diplomacy ended. Gasparri was probably the most outstanding and important Secretary of State since Ercole Consalvi in the early period after the ending of the Napoleonic War.[178] Of Cardinal Antonelli (1848–76), Rampolla (1883–1903), or Merry del Val (1903–14), none could claim the diplomatic successes of Gasparri, who had helped steer Vatican diplomacy successfully through the First World War and had then worked on building up the network of relations between the Holy See and the powers during and after it, especially with regard to the successor states. Like Consalvi, Gasparri had also achieved the restoration of the temporal power, albeit in a very minute, miniscule form—Consalvi had succeeded in persuading the statesman at the Congress of Vienna to restore the Papal States in their entirety.[179] The Lateran Pacts, which brought about that restoration, and, almost as important, the restoration of good relations with Italy must, along with the successful completion of the Code of Canon Law, be regarded as some of the greatest achievements in the history of the modern papacy. But Gasparri was probably lucky to be able to go when he did because the 1930s, even the early 1930s, brought challenges to the Holy See for which he was much less well equipped to cope.

[175] R. Gannon, SJ, *The Cardinal Spellman Story*, New York, 1963, 67; see also Alvarez, *Spies in the Vatican*, 159.

[176] Pagano, Chappin, and Coco, *I 'Fogli di Udienza'*, 55.

[177] ASV, AES, Sessioni, 1292. 18 July 1926. Messico. Stampa 1155.

[178] Hales, *Revolution and the Papacy*, ch. 15.

[179] Hales, *Revolution and the Papacy*, 231–238.

7

Pius XI and the Dictators, 1930–9

INTRODUCTION

In January 1930, Mgr Eugenio Pacelli, having been recalled from Berlin and made a cardinal, was appointed Secretary of State in succession to Gasparri. There was some surprise in Rome that the choice of successor did not fall upon Cardinal Bonaventura Cerretti, who had had a distinguished diplomatic career, culminating in his role as nuncio in Paris, the most prestigious Vatican diplomatic posting, where he had carried out the difficult task of enforcing the condemnation of L'Action Française.[1] But, like Gasparri, Cerretti had a reputation for being pragmatic and ruthless and seemed likely to continue Gasparri's policies. Again, he also seemed too pro-French, pro-democracy, and *pro-popolare*, that is, a supporter of the former Partito Popolare Italiano, to be persona grata with the Fascists.[2] There was even a whiff of scandalous worldliness around his name in France which had generated libels and defamatory statements.[3] Eventually, Cerretti was appointed to the Supreme Tribunal of the Segnatura in 1931, not an office of the first rank in the Roman Curia.[4]

On the other hand, though Mgr Eugenio Pacelli was also a pupil of Gasparri's, inasmuch as he had worked with him on the commission to codify Canon Law, he was considerably younger than Gasparri—54 years of age—and seemed likely to prove to be a more docile subordinate for the pope.[5] He had also had a fairly distinguished career in Germany, first as nuncio in Munich and then in Berlin, and had successfully negotiated concordats with two German states, Bavaria, 1924, and Prussia,1929, and begun negotiations

[1] Pagano, Chappin, and Coco, *I 'Fogli di Udienza'*, 78.

[2] Pagano, Chappin, and Coco, *I 'Fogli di Udienza'*, 79.

[3] Pagano, Chappin, and Coco, *I 'Fogli di Udienza'*, 81–82.

[4] Pagano, Chappin, and Coco, *I 'Fogli di Udienza'*, 50–51.

[5] Pagano, Chappin, and Coco, *I 'Fogli di Udienza'*, 50, 'For papa Ratti . . . mons. Pacelli looked like an able, diligent and extremely patient negotiator of concordats.' He also says that Pacelli was very much of the same mentality and spirituality as the pope.

for a third, Baden (see Chapter 6). All in all, Pacelli seemed a safer bet for Pius XI than Cerretti.

However, as has been suggested earlier, the 'changing of the guard' at the top of the Vatican hierarchy made no great difference to papal diplomatic policy in the short term. In particular, like Gasparri, Pacelli was to prove more conciliatory towards the Italian Fascist regime than his boss, Pius XI. While there remained an interesting tension between the two men in the formulation of Vatican policy towards states in the 1930s, which would manifest itself in a number of crises, it never led to a rupture and was certainly not always evident to contemporary 'Vatican watchers'. From the point of view of the historian of the modern papacy, the fact that Pacelli thereafter kept a careful record of his audiences with Pius XI certainly makes study of the Vatican's policymaking in the 1930s a very different proposition from that of the previous decade.[6] Pacelli would prove a faithful and diligent servant of Pius XI in the conduct of the Vatican's relations with states, especially the totalitarian dictatorships, and in the broader administration of the Roman curia, the central government of the worldwide Roman Catholic Church.

On the other hand, the management of the Vatican's diplomatic and administrative structures did change under Pacelli, who centralized into his own hands, always of course with the consent of the pope, the decision-making power in the Secretariat of State and the Congregation for Extraordinary Ecclesiastical Affairs, utilizing the services of two close assistants, Mgr Pizzardo and Mgr Malusardi.[7]

The new head of Vatican diplomacy had a turbulent decade ahead of him. In the 1930s barely a year went by without some international crisis or another, or some new, grave threat to the Roman Catholic Church. A key date was the proclamation of the Second Spanish Republic in May 1931, following which the Vatican was quickly confronted with the horrors of a Mexican situation, and worse, in its European backyard. The advent to power of the Nazis in Germany in January 1933 turned out to be an even more significant event than all the preceding ones. The triumph of National Socialism very quickly changed the whole atmosphere in Europe and the world and presented Pius XI with even greater problems. Thus, by1937, Pius XI faced the challenges posed by *two* totalitarian dictatorships—those of Stalin in the Soviet Union and Hitler in Germany, *and* the continuing, if lessened, persecution of the Church in Mexico and escalating anti-clerical violence in Spain as the civil war got under way. By the time of his death in February 1939, the pope also

[6] ASV, AES, IV Periodo, 430 (1930–1938), 348, 1931, Taccuini di S.Emo. Cardinale Pacelli, Segretario di Stato di Sua Sanita.

[7] Giovanni Coco, 'Eugenio Pacelli', in Pagano et al., *I 'Fogli di Udienza'*, 132.

had to contend with the consequences of Mussolini's systematic attempts to transform his regime into a totalitarian one and the clearest portents yet of another general European war.

PIUS XI AND THE GREAT DEPRESSION

The Wall Street Crash of October 1929 is usually regarded as *the* watershed in the history of interwar Europe since it was quickly followed by the onset of the Great Depression with its catastrophic effects on Weimar Germany, leading to the rise of Hitler and National Socialism and all the international consequences that that would bring. As a result of the fortnightly audiences with his investment manager, Bernardino Nogara, who was constantly travelling between the various financial capitals of Europe seeking investment opportunities for the Vatican, Pius XI was kept well informed about the various developments of the economic crisis that followed the collapse of the New York Stock Exchange. Thus, in June 1933, Nogara gave his analysis of the World Conference on Economic and Monetary Matters. Nogara doubted that it would have positive results, and he was proved right.[8] Pius also received first-hand accounts of the worsening economic crisis from other sources; as far as the United States were concerned, from American bishops in the letters accompanying their submission of diocesan Peter's Pence collections.[9] In late 1932, in a letter which Pius sent to Cardinal Mundelein of Chicago, thanking him for a 'conspicuous sum' which the latter had sent, he wrote:

> I would not have made that request [for an advance on the Peter's Pence collection] if I had known before what I have learnt in recent weeks about the terrible dimensions of the impact of the world crisis in the United States.[10]

As the worldwide depression deepened, Pius described it as 'the greatest human calamity since the flood' and though he could not have foreseen its longer-term political effects any more than his contemporaries, he deplored its more immediate economic and social effects in several speeches and also in no less than three encyclicals, *Quadragesimo Anno* of May 1931, *Nova Impendet* of October 1931, and *Caritate Christi Compulsi* of May 1932.[11]

[8] AFN, Nogara's diary, entry for 23 June and 6 July 1932.

[9] Pollard, 'American Catholics', 199 and 202.

[10] AAC, Mundelein papers, 1872–1939, 3/36, Pius to Mundelein, 12 December 1932.

[11] For the texts of these encyclicals, see Carlen, *The Papal Encyclicals*, III, 391–414, 459–460, and 475–483.

QUADRAGESIMO ANNO

Quadragesimo Anno was the most systematic and sustained of Pius XI's responses to the Great Depression, but it should be remembered that the timing of the encyclical, at the height of the Great Depression, was largely fortuitous. Pius XI would almost certainly have published a major encyclical on the 'social question' even if there had not been a depression because *Quadragesimo Anno* was supposed to be the fortieth anniversary commemoration of Leo XIII's encyclical *Rerum Novarum* and, consequently, a review of the significant developments in the economic, political, and social fields which had taken place since then, most particularly the First World War and the Bolshevik Revolution in Russia.

Like other encyclicals published during Pius's reign, the encyclical was largely the work of one hand, in this case the German Jesuit Fr Oswald Nell-Breuning, who consulted another Jesuit of the German school of Catholic Social Thought, Gustav Gundlach, though the pontiff reviewed it paragraph by paragraph.[12] The only part of the encyclical which was definitely from the pen of Pius XI himself was sections 91 to 96, those which dealt with the thorny question of the 'Corporate State' which the Fascists were rather slowly constructing in Italy.[13]

Communism was unequivocally condemned as elsewhere in Pius XI's encyclicals, and while acknowledging the changes which had taken place in the Marxist working-class movement since 1891, in particular the split which occurred in the movement in 1919 between the faithful supporters of the Comintern parties on the one hand and the Socialists, Social Democrats, and Labour parties who adhered to the Second International on the other, *Quadragesimo Anno* nevertheless reiterated the formal condemnation of the latter on the grounds that they had not fundamentally changed in their ideological hostility to Christianity.[14] Coleman argues that this had the effect of preventing Catholic–Socialist collaboration against both Fascism and Communism, and in particular hindered such cooperation between the Centre Party and the SPD against the Nazis in Germany.[15] This would seem to be something of an exaggeration: the progressive collapse of Weimar

[12] O. von Nell-Breuning, 'The Drafting of *Quadragesimo Anno*', in Charles E. Curran and Robert McCormick (eds), *Readings in Moral Theology No. 5*, New York, 1986; Fr Nell-Breuning slightly confuses the issue in the article when he says, on the one hand, that 'I could not consult anyone and was left wholly on my own'(p. 61) and, on the other, that 'I decided to incorporate his [Gundlach's] contributions un-shortened into the draft of the encyclical'(p. 62).

[13] For a fuller analysis of the encyclical, see the entry for *Quadragesimo Anno* in Judith A. Dwyer (ed.), *The New Dictionary of Catholic Social Thought*, Collegeville, MN, 1994, 802–813.

[14] Carlen, *The Papal Encyclicals*, III, 432–435.

[15] J. Coleman, 'Development of Catholic Social Teaching', in Curran and McCormick (eds), *Readings in Moral Theology No. 5*, 73–85.

democracy between 1930 and 1933 was due to a much more complex set of factors, not least of which were the inability of the Centre and the SPD to agree on a common policy to deal with the effects in Germany of the Great Depression and the meddling of President Hindenburg and his clique.[16] The hostility towards capitalism, the 'evil child of liberalism', was scarcely lessened; sections of the encyclical explicitly condemned the latest forms of anonymous, monopoly finance capital, like this passage:

> an immense and despotic dictatorship is consolidated in the hands of a few, who are often not owners but only the trustees and managing directors of invested funds which they administer according to their arbitrary will and pleasure.[17]

In a broader sense, *Quadragesimo Anno* reflected the feelings prevalent among Catholics at the time. While rejecting the 'Socialism in One Country' of Stalin's Russia, with its forced collectivization of the land, famines, and the horrors of breakneck industrialization, like many European Catholics Pius XI assumed that, as a result of the Great Depression, bourgeois capitalism, and the political system with which it was bound up, was moribund, and that new forms of economic and social organization were now called for. This was a natural response to the crisis for an Italian priest of deeply anti-liberal, conservative instincts. Hence, the encyclical invoked the solution to the problems of economic organization advocated by Leo XIII—a corporate system in which employers and employees would be brought together in syndicates which would jointly manage their sector of economic life. In common with Catholic social thinkers elsewhere, the author of *Quadragesimo Anno* looked back to the *Ordines* and guilds of the medieval 'golden age' of Christendom as a model of economic and social organization which would avoid the mistakes of both capitalism and communism. Even if this 'nostalgia' was limited to the historically more recent *ancien régime* organization of economic and social affairs of the eighteenth century, it was equally romanticized and unrealistic. European and North American society had been dramatically transformed by industrial capitalism since the eighteenth century. It is perhaps surprising that the mill manager's son from Lombardy, Italy's industrial heartland, should have been so accepting of this sort of solution to the economic crisis.

Against the background of a deepening of the capitalist crisis, and the mounting fear of world Communism, *Quadragesimo Anno* had a big impact. Catholics in several countries in Europe—for example, Austria, Ireland, and Portugal—and the United States of America were strongly influenced by the pope's words.[18] Austria was probably the state in which Catholic politicians most diligently attempted to enact the principles set out in the encyclical.

[16] See Sir Ian Kershaw, *Hitler, 1889–1936: Hubris*, London, 1998, ch. 9.
[17] Carlen, *Papal Encyclicals*, III, 431.
[18] See Dwyer, *New Dictionary of Catholic Social Thought*, 810.

According to Robert Pyrah, the new constitution of the 'Second' Austrian Republic, which Chancellor Dollfuss proclaimed in 1934, established Austria as an 'authoritarian, Christian state with a corporatist base'.[19] He further argues that, though Austrian corporative institutions 'went against the spirit of "subsidiarity" in *Quadragesimo Anno* . . . there can be no doubt that the regime at least attempted to act in the *spirit* of *Quadragesimo Anno*. . . .'[20]

Portugal, where Catholic academic António Salazar had also consolidated his dictatorship by 1932 with a new constitution, was another European country which claimed to be following the tenets of Catholic corporatism as established in the 1931 encyclical, and openly proclaimed its debt to *Quadragesimo Anno*. According to António Costa Pinto, 'Corporatism was one of the fundamentals of the Salazarist new order. . . .'[21] The debate on corporatism in Portugal pre-dated the emergence of fascist models, and even *Quadragesimo Anno*, but Catholics enthusiastically welcomed it, and corporate institutions were developed in Portugal in the context of a state which had been progressively 're-Catholicized' in reaction to the effects of the 1910 Republican Revolution.[22]

In the Irish Free State, an overwhelmingly Catholic country where the Church was a powerful influence on the two major political parties, *Quadragesimo Anno* was received with enthusiasm in both clerical and lay circles. Ironically, the state's overwhelmingly rural, agrarian economy meant it presented few of the industrial relations problems for which corporatism was meant to be the remedy, and consequently faced little threat from Communism. But the encyclical had a particular effect on General Eoin O'Duffy's Blueshirts, a 'para-fascist' political organization as Griffin would describe it, but a solidly Catholic one, nevertheless, thus also earning for itself the epithet of 'clerical Fascist'.[23]

But there was a real danger that, despite Pius XI's strictures in articles 91–96, less well-informed Catholics would fail to appreciate the essential differences between Catholic corporatism as enunciated in *Quadragesimo Anno* and the Fascist corporatism of Mussolini's Italy, and Nell-Breuning was seriously worried about that. Thus he wrote, 'When, three years later [after the publication of *Quadragesimo Anno*], Pius XI expressed high appreciation of the "QA" state allegedly established in Austria through the Constitution of May, 1934, I was completely dismayed.'[24] The confusion helped render

[19] R. Pyrah, 'Cultural Politics and "Clerical Fascism" in Austria, 1933–1938', *TMPR*, 8(2) (June 2007), 274.

[20] Pyrah, 'Cultural Politics', 274.

[21] Costa Pinto and Rezola, 'Political Catholicism', 360.

[22] Costa Pinto and Rezola, 'Political Catholicism', 360.

[23] See M. Cronin, 'Catholicising Fascism, Fascistising Catholicism? The Blueshirts and the Jesuits in Ireland', *TMPR*, 8(2) (June 2007), 189–200.

[24] Nell-Breuning, 'The Drafting of *Quadragesimo Anno*', 64.

Catholics in several countries, including Britain before Mussolini's invasion of Ethiopia in 1936, sympathetic to Fascism.[25] The difference between Catholic and Fascist variants of corporatism, as spelled out in sections 91–96 of *Quadragesimo Anno*,[26] was essentially founded on the Catholic social principle of 'subsidiarity', that a higher level of authority, in this case the State, should not usurp the functions of lower-level institutions in civil society such as the family, the Church, local authorities, and corporative syndicates. Pius criticized the fact that:

> the State itself has taken over the functions of the free organizations . . . The new system is excessively bureaucratic and political: despite the general advantages referred to, it is more likely to serve particular interests rather than lead to a better social order.[27]

As Pyrah admits, even Austrian corporatism, the apple of Pius XI's eye, was guilty of creating a more 'fascist' form of corporatism because it permitted the 'vertical' organization of authority prohibited in *Quadragesimo Anno*.[28] That may have been because Dollfuss sought to engage the sympathy of Mussolini, his major 'protector', against his overweening northern neighbour, Nazi Germany, after January 1933. Despite the deviations from the 'norms' of Catholic corporatism, as set out in *Quadragesimo Anno*, including the suppression of the trade unions, the Vatican looked benevolently on the Austria of Dollfuss, and, to a lesser extent, the Portugal of Salazar, which imitated some of the Austrian policies as models of political, economic, and social organization for Catholics.

Franco's Spain, after 1939, would also adopt corporative institutions but their Catholic, rather than Italian Fascist, inspiration is debatable.[29] Despite Pius XI's strictures, the Fascist corporate state would continue to evince a great deal of interest from Catholics in Europe and even from Roosevelt in America.[30]

There is one particular aspect to Pius XI's response to the Great Depression which is more than a little puzzling. On the one hand, as has been seen, he had deplored the forces of monopoly finance capital in *Quadragesimo Anno*, a censure repeated in the encyclical *Caritate Christi Compulsit* of 1932. The latter was a sort of omnibus condemnation of the ills of the age—including anti-clericalism (in Spain, in particular) and Communism—coupled with exhortations to penance and prayer, but it also harps on the theme of

[25] Tom Buchanan, 'Great Britain', in Buchanan and Conway (eds), *Political Catholicism*, 267–268.

[26] Carlen, *The Papal Encyclicals*, III, 430.

[27] Carlen, *The Papal Encyclicals*, III, 430.

[28] Pyrah, 'Cultural Politics', 274.

[29] C. Delzell (ed.), *Mediterranean Fascism, 1919–1945*, New York, 1971.

[30] See Giulia D'Alessio, 'The United States and the Vatican (1936–1939)', in Gallagher et al. (eds), *Pius XI and America*, 129–130.

monopoly capitalism: ' these very few men, very few indeed . . . who being addicted to excessive gain . . . were and are in great part the cause of these evils . . . The desire for money is the root of all evil.'[31]

How then did he reconcile this with Nogara's financial speculation on behalf of the Vatican? Was this not also a case of 'trustees and managing directors of investment funds which they administer to their arbitrary will and pleasure', against which he had argued in *Quadragesimo Anno*?[32] According to Mgr Tardini, in the 1930s Pius was always looking for new sources of money.[33] In this desperate search for money to pay for his ambitious building projects and to meet the requests contained in the many begging letters he received from Catholics and non-Catholics all over the world, Pius happily encouraged Nogara in his various financial operations, including *arbitrage*. Thus, in February 1932, Nogara reported to the pope:

> We have sold $220,000 worth of North American bonds: meanwhile we have bought $240,000 worth of first class bonds at a price of $188,000 . . . Another arbitrage operation is in progress to sell £100,000 of Australian loan stock in order to buy £300,000 of Australian stock. The purpose of this operation is to profit from the greater depression of the New York market in comparison with the London one.[34]

Could not these operations also be said to constitute an example of administering invested funds 'at arbitrary will and pleasure'? Furthermore, while the Roman Catholic Church had more or less abandoned its moral condemnation of moneylending at interest as equivalent to usury by this time, the Code of Canon Law of 1917 restricted the forms of investment open to the administrators of ecclesiastical property.[35] On the face of it, *arbitrage* would appear to be one of these.

THE VATICAN AND THE DISARMAMENT CONFERENCE OF 1932

One of the key features of Pius XI's analysis of the causes of the Great Depression, as outlined in *Nova Impendet* of October 1931, was his emphasis on the need for disarmament. In it he bemoaned ' an insensate competition in armaments which, in its turn, becomes the cause of enormous expenditure, diverting large sums of money from the public welfare; and this makes

[31] Carlen, *The Papal Encyclicals*, III, 475.

[32] Carlen, *The Papal Encyclicals*, III, 432.

[33] Casula, *Domenico Tardini*, 292.

[34] AFN, Nogara's diary, entry for 15 February 1932.

[35] For a discussion of this issue, see Pollard, *Money*, 64–166.

the present crisis more acute'.[36] This was not a new policy. The Vatican had urged disarmament since the end of the First World War. By the end of the 1920s, the papacy had achieved strong international standing and respect, not least because of its insistent calls for disarmament throughout the decade, and this was demonstrated by the démarches made to the Vatican by various organizations in anticipation of the Disarmament Conference of 1932, which was regarded by its supporters as a 'make or break' attempt for world peace. In November 1931, Daniel de Montenach, in charge of the political section of the League of Nations Secretariat, wrote to Mgr Pizzardo soliciting the public support of the pope for the conference.[37] In December, Fr André Arnou, SJ, a special adviser to the director-general of the ILO, passed another appeal for papal support to the Secretariat of State.[38] A third appeal was received by Mgr Ritter, counsellor at the Berne nunciature, from Lord Cecil of Chelwood, British leader of a coalition of international peace organizations, who requested an audience with the pope.[39] Though the Disarmament Conference was not a success, Pius XI continued to appeal for the necessity of peace-making efforts, as in his encyclical *Nova Impendet* of May 1932, issued between the opening of the conference in February at Geneva and its reopening in July at Lausanne, in which he coupled the need for a reduction in armaments with that of reducing worldwide unemployment, which had reached catastrophic proportions by then.[40] While papal peace efforts yielded no fruits in this period, on a more limited scale the Holy See had at least some success by helping to arbitrate a border dispute between Haiti and Santo Domingo in 1938.[41]

THE NAZI SEIZURE OF POWER AND THE *REICHSKONKORDAT* OF 1933

Because Pacelli had been nuncio in Germany for over thirteen years, when he became Secretary of State the responsibility for German affairs continued to rest with him, and thus he followed closely the negotiations for the concordat with Baden pursued by his successor. He also followed the politics of the Weimar Republic, 1930–3, with growing concern. The decline of the Weimar coalition of the Catholic Centre Party, Social Democrats (SPD) and Liberals (DDP)—after the death of Stresemann in 1929—was paralleled by

[36] Carlen, *The Papal Encyclicals*, III, 460.
[37] ASV, AES, IV Periodo, Stati Eccl, Pos. 467, Fasc. 486, f. 23.
[38] ASV, AES, IV Periodo, Stati Eccl, Pos. 467, Fasc. 468, sf. 43.
[39] ASV, AES, IV Periodo, Stati Eccl, Pos. 467, Fasc. 486, sf. 44.
[40] Carlen, *Papal Encyclicals*, III, 476.
[41] See ASV, IV Periodo, AES, IV Periodo, pos. 121–122 (P.O.), fasc. 15–18.

the electoral rise of the extremes of left and right: the Communists (KPD) and the Nazis (NSDAP). Under the impact of the effects of the Great Depression in Germany, between 1930 and the first Reichstag election of 1932, Hitler and the Nazis were transformed from a minor, peripheral political group into the largest party in the Reichstag.[42] Electoral polarization and the impossibility of finding a consensus on economic policy within the coalition made Germany virtually ungovernable: the fact that Chancellor Heinrich Brüning had no clear majority in the Reichstag and was thus dependent upon the president's use of article 48 of the constitution meant that parliamentary government in Germany had effectively ended in 1930. The Vatican particularly regretted Brüning's resignation in 1932.[43] Meanwhile, the Centre Party drifted towards the right and showed increasing signs of disunity, especially after its most right-wing leader, Franz Von Papen, became chancellor in 1932. The Vatican was alarmed by both the rise of the Nazis *and* its older enemy, Communism, in Germany. Pacelli, as an old Germany 'hand', was deeply apprehensive about Hitler's motives and policies. In 1923 he described the future *Fuehrer* as 'a notorious agitator', and in 1924 he presciently described National Socialism as 'perhaps the most dangerous heresy of our time'.[44] Pius XI was also neurotically obsessed by the Communist threat. The British minister to the Vatican, Ogilvie-Forbes, had it about right when he said that in the Vatican in 1932 there was a 'certain apprehension felt at the prospect of Germany going Communist . . . This consideration no doubt influenced the Vatican not to go too far towards the condemnation of the Nazi party.'[45] Indeed, the mixed feelings in the Vatican towards the German situation were summed up by Cardinal Michael von Faulhaber, archbishop of Munich and Freising, who, in March 1933, exclaimed:

> Let us meditate upon the words of the Holy Father, who, in a consistory, without mentioning his name, indicated before the whole world in Adolf Hitler the statesman who first, after the Pope himself, has raised his voice against Bolshevism.[46]

At this juncture, when Hitler was dissembling his real feelings towards the Church and before the nature of Nazi policies had yet become apparent, Pius XI's (albeit muted) enthusiasm for Nazi anti-Bolshevism is understandable.

The fact remained that Nazi attitudes to Catholicism were clearly hostile. There was present in German National Socialism, especially at the highest levels of leadership, a strange mixture of anti-clerical, anti-Catholic, anti-Christian, pagan, and even occult tendencies. The anti-clericalism manifested itself in hostility to all forms of organized, institutional religion. Although Hitler personally had strong anti-Catholic feelings, he wisely remained above the fray

[42] Kershaw, *Hitler*, ch. 9. [43] Hachey, *Anglo-Vatican Relations*, 234.
[44] As cited in Wolf, *Pope and Devil*, 135. [45] Wolf, *Pope and Devil*, 209.
[46] Falconi, *The Popes*, 194.

because of his fears that the religious question would be divisive for the party, especially during the *Kampfzeit*, the period of struggle before 1933. There were Nazis, like Artur Dinter, who campaigned strongly against the papacy, but they were isolated within the party. Dinter declared that 'The Roman Pope's church is just as terrible an enemy of a *volkisch* Germany as the Jew.'[47] Hitler, Himmler, and Goebbels, precisely because they were apostates from Catholicism, were also extremely hostile to it. Yet theirs was an equivocal attitude, hostility tinged with a certain admiration, maybe even envy, for the way in which the Roman Catholic Church managed to enforce its authority, exact obedience, and operate efficiently as an international institution: Himmler was known to have a particular admiration for the Jesuits.[48] These feelings of hostility towards the Church belied the cleverly opportunistic and duplicitous policies which the Nazis adopted after coming to power.

The German bishops had, individually and severally, condemned various aspects of Nazi ideology on more than one occasion,[49] prompting Hermann Göring, Hitler's right-hand man, to seek an audience with Pacelli in May 1931, in order to ask him to persuade them to lift the ban on Catholic membership of and support for the Nazi Party. The Vatican emasculated the visit by sending him to see Mgr Pizzardo, the under-secretary of state.[50] However, President Hindenburg's appointment of Adolf Hitler as Chancellor of Germany at the end of January 1933 forced the Vatican to take serious cognizance of the Nazis. It was kept up to date regarding political developments in Germany by reports from its nuncio in Berlin, Mgr Orsenigo, and pleas from Prince Albrecht of Bavaria, and other conservative Catholics, that the episcopal ban on the NSDAP be relaxed in order to 'save Germany from Communism'.[51] But neither the pope nor his Secretary of State took any action to influence the German bishops in this matter: the bishops did not seek the advice of the Vatican and the Vatican did not proffer any.[52] On 31 March, the German bishops lifted their ban; Pacelli and the pope grudgingly approved, but lamented the fact that the bishops had received nothing in return for their goodwill gesture.[53]

The first hint that the Nazi government was interested in negotiating a Reich-wide concordat came in a report from Orsenigo to Pacelli in April 1933, in which the former described a discussion which he had had with Von Papen, who then proceeded to Rome to open talks.[54] A *Reichskonkordat*, the ultimate diplomatic agreement with Germany which had eluded Pacelli during his long nunciature in Germany, was a

[47] As quoted in Pollard, 'Fascism and Religion', 144.

[48] Pollard, 'Fascism and Religion', 145.

[49] Wolf, *Pope and Devil*, 142–143.

[50] ASV, AES, IV Periodo, 430 (1930–1938), 348, 1931, Taccuini, f. 341.

[51] Wolf, *Pope and Devil*, 165.

[52] Wolf, *Pope and Devil*, 167–168.

[53] Wolf, *Pope and Devil*, 169.

[54] AES, AES, IV Periodo, Germania, IV Periodo, 643 P.O., f. 157, Orsenigo to Pacelli, 8 April 1933.

crucial part of Hitler's strategy for consolidating power. Formal agreement with the Holy See would both confer some reassuring legitimacy on the new regime in the eyes of foreign governments concerned about Nazi extremism, and eliminate the potential political threat from German Catholicism. Equally, as the ruthless, brutal nature of the new Nazi regime manifested itself during the first months after it came to power, it seemed prudent to the men in the Vatican to secure some cast-iron legal guarantees for the German Church, in particular for its schools and its lay associations, for fear that there might be another *Kulturkampf*.[55] The negotiations proceeded relatively quickly—there were no long-standing and difficult issues to be settled, as in the case of the negotiations for the Lateran Pacts with Italy in 1929—and there were already three concordats in place with individual German states to provide some sort of blueprint for a concordat with the Reich as a whole. Indeed, given the likelihood of the virtual disappearance of the individual German states as part of the process of *Gleichschaltung* (consolidation of power), and the consequent doubtful legal status of the concordats concluded with those states, a *Reichskonkordat* was a real necessity for the German Church.

The negotiations were conducted by Von Papen, Hitler's Vice-Chancellor, on the German side, and by Pacelli for the Holy See, but the latter was subject to the close, careful scrutiny of the pope, every clause and comma being examined by Pius XI.[56] Though the views of the German bishops on the matters covered by the *Reichskonkordat* were not sought during the course of the negotiations, they seemed to have given broad support precisely in order to avoid a 'second *Kulturkampf*'.[57] The Scholder claim—repeated by John Cornwell—that, in return for the *Reichskonkordat*, the Vatican agreed to the dissolution of the Centre Party, is not borne out by the documents now accessible in the Vatican Archives.[58] Indeed, Pacelli is on record as regretting that the dissolution of the German Catholic party left him less room for manoeuvre in his negotiations with the Nazis.[59] As Wolf states, the sudden demise of the party deprived him of a major bargaining chip in the particularly difficult negotiations to protect Catholic organizations, with the result that the exact definition of protected organizations was never agreed upon in the *Reichskonkordat*, laying them wide open to attack later on.[60] Hitler is

[55] The *Kulturkampf* was the name given to the campaign of legislative and administrative harassment of the Catholic Church in Prussia by Bismarck and Rudolf Virchow of the Progressive Party in the 1870s and early 1880s: for an overview of the *Kulturkampf*, see M. Valente, *Diplomazia Pontificia e Kulturkampf: La Santa Sede e la Prussia tra Pio IX e Bismarck, 1862-1878*, Rome, 2010.

[56] ASV, AES, IV Periodo, 430 (1930–1938), 348, 1931, Taccuini, f. 341, notes for audiences of 2 (morning and evening), 4, and 18 July 1933.

[57] Wolf, *Pope and Devil*, 174–175.

[58] Cornwell, *Hitler's Pope*, 149–150.

[59] Wolf, *Pope and Devil*, 174.

[60] Wolf, *Pope and Devil*, 174.

recorded as saying that the German negotiators could agree to anything so long as the concordat was signed. Later he could change or negate individual clauses.

As the introduction to the *Reichskonkordat* states, it was intended as a supplement to the concordats already signed with Bavaria, Prussia, and Baden, which covered roughly 77 per cent of the German population and all the Catholic dioceses except three—Limburg, Meissen, and Rottenburg, because they lay in states (Hesse, Saxony, and Wurttemberg) with which the Holy See had no agreements—consequently, it largely reiterated existing arrangements. The *Reichskonkordat*, however, did deal with some key issues on a Reich-wide basis: religious instruction in state schools (article 21), Catholic denominational schools (article 23), the provision of chaplains for the *Reichswehr* (article 27), the rights of Catholic members of non-German minorities (29), and the rights of Catholic associations (31).[61] Wolf has argued that the *Reichskonkordat* was:

> a forward defensive wall, which the National Socialists continually attempted to chip away over the next twelve years of their regime. They never completely succeeded. The Catholic Church in Germany was the only large-scale institution in Germany that Hitler never managed to co-opt.[62]

That may be so, but, as very quickly became apparent, it proved insufficient to defend the Church from Nazi attacks in the future.

When that became clear, and tension between the Vatican and Nazi Germany accordingly increased, Pius moved away from his enthusiasm for Hitlerian anti-Communism. Such had been his concern about Communism, that, in the run-up to the Disarmament Conference he had quietly suggested to the ambassadors of the Western powers that they should not disarm *too much*, for fear of the threat of Communism. In March 1933, he told British prime minister, Ramsay MacDonald, who was one of the chief advocates of disarmament, 'Do not disarm order to the profit of disorder.'[63] Whereas in June 1933 the Vatican had welcomed the Four-Power Pact between Britain, France, Germany, and Italy as a guarantee of international stability, a means of ensuring peaceful revision of Versailles, *and* an alliance against Soviet Communism, and had indeed used its diplomatic muscle to encourage it, by the end of the year it had become disillusioned with Hitler and concerned about his designs on Austria, whose independence the pope strongly favoured. The Vatican now recognized that Communism, and attendant anti-clericalism, were not the only threats to the Church and its interests.[64]

[61] For the text of the *Reichskonkordat*, see Coppa, *Controversial Concordats*, 205–214.

[62] Wolf, *Pope and Devil*, 178.

[63] As quoted in Kent, *The Pope and the Duce*, 154.

[64] Kent, *The Pope and the Duce*, 156.

Austria was one of the keys to this sea-change in Papa Ratti's policy. With the succession of Dollfuss as Austrian Chancellor following Mgr Seipel's death in 1932, Austria seemed to have become an almost perfect Catholic state. As well as apparently adopting much of the essence of *Quadragesimo Anno*, Dollfuss concluded a new concordat with the Holy See. The Austrian Concordat of 1933 was undoubtedly a triumph for the Vatican since it ensured the pope was able to choose Austrian bishops, as well as ensuring freedom for Catholic Action, and increased state financial aid to the Church.[65] Furthermore, religious instruction was reintroduced into state schools—and headmasters were required to be 'Christian'—and crucifixes were reintroduced into public institutions.[66] But, as with the German *Reichskonkordat*, this came at a price: the exclusion of the clergy from politics and the incorporation of the Catholic Christian Social Party, along with the Catholic paramilitary Heimwehr, into the Vaterlandfront, the ruling body of Dollfuss's one-party, authoritarian state.[67] Dollfuss, in his efforts to contain the threat from the Socialist working-class movement and the Austrian Nazis, played a delicate balancing act with his chief backers, the Vatican and Fascist Italy. Still, Pius conferred on him the prestigious papal order of the Golden Spur for his 'well-known devotion to the Catholic religion'.[68] In his turn, Dollfuss's successor, Schuschnigg, would also receive it.

When Dollfuss was murdered by Austrian Nazis in their failed *putsch* in August 1934, Pius was at one with Mussolini in his condemnation, and he supported the decision to send the Italian Army to the Brenner frontier with Austria in order to dissuade Hitler from any plan for immediate *Anschluss* of Austria with Germany.[69] Indeed, cooperation in defence of Austrian independence against German attempts at *Anschluss* in 1934–5 represents the high point in relations between the Vatican and Italian Fascism in the 1930s, Mussolini having a strategic concern about the danger of a rearmed Germany appearing on the northern, Brenner frontier of Italy. It also resulted in an extraordinary claim in the Fascist Party daily, *Il Popolo D'Italia*, that there was an identity of interests between the Church and Italian Fascism in Austria:

> The tasks of Austria are therefore twofold; first defence of the values of Teutonic culture, humanised through its contact with Latin culture; second to act as the vanguard of Catholicism in north-east [sic] and central Europe . . . Her absolute independence is therefore of the highest importance.[70]

[65] Rhodes, *The Vatican*, 148–149.
[66] Rhodes, *The Vatican*, 148–149, and Pyrah, 'Cultural Politics', 161–162.
[67] Pyrah, 'Cultural Politics', 162.
[68] Rhodes, *The Vatican*, 148.
[69] Kent, *The Pope and the Duce*, 172.
[70] As quoted in Rhodes, *The Vatican*, 150.

Henceforth, Vatican diplomacy would seek even more vigorously to promote Franco-Italian harmony, encouraging both sides to achieve a better understanding of the other's interests and problems.[71] It thus welcomed the agreement reached at the Stresa Conference of April 1934, which followed the German decision to abandon the Disarmament Conference and rearm in violation of the Versailles Treaty. The agreements concluded at Stresa committed Britain, represented by Ramsay MacDonald, France, represented by her foreign minister, Laval, and Italy, represented by Mussolini, to cooperate against further German violations of Versailles and, in particular, any further attempts on the independence of Austria.[72]

According to Kent:

> For the Holy See, the Franco-Italian rapprochement of 1935 represented the ideal diplomatic organisation of Europe, uniting European Catholicism, as it did, initially against the anti-clerical Nazis and ultimately against the anti-Christian Bolsheviks.[73]

THE ETHIOPIAN WAR AND THE ORIGINS OF THE AXIS

The long-term origins of the colonial war of conquest which Mussolini waged in East Africa from October 1935 until May 1936 lay in the humiliating defeats which Italy had suffered at Dogali (1888) and Adowa (1896) at the hands of Ethiopian forces, and, more recently, in the militaristic, expansionistic ideology of Italian Fascism. Mussolini's intentions in East Africa had been fairly clear since the middle of 1934. Having disposed of a German threat to Austrian independence after the murder of Dollfuss by Austrian Nazis, and entered into the Stresa Pact with Britain and France to contain Nazi military expansion, he was ready to carry out his war of conquest.

The Vatican at first probably did not take the threat too seriously, but when it became apparent that Mussolini was determined on a war, it began attempts to avoid a conflict. There was a proposal to send a papal letter to Mussolini asking him to abandon his invasion of Ethiopia, but after various modifications and moderations of the letter it was decided not to send it and Fr Tacchi-Venturi was sent to see Mussolini instead, albeit to no avail.[74] In July, the pope sent a personal appeal to King George V of Britain for assistance

[71] Kent, *The Pope and Duce*, 180. [72] Kent, *The Pope and Duce*, 180.

[73] Kent, *The Pope and Duce*, 180.

[74] L. Ceci, 'Santa Sede e impero fascista: contrasti, silenzi e fiancheggiamenti', in A. Guasco and Rafaella Perin (eds), *Pius XI: Keywords. International Conference, Milan 2009*, Berlin and Vienna, 2010, 139.

in averting war, via the newly appointed archbishop of Westminster, Mgr Hinsley.[75] Plans for suggesting a territorial compromise were also abandoned.

In the months leading up to the declaration of war, huge numbers of letters from all over the world reached Vatican pleading for the pope to speak out about Italy's threatened aggression.[76] This, and the fact that relations between the papacy and the recently crowned Emperor of Ethiopia, Haile Selassie, had improved in the early 1930s and that Catholic missionary activity was flourishing not only in the adjacent Italian colonies of Eritrea and Somalia, but in the empire itself, induced Pius XI to take a stand. In a famous speech to an audience from the Congress of Catholic Nurses, at his summer residence of Castel Gandolfo on 27 August, the pope vigorously condemned what he saw as the imminent Italian war of aggression: ' an unjust war is something which beggars the imagination, a most tragic, sad thing, something which is indescribably horrible'.[77] The speech elicited strenuous Italian protests, one of which the nuncio, Mgr Borgoncini-Duca, did not deliver to the pope for fear of upsetting him and thus precipitating a crisis. Attempts were also made by Pizzardo and Tardini to attenuate the strength of the condemnation as it appeared in *L'Osservatore Romano*, most of which met with Pius XI's approval.[78]

But there were no more Vatican public statements on the war. Two major factors forced the pope to remain silent on this question until victory was achieved by Italy seven months later. Firstly, the Vatican came under enormous pressure from the Italian government not to condemn further its act of aggression.[79] Secondly, the Italian Church—cardinals, bishops, clergy, and laity—all joined in this 'national patriotic' war, one which was quickly presented by leading Italian churchmen, like Cardinal Schuster of Milan and Fr Agostino Gemelli of the Catholic University of the Sacred Heart, as a 'Christian crusade' to free the inhabitants of Ethiopia from slavery, despite the fact that the country had long been a Christian empire. According to the British minister, Pius was annoyed with Schuster's enthusiasm for the war,[80] and Tardini also thought that the reaction of the Italian clergy was completely unbalanced.[81] Via Mgr Roveda, Pius XI urged the Italian bishops to moderate their language.[82]

75 Moloney, *Westminster, Whitehall and the Vatican*, 43–48.

76 Ceci, 'Santa Sede e impero fascista', 137–138.

77 Ceci, 'Santa Sede e impero fascista', 137–138.

78 Ceci, 'Santa Sede e impero fascista', 139.

79 L. Ceci, *Il Papa non deve parlare: Chiesa, fascismo e guerra d'Etiopia*, Rome and Bari, 2010; and C.-F. Casula, 'Santa Sede e Guerra d'Etiopia: a proposito di un discorso di Pio XI', *Studi Storici*, 46(2) (2003), 512–525.

80 Hachey, *Anglo-Vatican Relations*, 291–342.

81 Ceci, 'Santa Sede e impero fascista', 141.

82 Ceci, 'Santa Sede e impero fascista', 142.

The virtually complete alignment of the Italian Catholic world with Mussolini, especially after the imposition of League of Nations sanctions, left the Vatican with little room for manoeuvre. Benedict XV, that most pacifist of popes, had been unable to prevent 'patriotic excesses' on the part of Italian Catholics during the First World War, even before Caporetto turned the war into one of national survival for Italy, so it was unlikely that Pius XI would be able to dissuade Italian Catholics from following their patriotic instincts in this struggle by any number of condemnations: here were the limits of Italian Catholic allegiance to the Holy See.

Apart from ethical considerations—Italian aggression in Ethiopia could not be covered by any interpretation of 'just war' theory—the Holy See was concerned about three very serious possible outcomes to the war. First, that Mussolini would lose and that the regime would thus be destabilized, leaving the way open to a resurgence of Communism in Italy and untold future perils. This would also have put the Vatican's considerable investments in Italian industry, banking, and government bonds at risk (see Chapter 4). Second, that the invasion of Ethiopia would lead to a general European, or at least Mediterranean, war, given the intransigent hostility of the British to Mussolini's enterprise and their consequent deployment of the Royal Navy to the area, and, third, the war would destroy the recently established Italian alignment with Britain and France against Nazi Germany and thus provide Hitler with more room for manoeuvre, possibly even an alliance with Mussolini. By now, Hitler had become public enemy number two, after Stalin, for the Vatican, on account of his violations of the *Reichskonkordat* and persecution of the Church in Germany.

In an endeavour, therefore, to bring the war to an end as speedily as possible, the Vatican explored a number of different diplomatic avenues, in particular those leading to Washington. Bernardino Nogara, the Vatican's investment manager, had close links with American finance, especially J.P. Morgan's bank in New York. Nogara's idea, which was accepted in principle by the pope, was to persuade the Roosevelt administration to use its influence with Britain in order to bring about an agreement between Italy and Ethiopia.[83] This and other attempts by the Vatican to induce the US government to take a leading role failed.[84] The United States was still in isolationist mode and Ethiopia was not one of her priorities.

The war, the fervent Italian Catholic enthusiasm for it, and the silence of Pius XI had unfortunate consequences for the Holy See. While some Italian Catholic emigrant communities, especially in the USA, cheered the conquest

[83] For an account of this attempt, see R. De Felice, 'La Santa Sede e il conflitto Italo-Etiopico nel diario di Bernardino Nogara', *Storia Contemporanea*, 8(4) (1974), 823–834.

[84] Lucia Ceci, 'The First Steps in "Parallel Diplomacy": The Vatican and the U.S. in the Italo-Ethiopian War, 1935–6', in Gallagher et al. (eds), *Pius XI and America*, 88–105.

of Ethiopia, the stories of Italian atrocities against the civilian population, including the use of poison gas and splinter bombs, outraged world opinion, including that of liberal Catholics.[85] For example, it placed British Archbishop Hinsley of Westminster, the leader of Catholics in the country most opposed to Italian aggression, in an untenable position. In his attempts to excuse the silence of Pius XI he actually referred to the pope as 'an impotent, old man', which did not go down well in the Vatican and almost certainly delayed his receipt of the cardinal's hat normally given to his archiepiscopal see.[86]

At war's end, the Holy See was the second power (after the German Reich) to immediately recognize Victor Emmanuel III as emperor of Ethiopia, and after Mussolini had sent the French Catholic missionaries and Swedish Protestants packing on 24 March 1937 the Holy See ordered the complete Italianization of the missions in Italian East Africa (Eritrea, Ethiopia, and Somalia).[87] At this point Pius XI seemed to have reversed the stance he had taken at the outset of the conflict. In his speech at the inauguration of World Exhibition of Catholic Press in the Vatican on 12 May 1936, he uttered the infamous words, 'the happy triumph of a great and good people'.[88] This time it was the turn of the British and French ambassadors to protest.[89] The Vatican also caved in when, in the aftermath of the war, it had its first experience of Fascist racialism in colonies, with the introduction of the laws on the *meticciato* (miscegenation) which banned sexual relations between Italians and the indigenous population. Despite the fact that this was, effectively speaking, a system of a*partheid*, the Vatican Congregation of the Sacraments, led by Cardinal Jorio, took an extremely accommodating line towards the Italian legislation.[90]

In the short term, the Italo-Ethiopian War was a disaster for the Vatican. It strained the credibility of the Holy See as a neutral and impartial actor in international relations to breaking point. Furthermore, it raised serious doubts about the degree of real independence which the Holy See had achieved from Italy as a result of the Lateran Pacts of 1929. On the one hand, it seemed to reverse one of the great benefits of the *Conciliazione* of 1929, the affirmation of the Holy See's territorial and diplomatic independence from Italy. On the other hand, the struggle over sanctions drove Mussolini into the arms of Hitler.

Yet the Vatican recovered surprisingly quickly from the damage done to its international reputation and prestige by the Italo-Ethiopia War, probably

[85] D'Agostino, *Rome in America*, 263–265.

[86] Moloney, *Westminster, Whitehall and the Vatican*, 50–51.

[87] Ceci, 'Santa Sede e impero fascista', 43: she also makes the point that the Pope sent his greetings to Graziani 'the butcher of Ethiopia'.

[88] Ceci, 'Santa Sede e impero fascista', 142.

[89] Ceci, 'Santa Sede e impero fascista', 142.

[90] Ceci, 'Santa Sede e impero fascista', 143–145.

because the end of hostilities was followed, and was very soon overshadowed, by the outbreak of the Spanish Civil War in July 1936. While Mussolini had survived, and indeed his popularity and prestige in Italy were at an all-time high as a result of his African victory, the fears for the impact of the war on international relations which so concerned people in the Secretariat of State were largely realized. It disrupted the Stresa agreement between the Western democracies and Mussolini. Because Nazi Germany had helped bust League of Nations sanctions by providing Fascist Italy with coal during the war, Mussolini felt a certain gratitude towards his fellow fascist dictator, and in this can be seen the beginnings of that 'Rome–Berlin Axis' which would become the Pact of Steel between Italy and Germany of May 1939. This, and Mussolini's publicly declared 'understanding' of the German position on Austria, whose independence he had hitherto regarded as a *sine qua non* of Italian foreign policy, alarmed the Vatican. Now the only hope for Pius XI, Pacelli, and Tardini was that they could, in some way, use Mussolini to hold back Hitler from excesses.

One of the consequences of the cooling of relations between Britain and France on the one hand and Italy on the other, following the invasion of Ethiopia, was that this gave Hitler much more room for manoeuvre in Central Europe. A month after his success in the Saarland plebiscite, when the overwhelming majority of the population there voted to return to Germany in February 1935, Hitler had felt emboldened to reintroduce conscription. Now, a year later, he remilitarized the Rhineland, arguably the greatest blow to both the Treaty of Versailles and the Treaty of Locarno yet. This was done, of course, with Mussolini's tacit acceptance, thus the Stresa Front was no more. Pius XI was shocked by events in the Rhineland and he vented his frustration to the British minister to the Vatican, to whom 'he expressed the unhappy conviction that no signature of the present German government was worth the paper it was written on'.[91]

The Vatican's general unease and unhappiness with the international situation following the end of the Italo-Ethiopian War would help to explain the extraordinary, allegedly 'private', visit made by Secretary of State Pacelli to the United States of America, carefully choreographed by his friend Bishop Francis Spellman, which included a whistle-stop tour of twelve out of the then sixteen American Catholic ecclesiastical provinces in the autumn of 1936.[92] The visit should also be seen in the context of a succession of events—including Pacelli's visits to Lourdes in 1936, and later the Budapest Eucharistic Congress of 1938—which were designed to bring Pius XI closer to the Catholics of the world. They may also have been intended to show off

[91] As quoted in Hachey, *Anglo-Vatican Relations*, 356.

[92] For accounts of the visit, see Gannon, *The Cardinal Spellman Story*, ch. 8; and J. Cooney, *The American Pope*, New York, 1983.

his alleged 'dauphin' to the Catholic world. But the American visit had other purposes. It was, in the years before the papal 'pilgrimage' journeys of Paul VI, John Paul II, Benedict XVI, and Francis I to meet Catholics around the world, a very serious effort on the part of the Holy See to manifest its recognition and blessing to American Catholics and to demonstrate that American Catholicism had come of age.[93] Much of this had to do with money, American money, the enormous sums that continued to flow across the Atlantic from American Catholics, despite the Great Depression (see Chapter 5). It also gave the Secretary of State the opportunity to meet the Mexican Episcopal Commission in exile in the United States and to see at close hand the situation created by Fr Charles Coughlin, 'the radio priest', whose broadcasts were directed against both Jews and President Franklin Roosevelt's 'new deal' of measures to bring America out of recession.[94]

Deciding how to deal with Fr Coughlin was, in its turn, part of an attempt to establish a closer relationship with President Roosevelt, who was increasingly seen in the Vatican as a hope for peace at a time when war clouds were beginning to gather in Europe, and part of a broader papal diplomatic 'offensive' to get closer to the Western democracies. In this regard, it worked because Pacelli's conversations with the president at his private home, Hyde Park, upstate New York, helped create a personal relationship between Roosevelt and Pacelli that would provide the foundation for the 'special relationship' which the Vatican was able to establish with the White House during the Second World War. The possibility of re-establishing diplomatic relations between the USA and the Holy See was also discussed at the Hyde Park meeting.[95]

THE SPANISH CIVIL WAR

The Spanish Civil War which broke out in July 1936 was one of the greatest trials which the papacy faced in the interwar period. The Vatican was aware, long before the coming of the Second Republic in 1931, of the weaknesses of the Spanish Church and the consequent dangers to it under a republican regime. There was a high degree of complacency among the episcopate and clergy, a lack of commitment on their part to engage with the very serious

[93] For a succinct overview of American Catholicism between the wars, see Colleen McDannell, 'The United States during the Inter-war Years', in Hugh McLeod (ed.), *The Cambridge History of Christianity*, vol. 9, Cambridge, 2009, 236–251.

[94] See G. Fogarty, 'The Case of Charles Coughlin', in Gallagher et al. (eds), *Pius XI and America*, 107–127.

[95] Luca Castagna, *Un ponte oltre l'oceano: Assettti politici e strategicie diplomatiche tra Stati Uniti e santa Sede nella prima metà del novecento (1915–1940)*, Bologna, 2011, 318.

social tensions in both town and country, which had given rise to a militant and violent working-class movement, and a failure to develop an effective form of Catholic social activism, such as Catholic Action.[96] Spanish Catholicism, leaving aside its regional variants, was deeply divided between integralists and 'possibilists', the former led by Cardinal Segura, archbishop of Seville and the primate of Spain. As a result of Segura's influence, the Spanish Church was also closely associated with the monarchy and, more worryingly, with the 'Directory' (dictatorship) of General Miguel Primo de Rivera (1923–30).[97] In April 1924, Mgr Tedeschini, the apostolic nuncio in Madrid (1924–36), had reminded King Alfonso XIII of the ' support which the Episcopate had given to the Directory'.[98] Nevertheless, when the fall of Primo de Rivera was followed by the fall of the monarchy a year later, neither Tedeschini nor the Vatican was very surprised. King Alfonso XIII's precipitate flight from Madrid in April 1931 had been provoked by months of mounting popular disaffection and the early republican victories recorded in municipal elections.[99] But despite the fact that the Spanish king did not actually abdicate, the Holy See gave *de facto* recognition to the Republic almost immediately, something which drew withering scorn from Mussolini (see Chapter 4).

Relations with the Republic were difficult from the start as its government, strongly supported by anti-clerical elements of the liberal, radical, socialist (Communists, Trotskyites, and Anarcho-Syndicalists) left, started a legislative process to separate Church and State, confiscate the property of foreign religious orders, expel the Jesuits from Spain, and introduce divorce, amongst other measures.[100] Relations began to deteriorate under the impact of two factors, the intransigent and vocal opposition to the Republic of Cardinal Segura, and a wave of arson attacks against churches and other ecclesiastical property by the Anarchists.[101] Segura was bundled out of Spain by the authorities and the Vatican sought to keep him under surveillance in Rome.[102]

Under the Republican regime Tedeschini, supported by Cardinal Vidal y Barraquer, archbishop of Tarragona, attempted to preserve good relations with the more amenable of the ministers of the Republic and to seek some sort of

[96] Lannon, *Privilege, Persecution and Prophecy*, 148–149: ch. 6 provides an excellent analysis of the Catholic movement in Spain.

[97] F. Montero, 'La Iglesia y el catolicismo español durante el pontificado de Pio XI: la historiografia español y la investigación actual', in Guasco and Perin (eds), *Pius XI: Keynotes*, 72–75.

[98] ASV, ARP, IV, Periodo, Madrid, 831 fasc. 203–206, Tedeschini to Gasparri, 3 April 1924.

[99] Paul Preston, *Concise History of the Spanish Civil War*, London, 1997, ch. 3; see also José M. Sanchez, *The Spanish Civil War as a Religious Tragedy*, Notre Dame, IN, 1987, 7–8.

[100] Vicente Cárcel Ortí, *Pío XI entre la republica y Franco: Angustia del Papa ante la tragedia española*, Madrid, 2008, is the most up-to-date account of the Vatican's policy from the proclamation of the Second Spanish Republic in April 1931 to the end of the civil war in March 1939, accompanied by nearly a hundred key documents.

[101] Cárcel Ortí, *Pío XI entre la republica y Franco*, 23–35.

[102] Cárcel Ortí, *Pío XI entre la republica y Franco*, 35–37.

agreement that would permit an amicable separation of Church and State: he also supported the efforts of laymen to establish both a more progressive Catholic Action movement and a Catholic-conservative party.[103] This strategy seemed to pay off. In the November 1933 elections, a considerable number of deputies were returned to the Cortes for the CEDA, a Catholic and conservative political grouping, so Parliament and government moved to the right. It is indicative of the change in atmosphere that, a year later, Cardinal Pacelli was received with full honours by the civilian and military authorities in Barcelona, a city which had experienced great anti-clerical turmoil over the preceding two years.[104]

In these circumstances, Tedeschini sought to reach some sort of *modus vivendi* with the Republic. The documentary evidence suggests that this failed due to the Secretariat of State's delaying tactics. Pacelli believed that no agreement would have any guarantee of survival unless the offending articles of the Republican constitution were first repealed, and that such was possible by negotiating toughly with the government of the centre-right, so he more or less stalled throughout most of 1935 in the hope that a government of a more clearly conservative and Catholic hue come to power.[105] Unfortunately, the reverse happened. The political situation shifted to the left in late 1935 and early 1936, with the result that the general elections in the spring of 1936 brought about the narrow victory of the Popular Front of left-wing parties, including the Communists. Thereafter, the Spanish political situation continued to polarize and become more violent, and the murder of José Calvo Sotelo, a monarchist politician, by left-wing extremists, provided the signal in July for the *pronunciamento*, the attempted military coup, of Franco and his fellow generals. Resistance from forces loyal to the Republic led to a civil war, the passing of effective governmental power to the anarchist, communist, socialist, and Trotskyite left, and the beginning of a systematic persecution of the Church in Republican Spain on a scale and with a ferocity which surpassed that in Mexico and possibly even Russia.[106]

After the outbreak of the civil war the Vatican position towards Spain continued to be complex, and certainly more nuanced, than that of the Spanish bishops. The ambiguity of Pius XI's position came out very clearly in an address to Spanish pilgrims at Castel Gandolfo in September 1937, such that several of his listeners 'threw their copies [of the address] to the floor as they left . . .', an unheard of gesture at a papal audience.[107] The nuncio

[103] Montero, 'La Iglesia', 70–71.

[104] N. Padellaro, *Portrait of Pius XII*, trans. M. Derrick, London, 1956, 116.

[105] See ASV, AES, Sessioni, 1365, 2 February 1935, Proposta di Modus Vivendi.

[106] For an account of the outbreak of arson, murder, and violence in Madrid which followed the news of the Nationalist rising, see Vicente Cárcel Ortí, 'La Nunciatura de Madrid Durante la Guerra Civil (1936–1939)', *AHP*, 46 (2008), 163–356, where he cites the eye-witness reports of the Vatican chargé d'affaires, Fr Silvio Sericano.

[107] Sanchez, *The Spanish Civil War*, 123–124.

remained accredited to Madrid, rather than Burgos, the Nationalist capital, on the grounds that the Republic was still the legal regime, though Mgr Tedeschini himself returned to Rome and left a chargé d'affaires in his place. Consequently, Pius XI was extremely cautious about publishing the appeal of the Spanish bishops for Catholics to support the Nationalists. Another reason was that some bishops, most significantly Cardinal Vidal y Barraquer, refused to sign. The complication created by the support of the Basque clergy for the Republican regime was a further reason for preserving diplomatic relations with the Republic. It was in order to deal with this that, in July, Ildebrando Antoniutti, Apostolic Delegate to Albania, was sent on a special mission to Spain.[108] Fourteen Basque priests had been executed by Nationalist firing squads, along with Catholic laymen,[109] and during the course of his mission Mgr Antoniutti was to save several Basque priests from Nationalist firing squads and secure the release of others from prison, to plead on behalf of some Catholic laymen in military custody, and assist in the return of the many thousand Basque children sent abroad just before the conquest of the Basque Country by Franco's forces.[110]

The Holy See was reluctant to open relations with Franco, though the repeated massacres of bishops, clergy, religious, and laypeople, some 6,800 persons in all at the hands of Republican militias, left it with little option. In any case, for most Spanish Catholics the Nationalist cause had become a crusade, a *reconquista* of their country from violently anti-Christian barbarians, so, by the autumn of 1937, pleased with the outcome of Mgr Antoniutti's mission, the Vatican felt the need to establish more formal relations with the Nationalist government. Thus, in September 1937 Mgr Antoniutti was accredited to Franco as the first papal chargé d'affaires, and in June I938 there was an exchange of full diplomatic envoys between the Nationalist regime and the Vatican.[111]

Yet, during the remaining months of the civil war (which ended in March 1939), the Vatican had difficulties with the Franco regime, which was unwilling to release some Catholic civilian prisoners and claimed the right to vet episcopal nominations, despite the fact that the 1851 concordat with Spain had been abrogated as a result of the fall of the monarchy and the anti-clerical legislation of the Republic.[112] Another reason for the Vatican's initial desire to keep a prudent distance from Franco was the involvement, from virtually

[108] For an account of the mission of Mgr Antoniutti, see Vicente Cárcel Ortí, 'Notas sobre la misíon pontificia Mgr Ildebrando Antoniutti en Espana nacional durante la Guerra civil (1937-1938)', *AHP*, 42 (2004), 51–84.

[109] Sanchez, *The Spanish Civil War*, 79–80.

[110] Cárcel Ortí, 'Notas sobre la mission pontificia', 63–68, 74–77, and 83–84.

[111] For an account of the complicated quadrille leading to reciprocal recognition, see Cárcel Ortí, *Pio XI*, ch. 3.

[112] Cárcel Ortí, 'Notas sobre la mission pontificia', 80–81.

the beginning of the conflict, of Fascist Italy and, above all, Nazi Germany, which contributed amounts of military materiel and men to the Nationalist effort. By the mid-1930s, the Vatican was increasingly concerned about the neo-pagan influences which Hitler and the Nazis might bring to Spain. In 1937, during an audience granted to Mgr Antoniutti, the Vatican's chargé d'affaires to Franco's government, Pius urged him, 'If necessary, tell Franco not to trust the German Nazis.'[113]

Though Franco and the Nationalists won, and this was obviously welcomed in the Vatican, in the eyes of Pius XI the Spanish Civil War had serious long-term consequences. It divided Catholic public opinion in most countries: the official Church was on the side of Franco—in the Italian case the clergy viewed the Nationalist cause as little less than a 'crusade'—whereas some Catholic left-wing elements were deeply unhappy, especially figures like Jacques Maritain, François Mauriac, and Emmanuel Mounier in France.[114] On the other hand, Republican atrocities against the Church and the Spanish Catholic population, and the fact that the only effective supporters of the Republic were the Soviet Union and Mexico, whereas Hitler and Mussolini supported Franco, drove many Catholics into the arms of fascism. As a result, 'Catholic Fascism' or 'clerical-fascism' became much stronger during this period.[115]

Worst of all, the experience of the Spanish Civil War strengthened the bonds between Hitler and Mussolini, now comrades-in-arms in the conflict. In September 1937, after a visit to Berlin, the Duce signed the Anti-Comintern Pact with Germany and Japan. This was not a welcome development for Pius XI when the German Church was suffering a persecution of its own at the hands of the Nazis.

THE MONTH OF THE THREE ENCYCLICALS: MARCH 1937

In the space of a few weeks—that is, between 14 and 28 March 1937—Pius XI issued three encyclicals, each of which was a condemnation of the persecution of the Church in different parts of the world, and two of which also contained condemnations of the ideology behind the persecutions.

[113] Cited in Cárcel Ortí, 'Notas sobre la misiòn pontificia', 74, n. 47.

[114] Chiron, *Pio XI*, 409; for the divisive effects on British Catholicism of the Spanish war, see Buchanan, 'Great Britain', 267–269.

[115] See Pollard, 'Fascism and Religion', 154–155, and M. Mann, *Fascists*, Cambridge, 2004, 33.

A 'Second Syllabus of Errors'?

The first two encyclicals need to seen in the context of the fact that there is a considerable amount of evidence, mainly documents to be found in the archives of the Holy Office, that serious consideration was being given to the publication of a general condemnation of the chief 'materialist heresies' of the twentieth century, the ideologies of German National Socialism and Soviet Communism, and possibly even that of Italian Fascism, during the early to mid-1930s in the Vatican.[116] Such a condemnation was described by its proponents as a sort of new 'Syllabus of Errors', recalling the condemnation which Pius IX had pronounced in 1864 against democracy, liberalism, nationalism, and all their works.[117]

The Supreme Congregation of the Holy Office specially commissioned the Jesuit fathers, Hürth, Batt, Rabeneck, and Chagnon to examine various aspects of racialist doctrine as expressed in various Nazi publications—including those of Alfred Rosenberg and Hitler's *Mein Kampf.* Two further ecclesiastics, Padre Gillet O.P. and Mgr Ernesto Ruffini, a permanent consultor of the Holy Office, were also involved.[118] Though Communism is mentioned in some of the documents produced by this group, it was not separately considered in this context: in fact, as is clear from the documents in the archives of the Congregation for Extraordinary Ecclesiastical Affairs, that dicastery was already examining the issue. The doctrines of Italian Fascism, as expressed by Mussolini, Mario Missiroli, and other journalists, were also under scrutiny by the Holy Office at this time.[119]

It was Mgr Domenico Tardini, Under-Secretary in the Secretariat of State, who suggested that these 'materialist heresies . . . needed to be condemned by the Holy See both in the solemn form of an encyclical and also as a modern

[116] See ACDF, R.V. 1934/ n. 29 (Prot. 3373/34 RAZZISMO. Stampa Luglio 1935 N. 3373/34 Nazionalismo, Razzismo, Stato Totalitario, Relazione, Voto ed Elenco di proposizioni erronee formulate dai Rmi Padri Professori Francesco Hürth, G.Batt. Rabeneck e Luigi Chagnon).

[117] For an analysis of Pius IX's Syllabus, see E.E.Y. Hales, *Pio Nono: A Study in European Politics and Religion in the Nineteenth Century*, London, 1956, ch. 7.

[118] ACDF, R.V. 1934/n. 29 etc. (Prot. 3373/34 RAZZISMO. Stampa Luglio 1935 N. 3373/34 Nazionalismo, Razzismo, Stato Totalitario, Relazione, Voto ed Elenco di proposizioni erronee formulate dai Rmi Padri Professori Francesco Hürth, G.Batt. Rabeneck e Luigi Chagnon) 5 (in pencil) Maggio 1935 Nazionalism, Razzismo e Stato Totalitario, Premiere Partie Quelques Définitions Préliminaires Orthodoxes (P.Gillet, O.P.) and Breve Voto di Mons. Ruffini, Consultore. L'ultranazionalism = l'eresia dei nostril tempi.

[119] For the analysis of these writings, including Mussolini's 1932 'Doctrine of Fascism', which became the official statement of Italian Fascist ideology, see ACDF, R.V. 1934/n. 29 etc. (Prot. 3373/34 RAZZISMO. Stampa Luglio 1935 N. 3373/34 Nazionalismo, Razzismo, Stato Totalitario, Relazione, Voto ed Elenco di proposizioni erronee formulate dai Rmi Padri Professori Francesco Hürth, G. Batt, Rabeneck e Luigi Chagnon) 8 (in pencil) Stampa Maggio, 1936, N 3373/1934 Nazionalismo, Razzismo, Stato Totalitario Avvertenza.

form of the Syllabus of Pius IX'.[120] The process was moving in the direction indicated by Tardini but was halted by a decision of the cardinals of the Holy Office in November 1936 to postpone the production of a syllabus *sine die*.[121] The pope, prefect of the Holy Office, confirmed this decision in June 1937.[122] There would have been some good grounds for such a decision, notably the grave risks which would have arisen from effectively having to condemn Hitler's *Mein Kampf* since its author was the German head of state and government. Nevertheless, Alfred Rosenberg's *Myth of the Twentieth Century*, a treasury of racialist and pagan thinking, was put on the Index in 1934,[123] presumably because the Holy Office had fewer concerns about condemning the work of person of rather lesser standing in the Nazi hierarchy. There were also, obviously, only less serious risks associated with condemning key elements of the ideology of Italian Fascism when that regime was an uncomfortably close neighbour of the Vatican. No doubt, Eugenio Pacelli, ever the diplomat, advised against such a course, since he would have had to bear the brunt of the diplomatic consequences of such a proceeding. It is interesting, therefore, to note that his direct subordinate, Tardini, was the leading advocate of it.

So, in the end, the strategy adopted was to abandon a blanket condemnation of these political heresies, a twentieth-century version of the historic Syllabus of Errors, and to concentrate instead on dealing with two separate situations—the persecution of the Church in Nazi Germany and the threat to the Church from the international spread of Communism in the form of appropriate encyclicals. While at this stage, in late 1936 and early 1937, racialism was not yet an official part of the doctrine of Italian Fascism, Mussolini was already moving in that direction, and it is legitimate to speculate whether, if the papacy had publicly condemned racialist doctrine in the solemn form of a Syllabus of Errors in 1937, Mussolini would have continued along that path.

Mit Brennender Sorge: The Encyclical on Nazi Germany

On 14 March 1937, Pius XI published his protest against Nazi persecution of the German Church in the encyclical *Mit brennender Sorge* ('With Burning Anxiety'), a final response to nearly four years of attacks by the Nazis on the Church and Catholics in Germany. As Pacelli had bitterly admitted to the British minister at the Vatican shortly after the signing of the *Reichskonkordat*, 'The Nazis probably would not violate all of the clauses of the concordat at

[120] ACDF, R.V. 1934/n. 29 etc. (Prot. 3373/34 RAZZISMO. Stampa Luglio 1935 N. 3373/34 Nazionalismo, Razzismo, Stato Totalitario, Relazione, Voto ed Elenco di proposizioni erronee formulate dai Rmi Padri Professori Francesco Hürth, G.Batt. Rabeneck e Luigi Chagnon), 5.

[121] Wolf, *Pope and Devil*, 262. [122] Wolf, *Pope and Devil*, 262.

[123] *Index Librorum Prohibitorum*, 157.

the same time.'[124] By 1937, they had violated the most important ones. Hardly was the ink dry than violations began with an attack on Catholic schools and youth organizations. More seriously, the Nazis introduced a voluntary sterilization bill as part of the prelude to the transformation of Germany into a state completely based on the doctrine of race.[125] Sterilization was, of course, in complete contradiction with long-established Catholic doctrine, as reiterated in *Casti Connubii* (Chapter 5). Over the next few years, the Nazis attacked and largely destroyed precisely those Catholic institutions—schools, youth groups, and the press—which the *Reichskonkordat* was supposed to protect. The Nazis went on to confiscate church property and imprison Catholic clergy, especially members of the religious orders: male religious were found guilty of what would now be called paedophilia in 'show trials' and female religious were accused of serious violations of currency regulations.[126] Other priests were sent to concentration camps, some dying there, simply for criticizing the regime.[127]

As the pope explained in the encyclical itself, those German cardinals and bishops present in Rome in January 1937 were consulted about a proposed encyclical, and Cardinal Faulhaber was instructed to write the first draft in German, which was then developed and modified by the pope and Pacelli, with the advice of the General of the Jesuits, Ledóchowski.[128] At the core of the encyclical was a strong protest against Nazi violations of the *Reichskonkordat* and the more general persecution of the Church in Germany.[129] In particular, Pius protested against the closure of Catholic schools,[130] and the dissolution of Catholic associations,[131] as well as the treatment of Catholics and the Church in the propaganda of the Hitlerjugend and the insidious ways in which Catholics were encouraged, and sometimes bullied, into apostasy.[132] He then went on to condemn the persecution of individual priests and laity.[133]

But what is particularly striking about *Mit brennender Sorge* is the fact that it is not only a protest against the persecution of the German Church: it is much more than that. Well *over half* of the encyclical is devoted to an explicit refutation of almost all the key tenets of National Socialist ideology—the myth of race and blood (in four separate paragraphs),[134]

[124] Hachey, *Anglo-Vatican Relations*, 251–252.

[125] Gunter Lewy, *The Catholic Church and Nazi Germany*, London, 1964, ch. 5; and J. Conway, *The Nazi Persecution of the Churches, 1933–1945*, London, 1968, 40 and 272.

[126] Conway, *The Nazi Persecution of the Churches*, 155–156.

[127] Conway, *The Nazi Persecution of the Churches*, 309.

[128] Wolf, *Pope and Devil*, 166.

[129] For the text of the encyclical, see Carlen, *The Papal Encyclicals*, III, 525–535.

[130] Carlen, *The Papal Encyclicals*, III, 526.

[131] Carlen, *The Papal Encyclicals*, III, 532.

[132] Carlen, *The Papal Encyclicals*, III, 526, 529, and 532.

[133] Carlen, *The Papal Encyclicals*, III, 533.

[134] Carlen, *The Papal Encyclicals*, III, 527, 528, and 530.

the totalitarian state,[135] the superiority of the morality of race and the Nietschean will to power over Christian morality and Social Darwinism in international relations,[136] Nazi neo-paganism and pantheism,[137] and more generally the tendency to present National Socialism as a political religion and tendencies towards 'Aryan Christianity', including the discounting of the 'Semitic' Old Testament as an essential part of Christian revelation.[138] Pius's thunderous condemnation of Nazi ideology can be summed up by this one passage:

> Whoever exalts race, or the people, or the State, or a particular form of State . . . whoever raises these notions above their standard value and divinizes them to an idolatrous level, distorts and perverts an order of the world planned and created by God.[139]

The only element of Nazi ideology which was not explicitly condemned by name, racial anti-Semitism, is implicitly covered by the more general condemnations of Nazi racial theory: probably Ledóchowski, a notorious anti-Semite, advised against this. The pope made it clear that all of these ideas were condemned as *heresies*, so the encyclical served as an effective substitute for the greater part of the 'syllabus' which had not materialized. While Hitler, other Nazi leaders, and the Nazi Party were never named, they were clearly the targets of his prophetic ire. Who else could be?

Despite the best efforts of the Gestapo, the encyclical was smuggled into Germany and read from pulpits. The Secretariat of State instructed papal envoys in all countries to publicize it,[140] and Vatican Radio was also used to broadcast the text in various languages, resulting in formal protests by the German ambassador at the Vatican, von Bergen.[141] It is not known how the average German reacted to this broadcast, because Vatican Radio was jammed in Germany, but it infuriated the Nazi leadership.[142]

The Vatican made sure that the text of *Mit brennender Sorge* was widely distributed to Catholics in Europe and North America, thus Nazi Germany's persecution of the Church became widely known, prompting American cardinal, George Mundelein, archbishop of Chicago, to make his famous speech scorning Hitler as, 'an Austrian paperhanger, and a poor one at that'.[143] Hitler was inevitably outraged, yet Pacelli did little to

[135] Carlen, *The Papal Encyclicals*, III, 532.
[136] Carlen, *The Papal Encyclicals*, III, 532.
[137] Carlen, *The Papal Encyclicals*, III, 526 and 527.
[138] Carlen, *The Papal Encyclicals*, III, 527–528.
[139] Carlen, *The Papal Encyclicals*, III, 527.
[140] ASV, ARdP, IV Periodo, Archivio della Nunziature D'Irlanda (1929, 1939), Busta 4, Titolo 1, SantaSede, Segret. Di Stato, 1937, 15 March, proto. 1980, telegram from Vatican instructing the nuncio to make sure that the press gives maximum coverage to *Mit brennender Sorge*.
[141] Pollard, 'Electronic Pastors', 187.
[142] Rhodes, *The Vatican*, 205–206.
[143] As quoted in Fattorini, *Hitler, Mussolini and the Vatican*, 134.

assuage his anger, such was the sense of grievance in the Vatican towards Nazi Germany.[144]

Divini Redemptoris and Communism

From the end of the 1920s, the Vatican had become increasingly concerned about the spread of Communism outside of Russia, through the activities of Communist parties worldwide, coordinated by the Comintern in Moscow. It saw not only the persecutions of the Church in Russia as being instigated by the Communists, but also the ongoing persecution in Mexico, the persecution in Spain which reached horrendous heights in the massacres of clergy, religious, and laity during the civil war, and the sporadic attacks on Catholic and other Christian missions in China, as part of a concerted plan. Papal warnings about the dangers of Communism were contained in a succession of encyclicals dealing primarily with other subjects, *Miserentissimus Redemptor* (1928), *Quadragesimo Anno* (1931) on the fortieth anniversary of *Rerum Novarum, Caritate Christi* (1932) on the world economic situation, *Acerba anima* (1932) on the persecution of the Church in Mexico, and *Dilectissima Nobis* (1933) on the persecution of the Church in Spain.[145]

From about 1933 the Secretariat of State, either via the apostolic delegates or nuncios, or directly through chairmen of local bishops' conferences, sought information about the spread of Communism in a variety of countries, and about the activities of Communist parties. The responses which this circular elicited were mixed, but not reassuring.

The USA, Canada, and Australia were an especial object of the Vatican's anxieties concerning the spread of Communism, as Pizzardo's correspondence shows. Mgr Sassuolo, apostolic delegate in Canada, wrote to him that Communists were no great threat except in Ontario and British Columbia, that those most susceptible to their propaganda were immigrants, and that various organizations, like the Catholic Youth League, the Catholic Welfare Bureau, and the Knights of Columbus were active in combating them.[146] As far as the USA was concerned, the Vatican, and Italians generally, tended to exaggerate the threat of Communism there because of the 'democratic and egalitarian nature' of American society whereas, in fact, these two characteristics of America probably made the growth of Communism much less likely.[147]

[144] Fattorini, *Hitler, Mussolini and the Vatican*, 135–136; see also Robert Trisco, 'The Holy See and Cardinal Mundelein's Insult of Hitler (1937)', in Gallagher et al. (eds), *Pius XI and America*, 155–191.

[145] See Carlen, *Papal Encyclicals*, III, 415–444 and 475–490.

[146] ASV, AES, IV Periodo, 267 P.O. Canada, Propaganda Communista, Apostolic delegate, Msgr Sassuolo, to Pizzardo, 25 July 1933.

[147] *L'Avvenire*, 'Vita Sociale in Canada: L'Avanzata Communista', 12 July 1936.

In the case of Australia, the 'papal inspector of Catholic Action', Christine de Hemptinne, on her visit there was alarmed by signs of Communist 'activity and propaganda, at the University, amongst women in the street, in the ports', as she pointed out in a letter of November 1936, to Mgr Panico.[148] Many Australians shared her fears: the establishment of a national Catholic Action secretariat under the lay leadership of Santamaria and Mather in Melbourne in 1938 was, in large part, prompted by fears of Communist 'entryism' into the trade unions (ACT) and the Australian Labor Party (ALP): a strong national secretariat was seen as a means of combating this.[149] In 1930, Madame Steenberghe-Engheringh explained to Pizzardo that in Portugal there was a real Communist threat in some cities—especially Porto, where only one Catholic union operated in competition with Communists and Socialists active in the field.[150] Concern about Communism even reached the director of Vatican Radio, which had been founded in 1931. According to Ferdinando Bea, 'From Latin America came repeated requests for (radio) programmes of a social character with which to challenge Nazi and Soviet propaganda.'[151]

By the mid-1930s, in response to the Vatican's circulars, individual bishops and bishops' conferences were issuing pastoral letters on the perils of Communism, like those of England and Wales, Scotland, and Australia.[152]

Fr Ledóchowski and the Jesuits were in the forefront of the battle against the mortal enemy. In 1932, a Secretariat on Atheism was established in Rome, lodged in the same building as the Institute for Oriental Studies, run by another Jesuit, Fr Ledit, and 'Centres of Religious Defence' were set up in each society's provinces, the most prominent of which was that at Vanves, France.[153] The vast amounts of information accumulated by the Secretariat on the progress and expansion of Communist activity throughout the world was processed and then distributed to the Catholic world in the form of a periodical, *Lettres de Rome sur l'athéisme moderne*.[154] Ledóchowski took advantage of the World Exhibition of the Catholic Press held in the Vatican in May 1936 to summon a meeting in Rome of those Jesuit fathers responsible in their

[148] ASV, AdRP, Australia, Box 152, 603/36, Societa Cattoliche, 1936–7, letter from de Hemptine to Msgr Panico, 28 December 1936.

[149] ASV, AdRP, IV Periodo, Australia, Box 152, 603/36, Società Cattolica, 1936–7, letter from de Hemptinne to Msgr Panico, 28 December 1936.

[150] ASV, AES, IV Periodo, Stati Eccl., 437, 390–397, Unione Internazionale delle Leghe Femminili, 390, Steenberghe to Pizzardo, 30 September 1930.

[151] F. Bea, *Qui Radio Vaticana: mezzo secolo della radio del Papa*, Vatican City, 1981, 96–97.

[152] Westminster Diocesan Archives, Hi. 2, 55, 1930–1940 Communism, C.T.S. pamphlet, *What is Communism?*, October 1936; Scottish Catholic Historical Archives, ED 29/91, Scottish Hierarchy Minute Book, 11 May 1936, Pastoral of the Archbishop of Glasgow.

[153] G. Petracchi, 'I Gesuiti e il Communismo tra le due Guerre', in Vincenzo Ferrone (ed.), *La Chiesa Cattolica e il Totalitarismo. Atti del Convegno di Torino, 25–26 ottobre 2001*, Florence, 2004, 141–144.

[154] See Philippe Chenaux, 'Pie XI et le Communisme (1930–1939) D'auprès les Archives du Vatican', in Delville and Jacov (eds), *La Papautè Contemporaine*, 480.

own countries for the battle against Communism in Rome, to discuss review progress.[155]

In 1936, the Communist threat seemed to have assumed a particularly perilous form because of the advent of Popular Front governments, formed with Communist support, not only in Spain in February, but then in France in May. In Spain, the chief ringleaders of the bloody anti-Catholic campaigns were either Anarchists or Trotskyites, but the Vatican lumped them all together with the Spanish Communist Party (PCE) under the title of 'Communists'. In the case of France, even though Léon Blum's Popular Front government did not in fact adopt a hostile attitude towards the Church,[156] the situation was seen as especially dangerous. The danger was due to the insidious Communist campaign of *rapprochement* towards social Catholicism, the so-called '*main tendue*' ('outstretched hand') strategy as represented by the radio speech of Maurice Thorez, leader of Parti Communiste Français on 7 April 1936, in which he extended the hand of friendship to Catholics in the battle against fascism.[157]

The positive response of some French Catholic intellectuals and trade unionists eventually led to the periodicals *Terre nouvelle* and *Sept* being banned by the Holy Office late in 1937.[158]

Divini Redemptoris

The encyclical against Communism, *Divini Redemptoris*, was the work of many hands. The first draft, and most amendments, were the work of Mgr Valentini, Rector of the Minor Roman Seminary, but Mgr Pizzardo produced another draft, and Mgr Ottaviani, Assessor in the Holy Office, and Fr Ledóchowski contributed to it as well (see Chapter 5).[159]

Divini Redemptoris is, first and foremost, a comprehensive and systematic analysis and refutation of Communist ideology, all the way down to its Hegelian and Darwinian roots, then an exposition of the causes of the successful worldwide spread of Communism, and finally a restatement of Catholic social teaching as an answer to it. The essence of Marxism, dialectical materialism, and its consequences, atheism and economic determinism, are condemned along with the denial of the natural right to private property,

155 Petracchi, 'I Gesuiti e il Communismo', 143–144.

156 Blum had good relations with Mgr Valeri, nuncio in Paris, and excused himself with him for not having prevented an article hostile to the papacy being published in *Il Populaire*, a Socialist periodical: see ASV, AES, IV Periodo, Stati Eccl., 576, fascicoli 47–48, Valeri to Pacelli, 12 May 1937.

157 Petracchi, 'I Gesuiti e il Communismo', 146–147.

158 See Chenaux, 'Pie XI et le Communisme', 480.

159 ASV, AES, IV Periodo, Stati Eccl., 548, 571, Enciclica sul Communismo and 571 bis, Alcune Note Esplicative Sullo Schema dell'Enciclica sul Communismo.

the pursuit of the class struggle, the denigration of the family as a superseded 'bourgeois' institution, and the statolatry of 'real socialism' in the form of the Soviet state.[160] So Communism, in both theory and practice, was comprehensively and irrevocably denounced. But whereas over 40 per cent of *Mit brennender Sorge* consists of a detailed denunciation of Nazi persecution of the German Church, there is only one passing reference to the persecution of the Catholic Church in Russia in *Divini Redemptoris*.[161] By 1937, there was not much left of the Church in Russia to defend by comparison with Germany. *Divinum Mandatum*, of five years earlier, was much more of a condemnation of Communist anti-religious persecution than of Communism itself (see Chapter 5).

The explanation of this, and other differences, between the two encyclicals is to be found in the nature of the ideologies of the two regimes with which they dealt. Communism was a universalistic political religion which explicitly challenged the very essence of Catholic universalism because of its atheistic materialistic ideological base and was, as *Divini Redemptoris* so lamented, achieving massive worldwide expansion thanks to the era of economic, political, and social turbulence inaugurated by the Wall Street Crash. In this regard, the increasing power and influence exerted by the Communists in Spain, due to Stalin's intervention on the side of the Republic in the Spanish Civil War, must have been at the forefront of the pope's mind. In contrast, German National Socialism was, as yet, just that, an ideology, movement, and regime whose appeal, by virtue of its biological racial ideological core, was strictly confined within the frontiers of the German Reich, and possibly to Austria, Czechoslovakia (the Sudeten Lands), and Danzig. That said, many were already wondering how long it would be before it burst these boundaries, as witnessed by its involvement on the side of Franco and the Nationalists in the Spanish conflict. While its leaders may already have been thinking of world domination, they were not yet working to subvert the worldwide Catholic Church. While National Socialism was, of its ideological essence, pagan and anti-Christian, and in Germany was increasingly revealing itself to be so, it was not promoting atheistic materialism and attacks on the Church throughout the world. Finally, whereas Pius XI had nothing to lose any more by a root-and-branch condemnation of Communist theory and practice, the situation of German Catholics demanded that he show more caution and leave some doors open to a diplomatic reconciliation with the Third Reich.

The almost simultaneous publication of the two encyclicals is, of course, no accident: there was an obvious reason for dating *Divini Redemptoris* on 19

[160] Arthur F. McGovern, 'Marxism', in Dwyer (ed.), *The New Dictionary of Catholic Social Thought*, 576.

[161] Carlen, *Papal Encyclicals*, III, 541.

March for this was the feast of St Joseph, whose patronage Pius XI invoked in the crusade to preserve the 'Christian Social Order' against the assaults of Communism. It was felt in the Vatican that both encyclicals were urgent and necessary, but there was also an obvious concern that the one should not overshadow the other. On the other hand, German National Socialism and Soviet Communism were regarded as posing, each in their different ways, a mortal threat to the Catholic Church in 1937.

Nos es Muy Conocida (aka *Firmissimam constantiam*)

The *modus vivendi* of 1929 with the Mexican government had indeed become, as Cardinal Pio Boggiani, a former apostolic delegate in Mexico, described it, a '*modus morendi*', by the early1930s,[162] with no sign of any let-up in the persecution of the Church.[163] In 1935, however, the new president, General Lazaro Cárdenas, sought to placate Catholics by a return to the *modus vivendi*; he was also 'not wishing to embarrass Roosevelt with his Catholic constituents', as Roosevelt had been putting renewed pressure on Congress to intervene in Mexico 1936.[164] Cárdenas stopped the most violent religious persecution and dissolved some of the groups that had perpetrated it, like the infamous 'Red Shirts'.[165] Pacelli, during his visit to America in 1936, took the opportunity to talk face to face with representatives of the Mexican Church in exile. In the documentation which Pacelli saw before that meeting there is clear evidence of a continuing divergence of views between the Secretariat of State and the Mexicans.[166] A meeting of the Mexican Commission chaired by the bishop of Chiapas insisted that 'Catholic Action is insufficient for the good of an oppressed religion: there also needs to be civic action'.[167] By 'civic action', the Commission meant freedom for the Mexican laity on the ground to take whatever action they thought necessary to oppose the government's persecution of Catholics, including violence where necessary—'civic action, legal or illegal'.[168]

On the other hand, the advice which the Vatican received was the opposite. In particular, Mgr Guglielmo Piani, formerly Apostolic Delegate in Mexico, who conducted an apostolic visitation of the country in 1936, warned that the inevitable logic of the Mexican position was support for armed resistance against the government, in other words a renewal of the

[162] ASV, AES, Sessioni, 1346, Messico Situazione Religiosa, 20 December 1931, 5,

[163] Fogarty, *The Vatican*, 236, claims that there was an intensification of the persecution prompted by Roosevelt's election as president in 1932.

[164] Fogarty, *The Vatican*, 236.

[165] Nicholas Cheetham, *Mexico: A Short History*, New York, 1971, 252.

[166] ASV, AES, IV Periodo, Messico, 1936–1939, pos. 590–591 P.O., f. 388.

[167] ASV, AES, IV Periodo, Messico, 1936–1939, pos. 590–591 P.O., f. 388.

[168] ASV, AES, IV Periodo, Messico, 1936–1939, pos. 590–591 P.O., f. 388.

Cristiada. But, as he said, how could the Holy See approve of a movement which 'had defended the faith by cutting off government school masters' ears and raping school mistresses?'[169] In the end, Piani's advice was followed almost word for word in the pontifical letter or encyclical which Pius XI sent to the Mexican bishops in March 1937. *Nos es muy Conocida* is essentially devoted to the means of *reorganizing* the Mexican Church, putting great emphasis on the spiritual formation and training of priests and the development of Catholic Action.[170] Pius also laid great stress on the question of social justice, urging the bishops to give their attention to the land problem and the need to improve the living conditions of working men and their families, and to provide religious and economic assistance to the *campesino*.

By comparison with the two other encyclicals which Pius issued in March 1937, *Mit brennender Sorge* and *Divini Redemptoris*, that on Mexico was pastoral rather than polemical. It said nothing about the iniquitous clauses of the constitution and little about the anti-clerical laws, and rarely, and then only obliquely, referred to persecution: it was clearly premised on the assumption that the worst of the persecution was over. It is, therefore, rather paradoxical that the encyclical dwells at length upon the theoretical issue of what forms of resistance are available to Catholics against the unjust actions of secular governments.[171] This does not seem to be appropriate to the situation of the Church in Mexico in 1937. Paolo Valvo offers a very plausible explanation of this paradox, that this section of the encyclical was, in that very circumlocutory way of Vatican discourse, actually addressed to Catholics in *Spain* rather than Mexico.[172] Given the Vatican's formal neutrality in the Spanish Civil War, and its anxiety to avoid inciting the Republican militias to even more violence against Catholic clergy, it could not make such a direct statement to Spanish Catholics. But it could do so *indirectly*, in the context of a papal pronouncement on Mexico.

The Vatican was clearly grateful for the improvement in the Mexican situation by 1937 and hopeful of reaching some sort of more formal agreement with the Mexican government in the fullness of time. Certainly, thereafter, the situation in Mexico continued to improve. By the end of the decade, many churches had reopened and priests and bishops returned to their cures, and, in 1940, a presidential candidate, General Emmanuel Avila Camacho, felt able to declare, 'I am a believer.'[173]

169 ASV, AES, IV Periodo, Messico, 1936–1939, pos. 590–591 P.O., f. 388.

170 Carlen, *Papal Encyclicals*, III, 555–557.

171 Carlen, *The Papal Encyclicals*, III, 559–560.

172 Valvo, 'Difendere la fede', 215–218.

173 Cheetham, *Mexico*, 261.

Latin America in the 1930s

Despite the uncertainties and perils of the Mexican situation, the outlook for the Roman Catholic Church as a whole in Latin America in the 1930s was far from gloomy. There were no more major Church–State disputes and no more sudden and painful ruptures in relations between the Latin American states and the Vatican.

Relations with Argentina had been steadily improving since the election of General Justo as president in 1932 and this was confirmed by Pacelli's visit, as cardinal legate, to the Eucharistic Congress in Buenos Aires in October 1934. Pacelli was received with great pomp and ceremony by the Argentine president. As Pacelli's biographer, Nazareno Padellaro, explains:

> the General saluted the Legate in words which, if not strictly accurate, at least expressed his own great devotion to the Vicar of Christ: Your Eminence, I salute in the person of the Papal Legate the foremost sovereign of the world, before whose spiritual authority all other sovereigns prostrate themselves in veneration.[174]

Ignoring the hyperbole, the visit and the congress were a great success. They strengthened the papacy's relations with Argentina and also with Latin American Catholics in general. Many of the faithful came to the congress from other parts of the continent and were greeted not only by Pacelli, but by a speech from the pope himself, relayed, as was now the routine for major national or regional Catholic congresses, by Vatican Radio.[175]

Pacelli's visit demonstrated, in another way, Pius XI's concern for the Catholics of the whole of Latin America, since Buenos Aires was but the first of three stops made by the Secretary of State in Latin America. The next major stop was Brazil, where he was greeted with the same sort of pomp as in Buenos Aires by President Getulio Vargas in Rio De Janeiro.[176] In 1930, following the failed Communist–military coup, the Church was poised to become one of that country's most powerful pressure groups.[177] Between 1932 and 1947 there were discussions of a possible concordat, though one did not materialize.[178] Nevertheless, whereas the constitution of the First Republic, which was born after the overthrow of the monarchy in 1889, was secular in both spirit and letter, the constitution of the Second Republic created by Vargas was heavily influenced by Catholic principles, including those relating to the indissolubility of marriage, religious instruction in schools, and

[174] Padellaro, *Portrait of Pius XII*, 114. [175] Pollard, 'Electronic Pastors', 185.

[176] Padellaro, *Portrait of Pius XII*, 115–116.

[177] Carlo Felice Casula, 'La Santa Sede e il tentativo di sollevazione militare-comunista in Brasile nel 1935', unpublished paper presented to the 'Pius XI and America' conference, Brown University, 28–30 October 2010.

[178] ASV, AES, Brasile, IV Periodo, 509, 525, 533, 32 1930–1947 Eventuale Concordato.

Catholic chaplaincies to the armed forces. Moreover, the *Patronato*, state control over the appointment of bishops, which had been exercised by both imperial and republican governments, now vanished forever. On the other hand, the price which the Church had to pay was more or less open support of the increasingly authoritarian, even fascist, direction which the regime of Vargas took as the 1930s drew to a close. Not surprisingly, in the new political order a Catholic Action organization based on the Italian model was seen as the major means of mobilizing Catholics in public life, including elections.[179] In this way, a new sort of 'throne and altar' alliance seemed to be emerging in the subcontinent's two greatest states.

When the Bolivian government proposed to separate Church and State and suppress foreign religious orders in 1932, the Vatican was able to reach an accommodation.[180]

It was equally successful with Ecuador. As Cardinal Sibilia stated in a meeting of the Congregation for Extraordinary Ecclesiastical Affairs, 'After forty years of persecution a Modus Vivendi is necessary' with that country.[181] Eventually, in July of that year a Modus Vivendi was signed and a nuncio was despatched to Quito.[182] Even in Uruguay, where Church–State relations had not been good for a long time, where there had been no formal link with the Vatican for decades, and where there had been threats to introduce both abortion and euthanasia, the situation had greatly improved by the end of the 1930s, so much so that, in 1934, Pacelli made a short visit to the capital, Montevideo, after his triumph in Buenos Aires. In 1939 the government of Uruguay entered into negotiations for the reopening of diplomatic relations.[183]

Pius XI, Mussolini, and the Racial Laws

The racialist 'contagion' reached Fascist Italy in 1938. While Mussolini's claims that he had always been a racialist and anti-Semite can be dismissed as pure rhetoric, the move towards racialism on his part certainly began two or three years earlier with the invasion and occupation of Ethiopia. The regime introduced laws against miscegenation in order, as it claimed, to preserve the purity and authority of the imperial Italian race, and instil into it a sense of racial superiority over the Africans. The reaction of the Roman curia, in

[179] Casula, 'La Santa Sede', 5.

[180] ASV, AES, IV Periodo, 43 (1930–1938), 348, Taccuini, 24 June 1932.

[181] ASV, AES, Sessioni, 1373, Stampa 1267, Equatore, 3 January 1937, 6.

[182] ASV, AES, Sessioni.

[183] ASV, AES, Sessioni, AdRP, Uruguay, 1236. 1900–1939, Mons. Giuseppe Fietta (1936–1939), fasc. 36, 1, Ripresa delle relazioni diplomatiche, 18 Accreditato il Dott. Secco Illa a Ministro Plenipotenziaro presso la Santa Sede (1939) and 20 Acquisto di una casa a Montevideo per la Nunziatura Apostolica in Uruguay (1939–1940).

this case the Congregation for Sacraments to the law on *madamato*, banning sexual relations between white Italians and 'natives', was extremely muted. The congregation's prefect, Cardinal Domenico Jorio, commented on the proposed legislation that the Church had no objections to it because the ban did not extend to marriage, it merely dissuaded people from having sexual relations which it regarded as a wise thing to do.[184] While enslavement of people of non-white races had been condemned by a succession of popes, racial segregation had not.

This was the background to the situation in which, by 1937, racialist ideas were being openly discussed by Fascist academics and journalists.[185] The Vatican signalled its discomfort with the growing interest in racial doctrines on the part of the Regime by putting Guido Cogni's book, *Il Razzismo*, on the Index in June 1937.[186] Ironically, Mussolini largely ignored Cogni's 'Mediterranean' theories of race; the theories set out in the Manifesto of the Radical Scientists were a more Nordic, Aryan version and were clearly targeted against Italy's native population of 40,000 Jews and several thousand Jewish refugees.[187]

But the adoption of a form of racial anti-Semitism by the Fascist regime was chiefly prompted by Mussolini's growing relationship with Hitler's Germany. Mussolini's infatuation with Nazi Germany had been triggered by his official visit to Berlin in September 1937, which was followed two months later by his adherence to the Anti-Comintern Pact with Germany and Japan. The Duce perceived that only in alliance with the military might of the Third Reich could he realize his imperial ambitions in the Mediterranean, Africa, and the Middle East.

The first fruit of Mussolini's closer relationship with Hitler was Austrian *Anschluss* in March 1937 when the Italian dictator abandoned his 'Watch on the Brenner' and stood by while German troops invaded and occupied Austria and Hitler declared it annexed to the German Reich. Mussolini's acquiescence in the *Anschluss* was almost as much of a shock to the Vatican as the event itself. The loss of Catholic Austria to neo-Nazi paganism was a terrible blow to Pius XI, finally sweeping away all illusions about the possibility of using Mussolini to oppose, or at least restrain, Hitler.[188] The reaction of Cardinal Innitzer, archbishop of Vienna, and the rest of the Austrian episcopate to *Anschluss* was badly received in the Vatican. Innitzer's speech of welcome to the *Fuehrer* and his use of the Hitler salute sent Pius XI into a paroxysm of rage which was partially assuaged by summoning the wretched cardinal to Rome and giving him a serious dressing-down.[189] To set the record

184 Ceci, 'Santa Sede e impero fascista', 144–145.

185 Aaron Gillette, *Racial Theories in Fascist Italy*, London and New York, 2002, ch. 4.

186 *Index Librorum Prohibitorum*, 121, 9 June, 1937.

187 Gillette, *Racial Theories*, 69–70.

188 Rhodes, *The Vatican*, 150.

189 Rhodes, *The Vatican*, 150.

straight, *L'Osservatore Romano* and Vatican Radio published a statement dissociating the Holy See from the actions of the Austrian bishops.[190]

It was shortly after *Anschluss* that there occurred a rather curious incident in which Mussolini urged the Vatican to excommunicate Hitler, allegedly as a way of responding to the persecution of the Church in Germany.[191] The pope did not take up the suggestion. Wolf suggests that Mussolini was concerned that Nazi anti-clericalism threatened the common front against Communism.[192] It may also be surmised that Mussolini was experiencing one of his regular fits of resentment against the *Fuehrer* and concern about his ever-growing power in Europe. On this occasion, the feelings were not shared by his son-in-law and foreign minister, Galeazzo Ciano, whose fears and suspicions of Hitler and the Nazis would, however, develop with intensity over the coming months.

But Hitler marched on, and Mussolini began to settle into his role as junior partner to the German dictator. Thus, in May 1938, the *Fuehrer* paid a state visit to Italy. Hitler's refusal to make the customary visit to Vatican angered Pius XI who was willing to receive him, in order, no doubt, to give the *Fuehrer* a piece of his mind. When Pius discovered that members of Hitler's entourage had obtained free tickets to visit the Vatican museums and galleries the pope had them closed and he himself withdrew to Castel Gandolfo for the duration.[193] The Vatican even refused the request made by the Fascist governor (mayor) of Rome that its properties on the Via della Conciliazione be decorated with the flags of Italy and Germany.[194] It can be no coincidence that, on 3 May, the date of Hitler's arrival in the Italian capital, Pius, who had assumed the role of prefect of the Sacred Congregation of Catholic Universities and Seminaries following the death of Cardinal Sincero, instructed the congregation to issue a warning against the heresy of racialism to all Catholic institutions of higher education and for priestly training. The Congregation's decree condemned the proposition that: 'human races, by their natural and immutable character, are so different that the humblest among them is furthest from the most elevated than from the highest animal species'.[195] To underline the point he was making, Pius XI also uttered his memorable denunciation 'of a cross which is not the cross of Christ' flying over Rome: a reference to the swastika on the German flags decorating Rome in the *Fuehrer*'s honour.[196] It was also in the aftermath of Hitler's visit, in June, that Pius made the decision to commission three Jesuits, Frenchman Gustave Desbuquois, the American John Lafarge, and the German Gustav Gundlach, to prepare drafts of an

[190] Rhodes, *The Vatican*, 150. [191] Wolf, *Pope and Devil*, 270–271.
[192] Wolf, *Pope and Devil*, 270.
[193] Fattorini, *Hitler, Mussolini and the Vatican*, 143–147.
[194] Baxa, *Roads and Ruins*, 147.
[195] As quoted in Passalecq and Suchecky, *The Hidden Encyclical*, 114.
[196] Passalecq and Suchecky, *The Hidden Encyclical*, 114.

encyclical condemning biological racialism.[197] Apart from the Jesuit Father General Ledóchowski, no one else in the Vatican, not even the secretary of state, was let into the secret.

Just two months after Hitler's visit the first serious step was taken towards the introduction of racialism into Fascist Italy with the publication of the *Dichiarazione della Razza* ('Declaration on Race') on 14 July, followed by the 'Manifesto of the Racialist Scientists' on 5 August 1938.[198] The *Dichiarazione* was a 'decalogue' of principles, based on the assumptions that there was 'a pure Italian race' and that this race was Aryan in origin and civilisation, on which the regime would later base its racial anti-Semitic legislation a few months later.[199] Pius XI's response to the *Dichiarazione* was immediate and strong. Firstly, he denounced racialism in a speech to a General Chapter of the Sisters of the Cenacle, describing the Manifesto 'as a real form of apostasy . . . It is not just one or another idea which is wrong it is the whole spirit of the doctrine which is contrary to the faith of Christ.'[200] Then, on 21 July in a speech to the chaplains of Azione Cattolica Italiana, the pope declared 'There is something peculiarly loathsome about this spirit of separatism . . . which, precisely because it is un-Christian and irreligious, ends by being inhuman.'[201] Finally, in a speech to students of the College of Propaganda Fide on 28 July he uttered the famous phrase, 'spiritually we are all Jews' and accused Mussolini of imitating Hitler, provoking a predictable reaction on the part of the Duce.[202] In a later speech at Trieste, Mussolini denounced as 'poor half-wits, to whom we do not know whether to extend our contempt or our pity' those who claimed he had imitated Hitler.[203] Pius took this barb in remarkably good part.[204]

The Vatican organs, *L'Osservatore Romano* and *La Civiltà Cattolica* also inveighed against Nordic racialism, though the Jesuit journal had some difficulty distinguishing between 'good' and 'bad' anti-Semitism, between Catholic suspicion and diffidence towards the Jews and the racial biological version of the Nazis, and now the Italian Fascists: the fundamental problem was that *La Civiltà Cattolica* had been attacking the Jews in the most vituperative terms since its very inception, back in the 1850s. *L'Osservatore Romano* also went to great lengths to explain to its readers that the pope in his remarks was not 'philo-Semitic'.[205]

[197] Passalecq and Suchecky, *The Hidden Encyclical*, 39–40,

[198] For the text, see Delzell, *Mediterranean Fascism*, 174–176.

[199] Delzell, *Mediterranean Fascism*, 178–183.

[200] As quoted in Binchy, *Church and State*, 616.

[201] Binchy, *Church and State*, 616–617.

[202] Binchy, *Church and State*, 617–618.

[203] Susmel, Edoardo and Duilio (eds) (1951–1989), *Opera Omnia di Benito Mussolini (1883–1945)*, 44 vols (Florence), 19.ix.1938.

[204] ASV, AES, IV Periodo, Diario Tardini, 23 maggio–1 giugno 1938, note to Secretary of State of 21 September 1938.

[205] Binchy, *Church and State*, 615.

The dilemma of *La Civiltà Cattolica* reflects the profound ambivalence of many Catholics, and not only Italians, to the Jews. Catholicism in most European countries—especially France, Poland, and Hungary—was heavily tainted by anti-Semitism. As Richard Evans has pointed out, there were increasing campaigns against the Jews in Poland, under the influence of the colonels' junta that ruled the country. There was exclusion from public sector jobs and reduced entry to universities, and in 1939 Jews were barred from all the professions.[206] Referring to the hostility of the Catholic Church, he says, 'Polish anti-Semitism was thus by and large religious rather than racist, although the boundaries between the two inevitably became more blurred in the violence of anti-Semitic rhetoric and following the German example.'[207] In Romania 270,000 Jews were expelled from the judiciary, police, teaching, and officer corps and were coming under increasing pressure to emigrate.[208]

Added to the fundamental theological hostility of Catholicism towards the Jews for crucifying Christ (hence the term 'the deicide people') and rejecting him as Messiah, were centuries of anti-Jewish bigotry, paranoia, and violence. Consequently, Catholic anti-Semitism could hardly be described as principled discrimination, but contained an admixture of economic, cultural, and political prejudices which only fell short of the anti-Semitism of the Nazis by reason of the latter's biological, racial component. Giovanni Miccoli offers a crucial insight into Catholic anti-Semitism in the nineteenth century: 'For Catholic anti-Semitism, the Jews became the symbol of the hated modernisation which was in train, the inspirers and protagonists of the processes of secularisation.'[209] And it could be argued that the Jews had profited most from those processes. But however hostile Catholicism might be to the Jew, there was a simple remedy which was not available to Jews faced by Nazi biological, racial anti-Semitism: conversion. This explains in part the considerable efforts made by the Church authorities to help non-Aryan Christians both before and during the course of the Holocaust.

Catholic hostility towards the Jews—as 'Catholic anti-Semitism' or anti-Judaism—was strongly present in Hungary.[210] In 1938, several months before the Italian legislation, bills were introduced in Parliament which imposed quotas on Jewish participation in various areas of national life—public service, professions, artistic fields and cultural.[211] The Hungarian bishops, meeting in January 1939, declared that the laws had been adopted by the

[206] R. Evans, *The Third Reich in Power*, London, 2005, 606–607.

[207] Evans, *The Third Reich in Power*, 606–607.

[208] Evans, *The Third Reich in Power*, 608.

[209] G. Miccoli, 'Santa Sede, questione ebraica e antisemitismo fra Otto e Novecento', in C. Viviani (ed.), *Storia d'Italia; annali 11. Gli ebrei in Italia*, Turin, 1997, 1367–1374.

[210] See Paul A. Hanebrink, *In Defense of Christian Hungary: Religion, Nationalism and Anti-Semitism, 1890–1944*, Ithaca, NY, and London, 2006, especially 4–5.

[211] ASV, AES, IV Periodo, 77, P.O., 57, Ungheria, the nuncio Rotta to Pacelli, 12 April 1938.

Royal Hungarian government 'to defend the interests of Christian society in the face of the usurpations of the Jewish spirit'.[212] The idea that Christians had a legitimate right to defend their interests against Jewish aggression and 'usurpations' was common in both the Vatican and other Catholic circles in the interwar years, and can be attributed to the long-standing Catholic belief that the Jews were the chief promoters of Freemasonry, anti-clericalism, and secularization.[213] Nevertheless, both the nuncio in Budapest, Mgr Rotta, and Secretary of State Pacelli, in their correspondence on the matter, were concerned that, despite assurances to the contrary, Nazi influences could be detected behind the Hungarian laws as a consequence of the *Anschluss*, and that further legislation might reflect the severity of the Nuremberg Laws.[214] A further worry was the uncertain position of Jewish converts to Catholicism; this would become a serious problem in 1940.

It was probably precisely in order to contest growing German influence in Hungary that Pius sent Cardinal Pacelli as his legate to the International Eucharistic Congress held in Bucharest in June 1938. In his major speech to the congress, Pacelli spoke of 'the capital of Hungary . . . the bulwark Christian Europe, in tragic times, when the valour of the Magyar troops, lined up in defence of Christian civilisation, destroyed the pride of the infidels'.[215] He was, of course, referring to the defeat of the Turks but it was also clearly a reference to Hungarian Catholic values versus the paganism of the German Nazis.

In the light of Pius XI's growing hostility to Mussolini's policy of racial anti-Semitism, it is interesting to note that the Vatican was not represented at the Evian Conference, 6–12 July 1938, where the representatives of thirty-two European, North and South American, and even Australasian nations, and as many voluntary organizations, met to discuss how to resolve the humanitarian crisis provoked by the intensification of the Nazi persecution of the Jews in Germany.[216] While American, Belgian, British, Dutch, French, and Swiss Catholic committees for Aid to Refugees were present, the Vatican did not even send an observer. The Vatican under both Benedict XV and Pius XI had always given a high priority to humanitarian matters—witness Benedict's humanitarian efforts for POWs, civilian detainees, and famished populations during the after the First World War, which were then carried forward by his

[212] ASV, AES, IV Periodo, 77, P.O., 57, Ungheria, Rotta to Pacelli, 16 January 1939.

[213] ASV, AES, IV Periodo, 77, P.O., 57, Ungheria, Rotta to Pacelli, 12 April 1938, where he says that the 20% quotas imposed on the Jews were not unjust because they only constitute 5% of the population.

[214] ASV, AES, IV Periodo, 77, P.O., 57, Ungheria, Pacelli to Rotta, 8 May 1938.

[215] LaCC 89, 2 (1938), 2112.

[216] For an account of the proceedings of the conference as seen by the Vatican's man in Switzerland, see ASV, AES, Germania, 1936–9, 706–7 P.O, 272, 1936, Conferenza di Evian, Assistenza dei Cattolici tedeschi rifugiati a Parigi ecc., Nuncio apostolico a Berna a pacelli, 27 luglio 1938, Conferenza di Evian.

successor and then extended to seeking to alleviate the effects of famine in Soviet Russia. Why then it did not participate in the efforts to find places of refuge outside of Germany for the hundreds of thousands of victims of Nazi persecution? Perhaps the tragedy of the Jews' plight was not brought home to the Vatican until discriminatory legislation was passed in Italy itself?

The developing conflict between Pius XI and Mussolini over race during the summer of 1938 took place against the background of a recurrence of the old dispute over Italian Catholic Action.[217] Membership of Catholic Action and its youth organizations had been declared to be incompatible with that of the Fascist party and its youth organizations. Pius, now a sick man, was outraged by the series of incidents and, in an audience with Pacelli, he said he had instructed Fr Tacchi Venturi to tell Mussolini that if he wanted to kill the pope he was going about it the right way about it.[218] Of course, Tacchi Venturi said no such thing to the Duce and both he and the nuncio to Italy worked hard prevent an escalation of the crisis, with the result that a 'subsidiary agreement' on ACI was reached on 20 August. While it is certainly true that Mussolini used ACI as a bargaining point in his conflict with Pius XI over the racial question, the Catholic organization was seen as a problem in its right for the Fascist authorities, especially at a local level. ACI had been growing in numbers in the mid to late 1930s, arousing fears among ardent Fascists of the threat it posed to the totalitarian state they were trying to build in Italy.[219] In July 1935, the prefect of Treviso, a *very* Catholic province in north-eastern Italy, had warned about the way in which FUCI, the Catholic students' organization, in particular was creating 'cadres that will guide future [Catholic] formations ready for any and every eventuality': which was precisely what Pius XI intended.[220] The problem of ACI would resurface at the beginning of 1939 when the dispute over race between Mussolini and Pius reached a particularly delicate stage.

Pius XI and the Munich Crisis

Pius XI was seriously concerned about the dangers of a general European war over Czechoslovakia in the weeks leading up to the Munich Crisis of September 1938. On 29 September, he made an emotional radio broadcast

[217] For a description of the conflict, see Binchy, *Church and State*, 533–534.

[218] ASV, AES, IV Periodo, 430 (1930–1938), 355 (1938), Taccuini, 21 August 1938.

[219] As early as 1933, the Rome political police had warned the Ministry of the Interior about the renewed growth of Catholic Action and its 'professional associations': see ACS, Ministero dell'Interno, Direzione Generale della Pubblica Sicurezza, G.I., b. 146, 'Azione Cattolica', sf. III, 9 September 1933.

[220] ACS, Ministero dell'Interno, Direzione Generale della Pubblica Sicurezza, G.I., b. 146, 'Azione Cattolica', sf. III, 9 July 1935.

from Castel Gandolfo, warning of the danger to the peace of Europe and begging governments to act: he ended by offering his own life to God for the salvation of the world from war.[221] The Portuguese ambassador to the Vatican said that when he and his family heard the broadcast they wept.[222] The pope was not impressed, however, by the result of the eventual conference held in Munich on 29 and 30 September where Mussolini played the role of mediator between Hitler on the one hand and France and Britain on the other. He described it as 'not so much a capitulation as a complete collapse in face of Hitler's demands . . . Never has Germany been more powerful than it is today.'[223] His contempt for Chamberlain, whom he later received in audience along with Foreign Secretary Halifax, knew no bounds. By giving in to all of Hitler's demands on Czechoslovakia, the pope said that the British prime minister had 'put Hitler on a pedestal of gold . . . The Opposition [in Britain] were right.'[224] As he explained to Tardini, 'the Four [France, Germany, Britain, and Italy] had divided Czechoslovakia up without hearing her case'.[225] While the Czech anti-clericals had given the Holy See real grief over the years, Pius sympathized with them in their plight and obviously deplored the fact that over 3 million people in the Sudeten borderlands of Czechoslovakia were to be handed over to the Nazi rulers of the Great German Reich. Since they were mostly Catholics, this was a sort of *Anschluss* all over again.

Pius XI's Last Battle: The *Vulnus* in the Concordat

On 11 November 1938, there took place in Berlin and other German cities the infamous *Kristallnacht* (Night of Glass), the Nazi pogrom in which Jewish businesses were destroyed, synagogues burnt, Jews sent to concentration camps, and others beaten up and even murdered, as punishment for the murder of a German diplomat, Ernst Eduard vom Rath, by a Polish Jew; to add insult to injury, the Jews of Germany were 'fined' as a punishment for Roth's murder.[226] Amidst the international outrage, the Vatican, like other governmental authorities, maintained a diplomatic silence. On the other hand, Cardinal Archbishops Verdier of Paris, van Roey of Malines-Mechelen, Cerejeira, Patriarch of Lisbon, and closer to home, Cardinal Schuster of Milan, all protested.[227] A number of American bishops also organized public

[221] Bellocchi, *Tutte le Encicliche*, IX, 341–342.

[222] ASV, AES, IV Periodo, 560, f. 590, Diario di S.E. Mons. Tardini, 27 settembre al 29 ottobre 1938, entry of 29 September.

[223] ASV, AES, IV Periodo, Stati Eccl., 560, f. 592, Tardini, diary note for 7 October 1938.

[224] ASV, AES, IV Periodo, Stati Eccl., 560, f. 592, Tardini, diary note for, 14 October 1938.

[225] ASV, AES, IV Periodo, Stati Eccl., 560, f. 592, Tardini, diary note for, 1 October 1938.

[226] Evans, *The Third Reich in Power*, 593.

[227] John Pollard, 'Catholicism and Fascism', in R.J.B. Bosworth (ed.), *The Oxford Handbook of Fascism*, Oxford, 2010, p. 73.

protests. This was the background to the promulgation on 17 November 1938 by the Fascist government of the decree law outlining the discriminatory measures to be imposed upon Italy's native and foreign-born Jews.[228] The law declared that the Jews were not part of the Italian race and, in line with the Nuremberg decrees, it excluded Jews from public service and the professions and from access to state education, as well as limiting their right to carry certain kinds of business and own property: unlike Germany, exemptions were made for World War I veterans, 'Fascists of the first hour', and others with 'exceptional merits' and their families.[229] From the Church's point of view the worst aspects of the law were that Jews who had converted to Catholicism were not necessarily exempt from its provisions, a curiously illogical decision bearing in mind that many Jews who had not converted were, and that marriages between Gentiles and Jews, even when the latter were converts to Catholicism, were forbidden, which was a clear breach of article 34 of the 1929 Concordat, which set out the grounds for eligibility to marry.

The Vatican had anticipated these measures for some months and behind the scenes had battled to avert them. In September Tacchi Venturi was employed to dissuade Mussolini from the measures being proposed and to tell the Duce: 'The Holy Father is truly ashamed to be Italian when he sees the whole history of Italian good sense forgotten by the decision to open the window to a wave of German anti-Semitism', a statement which did not go down well.[230]

According to historian of Fascism Renzo De Felice, the Vatican even feared that the Racial Laws 'would introduce divorce into Italy, the annulment of marriages between Italians and Jews and the sterilisation of Jews', as had happened in Nazi Germany (see Chapter 5).[231] Once it became clear that these and other eugenic measures like prenuptial health tests were not being considered, the Vatican concentrated on the issue of marriages between Aryan and non-Aryan Catholics. According to Giovanni Sale, this was the result of a battle within the curia to decide how to respond to the Racial Laws which the 'doves'—Borgoncini-Duca, Jorio, Ottaviani, and so on—won. At a meeting of the Congregation of the Sacraments, Tardini had proposed a stronger motion which included the following:

> It is necessary that it should be made public that the Holy See does not approve of the racist principle which inspires the Laws and that because it cannot prevent the new Law, the Holy See has intervened simply in order to mitigate the effect of the said law, especially in the most serious cases. . . .[232]

[228] For the text of the Law, see R. De Felice, *The Jews in Fascist Italy: A History*, New York, 2001, 700–705.

[229] Delzell, *Mediterranean Fascism*, 284.

[230] ASV, AES, IV Periodo, Taccuini, 355 (1938), audience of 9 September 1938.

[231] De Felice, *The Jews*, 11–12.

[232] As cited in Sale, *Le Leggi Razziali*, 221.

Eventually, the Holy See obtained a small victory by having an article of the law of 17 November, which practically declared that marriages between Aryans and non-Aryans were 'concubinage', removed, but failed in regard to the invalidity of marriages between converts and Catholics.[233] Pius addressed personal letters to both the King and the Duce protesting against the ban on mixed marriages, in response to which he received a polite but evasive answer from the former and nothing from the latter.[234]

With the publication of the letters in *L'Osservatore Romano*, the dispute between the Vatican and the regime over the *vulnus nel concordato*, the violation of the Concordat, now became public knowledge.[235] There have been claims that some sort of compromise between the Vatican and the Regime was proposed which would have allowed mixed marriages to go ahead in church and ensured their registration with the civil authorities, leaving the parties to such marriages to take the risk of prosecution by the State.[236] No such agreement was ever publicized and there is no evidence that Church ever had recourse to it. On the other hand, marriages between Catholics and converts did continue to be celebrated in some Italian churches.[237]

Towards the end of the year, the Vatican seems to have accepted the inevitable as far as the application of the Italian Racial Laws was concerned and turned its attention to ameliorating their human consequences. So, at the end of November 1938, the Secretariat of State sent out the following telegram under the signature of Cardinal Pacelli, to all papal nuncios and apostolic delegates:

> Many Italian and German Jewish converts are forced by the well-known law to abandon their country and ask whether they may exercise their professions specifically medicine and teaching. His Eminence Cardinal Mercati is also willing to identify illustrious professors (of) various branches (of) science (suitable) for university teaching. We request that Your Excellency communicate with opportune information whether there are universities, Catholic institutes, hospitals or other institutions willing to appoint such persons and on what conditions.[238]

The responses were, inevitably, disappointing. The Canadians were worried about Jews without jobs and suggested settling them in Africa.[239] In Australia

[233] Sale, *Le Leggi Razziali*, 281.

[234] For the text of the letters, see De Felice, *The Jews*, 687–688.

[235] According Sale, *Le Leggi Razziali*, 183–184, Pius wanted the whole of official Holy See protest to be published by *L'Osservatore Romano* but 'the curia', presumably Pacelli et al., 'for reasons of prudence and so as not to embitter the conflict with the Fascist government any further, went over the pope's head and published a less compromising text'.

[236] See De Felice, *The Jews*, 631, fn 4.

[237] De Felice, *The Jews*, 631, fn. 4.

[238] ASV, AES, IV Period, Stati Eccl., 575, Aiuto e assistenza ai profughi per motive di razza e religione: Mercati was the prefect of the Vatican Library.

[239] ASV, AES, IV Period, Stati Eccl., 575, Aiuto e assistenza ai profughi per motive di razza e religione, reply of the Apostolic Delegate, 2 December 1938.

the problem was of continuing high levels of unemployment.[240] The Argentine responded in a similar fashion.[241] Just about the only gleam of hope was an offer from Lima, Peru, to set up university teaching posts in Italian.[242] None of this is surprising, bearing in mind the resistance displayed by national and humanitarian representatives attending the Evian Conference to the idea of accepting Jewish refugees. On the other hand, Catholic relief committees to raise funds for Jewish refugees were quickly set up in several dioceses across the world.[243]

In January, the pope himself addressed an appeal to the American and Canadian cardinals, and the cardinal archbishops of Westminster and Armagh on behalf of various Jewish professors, while Cardinal Mercati contacted various members of the Pontifical Academy of Sciences.[244] Eventually, the pope's telegram was sent to archbishops in England and Wales, Canada, Scotland, the USA, Latin America, the Netherlands, and Luxembourg, sixty bishops and archbishops in all.[245]

The End

Pius XI had never really recovered from his long illness of 1936–7, when he was bedridden for several months with diabetes and severe cardiac problems.[246] By December 1938, the signs of ill health had reappeared. A photograph, probably the last to be taken of him, on 3 February 1939, shows clear signs of tiredness, illness, and a significant loss of weight for a man who, in adulthood, had always been both robust and fleshy. Though the pope tried to continue the routine of work which he had always followed, by February the number of his *audiences* had shrunk to a trickle (see Mgr Venini's diary). But he was still ready to fight, this time with Mussolini's government. Relations with the Duce were tense throughout January and into February, with

[240] ASV, AES, IV Period, Stati Eccl., 575, Aiuto e assistenza ai profughi per motive di razza e religione, Mgr Panico to Pacelli, 13 December 1938.

[241] ASV, AES, IV Period, Stati Eccl., 575, Aiuto e assistenza ai profughi per motive di razza e religione, reply of the nuncio, 10 December 1938.

[242] ASV, AES, IV Period, Stati Eccl., 575, Aiuto e assistenza ai profughi per motive di razza e religione, reply of nuncio, 18 December 1938.

[243] ASV, AES, IV Period, Stati Eccl., 575, Aiuto e assistenza ai profughi per motive di razza e religione, reply of Mgr Robinson, nuncio Dublin, 13 December 1938, in which he says that the St Vincent de Paul Society is doing its best.

[244] ASV, AES, IV Period, Stati Eccl., 575, Aiuto e assistenza ai profughi per motive di razza e religione, 3 January 1939.

[245] ASV, AES, IV Period, Stati Eccl., 575, Aiuto e assistenza ai profughi per motive di razza e religione, 9 January 1939.

[246] C. Confalonieri, *Pio XI visto da vicino: nuova edizione con l'aggiunta di due appendici a cura di Giuseppe Frasso*, Cinisello Balsamo, Milan, 1993, 204–215; Confalonieri was his secretary from 1921 to 1939.

Mussolini being offended by what he took to be sarcasm in a letter of the pope to the King in which he talked of the latter's 'incomparable minister', prompting a threat by the Duce to order Italian abstention from the celebrations for the tenth anniversary of the signing of the Lateran Pacts.[247]

The pope prepared in his own hand the commemorative speech to be given to an assembly of the Italian bishops on 12 February,[248] the first official gathering of the Italian episcopate in history.[249] The speech was, in a very real sense, his last testament, reflecting his joys, satisfactions, priorities, and anxieties. In it the dying pope talked about his experiences as priest, bishop, and pope, what he believed were the really important elements in the Church, and expressed his continued joy for the successful conclusion of the *Conciliazione*.[250] But he also expressed his dissatisfaction with the Italian government over the Racial Laws and with the way in which his statements were so frequently distorted and misrepresented:

> There is a press which it can be truly said is against US and against our interests, reporting and interpreting in a false and perverse sense the recent and past history of the Church, to the extent of denying any persecution in Germany. . . .[251]

In addition, he warned his brother bishops about the dangers which surrounded them and their pastoral ministry, especially the spies and informers who eavesdropped on their conversations in order to report them to the police and what he described as 'pseudo-Catholics' who looked for 'differences of opinion between one bishop and another and between a bishop and the pope'.[252] He was particularly concerned about police interception of the telephone: 'never trust to the telephone what you feel and know . . . your words will be intercepted. We have not used the telephone for years.'[253] Finally (the text is unfinished) he urged them to preach and prophesy:

> the return to the Faith of all peoples, all nations, all races, united and conjoined in the link of the common blood of the great human family; prophesy order, tranquillity, peace, peace, peace to the whole of the world, even though it seems to have been taken hold of by a homicidal and suicidal folly of armaments.[254]

The speech was not, of course, given, because Pius died on 10 February.

[247] Fattorini, *Hitler, Mussolini and the Vatican*, 184.

[248] ASV, AES, IV Periodo, Pos. 576, f. 607 contains a collection of documents relating to Papa Ratti's final days, including the draft of his speech to the Italian bishops and the instructions which Tardini received.

[249] Gian Franco Pompei, *Un Ambasciatore in Vaticano. Diario 1969–1977*, ed. Pietro Scoppola, with notes by Roberto Morozzo della Rocca, Bologna, 1994, 387, fn. 21, where he cites a speech of Pope Paul VI on 10 February 1974.

[250] ASV, AES, IV Periodo, Pos. 576, f. 607, 161–163.

[251] ASV, AES, IV Periodo, Pos. 576, f. 607, 167–168.

[252] ASV, AES, IV Periodo, Pos. 576, f. 607, 167–168.

[253] ASV, AES, IV Periodo, Pos. 576, f. 607, 169–170.

[254] ASV, AES, IV Periodo, Pos. 576, f. 607, 171–172.

The fate of the text of the speech has generated serious historiographical controversy. After the death of Pius XI, Cardinal Pacelli, who, though no longer Secretary of State, was Cardinal Camerlengo of the Holy Roman Church, and therefore responsible for presiding over the Holy See during the *sede vacante*, gave strict orders to Tardini that all copies of the text of the speech, including proofs, were be destroyed.[255] In the light of what is known about the penetration of the offices of the Roman curia and the Vatican administration by Italian police spies, some precautions were almost certainly necessary.[256] Nevertheless, Tardini, for his own good reasons, did manage to save one copy of the speech, now preserved in the Vatican Archives. Emma Fattorini argues that Pacelli's action was a 'betrayal' of the Ratti pontificate, demonstrating that he thus wished to make a break with the policy of Pius XI.[257] The fact that, according to Tardini, Pacelli tried to dissuade Pius XI from talking about the persecution of the Church in Germany in the speech would appear to bear this out and perhaps even support the argument that there was some kind of conspiracy among the top echelons of the Vatican to undermine the pope's policy.[258] Fattorini also points to the 'hiding' of the drafts of the encyclical on racialism, *Humani Generis Unitas*, which, though it reached the Vatican in September 1938, was still lying in draft form on the pope's bedside table at the time of his death.

It is just as plausible to argue that Pacelli only did what anyone else in his position would have done, thus avoiding a serious row with Italy and Germany during the Conclave. Apart from the fact that *Humani Generis Unitas* was not, in any case, in a final draft form, to have published it on the eve of the Conclave might have precipitated a rupture in relations with Italy and Germany, thus rendering the position of the Holy See, always weak during an interregnum, extremely difficult. Given that Ledóchowski and others had added the usual rider to the Lafarge draft about 'perfidious Jews', it would not have been well received in Western democratic countries either. Furthermore, as Camerlengo, Pacelli was only 'caretaking' the Church so he was not authorized to take such initiatives as publishing the documents of the previous pontificate, particularly when there is no evidence that he had been instructed by Pius XI to do so. In all these circumstances the decision he took was undoubtedly the wisest course.

On 9 February, Tardini said a Mass *pro infermo* in the chapel adjacent to the pope's bedroom which was broadcast by Vatican Radio.[259] On the 10, the pope expired. The fact that daily medical bulletins, the Mass, and the funeral

[255] ASV, AES, IV Periodo, Pos. 576, f. 607,164.

[256] Alvarez, *Spies in the Vatican*, chs 4 and 5.

[257] Fattorini, *Hitler, Mussolini and the Vatican*.

[258] ASV, AES, IV, Pos. 576, f. 607, Tardini's note of 17 March 1939.

[259] Confalonieri, *Pio XI visto da vicino*, 241, says that Mgr Diego Venini, Pius XI's other secretary, celebrated the Mass.

rites of Pius XI were all broadcast by Vatican Radio, and then relayed via other national broadcasting services, were a fitting tribute to the first 'electronic pope'.[260]

AN EVALUATION OF PIUS XI

Everything, or nearly everything, about Pius XI and his pontificate seems to be clear and straightforward. His vigorous, 'high church' ecclesiology runs through his pontificate like a river. His emphatic reassertions of the teaching of Catholic faith and morals, even if most of the relevant encyclicals were written by attendant Jesuit and Dominican theologians, were an essential part of his vision of the papal office. His enormous capacity for hard work, his organizational powers, and his centralizing tendencies were also part of that vision. His angry outrage towards the misbehaviour of the dictators, especially Mussolini and Hitler, and his yearnings for peace all fit a personality that was essentially one of conventional Christian decency, which marries well with his intense devotion to St Teresa of Lisieux, suggesting a gentle, inner spirituality. In this regard, Emma Fattorini's portrait of Papa Ratti in old age as a 'lion at bay', surrounded by arch-appeasers—Pacelli, Pizzardo, Borgoncini-Duca, Tacchi-Venturi, and probably Tardini—also rings true.

Yet, there is still something just slightly mysterious about Pius XI. There is the feeling that, despite his very open, almost bullish, personality, the intellectual side of man has not been entirely revealed to us, in the way that the personalities of Benedict XV and Pius XII were. His silences during the 'modernist' crisis might suggest a lack of interest in the dangerous, avant-gardist, 'modernist' ideas about ecclesiastical history, theology, and exegetics that were emerging in his youth, that is, in the 1890s, on the part of a man buried in his books. On the other hand, the fact that Duchesne welcomed Pius XI's election (see Chapter 4) suggests that Achille Ratti may well have flirted with those ideas. After all, during his youth he was a scholar, working by essentially the same scientific methods as those employed by the 'modernists'. But by the time of his election, he must have returned to the path of orthodoxy, if he ever seriously strayed from it.

This view of the development of Pius XI's religious ideas would fit with his famous remark that 'faith, religion and piety (in which we are competent) are one thing, science is something else'.[261] It would also suggest a fascinating divide between the intellectual and academic man that he fundamentally was, and the priest, the man of religion. He remained a scholar manqué long

[260] Pollard, 'Electronic Pastors', 188.

[261] As quoted by Durand, 'Lo stile di governo di Pio XI', 56.

after he had left the Vatican Library, as is demonstrated by his continuing attention to the needs of the Library, in particular his equipping of it with the most up-to-date steel shelving imported at great cost from America. It would also seem plausible to suggest this sort of 'mental dualism' helps explain why, during his pontificate, the Holy Office held off from more formally condemning Darwin and evolution, and did not take up a more public and critical stance towards Freud, whereas his successor condemned 'polygenism' in two different encyclicals (see Chapter 9). Similarly, Pius XI had a much more sceptical attitude towards Padre Pio than Pius XII. The declining influence of Padre Gemelli after 1945 helps, in part, to explain these discrepancies. Gemelli was strongly supported by Papa Ratti—witness his appointment as President of the Pontifical Academy of Sciences, hence his influence in the Holy Office. After 1939 he was rather less influential and even less so after his brush with the Epurazione Commission in 1945 (see Chapter 10). Thus, Gemelli's change of heart over Freud could do nothing to slow the general acceptance of Freudian psychoanalysis in post-Fascist Italy.

We are left with a personality, a pope who is much more complex than either his predecessor or his successor. But his response to the challenges of the papacy was always assured, confident, and efficient. Thus, Pius XI left the papacy much stronger—diplomatically, ideologically, and institutionally—in 1939 than he received it in 1922. Upon the foundations laid by Benedict XV, he built up the papacy in such a way that it would survive the terrible challenges of the Second World War, despite Pius XII's indecision and mistakes.

8

Pius XII: Peace Diplomacy and War

EUGENIO PACELLI, 1876–1939

Eugenio Pacelli was born in Rome on 2 March 1876, into a family which, though strictly speaking not part of 'the Black Nobility', nevertheless had some claim to noble status as part of the patriciate of Acquapendente, near Viterbo, north-west of Rome.[1] The papal title of marquis was conferred on Eugenio's brother, Francesco Pacelli, in 1930, in recognition of his work during the negotiations for the Lateran Pacts, and the Italian title of prince on his sons Giulio, Marcantonio, and Carlo in 1941.[2] The family had already served the papacy for decades and its members refused to abandon it at the fall of Rome in 1870. Eugenio's grandfather, Marcantonio, had served in the government of the Papal States as Under-Secretary in the Ministry of Finances, then as Secretary for the Interior, 1851–70, and was a founder of *L'Osservatore Romano*, the Vatican newspaper.[3] Eugenio's father, Filippo, was a lawyer who practised in the papal courts of the Sacra Rota and the Segnatura. His elder brother, Francesco, would follow in their father's footsteps, becoming chief legal adviser to the Roman Curia after the First World War and the pope's representative during the negotiations which led to the signing of the Lateran Pacts of 1929. Probably the most important member of the Pacelli family in the last decades of the nineteenth and first two of the twentieth was Ernesto, Eugenio's uncle, who went into banking and ended up as President of the Banco di Roma, effectively speaking, the pope's bank, in 1903.[4]

Pacelli was first placed by his mother, Virginia Graziosi, in a nursery at the age of four, and later in a small private school run by the Marchi family: Signor Marchi was allegedly a vociferous anti-Semite, something which has bulked large in the debate over 'Hitler's Pope'.[5] The young Pacelli would

[1] Lai, *Finanze*, 146, n. 4.   [2] Padellaro, *Portrait of Pius XII*, 6–7.

[3] C. Pallenberg, *Inside the Vatican*, London, 1961, 13–15.

[4] Lai, *Finanze*, 147: on Ernesto's role in the finances of the Vatican, see Pollard, *Money*, chs 4 and 5.

[5] Padellaro, *Portrait of Pius XII*, 10–11.

certainly been aware of the Jewish community of Rome, because it was easily the largest in Italy, and of the anti-Semitism which was still rife in the city and especially in the Roman Curia. At the age of ten, Eugenio went to the Liceo Ennio Quirino Visconti, one of the most prestigious secondary schools in Rome.[6] Pacelli was a brilliant student, excelling especially in classical and modern languages, and consequently went on to study at Rome's university, La Sapienza.[7] Secondary school and university were both secular, state institutions in a city where the great struggle between Church and State, Catholicism and Liberalism, was being fought out in the last few decades of the nineteenth century.[8] This does not seem to have impacted much on the young Pacelli who, after a year in the university, decided that he had a vocation for the priesthood. So, in 1894, he was admitted to the Capranica, the major seminary for the Rome diocese.

But he left after a year. He seems to have been a sickly child, always needing care, and, as such, continued his studies in theology and philosophy at the Apollinare (now the Pontifical Roman Seminary) as an 'external student'. According to Padellaro, 'At the Apollinare he became an intellectual.'[9] Such was the precarious state of Pacelli's health that he was not publicly ordained with along with his fellow students—he was not thought to be strong enough to endure the five to six-hour ceremony in St John Lateran, the Cathedral of Rome, on Easter Saturday 1899. Instead, he was ordained next day by Mgr Paolo Cassetta, Latin Patriarch of Antioch, in his private chapel on the Esquiline Hill, and said his first Mass in the Chiesa Nuova, church of St Philip Neri.[10]

Pacelli's precarious physical health has also given rise to speculation about the state of his mental health. Paul Murphy and, more recently, Gerard Noel, have alleged that he suffered from some psychological problem, possibly bouts of depression.[11] He certainly seems to have withdrawn from the world at various times throughout his career to 1939; indeed, it is notable that he insisted on an annual *six-week* withdrawal to the convent of Einsiedeln every autumn, including that of 1938, as a result of which Mgr Tardini was obliged to hold the fort in the Secretariat of State during the tumultuous Munich crisis of September of that year (see Chapter 7).

For the next couple of years, Pacelli worked to achieve doctorates in theology and in *utroque iure* (i.e. civil and canon law) while teaching canon law at the Apollinare. It was in this period that he also had his one and only experience of parochial pastoral work, teaching the catechism at the Chiesa Nuova

[6] Padellaro, *Portrait of Pius XII*, 10–12. [7] Padellaro, *Portrait of Pius XII*, 14–15.

[8] See A. Ciampani, *Cattolici e Liberali durante la trasformazione dei partiti. La 'questione romana' e lapolitica nazionale e progetti vaticani (1870–1883)*, Rome, 2000.

[9] Padellaro, *Portrait of Pius XII*, 18. [10] Padellaro, *Portrait of Pius XII*, 19.

[11] P. Murphy, *La Popessa*, New York, 1983; and G. Noel, *The Hound of Hitler*, London, 2008, 12–14.

and also ministering to nuns of the Cenacle and the Assumption. Then, in 1901, he took his first career step, becoming a *minutante* in the Congregation of Extraordinary Ecclesiastical Affairs. Quite probably his Uncle Ernesto, a very influential figure in the Vatican at the turn of the century, put in a good word for him. The Congregation was at that time under the rule of Secretary of State, Cardinal Mariano Rampolla del Tindaro, the austere, ascetic Sicilian aristocrat, aided by Mgr Giacomo Della Chiesa (later Benedict XV) as Under-Secretary. With the death of Leo XIII in 1903, Rampolla was out, replaced by Mgr Rafael Merry del Val, so, all in all, the young Pacelli learnt the Vatican diplomatic trade from some very skilled practitioners. His skills and expertise were extended by working with Monsignor, later Cardinal, Pietro Gasparri, on the *white book*, an account of the Vatican's dealings with the French Republic during the crisis over the separation of Church and State and France's rupturing of diplomatic relations with the Holy See in 1905.[12]

A further formative experience during Pacelli's early career was his role as first principal assistant and then secretary to Gasparri on the commission which Pius X set up for the Codification of Canon Law (see Chapter 1). His career progress thereafter was rapid. In 1911, at the relatively early age of 35, he was appointed Assistant Secretary of State and visited London with Mgr Gennaro Granito Pignatelli di Belmonte for the coronation of King George V. A year later, he was pro-Secretary of State, and in 1914 Secretary to the Congregation of Extraordinary Ecclesiastical Affairs and the chief author of the concordat with Serbia—the first he was to negotiate in a diplomatic career that would span thirty-eight years in total. Pacelli's experiences in Germany between 1917 and 1930 and as Secretary of State between 1930 and 1939 have been dealt with elsewhere (see Chapters 6 and 7). Despite this smooth, easy career ascent, we are told that he didn't really want a diplomatic/curial career but a pastoral one, though he did want to go to Washington as professor of Canon Law at the Catholic University of America.[13]

CONCLAVE, ELECTION, AND CORONATION

Pacelli was the Camerlengo at his own election. In 1939 there were sixty-two cardinals: thirty-five of which were Italians and rest from Europe and North America. There were twenty-seven curial cardinals, 44 per cent of the total (all Italians except Eugène Tisserant, a Frenchman).[14] It was claimed at the time that Pacelli had been elected unanimously, which was not true. A minority of mainly Italian cardinals supported the saintly Elia

[12] Padellaro, *Portrait of Pius XII*, 23–24.

[13] Falconi, *The Popes*, 244.

[14] Zizola, *Il Conclave*, 206–207.

Dalla Costa, archbishop of Florence; others supported the more 'political' Cardinal Luigi Maglione.[15] Dalla Costa was regarded as too cold and aloof and Falconi says that his appointment was blocked because he was thought to be too anti-fascist, which would have been a serious handicap as pope for obvious reasons.[16] Maglione, because of his long sojourn as nuncio in Paris, was seen to be too pro-French and 'democratic'.[17] The French curial cardinal, Eugène Tisserant, opposed Pacelli until the end, declaring him to be too indecisive so would be 'destined to reign in torment'.[18] His prophecy was not far off the mark. Despite these countercurrents, Pacelli was elected quickly, on the third count of the second day, which was a record in three centuries.[19] This could be ascribed to the pressure imposed by worries about the likely imminence of war in March 1939.

Pacelli's election was probably inevitable. His prestigious role as Secretary of State, plus his numerous travels in Europe and in North and South America, had made him very widely known. Zizola says that he guided the Church during the last few months of Pius XI's reign when the pope had his activities restricted by illness.[20] Plus, there was his reputation as Papa Ratti's designated heir. According to Tardini:

> One day, while his Eminence [Pacelli] was in the United States, in October–November, 1936, he praised his Secretary greatly to me and concluded, looking me straight in the face with his keen eyes: 'He will make a magnificent Pope!' He did not say 'he would' or 'he could be', but 'he will be', making no allowance for uncertainty. These words were pronounced on November 12.[21]

Ironically, given the interest and anxiety of the foreign press in Rome, and that in the chancelleries of the European powers, Pacelli's election was greeted with relief by *all* the great European powers (except Russia, of course). Mussolini feigned indifference to the choice but clearly would not have been happy if a more pro-French cardinal like Maglione had been elected, and Ciano, Italy's foreign minister and Mussolini's son-in-law, was delighted by the election, having been reassured by Pacelli when Camarlengo during the late pope's obsequies that the Vatican was anxious for good relations with both Axis powers.[22] Even Germany was not dissatisfied with the election, because Pacelli was seen as being more conciliatory towards the Reich than

[15] Zizola, *Il Conclave*, 208.
[16] Falconi, *The Popes*, 245.
[17] Chadwick, *Britain and the Vatican*, 46.
[18] Chadwick, *Britain and the Vatican*, 43; see also E. Fouilloux, *Eugène, cardinal Tisserant (1884–1972)*, Paris, 2011, 280–284.
[19] Zizola, *Il Conclave*, 208.
[20] Zizola, *Il Conclave*, 201.
[21] Pierre Blet, Angelo Martini and Burkhart Schneider (eds), *Records and Documents of the Holy See Relating to the Second World War; the Holy See and the War in Europe, March 1939–August 1940*, English edition by Gerard Noel (henceforth *The Holy See and the War in Europe*), Dublin, 1968, 5; see also *La Revue Nouvelle*, November 1958, 375.
[22] *Ciano's Diary*, 37, entry for 2 March 1939.

Papa Ratti.[23] Perhaps the Italians and the Germans were cutting their losses because there is some evidence that the German ambassador, Bergen, had campaigned against Pacelli, and that some Fascists had considered Dalla Costa less 'political' and therefore more malleable to their wishes.[24] What was remarkable was that the French and the British had also wanted Pacelli as pope and had 'campaigned' for that outcome.[25] Only the Portuguese and the Spaniards were put out, the former because they had expected the election of the Patriarch of Lisbon, Cardinal Cerejeira, as a 'neutral', and the latter because of Pacelli's slowness in recognizing the Burgos government in 1938.[26] One American reaction was quite wrong: according to *The New York Times*, 'Pius XII—not the pope the totalitarians desired. This ally of Western democracy will uphold the claims of human personality against a sea of enemies.'[27] Given the very difficult international situation, Pacelli's election was probably the best for the Holy See, at least in the short term.

The coronation of the new pope on March 1939 was an elaborate affair, the first since 1846: the full panoply of the crowning being carried out on the external balcony/loggia of St Peter's before the crowds, and the Italian troops, present in the square below. According to Falconi, on the day of his coronation, Pacelli 'advanced between the feathered fans in his gestatorial chair with a hieratical solemnity that already seemed completely habitual'.[28] This, his election, and the funeral of his predecessor, were broadcast on radio: the coronation was also filmed and would form part of biographical film sketch of Pius XII, *Pastor Angelicus*, produced in 1942.[29] So, for the first time in the history of the papacy, the death of the pope and the election and coronation of his successor were major media events, raising the world profile of the Roman Catholic Church as a result.

THE NEW POPE: INTERPRETATIONS AND APPRECIATIONS

Pacelli's contemporaries seem to have got the measure of the new pope. Harold Macmillan, who visited him after the liberation of Rome in 1944, described him as '[the] little saintly man, rather worried, obviously quite selfless and holy—at once a pathetic and a tremendous figure.'[30] In 1946, Ernesto

[23] *Ciano's Diary*, 37, entry for 2 March 1939; Chadwick, *Britain and the Vatican*, 48–49, confirms this.

[24] Rhodes, *The Vatican in the Age of the Dictators*, 224.

[25] Chadwick, *Britain and the Vatican*, 41–43.

[26] Chadwick, *Britain and the Vatican*, 48–49.

[27] Rhodes, *The Papacy*, 225.

[28] Rhodes, *The Papacy*, 225.

[29] Pollard, 'Electronic Pastors', 188 and 197.

[30] Harold Macmillan, *The Blast of War: 1939–1945*, London, 1967, 556.

Buonaiuti, an unfrocked priest, and therefore not a natural friend and admirer, wrote of him:

> His whole career is characterised by a rigid sense of ascetic piety and exemplary morality. A fine figure of a priest, imbued with a sense of mission and the holiness of his office, Eugenio Pacelli cannot but arouse honest and sympathetic admiration for the dignified moral figure he presents and his proud composure as a prelate.[31]

Ten years later, Marcus Cheke, HM's Minister to the Holy See, penned this portrait of the pope in his Annual Report for 1957:

> Pius XII has none of the rugged, uncompromising, indomitable masculinity of Pius XI. He is gentle, simple, kindly and courteous: warm-hearted, charitable, and generous; his unmistakable saintliness is relieved by great personal charm and a sense of humour. Against this compendium of virtues must be set a very human vanity, particularly in respect of his speeches, to the composition, polishing and over-ornamentation of which he devotes much of his working time . . . [he has an] acute sensitivity to criticism, susceptibility to flattery and a meticulous preoccupation with form and detail. Politically he appears to be averse to irrevocable decisions and action, but he does not fail to proclaim the Church's uncompromising hostility to Communism. He has an active, supple and receptive intelligence, considerable learning, wide political experience and a modern sense of publicity values.[32]

While the 'compendium of virtues' is reassuring, that of his 'vices' is alarming in an absolute ruler.

THE VATICAN UNDER PIUS XII

In terms of the top echelons of the Vatican hierarchy, there was not only an essential continuity between the pontificates of Pius XI and his successor, but a remarkable stability across nineteen years, broken only by the death of Cardinal Maglione in 1944 and the 'defenestration' of Mgr Giambattista Montini from the Secretariat of State ten years later. While, inevitably, the cry went up among some of the Romans in the Vatican bureaucracy, 'Fuori I milanesi dal Vaticano' ('The Milanese out of the Vatican!'), this did not translate into any major changes in staffing. There was an enquiry into the management of the ASSS, probably prompted by the fact that Pius XI had insisted on dealing directly with Nogara and in strict secrecy, but the Milanese banker emerged completely vindicated and would remain in his post for most of the rest of Pius XII's reign.[33] Cardinal Caccia-Dominion

[31] E. Buonaiuti, *Pio XII*, Rome, 1946—quoted in Falconi, *The Popes*, 244.
[32] TNA/PRO, FCO, Annual Report of HM Minister to the Holy See, 1958, 5.
[33] Pollard, *Money*, 181.

and Mgr Arborio Mela di Sant'Elia, both Pius XI's appointees, and his two secretaries, Mgrs Carlo Confalonieri and Diego Venini, both remained too, though Confalonieri went as archbishop to L'Aquila in the Abruzzi in 1941, only to resume his career in the Roman curia in 1951 and be created cardinal by John XXIII in 1958.[34]

As his successor in the Secretariat of State, Pius chose Cardinal Luigi Maglione, a Vatican diplomat of considerable experience. This appointment of an alleged Francophile was perhaps intended to balance a Germanophile pope. Unlike Pacelli, in 1905–7 Maglione had had pastoral experience in Rome and the Agro Romano (the countryside south of Rome), but like Pacelli he then taught at the Pontifical Academy of Noble Ecclesiastics (1910–18). His most notable postings were as apostolic delegate and then nuncio in Berne (1913–26) where he did a lot of work at Benedict's behest to help victims of war and to facilitate the exchange of prisoners. He served as nuncio in Paris (1926–35), trying to renew the French episcopate in the aftermath of the condemnation of Action Française, which mounted vicious press attacks upon him: he was even accused of having been a German spy in Switzerland. He also succeeded in negotiating the return of much property to the management of the Church and permission for missionary congregations to use the property of dissolved religious orders in France. In 1935, he returned to the Roman curia as cardinal and later head of the Congregation of the Council (of Trent).[35]

Giuseppe Dalla Torre, editor of *L'Osservatore Romano,* said that he was slightly hesitant about becoming Secretary of State because he didn't entirely share Pacelli's ideas.[36] Certainly, Maglione did not always see eye to eye with his boss on how to handle Nazi aggression during the Second World War.

Pacelli's two lieutenants in the Secretariat of State also remained in office, Monsignori Domenico Tardini and Giambattista Montini, while Cardinal Giuseppe Pizzardo continued his ascent, being appointed as prefect of the important congregation of Seminaries and Universities—he became a powerful presence on other key Congregations as well. Another survivor from the previous pontificate, and indeed from that of Pius X, Cardinal Nicola Canali, became very powerful under the new pontiff as effectively the boss of the Vatican State. Though there were no other changes in the bureaucratic structure of the Roman Curia, that in the government of the State of the Vatican City, which was not, strictly speaking, part of the Roman curia, was significant. A new Pontifical Commission was set up to supervise all aspects of the running of the State, and Canali became its president. He was also the

[34] Giuseppe Sicari, *Cenni biografici su tutti I Cardinali (1198–2001),* Rome, 2001, 71.

[35] *Dizionario Biografico degli Italiani,* 67, Maglione, Luigi cardinale, 433–436.

[36] G. Dalla Torre, *Memorie,* Milan, 1965, 141.

president of the cardinalatial commission supervising the ABSS—though not the ASSS—and Grand Penitentiary. According to Cheke:

> He wielded great power and although reputed pious, he was just as much feared and disliked. Close friend of the present pope since they were in the Secretariat of State together at the beginning of the century.[37]

He became a figure of great importance during the Second World War when Allied diplomats, and sometimes escaped POWs, were inside the Vatican. He was allegedly pro-Fascist.[38]

A curial cardinal of exactly the opposite political point of view was Eugène Tisserant, now Secretary of the Congregation for the Oriental Churches. In part no doubt because of his fairly well-known opposition to the election of Pacelli but also because of his hostility to Italian Fascism and devotion to the cause of France, even after its defeat in June 1940, Tisserant's position in the Vatican was a difficult one during the war, and in consequence, his influence on the Secretariat of State in particular, rather limited.[39] Tisserant would find himself at odds with some of papa Pacelli's wartime policies (see Chapter 9). Though somewhat isolated among the Italian cardinals and prelates, he was close to his fellow-countryman Mgr Fontanelle of the Chapter of St Peter's and to the Allied ambassadors immured within the Vatican after June 1940, especially D'Arcy Osborne, the British minister.[40] With the fall of Fascism, the liberation of France, and the defeat of Hitler, Tisserant recovered ground in the Curia after the war. In consequence, he was appointed to the suburbicarian dioceses of Ostia, Porto, and Santa Rufina and created Dean of the Sacred College, and had thus become an *éminence grise* by the end of Papa Pacelli's reign.

Two other figures acquired increasing influence under Pius XII, Mgr Alfredo Ottaviani, who eventually became secretary of the extremely powerful Holy Office and Adeodato Piazza, who became a curial cardinal in 1935 and was appointed to the Consistorial Congregation in 1948.[41] After the Second World War, Montini became increasingly influential, representing the more 'liberal', more open tendency in the Vatican; his battles over Italian political, and other, matters with other powerful personalities there, like Ottaviani and Mgr Roberto Ronca, rector of the Roman Seminary, would lead to his exile to Milan in 1954 (see Chapter 11).

Like Papa Ratti with his Milanese friends, Pius XII also brought his own entourage into the Vatican, but this time they were mainly Germans. Fr Augustin Bea, SJ, who worked in the Pontifical Biblical Institute and was also Pius XII's personal confessor, Mgr Ludwig Kaas, Fr Robert Leiber, SJ, and Sister

[37] TNA/PRO, FCO, Annual Report of HM Minister to the Holy See, 1958, 5.
[38] Chadwick, *Britain and the Vatican*, 125.
[39] Fouilloux, *Eugène, cardinal Tisserant*, ch. 3.
[40] Fouilloux, *Eugène, cardinal Tisserant*, 360; and Chadwick, *Britain and the Vatican*, 157.
[41] Sicari, *Cardinali*, 185.

(otherwise called 'Mother') Pascalina Lehnert. The presence of these Germans at his side helped to consolidate the legend that Pius XII was 'soft on Germany'. Kaas, former chairman of the Catholic Zentrum Party, had actually arrived in 1933, effectively as a political refugee from the Nazis, and became secretary of the congregation which administered St Peter's Basilica, and supervised the archaeological excavations to find the tomb of St Peter.[42] He functioned as a close adviser of Pacelli, when Secretary of State and pope, on German affairs. Leiber had acted as private secretary to Pacelli when nuncio, had arrived in the Vatican with him, and continued to serve him when he was the Secretary of State and then pope. Though Leiber was ostensibly a professor of ecclesiastical history at the Gregorian, he was also a close personal assistant and confidant of the new pope.[43] Sister Pascalina, who had also served Pacelli when he was nuncio in Germany and then Secretary of State, was his housekeeper and leader of the little band of German nuns who assisted her. It is difficult to distinguish fact from fiction in the story of Sister Pascalina, but by any standards she does seem to have exercised considerable influence over Pius XII, especially during the war. Whether she was truly 'La Signora dei Sacri Palazzi' ('Mistress of the Sacred Palaces') as one author has, presumably unintentionally, rather ambiguously described her, is open to question.[44] She certainly seems to have entertained close relations with two friends of Pacelli, Archbishop (later Cardinal) Francis Spellman of New York and Count Enrico Galeazzi who was high up in the Vatican City administration, as well as the Pacelli nephews, Marcantonio, Carlo, and Giulio, who were themselves influential in the Vatican, especially in the last years of Pius XII's reign. Giuseppe Dalla Torre continued to occupy an important role as editor of *L'Osservatore Romano* as did Fr Ledóchowski until his death in 1942 after several years of infirmity.[45] Another leading player during the Ratti years, Fr Tacchi-Venturi, SJ, seems to have been rather less influential during Pacelli's reign after he fell out of favour with Mussolini during the disputes over the Racial Laws.[46]

Throughout the pontificate of Pacelli, an American, Francis Spellman, and one who was not even based in the Vatican but in New York, exercised an immense influence on the pope, reflecting the greater overall weight of American Catholicism in the Church after the First World War. A friend of Pacelli from the 1930s, he played a key role in the distribution of Pius XI's encyclical *Non Abbiamo Bisogno* in 1931 and in organizing Pacelli's trip to the USA in 1936.[47] He thus quickly established standing with Roosevelt, and his appointment as

[42] *NCE*, 8, 107.

[43] Martha Schad, *La Signora del Sacro Palazzo: Suor Pascalina e Pio XII*, Cinisello Balsamo, Milan, 2008, 24–25 and 62–63.

[44] See Murphy, *La Popessa*; and Schad, *La Signora del Sacro Palazzo*, especially 111–208.

[45] Malachy Martin, *The Jesuits and the Betrayal of the Roman Catholic Church*, Linden, NJ, 1987, 221–222.

[46] Sale, *Le Leggi Razziali*, 185.

[47] Gannon, *The Cardinal Spellman Story*, ch. 8.

Archbishop of New York, one of the first actions of Pius XII's pontificate—on 15 April 1939—and later as 'military bishop' for the Catholics in America's armed forces during the Second World War, also gave him enormous political influence in the USA itself. As will be seen, he played a key role in bringing about the appointment of Myron Taylor as Roosevelt's personal representative to the pope. Spellman also developed a strong relationship with leading players on Wall Street and thus had control of some of the pope's accounts in New York City banks.[48] Such was his dominating personality and powerful outreach that, after his elevation to the sacred purple, he was dubbed 'The American Pope'.[49]

The first major change in the Vatican hierarchy came in June 1944 with the death of Maglione. There is some evidence to suggest that, at this point, Pacelli considered appointing Spellman as his successor, but it was out of the question for a national of one of the major belligerent powers to be head of Vatican diplomacy. The change after Maglione's death was more apparent than real. In the end, Pius XII refused to appoint a new Secretary of State, leaving Tardini and Montini as pro-Secretaries, which of course gave him more direct control over the key dicastery of the Roman curia. This new arrangement did not always work well. American diplomats in particular complained that it was difficult and slow to get decisions from the Secretariat of State because Tardini and Montini felt obliged to refer everything to the pope, which was what Pius XII wanted: he told Tardini that he 'I do not want collaborators but executors'.[50] Like Pius XI with Gasparri in 1930, he was probably glad to see the back of Maglione, because both Gasparri and Maglione were the intellectual equals of their respective bosses.

Ten years after Maglione's death, Montini was ousted from his post and despatched to Milan as archbishop, in much the same way as Della Chiesa had been 'exiled' to Bologna in 1907 (Chapter 11). The departure of Montini signified the victory, or at least consolidation, of the power of the conservative 'Pentagon' of cardinals—Pizzardo, Canali, Micara (Vicar General of Rome), and Ottaviani and Piazza, assisted by Tardini, who was now effectively Secretary of State.

THE VATICAN PEACE EFFORTS AND THE APPROACH OF WAR

Pius XI's reign began under bad auspices: Hitler's occupation of Prague on 15 March 1939 followed the papal coronation by only four days. The consequences were the further dismemberment of Czechoslovakia, with

[48] Tittman, *Il Vaticano di Pio XII*, 47–48. [49] Cooney, *The American Pope*.
[50] A. Riccardi, *'Il Partito Romano' nel secondo dopoguerra (1945–1954)*, Brescia, 1983, 32.

Bohemia and Moravia becoming a Reich 'protectorate' subject to all the odious laws of Nazi Germany, the secession of Slovakia and the Hungarian takeover of Ruthenia, the easternmost section of the former Czechoslovak state. While the creation of an independent 'Catholic' Slovak Republic induced some optimism in the Secretariat of State, and occasioned the transfer of the nunciature from Prague to Bratislava, these events created problems for the Vatican, with yet more Catholics falling under Nazi rule and huge difficulties over diocesan boundaries and other issues. The final destruction of Czechoslovakia was followed by a peremptory German ultimatum to Lithuania to cede the Memel territory, which had been given to the Baltic state with a large German-speaking minority by the Treaty of Versailles: Lithuania complied. Then it was the turn of neighbouring Poland when Germany began to make menacing noises about Danzig, a thoroughly German city, taken from the Reich and made into an independent 'Free City' by the Versailles Peace Settlement in order to provide Poland with an outlet to the Baltic. German–Polish relations steadily deteriorated thereafter.

Further Axis aggression came on Good Friday, 7 April, with the Italian invasion of Albania, a response to the German takeover of Bohemia and Moravia. It was against this background that Pius XII made the first of what would be many public appeals for peace. In his radio message for Easter of 9 April 1939, he deplored mass unemployment, the arms race, and the violation of 'solemn treaties and pledges of faith', urging in fairly generic terms for justice and peace.[51] He followed up his words with a 'peace initiative' and invited Britain, France, Germany, Italy, and Poland to a conference to discuss outstanding issues between France and Italy and Germany and Poland, hoping also to involve the USA in some way given Roosevelt's own efforts to preserve the peace in Europe.[52] On 3 and 4 May the Vatican put out feelers to all five powers and Washington was kept informed.[53] The initiative was a failure. On the one hand, Britain and France were anxious to avoid a repeat of Munich, whereas the Germans knew that it was unlikely they would be able to repeat their success at that meeting.[54]

Despite this failure, Pius continued to engage in active peace diplomacy in the hope that he could help avert the outbreak of another European war. The prospects were not good. The polarization of Europe proceeded and was

[51] *The Holy See and the War in Europe*, doc. 7, the Pope's Easter Sermon to the Catholic World, 9 April 1939.

[52] For a summary of Pius's peace initiatives, see *The Holy See and the War in Europe*, doc. 7, 10–17.

[53] *The Holy See and the War in Europe*, doc. 19, Maglione to the Paris, Berlin, Warsaw nuncios, and to the Apostolic Delegate in London, 3 May 1939, and 20, Pius XII to Victor Emmanuel III, 4 May 1939.

[54] *The Holy See and the War in Europe*, 14–16.

reinforced, on the one hand, by the Anglo-French guarantees to Poland (31 March), Greece and Romania (13 April), and Turkey (12 May), and, on the other, by the Pact of Steel, which Ribbentrop for Germany and Ciano for Italy signed in Berlin on 22 May. The Vatican followed three paths. Firstly, it urged moderation on the Poles in their responses to German provocations over Danzig, the Polish Corridor, and the German minority.[55] Secondly, on more than one occasion it relayed to the German government, via Italy, the message of Sir D'Arcy Osborne, British minister to the Holy See: that Britain was in deadly earnest when it stated that it would stand by Poland.[56] Thirdly, Italy became the focus of papal peace diplomacy after the signing of the Pact of Steel with Germany in May on the assumption that she now had greater influence upon Germany and was thus able to restrain Hitler from war. As late as 29 August, Pius XII personally made a last-ditch appeal to Mussolini to intervene in the German–Polish crisis, as he had done at Munich.[57]

On 24 August, the pope transmitted another appeal to the powers on Vatican Radio in which he declared:

> The danger is imminent, but there is still time. Nothing is lost by peace, everything is lost by war. Men must seek to understand one another. They must resume negotiations.[58]

As Osborne recognized, 'the Holy See had done all that was possible for the sake of peace'.[59] Yet, despite the goodwill of at least the Western powers, the Holy See's involvement in the nitty-gritty of the issues in dispute endangered its neutrality and could easily be exploited by the Germans, as Tardini warned Maglione.[60] Furthermore, the Vatican had come under strong pressure from the French ambassador to abandon its neutrality and issue a message of support for the Poles in the event of a German attack upon them. Tardini swiftly replied:

> His Holiness says this is too much. We should not forget that in the Reich there are 40 million Catholics. To what might they not be exposed after such action by the Holy See! The Pope has already expressed himself and clearly.[61]

[55] *The Holy See and the War in Europe*, doc. 50, Maglione's Notes (of a meeting with the French Ambassador), 20 May 1939, and doc. 153, Cardinal Maglione to Warsaw Nuncio, Cortesi, 30 August 1939.

[56] *The Holy See and the War in Europe*, doc. 83, Mgr. Tardini's Notes, 4 July 1939.

[57] *The Holy See and the War in Europe*, doc. 148, Mgr. Tardini's Notes, 29 August 1939, and doc. 151, Fr. Tacchi-Venturi to Cardinal Maglione, 30 August 1939.

[58] *Allocuzioni e radiomessaggi di S.S. Pio XII, con commento degli scrittori della Civiltà cattolica*, Rome, 1943, 59.

[59] *The Holy See and the War in Europe*, doc. 197, British Minister Osborne to Maglione, 9 September 1939.

[60] *The Holy See and the War in Europe*, doc. 152, Mgr Tardini to Cardinal Maglione, 30 August 1939.

[61] *The Holy See and the War in Europe*, doc. 144, Mgr Montini and Mgr. Tardini's Notes, 28 August 1939.

Attempts by both sides, especially the Western Allies, to elicit condemnation of the enemy would dog the papacy throughout the Second World War. An additional anxiety for the Vatican was the apparent rapprochement taking place between Britain and France on the one hand, and the USSR on the other. There were fears in the Vatican of an Anglo-Franco-Soviet military pact due to the presence in Moscow of military leaders from the two Western powers in both April and August. Ironically, thanks to British foot-dragging, what emerged in August was not an Anglo-Franco-Russian alliance but the Molotov–Ribbentrop Pact, an unholy alliance of Catholicism's mortal enemies, German National Socialism, and Soviet Communism. All told, the pope's peace diplomacy during the first few months of his reign had been neither easy nor successful.

PIUS XII AND POLAND

Within the space of eighteen months, that is, between March 1938 and September 1939, *three* Catholic countries fell under the Nazi yoke—Austria, Czechoslovakia (Bohemia and Moravia), and Poland—with a total Catholic population approaching 45 million. But the tragic fate of Catholic Poland, crushed between the armies of pagan Nazi Germany and the atheistic Soviet Union, was naturally the matter of gravest concern in the Vatican. Despite the long preliminaries, the German invasion of Poland on 1 September was still a terrible blow to the pope, particularly when he became aware of the appalling suffering of the Poles, Jews and Gentiles alike. The problems which the Vatican faced in handling the Polish situation were aggravated by the increasing difficulties in communicating with the Polish hierarchy, as a result of the flight of the nuncio with the Polish government to Romania, and the flight of some bishops from their sees, most notably Cardinal Hlond, archbishop of Poznan-Gniezno and primate of Poland.

On September 1939, Cardinal Hlond, now in exile, made an emotional speech on Vatican Radio:

> Martyred Poland, you have fallen to violence while you fought for the sacred cause of freedom . . . Your tragedy arouses the conscience of the world . . . On these radio waves, which run across the world, carrying truth from the Vatican hill, I cry to you. Poland, you are not beaten! By the will of God you will rise with glory, my beloved, my martyred Poland.[62]

It is not absolutely clear whether Pius XII authorized this speech, but the fact that the Father-General of the Jesuits, Ledóchowski, was a Pole may explain

[62] As quoted in Chadwick, *Britain and the Vatican*, 80–81.

why Vatican Radio broadcast it. Owen Chadwick says that 'Nothing like this broadcast was ever allowed to happen again',[63] but in fact the Nazis would have reason to object to Vatican Radio broadcasts on many more future occasions. As he himself also says, there were further broadcasts about the appalling German atrocities in Poland during the winter of 1939–40, and because they were in both English and French they had a wider and more powerful impact.[64] Broadcasts on Vatican Radio were also directed at the American people. A very effective critic of the Germans was the American Jesuit, Fr J.E. Coffey, who broadcast in English primarily for North America. In one broadcast he described the conditions in which the Nazis treated the people of Poland, 'Jews and Poles were herded together in separate ghettoes, hermetically sealed, with miserably inadequate means of economic sustenance provided for those who had to live inside.'[65] It is hard to assess whether these broadcasts ever reached Germany and the territories it occupied because the German jamming of airwaves operated against Vatican Radio, but they and those of the Belgian priest, Fr Mistiaen, naturally infuriated the Nazis, leading to protests from their embassy to the Holy See.[66]

The fate of Poland under German rule between 1939 and 1945 can only be fully understood in terms of Nazi racial theory—the Slavs, including the Poles, were deemed to be *untermenschen* (subhuman)—and the Nazi project for the racial reorganization of Eastern Europe in search of *Lebensraum*, especially after the launch of 'Operation Barbarossa', the racial war against 'Judaeo-Bolshevism', in June 1941. In the latest phase of the millennial German *Drang nach Osten*, the Nazis sought to turn Eastern Europe as far as the Urals into their version of the 'Wild West'. In consequence, millions of Poles were uprooted from their homes and deported further east, millions of young men and women were sent to Germany as forced labour, and a total of 3 million Gentile Poles and nearly 3 million Polish Jews were murdered, or died from death or starvation, during the course of the Second World War.[67] Poland was now divided into a number of jurisdictions: the Warthegau, the former Polish Corridor, and Suwałki, the area south of Lithuania, with substantial German minorities, were directly subject to the Reich; Vilnius and its hinterland was annexed to Lithuania; and the rest of Poland was made into a 'Government General' under Hans Frank. In addition, a huge slice of eastern Poland passed under the rule of the Soviets after their invasion in September 1939.

[63] Chadwick, *Britain and the Vatican*, 143.

[64] Chadwick, *Britain and the Vatican*, 143.

[65] As quoted in R. Graham, SJ, 'La Radio Vaticana tra Londra e Berlino, Un dossier della Guerra delle onde: 1940–1941,' in *LaCC*, 127 (1976), 139.

[66] See Pollard, 'Electronic Pastors', 189.

[67] Timothy Snyder, *Bloodlands: Europe between Hitler and Stalin*, New York, 2010, especially chs 4 and 5.

From the Church's point of view, the area of Poland worst affected by Nazi oppression was undoubtedly the Warthegau. This area had been under German rule from 1793 to 1918, and in the late nineteenth and early twentieth century had both borne the brunt of the *Kulturkampf* and a later policy of 'Germanization' in order to assimilate it into the Kingdom of Prussia.[68] The Nazis reannexed the area to the Reich and repeated the experiment, more ruthlessly, brutally, and on a much bigger scale after the conquest in September 1939, under the leadership of Gauleiter Arthur Greiser. Greiser struck hard at the Catholic Church. As well as establishing *apartheid* between German and Polish Catholics, even in church, he imposed a series of restriction on the Church reminiscent of those of the Third Republic in the early 1900s, or even Soviet Russia after 1917. Many cathedrals and churches were closed, the Catholic Church and the various Protestant churches were reduced to the status of 'private clubs': only adults could be members. All monasteries and convents were abolished ('since these do not correspond to German morality and the politics of the population'), social, educational, and welfare activities were forbidden to the churches, all property not strictly employed for the purposes of worship was confiscated, and all external links, including to the Reich (Protestant) Church were banned.[69] As in the Government General, some bishops and priest were imprisoned in concentration camps, died there, or were simply murdered like other elements of Poland's intelligentsia.[70] This policy was not just one directed against the role of the Catholic Church as the pillar of Polish nationhood, which the Nazis were attempting to destroy, it was also an attack upon Roman Catholicism per se since Greiser stated that he wanted to establish a 'Catholic Church of the German nation'.[71] Both Polish and German Catholic leaders in the *Reichsgau* were convinced that Greiser was seeking something even more sinister than that, nothing less than the destruction of the Church itself, using the Wartheland Reichsgau, for whose government he was answerable to only Hitler himself, as a sort of laboratory for the future of Christianity in the Greater German Reich.[72] This bears out Jill Stephenson's claim that, during the war, 'in Nazi Germany the churches were to be marginalised, kept under surveillance and, eventually, perhaps hounded out of existence'.[73]

[68] C. Clark, *The Iron Kingdom: The Rise and Downfall of Prussia, 1600–1947*, London, 2006, 579–583.

[69] Ordinance of Gauleiter Walter Greiser, quoted in Martyn Housden, *Resistance and Conformity in the Third Reich*, London, 1997, 56–57.

[70] ADSS, 3, La Saint-Siège et la Situation Religieuse dans La Pologne et les Pays Baltes, 1939–1945, 1 Partie, 12–14.

[71] ADSS, 3, La Saint-Siège et la Situation Religieuse dans La Pologne et les Pays Baltes, 1939–1945, 1 Partie, 34–35.

[72] ADSS, 3, La Saint-Siège et la Situation Religieuse dans La Pologne et les Pays Baltes, 1939–1945, 1 Partie, 34–35.

[73] J. Stephenson, *Hitler's Home Front: Wurttemberg under the Nazis*, London, 2006, 231.

Conditions were little better in the regions of Poland occupied by the Soviets, where the new rulers imported their 'Godless' policies wholesale, closing churches, convents, and monasteries, and imprisoning clergy and religious of both sexes. The only consolation was that the Soviet occupying authorities treated Metropolitan Szeptyckyj and Bishop Chomyszyn of the Greek Catholic Church in the Western Ukraine with caution because of their standing among the people.[74] The situation for the Greek and Latin churches would get worse in these regions and the Baltic States, after the Red Army succeeded in driving back the Wehrmacht and reconquering them in 1944 and 1945.

The principal difficulty for the Vatican in its handling of the tragic Polish situation was communication. The German occupying authorities were naturally anxious to prevent all communication between the Catholic bishops and clergy and Rome. The Soviet block on such communication was even more complete. The chief Polish interlocutor for the Vatican, apart from Szeptyckyj, was Adam Sapieha, archbishop of Cracow, Poland's former capital and now the seat of Hans Frank's brutal regime. On one occasion Sapieha wrote a letter to the pope which he entrusted to an Italian priest, Don Pirro Scavizzi, who was passing though Poland on a hospital train to the Eastern Front. Then he changed his mind and, fearing the Gestapo would intercept it, he sent a Dominican to tell Scavizzi to burn the letter.[75] He did, but fortunately made a copy of it. Another problem arose from the fact that, in order to make more adequate provision for spiritual oversight in the absence of most of the bishops in prison or exile, the Vatican felt obliged to entrust some Polish dioceses to apostolic administrators who were bishops of neighbouring German sees, Splett, bishop of Danzig, for Chełmno-Peplin, Bertram, archbishop of Breslau, for Katowice, and Schneidemühl for Poznan.[76] This, while pleasing the Nazis, inevitably upset many Poles. It was yet one more grievance against the Holy See which Poles could now add to their list. Despite Hlond's and other broadcasts, and Pius XII's Christmas 1940 broadcast, many felt that the pope had abandoned Poland and the Vatican was inundated with aggrieved appeals from Poles in Poland and others in exile, including Polish President Raczkiewicz and the Polish Ambassador in the Vatican, Papée, that he take a firmer stance on Poland. Sapieha urged Maglione that, because of the severity of the religious persecution, a 'voice of protest and condemnation was indispensable on the part of the Holy See'.[77]

[74] ADSS, 3, Part I, 25.

[75] ADSS, 3, Part I, doc. 357, L'archeveque de Cracovie Sapieha au pape Pius XII, 28 février 1942.

[76] ADSS, 3, Part I, 5–12.

[77] ADSS, 3, Part II, 323, L'archevêque de Cracovie Sapieha au cardinal Maglione, 3 novembre 1941.

The Vatican, in its communications with the Poles, both in their homeland and in exile, stoutly rebutted claims that it had abandoned Poland, explaining the problems which it faced. When the pope's speech for his saint's day, Sant'Eugenio was broadcast on Vatican Radio, on 2 June 1943, its dedication to the people of Poland helped quieten some critics.[78]

Virtually all of the Vatican's attempts to persuade the Germans to ameliorate conditions in their occupied territories, in particular to stop the imprisonment and shootings of individual clergy and laity, and ensure the smooth flow of Vatican humanitarian aid, failed.

THE VATICAN'S HUMANITARIAN AID

On 18 September 1939, the Secretariat of State set up an Ufficio d'Informazioni, 'information bureau', to assist in attempts to put people in touch with their missing relatives—POWs, civilian refugees, concentration camp inmates, or similar—on the lines of Benedict XV's humanitarian initiative in the First World War.[79] Once it became known that the Holy See was engaged in this work, hundreds of thousands of letters were received in the Vatican and were then filed and indexed. Then an appeal was made over Vatican Radio for information about missing or detained persons, papal envoys being instructed to make enquiries in the countries concerned. According to Padellaro, 'In the year 1943 alone, 244,692 messages were relayed by the Vatican radio.'[80] All told, between 1940 and 1945 it broadcast 1,240,728 messages.[81]

But this work was not easy. It was frequently obstructed by the belligerent powers. The Italians were especially concerned about the humanitarian broadcasts, claiming that they were revealing details of the Italian order of battle by mentioning the location of ships, submarines, planes, and army units to which Italian POWs belonged.[82] The Germans gave little or no cooperation with papal humanitarian initiatives; unlike in the First World War, they refused virtually all attempts by the nuncio, Mgr Orsenigo, to visit POW camps.[83] Furthermore, they refused to cooperate with the Ufficio d'Informazioni, claiming that only the International Red Cross could carry out this kind of work in Germany. Consequently, thousands of messages to Allied POWs in camps in Germany, which had come via the Vatican, were

[78] ADSS, 3, Part II, 50–54.

[79] Blet, *Pius XII and the Second World War*, 139.

[80] Padellaro, *Portrait of Pius XII*, 195.

[81] Bea, *Qui Radio vaticana*, 134.

[82] ACS, MdI, Direzione Generale della Pubblica Sicurezza, letter from the Ministry of Foreign Affairs, 11 January 1941.

[83] ADSS, 8, Le Saint-Siège et les Victimes de la Guerre, janvier 1941– décembre 1942, doc. 55, Le nonce à Berlin Orsenigo au cardinal Maglione, 27 mars 1941, and doc. 571 Le nonce à Berlin Orsenigo au cardinal Maglione, 19 décembre 1942.

never delivered.[84] When the German authorities became aware that the work of the Ufficio d'Informazioni was actually being publicized in German Catholic periodicals and from the pulpit, they ordered it to cease, and persuaded Cardinal Bertram to circularize a directive among the German bishops to this effect.[85] The Vatican was especially outraged that Bertram and the secretary of the Fulda Bishops' Conference had effectively carried out the German government's instructions.[86] Despite all its prevarications, the only possible explanation for the government's obstructionism was to prevent, as far as possible, the German public, especially German Catholics, from learning about the Vatican's humanitarian activities.

Another belligerent, Great Britain, was not entirely cooperative either. Anthony Eden repeatedly refused the Vatican's request, transmitted via Osborne, to provide lists of the German and Italian POWs in British hands.[87] The excuses were that it would take too much work copying the details of 200,000 prisoners; that in any case the International Red Cross acted as intermediary between the POWs and their relatives; and that the Germans did not do it either.[88] On the other hand, the British allowed the Vatican to facilitate exchanges of messages between Italian POWs and their families,[89] and permitted free access to their POW camps to the relevant Vatican envoys—Mgr Testa in the Middle East and Mgr Panico in Australia. Testa was particularly appreciative of the cooperativeness of the British military authorities on the ground.[90] That did not, however, prevent British complaints about him being Italian.[91]

PIUS XII'S FIRST ENCYCLICAL: *SUMMI PONTIFICATUS*

Pius XII's first encyclical, *Summi Pontificatus*, was published in October 1939 to coincide, as the pope declared, with the celebration of the feast of Christ the King, but it was inevitably conditioned by the dramatic and tragic events

[84] ADSS, 8, Le Saint-Siège et les Victimes de la Guerre, Janvier 1941–décembre 1942, 6–8.

[85] ADSS, 8, Le Saint-Siège et les Victimes de la Guerre, janvier 194–décembre 1942, doc. 341, Le nonce à Berne Bernardini à Mgr Montini, 8 avril 1942.

[86] ADSS, 8, Le Saint-Siège et les Victimes de la Guerre, janvier 1941–décembre 1942, doc. 376, Le cardinal Maglione au nonce à Berlin Orsenigo, 13 mai 1942.

[87] ADSS, 8, Le Saint-Siège et les Victimes de la Guerre, janvier 1941–décembre 1942, 12–16.

[88] ADSS, 8, Le Saint-Siège et les Victimes de la Guerre, janvier 1941–décembre, 15.

[89] ADSS, 8, Le Saint-Siège et les Victimes de la Guerre, janvier 1941–décembre 1942, doc. 361, Le minister de Grand Bretagne Osborne au cardinal Maglione, 27 avril 1942.

[90] ADSS, 8, Le Saint-Siège et les Victimes de la Guerre, janvier 1941–décembre 1942, doc. 290, Le Délégué apostolique au Caire Testa au cardinal Maglione, 21 février 1942.

[91] Chadwick, *Britain and the Vatican*, 188.

of the preceding few months and very largely prompted by them.[92] If there is still doubt as to the essential continuity between the pontificates of Pius XI and Pius XII then the encyclical emphatically demonstrates it. At the height of the 'phoney war' between Germany on the one hand and Britain and France on the other, Pius XII reiterated the condemnations of racialism, 'statolatry', and international immorality as contained in *Mit brennender Sorge* and *Humani Generis Unitas*. Thus, his declarations on 'The Equality of Races',[93] 'Deification of the State',[94] and 'Christian Charity and the Love of Country',[95] could only apply to Nazi Germany and, to a lesser extent, Fascist Italy. To buttress his arguments against racialism he used exactly the same scriptural quotations, such as the Pauline precept '. . . there is neither Gentile nor Jew, circumcision nor un-circumcision, barbarian or Scythian etc.'[96] In order to underline this teaching, he announced that:

> In accordance with these principles of equality . . . And in order to give expression to these, Our intentions, We have chosen the forthcoming Feast of Christ the King to raise to the Episcopal dignity at the Tomb of the Apostles twelve representatives of widely differing peoples and races. . . .[97]

Arguing that international relations should once more be based upon international law, which in turn derived its force from natural law, he declared that the law of nations had been torn away from the 'Divine Law'.[98] This statement, and a further one that 'The blood of countless human beings, even non-combatants, raises a piteous dirge for a nation such as Our dear Poland',[99] could only be directed against the two powers, Nazi Germany and Soviet Russia, which had invaded and occupied Poland. He reminded his readers of his own attempts at mediation in the months leading up to the outbreak of war and restated his willingness do so again.[100]

Two months later, in his consistorial allocution on 24 December to the Sacred College of Cardinals he reiterated his calls for peace. But first of all, he condemned what would now be called 'war crimes':

> Among such crimes We must include a calculated act of aggression against a small, industrious, and peaceful nation, on the pretext of a threat which was neither real nor intended, nor even possible; atrocities (by whichever side committed) and the unlawful use of destructive weapons against non-combatants and refugees, against old men, women and children. . . .[101]

[92] For the text of the encyclical, see Carlen, *Papal Encyclicals*, III, 5–22.
[93] Carlen, *Papal Encyclicals*, III, 11.
[94] Carlen, *Papal Encyclicals*, III, 13.
[95] Carlen, *Papal Encyclicals*, III, 13.
[96] Carlen, *Papal Encyclicals*, III, 11.
[97] Carlen, *Papal Encyclicals*, III, 11.
[98] Carlen, *Papal Encyclicals*, III, 15.
[99] Carlen, *Papal Encyclicals*, III, 19.
[100] Carlen, *Papal Encyclicals*, III, 19.
[101] *The Pope's Five Peace Points: Allocution to the College of Cardinals by his Holiness Pope Pius XII on December 24th 1939*, London, 1940, 9.

This was clearly an allusion to the Russian invasion of Finland, which precipitated the 'winter war' that the Kremlin nearly lost due to the intrepidity and courage of the Finnish troops.

Towards the end of the allocution, he set out his 'Five-Points', the 'Requisites for a Just and Honourable Peace':

1. Guarantees of the inviolability of national sovereignty for all countries, large or small
2. Mutually agreed and progressive disarmament
3. Creation of an international judicial body to enforce treaties
4. Guarantees for national minorities
5. Agreed system of international law based on principles of justice.[102]

The pope's proposals were well received in America, France, and Britain. In the latter, it elicited support of both the archbishops of Canterbury and York, in the House of Lords, and of the Moderator of the Free Church Federal Council. It was praised in a *Times* editorial.[103] After all the disappointments of the previous twelve months, it seemed that the Vatican was once again in the forefront of the peace-making lobby.

THE MYRON TAYLOR MISSION TO THE VATICAN, 1940

But the New Year did not bring much cheer on the peace-making front. A papal attempt to broker a Christmas truce was rejected by all sides, as in 1914.[104] The 'phoney war' continued but no prospect of peace appeared. Amidst the gathering gloom of early 1940, however, as the Vatican awaited what seemed, by now, to be the inevitable German offensive in the West, one glimmer of hope was the re-establishment of diplomatic relations with the United States. On 27 February, Mr Myron Taylor presented his credentials as President Roosevelt's 'Personal Representative' to the pope, though he was received with all the honours of an envoy of ambassadorial rank.[105]

[102] *The Pope's Five Peace Points*, 9.

[103] *The Times*, 24 December 1939.

[104] *The Holy See and the War in Europe*, doc. 225, Cardinal Maglione to the Ambassadors of Germany and France and to the Minister of Great Britain, 13 December 1939; for the replies see doc. 227, the French Ambassador Charles-Roux to Cardinal Maglione, 14 December 1939; doc. 228, Cardinal Maglione's Notes, 16 December 1939 (British reply); and doc. 229, Cardinal Maglione's Notes, 17 December 1939 (German reply).

[105] ADSS, 8, Le Saint-Siège et les Victimes de la Guerre, janvier 1941–décembre 1942, 52, which says that *L'Osservatore Romano* made 'as much headline news as possible of the arrival of the American representative, whose solemn audience appeared on the front page', compared with the very limited coverage reserved for the visit of Ribbentrop a fortnight later.

As has been seen (Chapter 7), the origins of this event lay some years earlier, arguably as far back as Pacelli's visit to America in 1936. There was, therefore, already plenty of goodwill on both sides for a resumption of diplomatic relations between the Holy See and the United States of America when Pacelli became pope at the beginning of March 1939, and this was confirmed by Roosevelt's extremely cordial letter of congratulations to 'his dear and old friend' on his election. This was followed by the President's decision to send an official US representative, the ambassador in London, Joseph Kennedy, to Pius XII's coronation in March 1939, the first such gesture in US history.[106] The influence of Mundelein can be seen in this episode. With the Chicago cardinal's death on 2 October 1939, Francis Spellman, who had been nominated archbishop of New York on 15 April, was able to take over the task of acting as the new pope's spokesperson to Roosevelt, one which he had already carried out on previous occasions.

Much of the pressure for a resumption of relations came from within the USA itself. As a result of Pius XII's peace offensive in relation to the Polish situation, which was to have involved the USA, the State Department began to support the idea of diplomatic relations with the Holy See. Thus, in July 1939 Under-Secretary Welles wrote to US Ambassador Philips in Rome of the desirability of such a link.[107] Sometimes support came from unexpected quarters, like that from the Jewish Congressman, Emanuel Celler, who wrote to the State Department arguing for a resumption of relations with Vatican in that same month. Within a few weeks, Secretary Cordell Hull had found the solution to the political and protocol difficulties of a resumption of relations, suggesting to Roosevelt the appointment of a 'Personal Representative' which would not require the approval of the Senate.[108]

Thus the way was clear for Francis Spellman, in a letter to Maglione, via Cicognani, of 24 October, to sound out the Vatican on Roosevelt's decision to send a special representative and to announce it over Christmas when Congress was not in session, a decision which the pope readily accepted.[109] He also happily accepted the choice of Myron Taylor, an Episcopalian, large-scale industrialist and financier, and the US representative at the Evian Conference of the previous year.[110] Roosevelt then announced the appointment formally to the pope in his Christmas message of 23 December.[111] Despite the inevitable

[106] Fogarty, *The Vatican*, 257.

[107] E. Di Nolfo, *Vaticano e Stati Uniti 1939–1952 (Dalle carte di Myron C. Taylor)*, Milan, 1978, doc. 1, Welles a Roosevelt, 1 agosto 1939.

[108] Fogarty, *The Vatican*, 258–259.

[109] *The Holy See and the War in Europe*, doc. 233, President Roosevelt to Pope Pius XII, 23 December 1939.

[110] Tittman, *Il Vaticano di Pio XII*, vii.

[111] *The Holy See and the War in Europe*, doc. 246, President Roosevelt to Pope Pius XII, 14 February 1940.

furore of Protestant protest in the United States, the appointment was enormously advantageous to both sides. For Roosevelt it was, in part, a way of hopefully bringing US Catholics, especially those of German and Italian immigrant origin, on side in the event of America entering the European war, and, more immediately, of securing their support in the presidential elections due in November 1940. Through Taylor, he hoped to gain the support of the Vatican against certain bishops like Stritch of Chicago, whom he accused of being 'pro-Fascist', and those dioceses such as Brooklyn, Baltimore, and Detroit, where he believed anti-Semitism was strong.[112] It was, above all, a means of securing permanent contact with the Holy See of whose diplomatic prestige and importance, and consequently key role in any peace offensives, Roosevelt was convinced.[113] For Pius XII, it was also obviously a tremendous fillip to Vatican diplomatic prestige, vis-à-vis both Germany and Italy, to have relations with 'the great neutral'.

While Myron Taylor's mission was ostensibly to treat with the Vatican on largely humanitarian questions—refugees, civilian internees, and POWs—it was clearly also intended as a way of preparing and supporting joint peace initiatives with the Vatican. In particular, with the inevitability of the end of the 'phoney war' between the Western powers on the one hand and Nazi Germany on the other, its major purpose was to promote joint action to keep Italy out of the imminent armed conflict. Even when that objective failed, and Italy not only entered the war against Britain and France, but the USA as well, Roosevelt kept on with the Myron Taylor mission, entrusting it to a career diplomat with experience of Rome, Harold Tittman, who was appointed chargé d'affaires for Taylor in February 1941.[114]

PIUS XII AND THE GERMAN GENERALS' PLOT AGAINST HITLER

Between September 1939 and May 1940 there took place one of the most extraordinary episodes in the history of the modern papacy. In this period, Pius XII acted as intermediary in a series of secret 'conversations' between German generals plotting to overthrow Hitler on the one hand, and the British government on the other.[115] The generals, led by Ludwig August Beck, were plotting to remove Hitler and the Nazis from power before the latter could

[112] Di Nolfo, *Vaticano e Stati Uniti*, docs 4 and 5.

[113] Di Nolfo, *Vaticano e Stati Uniti*, doc. 2.

[114] See Tittman, *Il Vaticano di Pio XII*, 36–46.

[115] For a full account of the episode, see David J. Alvarez and Robert A. Graham, *Nothing Sacred: Nazi Espionage against the Vatican, 1939–1945*, London, 1997, 25–33; and Chadwick, *Britain and the Vatican*, 86–98.

unleash what the generals regarded as a suicidal offensive against the Benelux countries and France. They sought assurances from the British government that, if they did so, the post-Hitler regime would be allowed to retain the borders of the Reich as established by the Munich conference of September 1938, that is, including Austria and the Sudeten lands. Their supporters in the Abwehr (the German Army intelligence service) sent Josef Müller, a devout Catholic lawyer and anti-Nazi, to Rome to establish contact with the pope. Müller did so via Mgr Kaas and Fr Leiber, who passed on the generals' proposals to Pius XII, who, in his turn, discussed these approaches with D'Arcy Osborne.

Osborne was naturally sceptical but conveyed the proposals to the Foreign Office in London.[116] The contacts failed because Halifax and Chamberlain, like Osborne, were sceptical of the generals' ability to deliver on the promise to overthrow Hitler. They were also unwilling to agree to the 1938 borders and to contemplate the continued existence of the mighty German Army in the centre of Europe. Whether or not the British attitude was a factor, ultimately the generals failed to go ahead with their putsch and the German offensive in the West took place in May 1940.

Pius XII worked in great secrecy—no one in the Secretariat of State, even Maglione, Tardini, or Montini, was let into the secret. Nevertheless, it was nearly discovered and reported to Hitler.[117] It was incredibly risky, because if the Nazis had found out then it would, of course, have completely destroyed the Holy See's official position of neutrality and impartiality, confirmed Nazi suspicions of the Vatican, and made relations with Mussolini's Italy extremely difficult. Chadwick argues that the pope felt he had to take this risk because it seemed to be the only chance to bring the war to an end.[118]

THE VATICAN AND THE GERMAN OFFENSIVE IN THE WEST, APRIL TO JULY, 1940

The unleashing of the German offensive in the West—first Denmark and Norway on 9 April and then Belgium, Holland, Luxembourg, and France on 10 May, did not, of course, come as a surprise in the Vatican. It had been forewarned by Müller, the German generals' envoy to the Vatican, months before. The Secretariat of State had already given warnings to the Belgian and Dutch monarchs of German intentions towards those two neutral states via

[116] Chadwick, *Britain and the Vatican*, 90–98

[117] Alvarez and Graham, *Nothing Sacred*, 28–33.

[118] Chadwick, *Britain and the Vatican*, 97–98.

the nuncios in Brussels and The Hague respectively, on 3 May.[119] Following the opening of the German offensive, the Belgian, British, and French envoys to the Vatican demanded, on behalf of their governments, that the pope condemn the brutal and unjustified violation of the small neutral nations.[120] In response, the pope limited himself to telegrams to Belgian King Leopold and Dutch Queen Wilhelmina, which expressed a prayer for the 're-establishment of full liberty and independence to Belgium',[121] and 'the return of justice and liberty' for the Netherlands.[122] Of course, that was not exactly what those monarchs, or the British and French, wanted. For them, the telegrams did not constitute an unequivocal condemnation of naked aggression, even though the officials in the Secretariat of State, including the ever-realistic Tardini, genuinely believed that they did.[123] The Germans and the Italians, on the contrary, saw them as an unjustified and provocative interference in their affairs, and protested accordingly. Mussolini was particularly infuriated because he saw the telegrams as an attack upon his alliance with Germany and a scarcely veiled indication of how the Holy See would view his entry into the war on the side of Hitler.[124]

Pius was deeply anguished by the fate of the Benelux countries and France. Once more the nuncios were forced to abandon their positions in predominantly Catholic countries and it was difficult to predict how those populations would be treated by the German occupying forces. In France, at least, a semblance of independence had been guaranteed for the non-occupied, south-eastern zone, which remained under the direct authority of Marshal Pétain's government at Vichy, where the nuncio, Mgr Valerio Valeri, now stationed himself. The ultra-conservative, even Catholic tendencies of this new regime, which committed itself to the motto 'Famille, Travail et Patrie', commended themselves to the French episcopate, one of whom, Cardinal Gerlier, archbishop of Lyons and Primate of the Gauls, rather obsequiously and blasphemously described Pétain as the 'incarnation of suffering France'.[125] As Pétain unveiled the aims of his 'National Revolution', it became clear that this involved a rolling back of the 1904 separatist legislation, including the reintroduction of religious instruction into state schools and state subsidies to

[119] *The Holy See and the War in Europe*, doc. 293, Cardinal Maglione to Brussels Nuncio Micara and to Hague Internuncio Giobbe, 3 May 1940.

[120] *The Holy See and the War in Europe*, doc. 293, Cardinal Maglione to Brussels Nuncio Micara and to Hague Internuncio Giobbe, 3 May 1940, 74–75

[121] *The Holy See and the War in Europe*, doc. 301, Pope Pius XII to Leopold, King of the Belgians, 10 May 1940.

[122] *The Holy See and the War in Europe*, doc. 302, Pope Pius XII to Queen Wilhelmina of the Netherlands, 10 May 1940.

[123] *The Holy See and the War in Europe*, doc. 302, Pope Pius XII to Queen Wilhelmina of the Netherlands, 10 May 1940, 76.

[124] *Ciano's Diary*, 1939–1943, 248–249.

[125] As cited in Cobban, *A History of Modern France*, vol. 3, 185.

private schools, to the great joy of the Church and Catholics.[126] The Vatican's attitude was much more cautious than that of the French hierarchy, albeit initially sympathetic. The powerful influence wielded by Charles Maurras and Action Française inside the Vichy regime was one reason for the Vatican's coolness.[127] The development of Vichy's collaborationist policies towards Nazi Germany, and in particular its introduction of anti-Semitic legislation was another cause of increasing disquiet in the Secretariat of State.[128] Following Gerlier's visit to the Vatican in January 1941, the attitude of the French hierarchy moved more into line with that of the Secretariat of State, so much so that Pétain dubbed the archbishop of Lyons, 'Son reticence'.

There is clear documentary evidence that, in July 1940, after Dunkirk and the fall of France and following Hitler's Reichstag speech of 19 July offering peace, the Vatican was anxious that Britain should negotiate with Hitler. It explored the possibility of a démarche to the British government via the Apostolic Delegate in Britain, Mgr Godfrey, and the archbishop of Westminster, Cardinal Hinsley. D'Arcy Osborne even supported the idea, up to a point.[129] Over a month earlier, on 10 June, in a long note, Godfrey had already explained in the clearest possible terms the high state of morale in Britain and the hostility of public opinion to peace negotiations with Hitler.[130] Nevertheless, at this stage, the Vatican would not be dissuaded from its peace-making efforts and began discreet soundings in Berlin, London, and Rome.[131] In addition, there had been contact with the French ambassador.[132] There is evidence that the Secretariat of State was encouraged in pursuing its plan for a general negotiated peace by the Germans,[133] and also by John Cudahy, American ambassador in Belgium.[134] On 26 July, Maglione instructed Godfrey to approach the British government with the proposal that it (the Secretariat of State) 'ask the German Government to specify a concrete basis for eventual negotiations'.[135] The Foreign Office gave this idea very short shrift, as did Cardinal Hinsley,

[126] Rhodes, *The Vatican*, 312. [127] Rhodes, *The Vatican*, 312.

[128] See ADSS, 5, doc. 114, Le nonce en France Valeri au cardinal Maglione, 7 October, 1941, in which Valeri recounts the attempt by Bouthillier, Pétain's Minister of Finances and National Economy, to reassure him that Vichy was *not* influenced by Nazi or other totalitarian ideologies.

[129] Chadwick, *Britain and the Vatican*, 139.

[130] *The Holy See and the War in Europe*, doc. 342, London Apostolic Delegate Godfrey to Cardinal Maglione, London, 10 June 1940.

[131] *The Holy See and the War in Europe*, doc. 360, Cardinal Maglione to the German Ambassador, the Apostolic Delegate in London, to the Nuncio to Italy, and to the Italian Ambassador, 27 June 1940.

[132] *The Holy See and the War in Europe*, doc. 359, Mgr Tardini's Notes, 29 June 1940.

[133] *The Holy See and the War in Europe*, doc. 367, Berne Nuncio Bernardini to Cardinal Maglione, 16 July 1940, and 372, Berlin Nuncio Orsenigo to Cardinal Maglione, 27 July 1940.

[134] *The Holy See and the War in Europe*, doc. 369, Mgr Montini's Notes, 25 July 1940.

[135] *The Holy See and the War in Europe*, doc. 370, Cardinal Maglione to the London Apostolic Delegate Godfrey, 26 July 1940, and 371, Tardini's Notes, same date.

who pointed out that Hitler's Reichstag speech of 19 July contained none of the 'Five Points for Peace' which the pope had enunciated in his Christmas allocution of the year before but many insults to Britain: hardly a basis for peace talks.[136] That was it. The Vatican now had to reconcile itself to the fact that it was going to be a long war.

THE VATICAN, MUSSOLINI, AND WAR

The dispute between the Holy See and Italy over the Racial Laws had largely petered out by the time of Pius XI's death in February 1939. But the clash over ACI was still a problem and one which was solved by his successor. After negotiations between Tacchi-Venturi and Mussolini, further restrictions were placed upon the organization. In his attempts to defuse the tension with the Regime, in April Pius XII agreed to dismantle the national associations of Catholic Action, and he removed the greatest exponent of the Italian model, Cardinal Pizzardo, from his post as head of the organization, and decentralized control to local archbishops and bishops.[137] This would explain why the Ufficio Centrale dell'Azione Cattolica disappeared from *L'Annuario Pontificio* after 1939. Pizzardo, who had always been somewhat of a controversial figure for the Fascists (see Chapter 4) was sent to head the congregation of Seminaries and Universities.

In fact, Eugenio Pacelli had been trying to mend fences with Fascist Italy since before he was actually elected pope. On 10 February 1939, Ciano reported in his diary that, during the course of his visit to the Vatican to view the corpse of Pius XI, Pacelli, who, as Camarlengo, accompanied him on the visit, 'spoke in a very agreeable and hopeful tone about relations between State and Church'.[138] Though he was eventually persuaded to attend some of the obsequies for the dead pontiff, Mussolini remained hostile to the Vatican, remarking to Ciano that he was 'not at all interested in the Conclave. "If the Pope is an Italian, all right, if he is a foreigner, all right just the same." '[139] This was bluff and bluster, he was *very* interested in what transpired in the Vatican at this juncture, in particular he was concerned about rumours which had reached him regarding Pius XI's last, undelivered, speech, wanting to know exactly what it contained.[140] Pacelli's eventual election as successor to Pius XI was well received in Italy and Ciano reported Mussolini's reaction: 'He is

[136] *The Holy See and the War in Europe*, doc. 374, London Apostolic Delegate Godfrey to Cardinal Maglione, 28 July 1939.

[137] *Ciano's Diary*, entry for 18 March 1939, 49.

[138] *Ciano's Diary*, entry for 10 February 1939.

[139] *Ciano's Diary*, entry for 10 February 1939.

[140] *Ciano's Diary*, entry for 12 February 1939.

satisfied with Pacelli's election.'[141] There could now be no unpleasant surprises in Vatican policy but rather a strengthening of the same conciliatory attitude towards Italy which Pacelli had sought to pursue as Secretary of State.

Pius XII sought closer relations with Fascism in the hope that Mussolini still be able to exercise some restraining influence on Hitler. The Duce's decision to remain neutral at the outbreak of war between Germany and the Western powers in September 1939—what he called 'non-belligerence', neutrality was too craven a word for the warlike Fascist regime and smelled too closely of Liberal Italy's declaration of neutrality at the outbreak of the First World War in July 1914—gave some grounds for believing that such a hope was not an illusion. But, as the months passed, Mussolini became increasingly restless, impatient, and, even in some degree, humiliated with 'non-belligerence'. It was clearly not the 'Fascist style', and when it became clear that Hitler had not bitten off more than he could chew by invading Poland, that Britain and France had been powerless to intervene in defence of their Eastern European ally, his tone became more belligerent. Nevertheless, it was an open secret that the monarchy, many in the armed forces and business circles, and many of Italians at large were not keen on joining a war on the side of Nazi Germany.[142] Accordingly, the new pope sought to strengthen ties with the monarchy, the court being the centre of a web of forces not entirely committed to Mussolini's foreign policy. After the Italian monarchs had paid a state visit to the Vatican on 21 December 1939, the pope reciprocated by making a state visit to the Quirinale on 27 December. It was by any measure an historic moment—no pope had set foot in the Quirinale since 1870 and Pius XI had not returned the Italian monarchs' state visit of 1929. In theory, he could also count on Italian Catholic opinion which was still 'pacifist', or at least neutralist at this point. As Giorgio Rumi pointed out, when war came, 'Catholics, bishops, priests and lay people gave their outward obedience to the State because there was no alternative.'[143]

Pius also activated the Vatican–Washington 'alliance', cooperating with Roosevelt in an attempt to dissuade Mussolini from going to war. As early as mid-March, when US Under-Secretary of State Sumner Welles was received in audience by the pope and also by Cardinal Maglione as part of his tour of European capitals, the issue of joint US–Vatican peace initiatives had been discussed, although it was not immediately pursued.[144] The situation changed

[141] *Ciano's Diary*, entry for 3 March 1939.

[142] *Ciano's Diary*, entry for 31 August 1939, with reference to the report of Arturo Bocchini, chief of police, about Italian public opinion.

[143] G. Rumi, 'La Santa Sede e la Politica di Potenza', in E. Di Nolfo, R. H. Rainero, and B. Vigezzi (eds), *L'Italia e la politica di Potenza, 1938–1940*, Settimo Milanese, 1975, 17.

[144] Di Nolfo, *Vaticano e Stati Uniti*, doc. 15, Taylor al Dipartimento di Stato, 18 marzo 1940, and 16, Taylor to Roosevelt, 29 marzo 1940; see also *The Holy See and the War in Europe*, 268, Cardinal Maglione's Notes, 18 March 1940.

in April as it became clear from the bellicose behaviour of the Italian press and certain leading Fascist figures that Mussolini was seriously considering entering the war.[145] Consequently, at the end of the month both Pius and the President launched peace offensives against Italy. On the 24th, Pius sent a personal letter to the Duce urging him to remain out of the conflict.[146] Inevitably, Mussolini's reply to the pope was not encouraging: the Duce blamed Britain and France for the failure of his proposed 'peace conference' the previous year and made it clear that he could not guarantee the continuation of Italian 'non-belligerence in view of the rapidly changing European situation.[147] Roosevelt's own démarche at Palazzo Venezia, via US ambassador Williams Phillips, was equally fruitless. In the end, Mussolini could not resist the temptation to seek some easy pickings as a result of Germany's walkover of Denmark and Norway, the Benelux countries, and even France in the spring of 1940. Consequently, he declared war upon Britain and France on 10 June.

THE IMPACT OF ITALY'S DECLARATION OF WAR ON THE VATICAN

Italy's entry into the war was bound to have serious consequences for the Vatican, but the fate of embassies to the Holy See from countries at war with Italy was very different in June 1940 from what it had been in May 1915 (see Chapter 2). Thanks to the terms of the Lateran Treaty, the embassies of Britain and France were permitted to transfer into the sovereign and neutral State of the Vatican City. There is evidence that the Secretariat of State was not happy with this solution, that it would actually have preferred a repeat of 1915, but it later came to appreciate the advantages of having the Allied ambassadors close to hand.[148] The French ambassador, Léon Bérard, remained there after the July 1940 armistice between Italy and France as the representative of the Vichy government of Marshal Pétain because the two countries remained in a formal state of war with each other.[149] The Belgian ambassador, Adrien Nieuwenhuys, also initially chose to enter the Vatican, even though his country and Italy were not at war.[150] After the invasion and destruction of Yugoslavia by German troops in May 1941, and the recognition of the Independent State of Croatia by the Axis, the Yugoslavian ambassador to the

[145] See Di Nolfo, *Vaticano e Stati Uniti*, doc. 21, Roosevelt to Taylor, 30 aprile 1940.
[146] *The Holy See and the War in Europe*, doc. 284, Pope Pius XII to Mussolini, 24 April 1940.
[147] *The Holy See and the War in Europe*, doc. 290, Mussolini to Pope Pius XII, 20 April 1940.
[148] Chadwick, *Britain and the Vatican*, 114–117.
[149] Tittman, *Il Vaticano di Pio XII*, 98.
[150] Tittman, *Il Vaticano di Pio XII*, 23–24.

Holy See, Niki Mirošević Sorgo, was informed that the Italian authorities would allow him to remain on Italian soil on the grounds that Italy was not at war with Yugoslavia. Then it changed its mind, accusing him of espionage and, despite strong protests from the Secretary of State, he was deported from Italy and his subordinate, Kosta M. Zukic, transferred into the Vatican.[151] In December 1941, following Italy's declaration of war on the United States, Myron Taylor's chargé d'affaires, Harold Tittman, entered the Vatican.[152] The number of diplomats inside the Vatican was further swelled in March 1942 by the representatives of Brazil, Bolivia, Colombia, Cuba, Ecuador, Peru, Venezuela, and Uruguay, following their governments' declaration of war on Italy and by the entry of the Chinese minister in March 1943.[153] When the Allies liberated Rome in June 1944, it was the turn of the ambassadors of Germany, Hungary, Finland, Japan, and Slovakia to go to the Holy See to seek refuge there. Life inside its narrow confines was neither comfortable nor easy. At the height of the war there were not only representatives of the various powers, but also their families and staffs, all crowded inside the walls. Despite an initial scepticism about the usefulness of Osborne 'hiding' in the Vatican, the British Foreign Office eventually came to the conclusion that it was a matter of the utmost importance that its envoy should remain inside the Vatican, if only to assert its neutrality: later, it would come to regard the Vatican as a crucial 'listening-post' in Nazi-occupied Europe.[154]

There were certainly difficulties, both for the Holy See and the ambassadors. Even before Mussolini's declaration of war, the hostility of certain Fascist elements, no doubt stirred up by the party, had manifested itself on the streets of Rome, including burnings of *L'Osservatore Romano*, and culminated in an incident in May 1939 when Fascist youths mobbed the car carrying the pope to a ceremony in a Roman church.[155]

The Achilles heel of the Vatican after Italy entered the war was that it remained dependent on Italy for its material survival. Surrounded by Italian territory, it was at the mercy of the Italian government as far as food, water, and energy supplies were concerned. And also in regard of communications with the rest of the world as far by telegraph and telephone. As Chadwick points out, 'The Italian Government could switch off its [the Vatican's] electric light, or its water supply or even its

[151] Tittman, *Il Vaticano di Pio XII*, 52–54; see also ADSS, vol. 7, 216, n. 1, which says that the Chilean ambassador to the Holy See moved into the Vatican following his country's declaration of war on the Axis powers.

[152] For an account of the experience of the US chargé d'affaires, Harold Tittman, see Tittman, *Il Vaticano di Pio XII*, 71–81.

[153] Tittman, *Il Vaticano di Pio XII*, 100–101.

[154] Chadwick, *Britain and the Vatican*, 118.

[155] Alvarez and Graham, *Nothing Sacred*, 182.

food.'[156] However, his further claim that, 'It could refuse it banking facilities and bankrupt the pope's government', is a little wide of the mark.[157] By 1939, Nogara had set up banking facilities for the Vatican abroad, in order to finance its diplomatic network and its humanitarian and investment activities, including accounts in banks in Latin America, New York and Washington, and Switzerland.[158] Nogara took the further step of removing Vatican gold and securities lodged in London banks, and transferring the gold, worth 7.665 million dollars to the US Federal Reserve in May 1940.[159] By transforming some bullion into the currencies of various neutral states—chiefly Swiss francs—Nogara was able to meet the Vatican's wartime financial needs.[160] Despite some misgivings, the Federal Reserve thus effectively became the Vatican's major international banker for the duration of the war, on the grounds that the possible economic disadvantages to the Allied cause were trivial and outweighed by other important policy considerations: an indication of the special place which the Holy See occupied in Roosevelt's diplomacy.[161]

The real problems arose in other fields. The Vatican's diplomatic codes were largely cracked by Italian military intelligence, as in the First World War, and despite the use of couriers, Vatican was unable to guarantee the mail it sent to Switzerland, or be certain that the Italians did not open mail addressed to it when it passed through Italy.[162] The Germans had less success, though the *Forschungsamt* of Göring's Air Ministry very effectively monitored the Vatican's communications with the Berlin nunciature.[163] Both Axis powers also read the codes of the diplomatic envoys inside the Vatican. As early March 1939, in an extraordinary act of indiscretion, Ciano admitted as much to the papal nuncio to Italy, Borgoncini-Duca, in an audience at the Foreign Ministry:

> Do not trust the diplomats accredited to the Holy See who in their telegrams and reports give information about Italy as heard in the Vatican and also mention my name. We read everything and Mussolini reads everything.[164]

[156] Chadwick, *Britain and the Vatican*, 132.

[157] Chadwick, *Britain and the Vatican*, 132.

[158] Pollard, *Money*, ch. 9, and 'American Catholics'.

[159] Pollard, *Money*, 187–188.

[160] Pollard, *Money*, 187–188; see also P.M. McGoldrick, 'New Perspectives on Pius XII and Vatican Financial Transactions during the Second World War', *Historical Journal*, 55(4) (December 2012), 1029–1048.

[161] College Park, MD, USA, National Archives and Records Administration, RG, 131(Dept. of Justice, Foreign Funds, and Control Records), box 487, letter of J.W. Pehle to Morgenthau (Secretary of the Treasury), 21 April 1942.

[162] Alvarez and Graham, *Nothing Sacred*, 164–165.

[163] Alvarez and Graham, *Nothing Sacred*, 160–161.

[164] *The Holy See and the War in Europe*, doc. 274, the Nuncio to Italy Borgoncini-Duca to Cardinal Maglione, 31 March 1940.

D'Arcy Osborne cottoned on to the effectiveness of the Axis secret services in the matter of interception and decrypting and warned the Foreign Secretary, Anthony Eden, accordingly:

> [For all these reasons] I am careful not to say anything of sentiments or expressions of opinion here that might be incriminating. And my style is somewhat cramped in representing the Vatican attitude.[165]

Vatican Radio now became crucial to the functioning of the papacy as an international religious centre during the Second World War. It served as a communications medium for papal envoys—apostolic delegates and nuncios—and therefore to national hierarchies via its radio telegraph facilities, and to the peoples of the world, Catholic and non-Catholic, through its radio broadcasts, which included news, the pope's speeches, and information about missing civilians and soldiers of the conflict.[166] But it was subject to pressure from the Axis powers to restrict its broadcasts. The German embassy to the Holy See repeatedly complained to the Secretariat of State and the pope himself about Vatican Radio broadcasts, especially those of Fathers Muckermann (Swiss), Coffey and Hurley (American), and Mistaen (Belgian), who all criticized the brutally oppressive occupation regime of the Nazis in various parts of Europe.[167] In a broadcast of January 1941, Mistaen declared:

> the Church will never submit to the claim that might is right. There is an order of slavery and death, quite unsuitable for the whole of humanity. Is that what those who talk about the *new orders* mean?[168]

Listeners could have been in little doubt that these criticisms were levelled at the 'New Order' which Germany had established in Europe. The Italians supported the diplomatic protests of their ally and repeatedly warned the Vatican of the risks which its radio station was running.[169]

On the other hand, the British propaganda machine regarded Vatican Radio as a godsend: they repeated its descriptions of Germany's brutal occupation policies, often embellishing and exaggerating them. The British even went so far as to establish a fake radio station of their own called 'Radio Christ the King', which purported to be Vatican Radio, and broadcast anti-Nazi propaganda in its name.[170] According to Sir Alec Randall, a British diplomat who worked in the Vatican, 'Vatican Radio has been of the greatest use to our propaganda and we have exploited it to the full.'[171]

[165] As quoted in Chadwick, *Britain and the Vatican*, 182–183.

[166] Pollard, 'Electronic Pastors', 194.

[167] Pollard, 'Electronic Pastors', 188–196.

[168] As quoted in Jacques Adler, '"The Sin of Omission"? Radio Vatican and the Anti-Nazi Struggle, 1940–1942', *Australian Journal of History and Politics*, 50(3) (2004), 402.

[169] Chadwick, *Britain and the Vatican*, 132.

[170] Alvarez and Graham, *Nothing Sacred*, 144.

[171] As quoted in Graham, 'La Radio Vaticana', 148 and 150.

In these circumstances, the pressure on the Secretariat of State from Germany and Italy to curtail or censor the broadcasts of Vatican Radio was considerable and sometimes had its effects. The pope, Maglione, Tardini, and Montini used every pretext to wriggle free from the accusations of the German and Italian ambassadors about the partiality of Vatican Radio, ultimately pretending that it was 'independent' of their control, an implausible argument from the rulers of an absolute monarchy.[172] The Vatican finally bowed to Axis pressure in the spring of 1941 and effectively discontinued Vatican Radio protests about conditions in Nazi-occupied Europe. Then it was the turn of D'Arcy Osborne to protest on behalf of the British government, claiming that the Vatican had compromised its independence.[173]

Another consequence of Italy's entry into the war against Britain in the Mediterranean, Africa, and potentially the Middle East was that the Foreign Office became extremely suspicious of Vatican diplomats and other prelates of Italian extraction working there.[174] Between August 1941 and the October 1942, Britain, through its minister at the Vatican, Osborne, put increasing pressure on the Vatican to remove from their posts all Italian nationals working for it, even if they had Vatican citizenship.[175] Eventually, it secured the 'heads' of Mgr Testa, apostolic delegate in Jerusalem, Mgr Riberi, apostolic delegate in Mombasa responsible for the African missions, Fr Jacopozzi, vicar apostolic in Alexandria, Mgr Nuti, vicar apostolic in the rest of Egypt, Mgr Mozzoni, an official in the Apostolic Delegation in London, and Mgr Castellani, apostolic delegate in Ethiopia.[176] The Vatican fiercely resisted what it regarded as infringements of its rights as a sovereign neutral power. It was even more incensed when the Foreign Office refused to permit another Italian, Mgr Alfredo Pacini from taking up his post as chargé d'affaires in the nunciature to the Polish government-in-exile in London.[177] The Foreign Office did not bend to these protests, indeed, in August 1942 it was demanding that *all* Italian missionaries, priests, or sisters be removed from Africa and the Middle East because of the 'general Fascist and pro-Axist attitude and activities of the Catholic Church' there.[178] While there may well have been an element of anti-Catholic bigotry on the part of Anthony Eden, the foreign secretary, as Tardini alleged,[179] it is also the case that the Vatican had left itself wide open to this kind of difficulty because of its failure to 'internationalize'

[172] ADSS, 3, I, doc. 108, Notes de Mgr Montini, 27 janvier 1940.

[173] ADSS, 4, doc. 313, Mémorandum du Légation britannique, 10 juin 1941.

[174] Chadwick, *Britain and the Vatican*, 187–190.

[175] ADSS, 5, juillet 1941–octobre 1942, 28–33.

[176] Chadwick, *Britain and the Vatican*, 188: on page 190, he says that when the British searched Mgr Castellani's house, they found a wireless transmitter, which admittedly was usual for a Vatican envoy, and 'a large store of arms and ammunition', which was not. . . .

[177] ADSS, 5, doc. 424, Notes de Mgr Tardini, 2 aout 1942.

[178] ADSS, 5, doc. 428, La Légation de Grande Bretagne à la Secrétaire d'État, 5 août 1942.

[179] ADSS, 5, doc. 424, Notes de Mgr Tardini, 2 août 1942.

the papal diplomatic service, hence its dependence upon diplomats of Italian nationality. Both Osborne and Accioly, Brazilian ambassador to the Holy See and dean of its diplomatic corps, had urged this necessity upon the pope.[180] As a footnote to this struggle between the Vatican and Britain, it is interesting to note that, for more than a decade, the Colonial Office anguished over the appointment of a replacement for Archbishop Caruana of Malta. They rejected the Vatican's proposal of Mgr Gonzi, bishop of neighbouring Gozo, on the grounds that he was too pro-Italian: in 1940, this was obviously a serious consideration.[181] Eventually, they agreed to his appointment and he turned out to be so much of a patriotic and pro-British leader of his people during the very painful siege of Malta by the Italians and Germans from 1940 to 1943 that he was made a knight of the Order of the British Empire!

OPERATION BARBAROSSA AND DETERIORATING RELATIONS WITH NAZI GERMANY

The launch of 'Operation Barbarossa', the German invasion of the Soviet Union, in June 1941, obviously marked a major turning point in the Second World War: the start of Hitler's crusade against 'Judaeo-Bolshevism' which was but part of a broader war of racial annihilation and territorial expansion. Soon Mussolini joined in, sending a division of Italian troops to fight on the Eastern Front. Hungary, Slovakia, and Romania were also induced to participate in the war against the Soviet Union, and Franco sent the 'Blue Division' as a contribution to the struggle against the Great Beast. The Axis powers were naturally anxious to enlist the support of the papacy in their 'crusade', believing that they all had a common objective in the destruction of Communism.[182] The fact that Hungary, Italy, Slovakia, and Spain were all predominantly, or overwhelmingly, Catholic states underlined the crusading nature of the war against Communism. But the Vatican firmly resisted any association with anti-Communist war coalition. In November 1941, Mgr Tardini drew up a memorandum about the requests received from the German and Italian ambassadors for Vatican support in the anti-Bolshevik 'crusade' shortly after the launch of Operation Barbarossa.[183] In reply to the insistent demands of the Italian ambassador, Attolico, with regard to this, Cardinal Maglione retorted that Nazism was persecuting the Church,

[180] Chadwick, *Britain and the Vatican*, 305.

[181] ADSS, 4, 11, doc. 59, Notes du cardinal Maglione, 25 août 1940, and doc. 63, Mgr Tardini au ministère de la Grande Bretagne Osborne, 31 août 1940.

[182] ADSS, 5, 8–13.

[183] ADSS, 5, doc. 151, Notes de Mgr Tardini, 27 novembre 1941.

that until June 1941 the Third Reich had been an ally of Russia, that the papacy had always condemned Bolshevism, and consequently it had nothing to add to that.[184] This silenced Attolico. Nevertheless, the Vatican was concerned about the way in which Nazi propaganda abroad, especially in Spain and Latin America, was seeking to cover up its own persecution of the Church by protesting about the Russian persecution of it.[185]

Meanwhile, the Vatican's relations with Nazi Germany had deteriorated throughout 1941. The Nazis embarked upon further measures against the Church in the 'Greater German Reich' (Germany, Austria, Alsace-Lorraine, Bohemia, and the Warthegau): convents and monasteries in Germany and Austria were requisitioned and their inmates ejected, Catholic colleges and seminaries were closed, a Catholic printing press closed down for printing 'defeatist' literature, confiscations of monies collected for Catholic causes, and all Jesuits banned from serving as chaplains to the Wehrmacht.[186] The bishop of Münster, Mgr von Galen protested vociferously and energetically to any government official he could find, including the local garrison commander, but in vain.[187] The Nazis seem to have believed that their invasion of the Soviet Union on 22 June had put them in an unassailable position: having embarked upon their 'crusade' against Godless Bolshevism, the Church would be unable to gainsay them anything. Indeed, at this point the German government was emboldened to make a most extraordinary demand, that it should have a veto power on all episcopal appointments—not just archbishops, bishops, and coadjutors as set down in the *Reichskonkordat*—but also auxiliary bishops, abbots nullius, apostolic administrators and vicars capitular (both temporary administrators of sees), and not only in the 'old' Reich, but also in Alsace-Lorraine, Luxembourg, the Government-General of Poland, and the Warthegau.[188] Already in September 1940, the government of the Reich had demanded the right to vet the appointment of prelates to fill the vacancy at Budějovice, in what was now the 'ReichsProtektorat of Bohemia' (ex-Czechoslovakia).[189]

In August 1941, in the flush of the seemingly unstoppable invasion of the Soviet Union, the German chargé Menshausen presented a nota verbale containing all of the Reich government's demands in respect of episcopal nominations.[190] Tardini's initial response was generic but negative, essentially

[184] ADSS, 5, doc. 151, Notes de Mgr Tardini, 27 novembre 1941.

[185] ADSS, 5, doc. 151, Notes de Mgr Tardini, 27 novembre 1941.

[186] ADSS, 5, doc. 1, Orsenigo au cardinal Maglione, 2 juillet 1941; doc. 37, Le Cardinal Maglione au Délégué Cicognani and Spellman, 6 aout 1941; and doc. 38, Le nonce à Berlin Orsenigo au cardinal Maglione, 6 août 1941.

[187] ADSS, 5, doc. 46, Le nonce à Berlin Orsenigo au cardinal Maglione, 19 août 1941.

[188] ADSS, 3, doc. 435, Note Verbale du Ambassade de l'Allemagne, 29 août 1941; ADSS, 7–8 and Le cardinal Maglione au primat de Pologne Hlond, 24 octobre 1942; and ADSS, 4, 14–16.

[189] ADSS, 5, 7–8 and doc. 92, Le nonce à Berlin Orsenigo au cardinal Maglione, 21 septembre 1940, Note de Mgr Tardini.

[190] ADSS, 5, 7–8 and doc. 92, Le nonce à Berlin Orsenigo au cardinal Maglione, 21 septembre 1940, Note de Mgr Tardini.

a prevarication. He retorted that the request went far beyond the terms of the *Reichskonkordat* and that because it could set a precedent in dealings with other governments, it would have to be discussed at the highest level at length.[191] It was indeed discussed at the highest level, by the pope and a session of the Congregation for Extraordinary Ecclesiastical Affairs on 27 November. The Vatican's official reply was, in fact, a clear and firm rejection of the German demands on all points.[192] The Secretariat of State began with a lengthy recapitulation of the efforts which the Holy See had gone to since the election of Pius XII to maintain good relations with the Third Reich, and, on the other hand, the violations which the Church had suffered to its legal rights and property both in the 'old Reich' and in the occupied territories. It reminded the Germans that in no concordat and for no country had the right to vet temporary episcopal administrators (apostolic administrators and vicars capitular) ever been conceded by the Holy See. Moreover, it reiterated its long-standing practice of never making new agreements on religious matters in occupied or annexed territories until the status of those territories had been regularized in international law, that is, by peace treaties, citing the example of Alsace-Lorraine between the November 1918 armistice and the signature of the Treaty of Versailles, which sanctioned its return to France. For these reasons, but in the usual diplomatic style of the Vatican, the German demands were rejected.

This was probably the worst crisis in the relations between the Holy See and Nazi Germany during the whole of the war. When their note was delivered, in August 1941, the Germans were at the height of their military success—that is, before they were repulsed by the Red Army in front of Moscow, and before the entry of the United States into the war—and Italy was now a full accomplice in the Nazi war of aggression, and so the triumph of the Axis seemed almost inevitable. At this point the temptation to yield to the German demands was, therefore, very strong indeed. But the men in the Vatican did not do so. The Germans refused to 'receive' the note and thus Vatican–German relations reached their lowest point in January 1942.[193]

[191] ADSS, 5, doc. 54, notes de Mgr Tardini, 29 août 1941.

[192] ADSS, 3, doc. 347, La Secrétairie d'Etat à l'Ambassade d'Allemagne près le Saint Siège, 18 janvier 1942.

[193] ADSS, 3b, doc. 390, Le nonce à Berlin Orsenigo au cardinal Maglione, 27 janvier 1942.

9

Pius XII: War and Fascist Genocides

THE PAPACY AND THE GRAND ALLIANCE

Probably the most important turning point in the Second World War came when the Grand Alliance between Britain and the Soviet Union was consolidated by the adherence of the United States, following the Japanese attack on Pearl Harbor and subsequent declaration of war by Germany and Italy on America in December 1941. With this new development, the strains on the papal policy of impartiality and neutrality grew apace.

The US State Department had already applied pressure on the Vatican before Pearl Harbor, via both the Apostolic Delegate in Washington, Cicognani, and Harold Tittman, Myron Taylor's chargé d'affaires, regarding the hostile attitude of certain American bishops, most notably those of Irish extraction like Archbishop McNicholas of Cincinnati and Cardinal O'Connell of Boston, regarding American benevolence towards Britain.[1] The issue had first arisen in July 1941, when Mgr Hurley, formerly an official in the Secretariat of State, and now a member of the US hierarchy as bishop of St Augustine, Florida, made a radio broadcast denouncing 'the murderous hosts of Nazi Germany' and supporting the right of President Roosevelt to take the United States to war.[2] As Mgr Cicognani reported to Maglione, the broadcast, along with Hurley's other pro-war broadcasts and speeches, had aroused a chorus of protests in American Catholic circles, including those of McNicholas and O'Connell.[3] The US government's decision to extend the 'lend-lease' system of providing military aid to Britain to Russia provoked further protest from Catholic prelates and also from sections of the Catholic press. Citing a passage from Pius XI's encyclical *Divini Redemptoris*—'Communism is

[1] Tittman, *Il Vaticano*, 49, also lists Archbishops Curley of Baltimore and Beckman of Dubuque, Iowa.

[2] Cited in Gallagher, *Vatican Secret Diplomacy*, 120–121. See also ADSS, 5, doc. 61, L'archevêque de New York Spellman au Pape Pie XII, 4 septembre 1941, for a bird's-eye view of the furore generated by Hurley's broadcast.

[3] ADSS, 5, doc. 35, Le délégué apostolique à Washington Cicognani au cardinal Maglione, 4 August 1941, 115–30.

intrinsically perverse and no one who would save Christian Civilisation may collaborate with Communism in any undertaking whatsoever'—they argued against military aid to the Soviets.[4] Myron Taylor, during his three-week stay in the Vatican in September 1941, requested Pius XII to instruct the American hierarchy to reassure the faithful not to confuse the Russian people with Communism. Eventually, through Mgr Cicognani in Washington, it was arranged that no less a person than Mgr McNicholas, archbishop of Cincinnati, would publish a pastoral letter on 30 October which, based on the same distinction in *Mit brennender Sorge* between the Nazi regime and the German people, drew a clear line of demarcation between the Communist government of the Soviet Union and the Russian people, and concluded by saying that Pius XI's ban on collaboration with Communism did not apply in the existing situation of world conflict.[5]

This important gesture on the part of the Vatican to assist Roosevelt in his efforts to get an extension of lend-lease through Congress is all the more remarkable given the complete failure of the administration to extract even the smallest concession from the Soviets on the matter of freedom of religion, despite overly optimistic promises to the contrary. During his same September visit, Taylor had had long discussions with both Maglione and Tardini over precisely this vexed issue. Tardini's 'bill of indictment' against religious persecution in Russia, or at least of the Roman Catholic Church there, was overwhelming and clearly impressed Taylor.[6] In a long memorandum on this subject—there were others—Tardini gave a response to a letter of Roosevelt delivered by Taylor, in which he stated that:

> I believe that there is a real possibility that Russia may as a result of the present conflict recognise freedom of religion in Russia, although, of course, without recognition of any form of official intervention on the part of the church in education or political matters within Russia.[7]

Roosevelt's further claim that, 'In my opinion . . . Russia is governed by a form of dictatorship as rigid . . . as the dictatorship in Germany. I believe, however, that this Russian dictatorship is less dangerous to the safety of other nations than is the German dictatorship',[8] prompted a detailed written response on the part of Tardini, but one which he put rather more succinctly face to face. The Vatican Under-Secretary of State questioned Taylor as to what the USA would do at war's end, following the defeat of Nazi Germany, when faced by a

[4] ADSS, 5, doc. 59, Le délégué apostolique à Washington Cicignani au cardinal Maglione, 1 septembre 1941: see also, Tittman, *Il Vaticano*, 59–60.

[5] ADSS, 5, doc. 131, Le délégûé apostolique à Washington Cicognani au cardinal Maglione, 28 octobre 1941.

[6] See ADSS, 5, doc. 194, Mgr Tardini à Mr Taylor, 20 septembre 1941.

[7] ADSS, 5, doc. 59, Le Président des Etats Unis Roosevelt au Pape Pie XII, 3 septembre 1941.

[8] ADSS, 5, doc. 59, Le President des Etats Unis Roosevelt au Pape Pie XII, 3 septembre 1941.

massively armed Soviet Union triumphant in Europe; that is, how it would stop the further spread of Communism. Roosevelt's Personal Representative 'seemed surprised by my question, as if he had never even thought about it . . . Mr Taylor had nothing to add and nothing to explain'.[9] America's rather complacent attitude towards Soviet Communism would remain a major bone of contention with the Vatican for some years to come.

Another bone of contention between Pius XII and Britain and the United States was the question of the likely bombing of Rome, and the pope's efforts to avoid such a situation by obtaining 'open city' status for the Eternal City. There seems to have been a major failure of imagination on the part of Pius XII in this matter. He penned a note deploring the British bombing of Italian cities—Turin, Genoa, and Milan—which seems totally parochially minded and out of place considering that he had never expressed regret for German (and sometimes, Italian) bombing of Warsaw, Rotterdam, London, Coventry, and so on. The pope's virtual paranoia about the possibility of the bombing of Rome excited the criticism of some of his own subordinates like Cardinal Tisserant and the American Jesuit Fr McCormack, rector of the Gregorian University, who deplored the fact that, in 1942, Pius had sent a letter of sympathy to the archbishop of Palermo for the Allied bombing of his city. Moreover, 'yet, though knowing about the sufferings of the Croats, Greeks and Slovenes (victims) of Italians, he says nothing'.[10] On the other hand, Roberto Farinacci, Mussolini's one-time rival for the leadership of Fascism and the violently anti-Semitic boss of Cremona, in his newspaper *Il Regime Fascista*, attacked Pius XII for failing in his duty as Primate of Italy, by not condemning Allied bombing of Italian cities.[11] Such were the perils of impartiality and neutrality.

Pius sought to protect Rome from bombing by having Rome declared an 'open city', as Paris had been in May 1940, but as Osborne rather tartly pointed out in December 1941, 'The city and district of Rome cannot be at one and the same time an open city for the Catholic world and an important military centre for the armed forces of the Axis.'[12]

Early in 1942, another issue shook the Holy See's relations with the Grand Alliance, and especially the United States—its decision to establish relations with Japan. As has been seen, relations between the Vatican and Japan were good throughout the interwar period and only Buddhist opposition in Japan prevented them from being placed on an official, diplomatic basis (Chapter 6). A new approach in this sense was made by the Japanese in January 1942, via the Italian embassy to the Holy See.[13] In the context of the rapid conquest by the

[9] ADSS, 5, doc. 80, Notes de Mgr Tardini, 16 septembre 1941.

[10] James Hennessy, 'American Jesuit in Rome: The Diary of Vincent McCormick 1942–1945', *Mid-America*, 56(1) (1974), 36.

[11] Chadwick, *Britain and the Vatican*, 134 and 140.

[12] ADSS, 5, doc. 155, Le ministre britannique Osborne au cardinal Maglione, 2 décembre 1941.

[13] ADSS, 5, doc. 212, Notes de Mgr Tardini, 21 janvier 1942.

Japanese in 1941 and 1942 of large areas of South-East Asia, containing substantial Catholic communities in the Philippines and French Indochina, the establishment of diplomatic relations made a great deal of sense for the Holy See. The decision, which as a courtesy was communicated in advance to both the British and American representatives in the Vatican, obviously did not go down well in Washington.[14] The White House and the State Department were appalled and expressed disbelief in the reasons advanced by the Vatican for the link with Japan.[15] It took a personal letter from the pope to Roosevelt and a visit by Archbishop Spellman to the White House to calm the waters.[16] Meanwhile the Church in the USA had to endure the inevitable storm of protest in the press.[17] A Japanese minister, Ken Harada, stationed in the embassy at Vichy, was accredited to the Holy See on 27 March, though the Vatican's representative in Tokyo remained only an apostolic delegate so as not to inflame Buddhist opinion.

As a 'bonus' for standing firm on the Japanese link the Holy See was rewarded with the establishment of relations with Nationalist China and the decision of the Dutch government-in-exile to send a diplomatic representative to the Vatican, nearly twenty years after they had withdrawn him: this was clearly inspired by concerns over the Japanese-occupied Dutch East Indies (now Indonesia).[18] Both moves were clearly intended to counter what was perceived to be dangerous Japanese influence in the Vatican. This, in turn, caused some offence among the Japanese, who demanded that the government of Nanking, which was effectively their puppet, should also be represented in the Vatican, and in this they were aided and abetted by the Italians.[19] Maglione only managed to elude this quite dangerous manoeuvre, and attempts by Italy and Japan to prevent the accreditation of a Chinese envoy, by citing the Vatican's diplomatic practice of not recognizing a government created during and because of a war, in this case that between Japan and China which had begun in 1936. Eventually, Japanese honour was satisfied by an informal agreement that the apostolic delegate in Peking should visit Catholic missionaries in the territory of the Nanking government.[20] The Vatican also evaded demands that it recognize another Japanese puppet state,

[14] For the American side of the affair, see Tittman, *Il Vaticano*, 101–109.

[15] Tittman, *Il Vaticano*, 104–105.

[16] ADSS, 5, doc. 293, Le Cardinal Maglione au délégué apostolique à Washington Cicognani, 13 mars 1942.

[17] ADSS, 5, doc. 303, Le Delélégué apostolique à Washington Cicognani au cardinal Maglione, 18 mars 1942, and Fogarty, *The Vatican*, 280–283.

[18] Tittman, *Il Vaticano*, 107, and ADSS, 11, doc. 258, Le délégué apostolique à Londres Godfrey au cardinal Maglione, 11 juin 1944, where he says that Dutch government had agreed to send a minister plenipoteniary back in August 1943 but hitherto had been impeded by unforeseen developments.

[19] See ADSS, 11, doc. 387, Le délégué apostolique à Tokyo Marella au cardinal Maglione, 5 juin 1942.

[20] ADSS, 11, doc. 393, Le délégué apostolique à Tokyo Marella au cardinal Maglione, 11 juin 1942.

the Empire of Manchukuo.[21]As during the First World War, so during the Second, the Holy See benefited from the anxious desire of belligerents on both sides not to lack influence in the Vatican. The only major power now not represented in the Vatican was the Soviet Union but, as both Maglione and Montini explained, that was unlikely to happen unless the Soviets changed their religious policy.[22]

A further cause of dispute between the Holy See on the one hand and the British and Americans on the other was financial. Bernardino Nogara, in the complicated series of transactions and arrangements which he had created to sustain the finances of the Vatican, continued to operate a number of companies in the German-occupied zone of France through Profima, the Vatican's Swiss-based holding company. As a result, during the course of 1941–2, he was accused of 'shady activities' and of being 'up to some dirty work' by the British Ministry of Economic Warfare.[23] Worse was to come. In order to help his colleagues in the Banca Commerciale Italiana (of which he was still a director), in late 1942 Nogara used Profima to buy a controlling interest in the South American subsidiary of the bank, SUDAMERIS, in order to evade its confiscation at the hands of those governments who had declared war on the Axis, like Brazil.[24] This time, he aroused the wrath of the American authorities as well. The envoys of the Western Allies protested to the Secretariat of State about what they regarded as Nogara's violations of wartime economic controls and there is evidence to suggest that Maglione genuinely did not know the extent of the Vatican stake in SUDAMERIS.[25] Being *financially* impartial was not easy for the Vatican in time of war, especially when Nogara was heavily involved in a major Italian bank. In any case, it was difficult for British and American bureaucratic mind to conceive of how Nogara, by nationality an Italian, operating in a sovereign enclave completely surrounded by Italian territory, could be regarded as 'neutral'.[26]

Almost exactly a year after his 1941 visit, in September–October 1942, Taylor made another long sojourn in the Vatican, one which was designed by Roosevelt to make absolutely clear to Pius XII several key elements in US policy. Firstly, Taylor wanted the pope to understand that the USA was in the war to win and that win it would, demonstrating how the country had become, in the President's own words, 'the arsenal of democracy'.[27] Secondly, he made it clear that there could be no compromise peace with Nazi Germany: the purpose of American involvement in the Europe was nothing less than the

[21] ADSS, 5, doc.358, le délégué apostolique à Tokyo Marella au cardinal Maglione 11 juin 1942.

[22] ADSS, 5, doc.358, le délégué apostolique à Tokyo Marella au cardinal Maglione 11 juin 1942.

[23] TNA/PRO, FCO, 37150078, Financial Activities of the Vatican, Crump, Ministry of Economic Warfare, to Hebblethwaite at Foreign Office, 29 March 1945.

[24] Pollard, *Money*, 191–193.

[25] Pollard, *Money*, 192.

[26] For further analysis of the Vatican's wartime financial activities, see McGoldrick, 'New Perspectives', 1029–1048.

[27] ADSS, 5, doc. 472, L'ambassadeur Myron Taylor au pape Pie XII, 19 septembre 1942.

destruction of Nazism, and the Vatican should avoid any attempt by the Axis powers to exploit its neutrality and authority to seek a way out of the war.[28] However, Taylor made a point in several conversations that the Americans were not hostile to the Italian people: a coded way of saying that they looked to the fall of Mussolini's government and peace with his successor, possibly via the good offices of the Holy See. Further, he set out the basis on which the members of the Grand Alliance were fighting the war—the four elements of the Atlantic Charter agreed between Roosevelt and Churchill in August 1941 which, he claimed, were effectively the same as those which Pius XII had set out in his appeals for peace, most notably that of the Christmas allocutions of 1939 and 1940 (see Chapter 8). Taylor also set out American concerns and hopes for a reconstructed, post-war Europe.[29] While much of this was welcome to the men in the Secretariat of State, some of the proposals caused perplexity and Tardini at least was very doubtful about the American capacity to understand Europe and the Europeans.[30]

Consequently, the visit quickly revealed differences of opinion between the Holy See and the USA, first in relation to attitudes towards Russia and second in relation to the Allied notion of 'unconditional surrender'. Tardini, with all the scepticism of a hardened Roman diplomat, thought that the American attitude towards religious freedom in Russia, as set out in the various documents which Taylor submitted to the pope, was naïve and deluded.[31] This was in response to Taylor's claims that, in the struggle against the Nazi evil, the Soviet Union 'is asked to surrender, in return for the advantage of security, only that she cease her ideological propaganda in other countries, and make religion truly free within her borders'.[32] In further conversations with both the pope and Tardini, Taylor insisted that Soviet politics was 'evolving' and that 'the United States Government was constantly working to bring about a modification of Soviet policy towards religion'.[33] Tardini's 'final shot' was a short memorandum which he delivered to Taylor in his last meeting, detailing the almost total lack of any change in the Soviet policy on religion, despite a few cosmetic changes to its propaganda.[34] In a private memorandum, however, his opinion of the Americans was scathing:

> [They] believe that once the Communists have won the war they will enter like a gentle lamb into the family of the European nations. The truth is rather different. If Stalin wins the war he will be the lion that devours all of Europe.[35]

[28] ADSS, 5, doc. 473, L'ambassadeur Myron Taylor au pape Pie XII, 19 septembre 1942.
[29] ADSS, 5, doc. 478, L'ambassadeur Mryon Taylor au pape Pie XII, 22 septembre 1942.
[30] ADSS, 5, doc. 480, Notes de Mgr Tardini, 22 septembre 1942.
[31] ADSS, 5, doc. 695, note 1 containing a brief memorandum written by Tardini.
[32] ADSS, 5, doc. 477, L'ambassadeur Myron Taylor au pape Pie, 22 septembre 1942.
[33] ADSS, 5, doc. 481, Notes de Mgr Carroll, 22 septembre 1942.
[34] ADSS, 5, doc. 492, Mgr Tardini à l'ambassadeur Myron Taylor, 26 septembre 1942.
[35] ADSS, 5, doc. 492, Mgr Tardini à l'ambassadeur Myron Taylor, 26 septembre 1942, 695, note 1.

On this issue the Vatican was proved right and the USA wrong by the events that followed in Eastern Europe at the end of the war, but the Holy See's scepticism towards Roosevelt's belief that the Soviets could be persuaded to introduce religious toleration in no way undermined their willingness to encourage the US hierarchy's support for aid to USSR.[36]

The Taylor visit was clearly important from several points of view. First, it demonstrated that the Vatican was truly independent, neutral, and impartial, and that it could thus insist on the passage of an enemy alien diplomat across Italian territory in time of war. Secondly, it raised its standing with the powers to receive a visit from the Personal Representative of the US president, and for the president, in this way, to share his thoughts with the pope about the future of Europe. Thirdly, it was a reminder to the Italians that, in the event of Italy seeking a separate peace with the Allies, the Vatican had the means to facilitate it. It also clearly rattled the Germans, whose ambassador was constantly dropping into the Secretariat of State in order to find out what was going on. In an attempt to trump Taylor's visit, the German ambassador, Von Bergen, asked the pope to appeal to the Allies to stop bombing German cities, a request which fell on deaf ears.[37]

PIUS XII, THE HOLOCAUST, AND OTHER FASCIST GENOCIDES

The Vatican probably first became aware of the beginning of what would eventually develop into the Holocaust, the Nazis' systematic extermination of the Jews of Europe, from the reports of Don Scavizzi (see Chapter 8). The report which he conveyed from Archbishop Sapieha of Cracow gave a clear idea that Jews in Poland were being singled out for mass execution by the beginning of 1942.[38] In February 1942, Metropolitan Szeptyckyj of Lvov complained that, after the launching of Operation Barbarossa, and the consequent German occupation of the region in the Western Ukraine, the Nazis were a degree worse in their behaviour than the Soviets, that they committed, 'horrible crimes, murders, robberies and rapes, confiscations and extortions. The Jews are the first victims—200,000 and more were killed in the first weeks.'[39] This was again

[36] Riccardi, '*Il Partito Romano*', 33.

[37] See ADSS, 5, 691, note 1, 714 ; note 1 to doc. 486, Notes du cardinal Maglione, 25 septembre 1942; and doc. 488, Le papa Pie XII à l'ambassadeur Myron Taylor, Annex and note 2.

[38] ADSS, 3, II, doc. 357, L'archeveque de Cracovie Sapieha au pape Pie XII, 28 février 1942, note 1.

[39] ADSS, 3, II, doc. 406, Le métropolite de Léopol des Ruthenes Szeptyckyj au pape Pius XII, 29–31 août 1942.

one of the first direct pieces of evidence received in the Vatican to testify to the beginning of the Holocaust. A further report, sent by Richard Lichtheim and Gerhard Riegner via the nuncio in Berne, outlining the anti-Semitic measures adopted under pressure from the Nazis in Croatia, Slovakia, Hungary, and Vichy France, was received in the Vatican the following month.[40] As far as Slovakia concerned, these facts were confirmed by several reports from the chargé d'affaires, Mgr Giuseppe Burzio, the first in March 1941.[41] By this time, they could be no doubt that Jews deported east from any country were being sent not 'to work' but to be killed: as Hitler said himself in a broadcast at this time: 'The Jews will be liquidated for at least a thousand years.'[42] In addition, Osborne, who carefully listened to the BBC, was able to pass on information about the unfolding of the Holocaust to the pope on a regular basis in 1942, 1943, and the first half of 1944.[43]

Like other observers at the time, including the Allied governments,[44] the Vatican was rather incredulous when faced with the first evidence of the Holocaust. Additionally, after its experience of the claims and counterclaims of belligerents during the First World War about the atrocities allegedly committed by the other side (Chapter 2), it was a little wary when reports came from the Allies about the massacre of Jews. But by the end of 1942, few in the Allied countries could seriously doubt that the Germans had, indeed, embarked on a final solution of the Jewish 'problem', as they called it. News reports were appearing in British and American newspapers, and in both countries rallies and demonstrations of protest were being organized.[45] The full horror of what was happening in the Nazi death camps finally came home to the pope and his subordinates in the Secretariat of State.

At no time did Pius specifically mention the plight of *the Jews* in a public statement after he had learnt of the Holocaust, though on a number of occasions he did indirectly refer to the victims of Nazi policies. In his Christmas allocution of 1939 (see Chapter 8), he had already condemned 'a series of acts incompatible with . . . the principles of natural law and the most elementary sentiments of humanity'.[46] It should also be noted that he never said anything about the murder of gypsies either, though arguably they too

[40] S. Friedlander, *Pius XII and the Third Reich: A Documentation*, London, 1996, 104.

[41] W. Brandmueller, *L'Olocausto nella Slovacchia e La Chiesa Cattolica*, Vatican City, 2004, 32, fn. 19.

[42] Martin Gilbert, *Auschwitz and the Allies*, New York, 1981, 13.

[43] Chadwick, *Britain and the Vatican*, 208–211.

[44] Chadwick, *Britain and the Vatican*, 211.

[45] Chadwick, *Britain and the Vatican*, 211–214.

[46] *The Holy See and the War in Europe*, doc. 235, Christmas message of Pope Pius XII (Extracts), 24 December 1939.

could be covered by the reference to 'race'. His Easter message, on 13 April 1941, which contained a plea to the occupying powers to exercise humanity, evoked a furious response from Goebbels because only Germany, and its ally the Soviet Union, were occupying territory in Europe at that time. The German Propaganda Minister exclaimed that, 'The Vatican continues to attack us through the Radio' and insisted that Vatican Radio had to be silenced.[47] As on previous occasions, there were formal German and Italian protests to the Secretariat of State, the pope told Vatican Radio to stop talking about Germany and persecution, and, as usual, Osborne protested. On the other hand, the message was well received in the British and American press. *The New York Times* printed the message in full, with a photograph of the pope, and in its editorial it argued that, 'Despite the impartiality imposed upon him as the head of a Church with congregations in every warring nation, Pope Pius XII gave the world an Easter message which could be of small comfort to the Nazis.'[48]

The pope's Christmas message for 1941, long and prolix as it was, while it dwelled briefly on the horrors and victims of war—'the unhappy fate of the wounded and prisoners of war, the destruction and ruin which aerial bombardment has wrought on big, populous cities'—was essentially focused on causes of the war.[49] Pius attacked the usual targets, 'materialism', 'de-Christianization', and, above all, 'an atheistic or anti-Christian conception of the state'.[50] There is the sense that this was really intended for a (Latin?) American, rather than a European, audience.

The closest Pius XII came to actually identifying the victims of Nazi terror was in his Christmas message of 1942 when he declared:

> Humanity owes this vow to those hundreds of thousands who, without any fault of their own, sometimes only by reason of their nationality or race, are marked down for death or gradual extinction.[51]

The pope was undoubtedly talking principally about the Jews, among others, and the speech hit its target, the Germans being predictably furious about its content, seeing, quite rightly, that the message was 'virtually accusing the German people of injustice towards the Jews and [the pope] makes himself a mouthpiece of the Jewish war criminals.'[52] Nevertheless, it was not enough to satisfy Allied observers, prompting an official protest from the Belgian,

[47] *Goebbels' Diaries, 1939–1941*, trans. and ed. Fred Taylor, London, 1983, 332, entry for 25 April 1941.

[48] *New York Times*, 15 April 1941, 3.

[49] ADSS, 5, doc. 172, Message de Noel du papa Pie XII (n.d.).

[50] ADSS, 5, doc. 172, Message de Noel du papa Pie XII (n.d.).

[51] ADSS, 7, La Saint Siège et la Guerre Mondiale, novembre 1942–1 décembre 1943; doc. 71, Radio-message du papa Pie XII, 24 décembre 1942 (no doc. number, 732).

[52] SS report of January 1943, quoted in Rhodes, *The Vatican*, 273.

British, Polish, and Brazilian ambassadors to the Holy See for its vagueness.[53] Arguably the most explicit and public condemnation by the Vatican of Nazi atrocities had come *before* the onset of the Holocaust proper on Vatican Radio when, in 1940, 'an unnamed speaker' said, 'In Germany the Jews are killed, brutalised, tortured.'[54]

The representatives of Britain, American, and other Allied powers urged the pope to speak out about the Nazi persecution of the Jews and their other atrocities on several occasions. In September 1942, on the occasion of Myron Taylor's lengthy visit to the Vatican, courtesy of the Italians, there had been an orchestrated campaign among the diplomatic corps in the Vatican to pressurize the pope into making a public statement. The first was a joint effort on the part of the representatives of the governments-in-exile of Belgium, Czechoslovakia, Luxembourg, the Netherlands, Norway, Poland, and the National French Committee (De Gaulle's Free French), drawing attention to Nazi war crimes, and calling upon the pope to speak out.[55] They were followed by a note from the Brazilian ambassador in the same vein two days later.[56] Neither of these protests contained an explicit reference to the persecution of the Jews, though they did mention the taking and execution of hostages, the razing of towns and villages to the ground, and other acts of terror against civilian populations. The note from the Brazilian ambassador, Accioly, also mentioned German torpedoing of commercial craft and religious persecution.[57]

When Osborne made his approach to the Secretariat of State on the subject, on the same day as Accioly, he explicitly mentioned not only the horrors of the whole Nazi racial project, but specifically: 'the merciless persecution of the Jews throughout Europe'.[58] Osborne concluded his note in an admonitory, and slightly menacing, tone:

> A policy of silence in regard to such offences must necessarily involve a renunciation of moral leadership and a consequent atrophy of the influence and authority of the Vatican: and it is upon the maintenance and assertion of such authority that must depend any prospect of a Papal contribution to the re-establishment of world peace.[59]

In his turn, Myron Taylor did not fail to take advantage of his visit to the Vatican to press home the demands of his colleagues. In several audiences

[53] Rhodes, *The Vatican*, 272.

[54] As quoted in Adler, 'The Sin of Omission', 404.

[55] ADSS, 5, doc. 465, L'ambassadeur de Belgique Nieuwenhuys et l'ambassadeur de Pologne Papée au cardinal Maglione, 12 septembre 1942.

[56] ADSS, 5, doc. 466, L'ambassadeur du Brésil Accioly au cardinal Maglione, 14 septembre 1942.

[57] ADSS, 5, doc. 466, L'ambassadeur du Brésil Accioly au cardinal Maglione, 14 septembre 1942.

[58] ADSS, 5, doc. 467, Le ministre de Grand Bretagne Osborne au cardinal Maglione, 14 septembre 1942.

[59] ADSS, 5, doc. 467, Le ministre de Grand Bretagne Osborne au cardinal Maglione, 14 septembre 1942.

with the pope, Maglione, and Tardini he drew attention to Nazi war crimes, and in his meeting with Maglione of 25 September 1942 he pointed out that:

> there is a general impression, both in America and Europe, an impression which Taylor himself had observed without any danger of error, that it is now necessary for His Holiness to again condemn the inhuman treatment of refugees, of hostages and particularly of Jews in the occupied territories. This condemnation is requested not only by Catholics, but also by Protestants.[60]

Tardini's response was that the pope had already condemned war crimes but that 'in several quarters they want the Pope to condemn Hitler and Germany by name, which is impossible'; Taylor then denied that he had ever asked for a condemnation of Hitler but that the pope could still repeat his condemnations, to which Tardini agreed.[61] A point that Tardini would also make on several occasions was that the Soviet Union was also committing acts of oppression, persecution, and murder at this time, but certainly not on the scale of the Nazis. In order to adhere to its impartiality and neutrality, the Vatican would have been obliged to condemn Stalin's crimes, as well as those of Hitler. An obvious example would have been the massacre by the NKVD of Polish Army officers at Katyn and other atrocities in the Baltic States.[62]

Given the papacy's claims to be infallible in matters of faith and morals, and its consequent presentation of itself as the world's supreme moral authority, the proverbial 'oracle of God', Osborne felt entitled to expect that Pius would speak out clearly against the greatest evil of his day, the atrocities of Nazi racialism, and, above all, the Holocaust. Indeed, one might have expected the Holy Office to excommunicate Hitler, Goebbels, and Himmler, all nominal Catholics, as well as their German, Hungarian, Croatian, Lithuanian, and Slovakian collaborators in various genocidal activities, as it was to do in 1949 when it excommunicated all those who voted for or in any other way assisted Marxist parties (see Chapter 10).

However, Pius XII did not understand the criticisms made of him, as is clear from a letter to Bishop Preysing of Berlin in April 1943:

> As far as what is happening to the non-Aryans in the territories occupied by the Germans is concerned, we made reference to this in our Christmas message. It was brief, but it was clearly understood. We do not need to assure you that Our love and Our paternal solicitude leans towards the non-Aryans and half Aryans . . . we have decided that when the circumstances advise or permit to raise our voice on their behalf again.[63]

[60] ADSS, 5, doc. 487, Notes de Mgr Carroll, 25 septembre 1942.

[61] ADSS, 5, doc. 480, Notes de Mgr Tardini, 22 septembre 1942.

[62] For the former, see G. Weinberg, *A World at Arms*, Cambridge, 1994, 107 and 468.

[63] ADSS, 2, Lettres de Pie XII aux Evêques Allemands, 1919–1944; doc. 105, A l'Eveque de Berlin, 30 avril 1943.

In remarks to his collaborators and to Allied ambassadors Osborne, Accioly, Myron Taylor, and Tittman, and in letters to various prelates, Pius XII explained his reluctance to condemn the Holocaust more explicitly on a variety of grounds. Thus, he argued that more explicit condemnations would either have no effect or make the situation even worse, citing the case of the Dutch bishops: when they broke ranks with the leaders of the Dutch Reformed churches and made public a denunciation of Nazi deportation of their country's Jews in 1942, the German occupation authorities responded by extending the deportations to non-Aryan Catholics, including Edith Stein.[64] Mother Pascalina claimed the pope eventually decided to burn a public protest he had been drafting precisely for fear that it would provoke further German reprisals.[65] In 1943, when Maglione sent a list of protests to Ribbentrop against maltreatment of Poles by Germans,[66] the German Foreign Office refused to receive the note, arguing that this and Nuncio Orsenigo's complaints were out of order since they touched on German internal affairs.[67]

Pius believed that he was doing as much as was possible within the limits imposed upon him by his other responsibilities, his government of the universal Church. He was afraid that if he spoke out too strongly or frequently, the Nazis would retaliate by intensifying their persecution of Catholics and the Church in Germany and in the territories under their occupation.[68] Certainly, fear of a new, sustained Nazi *Kulturkampf* haunted the minds of German bishops throughout the life of the Third Reich. Yet Nazi persecution of the German Church, albeit spasmodic and patchy, had been going on since 1933 and was arguably intensifying anyway. It also has to be said that when Bishop Von Galen of Münster denounced the Nazi euthanasia programme against the mentally and physically handicapped and the chronically sick, from the pulpit of his cathedral in August 1941, no subsequent action was taken against him and the sermon contributed to the programme being temporarily halted.[69]

It also seems that Pius feared placing German and other Catholics in a grave moral dilemma, forcing them to choose between their loyalty to

[64] Blet, *Pius XII*, 148.

[65] P. Lehnert, *Pio XII: Il privilegio di servirlo*, Milan, 1984, 148–149.

[66] ADSS, 3b, doc. 480, Le cardinal Maglione au ministre des Affaires Etrangers du Reich von Ribbentrop, 2 mars 1943.

[67] ADSS, 7, doc. 145, Le nonce à Berlin Orsenigo au cardinal Maglione, 17 mars 1943; after a session of the Congregation for Extraordinary Ecclesiastical Affairs, Maglione replied was that this was an unfriendly act and that as far as Holy See was concerned, the document had been received. See, ADSS, 7, doc. 171, Le cardinal Maglione au nonce à Berlin Orsenigo, 17 avril 1943.

[68] ADSS, 2, doc. 105, à l'Evêque de Berlin, 30 avril 1943.

[69] Beth A. Griech-Polelle, *Bishop Von Galen: German Catholicism and National Socialism*, New Haven, CT, and London, 2002, 92.

the Church and to the State, a very difficult choice in a time of war. Such a concern was compounded by the fear that, in the event of Germany losing the war, the pope and the Church would be held responsible for this. Thus Tittman, in a despatch to the US Secretary of State in October 1942 explained that:

> another motive, possibly the controlling one behind the Pope's disinclination to denounce Nazi atrocities is his fear that if he does so now the German people, in the bitterness of their defeat, will reproach him later on for having contributed, if only indirectly to this defeat . . . just such accusations were directed against the Holy See by the Germans after the last war, because of certain phrases and attitudes adopted by Benedict XV while hostilities were in progress.[70]

Tittman made the further point that Pius was particularly sensitive to this argument because of his long experience in Germany.[71]

The pope's response to war crimes was also criticized from inside the Vatican. As early as June 1940, appalled by the papal response to Nazi crimes in Poland, Cardinal Tisserant wrote this to Cardinal Suhard of Paris:

> I fear that history will reproach the Holy See with having practised a policy of selfish convenience and not much else. This is extremely sad, especially for those [of us] who have lived under Pius XII. Everyone [here] is confident that, after Rome has been declared an open city, members of the Curia will not have to suffer any harm; this is a disgrace.[72]

As has been seen, Tisserant had never been a fan of Eugenio Pacelli, but his prophesy was extremely accurate, and arguably valid also for Pius XII's response to the Holocaust. Three years later, in May 1943, another Vatican official, Mgr Respighi, the Master of the Papal Ceremonies, demanded of Maglione a public pronouncement by the pope in defence of humanity:

> One is sadly shocked by having contacts with populations that remain not only astonished but disgusted by the lack of action on the part of the Holy See . . . It is said that the pope is afraid of upsetting rulers . . . and for this reason permits the destruction of humanity . . . The Holy See is expected to act with great courage before the whole world.[73]

Some of Pius XII's critics have attributed his failure to speak out explicitly in defence of the Jews as cowardice.[74] This is hardly tenable in the light of the risks he took during the German generals' plot (see Chapter 8) and his

[70] FRUS, 740.00116 European War, 1939/1942, Tittman to the Secretary of State, 6 October 1942.

[71] FRUS, 740.00116 European War, 1939/1942, Tittman to the Secretary of State, 6 October 1942.

[72] As quoted in Lewy, *The Catholic Church*, 307.

[73] ADSS, 9, La SS et les Victimes de la Guerre, doc. 184, Mgr Respighi to Cardinal Maglione, 10 May 1943.

[74] Hochhuth, *The Deputy*, 201–203.

warnings to Ciano and the Italian ambassador. Again, when confronted by what appeared to have been the very real danger of a Communist/Socialist takeover in Italy, were they to gain a parliamentary majority in the 1948 general elections, Pius seems to have faced the admittedly rather implausible possibility of ending up on trial in a 'People's Court', like Stepinaz, Mindszenty, and Beran, with equanimity (see Chapter 10). He has also been accused of anti-Semitism and this is presented as an explanation for his silence, like the claim of Cornwell that his experience as nuncio in Munich of the Bavarian Soviet Republic in 1919, when armed Bolsheviks, apparently all Jews, invaded the nunciature, confirmed his dislike of the Jews.[75] At most, Pius could be held to have been anti-Jewish in the same way that he shared in the typical anti-Jewish and anti-Protestant prejudices of Italian Catholic clergy at this time. In this regard, the most serious claim about Pius XII's 'silence' on the Holocaust comes from Richard Rubinstein:

> *could it be that Pius regarded the demographic elimination of Europe's Jews as a benefit for European Christendom? Put differently, did the pope recognise any moral obligation whatsoever to rescue Jews?* It is my conviction that the pontiff recognised no such obligation and that he did regard the demographic removal of Europe's Jews as a benefit for European Christendom.[76]

There is not a scrap of evidence that Pius XII thought in such terms. As he said to Cardinal Gerlier, archbishop of Lyon, 'I believe that if Germany were to be victorious, it would be the greatest misfortune to befall the Church for centuries',[77] but as has also been seen he and others in the Secretariat of State dreaded the consequences of a *Soviet* victory over the Third Reich. As Tardini reiterated to Weizsäcker, the German ambassador, in February 1945, 'The Holy See has always regarded the danger [to Europe] as two-fold: Nazism and Communism.'[78] For the pope, these were 'the enemies of European Christendom', not European Jewry.

A further argument has been that Pius was so concerned about the consequences for Europe of a Soviet victory over Nazi Germany that he hoped the Soviets would be beaten by the Nazis first and they in turn defeated by the Western Allies, hence his unwillingness to condemn the Nazis for their persecution of the Jews.[79] He probably did indeed hope that but he was not alone in this. Some leaders of the Western Allied camp, most notably Churchill, shared this concern, especially after Stalingrad.[80] In this regard, it

[75] Cornwell, *Hitler's Pope*, 295–298.

[76] R. Rubinstein, 'Pius XII and the Shoah', in Carol Rittner and John K. Roth (eds), *Pope Pius XII and the Holocaust*, London and New York, 2002, 177, author's italics.

[77] Jacques Duquesne, *Les Catholiques français sous l'Occupation*, Paris, 1966, 276.

[78] ADSS, 11, doc. 504. Notes de Mgr Tardini, 20 février 1945.

[79] Rubinstein, 'Pius XII and the Shoah', 179.

[80] Katz, R. *Fatal Silence: The Pope, the Resistance and the German Occupation of Rome*, London, 2003, 137.

is significant what Holocaust survivor, Alexander J. Groth, says of the pope's stance on the Holocaust:

> As the Vicar of Christ, perhaps the Pope should have spoken out on behalf of the murdered Jews, in order to condemn one of the greatest crimes in all history, no matter the costs. But the Pope did not have the enormous material resources of the Western Allies or their personal security. Churchill and Roosevelt were never threatened with martyrdom.[81]

William D. Rubinstein is also dismissive of claims that:

> In all likelihood—a likelihood probably amounting to a bare certainty—Hitler would have paid no heed to any pronouncements on the Jews made by the Vatican . . . Theoretically, and in hindsight, the Pope might have excommunicated all Catholic members of the SS (or the Nazi Party) although the only effect would have been that the Nazis denounced the pope as an agent of 'Judeo-Bolshevism' . . . .[82]

The most that he will concede is that only repeated condemnation from Pius, Churchill, and Roosevelt, coupled with a threat of punishment, could have saved some Jews by alerting Jews in Europe to the danger and possibly persuading the SS to abandon their extermination campaign earlier.[83]

Pius, Maglione, Tardini, and Montini all argued to the Allied and neutral envoys to the Vatican that if they were to condemn Nazi German atrocities, then they would have to condemn atrocities on the other side—like the Katyn massacre of Polish officers by the Soviets in 1940 and the Soviets' crimes in the Baltic States in the same period, and perhaps even Allied 'terror bombing' which Pius found so especially deplorable. Here was the rub: if the Holy See was to maintain good diplomatic relations with both sides in the conflict, it had to preserve its position of absolute neutrality and impartiality. Condemnations of the acts of one side or another would destroy that. This was exactly the same dilemma that the papacy had faced in the First World War. Furthermore, the Secretariat of State felt particularly constrained from criticizing Italy by the terms of the Lateran Pacts, which enjoined neutrality upon the State of the Vatican City.

Pius continued to believe, almost to the end of the war, and despite the Allies' commitment to unconditional surrender, that the Holy See had the capacity to act as an intermediary to bring about peace, even if that might only be a separate peace for Italy.[84] In consequence, the diplomat in Papa

[81] Alexander J. Groth, *Accomplices: Churchill, Roosevelt and the Holocaust*, New York, 2011, 87.

[82] William D. Rubinstein, *The Myth of Rescue: Why the Democracies Could Not Have Saved More Jews from the Nazis*, London and New York, 1997, 101.

[83] Rubinstein, *The Myth of Rescue*, 209.

[84] Pirelli, *Taccuini, 1922–1943*, 422–423 (Pirelli's conversation with Cardinal Maglione).

Pacelli triumphed over the prophet, the papacy's international diplomatic role over its moral primacy.

THE CHURCH'S CONTRIBUTION TO THE SAVING OF EUROPEAN JEWS

During the course of the Second World War, Catholics saved many thousands of Jews—and other civilian and military victims of fascist persecution as well. According to Pinchas Lapide:

> the Catholic Church saved more Jewish lives during the war than all the other churches, religious institutions and rescue organisations put together. Its record stands in startling contrast to the achievements of the International Red Cross and the Western democracies . . . the Holy See, the nuncios and the entire Catholic Church saved some 400,000 Jews from certain death.[85]

Whether the Catholic Church really did save more lives than all other rescuers put together is doubtful. In any case, it would be impossible to prove it. But the documents contained in the *Actes et Documents du Saint Siège relatifs au Seconde guerre mondiale*, especially in volumes 6, 8, 9, and 10, prove beyond all doubt that the Roman Catholic Church and Roman Catholics, at all levels and in all countries, saved tens, possibly hundreds of thousands of Jews from death during the Second World War and that the Vatican was heavily involved in those actions. One criticism of Pius XII is that he never *personally* gave the order to those Catholic clergy, religious, and laity who helped save Jews.[86] However, Lapide claims that when he was received in audience by Papa Roncalli to thank him for his work in saving Jews as Apostolic Delegate in Turkey, John XXIII interrupted him to say that he had done so on orders from the pope, that is, Pius XII.[87] There is other evidence that Pius XII gave specific orders to save the Jews in the form of several documented examples of decisions taken in the Secretariat of State, with which he would undoubtedly have been aware and which he sanctioned, or taken with his nephews, the princes Marcantonio and Carlo, which resulted in the protection of Jews in Rome.[88]

[85] Lapide, *Three Popes and the Jews*, 214–215.

[86] For example, S. Zuccotti, *Under His Very Windows: The Vatican and the Holocaust in Italy*, New Haven, CT, 2000, 307.

[87] Lapide, *Three Popes and the Jews*, 17.

[88] See A. Riccardi, *L'inverno più lungo 1943–44: Pio XII, gli Ebrei e I Nazisti a Roma*, Rome and Bari, 2008, 81–82.

Inevitably, the priority for the Church was the rescue of non-Aryan Catholics. Though classified as Jews by the Racial Laws of Germany and other countries, non-Aryan Catholics, particularly those of recent conversion, for obvious reasons could not count on any help from Jewish organizations. As has been seen (Chapter 8), when racial legislation was introduced into Italy and Hungary the Church authorities there, supported by the nuncios, sought to extract exemptions for non-Aryan Catholics: it tried to do the same in Slovakia as well.[89] Various organizations were specifically involved in trying to save non-Aryan Catholics by facilitating their emigration to the Americas and the money from American Catholics played a large part in these efforts.[90]

But the Church was involved in much wider operations to save Jews. Hungary was a case in point. After German occupation of the country in March 1944 and the arrival of Adolf Eichmann, the collection and deportation of Hungarian and other Jews began. The Vatican sought to galvanize the Cardinal Primate, Serédi, and other Hungarian bishops into action. Mgr Angelo Rotta, nuncio in Budapest, who was to earn his place among the official 'righteous Gentiles' for his work in saving Hungarian Jews through the issue of 'Immigration Certificates' and other stratagems, telegraphed Maglione in June 1944 to say that 'Only energetic action [on the part of the Hungarian] episcopate can perhaps put a brake [on the persecution]' and that 'Catholics and priests [were] scandalised [by the] abject conduct [of the] episcopate [which is] dictated by excessive prudence.'[91] According to Bèla Bodó, 'The Vatican strongly denounced the deportation of Hungary's Jew; the Vatican's opposition finally gave the Hungarian church elite enough courage to take a stand against the government on this issue. The church protested against the law that ordered the Jews to wear yellow star on 5 April 1940.'[92]

By the middle of June 1944, the situation for Hungarian Jews was becoming catastrophic and on the 25th of that month Pius sent a telegram to the Regent Horthy appealing to him to desist from the deportation of Hungarian Jews, and foreign Jews who had seen the country as a refuge.[93] The text of this telegram, *en clair*, to Admiral Horthy, at the height of the deportations

[89] W. Brandmüller, *L'Olocausto nella Slovacchia e la Chiesa cattolica*, Vatican City, 2004, 22–23.

[90] See, for example, ADSS, 8, Le Saint Siège et les Victimes de la Guerre, janvier–décembre 1942 ; doc. 15, Le cardinal Maglione au cardinal-archevêque de Vienne Innitzer, 6 février 1941.

[91] ADSS, doc. 242, Le nonce à Budapest Rotta au cardinal Maglione, 24 juin 1944; Paul A. Hanebrink, *In Defense of Christian Hungary: Religion, Nationalism and Anti-Semitism, 1890-1944*, Ithaca and London, 2006, ch. 7, gives an illuminating account of the moral failure of the leadership of all of Hungary's Christian communities in the face of the Holocaust.

[92] Bèla Bodó, '"Do Not Lead us into (Fascist) Temptation": The Catholic Church in Inter-war Hungary', in M. Feldmann and M. Turda (eds), *Clerical Fascism in Inter-war Europe*, Abingdon, Oxford, 2008, 214.

[93] Text in ADSS, 10, Le Saint Siège et les Victimes de la Guerre, doc. 243, le pape Pie XII au Regent Horthy, 25 juin 1944.

of Hungarian and other Jews, again made no explicit mention of them, talking about 'the grievous sufferings endured by a great number of unfortunate people because of their nationality or their race':[94] presumably, the pope was still afraid of upsetting the Nazis at this juncture. Despite the apparent vagueness of the wording, the appeal of Pius had effect: Horthy intervened in July to stop the deportations, though his action was probably also influenced by the belief that the Germans were going to lose the war.[95] When Horthy was arrested by the Nazis in October and deported from Hungary, the government of the fanatically anti-Semitic Arrow Cross Movement, led by Ferenc Szálasi, took over and embarked upon an even more cruel persecution of the Jews inside the country. Towards the end of the month, under pressure from America, Pius sent a message, to be read in all Hungarian churches, calling upon Hungary's Catholics to provide assistance to Jews and refugees.[96] Despite his and Nuncio Rotta's efforts, in the end only a small percentage of Hungary's Jews were saved from the Nazi extermination machine.

The Vatican was particularly active in the case of the Slovak Republic, an overwhelmingly Catholic country but one which, entirely surrounded by Germany, German-occupied territories, or minor Axis allies like Hungary and Romania, was effectively a client state of the Third Reich. Following the Nazi occupation of the western parts of Czechoslovakia, the 'Protectorate of Bohemia and Moravia', and the Slovak declaration of independence, Mgr Burzio, the nuncio in Prague, transferred his office to Bratislava, the Slovak capital, where he acted as chargé d'affaires for the Holy See to the government there. The president of the Republic, Mgr Joseph Tiso, was the leader of the moderate wing of the ruling Catholic party, while the prime minister, Adalbert Tika, and his minister of home affairs, Alexander Mach, were more radical and closer to the Germans.[97] Thus, under Nazi pressure, they introduced a 'Jewish Code', discriminatory legislation against the Jews in September 1941 on the pretexts that the Jews had a stranglehold on the economy of Slovakia and that they were pro-Hungarian.[98] The reaction of the Slovakian clergy, and in particular Bishop Vojtaššák of Spiš (who was also vice-president of the Council of State a sort of upper house of parliament), to the new laws was ambiguous, revealing the deep-seated anti-Semitism of Slovakian Catholicism.[99] Subsequently, Tuka and Mach bowed to Nazi demands and, in September 1942, began the deportation of Slovakian Jews

[94] Text in ADSS, 10, Le Saint Siège et les Victimes de la Guerre, doc. 243, le pape Pie XII au Regent Horthy, 25 juin 1944.

[95] Text in ADSS, 10, Le Saint Siège et les Victimes de la Guerre, doc. 243, le pape Pie XII au Regent Horthy, 25 juin 1944; the intervention at this point of the King of Sweden, Gustav V, also appears to have weighed in the balance. See Blet, *Pius XII*, 195.

[96] Blet, *Pius XII*, 195.

[97] Brandmüller, *L'Olocausto nella Slovacchia*, 20–21.

[98] Brandmüller, *L'Olocausto nella Slovacchia*, 30–32.

[99] Brandmüller, *L'Olocausto nella Slovacchia*, 30–32.

and foreign Jews resident in Slovakia to Poland. In Slovakia, as in Hungary, it fell to the papal envoy to galvanize the local episcopacy into action on behalf of Jews, with the result that, in April 1942, it issued a fairly generic protest against the newly imposed laws against the Jews in the form of a pastoral letter and also made direct representations to the government.[100] This had no effect and the deportations of Jews to Auschwitz began a month later.[101] The Vatican repeatedly protested the deportations, either directly to Tiso or indirectly through Burzio or the Slovak ambassador to the Holy See, Karel Sidor, and had some success in slowing them down.[102] In this way, probably as many as a third of the Slovakian Jews were saved.[103] But, by late October 1944, Slovakia was firmly in the grip of the Nazi occupiers and Burzio reported that nothing more could be done because Tiso was carrying out orders in a servile manner.[104] The Slovakian experience was a painful one for the Vatican, prompting Tardini to exclaim, 'It is a great misfortune that the President of Slovakia is a priest. Everyone knows that the Holy See cannot bring Hitler to heel. But who will understand that we cannot control a priest?!'[105]

France, after the June 1940 defeat, also presented the Vatican with many problems. As with German occupation policies elsewhere, the division of the country—into Alsace-Lorraine annexed to the Reich, an area in the north ruled from Brussels, an occupied zone stretching from Dieppe to Bayonne and from the Swiss border to the Atlantic, another strip occupied by the Italians from almost Lake Geneva in the north to Nice in the south, and finally the unoccupied zone under Pétain—made communication with the French bishops difficult, despite the presence of the nunciature at Vichy. Certainly, the Church's life in the German zones was more difficult than under Vichy and, as elsewhere, on the whole the French bishops did not encourage resistance. But, generalizing from his study of the departments of Nantes, Angers, and Tours, Gildea argues that:

> the notion of resistance in the case of the Catholic Church has to be put in context. The defence of the Catholic Church as an institution was in itself a 'politics of presence' that offered a guarantee against the Nazification of France and the French.[106]

[100] Brandmüller, *L'Olocausto nella Slovacchia*, 30–31 and 34.

[101] Brandmüller, *L'Olocausto nella Slovacchia*, 32.

[102] See, for example, ADSS, 10, doc. 329, La Secrétaire d'Etat à la Légation de Slovaquie, 20 septembre 1944, and doc. 341, Le chargé d'affaires à Pressbourg Burzio à la Sécretaire d'Etat, 6 octobre 1944.

[103] Brandmüller, *L'Olocausto nella Slovacchia*, 95.

[104] ADSS, 10, doc. 377, Le chargé d'affaires à Pressbourg Burzio à la Sécretaire d'Etat, 26 octobre 1944.

[105] ADSS, 8, doc. 426, Notes de Mgr Tardini, 13 juillet 1942.

[106] R. Gildea, *Marianne in Chains: In Search of the German Occupation, 1940–1945*, Basingstoke and London, 2002, 215.

When the Vichy regime promulgated a 'Jewish Statute', shortly after its inception in September 1940, the Vatican made no objections. It had already made it clear in the cases of Hungary and Romania in the late 1930s that it was not opposed in principle to discriminatory legislation against Jewish communities (see Chapter 7), yet, in the autumn of 1942, the nuncio in France publicly contradicted Marshal Pétain when he declared that the Holy See approved of the passage of further anti-Semitic legislation.[107] The circumstances had changed. Most of Europe now knew that the Nazis were murdering the Jews and that anti-Semitic legislation was merely a preliminary to this. Following 'La Grande Rafle' of July 1942, the big round-up of nearly 8,000 foreign Jews in the occupied zone, who were arrested and held at the Paris Vélodrome, the assembly of cardinals and archbishops of France considered making a public protest but in the end decided that Cardinal Suhard, archbishop of Paris, should make their feelings known to Pétain in person. Valeri complained to Maglione that this French bishops' response was 'a rather platonic protest. . . .'[108] When Jews began to be deported from the unoccupied zone, only five out of the thirty-five bishops in the territory of Vichy publicly protested—Gerlier of Lyons, Théas of Montauban, Delay of Marseilles, Moussaron of Albi, and Saliège of Toulouse.[109] As a result, Laval, Pétain's prime minister, summoned Mgr Rocco, secretary of the nunciature, to protest about the protest of Archbishop Saliège of Toulouse regarding deportations of Jews. He said it could have terrible repercussions as the protest would be used by the British as propaganda and he claimed that the archbishopric of Toulouse was a hotbed of Gaullists.[110]

In September 1942, Laval announced the beginning of a policy of more active collaboration with the Nazis by declaring that he intended to 'cleanse France of its foreign Jewry', thus ensuring the extension of the raids to the unoccupied zone.[111]

Relations between the French hierarchy and Vichy subsequently deteriorated.[112] As the deportations continued, Vatican Radio condemned Laval's policy and Vatican diplomacy intervened on several occasions to save French Jews, and foreign Jews trapped in France.[113]

[107] Blet, *Pius XII*, 232.

[108] ADSS, 8, doc. 440, Le nonce en France Valeri au cardinal Maglione, 29 juillet1942; Rhodes, *The Vatican*, 316–317, gives a quotation from 'this protest to Vichy' but without providing its source. If what Rhodes cites is indeed the protest which Suhard conveyed to Pétain then it was far from being 'platonic'.

[109] J. Jackson, *France: The Dark Years, 1940–1944*, Oxford, 2001, 375.

[110] ADSS, 8, doc. 454, Le conseiller de nonciature Pacini au cardinal Maglione, 27 août 1942.

[111] As quoted in Rhodes, *The Vatican*, 316.

[112] Rhodes, *The Vatican*, 317–318.

[113] ADSS, 7, doc. 69, Le nonce Valeri au cardinal Maglione, 1 mars 1943, and doc. 308, Mgr Carroll au cardinal Maglione, 23 août 1943; in fact, there are several more instances in this volume alone.

Romania was another country where the papal diplomatic envoy was instructed to save Jews by all possible means, in this case as much from the tender mercies of the Romanians themselves as from their German masters. By 1941, Romania was thoroughly trapped in the vice-like grip of the Axis. Having been forced to concede territory to Bulgaria, Hungary, and Russia, she was nevertheless obliged to join in the war against Judaeo-Bolshevism after June 1941. Romanian anti-Semitism was easily as virulent as the German Nazi variety thanks to the presence in Romanian politics of two extreme right-wing parties, the Iron Guard/Legion of the Archangel Michael of Cornelius Codreanu and the National Christian Party of Alexander Cusa and Octavian Goga.[114] Under the dictatorship of Marshal Antonescu, the Romanians initiated the massacre of Jews in Romania in the summer of 1941.[115] Mgr Andrea Cassulo, the nuncio in Bucharest, did what he could to help the Jews in Romania, and especially those in Transniestria, the area of Russia occupied by the Romanians in 1941, but without a great deal of success.[116]

Of all Pius XII's alleged 'silences', arguably the worst was not over the Nazi extermination of the Jews, but over the murderous campaigns of the fascist Ustasha regime in Croatia against ethnic Serbs, Jews, and gypsies. This regime had come into being following the German invasion and dismemberment of Yugoslavia in April 1941, and was enthusiastically welcomed by the Croatian clergy led by Mgr Alojije Stepinac, archbishop of Zagreb. The 'Croatian Independent State', as it was called, did not inherit all of the historical Croatian territories, but its control over Slavonia and what is now Bosnia-Hercegovina, ensured that large numbers of Orthodox Serbs fell into its clutches.[117] Allied to Germany and Italy (an Italian prince was its nominal king as Tomislav II but he never took up his throne), Croatia was recognized by only the Axis powers and their satellites but not by the Holy See on the grounds that it was a state borne out of war and therefore not legitimate. The Secretariat of State stuck to this line, despite pressure brought by the Italians.[118] It refused to receive a permanent representative, either official or unofficial, from the new Croatian regime, though an emissary from Ante Pavelić, Ustasha leader or *Poglavnik* and head of the Croatian government, was received from time to time to discuss certain ecclesiastical matters.[119] On the same grounds, it would not even send an apostolic delegate to Zagreb,

[114] Christopher R. Browning, *The Origins of the Final Solution: September 1939 to March 1942, with Contributions by Matthaus Juergen*, London, 2004, 210.

[115] Browning, *The Origins of the Final Solution*, 276–277.

[116] Blet, *Pius XII*, 182–190.

[117] Alexander, *Church and State in Yugoslavia*, 19–40.

[118] ADSS, 4, doc. 400, Notes de Mgr Tardini, 13 juin 1941.

[119] ADSS, 5, doc. 242, Notes du cardinal Maglione, 7 février, 1942, and doc. 244, Le cardinal Maglione au minister Lorković (Foreign Minister of Croatia), février 1942.

instead posting an 'apostolic visitator', Abbot Giuseppe Marcone, O.S.B., of Monte Cassino, a sure sign of how temporary they regarded the Ustasha regime.

The Vatican's relationship with Croatia was, consequently, a difficult and ambiguous one. When the pope or Maglione received Pavelić in *private* audience, there were protests from the British and Yugoslavian representatives.[120] Pius argued that he could hardly refuse an audience since Pavelić was nominally a Catholic and the pope felt he could not refuse a Catholic. When another visit of Pavelić to Rome was announced in June 1943, the pope sought to avoid it altogether for fear of offending the Allies.[121] The Ustasha regime turned out to be as bloody as its Nazi overlords: its private police force, the Black Legion, a thinly disguised imitation of the SS, took the lead in murdering some 300,000 Serbs, including 128 Orthodox priests and 3 bishops, and destroyed 300 churches.[122] There was much sadism in these hate crimes and several Franciscan priests also participated—one even ran an Ustasha concentration camp for interning Serbs.[123]

There is clear evidence that Archbishop Stepinac protested against the Ustasha treatment of the Jews and gypsies, the massacres of the Serbs, and the forced conversion to Catholicism of thousands of Serbs which took place on Croatian territory.[124] There is also evidence that the Vatican was not unaware of the forced conversions and the massacres of Serbs.[125] On the other hand, there is absolutely no evidence of Vatican protests via official or unofficial channels, that is, through Abbot Marcone after the Ustasha started slaughtering Serbs, Jews, and gypsies. To make matters worse, Abbot Marcone, who, in Vatican terms, did not have a diplomatic rank but who was nevertheless treated as such by the Ustasha, was also frequently seen in the company of the Ustasha leadership.[126] The regime of Pavelić was clearly of the 'clerical–fascist' variety, the *Poglavnik* deliberately espousing Catholicism as the key element in Croatia's resurgence as an independent state. Stepinac and Marcone, and the Vatican in its turn, seem to have been seduced by this, and by the fact

[120] ADSS, 4, doc. 398, Aide-mémoire de la legation de Yugoslavie, 11 juin 1941; and 5, doc. 498, Le ministre de Grande Bretagne Osborne à Mgr Tardini, 3 octobre 1941.

[121] ADSS, 7, doc. 231, Notes de la Secréterie d'État, 5 juin 1943.

[122] O. Chadwick, *The Christian Church in the Cold War*, Harmondsworth, 1992, 63.

[123] Marco Aurelio Rivelli, *L'Arcivescovo del genocidio: Monsignor Stepinac, il Vaticano e la dittatura ustacia in Croazia, 1941–1945*, Milan, 1998, 39–144.

[124] ADSS, 8, L'archeveque de Zagreb Stépinac au pape Pie XII, 3 décembre 1941; doc. 253, L'archeveque de Zagreb Stépinac au cardinal Maglione, 9 janvier 1942; doc. 261, Le P. Tacchi-Venturi au cardinal Maglione, 20 janvier 1942; and doc. 289, Le cardinal Maglione au visiteur en Croatie Marcone, 21 février 1942.

[125] See, for example, ADSS, 5, doc. 95, Le nonce en Italie Borgoncini Duca au cardinal Maglione, 22 septembre 1941; and 8, doc. 162, La Secrétairie d'Etat à la Légation de Yugoslavie, 27 septembre 1941.

[126] See the photographs of their meetings reproduced in Rivelli, *L'Arcivescovo del genocidio*, 76–78.

that the partisan forces in Yugoslavia were led by Communists, most notably Tito (Josip Broz). But this cannot exculpate it from turning a blind eye to the systematic processes of ethnic cleansing carried out by Pavelić and his collaborators, of which the Vatican were clearly aware. Given that Independent Croatia, like the Republic of Slovakia, proclaimed itself a 'Catholic state', the failure of the Vatican to condemn Ustasha genocides is arguably more reprehensible than Pius XII's failure to speak out more clearly against the Holocaust. No doubt its policy of 'discretion' was influenced by the same considerations as that towards the activities of the Nazis: that Croatia was not only an ally of the Third Reich but of Fascist Italy as well and that to criticize it would be to condemn the latter regimes by association and thus complicate relations with them.

VATICAN RELIEF EFFORTS: THE GERMANS AND THE ALLIES

By 1943, the rescue and relief activities of the Holy See and its nuncios were known worldwide, prompting appeals from Jewish and other groups in occupied Europe, the neutral countries, Latin America, and the USA. From then onwards, there was a constant flow of such appeals until the end of the war.[127] These activities also extended to other groups, POWs, civilian internees, and refugees, all assisted by one Vatican organization or another, especially the Ufficio d'Informazioni. The pope was also frequently called upon to intervene to prevent the Germans from shooting hostages.[128] The only group from whom no appeals were received and on whose behalf the Vatican was not called upon to act were the gypsies or Roma and Sinti peoples.[129] Clearly, the gypsies were the forgotten victims of the Nazi and fascist racial projects.

As in the First World War, the Vatican sought to bring relief to whole starving populations in various parts of Axis-occupied Europe and territories

[127] See, for example, John F. Morley, 'The Holocaust in Hungary', in Carol Rittner and John K. Roth (eds), *Pope Pius XII and the Holocaust*, Leicester, 2002, 168–169. The examples in the volumes of the *Actes et Documents* are too numerous to cite.

[128] See, for example, ADSS, 8, doc. 191, La Secrśterie d'Etat à la Légation de Grande Bretagne, 31 octobre 1941; and doc. 192, Le nonce en France Valeri au cardinal Maglione, 31 octobre 1941.

[129] In all sixteen volumes of the *Actes et Documents* there is not a single reference to appeals for help for gypsies or attempts by the Vatican, the Church, or Catholics anywhere in Europe to save gypsies from their persecutors. See Zoltan Barany, *The East European Gypsies: Regime Change, Marginality and Ethno-politics*, Cambridge, 2002, 104, where he says: 'While there were numerous examples of righteous gentiles trying to and actually succeeding in saving Jews, few Roma received such assistance and no state or international organisation expressed concern with their fate.'

newly liberated by the Allies. Attempts to bring food relief to Poland and the Baltic States were thwarted by the Nazis.[130] There were also problems distributing the monies collected by American dioceses for people in occupied territories of Europe.[131] The policies of the Allies were another impediment to the Vatican's relief efforts, an attempt which was made to reprovision Belgium after the German invasion and occupation being rejected by the British government on the grounds that any food aid would be seized and used by Germany.[132] There was logic in the British position: the sooner the Germans were defeated, the better for everyone, and allowing precious food resources into their hands would only delay that defeat. In fact, Vatican relief efforts were another irritant in relations with the Allies, most particularly the British, which was thrown into sharp relief in the winter of 1941–2. One of the most serious cases of mass starvation in the European theatre during the Second World War was in Greece where, thanks to rapacious German economic policies, there was a famine which killed over 200,00 people in the winter of 1941–2.[133] The Secretariat of State intervened several times in efforts to persuade the British government to allow 350,000 tons of wheat, which the puppet Greek government had purchased and was waiting in the Suez Canal, to be despatched to Greece.[134] Though other neutral states, including Sweden, were allowed to send aid to Greece, the British rejected the Vatican plea on the grounds that, in international law, feeding the populations of occupied territories was the responsibility of the occupying powers, in this case Germany and Italy, but above all Italy.[135] The men in the Vatican, especially Tardini, were left feeling very bitter by British obduracy, not least because they felt that the Foreign Office believed that they were doing Italy's business in this affair when they were not.

THE VATICAN AND ITALY: FROM THE FALL OF MUSSOLINI TO THE LIBERATION OF ROME

The Vatican's relations with Fascist Italy after the latter's entry into war were correct, but often uneasy. On the one hand, Pius was scrupulous in avoiding giving offence to Italy and not only enforced a 'blackout' on the State of the

130 Chadwick, *Britain and the Vatican*, 190.

131 ADSS, 8, doc. 38, Le délegué apostolique à Washington Cicognani au cardinal Maglione, 6 mars 1941, and 237, Le délegué apostolique à Washington Cicognani au cardinal Maglione, 18 décembre 1941.

132 Chadwick, *Britain and the Vatican*, 191.

133 Weinberg, *A World at Arms*, 526.

134 For a brief summary of the incident, see Chadwick, *Britain and the Vatican*, 190–193.

135 ADSS, 8, doc. 198, Le ministre de Grande Bretagne Osborne à la Sécretaire d'Etat, 11 novembre 1941.

Vatican City in accordance with the air-raid precautions programme of the Rome authorities, but, out of sympathy with the wartime privations of the Italian people, he insisted on imposing strict limits on heating levels.[136] This did not go down well with all the Vatican's residents, particularly the 'incarcerated' diplomats.[137] At the level of officialdom, the Italians were cooperative towards Vatican needs; they even conceded Nogara the use of a first-class wagon lit car on the State railways for his various journeys throughout the peninsula to manage the Holy See's properties and investments.[138] But despite the Vatican's efforts to placate Mussolini, and the loyal, if unenthusiastic, commitment of many Italian Catholics to their country's war effort, the Duce continued to inveigh against the Church, particularly when the pope made 'peace broadcasts', as in December 1941.[139] After his declaration of war on the United States, Mussolini became increasingly irritated with the visits to the Vatican made by Myron Taylor, who, though a serving diplomat to the Holy See was also an enemy alien: Mussolini was forced to permit the visits by the terms of the Lateran Treaty.[140] In January 1942 he took a swipe at the Church in a violent speech to the Directory of the National Fascist Party:

> This Vatican will end by being reduced to what it was in the epoch of Celestino V. It has already lost many political opportunities (*possibilitá*). They are partially recoverable, but it will lose moral opportunities as well which are not so easily recoverable. One thing is the politics of the Italian people, another is the politics of the Vatican.[141]

Mussolini was grossly underestimating the international political importance of the papacy, and of the Church in Italy. Ironically, as Davide Rodogno points out, during the war 'Mussolini relied on the military chaplains to help sustain the [Italian] soldiers' morale.'[142] The morale of the Italian armed forces certainly needed sustaining as the war progressed. Italy suffered a series of military defeats—largely thanks to Mussolini's overambitious war aims and his strategic incompetence—in Greece in the winter 1940–1, in East Africa in 1941, where she lost the whole of her empire, including recently conquered Ethiopia, to British troops. Already, by the autumn of 1942, Ciano

[136] T. Abse, 'Italy', in J. Noakes (ed.), *The Civilian in War: The Home Front in Europe, Japan and the USA in World War II*, Leicester, 1992, ch, 7.

[137] Tittman, *Il Vaticano*, 93–94.

[138] ASMAE, Ambasciata presso la Santa Sede (ApSS), pacco 160.1.3, Embassy memo of 10 June 1942.

[139] *Ciano's Diary*, entry for 25 December 1941.

[140] *Ciano's Diary*, 8 and 26 October 1942.

[141] Susmel, *Opera Omnia*, XXX, 157; G. Miccoli, 'Chiesa Cattolica e Totalitarismi', in Vincenzo Ferrone (ed.), *La Chiesa Cattolica e il Totalitarismo, Atti del Convegno di Torino, 25–26 ottobre 2001*, Florence, 2004, 26; and R. De Felice, *Mussolini l'alleato (1940–1943)*, 1/2, *L'Italia in Guerra (1940–1943)*, tome 2, *Crisi e agonia del regime*, Turin, 1990, 755.

[142] D. Rodogno, *Fascism's European Empire: Italian Occupation during the Second World War*, Cambridge, 2006, 154–157.

was seeking a way out of Italy's predicament, some sort of separate peace with the Western Allies. The focus of his efforts was the Vatican because it had flexed its diplomatic muscle with both Britain and America in efforts to avert the bombing of Rome and obtain a declaration of its status as an 'open city'.[143] There is evidence that, as early as October 1942, the Vatican was putting out feelers to America, though it is not clear whether Ciano had explicitly asked for them. The Italian Foreign Ministry's helpfulness towards Nogara was undoubtedly influenced by an awareness of the Vatican's 'back channels' to the US administration and Nogara's own contacts in the highest financial circles in America.

As Italy's military situation deteriorated in the first few months of 1943, the Vatican proffered its services in pursuit of a separate peace with the Western Allies. The German catastrophe at Stalingrad in the winter of 1942–43 involved Italy, inasmuch as its 8th Army had effectively been destroyed, and in January 1943 the Italians were driven out of Libya. At this point, Ciano had a long conversation with Montini, who put himself at Italy's disposal, a fairly obvious way of saying the Vatican was willing to negotiate on its behalf. The latter also made clear the Vatican's concern about the dangers of growing Communist influence, a concern which would shape the Vatican's policy towards Italy for years to come.[144] The men in the Secretariat of State were well aware of the plotting going on in Italian court, military, and Fascist party circles in the spring and summer of 1943. Not long after the loss of Italy's North African colony, Mussolini gave a clear signal of his increasing political weakness and isolation by carrying out a cabinet reshuffle. One of the ministers who lost his job was Ciano, who accepted the embassy to the Holy See instead. In his diary entry for the day of his sacking from the Foreign Ministry, Ciano recorded, 'I choose to be Ambassador to the Holy See. It is a place of rest that may, moreover, hold many possibilities for the future.'[145] He was quickly proved right. Within a few weeks of the reshuffle Maglione was carefully considering whether to send Nogara to the USA, along with Giovanni Fummi, the representative of J.P. Morgan's bank in Italy, to take unofficial soundings on Italy's behalf.[146] Eventually, the project was abandoned as impractical.[147]

In fact, the Secretariat of State had not initially welcomed Ciano's appointment. It was felt that he was too 'political' and that the Allies would consider him to be too Fascist; the behaviour of his wife Edda, Mussolini's daughter, did not go down too well in the Vatican either and so the *agrément* was delayed.[148]

[143] Chadwick, *Britain and the Vatican*, 236–239.
[144] *Ciano's Diary*, entry for 13 January 1943.
[145] *Ciano's Diary*, 5 February 1943.
[146] Pirelli, *Taccuini*, 407–408.
[147] Pirelli, *Taccuini*, 407–408.
[148] Pirelli, *Taccuini*, 407–408.

The final Axis defeat in North Africa (Tunis) in April 1943, which left Italy vulnerable to Allied invasion, was, however, followed by a series of Vatican démarches to Italian leaders, including Mussolini himself. Tardini was concerned about the way in which such efforts should be made, arguing that in order to avoid compromising the neutrality and dignity of the Holy See it would be best to make an approach to the Duce via Maglione and Ciano, rather than through the Ministry of Foreign Affairs.[149] This procedure was followed, and in a letter of 12 May, the pope stated that he 'was, as always, ready to do all in his power to come to the aid of the people who suffer'.[150] The response was not positive. According to Ciano, Mussolini was intransigent: he would not budge and was determined to fight on. The king and Crown Prince Umberto would not move either, which was unfortunate because the Allies would not negotiate directly with the Duce.[151]

In June, Maglione sent Mgr Borgoncini-Duca, nuncio to Italy, to see the king to convince him that Roosevelt's declaration to the Italian people following the fall of the island of Pantelleria, the first piece of Italian soil to be captured by the Allies, was to be trusted. In his message to the pope, Roosevelt had declared that 'The soldiers of the United Nations have come to rid Italy of Fascism . . . and to drive out the Nazi oppressors who are infesting her.'[152] The king was sceptical and unforthcoming. Ultimately, he was afraid to take the initiative and persisted in this stance until after the Grand Council of Fascism meeting on 25 July. Nevertheless, before the meeting, Pius XII, despite the opposition of Maglione, considered sending Enrico Galeazzi, the pope's personal friend and a leading figure in the administration of the State of the Vatican City, and Fr Walter Carroll, an American in the Secretariat of State, to the USA to make direct contact with American officials: this was abandoned.[153] According to Giuseppe Bastianini, Under-Secretary to Mussolini at Palazzo Chigi, he approached Maglione on 17 July with a request that the Holy See contact the Allies on behalf of Italy: he claimed that Mussolini knew of this initiative and did not object.[154]

In the meantime, the film which the Vatican had commissioned about the pope in 1942, *Pastor Angelicus*, paved the way for Pius XII's emergence as the key personality in Italy after Mussolini's fall. *Pastor Angelicus* was entirely dedicated to Pacelli, on the twenty-fifth anniversary of his episcopal ordination. After brief footage of the Vatican during the last days of Pius XI, his funeral, and the conclave, the eighty-minute-long film showed scenes

[149] ADSS, 7, doc. 181, Les notes de Mgr Tardini, 10 mai 1943.
[150] ADSS, 7, doc. 185, Le papa Pie XII à Mussolini, 12 mai 1943.
[151] ADSS, 7, doc. 186, Notes du cardinal Maglione, 12 mai 1943.
[152] ADSS, 7, doc. 285, Le président Roosevelt au papa Pie XII, 10 juillet 1943.
[153] See ADSS, 7, 374, le Cardinal Maglione au délégué apostolique à Washington Cicognani, 28 août 1943, Annexe, Notes of Mgr Tardini, Vatican, 26 juin 1943.
[154] G. Bastianini, *Uomini, cose*, Milan, 1959, 115–118.

from the early life of Pacelli, his daily routine, and then the key moments of his three-year pontificate, including him making his first radio speech on 25 September 1939.[155] The film was initially shown in Rome and Italy, and Vincent McCormick, an astute observer of Roman life during the Second World War, said of its reception:

> Here in Rome it only ran for a few days, and was ordered off the screen by the civil authorities. [The] Pope became too popular, it is said: it occasioned shouts for peace. It is now on the Rome circuit [sic] and may return to Rome later.[156]

This confirms what one might well have surmised: during the last, increasingly difficult year of the Fascist regime (it fell in July 1943), Mussolini was extremely unhappy about any public manifestation of the papal charisma.[157] Mussolini's own 'cult of the Duce' always had to compete with two rivals: that still lingering around the Italian monarch, Victor Emmanuel III, and the other around the pope. Already, in July 1943, while Mussolini was at Feltre in northern Italy conferring with Hitler, the pope was able to upstage him following the first Allied bombing of Rome. The Americans attacked the San Lorenzo district, close to the central railway station (Stazione Termini) of the city and home to many railway workers. The pope quickly appeared among the ruins, bringing moral and financial succour to the mainly working-class victims.[158] Pius XII then strove to establish and maintain Rome's status as an 'open city,' thus sparing it further aerial bombardment, as well as street fighting.[159]

The Vatican's reactions to Mussolini's defeat in the Fascist Grand Council vote of 25 July, the king's dismissal, and the arrest of the Duce and the appointment of Marshal Badoglio as head of an interim government, were naturally cautious and circumspect, but Pius and his advisers must have been pleased at the prospect of Italy pulling out of the war. On the morning after the 'coup', Mgr Montini was asked to go and see Alberto De Stefani, Fascist ex-minister and one of the plotters of Mussolini's downfall, at the palace of Propaganda Fide in Piazza di Spagna. Here De Stefani explained to him what had happened in Grand Council meeting of the night before and raised the possibility of the Holy See approaching the Allies for a separate peace.[160] Two days later Luigi Federzoni, another plotter and former éminence grise of the regime visited Maglione to reiterate De Stefani's request.[161] All this is indicative of

155 *Pastor Angelicus*, 1943, Centro Cinematografico Cattolico, Filmoteca del Vaticano.

156 Hennessy, 'American Jesuit in Rome', 37.

157 According to Pirelli, *Taccuini*, 457, he ordered newspapers and radio to stop references to the pope's visit to the San Lorenzo quarter of Rome after it had been devastated in an air raid.

158 ACS, MdI, DGPS, Capo della Polizia (Chief of the Police), report for the Duce of 19 July 1943.

159 See Tittman, *Il Vaticano*, 173, where he says that the pope's visits to San Lorenzo enormously increased his popularity.

160 ADSS, 7, doc. 313, Notes de Mgr Montini, 25 juillet 1943.

161 ADSS, 7, doc. 313, Notes de Mgr Montini, 25 juillet 1943, note 6.

the strong position of the papacy in Italy after Mussolini's fall. The balance of power between the Italian state and the Church had decisively shifted in the latter's favour as a result of the fall of Fascism. The king and Badoglio desperately sought an armistice with the Allies as the latter advanced up the Italian peninsula while, correspondingly, Italy's erstwhile German allies took over control of more and more of the country. Vatican diplomacy sought to be of assistance in the process of negotiation by bringing together, in Maglione's office, first Harold Tittman and Francesco Babuscio Rizzo, a leading official in the Italian Foreign Ministry, and then D'Arcy Osborne and Raffaele Guariglia, Badoglio's new foreign minister. Both Tittman and Osborne felt obliged to refuse the pleas of the Italians to seek the agreement of their respective governments for the opening of peace negotiations with Italy because of the insecurity of their codes.[162] Nevertheless, the Badoglio government persisted in its efforts to obtain Allied recognition of its unilateral declaration of Rome as an 'open city' in mid-August.[163] These efforts failed, as did other efforts, again via the Vatican, on the part of the Italian Comando Supremo to obtain an immediate Allied seizure of Rome, before the Germans could complete their own occupation.[164] Between the announcement of the Italian armistice with the Allies on 8 September, and the subsequent flight of the King and Italian government from Rome, and the re-establishment of a fascist government in the north on 23 September, the Eternal City lived in a strange, uncertain, uneasy twilight world. Officially, it was under an Italian military administration, in reality it had been brought physically under the control of German occupying forces, whose presence ended any hopes of achieving 'open city' status.

After the armistice of 8 September 1943, Italy virtually ceased to exist as an international entity. On the one hand, post-Fascist 'king's' Italy, in the absence of a formal peace treaty, became a 'co-belligerent' with the Allies. On the other hand, following Mussolini's rescue from his royal prison and the establishment of the Fascist 'Italian Social Republic' (more commonly known as the Repubblica di Salò from the name of the small town on Lago di Garda which was its provisional capital) and the consequent civil war between the fascists and the anti-fascist Resistenza Armata, the Vatican assumed a position of enormous influence: the Church more generally was recognized as a major stabilizing force in Italy by the Allied authorities.[165] The Holy See never recognized Salò, but acted increasingly as an intermediary with the United States on behalf of the King's government, in virtue of Pius XII's 'special relationship' with Roosevelt. In all of its dealings on behalf of Italy, the Vatican was primarily concerned that the fall of Fascism should not open the way

[162] Tittman, *Il Vaticano*, 170–171. [163] Tittman, *Il Vaticano*, 175.
[164] ADSS, 7, doc. 391, Notes de Mgr Montini, 9/10 septembre 1943.
[165] D. W. Ellwood, *Italy 1943–45*, Leicester, 1985, 141 and 194.

to the victory of Communism, hence its support of the king's government. As Maglione explained to Cicognani in Washington, at the end of August 1943, 'In this situation, it is easy to see how difficult—not to say impossible—it would become for the Holy See to govern the Universal Church if Italy fell under the control of Communism.'[166]

ENEMY AT THE GATES: HITLER AND THE VATICAN, SEPTEMBER 1943 TO JUNE 1944

If it had been uncomfortable for the Vatican living with Fascist Italy after June 1940, it was much more so during the eight-month-long German occupation of Rome from September 1943 to June 1944. German troops now largely replaced Italians in their patrols around the Vatican's perimeter and in St Peter's Square. Hitler had already, from time to time, threatened to 'deal with' the pope: threats of having him kidnapped were averted by his wiser counsellors.[167] But Pius XII nevertheless feared the worst and there are suggestions of a 'worst-case scenario' plan which involved temporarily devolving leadership of the Church to Cardinal Cerejeira, the Patriarch of Lisbon in neutral Portugal.[168] In reality, as Alvarez points, only the Allies could have benefited from an attempt by the Germans to abduct the pope and occupy the Vatican. Such action would have outraged Catholic public opinion in Ireland, Portugal, Spain, and Switzerland, not to mention the Latin American states who remained neutral. The Vatican was now even more uncomfortably under surveillance by the German security services than it had been of those by Italy, though Alvarez demonstrates that the Germans were, in many ways, much more amateur, indeed sometimes almost clueless, about the Vatican, than the Italians.[169] If, prior to the German occupation, the Vatican, according to the Fascists, had been a 'nest of Allied spies', in actuality heavily penetrated by real Fascist ones, now those 'spies', that is, the Allied diplomats, continued to be tailed by the Fascist spies, plus many German agents as well.[170] And presiding over this miniature Lisbon, Tangier, or Casablanca, was the irascible, and allegedly pro-Fascist Cardinal Canali; and in a Vatican almost entirely staffed by Italians, clerical and lay, Canali was by no means alone in his sympathies.

It had been difficult to formulate an effective response to German war crimes throughout Europe, but it should have been easier when the Nazis

[166] ADSS, 7, doc. 374, Maglione au delegue apostolique à Washington Cicognani, 28 août 1943.

[167] Chadwick, *Britain and the Vatican*, 259–260; and Alvarez and Graham, *Nothing Sacred*, 85–86.

[168] Tittman, *Il Vaticano*, 178–179.

[169] Alvarez and Graham, *Nothing Sacred*, 43.

[170] Tittman, *Il Vaticano*, 179.

committed them in Rome, Pius XII's see city. The first test came in late September when the German occupying authorities demanded the handover of 6,000 Italian civilian hostages in reprisal for the alleged murder of wounded German soldiers. When Cardinal Maglione sought the intervention of the German ambassador to the Holy See, Ernst von Weizsäcker, who had formerly been Under-Secretary in the German Foreign Ministry, Weizsäcker quickly revealed his strategy for dealing with potential trouble between the Vatican and the German authorities. His preference was to avoid any contact, direct or indirect, between them, and to work in more roundabout ways to moderate German behaviour in the Eternal City likely to upset the Vatican: hence, to Cardinal Maglione's surprise and dismay, he refused to negotiate with the German authorities on the matter.[171] The problem was resolved when it became clear to the Germans that, in fact, no German wounded had been murdered, but Weizsäcker's policy caused concern and perplexity in the Vatican.

In October, an even greater threat arose when the Kappler, the SS–Gestapo chief in the city, demanded 35 kilos of gold otherwise members of the male Jewish population would immediately be deported, which prompted Rome's Grand Rabbi, Israel Zolli, to appeal directly to the pope for help in finding the 15 kilos which the Jews themselves had been unable to assemble.[172] Bernardino Nogara, as director of the ASSS, was designated to find the necessary quantity, presumably from the reserve held in the Vatican vaults, but on 29 September he was informed by Cardinal Maglione that Zolli had told him that various 'Catholic communities', presumably religious houses, had made up the difference.[173]

Two further episodes tested the relationship between the Vatican and Rome's new masters. The first was the Nazi raid on the Rome ghetto in October 1943. The pope has been heavily criticized by some authors for his response to the episode.[174] His response was certainly slow and initially ineffective: in the end, 1,023 were transported to Auschwitz and almost all were gassed.[175] At this point at least, Pius XII was on strong ground, his own ground, vis-à-vis the Germans. As Bishop of Rome he surely had the moral, and to some extent political, authority to defy Hitler. That said, the Vatican's concurrence in Weizäcker's 'softly-softly' policy towards German police action in Rome, does seem to have worked in the longer term. The diplomatic protest of Maglione to the anti-Nazi German ambassador, which implicitly included a threat that the pope would go public if forced to so, seems to have prevented further mass

[171] ADSS, 7, doc. 410, Notes du cardinal Maglione, 20 septembre 1943.

[172] ADSS, 9, doc. 349, Notes de la Secréterie d'Etat, 29 septembre 1943.

[173] ADSS, 9, doc. 353, Le délégué à l'Administration spéciale du Saint Siège Nogara au cardinal Maglione, 29 septembre 1943.

[174] See, for example, Zucotti, *Under His Very Windows*, 156–157.

[175] Zucotti, *Under His Very Windows*, 155–156.

raids.[176] The Germans, including Himmler himself, backed off from a public confrontation with Pius XII.[177]

A further trial came with the Ardeatine massacre of March 1944, when 389 Italian military and civilians, including 79 Jews, were murdered in retaliation for the killing of German troops by a Communist partisan unit, GAP, in Via Rasella.[178] Again, the Vatican's response was slow.[179] It is difficult to know whether the pope was unwilling to call the German bluff, to use the full force of his international authority, which allegedly the Germans feared, to prevent their atrocities, or whether the Vatican was not informed in time to prevent the executions. The Vatican's attitude towards the Italian Armed Resistance was, in any case, extremely diffident. Apart from the fact that the Resistance was dominated by the Communist Party—it controlled two thirds of the partisan bands—it was precisely the fear of the German reprisals on the civilian population for the actions of the partisans which the Church feared.[180] This attitude was common throughout the Italian ecclesiastical hierarchy, even if parochial, especially rural, clergy were often supportive of the Resistance.[181] But the Vatican did not allow those feelings to blind it to the need to have contacts with the Resistance, thus Bernardino Nogara, the Vatican's financial manager, and Mgr Ronca, the rector of the Roman Seminary, acted as its representatives to the Rome Resistance executive, the CLN (Comitato di Liberazione Nazionale), during the German occupation of Rome.[182] In fact, most of the CLN, including leading Communists, were quartered in the Lateran Palace complex, another extraterritorial enclave in Rome, which was effectively run by Ronca.[183]

Nogara liaised with the Rome CLN on the question of the thousands of escaped Allied POWS, Italian Army deserters (including some high-ranking officers), anti-Fascist politicians, Jews, and other civilian refugees who were hidden in monasteries and convents, Vatican extraterritorial properties like the Basilicas of the Lateran, San Paolo, and Santa Maria Maggiore, and even

[176] ADSS, 7, doc. 506, Notes du cardinal Maglione, 16 octobre 1943, where he says he warned the German ambassador that if raids on the ghetto continued, the pope would be forced to protest publicly.

[177] See Ventresca, *Soldier of Christ*, 202–207.

[178] For a detailed account of the Via Rasella operation and its repercussions, see Robert Katz, *Death in Rome*, London, 1967, especially chs 2, 3, and 4.

[179] Katz is extremely critical of the attitude taken by Pius XII towards the Via Rasella operation and the Ardeatine massacre; see Katz, *Death in Rome*, 190–204.

[180] ADSS, 11, doc. 210, Cardinal Maglione au cardinal Schuster, 4 juin 1944, in which he sets out the pope's instructions to bishops and clergy in the difficult times.

[181] See R. N. L. Absalom, *L'Alleanza inattesa. Mondo contadino e prigionieri alleati in fuga in Italia (1943–1945) [A Strange Alliance: Aspects of Escape and Survival in Italy, 1943–1945]*, Florence, 1991, especially 307–308 and 378–390.

[182] 'Morte di Bernardino Nogara', *Corriere della Sera*, 16 November 1958.

[183] See ADSS, 10, doc. 32, Notes de la Secréterie d'Etat, 31 janvier 1944, and doc. 37, Notes de Mgr Ronca, 6 fevriér 1944.

the Vatican itself during the German occupation.[184] None of these places was 100 per cent safe, perhaps not even the Vatican: the latter was bombed on 5 November 1943, almost certainly at the instigation of the Fascists.[185] There were frequent irruptions of Kappler's Gestapo–SS and also the Fascist police into Vatican extraterritorial premises, including the precinct of the abbey of San Paolo fuori le Mura and the Lateran complex.[186] There is ample evidence that Pius XII knew about and indeed authorized the provision of refuges for these people, including the hospitality extended by various ecclesiastics and diplomats in the Vatican itself.[187] Nogara was also responsible for the Vatican's relief operations, organizing food convoys of lorries with Vatican markings from rural areas as far away as Liguria and Tuscany in order to feed the starving Roman population: on occasion these vehicles were bombed or machine-gunned by Allied aircraft.[188] Meanwhile, the Vatican was faced by difficult moments outside of the city, in particular, the bombing of the papal villa of Castel Gandolfo by Allied planes, with substantial loss of life among the refugees sheltering there in February 1944.[189] The Allied liberation of Rome on 6 June 1944 was greeted with enormous relief in the Vatican, but it also brought problems. Now Axis diplomats had to take shelter in the place of their enemies. And Pius XII felt himself obliged to ask that coloured troops in the Allied armies not be allowed to enter Rome, such was the reputation for pillage and rape which had preceded them.[190]

PIUS XII AND DE GAULLE

Following D-Day, June 1944, and the subsequent Allied recapture of Paris in August, the Vatican was faced with a difficult situation in France. Whereas, after September 1943, it recognized Marshal Badoglio and the king as the legitimate, continuing government of Italy but regarded Mussolini's Fascist Social Republic as a child of war and as a 'rebel' government, the reverse was the case in France. After June 1940 Vichy was arguably the legal, legitimate government of France, having inherited its authority from the Third Republic as the result of a vote in the National Assembly, whereas General De Gaulles'

[184] For a full account of this phenomenon, see Riccardi, *L'inverno più lungo*, passim.

[185] Hebblethwaite, *Paul VI*, 192.

[186] Riccardi, *L'inverno più lungo*, ch. VIII.

[187] See, for example, ADSS, 9, doc. 356, Notes de Mgr Montini, 1 octobre 1943, annotated with the words 'Ex. Aud. SS.mi. 1.X.43', which refer to an audience with the pope.

[188] Pollard, *Money*, 195–196.

[189] ADSS, 11, 68, Le délégué apostolique à Washington au cardinal Maglione, 1 mars 1944; see Fogarty, *The Vatican*, 306, for Spellman's public protest against the bombings.

[190] Chadwick, *Britain and the Vatican*, 301.

Free French organization and their National Council were a child of war and in effect 'rebels'. In reality, sometime before the recapture of Paris, the Vatican had been obliged to break with diplomatic convention and establish contact with the Free French.[191] Even so, several serious issues were outstanding between Free France and the Holy See. As Larkin points out, 'the record of senior churchmen during the Occupation was not a heroic one—with certain remarkable exceptions'.[192] In spite of the fact that relations between Vichy and the French hierarchy had not always been good, the Gaullists regarded the French bishops as largely collaborationist and sought to remove twelve of them from their sees.[193]

To make matters worse, even the nuncio, Mgr Valerio Valeri, was regarded as *persona non grata* by the new French government because of his role as nuncio to Vichy. A tussle ensued between De Gaulle and Pius XII as the latter refused to give way over Valeri and the 'delinquent' bishops, indeed a stalemate ensued which lasted until late December 1944. Despite Cardinal Tisserant's pressure on the Secretariat of State in support of De Gaulle's government,[194] it was only at the end of November that Pius very unwillingly agreed to send Valeri on leave and appoint a chargé d'affaires in his place.[195] It was not until on 4 December that the Holy See finally recognized De Gaulle's provisional government.[196] With Valeri no longer acceptable, the post of acting doyen of the diplomatic corps, and therefore the person who would give the annual New Year's Day address on its behalf to the (acting) President of the Republic, General de Gaulle, fell to the Russian ambassador. It was unthinkable that such a thing be allowed to happen and so, against Tardini's better judgement, Mgr Angelo Roncalli was hastily summoned from his obscure but fruitful Turkish posting and despatched to Paris as replacement nuncio. Tardini did not have a very high regard for the diplomatic talents of Roncalli and said as much, a frankness that would come back to haunt him when Roncalli was elected pope, as John XXIII, in 1958.[197] In return, De Gaulle sent Jacques Maritain, a dissident Catholic intellectual (he had written in support of the Republican side in the Spanish Civil War and was author of *Humanisme Integrale*, a 'modernist' tract if ever there was one), as French ambassador to the Holy See. In retrospect, both appointments would prove to be little less than strokes of genius.

[191] Larkin, *Religion, Politics and Preferment*, 184.

[192] Larkin, *Religion, Politics and Preferment*, 174.

[193] Larkin, *Religion, Politics and Preferment*, 187.

[194] See Fouilloux, *Eugène, cardinal Tisserant*, 337–346.

[195] ADSS, 11, doc. 448, Mgr Tardini au nonce en France Valeri, 29 novembre 1944.

[196] ADSS, 11, doc. 456, La Secrétairerie d'État au ministre de France Guérin, 4 décembre 1944.

[197] Hebblethwaite, *John XXIII*, 289–290.

THE PAPACY AND THE ALLIES IN THE LAST YEARS OF THE WAR

Apart from precluding the possibility of papal involvement in a negotiated peace, the Allied policy of 'unconditional surrender' had, from the beginning, given rise to serious concerns in the Secretariat of State about the nature of the proposed post-war settlement. The principal concern was about the future of Germany, the fear that it would be treated harshly, as at Versailles, and that consequently this would lead to yet another major European war, despite Allied claims that unconditional surrender was designed precisely to avoid this outcome by demonstrating to the German people that they had been well and truly defeated and by eliminating the Nazis and removing all traces of militarism in Germany. Thus Pius, in his allocution to the Roman curia of 2 June 1944, just before the Allied liberation of Rome, made some very pointed references precisely to the policies of the Allies. After fairly mild complaints about the Allied air raids on Rome in February and March and about the refusal of the Allies to let him help starving populations, in pontifical vessels, he got down to the meat of the matter. He warned of the dangers of 'total victory' or 'complete destruction' and the dangers of policies which would only result in the 'unfortunate prolongation of the War', in other words, unconditional surrender.[198] According to the pope, 'Today, no less than in the past, it is difficult to apportion blame for war, particularly on peoples as such.'[199] This was a very obvious reference to the unfortunate precedent of the 'War Guilt' clause of the Versailles Treaty of 1919, which had laid the responsibility for causing the First World War squarely on the shoulders of Germany and thus provided a justification for the onerous reparations payments imposed upon her (see Chapter 6). Finally, after admitting the legitimacy of punishing war crimes, he declared:

> angry and vengeful instincts must be subordinated, *quae est inimica consilio*, to the majesty of justice and equanimity. In every war, if one of the belligerents were to succeed in reaching a clear and unequivocal victory, by the sword alone, or with other irresistible means, one could find oneself physically able to dictate a peace which is not equitable but imposed by force.[200]

This was indeed a shot fired across the bows of the Allies and it had its effect. Roosevelt was upset by the speech, as he made clear in a meeting with Mgr Spellman.[201] Thereafter, the US State Department strove to win the pope round

198 ADSS, 11, doc. 205, Pie XII au Cardinaux et prélats de la Curie romaine, 2 juin 1944.

199 ADSS, 11, doc. 205, Pie XII au Cardinaux et prélats de la Curie romaine, 2 juin 1944.

200 ADSS, 11, doc. 205, Pie XII au Cardinaux et prélats de la Curie romaine, 2 juin 1944.

201 ADSS, 11, doc. 256, Le délégué apostolique à Washington Cicognani au cardinal Maglione, 19 juin 1944; and Di Nolfo, *Vaticano e Stati Uniti*, 317. Fogarty, *The Vatican*, 309, implies that the real problem was the Morgenthau Plan, to starve the Germans and reduce Germany to a purely agricultural country.

to the Allied point of view: clearly they were concerned about the impact Pius XII's comments would have on Catholic opinion, especially in America. In a discussion with Mgr Cicognani, apostolic delegate in Washington, Cordell Hull emphasized that the Allies sought a complete victory but that they did not want 'the total destruction of the enemy', rather 'a complete destruction of the Nazi system but not the people'.[202] The president's personal representative to the Pope was despatched to Rome where he was received in audience by Pius XII, his Secretary of State, and Tardini, and on all occasions reiterated the Allies' absolute commitment to unconditional surrender and what it meant.[203] His interlocutors were equally firm in their opposition to it and Pius emphasized the need to distinguish between the Nazis and the Germans: 'A laborious people of 60–70 million souls should be able to become a respected member of the international community when they showed that they had renounced aggression and conquest.'[204]

Myron Taylor returned to the Vatican in November 1944 when he was again at pains to explain to the pope what unconditional surrender did and did not mean:

> Surrender. Unconditional surrender does not mean subjugation and destruction.
> Germany should deliver all rights and powers to the Allies jointly in short and simple terms.
> Signature by authorised German High Command and by the existing German Government. (In case of the existence at the time of a Nazi or quasi-Nazi Government, the signature of a highly-placed civilian would be equally desirable. A military signature would have to be authorised by whatever government was in power at the time).[205]

The pope's reply to Taylor, drawn up by Tardini, was based on 'democratic principles, a rather curious, even cynical, premise given the papacy's history of a notorious diffidence towards the theory and practice of democracy . . . According to Tardini's reasoning, only the people of a democratic country in a referendum could hand to foreigners power over them.'[206] Furthermore, the pope/Tardini argued that:

> The conditions which the victor has prepared for the loser are either just or unjust. In the first case no reason is seen why they cannot be known beforehand; in the second case, it is not seen how they could be approved by the human conscience.[207]

[202] ADSS, 11, doc. 256, Le délégué apostolique a Washington Cicognani au cardinal Maglione, 19 juin 1944.

[203] ADSS, 11, doc. 267, L'ambassadeur Taylor au pape Pie, XII, 29 juin 1944.

[204] As cited in ADSS, 11, doc. 267, L'ambassadeur Taylor au pape Pie, XII, 29 juin 1944.

[205] ADSS, 11, doc. 446, Myron Taylor au Pape Pie XII, 28 novembre 1944.

[206] ADSS, 11, doc. 463, Le pape Pie XII à Myron Taylor, 12 décembre 1944.

[207] ADSS, 11, doc. 463, Le pape Pie XII à Myron Taylor, 12 décembre 1944.

This produced stalemate: neither side would budge from their positions, so the Allies continued with their plans to occupy and disarm Germany and reorganize it regardless of the pope's concerns.

Throughout 1944 and early 1945, the Vatican became increasingly apprehensive about the ultimate consequences of the advance of the Red Army into Eastern and Central Europe, concerns which it communicated to both the American and British representatives and their governments. The future of both the Baltic States and Poland were particular causes of concern, thus, in June 1944, Taylor was to be advised that, 'The Holy See is looking with great concern at the war aims of the Soviet government. The intention of occupying the Baltic States, part of Poland and some Balkan countries would not be according to the Atlantic Charter. . . .'[208] When the Allied plans for post-war Germany, and Europe more generally, gradually became evident, though they were not unexpected, they still caused consternation in the Vatican. The Yalta conference between Churchill, Roosevelt, and Stalin in January 1945, at which the decision to divide Europe into spheres of influence and divide Germany into zones of occupation was confirmed, thus permitting the entry of the Soviets into the heart of Europe, was, for Pius XII, Tardini, and Montini the realization of their worst fears (see Chapter 10).

THE EMERGENCE OF THE UNITED NATIONS AND THE POST-WAR SETTLEMENT

The only seriously reassuring element in the emerging European post-war settlement was the clear commitment of Roosevelt to a continued American world leadership role and, in particular, to a role in Europe after the end of the war. The holding of the founding conference of the United Nations organization in San Francisco in April 1945, and thus the decision to transform the UN from a temporary wartime alliance into a permanent international organization including neutral as well as victor states, but not as yet the vanquished, all seemed to reinforce the impression in the Vatican that Britain, France, and the United States at least were determined to establish a truly new and democratic order in the post-war world, essentially founded upon the Atlantic Charter of 1941. Pius XII acknowledged this in his radio message of Christmas 1944. Commenting on the negotiations which had so far taken place, he offered his support for the decision to establish a 'supreme authority' (presumably the Security Council of the United Nations) whose purpose was to deal with threats of aggression and thus maintain

[208] ADSS, 11, doc. 260, Notes de la Secréterie d'Etat, 21 juin 1944, which were prepared in advance of the Myron Taylor visit.

peace.[209] There is even some evidence that the Vatican considered applying to join the UN but worries about the implications of the Lateran Treaty (which had dissuaded Pius XI from joining the League), the fact that the Vatican could not contribute to any military force, and also concern about hostile American public opinion led to the abandonment of the idea. However, in the late 1940s and early 1950s, the Vatican did join some of the associated organizations of the UN, like the Food and Agriculture Organization, UN High Commission for Refugees, and UN Economic, Social and Cultural Organisation.[210]

Nevertheless, in 1945, there is the sense of the same kind of pessimism for the future as that expressed by the Vatican in the immediate aftermath of the First World War. In the Secretariat of State, there was a very real fear that the peace would be worse than the war.

[209] *Pio XII Discorsi e radiomessaggi*, 20 vols, Milan, 1944, Il radiomessagio natalizio ai popoli del mondo intero, 245.

[210] Carlo-Felice Casula, 'Le segreterie di stato tra le due guerre', in De Rosa and Cracco (eds), *Il Papato e L'Europa*, 493 and 495.

10

Pius XII: Communism and the Cold War

THE VATICAN, THE ALLIES, AND POST-WAR EUROPE

In the thirteen years of 'peace' that were left of Pius XII's pontificate after the end of the war, the chief preoccupation of Vatican diplomacy was the international polarization which took place between the two newly emerged superpowers, the USA and the USSR, East and West, and the consequences which that 'cold war' had for the worldwide Church. In particular, the extension of the Soviet 'sphere of influence' into the centre of Europe, to the Elbe in fact, posed a mortal threat to the Roman Catholic Church in those countries behind the 'Iron Curtain'. The triumph of Communism in China in 1949, and the spread of Communism into the Korean Peninsula and Indochina, were to have similarly catastrophic effects on the nascent churches there. During the rest of Pius XII's pontificate the energies of the men in the Vatican, and consequently the efforts of Vatican diplomacy, were overwhelmingly directed towards combating Communism and seeking to protect the Church as far as possible from the damage inflicted upon it by Communist governments, not only in Europe, but elsewhere too.

The papacy itself had come through the war very well. Its prestige had probably never been higher, thanks to Pius XII's attempts to negotiate peace and his humanitarian efforts on behalf of POWs and civilians alike, despite some lingering suspicion inside the British Foreign Office about the Vatican's 'trimming during the war'.[1] In Italy, the Vatican's work to provision Rome in 1943 and 1944, as well as the hospitality given by religious institutions to thousands of escaped POWs, Jews, and members of the anti-Fascist resistance, earned Pius XII the title of *Defensor Civitatis*, defender of the city of Rome, from its

[1] As quoted in D. Kirby, 'Harry Truman's Religious Legacy: The Holy Alliance, Containment and the Cold War', in D. Kirby (ed.), *Religion and the Cold War*, Basingstoke, 2003, 77–102, 99, n. 31.

grateful citizens.[2] Criticism of his silences during the Holocaust and other fascist genocides was rare, and the writers who were exceptions to this general rule, like Avro Manhattan and Edmond Paris, were dismissed as extreme anti-clericals.[3] Not until 1963, with the publication of Rolf Hochhuth's play, *Der Stellvertreter*, was there a serious debate about Pius XII's wartime role. In some American Jewish circles, Pius XII tended to be seen as an unofficial 'righteous gentile' and some European Jews, like Pinchas Lapide, who actually converted to Christianity, also hailed him as their saviour.[4] A few months after the end of the war, in November 1945, a group of Jews came to visit the pope and express their gratitude for the efforts of Catholics to save members of their race from extermination.[5]

In 1945 the papacy surveyed a shattered Europe, far more physically devastated by the ravages of war than in 1918. Apart from the fact that most countries, east and west, including Italy, had actually been theatres of war for up to six years, most of Europe's great cities, with the exceptions of Lisbon, Madrid, Paris, and Rome, had been devastated by aerial bombardment. The 'reserves', so to speak, of Catholicism now definitely lay elsewhere, in North and South America, above all, in the United States, which would eventually play such a crucial role in the reconstruction of Europe through various forms of relief, and in its defence against the further spread of Communism.

After the First World War Benedict XV had made several appeals to Catholics to help the destitute of Central Europe (see Chapter 2), so, after 1945, the Holy See was heavily involved in humanitarian relief work in shattered Europe. Vatican relief agencies, especially the Pontificia Commissione di Assistenza and Mother Pascalina's 'Magazzino',[6] were employed to help refugees and other displaced persons, particularly in Italy, Austria, and Germany, but also Czechoslovakia, France, and Poland.[7] In the encyclical *Quemadmodum* of January 1946, the pope appealed to Catholics throughout the world to contribute, through their prayers and offerings, towards the relief of suffering in Europe and especially that of destitute children.[8] The

[2] See U. Gentiloni Silveri and M. Carli, *Bombardare Roma: Gli Alleati e la 'citta aperta' (1940–1944)*, Bologna, 2007.

[3] Avro Manhattan, *The Catholic Church against the Twentieth Century*, London, 1947 (Manhattan wrote a dozen books attacking the iniquities of Catholicism), and Edmond Paris, *The Vatican against Europe*, London, 1961.

[4] Lapide, *Three Popes and the Jews*, 34.

[5] *Pio XII Discorsi*, VII, 1945-195-46, Confortatrici parole in risposta all'omaggio riconoscente di ebrei profughi, 29 novembre 1945, 294.

[6] On Mother Pascalina's role, see Schad, *La Signora del Sacro Palazzo*, 142–159.

[7] See, for example, C. Falconi, *Chiesa e organizzazioni cattoliche in Europa*, Milan, 1960; A. Giovagnoli, 'La Pontificia Commissione di Assistenza e gli aiuti americani 1945–48', *Storia Contemporanea*, 5–6 (1978), 1091–1111; and Erwin Gatz, 'Charity and Ecclesiastical Works of Assistance', in H. Jedin, K. Repgen, and J. Dolan (eds), *History of the Church*, vol. X: *The Church in the Modern Age*, London, 1981, 436–459.

[8] Carlen, *Papal Encyclicals*, IV, 105–107.

efforts of Pius XII were strongly supported by Catholics in the New World—the USA, Brazil, Argentina, Mexico, and Canada. The US bishops set up the War Relief Services charity under the aegis of the NCWC and the French hierarchy created its own Secours Catholique. Not surprisingly, according to Gatz, 'The Papal and other Catholic charities depended largely on the generosity of American Catholics after the war, who contributed thirty million dollars over a very short period of time.'[9]

THE COMMUNIST ONSLAUGHT ON THE CHURCH IN EASTERN EUROPE

Though there was to be no formal peace with Germany until reunification in 1990, the three leaders of the Grand Alliance, Churchill, Roosevelt, and Stalin, had effectively settled the boundaries of post-war Europe at Yalta in January 1945. Those of Germany and Poland suffered the most drastic revision, with East Prussia being divided horizontally between the Soviet Union and Poland, and all of German territory east of the Oder–Neisse line being handed over to Poland, which in turn lost a large part of its eastern territories to Belarus and the Ukraine, now formally Soviet Republics with representation at the United Nations. In addition, the Baltic States were definitively incorporated into the Soviet Union. This was reason enough for the Vatican to oppose Yalta. The 'spheres of influence' principle established at Yalta resulted in so many Catholic countries, or ones with substantial Catholic minorities, passing under effective Soviet domination or Communist influence—Poland, Lithuania, Hungary, Czechoslovakia, Yugoslavia, and Romania. In addition, as a result of boundary changes, Poland suffered the permanent loss of the Western Ukraine, with its Latin and Greek Catholic communities handed over to the tender mercies of the Soviets.

Within a few months of the end of the war, there developed in Eastern and South-Eastern Europe the beginnings of what would turn out to be a terrible assault upon the Roman Catholic Church, and other churches, which was part and parcel of the process of 'Sovietization' in those areas. The Church came under attack in the Baltic States, Poland, Czechoslovakia, Hungary, Romania, Bulgaria, Albania, and Yugoslavia. Very similar policies were applied in all these countries, based on the ideology of atheistic materialism and the Soviet experience of three decades of the 'Godless campaigns'. This is hardly surprising since the native Communists who directed the Sovietization campaigns in Eastern Europe—like Boleslav Bierut and Wladislav Gomulka

[9] Gatz, 'Charity', 449.

(Poles), Mátyás Rákosi and Ernő Gerő (Hungarians), Georgi Dimitrov (Bulgarian), Klement Gottwald (Czechoslovak), Josip Tito (Yugoslav), and Walter Ulbricht (German)—were all 'Moscow Communists', that is, they had spent a preparatory exile in Stalin's Russia.[10] But the pace of the campaigns against the Roman Catholic Church (and the other Christian churches) varied from country to country, depending on the speed with which Communist regimes managed to establish and consolidate themselves and the resistance which Church leaders were able to offer.

Broadly speaking, the Catholic Church was not treated too badly in Eastern Europe before 1948 as the Communist regimes built up their power, but in 1948 Moscow pressed those regimes to clamp down on the Church, presumably as a consequence of renewed Stalinist repression in the Soviet Union itself.[11] The ferocity of the persecution of the Catholic Church in the territories now under Communist control also varied geographically: it was at its worst in Albania and at its mildest in the Soviet zone of Germany, what in 1949 became the German Democratic Republic.

For the Communists, the Church was not only a long-standing ideological foe, and one that was explicit and vociferous in its condemnation of Marxism, but an integral part of the 'old regime' which their revolutions were seeking to eliminate once and for all. In Hungary, for instance, the Church had traditionally been closely allied with the Habsburgs: the Primate had some claim to the role of Regent in the absence of the monarch and the Hungarian bishops had seats ex officio in the upper house of Parliament and had thus supported Admiral Horthy's regime between 1919 and 1944 (see Chapter 9). Moreover, the Church was the country's largest landowner, so its wealth and the relatively high standard of living of the parochial clergy by comparison with the mass of population played into the hands of Hungary's new Communist rulers.[12] The institutional position of the Church in other Eastern European countries may not have been as strong as it was in Hungary, or Poland, but it was still one of the most well-organized and influential institutions in civil society, and thus the most likely source of resistance to revolutionary change.

Inevitably, a first major target of the Communists was church schools, which were almost invariably nationalized. Religious instruction was abolished in state schools and sometimes, in even voluntary ones, religious instruction was proscribed for under-18 year olds. In some cases, in a pale imitation of Soviet practices, the new Communist regimes introduced secular rites of passage in competition with, or even in substitution of those of the

[10] See Anne Applebaum, *Iron Curtain: The Crushing of Eastern Europe, 1944–1956*, London, 2012, ch. 3.

[11] Peter C. Kent, *The Lonely Cold War of Pius XII: The Roman Catholic Church and the Division of Europe, 1943–1950*, Montreal and London, 2002, 203 and 218–220.

[12] J. Luxmoore and J. Babuich, *The Vatican and the Red Flag: The Struggle for the Soul of Eastern Europe*, London, 2000, 36.

Church. Thus the *Jugendweihe*, a sort of secular confirmation ceremony, was undergone by most children in East Germany by 1969.[13]

The land reform legislation initiated by the incoming regimes seriously affected the Church, most notably in Hungary. Under this land reform, the Church's holding was reduced from 500,000 to 1,100 hectares, though the State continued to pay a minimum wage to parochial clergy.[14] There was a similar measure in Poland where the Church was left with only 75,000 of the half a million hectares it had originally owned, leaving it dependent upon the offerings of the faithful and State subsidies.[15] The confiscation of the property of monasteries and convents affected the contemplative orders especially badly, because they had little in the way of other income, while non-contemplative religious were driven out of schools, hospitals, and so on, thus depriving them not only of income but also their major vocation: some male and female religious were even forbidden to wear their distinctive dress.[16] In Czechoslovakia in 1950, all male religious orders were completely abolished, leaving only a few convents of nuns,[17] and in Hungary all religious houses were dissolved in 1954, apart from leaving only three to provide teaching in schools.[18] The loss of, especially, landed property and the income derived from it clearly made the Church in Eastern European countries more dependent upon the State, as indeed it was intended to do.

In order to evade legal obligations to an international power centre—the papacy—the Communist governments of Poland, Lithuania, Hungary, and Romania unilaterally abrogated the existing concordats: the government of Czechoslovakia did the same with the *modus vivendi*. In the case of Lithuania, the Soviet Union, into which the Baltic country was finally incorporated in 1945, simply declared that the agreement with the Vatican was null and void, citing as a justification the Holy See's continuing diplomatic relations with the Lithuanian government-in-exile.[19] The case of the Polish concordat was not very different. The Vatican refused to abandon the London-based government instead of the Lublin, Soviet-sponsored government, which was eventually recognized by the Allies.[20] The fact that the Vatican had charged neighbouring German bishops with the administration of Polish sees in Nazi-occupied territories during the war, that it was unwilling to accept the new frontiers with Germany until a definitive peace treaty had been signed, that it refused

[13] Chadwick, *The Christian Church*, 25–28.

[14] Chadwick, *The Christian Church*, 68.

[15] Chadwick, *The Christian Church*, 68.

[16] Chadwick, *The Christian Church*, 29.

[17] Luxmoore and Babuich, *The Vatican*, 66.

[18] Chadwick, *The Christian Church*, 30.

[19] According to Kent, *The Lonely Cold War*, 100, 'In Lithuania, the Catholic Church was at the centre of the resistance movement to Soviet rule which gave Moscow difficulties from 1944 to 1952. Leading bishops, who had ignored a Soviet request to denounce the partisans were arrested. . .'.

[20] Kent, *The Lonely Cold War*, 36–37 and 123.

to appoint permanent, Polish, bishops to sees in former German territory like Breslau (now renamed Wrocław), were used as further excuses by Poland's new rulers to abrogate the 1925 concordat in September 1945.[21]

When the concordats had been abrogated, governments continued to claim the right to vet all episcopal and other higher ecclesiastical appointments. Then the dilemma for the Vatican was whether to acquiesce, and thus implicitly concede this power to the new Communist regimes, or to refuse and be faced by a situation in which episcopal sees were left vacant for an indeterminate period of time. Under Pius XII, the latter was the policy generally followed, but his successor became so concerned about the dangers of a 'withering away' in these countries of the apostolic succession, the guarantee of the sacramental lifeblood of the Catholic Church, that, assisted by Mgr Agostino Casaroli, he would choose to negotiate wherever possible to fill vacant sees.[22]

Despite their conflicts with the Holy See, not all Communist governments were in a hurry to do break relations with it. Preserving diplomatic relations with the Vatican could serve all sorts of purposes, most notably prestige and even, apparently, draping a thin covering of respectability over the new Communist regimes. Thus, when the Vatican and individual states were at constant loggerheads over most aspects of Church–State relations, even when the local Church leader was on trial, as in the case of Archbishop Stepinac in Yugoslavia, a break was avoided. In the latter case, the rupture only happened when Pius bestowed the cardinal's hat on Stepinac in 1952, a move which Tito chose to regard as an insult.[23]

A series of 'show trials' of leading prelates for 'treason' or 'collaborationism' with the former Nazis/fascist rulers of the countries concerned took place in Slovakia, Yugoslavia, Hungary, and Czechoslovakia with the purpose of discrediting the Church and disempowering the Catholic hierarchy there. The first was that of Mgr Tiso, the president of Slovakia, who was tried for collaboration with the policy of the Germans and more Nazi elements of his own party of deporting Slovak Jews to Auschwitz. He was also held to account for atrocities committed by government forces during the Slovak National Rising of 1944. He was inevitably found guilty and hanged on 18 April 1948.[24] There can be little doubt that Tiso was guilty as charged, and that his activities during the war had 'tarnished the image of Catholicism and provided a rich fund for Communist anti-Catholic propaganda'.[25] It is significant that the Vatican was less active in the defence of Tiso than in the trials of other Catholic leaders in Eastern Europe, and it has to be said that Tiso would have been tried and executed even if he not been a priest.

21 See the semi-official book by A. Piekarski, *The Church in Poland*, Warsaw, 1978, 84.

22 Stehle, *The Eastern Policies*, 313–315.

23 Stehle, *The Eastern Policies*, 260.

24 Chadwick, *The Christian Church*, 60–62; and Luxmoore and Babuich, *The Vatican*, 59.

25 Luxmoore and Babuich, *The Vatican*, 35.

Archbishop, later Cardinal, Alois Stepinac of Zagreb was arrested and put on trial in the winter of 1945–6. The situation in Croatia following the victory of Communist leader Tito (Josip Broz) and his partisans was chaotic and violent. It is estimated that 400 to 450 Catholic priests fled with Ustasha forces across the border into Austria, but were returned by US troops, and some were slaughtered; thirty-five Franciscans, members of an order of which some members had participated in the Ustasha genocide of Serbs, were murdered by the partisans, and the Bishop of Dubrovnik was also killed.[26]

Tito introduced the more usual Communist measures against the Church, giving civil marriage priority over the religious ceremony, confiscating Church property, dissolving monasteries and convents, abolishing RI in schools, and so on.[27] All this was accompanied by state propaganda against the Church and trials of other priests and nuns for collaboration with the Ustashe regime.[28]

The trial of Stepinac could be seen merely as one of these, but it became a much larger, public, international affair. The archbishop of Zagreb was much bigger fry for Tito, the impediment to the achievement of some sort of *modus vivendi* between the new Communist Yugoslavia and Croatian Catholicism, because Stepinac steadfastly and publicly opposed the anti-Church measures of Tito's government throughout 1945 and 1946. Another key factor which contributed to the magnification of the trial into a *cause célèbre* and the elevation of Stepinac into a martyr was the reaction of the Vatican. Initially, it had given Tito's request that Stepinac be removed from Zagreb serious attention then it changed its mind and plucked Mgr Joseph Hurley from his remote American bishopric and sent him to Belgrade as *reggente* of the nunciature there.[29] When Stepinac was arrested and tried for treason, collaboration with the Nazis and Ustashe, and for complicity in the forced conversion of Serbs and sentenced to sixteen years forced labour, Hurley used every means possible to make the trial into an international media event—and succeeded.[30]

Archbishop Mindszenty of Esztergom, primate of Hungary, was undoubtedly the most intransigent and dangerous enemy of Rákosi, the Communist who took power in 1948, despite the fact that the election had been won by the conservative Smallholders' Party.[31] Yet Mindszenty had an impeccable anti-Fascist past: made bishop of Veszprém in 1944, he had protested against the shutting of Jews in ghettos and their deportation, and had been imprisoned by the Nazis for his pains.[32] He was appointed primate in October 1945

[26] Chadwick, *The Christian Church*, 64.

[27] See Gallagher, *Vatican Secret Diplomacy*, chs 7 and 8; and Alexander, *Church and State*, 136–146.

[28] Alexander, *Church and State*, 131–136.

[29] Gallagher, *Vatican Secret Diplomacy*, ch. 8.

[30] Gallagher, *Vatican Secret Diplomacy*, 171–181.

[31] Applebaum, *Iron Curtain*, 219–227.

[32] Applebaum, *Iron Curtain*, 281.

and cardinal a year later. He would not compromise with the Communists in order to preserve Church's legal status. So he was tried for spying, treason, and currency manipulation. Tortured and beaten, he signed a confession and was found guilty in 1949. This provoked a massive international outcry, in part orchestrated by the Vatican and the USA, so much so that the UN condemned his trial.[33]

But the trial had its effect. It silenced Mindszenty and, without him, the remaining Hungarian bishops made peace with the regime, though they could not prevent it from dissolving the remaining religious houses. Mindszenty had his moment of triumph when he was released from prison in October 1956 and blessed the Hungarian Revolution. When the uprising was crushed by Soviet tanks in November, he took refuge in the US embassy where he remained, an embarrassing and unwelcome guest, until 1972. Even Archbishop Beran of Prague, who had spent three years in Dachau and other concentration camps for his opposition to the Nazis, was sentenced to sixteen years in prison in 1949.[34] Once again, a national hierarchy had effectively been 'decapitated'.

A particularly sinister and dangerous tactic of Communist governments was to seek to split the Catholic clergy. Associations of priests willing to cooperate with the regime were set up, their members often receiving favours in the form of preferment and administrative positions. Sometimes, they were specifically set up to further Soviet Bloc interests, like the various peace campaigns during the second half of the 1940s and the early years of the 1950s, when the Soviet Union did not as yet have the bomb and therefore was arguably in a weaker strategic position than the West. A classic example was the Hungarian movement of Catholic 'Priests for Peace'.[35] These pro-Communist priests sometimes held seats in parliaments, and in 1958 the Vatican excommunicated three such priests in Hungary.[36] The chief function of the associations was to provide tame priests whom the Communist authorities could insert into positions of power inside the Church in the hope of bringing it more fully under state control. From the Communist point of view, however, these organizations had limited success. In Yugoslavia, they were firmly and effectively contested by the bishops under the leadership of the papal envoy, Mgr Hurley.[37] Elsewhere they remained a thorn in the side of the Vatican. But for Pius XII, however, they raised the terrible spectre of attempts to found schismatic 'national' churches along the same line as those followed by Masaryk in Czechoslovakia a couple of decades earlier

[33] Applebaum, *Iron Curtain*, 282–283.
[34] Luxmoore and Babuich, *The Vatican*, 81–82.
[35] Applebaum, *Iron Curtain*, 287–290.
[36] Chadwick, *The Christian Church*, 36–37.
[37] Gallagher, *Secret Vatican Diplomacy*, 186–189.

(see Chapter 6). Kent has argued that the 1949 'Excommunication decree was prompted by fears of schism in eastern Europe',[38] and even in his last encyclical, *Meminisse Iuvat* of July 1958, Pius warned that 'The Unity of the Church is being attacked by false doctrines and by a variety of insidious stratagems.'[39] Luckily for the Vatican, the Communist regimes in Eastern Europe lacked the bottle, the energy, or the inclination to pursue this policy to its ultimate conclusion, unlike the Chinese Communists in the 1950s with their 'Catholic Patriotic Association'.

THE FATE OF THE GREEK CATHOLIC CHURCHES IN EASTERN EUROPE

The fate of the Greek Catholics in communion with Rome ('Uniats') in the areas conquered by the Red Army was catastrophic. They were forced to cut their ties with Rome and forced back into communion with the Orthodox churches, which pleased the local Orthodox who had always resented the reunions with Rome of the sixteenth century, like that of the Union of Brest-Litovsk of 1596, which the Orthodox claimed had been a 'shotgun marriage' brought about by Habsburg hegemony.[40] For the new Communist regimes, this killed several birds with one stone. It was a divide-and-rule policy, which strengthened the Orthodox, usually national, churches, and therefore strengthened national feeling, while it diminished the influence of Rome, that is, a Western power centre. It also increased ill feeling between Rome and the Orthodox churches, and between their adherents on the ground.

By December 1945, the situation of the Greek Catholic Church in the Western Ukraine or Galicia, the 'Ruthenians', was dire following the Soviet recapture of the region from the Germans and its incorporation into the Ukrainian Soviet Socialist Republic. Pius's encyclical *Orientales Omnes Ecclesias* of that month ostensibly commemorated the 350 years of reunion of Ruthenian Church with Rome, but was laced with fear and foreboding regarding its future.[41]

The Soviets carried out a forcible reunification of the Ruthenian Church with the Ukrainian Orthodox Church, as a way of reintegrating the Galicians into the Ukraine and reducing the influence of Rome. Their 'softening-up' process included the expulsion of the primate Mgr Slipyjy who had succeeded Metropolitan Szeptickyj, from his see of Lvov, and the imprisonment of other bishops and priests.[42] In 1946, in a Soviet-sponsored shotgun marriage, a

[38] Kent, *The Lonely Cold War*, 74.

[39] Carlen, *Papal Encyclicals*, IV, 375.

[40] Carlen, *Papal Encyclicals*, IV, 51–56.

[41] Carlen, *Papal Encyclicals*, IV, 91–103.

[42] Carlen, *Papal Encyclicals*, IV, 97.

hastily summoned clergy synod, the Council of Lvov, declared that the Greek Catholics had been reunited to the Autonomous Orthodox Church of the Ukraine, though many priests refused to comply, and a sort of underground church would remain in existence until the fall of Communism. According to Chadwick, Metropolitan Alexi of Moscow welcomed the news.[43]

A similar fate overtook the Ruthenian Church in the Carpathian region of the south-eastern tip of Czechoslovakia where a 'pseudo-synod' met in Prešov in 1950 and voted for reunification with the Orthodox Church. This was enforced by the Communist Czechoslovak state, which gave all the former church's property to the Orthodox. Those Ruthenian bishops who protested were imprisoned.[44] The 1.5 million Greek Catholics in Transylvania, Romania, also suffered in this way. After the consolidation of Communist power in Romania, following the abdication and exile of King Michael in 1948, a sustained press campaign was mounted against the Vatican, another 'pseudo-synod' met in Cluj at which 423 priests adhered to a reunion with the Romanian Orthodox Church.[45] Patriarch Justinian of Romania also welcomed it. Again, six bishops who refused to abjure their Roman allegiance were imprisoned. And an identical story can be told about the tiny Greek Catholic Church (10,000 souls) in Bulgaria, the 200,000 or so in Hungary, and also those in Poland after 1947.[46]

The Catholic Church in Albania deserves an especial mention. The small, Catholic minority was ferociously persecuted, as was the Orthodox Church. Archbishop Thaci of Scutari died in a camp, four other bishops were shot, and Archbishop Prenushi of Durazzo died serving a twenty-year jail sentence.[47] Places of worship were progressively closed, demolished, or turned to secular uses like museums, cinemas, cafes, and so on. Thus, the Vatican paid the price for allowing the Church in Albania to be dubbed 'Fascist' and friendly to Italy, because of the privileges which it had enjoyed during the Italian occupation of the country from 1939 to 1943.

PIUS XII'S RESPONSE TO PERSECUTION

The Vatican response to the deteriorating situation of the Church in Eastern Europe obviously developed over time, and varied in its application from country to country, but only up to a point: since there was not only a common

[43] Chadwick, *The Christian Church*, 52.

[44] Chadwick, *The Christian Church*, 55–56.

[45] Chadwick, *The Christian Church*, 51.

[46] Chadwick, *The Christian Church*, 59.

[47] Chadwick, *The Christian Church*, 46–48; Luxmoore and Babuich, *The Vatican*, 38, have higher figures.

ideology at work behind the campaigns, but the patterns of harassment and persecution were broadly similar, the Vatican response had equally common elements. Naturally, as long as they were able to remain in post, papal envoys in the capitals of Eastern Europe continually protested against violations of concordats and other agreements, and made efforts, almost always fruitless, to negotiate with incoming Communist regimes.

A key element in the Vatican response to the Communist persecution of the 'Church of Silence' was propagandistic. Pius XII himself regularly and vigorously denounced both Communist ideology and the persecutions in encyclicals, speeches, and radio messages, in which he spelt out the Catholic attitude towards materialistic atheism, Communism, and the persecution of the Church. The encyclical *Summi Maeroris* of July 1950, at the beginning of the Korean War, gives the flavour of the pope's many utterances on the subject:

> Indeed, in not a few countries, falsehood instead of truth has been presented under a certain guise of reasonableness; not love not charity have been fostered but hatred and a blind rivalry are being encouraged; not concord among citizens is exalted, but disturbances and disorder are being provoked. The proletarian classes [cannot] be guided, as they should, towards a better future . . . it is easy to conclude . . . how far removed from peace are those who trample underfoot the sacred rights of the Catholic Church.[48]

Then there was the battle which was conducted on a day-to-day basis through the transmitters of Vatican Radio with its regular programme *La Chiesa del Silenzio* ('The Church of Silence') edited by Jesuits, and, from 1957 onwards, *Radiogiornale* ('Radio News'), which was especially targeted at Eastern Europe.[49] Whether these broadcasts were any more effective than Vatican Radio's broadcasts against National Socialism is hard to tell: presumably the station was jammed behind the Iron Curtain as it had been in Germany and in the territories occupied by the Nazis during the war, though there is evidence that Archbishop Beran of Prague did use Vatican Radio to communicate with his clergy.[50] In 1949, Bishop Hurley, one of the Vatican's greatest 'cold warriors', spoke of the '. . . sepulchral ineptitude and incompetence of Vatican Radio'.[51] But its broadcasts almost certainly had a deeper impact on the peoples of the West.

The Vatican Excommunication of Communists

The most clamorous Vatican response came with the 1 July1949 decree of the Holy Office declaring that it was not lawful for a Roman Catholic to be a member of a Communist Party, to publish or write anything that advocated

[48] Carlen, *Papal Encyclicals*, IV, 171. [49] Bea, *Qui Radio vaticana*, 196.

[50] A. Rhodes, *The Vatican in the Age of the Cold War, 1945–1980*, Norwich, 1992, 118.

[51] As quoted in Gallagher, *Vatican Secret Diplomacy*, 191.

Communism, nor for a priest to administer the sacraments to those who violated the foregoing rules.[52] A further decree of 11 August required special dispensation for 'mixed' marriages between Catholics and Communists, and one in 1950 denied the sacraments to children who joined Communist youth groups.[53] Linked to this was the use of canonical sanctions against those officials in Eastern Europe involved in the arrest and imprisonment of bishops, as in the Consistorial Congregation's 1951 excommunication:

> of all those who violate the Church's rights by bringing a bishop before a secular judge, attacking his person, hampering the exercise of ecclesiastical jurisdiction, plotting against ecclesiastical authorities or occupying a post or function without legitimated appointment.[54]

The Vatican decrees enraged Communist rulers in Eastern Europe, providing them with a pretext to intensify the campaign against the Church. Thus, in Poland, the Communists declared it to be 'an act of aggression against the Polish state'.[55] In Romania, Bishop Augustin Pacha of Timisoara was arrested that same July, tried, and imprisoned for sixteen years; in Hungary Mindszenty's sentence was confirmed by an appeal court; in Bulgaria further measures were taken against religious orders and the Catholic seminary; and in Czechoslovakia the decree was used as an excuse to expel Mgr Verolino, the Vatican chargé d'affaires.[56]

All these measures would probably have been adopted anyway in the fullness of time. Certainly, the campaign against all the Christian churches in Eastern Europe had been stepped up from mid-1948 onwards, as part of a wider renewal of Soviet repression in the wake of the inauguration of Marshall Aid, the Berlin Airlift, and Tito's expulsion from the Comintern.[57] In this regard, it is significant that the trials of both Beran and Mindszenty were initiated before the publication of the excommunication decree. On the other hand, the most severe measures against the Church in Czechoslovakia, including the imprisonment of 1,000 priests and the dissolution of the religious orders, took place *after* the decree, in 1950 and 1951, and thus, 'the Vatican Decree appeared to reaffirm the stereotype—that all Catholics were enemies of Communism'.[58]

The decree had its critics inside the Vatican, first among them Mgr Tardini, who allegedly thought that it had not been preceded with

[52] Luxmoore and Babuich, *The Vatican*, 65–66.

[53] AAS, XXXXI, Serie II, XVI, Schemata, Actio Catholicae in Cecoslovacchia Damnatur, 1 July 1949.

[54] Luxmoore and Babuich, *The Vatican*, 103.

[55] Luxmoore and Babuich, *The Vatican*, 69.

[56] Luxmoore and Babuich, *The Vatican*, 66.

[57] Applebaum, *Iron Curtain*, 269–271; Kent, *The Lonely Cold War*, 73, says that in 1948 Moscow pressed the East European governments to clamp down on the Church.

[58] Luxmoore and Babuich, *The Vatican*, 70–71; and Hebblethwaite, *John XXIII*.

'sufficient psychological preparation'.[59] As both Luxmoore and Babuich, and Hebblethwaite, have argued,[60] the decree was counterproductive. It made life more difficult for Catholics, especially the hierarchy and clergy, in Eastern Europe, and far from dissuading Communist rulers from further repressive measures, as has been seen it provoked them into acts of even greater damage to the Church. Perhaps Pius XII *wanted* more martyrs? He most surely got them. On the eve of the April 1948 elections in Italy, when a Communist–Socialist victory seemed not unlikely, he told the Irish minister to the Holy See that he was prepared to be a martyr himself, to suffer the same fate as his Divine Master and his original successor in the Apostolic See.[61]

But was there an alternative response? It is noticeable that excommunication was never employed against the Nazis in response to their persecution of the Church, either in Germany itself or in the territories which they conquered during the Second World War. Certainly, German children had never been refused the sacraments because they belonged by law to the Hitlerjugend (like Pope Benedict XVI in his youth) or Bund Deutscher Mädel, but in fairness the 1949 decree exempted from excommunication those Catholics 'who joined Communist organisations to save their lives or their job'.[62] The Nazi persecution was in some ways milder and less systematic than that carried out by the Communists after the war—there had been no wholesale dissolutions of religious orders or seizure of their assets, there was no comprehensive nationalization of church property, no unilateral denunciations of the *Reichskonkordat*, and no 'show trials' of Cardinals Bertram, Innitzer, or Faulhaber, though thousands of priests were imprisoned. Perhaps the fundamental difference was ideological: neither National Socialism nor Italian Fascism *openly* and *explicitly* advocated atheistic materialism as a core doctrine.

It is also to be considered whether excommunication was the *right*, most effective response to the Communist onslaught. It was the *comprehensiveness* which was perhaps the mistake. The Polish case perhaps suggests that it would have been better to have dealt with problems on a country-by-country basis, whereas the Holy Office decree poisoned relations with *all* the new Communist states at the same time. The situation in Poland was very different from elsewhere in Eastern Europe. As a result of the Holocaust nearly all the country's 3 million Jews had been exterminated, and the westward shift of its boundaries meant the loss of millions of Orthodox Christians in the Western Ukraine, so that Poland was now an overwhelmingly Catholic

[59] Casula, *Domenico Tardini*, 153–168; and Riccardi, *Il 'Partito Romano'*, 97–98.

[60] Luxmoore and Babuich, *The Vatican*, 69, and Hebblethwaite, *John XXIII*, 225–226.

[61] O. Logan, 'Pius XII: romanità, prophesy and charisma', *Modern Italy: Journal of the Association for the Study of Modern Italy*, 3(2) (November 1998), 237–249.

[62] Luxmoore and Babuich, *The Vatican*, 66.

country (95% of the population was Catholics). Moreover, historically the Church had come to be the very symbol of the nation through all its trials and tribulations: the partitions of the last three decades of the eighteenth century, Russian occupation and oppression from 1814 to 1918, and then the martyrdom of the Second World War.

Despite the increasingly Socialist–Communist character of the new regime of the Polish United Workers Party, it had contributed money to reconstruct churches.[63] The 1949 Holy Office decree produced a strong Communist reaction in Poland; more church property was confiscated and clergy were jailed.[64] Only in 1950 was Cardinal Wyszyński, archbishop of Warsaw and Gniezno, able to reach an agreement with the government. In return for at least passive support by the Church for Communist policies, like the collective farms and the annexation of German lands, the State would permit RI in schools, maintain the faculties of theology in the State universities, preserve the independence of Lublin Catholic University, leave the religious orders alone, and maintain chaplains in the army.[65] The agreement eventually collapsed because the government did not keep its side of the bargain and some clergy spoke out against it. In 1953 Bishop Kaszmarek of Kielce was jailed and Wyszyński protested. He was then put under house arrest in a monastery for three years. By 1954, 2,000 priests were in prison, RI in schools and the theological faculties had been abolished, and more church property seized.[66]

Yet even though the 1956 Soviet invasion of Hungary to crush the revolution there seemed to have ominous, threatening implications for Poland as well, it actually strengthened the position of the Polish Church. As would happen again later under Polish pope Karol Wojtyła, John Paul II, Church and State cooperated to protect Polish independence.[67] Wyszyński was released, and 'Between them, Gomulka and Wyszynski almost certainly saved Poland from the fate of Hungary.'[68] Polish Catholicism remained strong enough to fend off further attempts from the Communist state to restrict it, and later would help sustain the Solidarity movement which, together with John Paul II, would do so much to overthrow Communism completely.[69]

Yet much of what the Poles achieved was done in the teeth of Vatican opposition. Pius XII did not approve of Wyszyński's policy of compromise with Polish Communism and demonstrated this disapproval by the cold reception

[63] Luxmoore and Babuich, *The Vatican*, 95.

[64] Chadwick, *The Christian Church*, 103.

[65] Chadwick, *The Christian Church*, 103.

[66] Chadwick, *The Christian Church*, 104.

[67] Naturally, there is no mention of this by Peikarski, and he describes Wyszyński's period of house arrest as the period when the cardinal 'ceased to perform Church duties. He resumed them towards the end of 1956.' *The Church in Poland*, 98.

[68] Chadwick, *The Christian Church*, 104.

[69] Eric O. Hansom, *The Catholic Church in World Politics*, Princeton, NJ, 1990, ch. 6.

afforded the latter when he visited Rome to receive the red hat in 1954.[70] Even Cardinal Hlond, that most loyal of prelates, who had returned to Poland with 'special powers', supported what would become the Polish hierarchy's policy by suggesting that the Vatican should have played a more subtle game with the new Communist regime.[71] Another East European prelate who found Vatican intransigence unhelpful was Mgr Beran, archbishop of Prague, who 'would have liked to see some kind of Church–State agreement, accepting the communist system in return for a guarantee of church rights'.[72] This was rendered impossible, in part admittedly because of Communist government policy, 'but also by Vatican pressure not to compromise'.[73]

THE PAPACY AND THE 'RATLINES'

Pius XII has been accused by a number of authors of being so obsessed with the Communism peril that he was party to efforts by organizations and individuals close to the Vatican to help Nazi and Ustasha war criminals escape justice by flight to Spain and South America, as part of his response to the Communist takeover of Eastern Europe.[74] These allegations should be seen against the background of Catholic resistance to incoming Communist regimes—in Lithuania, the Ukraine, and Yugoslavia—in the immediate post-war period, which often included former Nazi–fascist elements. In addition, there is some evidence to suggest that the pope believed the post-war threat from Communism could be more permanently contained by the creation of a sort of Catholic 'super-state' in Central Europe like the former Habsburg Empire.[75]

The means which it is alleged were used in the 'Ratlines' were the Pontifical Commission of Assistance, various religious houses in Rome, Latin American ecclesiastics, especially in Argentina, and the so-called Vatican 'Bank', the Istituto per le Opere di Religione. The pope's motives are alleged to have been a belief that helping Ustasha refugees in particular would have been a way to fight against Tito's oppressive Communist regime in Yugoslavia. Almost all

[70] Luxmoore and Babuich, *The Vatican*, 106.

[71] Luxmoore and Babuich, *The Vatican*, 62.

[72] Luxmoore and Babuich, *The Vatican*, 42.

[73] Kent, *The Lonely Cold War*, 232–233.

[74] See, for example, Aarons and Loftus, *Ratlines*, especially chs 1–6; Phayer, *Pius XII, the Holocaust and the Cold War*, ch. 7; Uki Goni, *The Real Odessa: How Peron Brought the War Criminals to Argentina*, London, 2002, chs 7 and 16; and Gerald Steinacher, *Nazis on the Run: How Hitler's Henchmen Fled Justice*, Oxford, 2012, ch. 3.

[75] Phayer, *Pius XII, the Holocaust and the Cold War*, 153–154.

of the war criminals the Vatican is alleged to have helped were Catholic and so compassion towards them was requisite.

There is clear evidence that ecclesiastics in Rome, in particular Bishop Hudal of the German College and priests of the Croatian College of St Jerome, were involved in assisting Nazis and Ustasha to escape justice.[76] The claims about the involvement of the Vatican 'bank', which have been aired on several occasions in recent years, are virtually impossible to verify.[77] They are based on a single US intelligence report which claimed that the Ustasha had sent 200 million dollars to the Vatican which then passed it on to Spain and Argentina.[78] The report has never been verified but, if it is true, then certainly the Vatican possessed the means to channel these funds to Latin America, though probably not via the Vatican 'bank'.[79]

Initially, the Americans and British were extremely critical of the Vatican's stance on these flights of war criminals and said so to both Montini and Tardini.[80] But, in 1947, as the world moved into Cold War 'mode', the Western Allies became less concerned about what was happening in Rome, because they were now 'recycling' their former enemies for their own purposes.[81]

Proving that the pope was complicit in these all activities is difficult. He does, however, seem to have known about the escape of some figures hunted by the Yugoslav authorities, including Bishop Rožman of Ljubljana.[82] Ventresca is undoubtedly right when he says '. . . the story of the ratlines with its many unanswered questions casts a long shadow on Pius XII's otherwise heroic efforts to help rebuild the Continent after a cataclysmic war'.[83]

PIUS XII'S COLD WAR DIPLOMACY

In its battle with Communism, above all else, the Vatican, especially Pius XII, counted on the diplomatic weapons at its disposal, particularly the 'special relationship' with America. In the early years of the Cold War, the Vatican and Washington cooperated closely against Communism. Thus, when Mgr Hurley was despatched to Belgrade as *reggente* of the nunciature in 1945, he established close relations with the American embassy there,

[76] Ventresca, *Soldier of Christ*, 257–258, offers the most carefully considered of all the evaluations of the Vatican 'Ratlines' phenomenon.

[77] See S. E. Eizenstat and W.Z. Slany, *Supplement to the Preliminary Study on US and Allied Efforts to Recover Gold and Other Assets Stolen during World War II*, Washington DC, 1998; and the court case *Alperin v. Vatican Bank*, 2006, US District LEXIS 42902 (N.D. Cal. June 15 2006).

[78] NARA, RG 226, entry 183, box 29, report from Bigelow, October 1946.

[79] See Pollard, *Money*, 197–202.

[80] Ventresca, *Soldier of Christ*, 262–265.

[81] Steinacher, *Nazis on the Run*, ch. 4.

[82] Ventresca, *Soldier of Christ*, 262.

[83] Ventresca, *Soldier of Christ*, 270.

sharing intelligence and even a diplomatic bag.[84] Myron Taylor, now Truman's Personal Representative to the pope, also encouraged the sharing of intelligence between the Vatican and America.[85] Though Hurley had a particularly strong relationship with the US State Department, thanks to his pro-Allied stance throughout the war, and thus the Yugoslavian situation may have been exceptional, it is significant that the Vatican employed another American prelate, Mgr Gerald O'Hara, bishop of Savannah–Atlanta, Georgia, as the *reggente* in the nunciature to Romania. In 1947, Mgr Cicognani, apostolic delegate in Washington, in a conversation with a State Department official claimed that the latter, 'all but stated that we [the United States] were the Church's greatest ally and greatest hope against Communism'.[86]

There was also close cooperation between Washington and Rome over Marshall Aid (the European Recovery Programme) which Myron Taylor persuasively argued for in the Vatican during his visits in 1946 and 1947.[87] According to Kirby, 'Pius XII took care to ensure that 17 different groups of Congressmen and Senators who visited Rome in this period received an audience. Pius XII made an allocution for all these groups.'[88] The State Department was well pleased with the implicit support which the pope gave ERP in these allocutions to the men who would be voting on it. By 1947, the relationship between Truman and Pius XII was 'sealed' by a much-publicized exchange of letters—which was translated into six languages. Through the exchange, according to Kirby, Truman:

> used the spiritual authority of the Pope . . . to dramatise and publicise the Cold War as a Manichean conflict, contributing to the onset and intensification of the Cold War and the shape it assumed, including a commitment to undermine the Soviet Union and roll back communism.[89]

From the point of view of the US administration, the American Church's hard-line anti-Communist stance, exemplified by the speeches and broadcasts of Cardinal Spellman and Bishop Fulton J. Sheen, was even more helpful. In 1947 Truman embarked on an attempt to create a broad 'religious front' against Communism, seeking to unite the Christian denominations against the great enemy. But working with the pope was one thing, trying to enlist him in a 'Holy Alliance' of other Christian leaders and organizations, like the Ecumenical Patriarch and the World Council of Churches, was quite another. As Kirby describes it, Truman 'was happily ignorant of the ancient

[84] Ventresca, *Soldier of Christ*, 118.

[85] Kirby, 'Harry Truman's Religious Legacy', 85.

[86] As quoted in Kirby, 'Harry Truman's Religious Legacy', 120.

[87] Kirby, 'Harry Truman's Religious Legacy', 88.

[88] *Pio XII Discorsi*, XI, 269–271, speech to American Congressmen and Senators, 7 October 1947.

[89] Kirby, 'Harry Truman's Religious Legacy', 93.

animosities and doctrinal conflicts which bitterly divided the Christian churches, never mind one religion from another, which were to deter his grand scheme'.[90]

Thus, Myron Taylor's efforts in both Rome and Geneva were not very fruitful. The World Council of Churches had less reason than the papacy to pursue an anti-Communist line. When the WCC approved the admission of 'Red China' to the UN that arch-cold warrior, Cardinal Spellman, told Madame Chiang Kai-Shek, 'See, here is the organisation which represents practically all the Protestants in the world and this is the way it thinks and acts, undercutting the staunchest foes of Communism',[91] a perfect expression of the symbiosis of Catholic anti-Communism with anti-Protestantism.

The US–Vatican 'special relationship' began to seriously fall apart in 1948, shortly after it achieved its greatest success, the rejection of the Communist–Socialist left in the Italian general elections, a success which was partly financed by the CIA. Apart from the increasing divergence between Vatican and American policies over Palestine, the cooperation in Yugoslavia turned sour. On 28 June 1948, Stalin expelled Tito from the Cominform. As Gallagher explains, 'Tito's expulsion from the Soviet Bloc was the abrupt blow that forced a complete fracture of the US–Vatican interests.'[92] The US State Department switched policy in order exploit the Tito–Stalin dispute for the purposes of splitting the Soviet Bloc, so it was no longer interested in taking a hard-line attitude towards Tito and his campaigns against the Catholic Church in Yugoslavia, and it became less and less sympathetic as persecution of the Church in Eastern Europe intensified in 1948–9.[93] The pope was forced to endure what Peter Kent has described as a 'lonely Cold War'.

Pius XII's position became even lonelier when the Vatican's 'special relationship' with Washington completely collapsed in 1952. Following Myron Taylor's resignation from the post of the president's personal representative to the pope, Truman went for broke, trying to get Congressional backing for the nomination of General Mark Wayne Clark as fully fledged ambassador to the Holy See, and failing. Despite the careful choice of a candidate who was not only a hero of the war in Italy, a Protestant (Episcopalian), and a 33rd Degree Freemason, the proposal aroused a storm of protest in Protestant circles and Clark was forced to withdraw.[94] With this disaster, the diplomatic channel between the White House and the Apostolic Palace came to an end. Truman's

[90] Kirby, 'Harry Truman's Religious Legacy', 92

[91] Archive of the World Council of Churches (henceforth AWCC), D/201.2.2/1, N.H. to Dr Frankelin C. Fry, 17/2/1956.

[92] Gallagher, 'The US and the Vatican in Yugoslavia, 1945–1950', in Kirby (ed.), *Religion and the Cold War*, 133.

[93] Kent, 'The Lonely Cold War', in Kirby (ed.), *Religion and the Cold War*, 68.

[94] Andrea Di Stefano, 'Stati Uniti-Vaticano: Relazioni Politiche e Aspetti Diplomatici, 1952–1984', doctoral thesis, University of Teramo, 2008, 12–16.

successor, Dwight Eisenhower, and his Secretary of State, John Foster Dulles, carefully and repeatedly stated their opposition to sending an envoy to the Vatican. They did, however, flirt with the idea that the ambassador they appointed to the Quirinale in 1954, the Catholic Clare Boothe Luce, might also act as a channel to the Vatican in the pursuit of shared anti-Communist policy.[95] The Vatican response to this idea was firmly but politely negative. It would be another thirty years before diplomatic relations were restored between the Vatican and Washington.

Pius XII's 'holy alliance' with America could not have lasted long anyway. He had reasons not to be too closely associated with American and the West. The very instinct and tradition of Vatican diplomacy going back over a hundred years obliged the Holy See to adopt a policy of impartiality and neutrality which was carried forward by Vatican diplomats like Rampolla del Tindaro, Benedict XV, Gasparri, Pius XI, and Pacelli, both as Secretary of State and as pope, hence the Vatican's careful abstention from involvement in international organizations like the League of Nations and the United Nations. Thus the emergence of NATO in 1949 presented Pius XII with a dilemma: Britain, America, and the other founding members expected and requested the new Italian Republic to join this defensive military alliance and there were many in the Italian political class who wished to do so, though there were also strong minority elements on both left and right who did not.[96] Such was Papa Pacelli's concern for the future of Italy and for the neutrality and safety of the Holy See, that he considered long and hard what option to support as the ruling Christian Democratic Party debated the pros and cons. Above all, despite Pacelli's obvious anti-Communism, he did not wish to be seen as the 'the Chaplain of NATO'. Of course, he would be seen as exactly that in the Soviet Bloc, but he was particularly anxious about the Holy See's reputation among what would become the 'non-aligned nations' of the post-colonial world. In the end, after much soul-searching, he opted for Italian membership, thus guaranteeing the victory of De Gasperi over the neutralists and pacifists inside the Catholic party.[97]

A further problem for Vatican diplomacy during the Cold War was what used to be called simply 'the bomb'. The explosion of the atomic bombs over Hiroshima and then Nagasaki in the summer of 1945 called into question the Roman Catholic Church's time-hallowed concept of a 'just war'. The horrors of conventional warfare between 1939 and 1945, and in particular the wholesale slaughter of civilian populations under the impact of aerial

[95] Di Stefano, 'Stati Uniti-Vaticano', 17–18.

[96] P. Hebblethwaite, 'Pope Pius XII: Chaplain of the Atlantic Alliance?', in C. Duggan and C. Wagstaff (eds), *Italy in the Cold War: Politics, Society and Culture*, Oxford and New York, 1995, 75–75; and J.F. Pollard, 'Il Vaticano e la politica estera Italiana', in Richard J.B. Bosworth and Sergio Romano (eds), *La politica estera italiana, 1860–1985*, Bologna, 1991, 226–268.

[97] Pollard, 'Il Vaticano e la politica estera Italiana', 226–268.

bombardment, had exercised the men in the Vatican and were decried in several of Pius XII's radio messages, though neither side in the conflict had been condemned on the basis of 'just war' doctrine. But how could any war be called 'just' if it involved the deployment of weapons of indiscriminate mass slaughter and destruction on a hitherto unimaginable scale as the use of the atomic bomb? Pius put forth several encyclicals, radio messages, and speeches which devoted attention to the moral implications of the atomic bomb. Representative of these were the encyclicals *Summi Maeroris* of 1950, which called for public prayers for peace during the Korean War,[98] and *Mirabile Illud* in December of the same year, which was inspired by fear of the consequences of an escalation of the same war.[99]

Just a few months before his death, in July 1958, when memories of the Korean War had begun to recede but problems over Berlin once again seemed to threaten the peace, in his encyclical *Meminisse uvat*, which was in fact essentially a call for prayers for the persecuted Church, the pope again reminded the world that 'human ingenuity has devised weapons so powerful that they can ravage and sink into general destruction, not only the vanquished, but the victors with them, and all mankind'.[100]

Yet, for all these dire prophecies, the Holy See did not actually condemn the use of nuclear weapons as immoral during Pius XII's pontificate, presumably because it would have morally 'disarmed' the West in its struggle against Communism.

WESTERN EUROPE AND THE PAPACY

Western Europe presented the Vatican with almost as many problems as the East in the aftermath of the war, and the overriding worry was, as in the East, the threat of Communism. In the 'Atlantic fringe', Portugal, Spain, and Ireland, however, the Vatican had few worries. The dictatorial regimes of Salazar and Franco were an embarrassment to the Western democracies, but the Vatican took a rather different view of them. Indeed, Pius XII continued to nurse a high regard for both 'Catholic' authoritarian regimes, considering their political systems and corporative institutions a possible blueprint for post-Fascist Italy. Certainly, with a few hiccoughs, Church–State relations in the two states were very satisfactory from the point of the Vatican. It was possible to conclude a new concordat with neutral Portugal in 7 May 1940, which brought many benefits to the Church. Catholic religious instruction was reintroduced into state schools, with children opting out if parents so

[98] Carlen, *Papal Encyclicals*, IV, 172.

[99] Carlen, *Papal Encyclicals*, IV, 183.

[100] Carlen, *Papal Encyclicals*, IV, 383.

desired; religious chaplaincies were provided in the armed forces, and other state establishments; churches and seminaries were exempt from taxes; most church property was returned; the Church was granted legal personality and the free exercise of its authority; the civil effects of religious marriage were recognized; and the indissolubility of marriage for Roman Catholics was re-established.[101] Thirty years on from the Republican Revolution, Cardinal Cerejeira was able to express his satisfaction that, through the Concordat, 'the state accepts the Church as it is', while, according to Salazar, the Concordat was an attempt 'to return to the better [sic] tradition and to reintegrate Portugal into the traditional direction of its destiny'.[102] Consequently, Pope Pius XII held Portugal up as a model: 'The Lord has provided the Portuguese nation with an exemplary head of government.'[103]

On the surface, the Vatican' attitude towards Franco's Spain was very like that towards Salazar's Portugal. Nevertheless, it was characterized by tensions of some kind or another for much of Pius XII's pontificate. Franco was touchy about his 'prerogative powers' over the Spanish Church, prerogatives which the Vatican claimed had lapsed with the abdication of Alfonso XIII in 1931 and the subsequent adoption of a Republican constitution. On the other hand, after 1939, Catholicism provided a cloak of legitimacy for Franco's dictatorship. For the Spanish Church, the civil war had been nothing less than a 'crusade' or *Riconquista*. The encomia which not only the Spanish primate, but even Pius XII himself, heaped upon Franco, were rewarded by the granting of a uniquely privileged position to the Church under the Nationalist regime.[104] Catholicism was once again the religion of the State, censorship and the persecution of Protestants were renewed, and marriage was declared indissoluble.[105] Franco repeatedly and insistently stressed that the New Spain was Catholic and he handed over to the Church control of virtually the whole of the educational system, including, effectively, the universities.[106] Thus the Church had become one of the pillars of the Franco regime, cunningly used by the Caudillo as a counterweight to the Falange, Spanish Fascism. Opus Dei, 'the holy mafia' led by Fr Escrivá, now assumed an important role in the regime, its cadres taking positions of power in various ministries and other state institutions, as the 'lay arm' of Catholic influence.[107] There really was not much more that the Vatican could have hoped for from a 'Catholic state'.

Franco's ambiguous relationship with the Axis during the Second World War had precluded the negotiation of a more permanent agreement with

[101] Costa Pinto and Inácia Rezola, 'Political Catholicism', 365; for the text of the Concordat, see Ciprotti and Talamanca, *I Concordati di Pio XII*, 18–35.

[102] Costa Pinto and Inácia Rezola, 'Political Catholicism', 366.

[103] Rita Carvalho, 'Concordata com la Santa Sè', *História*, 31 (1997), 4–15.

[104] M. Gallo, *Spain under Franco: A History*, London, 1973, 89–91 and 132–133.

[105] Gallo, *Spain under Franco*, 155–156.

[106] Gallo, *Spain under Franco*, 132–133.

[107] Gallo, *Spain under Franco*, 228–229.

Spain so, in June 1941, a provisional 'convention' was agreed whereby the Holy See reiterated its position that Franco had not 'inherited' the royal power of nomination, but, on the other hand, conceded a very big role for the Caudillo in practical terms.[108] Further conventions were signed in 1946 and 1950 to regulate other ecclesiastical nominations, seminaries and Catholic universities in Spain, and the military chaplaincies.[109]

The year 1953 was the turning point in the rehabilitation of Franco's Spain after its flirtation with the Axis powers, first during the civil war and then the Second World War. Not only was Spain formally recognized by the USA as 'the sentinel of the West', and given economic and military aid,[110] but the Vatican concluded a concordat, one of the few of Pius XII's reign. Franco was desperate for this recognition and therefore disposed to make considerable concessions. In fact, the Concordat was largely a reiteration on the level of international law of all the privileges which the Spanish Church had lost under the Republic but had already recuperated in practice under the Nationalist regime.[111] The sting in the tail was that Franco, as *de facto* Spanish head of state and therefore heir of the 'Most Catholic Kings', recovered the power to vet episcopal nominations: in the aftermath of the election of Pope Paul VI (Giambattista Montini) and work of the Second Council of the Vatican, and the emergence of Catholic dissent in Spain, this would prove irksome to the Vatican.[112] But for the moment, while Pius was pope and Mgr Ottaviani reigned supreme in the Holy Office, and especially after the 'banishment' of Mgr Montini to Milan in 1954, the situation in Spain was most satisfactory to the men in the Vatican. The Concordat formally restored the position which the Spanish Church had enjoyed under the *ancien régime*, re-establishing 'The rights and prerogatives which belong to it according to the divine law and canon law.'[113] In addition, Spain recognized the 'juridical personality of the Holy See and the State of the Vatican City in international law'. This was a new departure in concordatory negotiations but one repeated in the Colombian Concordat of 1954,[114] which was presumably part of a Vatican campaign to achieve international recognition of the Lateran Pacts in case Italy passed under a Communist regime. But what is unique about the Spanish concordat of 1953, setting it apart from concordats hitherto negotiated, is the commitment made to provide 'a convenient place in the State

[108] Ciprotti and Talamanca, *I Concordati di Pio XII*, 53–54, Art. VI.

[109] Ciprotti and Talamanca, *I Concordati di Pio XII*, 41–46

[110] Carr, *Modern Spain*, 169.

[111] Gallo, *Spain under Franco*, 222–223; for the text of the Spanish concordat, see Ciprotti and Talamanca, *I Concordati di Pio XII*, 52–72.

[112] Ciprotti and Talamanca, *I Concordati di Pio XII*.

[113] Ciprotti and Talamanca, *I Concordati di Pio XII*, 54.

[114] Ciprotti and Talamanca, *I Concordati di Pio XII*, 52 and 104 respectively.

media for exposition and defence of religious truth by priests and religious designated by the appropriate ordinary'.[115]

Ireland was another ideal Catholic state: 95 per cent of its population were practising Catholics.[116] According to Kissane, 'By 1937 the Irish state was the only stable Catholic democracy in the world.'[117] It remained so in the post-war period and was accordingly rewarded with papal benevolence, but given the fact that that it was on the geographical periphery of Europe and of marginal size, it counted for little in the universal Church except in the missionary field where the Irish punched vigorously above their weight. Internally, thanks to the energetic efforts of Archbishop McQuaid, 'the ruler of Catholic Ireland' as he has been called, Ireland was a model Catholic state enforcing papal teaching on such matters as contraception, eugenics, and the woman's place in the home, as well as abjuring state intervention in the social sphere during the attempt to establish a national health service in Ireland in 1952.[118] The Republic of Ireland, as it became in 1949, was also a loyal ally of the Holy See, particularly in the struggles of the Cold War when impoverished Catholic Ireland contributed financially to the anti-Communist campaign in Italy during the crucial 1948 general elections.[119] But even Catholic Ireland could rebel when pushed too far by Vatican diplomatic manoeuvres: when faced by the prospect of having an Italian, Mgr Felici, and not an Irishman, as the replacement for the gentle Pasquale Robinson, the Irish Foreign Ministry firmly resisted and only gave way after a long struggle.[120]

Beyond the Atlantic fringe, however, the Vatican had real worries about the future of the Church in Western Europe and the spread of Communism. The Communist Party was greatly strengthened in all Western European countries after the victory of the Red Army, and the Communists had played a central role in anti-Fascist and anti-Nazi resistance movements in the BENELUX countries, France and Italy. Another consequence of these events was the fact that in France and Italy 'Catholic' political forces, that is, Christian Democratic/Social Parties were forced into government coalitions with the Socialist/Social Democratic and Communist Parties as the price of continuing 'resistance unity'. The Vatican's concerns about the Communist threat inside Western Europe countries inevitably increased with the onset

[115] Ciprotti and Talamanca, *I Concordati di Pio XII*, 65.

[116] Bill Kissane, 'Éamon de Valéra and the Survival of Democracy in Inter-War Ireland', *JCH*, 42(2) (April 2007), 213–226.

[117] Kissane, 'Éamon de Valéra', 20.

[118] See John Cooney, *John Charles McQuaid, Ruler of Catholic Ireland*, Syracuse, NY, 2000, 298–307.

[119] I. Keogh, 'Ireland and the Vatican, 1921–1949', in Kent and Pollard (eds), *Papal Diplomacy*, 98–101.

[120] Keogh, 'Ireland and the Vatican', 98–101.

of the Cold War and the rolling out of the attack on the Church in Eastern Europe.

Germany, of all the Western European countries, presented the Vatican with the most intractable problems in the immediate post-war period. Apart from the territories east of the Oder–Neisse line which were now incorporated into Poland and Russia, there was the fact that what remained was divided into four zones of military occupation—American (Bavaria, Hesse, and Württemberg), British (Schleswig-Holstein, Lower Saxony and North Rhine Westphalia), French (Baden and the Rhine Palatinate), and Russian (Mecklenburg-Vorpommern, Brandenburg, Sachsen-Anhalt, Saxony, and Thuringia). Worse, as a result of the unconditional surrender of the German armed forces in May 1945, and the subsequent arrest and imprisonment of members of Doenitz's 'successor' government, there no longer existed an independent German state. Consequently, Mgr Orsenigo and the apostolic nunciature, now removed to Eichstätt in Bavaria, were left in diplomatic limbo. Orsenigo died in April 1946 and the Vatican sought to re-establish its links with the Catholic hierarchy in the former German Reich and make effective contact with its new military rulers. After three largely abortive missions, including that of Archbishop Chiarlo, the Vatican finally settled on a German-American, Aloisius Joseph Muench, the bishop of Fargo, North Dakota, the son of immigrants, as its representative in Germany.[121] When Muench arrived in Germany in June 1946, as Pius XII's personal choice, he came not only as apostolic visitator, but as liaison between the American Catholic hierarchy and the military administration (like his Jewish and Protestant counterparts), chief of the American chaplains in Germany, and chief of what remained of the Holy See's 'diplomatic mission' as well, a combination of roles which was arduous, conflicting, and aroused some criticism.[122]

After the end of the war, in his speech to the Sacred College on 2 June 1945, Pius launched into a powerful condemnation of National Socialism, quoting from his predecessor's encyclical *Mit brennender Sorge* and claiming that he had repeated the condemnations contained therein during the course of the war.[123] He also reminded his listeners that the Roman Catholic Church had been one of the principal victims of National Socialist persecution, arguing that German Catholics had, at various levels and in various forms, opposed National Socialism—'But not all!'[124] Nevertheless, the Catholic Church had always been seen by the Nazis as

[121] See Colman J. Barry, O.S.B., *American Nuncio: Cardinal Aloisius Muench*, Collegeville, MN, 1969, chs 1 and 2.

[122] Barry, *American Nuncio*, 93.

[123] *Pio XII Discorsi*, VII, 1945–1946, Al sacro collegio nel giorno dell'onomastico di Sua Santità, 2 giugno 1945, 67–78.

[124] *Pio XII Discorsi*, VII, 1945–1946, Al sacro collegio nel giorno dell'onomastico di Sua Santità, 2 giugno 1945, 71.

one of its principal opponents and the Nazis had 'always denounced the Church as the enemy of the German people'.[125] The whole speech reads as both a justification of Vatican policy towards Nazi Germany and a justification of the role played by the Catholic Church throughout the life of the Third Reich. It thus provided the basis for the distinction Pius had drawn between the guilty Nazis and the 'innocent' German people in his 1944 Christmas radio message (see Chapter 9): while accepting the need to punish those guilty of war crimes, he had warned that it was not acceptable to punish 'entire communities'.[126]

In these two speeches, the pope was at one with the feelings of the German bishops and probably the majority of German Caolics. Cardinal Faulhaber of Munich, in a speech of March 1946, seized on the fact that the Holy Father has never talked of the 'collective guilt of the German people' and declared that 'Our nation was not an active community in the fight.'[127] As Kent points out, the German bishops seem to have forgotten their constantly reiterated support for the German war effort,[128] unlike the representatives of the Evangelical Lutheran churches of Germany who, at their meeting in Stuttgart, October 1945, in the presence of foreign representatives, did make a declaration of collective guilt.[129]

Because they felt 'innocent' in the face of the many condemnations of Germany, the German bishops as a whole did not get on easily with the Allied military occupiers. There were many disputes between the latter and bishops, who repeatedly complained about the occupation policies pursued by the Western Allies: the lack of respect shown to the German hierarchy, including the censoring or suppression of pastoral letters by the Americans; arguments over the future of Catholic schools, initially a major source of dispute in Bavaria but which was eventually resolved; and the 'de-Nazification' programme which the bishops felt treated many innocent Catholics unfairly.[130]

In fact, despite the hierarchy's repeated complaints about de-Nazification and its effects on 'innocent' people, and their broader claim that the Nuremberg trials were 'being used to blacken the reputation of the whole German population',[131] the evidence is that the Western Allies at least, quickly abandoned a large-scale purge, for eminently practical reasons.[132] Nevertheless, as Barry states, 'The reaction of German churchmen to the

[125] *Pio XII Discorsi*, VII, 1945–1946, Al sacro collegio nel giorno dell'onomastico di Sua Santità, 2 giugno 1945, 74.

[126] *Pio XII Discorsi*, 1944, Radio messaggio di natale ai popoli del mondo, 248.

[127] Kent, *The Lonely Cold War*, 139.

[128] Kent, *The Lonely Cold War*, 139.

[129] Kent, *The Lonely Cold War*, 139.

[130] Kent, *The Lonely Cold War*, 142–151.

[131] Kent, *The Lonely Cold War*, 148.

[132] Frederick Taylor, *Exorcising Hitler: The Occupation and De-Nazification of Germany*, London, 2011, esp. chs 9–11.

De-Nazification Programme was strongly negative.'[133] And in December 1946, the Catholic hierarchy joined in a public letter by Presiding Bishop Wurm of the Evangelical churches, protesting at the fact that thousands of 'innocent' people were detained.[134]

Pius XII and the Secretariat of State supported the German bishops. Indeed, in the 1946 consistory the pope made three Germans cardinals, a number equal to the French appointees—Saliège of Toulouse, Petit de Julleville of Rouen, and Roques of Rennes—when Germany had traditionally had fewer cardinals than France because of very different religious demographics. Cardinals Von Galen of Münster and Preysing of Berlin could be regarded in some sense as anti-Nazi resisters, though the choice of Frings (Cologne) was necessitated by the great Rhineland archbishopric's established claim on a red hat. Archbishop Muench was, therefore, arguably only carrying out orders by supporting the German bishops in their disputes with the occupying powers. Muench worked like a Trojan at all the tasks imposed upon by the Vatican, including helping coordinate Vatican humanitarian relief. But he was not always wise in his judgements, thus sometimes making a bad situation worse.[135] He faithfully conveyed the unhappiness of the German bishops to the Allies, but his many interventions in de-Nazification proceedings against Catholics and in property disputes between Catholics and returning Jews, suggest that he was naïvely pro-German and that his own feelings reflected the still lingering anti-Semitism among German Catholics, even the bishops, which seem to bear out Susan Brown-Fleming's criticism of his mission in Germany between 1946 and 1950.[136]

The problems faced by the German bishops were at their worst in the Soviet zone. This part of Germany had always had the fewest Catholics—maybe 16 per cent of the population at the most—but now, thanks to the influx of expellees from east of the Oder–Neisse line, this Catholic population was massively swollen and the church hierarchy was at a loss how to cope.[137] And though the Soviets were not especially hard on the Catholic Church in their zone, both Muench and the bishops based outside Soviet zone—Fulda, Osnabruck, and Paderborn—were impeded from visiting the territories of their dioceses which lay in the east. In addition, the territory inside the Soviet zone belonging to the archbishopric of Breslau, now in Poland, was cut off from that see. The Soviets also abolished Catholic (and Protestant) schools, along with RI in state schools.[138]

[133] Barry, *American Nuncio*, 141.

[134] Barry, *American Nuncio*, 142–143.

[135] Barry, *American Nuncio*, 142–143.

[136] S. Brown-Fleming, *The Holocaust and the Catholic Conscience: Cardinal Aloisius Muench and the Guilt Question in Germany*, Notre Dame, IN, 2006, 123–125; in fact, the whole book is extremely critical of Muench for his complaisance towards the Germans and his scarcely veiled anti-Semitism.

[137] Barry, *American Nuncio*, 183–184.

[138] Barry, *American Nuncio*, 183–184.

When the two German republics, the German Federal Republic in the Western zones and the German Democratic Republic in the Soviet zone, were established in 1949, the Vatican refused to accept this division of German, nor the cession of the territories east of the Oder–Neisse line until 1972, on the grounds that these territorial changes had not been sanctioned in a peace treaty. Muench became nuncio to 'Germany', and not to the Federal Republic. In West Germany at least, Catholics were now a more substantial minority than they had been in the pre-war period, they were also, in consequence, more influential in political life, with Konrad Adenauer, the former lord mayor of Cologne, becoming the first post-war chancellor of Germany in 1949. The CDU (Christian Democratic Union) which he led was the first 'ecumenical' political experiment of European Catholics.[139] The merger of the former Zentrum Party with Protestant and non-sectarian elements from other former middle-class and moderate parties was a great success. In coalition with the CSU (Christian Social Union), which was the successor of the former Bavarian People's Party, Adenauer and his successor as leader of the CDU, Ludwig Erhard, ruled Germany until 1968. Pius XII demonstrated his satisfaction with the new Catholic-centred and conservative Germany by giving its first federal president, Theodor Heuss, an especially warm welcome on his state visit to the Vatican in June 1957.[140]

Austria was also briefly divided, like Germany, into zones of influence until the Austrian State Treaty of 1957. The small German-speaking state was seen by the Allies as a kind of 'victim' of Nazi Germany, and when they declared that they regarded the Nazi forcible *Anschluss* with Germany as 'null and void', in the Moscow Declaration of October 1943, and that they intended to re-establish Austria as an independent, sovereign state after the end of the war, the Vatican was delighted.

France was to give particular concern to the Vatican throughout the rest of Pius XII's reign, and the state of the French Church constituted a particular problem for the Holy Office. Yet, despite Tardini's doubts, Roncalli proved an effective choice as nuncio, doing much to deal with the difficult situation in France. His amiability and humility helped smooth over many difficulties with French government. With or without his efforts, the number of 'delinquent', 'Vichyite', bishops to be removed was whittled down to 'seven prelates of France and the Empire', and there the matter was laid to rest.[141] But France remained a big problem. As Roncalli himself said in 1947, 'I am concerned about the practice of religion, the unresolved question of the schools, the lack of clergy and the spread of socialism and communism.'[142] He was really

[139] The next was the fusion in the Christian Democratic Appeal of the Dutch Catholic Party with two Protestant parties in 1976: see Herman Bakvis, *Catholic Power in the Netherlands*, Kingston and Montreal, 1981, 2–3.

[140] TNA/PRO, FCO, 8, Report of the British Minister to the Vatican, Sir Marcus Cheke, 1957.

[141] Hebblethwaite, *John XXIII*, 210.

[142] As quoted in Hebblethwaite, *John XXIII*, 222.

concerned about the *lack* of practice of religion; in the 'secular and indivisible' Republic, the industrial working class had virtually abandoned the Church despite the efforts of ever fewer energetic priests, and the Jocistes. In 1943, Godin and Daniel had published a book with the title *La France, pays de mission?* ('France, mission country?'), setting out the extent of secularization in France.[143] Secularization and the powerful Communist presence between them spawned a third problem, the movement of 'worker-priests'. This experiment had begun with the *mission de France*, established by Cardinal Suhard, archbishop of Paris, in 1941 to meet the challenge of de-Christianization among the working masses.[144] Some priests had then been sent as undercover chaplains to accompany the mass of labourers from the occupied and unoccupied zones of France who went to work in Germany between 1940 and 1944.[145] In the post-war period the *mission de France* put the worker priests on an official footing. But, almost inevitably, so immersed were some of these priest in the working-class/Communist milieu that they began to go astray, some ending up as 'fellow travellers'.[146] The problem reached a pitch in November 1948 when Abbé Boulier publicly announced, in Warsaw of all places, 'Who are the Communists among us? All of us', and Suhard was later forced to denounce 'habitual and close collaboration with Communism among Catholics'.[147] The worker-priest experiment would be effectively closed down after Pius XII died.

The French Church was a problem in other ways too. Such was the ferment of new ideas in French Catholic intellectual circles, especially among theologians, exegetes, and patristic scholars, that to the men in the Vatican the traditional 'elder daughter of the Church' looked more like a proverbial 'enfant terrible' (see Chapter 11).

On the positive side, France in the late 1940s and early 1950s, despite the governmental instability of the Fourth Republic, was an example of 'the triumph of Christian Democracy' in Europe. At the end of the war, bathing in the afterglow of Stalin's victories and their powerful presence in the Maquis, the Parti Communiste Français was very strong politically: in 1945 it won 26 per cent of the parliamentary vote, though in 1946 only 15 per cent. This defeat for the Communists can be attributed to the emergence of a 'Catholic' party. After the retreat into isolation by de Gaulle in 1946, the Mouvement Républicaine Populaire (MRP) became the key element in a succession of coalition governments, bringing men such as Bidault, Schumann, and Monnet to the fore. By winning roughly 25 per cent of the

[143] A. Godin and Y. Daniel, *France: pays de mission?*, Paris, 1950.
[144] Hebblethwaite, *John XXIII*, 215.
[145] Hebblethwaite, *John XXIII*, 215.
[146] Hebblethwaite, *John XXIII*, 215.
[147] As quoted in Hebblethwaite, *John XXIII*, 222.

vote in the first three post-war elections it helped to keep the Communists at bay.[148] While the MRP was undoubtedly a basically 'Catholic' party, it was not a classic case of Christian Democracy as such. Though it contained a hard core of the pre-war Christian Democratic *Démocrates Populaires,* it was also heavily supported by more traditional right-wing Catholic elements, including ex-Vichyites.[149] With the return of the Gaullists to politics in the early 1950s, the MRP's electoral following fell to roughly 11 per cent and it lost its strategic place in parliamentary politics. But the fall of the Fourth Republic and the return to power of De Gaulle in 1958, which inaugurated a new era of political conservatism and stability in France with governments friendly towards the Church, neatly coincided with the death of Pius XII.

Italy, like France, had a difficult political inheritance from the resistance experience. Thanks to its major role in the anti-Fascist resistance and prestige accrued by the Soviet Union out of the military victories from Stalingrad onwards, the Partito Comunista Italiano (Italian Communist Party) was a very powerful force in Italian post-war politics, second only in size to the Parti communiste français (PCF) among European Communist parties. Worse, the Italian Socialist Party (PSI) was still a largely Marxian party in ideology and was closely allied to the Communists.[150] This strong Communist presence in the peninsula, coupled with the fact that Italy had a border with Communist Yugoslavia at Trieste, a city contested between the two countries until 1953, was a source of continual concern in the Secretariat of State. The Church's experience of the Communist predominance in the Resistance had not been a happy one. Twenty priests were murdered by Communist-led partisan groups in the 'Triangle of Death' in Emilia-Romagna between September 1944 and June 1946,[151] and some Communists were complicit in the 'foibe' killings of Italians by Tito's partisans in the border lands between Italy and present-day Slovenia in the same period.[152]

On the other hand, the re-emergence of political Catholicism in the form of the Christian Democratic Party in 1943, under the direction of the 'historic' leader of the Popolari, Alcide De Gasperi, gave cause for optimism for some leading figures in the Vatican, especially Mgr Montini. De Gasperi turned

[148] For the history of the MRP, see J. McMillan, 'France', in T. Buchanan and M. Conway (eds), *Political Catholicism: 1918–1965*, Oxford, 1996, 59–68.

[149] McMillan, 'France', 60.

[150] For a bird's-eye view of politics in Italy from 1945 to 1953, see P. Ginsborg, *Contemporary Italy: Society and Politics, 1943–1988*, London, 1990, chs 3–5.

[151] G. and P. Pisanò, *Il Triangolo della Morte: La Politica della Strage in Emilia durante e dopo la Guerra Civile*, Milan, 1992, 427–428.

[152] Ginsborg, *Contemporary Italy*, 103, and P. Morgan, *The Fall of Mussolini*, Oxford, 2007, 7–8 and 209–210.

out to be an astute, clever politician who successfully navigated Italy through very turbulent waters after he became prime minister in December 1945. First he led the Christian Democrats to victory in the 1946 general elections, in which it won 35 per cent of the vote and became Italy's largest political party. He also manoeuvred carefully through the minefield presented by the referendum on the monarchy which accompanied the elections and coped with the very difficult transition to the republic in its aftermath. Finally, in 1947 he achieved a remarkable hat-trick by ejecting the Communists from government, negotiating a Peace Treaty with the Allies that was rather less harsh than had been expected, and pushing through the Constituent Assembly the inclusion of article 7 in the new Republican constitution, which declared that:

> The State and the Catholic Church are, each in its own order, independent and sovereign. Their relations are regulated by the Lateran Pacts. Modifications of the pacts, which have been accepted by the two sides, do not require a constitutional amendment.[153]

He thus saved the Lateran Pacts from a feared anti-clerical backlash.

Much of the credit for this felicitous insertion of Catholicism into the post-war political settlement can also be attributed to the papacy. It was at the height of its prestige at the end of the war. Pius XII had used his influence in America to soften the terms of the 1947 Peace Treaty and had supported De Gasperi's efforts to get special American aid for war-torn Italy.[154] It was also the Vatican, through the organizations of Catholic Action, that had helped to mobilize the Catholic vote in the 1946 elections.

The next big test for De Gasperi was the 1948 general elections, the first under the newly promulgated Republican constitution. Against the backdrop of the Communist coup which had taken place in Prague, the Italian elections were seen by the Vatican in apocalyptic terms, a choice between 'God or Satan, Christ or Antichrist, civilisation or barbarism, liberty or slavery'.[155] Pius and his collaborators in the Secretariat of State were genuinely afraid that the formidable Communist–Socialist alliance would win in their own backyard, so to speak. So the Vatican pulled out all the stops in the election campaign, mobilizing the Catholic vote through the 'Civic Committees'—an emanation of Gedda's Catholic Action—and utilizing its diplomatic network to raise funds for the cash-strapped Christian Democratic machine, from countries as far apart as Ireland and the USA.[156] De Gasperi's success was also due to a genuine fear on the part of the more 'secularized' elements of

[153] As quoted in Pollard, *Catholicism*, 114.

[154] Pollard, 'Il Vaticano e la politica estera italiana', 226–227.

[155] G. Poggi, 'The Church in Italian Politics', in SJ Woolf (ed.), *The Rebirth of Italy, 1943–1950*, London, 1972, 147.

[156] For an account of the Vatican's role in 1948, see Pollard, *Catholicism*, 115–117.

the Italian middle classes of the consequences of a left-wing victory.[157] The Christian Democrats won 48 per cent of the votes and, thanks to a quirk in the electoral system, an absolute majority of the seats in the lower house, which assured them of control over the Italian Parliament for the next five years and ensured the marginalization of the left forces in Italian politics.

Despite his considerable early success, De Gasperi's relationship with the Vatican was far from being an easy or secure one. The fundamental problem was the deep divisions on political issues, especially those affecting Italy, inside the Roman curia. There was effectively a three-way split—between Ottaviani, the moderate reformers around Montini, with Pius XII and Tardini in the middle.[158] Ottaviani was very powerful because the Holy Office dealt with political questions with doctrinal implications—like the excommunication of those who supported communism. The intransigent, paranoid anti-Communism and Catholic integralism of Ottaviani was widely supported both inside and outside the curia. Leading Vatican and lay personalities like Cardinal Marchetti-Selvaggiani, the pope's vicar for Rome, Mgr Ronca, the rector of the Roman seminary, Mgr Baldelli, the head of ONARMO (Opera Nazionale Assistenza Religiosa e Morale agli Operai) which played a key role in the battle against Communist trade unions, Dr Luigi Gedda, the head of Italian Catholic Action and the Comitati Civici, and Padre Riccardo Lombardo, SJ, whose broadcasting and speechifying activities earned him the nickname of the *il microfono di Dio* ('the microphone of God') all tended towards Ottaviani. In addition, some Vatican diplomats, plus Cardinal Archbishops Siri of Genoa and Ruffini of Palermo were of the same opinion. According to Riccardi, Count Enrico Galeazzi, a personal friend of the pope, and Prince Carlo Pacelli, the pope's nephew, and possibly Suor Pascalina, were close to Ronca and therefore to Ottaviani and the so-called 'Roman party'.[159]

Montini and his allies were democrats, even Christian Democrats, and therefore committed to moderate reformism and, above all, to the political leadership of De Gasperi. Montini's power base lay in his section of the Secretariat of State, Ordinary Affairs, where he dealt mainly with Italy and its bishops. His allies included De Gasperi, Cardinal Tisserant, Padre Cordovano, Master of the Sacred Palaces and 'house theologian', Giulio Veronese, the man who succeeded Gedda as head of ACI in 1952, and many Italian bishops: it is significant that American diplomats believed it was Montini who counted as far as Italy and the bishops were concerned.[160]

Tardini did not share Ottaviani's more right-wing vision of Italy's political future, though, given his wartime experiences, he was not enamoured of the Anglo-Saxon version of democracy. He supported the Christian Democrats

[157] Pollard, *Catholicism*, 117. [158] Riccardi, *Il 'Partito Romano'*, 56.
[159] Riccardi, *Il 'Partito Romano'*, 55–56. [160] Riccardi, *Il 'Partito Romano'*, 39.

but worried about some of their more leftist currents. Above all, Tardini was concerned that the Church should not get too closely involved in Italian politics. Exactly where the pope fitted into this picture is unclear. Similarly, powerful curial cardinals like Pietro Fumasoni Biondi, prefect of Propaganda Fide, are difficult to pigeonhole, even if his concerns about the spread of Communism in Catholic mission fields in emerging nations of Third World, especially in the Far East, would have inclined him to Ottaviani's side. The same could be said of 'vast sectors of Vatican diplomacy, among which was the nuncio in Spain, Mgr Gaetano Cicognani'.[161] Riccardi suggests that confusion was beginning to creep into the everyday functioning of the Roman curia—sometimes the pope would give Tardini and Montini the same tasks.[162] If there was confusion, then this was due in part to the sharply conflicting forces present in the curia. It may also have been due to Pius XII's notorious hesitancy, which suggests that the pope was becoming charismatic rather than political or religious figure.

While Montini may have had his victories in the mid and late 1940s, the influence of his opponents increased in the early 1950s. The high points of their power were reached in 1949, 1952, and 1954. Meanwhile, in Italy the struggle against the Communists and Socialists continued at a variety of different levels, the most important being that of local government. Thus, the municipal elections in Rome in 1952 threw the Vatican into a panic. There was a real fear of a Socialist–Communist victory and Ottaviani and his collaborators persuaded the pope to impose on the Christian Democrats and their leader an alliance with the extreme, neo-Fascist right, a manoeuvre which was nicknamed 'operazione Sturzo' because of the fact that the former *popolare* chief lent the prestige of his support to the gambit.[163] De Gasperi managed to elude this political manoeuvre, which would have damaged the anti-Fascist credentials of his party: he also managed to successfully fight off the threat from the left.[164]

But Pius XII never forgave him for his 'disobedience' and treated the man who had effectively reconstructed Italy, politically and economically, after the disasters of Fascism, and saved her from the threat of a Socialist–Communism takeover, very shabbily.[165] This was not Papa Pacelli's finest hour. He, Ottaviani, Ruffini, and Siri continued to interfere at the highest level in Italian politics through their access to the Christian Democratic Party which, given its rather primitive organizational structures and limited finances, was heavily dependent upon the hierarchical Church and Catholic Action organizations for its electoral strength.[166] Not until the election of John XXIII in

161 Riccardi, *Il 'Partito Romano'*, 48.
162 Riccardi, *Il 'Partito Romano'*, 56.
163 N. Kogan, *A Political History of Italy: The Post-War Years*, New York, 1983, 60–61.
164 Kogan, *A Political History of Italy*, 60–61.
165 Falconi, *The Popes*, 125.
166 J. Pollard, 'Italy', in Buchanan and Conway (eds), *Political Catholicism*, 89–90.

1958 would the Vatican begin to 'disengage' from Italian politics, and then only reluctantly, half-heartedly, and never entirely.

The biggest victory of the 'Roman party' came in 1954 when Montini was effectively banished from the Vatican, being sent to Milan as its archbishop. Ironically, by 1953 he had reached the apogee of his power in the Vatican. The late Derek Worlock, Catholic archbishop of Liverpool, provided a graphic account of Montini's power of attraction in the worldwide Church at that time: 'His anteroom was packed. It was like a dentist's waiting room.'[167] But he turned down the red hat originally assigned to both him and Tardini for the 1953 consistory, presumably because it would have meant leaving the Secretariat of State. Either Tardini or Montini would have had to go, and this would have meant Montini, since Tardini was the senior of the two.

The vultures were already gathering, and 1954 provided them with more than one opportunity to bring about Montini's downfall—the French worker-priest movement, on which he was judged to be 'unsound', was condemned; the 'dissident' Dominican theologians, Congar and Chenu, were disciplined (see Chapter 11), and his disciple Mario Rossi, head of GIAC, was sacked (the commission who dismissed him ominously including Cardinal Pizzardo, one of Montini's mortal enemies).[168] It might be charitable to suggest that Pius XII sent Montini to Milan to get pastoral experience. But his appointment looks too much like a repetition of what had happened to Giacomo Della Chiesa in 1907 (see Chapter 2). Montini did not get the red hat and the red hat was *always* conferred on the archbishop of Milan, Italy's largest and most important diocese.

Falconi claims that, for Pius XII, Italians were a special, 'Levitical people' destined by history to serve the Universal Church and her chief pastor.[169] The insertion of article 7 into the Italian constitution of 1948 and the victory of the Christian Democrats in the same year led to a sort of Catholic 'Triumphalism' in Italy: what Richard Webster described as the 'Papal State of the Twentieth Century'.[170] By this statement he means that, until the mid-1960s, Italian politics and Italian civil society were heavily dominated by the Church and its values, which were propagated and enforced by Christian Democrat-dominated coalition governments and the revivified Catholic movement.[171] In these years, the Catholic subculture battled with a Socialist–Communist subculture for ultimate hegemony in Italy. Neither actually won in the long term, but in the short term the harassment of non-Catholic churches, the enforcement of the ban on divorce and contraception, and the huge influence which the Church even exercised on such things as labour relations certainly gave the impression that papal temporal power had been restored.[172] This Catholic hegemony

[167] As quoted in Hebblethwaite, *Paul VI*, 249–250.

[168] Hebblethwaite, *Paul VI*, 253–254.

[169] Falconi, *The Popes*, 272–273.

[170] Webster, *The Cross and the Fasces*, 214.

[171] Pollard, *Catholicism*, 117–124.

[172] Pollard, *Catholicism*, 118–119.

was unnatural, artificial and short-lived. It was already being undermined before Pius XII's death by the effects of the Italian economic 'miracle' and the impact of Anglo-American cultural influences.[173]

THE BENELUX COUNTRIES AND SWITZERLAND

The achievement of a post-war settlement in Belgium, the Netherlands, and Luxembourg was easier than in France, Germany, or Italy. The system of constitutional, parliamentary monarchy survived the Nazi invasions and the escape of their governments carried on the fight from London. In Belgium, however, there was the very serious problem of King Leopold III who had surrendered Belgian forces to the Germans in May 1940 while his government took ship to Britain. After the war the 'king question' would dominate and destabilize Belgian politics and would only be finally resolved in 1951 when Leopold abdicated and his son Baudouin succeeded him.[174] The Belgian Church was lucky to come out of that prolonged and painful crisis unscathed, in light of the very public moral support which Cardinal Van Roey had given to Leopold during the war.[175] Notwithstanding the ambiguous role which the nuncio to Belgium, Mgr Micara, had also played,[176] after the war cordial relations were resumed between the Vatican and Belgium, as they were also with Luxembourg and the Netherlands.

Unlike in France and Italy, in none of the BENELUX countries did the Communist Party achieve a significant share of the vote in post-war elections. The most it achieved in 1946 was 12.7 per cent in Belgium,[177] in the Netherlands 10.6 per cent,[178] and a similar result in Luxembourg.[179] This poor showing and the steady decline in the Communist vote thereafter made Communist participation in government in the BENELUX countries in the post-war period unnecessary and facilitated the rise of Catholic parties to a dominant position in politics. The Parti Social Chretien/Christelijke Volkspartij (PCC/CVP) won in excess of 40 per cent of the vote in Belgium throughout the 1940s and was thus its largest party,[180] the Chrëschtlech-Sozial Vollekspartei (PCS) in Luxembourg usually attained 50 per cent of the vote in the same period,[181]

[173] Pollard, *Catholicism*, 132–139.

[174] John Fitzmaurice, *The Politics of Belgium: Crisis and Compromise in a Plural Society*, London, 1983, 47–48.

[175] M. de Wilde, *L'Ordre Nouveau*, Paris, 1984, 75.

[176] De Wilde, *L'Ordre Nouveau*, 75.

[177] Fitzmaurice, *The Politics of Belgium*, 248.

[178] Rudy B. Andeweg and Galen A. Irwin, *Dutch Government and Politics*, Basingstoke, 1993, 119.

[179] *La Vie Politique au Grand-Duché de Luxembourg*, Luxemburg, 1995, 13.

[180] Fitzmaurice, *The Politics of Belgium*, 248.

[181] *La Vie Politique*, 13.

and the Katholieke Volkspartij (KVP) in the Netherlands also achieved more than 30 per cent of the vote.[182] Catholic parties participated in the governments of those countries throughout the 1940s and 1950s and frequently provided the prime minister. Thus the Vatican could feel confident that the position of the Church and Catholics was assured in the BENELUX countries after 1945, and that the danger of Communism was much less serious there than in their bigger neighbours.

THE PAPACY AND EUROPEAN INTEGRATION

The papal response to the emergence of such supranational European organizations as the abortive European Defence Community (EDC) of 1954, The European Coal and Steel Community in 1955, EURATOM in 1957, and the European Economic Community (EEC) of 1958, which all took place during Pius XII's reign, should be regarded as part and parcel of the Vatican's Cold War diplomacy. Pius undoubtedly regretted the fact that the moves towards European integration reflected, and arguably reinforced, the division of Europe created by Yalta. His anguish about Yalta is expressed obliquely in his encyclical on St Benedict, *Fulgens Radiator*, of March 1947. There the pope stressed that the monastic order which Benedict founded had helped the spread of Catholic Christianity after the fall of the Roman Empire, particularly in the East, '. . . not a few Slav nations also rejoice in these monks as their Apostles and consider them as their glory and the illustrious authors of their civilisation'.[183]

Pius made the further point that Benedictine monasteries brought the material benefits of improved animal husbandry, agriculture, and building methods to vast areas of European Christendom.[184] This was especially true in the countries of 'the Six'—France, Germany, Italy, Belgium, the Netherlands, and Luxembourg—around which the various European supranational institutions were built in the early years. It is no coincidence that all of these countries were ruled by Christian Democrats, albeit in coalition with other parties, which was a very positive development for the Vatican. Consequently, most of the 'fathers of Europe'—like Jean Monnet and Robert Schuman (France), Joseph Beck (Luxembourg), Konrad Adenauer (Germany), and Alcide De Gasperi (Italy)—were Christian Democrats and Catholics and were inspired to some extent by a vision of a renewed Christian polity. According to O. Hansom, 'The old medieval vision of a United Europe advocated by the Christian Democrats, seemed attractive to post-war Catholics who had

182 Andeweg and Irwin, *Dutch Government*, 115.

183 Carlen, *Papal Encyclicals*, IV, 116.

184 Carlen, *Papal Encyclicals*, IV, 116.

suffered two global wars within three decades.'[185] R. Vinen argued that, 'some began to feel that Europe was being built under the aegis of the Catholic international',[186] while others, like the leaders of the British Protestant Truth Society, have always believed that European integration is a 'Vatican plot'.[187] James McMillan says that Robert Schuman 'epitomised the European ideal in his own person, viewing it as a logical extension of his own commitment to a Christian civilisation which was threatened by Soviet domination and Communist subversion'.[188] Schuman was beatified in 2011 and may thus, very appropriately, be regarded, along with St Benedict, as one of the patron 'saints' of Europe.

The Vatican undoubtedly saw in the emerging European integration movement a major bulwark of Christian (albeit now only Western) Europe against Communism. Though initially it only very quietly and inconspicuously encouraged the efforts being made in this direction, in February 1948 it made a more public appeal for 'the great nations of the continent' to form 'a larger political association'.[189] Three months later, Pius XII sent a 'special representative' to the Congress (Council) of Europe meeting held in The Hague at which were represented various Europeanist organizations, including Churchill's United Europe Committee. Thus the Holy See was at the founding meeting of the Council of Europe and its various agencies, even though it did not join them. In September 1948 the authoritative Jesuit organ, *La Civiltà Cattolica* published two articles by Fr Brucculieri, SJ, hitherto a fan of Fascist corporatism, strongly supporting moves towards European integration.[190]

In June 1950, at the height of the controversy over the European Defence Union project, the French cardinals and bishops publicly 'called upon all Catholics to interest themselves in, and work for, European integration', thus making it clear that the Church as a whole was in support of it.[191] As the European project neared realization in 1957 with the Venice conference to create the EEC, the Vatican gave its official blessing. According to the British Minister to the Vatican Sir Marcus Cheke:

> Pius . . . missed no opportunity of advertising his sympathy with the cause of a United Europe notably in his address to the Members of the Congress of Europe in June, to Parliamentarians of the Coal and Steel Community in November, and his speech to President Heuss (of Germany) in the same month.[192]

[185] Hansom, *The Catholic Church in World Politics*, 139.

[186] R. Vinen, *A History in Fragments: Europe in the Twentieth Century*, London, 2000, 359.

[187] See Protestant Truth Society, *New Holy Roman Empire*, London, 1993.

[188] McMillan, 'France', 63.

[189] W. Kaiser, *Christian Democracy and the Origins of the European Union*, Cambridge, 2007, 181.

[190] *LaCC*, 'Per una migliore domani dell'Europa', 99, III, 1948, 32557, 449–462 and 2358, 602–612.

[191] *LaCC* 180–181.

[192] TNA/PRO, FCO, British Minister's Report, 1957, 8.

The Europe that emerged in late 1950s was probably not Catholic enough for Pius XII, too prey to dangerous Protestant influences from Germany and the Netherlands. It was also too much of an *economic* project, and thus prey to the deleterious moral influences of American capitalism; it simply did not have enough 'soul'. But while Pius almost certainly deplored all these dangerous tendencies, and the indisputable fact that it *did* reinforce Yalta, its great virtue was that, with US military backing, it undoubtedly provided another line of defence for what remained of Western European civilization, and therefore the Catholic Church, against the expansion of the Communist Bloc.

PIUS XII AND THE AMERICAS

America, North and South, was the only continent which had not been a major source of concern to the papacy during the course of the Second World War, primarily, of course, because there had been virtually no fighting in the Western hemisphere. The USA had, in many ways, been a great source of support, moral and material, to the papacy, and in consequence the links between the Holy See and both the American government and the American Church had been greatly strengthened. But even though, in the new situation presented by the advance of Communism in Europe and Asia, and the advent of the Cold War, Papa Pacelli had inevitably looked to the USA as the ultimate bulwark against a further expansion, there were aspects of the American way of life which he deplored. In one of the first encyclicals of his pontificate, *Sertum Laetititae* of November 1939, which was to celebrate the 150th anniversary of the establishment of the hierarchy in the USA, and therefore extolled the progress Catholicism had made, he had not failed to draw attention to peculiarly American evils.[193] The subtext of much of the encyclical is a warning against the dangers of the emphasis on individualism and *material* success, what is often called the 'American dream'. In consequence, Pius provided a catalogue of what he defines as 'American Problems':

> Thence there arise immoderate and blind egoists, that thirst for pleasure, the vice of drunkenness, immodesty and costly styles in dress, the prevalence of crime even among minors, the lust for power, neglect of the poor, base craving for ill-gotten wealth, the flight from the land, the levity of entering into marriage, divorce, the break-up of the family, the cooling of mutual affection between parents and children, birth control, the enfeeblement of the race, the weakening of respect for authority, or obsequiousness, neglect of one's duty toward one's country and toward mankind.[194]

[193] Carlen, *Papal Encyclicals*, IV, 23–30.

[194] Carlen, *Papal Encyclicals*, IV, 26.

This was a terrible indictment, even if the Second World War would suggest that Americans were not guilty of 'neglect of one's duty toward one's country and toward mankind'.

Under a further list of 'American Problems (continued) Social Problems', Pius made particular mention of 'Justice and Wages' of unemployment in the USA:

> We deeply lament the lot of those—and their number in the United States is large indeed—who though robust, capable and willing, cannot have the work for which they are anxiously searching.[195]

He further hinted that freedom to form and belong to trade unions was not entirely guaranteed there.[196] But he ended on a positive note, praising the recognition by some Americans of the merits of the social encyclicals of both Leo XIII and Pius XI and implicitly acknowledging the importance of Roosevelt's New Deal policies in his reference to 'U.S. and Social Reconstruction'.[197] Pius would have reason to lament the extension of 'American problems' to Europe, and even to Italy, in the 1950s as a result of the impact of a post-war cultural 'invasion'.[198]

As far as the people of Latin America were concerned, he had kept in touch with them throughout the war by means of radio broadcasts,[199] building on his visits—to Brazil, Argentina, and Uruguay during the late 1930s (see Chapter 7). After the war, Latin America seemed to present fewer of the problems which had so worried the Roman curia during the 1920s and 1930s. Now, the Holy See had diplomatic relations with nineteen out of the twenty southern and central American independent states—Mexico was the great absentee. But even the Mexican situation was a vast improvement on what it had been in 1920s and 1930s. The worst of the persecution was over: Mgr Piani was able to visit Mexico as Apostolic Visitor in 1948, and in 1951 he was able to return as Apostolic Delegate and stay until 1956.

Elsewhere, while political instability continued, there were no recurrences of the Church–State disputes of the interwar period. In the case of Haiti and the Dominican Republic, Church–State relations were further improved by concordats concluded in 1946 and 1953 respectively. There were also encouraging signs of new life at the level of the apostolate of the laity. According to Dussell, '. . . the awakening of the Catholic laity began in most countries of Latin America in about 1930'.[200] Consequently, by the 1950s Catholic Action was flourishing in Argentina, Costa Rica, Bolivia, Peru, and Uruguay, Catholic trade unions were being built up, and political parties of

[195] Carlen, *Papal Encyclicals*, IV, 29.

[196] Carlen, *Papal Encyclicals*, IV, 29.

[197] Carlen, *Papal Encyclicals*, IV, 29.

[198] See Pollard, *Catholicism*, 134–137.

[199] See various speeches in *Pio XII Discorsi*, VII–XX.

[200] E. Dussell, *A History of the Church in Latin America: Colonialism to Liberalism, 1492–1979*, Grand Rapids, MI, 1981, 115.

a Christian Democratic inspiration had emerged in Argentina, Brazil, and Peru.[201] Catholic universities played an important role in the training of the leadership cadres of these movements, eight—Lima (1942), Medellin (1945), Rio de Janeiro and Sao Paulo (1947), Porto Alegre (1950), Campinas and Quito (1956)—being established during Pius XII's pontificate, a remarkable achievement.[202] One of the most important characteristics of post-war Latin American Catholicism was a flowering of its intellectual life, ecclesiastical and lay, even if it owed much to European influences.[203] These developments, together, would ultimately help to give birth to the 'Liberation Theology' movement of the 1970s.

In the meantime, while Catholicism in the various Latin American states faced difficulties peculiar to those states, there were certain common challenges, most notably Communism and Protestantism. The fear of Communism was not alarmist. It was establishing itself among the industrial proletariat in the most economically developed states. The rural, agrarian, guerrilla movements would begin to develop later. The underlying danger was the continuing association between Church and local, especially landed, elites, and with some dictatorial and oppressive regimes. Financed by generous support from the USA, Protestant missionary organizations were already at work in Latin America. The Pentecostalists had made the most spectacular headway, especially in Argentina, Brazil, and Chile, but the Baptists, Bible Societies, Methodists, Presbyterians, and Seventh-Day Adventists, who were longer established, were also having success.[204]

The Vatican had a particular concern for Latin America at this time, even though Pius XII did not publish an encyclical on it. His cardinalatial creations represent a clear shift away from Europe towards America (and, to a much lesser extent, Asia). One of the clearest manifestations of his concern for the Americas is to be found in his appointments to the Sacred College. In North America he created six cardinals rather than his predecessor's four—Spellman of New York, Stritch of Chicago, and McIntyre of Los Angeles, plus Glennon of St Louis, McGuigan of Toronto, and Mooney of Detroit—in places which, previously, been not been 'cardinalatial sees'. In Latin America, apart from the usual cardinalatial sees of Buenos Aires and Rio di Janeiro, he set a precedent by raising the archbishops of San Paulo and San Salvador de Bahia (Brazil), Quito (Ecuador), Havana (Cuba), Lima (Peru), and Santiago (Chile) to the sacred purple.[205]

[201] Dussell, *A History of the Church*, 115.
[202] Dussell, *A History of the Church*, 108.
[203] Dussell, *A History of the Church*, 108, 111–113.
[204] Dussell, *A History of the Church*, 118.
[205] Dussell, *A History of the Church*, 109–110.

Cardinals nominated by continent of birth, 1914–58

Pope	Europe	Of whom in Italy	N. America	LA	Africa	Asia	Oceania	Total of Europeans
Benedict XV	31	18	3	0	0	0	0	97%
Pius XI	69	44	4	2	0	1	0	91%
Pius XII	36	13	6	9	1	3	1	64%

Taken from Graziano, *Il secolo cattolico*, 61

One of the most important events in the history of Latin American Catholicism was the meeting of CELAM, the General Conference of the Latin American Episcopacy in Rio de Janeiro, in 1955. Rome took it most seriously, sending Cardinal Adeodato Piazza, formerly Patriarch of Venice and now Prefect of the Congregation of Bishops, to chair some of the sessions and to convey a message to the assembled bishops.[206] Piazza identified two key problems facing Latin American Catholicism:

> I believe at this point it is well to note a serious problem which exists in all our countries, namely, the question of the conversion and Christian formation of the Indians and simultaneously of the coloured peoples. In the urban centres, where local wealth contributes to a prosperity 'whose appearance is materialistic, hedonistic and almost pagan', Christianity has been reduced to the formalism of good customs rather than something deeply felt.[207]

In his speech, Pius XII largely seconded Cardinal Piazza's sentiments. In the following decades Latin America would present huge problems to the papacy, as it would undermine efforts to meet the threats from Communism and Protestantism and carry out the Church's evangelistic mission.

PIUS XII, DECOLONIZATION, AND THE EMERGENCE OF THE NON-ALIGNED MOVEMENT

While the pope himself made no public statements about the 'colonial question', through the pages of *La Civiltà Cattolica* the Vatican made its position fairly clear in the late 1940s. In a series of articles on the transition from the

[206] *Pio XII Discorsi*, XVII, 1955–6, Per il Convegno dei Presuli dell'America Latina in Rio de Janiero, 29 giugno 1955, 594–606.

[207] As cited in *Pio XII Discorsi*, XVII, 1955–6, Per il Convegno dei Presuli dell'America Latina in Rio de Janiero, 29 giugno 1955, 114.

mandate system of the League of Nations to the trusteeship system of the United Nations, Fr Antonio Messineo, SJ, who was held in high esteem in the Vatican, strongly supported the trusteeship system.[208] In fact, he urged its extension from the colonies of the vanquished of the First World War (Germany and the Ottoman Empire) and those of the Second (Italy and Japan) to *all* the colonies of all the colonial powers to promote 'the political, economic, social and educational progress' of the colonial peoples as a prelude to decolonization.[209] While praising the United States for its efforts to insert into the United Nations covenant provision for a permanent international agency to scrutinize the colonial administration of the powers, he lambasted Britain and France, and to a lesser extent Belgium and the Netherlands, for their equally energetic, and ultimately successful, efforts to prevent such a development.[210] He concluded by arguing that the trusteeship system was effectively being used against Italy and Japan and expressed pessimism about the likely success of the arrangement.[211] Though he castigated the British and French for their 'colonial egoism',[212] he said nothing about the crimes that had been committed by the Italians or Japanese in their colonies. In this, he reflected the innate anti-British and anti-French prejudices of an overwhelmingly Italian Roman curia.

In practice, the Vatican was much more tactful and diplomatic than Fr Messineo in dealing with questions of colonial policy and decolonization during Pius XII's reign. Thus, as late as 1953 a convention was concluded with the Brussels government regarding the Belgian Congo, granting tax exemptions to the Church in the colony in return for Belgian government involvement in the erection of dioceses and a say in the appointment of bishops (mainly vicars apostolic).[213] All told, these arrangements constituted a very cosy Church–State relationship at the colonial level in which the 'particular services rendered by Belgium to Catholic missions in the Congo' were matched by 'the contribution of the missionaries to the promotion of the work of civilising' the local inhabitants.[214] In these circumstances, it is not surprising that both sides agreed that their agreement should 'remain strictly secret'.[215]

The pope was also initially very timid about supporting the aspirations towards independence of colonial peoples, particularly where violence was involved, and condemning colonial powers' repression of the same, like the French in Indochina, the Dutch in their East Indian Empire, and the British

[208] LaCC, anno 99, vol. IV, 18 December 1948, 2364, 583–585.
[209] LaCC, anno 99, vol. IV, 18 December 1948, 2364, 588.
[210] LaCC, anno 99, vol. IV, 18 December 1948, 2364, 586.
[211] LaCC, anno 99, vol. IV, 18 December 1948, 2364, 591–592.
[212] LaCC, anno 99, vol. IV, 18 December 1948, 2364, 585.
[213] Ciprotti and Talamanca, *I Concordati di Pio XII*, 5–8.
[214] Ciprotti and Talamanca, *I Concordati di Pio XII*, 7.
[215] Ciprotti and Talamanca, *I Concordati di Pio XII*, 6.

in Kenya and the Gold Coast. One factor was undoubtedly worries about the powerful role played by Communist parties in colonial liberation movements in Indochina, what became Indonesia, and also in the British protected states of Malaya.[216] In July 1950, a Vatican decree excommunicated 'Catholics who collaborated with Communists in Third-World anti-colonial movements.'[217] This had a particular resonance in the situation in Vietnam, and other parts of Indochina where Communist Ho Chi Minh and the Viet Cong were engaged in a national liberation struggle against the French colonial rulers. Thanks to the French colonial presence, Catholic missions had been strongly established in Indochina before the Japanese invasion in 1942. A network of sixteen apostolic vicariates covered Vietnam, with half a dozen more in Cambodia and Laos.[218] The Catholics, who comprised over 5 per cent of the population, were largely concentrated in the north and most tended to oppose Ho Chi Minh's national liberation struggle against the French precisely on the grounds that he and his supporters were Communists.[219] When the country was divided along the '17th parallel' in 1954, there was a large migration of Catholics from north to south, led by their bishops.[220]

Despite problems like these, after the Second World War the papacy came to accept decolonization as natural and inevitable. Even where there were wars, the Holy See never took the side of the colonial power and never condemned rebellions. But its policy evolved slowly. Whereas, in an address to the 1948 Semaine Sociale at Lyons, Pius declared that 'Changes, developments are coming overseas and they may be accompanied by violence etc., but Europe must use its influence to help them', in his Christmas message of 1954 he claimed that 'The explosive form some campaigns for and processes of independence are taking are partly the fault of the bad example set by Europe . . .', and a year later he stated emphatically that 'A just and progressive liberty should not be refused and it should not be impeded.'[221]

As with the European 'successor states' in 1919, the Vatican was quick to establish relations with newly independent states almost as soon as they achieved nationhood: Egypt, 1947 (strictly speaking it had been independent since the 1920s but subject to British neocolonial control throughout the Second World War), Lebanon, which achieved independence from France in 1947, and India, which won its freedom from Britain in 1947. Indonesia was a rather different story: it was only recognized by the Holy See in 1950, after fighting two wars of independence against the Dutch colonial power. Rather surprisingly, the Philippines, a largely Catholic country which was granted

[216] See Giovagnoli's comments on Pius XII and decolonization; and also C. Alix, 'Le Vatican et la décolonisation', in M. Merle (ed.), *Les Eglises chrétiennes et la décolonisation*, Paris, 1967, 20.

[217] Luxmoore and Babuich, *The Vatican*, 66.

[218] See *Annuario Pontificio*, 1948, 1101.

[219] ODCC, 1696.

[220] ODCC, 1696.

[221] As quoted in Alix, 'Le Vatican et la décolonisation', 117–112.

independence by the USA in 1946, only established relations with the Vatican in 1951. Even two overwhelmingly Muslim countries, Iran and Syria, though with small but significant Christian minorities, established relations with the Vatican in 1951 and 1953. This suggests that relations with the Vatican were still sought by newly independent states as a means of consolidating their legitimacy.

THE RISE OF COMMUNISM IN ASIA

Events in Korea and China in the late forties and early fifties constituted, in effect, cases of decolonization given that Japan had conquered and ruled the Korean Peninsula as a colony and that the triumph of the Communists marked the end of European, American, and Japanese quasi-colonialism in China. Their takeover meant the final dismantling of the 'unequal treaties' and thus the end of foreign possessions in ports like Canton, Shanghai, and so on. After 1949, only British Hong Kong and Portuguese Macau remained. But the spread of Communism into the Far East, where China was the first country to fall to a Communist victory in 1949, followed by Korea, also signalled an extension of the persecution which the Church faced in Eastern Europe.

During the early part of Pius XII's reign, the Vatican had moved both to strengthen its relations with the Nationalist authorities and construct a more clearly indigenous local church. Following the Chinese decision to establish relations with the Holy See (see Chapter 8), the first ambassador, Cheong Kang Sié, presented his credentials at the Vatican on 25 March 1943. Three and a half years later, the first Apostolic Nuncio to China, Mgr Antonio Riberi, was accredited to the government in Nanking. In the same year, by the apostolic constitution *Quotidie Nos*, a Chinese ecclesiastical hierarchy was established and China also received its first red hat, given to Thomas Tian Gengxin, archbishop of Peking. But it was all too late. In 1949, Mao Tse-Tung led the Chinese Communist Party to power by capturing Peking and proclaiming the People's Republic of China.

The Roman Catholic Church had long seemed to the Chinese Communists to be the ally of Chiang Kai-shek and his Nationalist forces or, even worse, the agents of the foreign countries which had bullied China since the mid-nineteenth century. Moreover, the Vatican was seen to be a close ally of US imperialism and Pius XII was well known for his strongly anti-Communist position.[222] The bulk of the clergy in China were still missionaries, drawn largely from those countries which had imposed the unequal treaties. The year

[222] Leung, *Sino-Vatican Relations*, 80.

1949 was also, unfortunately, the one in which the Holy Office chose to publish its decree against Communism. As a result, Chinese Christians were attacked as 'counter-revolutionaries' and Catholics were no exception. The Communists demanded that the Chinese Catholic Church, which had roughly 3.5 million members in 1949, should be become, like the other Christian religions in China, independent of foreign influence, control, and financial support.[223]

Riberi's nunciature to China was short-lived. In April 1949, only the representatives of the USA, India, the Holy See, Italy, and France remained in Nanking, but Riberi was ignored by the new Communist government. According Leung:

> The Korean War was the turning point . . . when the White House decided to freeze Chinese assets in the USA, strong anti-American feeling was aroused. Zhou Enlai demanded that all Christian churches and organisations immediately terminate all relations with American mission boards. Foreign missionaries, including the Papal Nuncio were expelled.[224]

They thus mounted a campaign against Riberi and finally, in June 1951, he was expelled from China. The Nationalist authorities in Taiwan refused to accept him. Land reform affected Catholic churches and monasteries; the Legion of Mary was disbanded because of the military connotations of its name; and accusations of spying against foreign bishops and priests—Americans and French—were used to thin the ranks of the missionary clergy.[225]

The first papal response to the Communists' religious policy came in the apostolic letter *Cupimus Imprimis* of 18 March 1952.[226] A more trenchant response came in October 1954 with the encyclical *Ad Sinarum gentem* ('To the Chinese People'), following the promulgation a month earlier of the new Communist constitution which established freedom of religious belief.[227] Addressed to all Chinese Catholics, the encyclical absolutely rejected the Chinese Catholic Patriotic Association which had been created to fulfil the authorities' demands for totally 'Chinese' religious organizations. Pius rejected the 'Three Autonomies' which formed the conceptual basis of the new organization.[228] Catholic bishops and priests who did not accept the new CPA were imprisoned; others, like Cardinal Tian Gengxin, went into exile. But most bishops, clergy, and laity accepted the new ecclesiastical order and, at a meeting in July 1957, with 241 representatives, clerical and lay, of 108 dioceses, the Association was inaugurated and the meeting declared that:

> The Congress believes that for the good of the Fatherland and for the future of the Church, the Chinese Catholic church . . . must maintain only purely spiritual relations with the Holy See of the Vatican.[229]

[223] Pighin, *Chies e Stato in Cina*, 85. [224] Pighin, *Chies e Stato in Cina*, 85.
[225] Leung, *Sino-Vatican Relations*, 89–90.
[226] For the text, see AAS XXXXIV, 18 March 1952, 153–157.
[227] Carlen, *Papal Encyclicals*, IV, 265–270. [228] Carlen, *Papal Encyclicals*, IV, 268.
[229] Quoted in Pighin, *Chiesa e Stato in Cina*, 94–95.

Worse, it decreed that in future all bishops should be elected, and in due course telegrams were sent to the Vatican requesting its approval of those thus chosen, for Hankow and Wuchan.[230] The Vatican's response was to excommunicate all such bishops.[231] This caused much bitterness among those Catholics belonging to the patriotic Association.[232]

In what turned out to be one of the last of his encyclicals, *Ad Apostolorum Principis*, of 29 June 1958, Pius XII warned that Patriotic Catholic Association would lead Roman Catholics to atheism, but, though denying the canonical legitimacy of episcopal consecration, he did not deny their sacramental validity.[233] Perhaps the very clear statement of this distinction was meant as a means of somehow holding on to Chinese Catholics in whatever circumstances and the hoped-for possibility of some sort of 'reunion' between the Catholic Patriotic Association and the Holy See in the future. Nevertheless, what had been the Vatican's worst nightmare throughout the 1920s and the 1930s and then the 1940s in Europe, had finally come to pass in China, a national, schismatic, 'Catholic' Church.

KOREA

The problems faced by the Roman Catholic Church (and other churches) were even worse in Korea. Korean Catholicism was unusual, if not unique, because 'The Korean Catholic church was established on the initiative of Koreans before foreign missionaries entered the country.'[234] By the 1948, there were three apostolic prefectures and four apostolic vicariates, plus one abbey nullius at Tokugen (Tae-gun) and roughly 258,000 Catholics out of a population of 30 million.[235] The outbreak of what was originally a civil war between the Communist and non-Communist forces, then the intervention of the United Nations which led to the Korean War of June 1950 until July 1953, followed by the definitive partition of the country more or less along the 38th degree of latitude, spelled disaster for the Korean Catholic Church. Thousands of Christians fled from North Korea to the South, and the Communist regime in the North set about destroying all religious institutions with a thoroughness that was only equalled in Albania. In his encyclical on the missions of 1951, *Evangelii praecones*, Pius

[230] Leung, *Sino-Vatican Relations*, 95.
[231] Leung, *Sino-Vatican Relations*, 97.
[232] Leung, *Sino-Vatican Relations*, 97.
[233] Leung, *Sino-Vatican Relations*, 384–371.
[234] *Catholic Korea: Yesterday and Today*, compiled and ed. Fr Chang-mun Kim and Catechist John Jae-sun, Seoul, 1964, 340.
[235] *Annuario Pontificio*, 1948, 1101.

made specific mention of Korea and China, 'There, what were the most flourishing of missions ripe for the harvest, are now, alas, reduced to the direst straits.'[236]

Africa was the only major continent where decolonization was not already in train; indeed, it would not start in earnest until 1957, a year before the end of Pacelli's pontificate, with the granting of independence to the British colony of the Gold Coast, renamed Ghana. Africa was also a major, if not the major, field of mission for the Catholic Church, and the Holy See was very aware of the great changes that were going on there. Consequently, in his encyclical *Fidei donum* of 1957, Pius declared that 'The Church . . . cannot help turning her attention to those nations that are now on the point of obtaining the rights of civil liberty' and he expressed the usual fears about the spread of atheistic materialism in Africa.[237] He ended on a positive note, 'For the people of Africa have made as much progress toward civilisation during the past few decades as required centuries among the nations of Western Europe.'[238] In this he was positioning the Church well for the wave of decolonization that would spread throughout the 'Dark Continent' in the late 1950s and 1960s. The Vatican also stood by the declaration of the South African episcopate against apartheid in 6 July 1957,[239] and in 1954 Pius had also elevated the first African cleric, albeit a Portuguese national, the archbishop of Lourenço Marques (now Maputo), Mozambique, to the Sacred College.

The establishment of relations with the Empire of Ethiopia in 1958 was a prescient gesture towards the State that would, by virtue of its long history of resistance to European colonialism, become the leader of the newly independent African states.

THE VATICAN AND THE PROBLEM OF PALESTINE

There was one process of decolonization, the British withdrawal from the Palestinian mandate, which presented the Holy See with particular problems, as is witnessed by the fact that Pius issued three encyclicals on the subject in just under twelve months. The British departure was a very messy and bloody 'scuttle', threatening the Holy See's interests in the Holy Land. First and foremost was the question of the access to, and the security of, the Holy Places in Jerusalem and elsewhere. In 1947 the Holy See was very

236 Carlen, *Papal Encyclicals*, IV, 194.

237 Carlen, *Papal Encyclicals*, IV, 323.

238 Carlen, *Papal Encyclicals*, IV, 325.

239 TNA/PRO, FCO, 1958, Rv1011/1, British Minister's annual report, 1957, 10, and L'OR, 6 July 1957.

alarmed by the mounting violence of the civil war in Palestine between Arabs and Jews and by the proposals of Britain's Peel Commission for the partition of Palestine because, despite continuing British administration of Jerusalem and Bethlehem, this would still have left some Holy Places in the proposed Muslim and Jewish-controlled areas.[240]

Then there was the future of the Christian Arab community in face of the Zionist project of setting up a Jewish state. There was rather less concern in the Vatican about the fate of the either Jewish community or the (mainly Muslim) Arab community as a whole. It is clear that the Vatican feared the consequences for the Holy Places, and the small Catholic community, whoever gained the upper hand in the struggle, Jews or Arabs. Thus, in January 1948, Mgr Montini told the British Minister that the Holy See preferred that 'a third power, neither Jewish nor Arab . . . have control of the Holy Land'.[241] While the UN plan for the partition of Palestine after British withdrawal into Jewish and Arab areas was not welcomed by the Vatican, it did at least envisage Jerusalem as a *corpus separatum* under international administration.

This long-standing preference, rather than Vatican unwillingness to challenge Zionism in the wake of the Holocaust or fear of destabilizing its 'alliance' with America, as has been suggested by Kreutz,[242] explains why the Vatican maintained a prudent neutrality as the Arab–Jewish conflict developed in the late forties. But the victory of the State of Israel at the end of the 1947–9 Jewish–Arab War, with 79 per cent of the territory of the former Palestinian mandate, and the flight of 75 per cent of the Christian Arabs from that territory, terrorized by massacres and by the profanation of some churches,[243] was inevitably viewed as nothing less than a catastrophe in the Vatican.

The three encyclicals, *Auspicia Quaedam* of May 1948, *Multiplicibus Curis* of October of the same year, and *Redemptoris Nostri Cruciatus* of April 1949, accurately reflect the development of Vatican policy during the Jewish–Arab conflict. *Auspicia Quaedam* was written at the end of the first phase of the conflict, when the increasingly better-organized and equipped Jewish forces had crushed those of the Palestinian Arabs, and the State of Israel was about to be proclaimed. But the situation was, as yet, far from stable and so Pius limited himself to calling for prayers, 'that the situation in Palestine may at long last be settled justly and thereby concord and peace be also happily established', but already it was evident that his chief priority was the Holy Places, which he claimed 'had long been disturbed'.[244]

[240] Giovanelli, *La Santa Sede e la Palestina*, 124.

[241] As cited in Andrej Kreutz, 'The Vatican and the Palestinians: A Historical Overview', in Kent and Pollard (eds), *Papal Diplomacy*, 172, and FO 371/68500, Perowne (Rome) to Burrows, 19 January 1948.

[242] Kreutz, 'The Vatican and the Palestinians', 172.

[243] Giovanelli, *La Santa Sede e la Palestina*, 184–187.

[244] Carlen, *Papal Encyclicals*, IV, 158.

By the time that he published *In Multiplicibus Curis*, on 24 October 1948, the second phase of the conflict, the war between Israel and the Arab states—Egypt, Iraq, Jordan, Lebanon, and Syria—was under way and the exodus or expulsion of Palestinian Arabs was virtually complete. Thus Pius talked of 'the distress of the unfortunate and the fear of the terrorised, while thousands of refugees, homeless and driven, wander from their fatherland in search of shelter and food'.[245] He was, of course, referring to the Palestinian Arabs and his concern for them was matched by the Vatican's coordination of efforts at refugee relief for the 'unhappy victims of the war', the establishment of the Pontifical Mission for Palestine.[246] But the bulk of the encyclical was still devoted to his concerns about the danger to the Holy Places.

The publication of *Redemptoris Nostri Cruciatus* in April 1949 followed the conclusion of armistices between Israel and all the Arab states except Syria, so it was by now clear that the *de facto* partition of Palestine, including the partition of Jerusalem between Israel in the west and King Abdullah of Jordan's troops in the east, was likely to be permanent. Consequently, though Pius again expressed concern about 'the exiles . . . driven far from their homes by the turmoil of war' and for the future of the specifically Catholic community in Palestine,[247] the thrust of his concern remained the Holy Places. Here he repeated his demand several times that the Holy Places 'should also be suitably protected by definite statute guaranteed by an "international" agreement'.[248] There is no explicit mention of either Jewish or Muslim sacred sites. Even less is there a reference to Israel. In the circumstances immediately following the end of hostilities a perfectly reasonable explanation is to be found in the Vatican's time-hallowed policy of not recognizing states which are the product of armed conflicts. But given the fact that, for the remaining nine years of his pontificate the situation in the Holy Land remained fairly stable, and was arguably reinforced by the outcome of the brief Arab–Israel conflict of 1956, the Vatican's refusal to recognize the Jewish state can only really be explained in terms of an unwillingness to offend those Arab states, with some of whom the Vatican had diplomatic relations and in whose territory lived substantial Catholic minorities. But it made negotiating with the Israeli authorities over the Holy Places infinitely more difficult and contributed to the cooling of the Vatican's relationship with the United States under the Truman administration.

The process of decolonization brought about the emergence of the 'Third World' and a group of new powers unwilling to take sides in the Cold War

[245] Carlen, *Papal Encyclicals*, IV, 161.

[246] Carlen, *Papal Encyclicals*, IV, 161; on pontifical relief efforts for Palestinian refugees, see Kreutz, 'The Vatican and the Palestinians', 172–173.

[247] Kreutz, 'The Vatican and the Palestinians', 163–164.

[248] Kreutz, 'The Vatican and the Palestinians', 163–164.

struggle. The importance of this phenomenon was underlined when 29 countries, 4 in Africa and the rest in Asia, representing a total 1.5 billion people, half the world's population, was held in Bandung, Indonesia, in 1955. The Vatican was anxious to establish and consolidate its relations with the emerging countries of the Third World and there would have been some logic for the papacy to associate itself with these 'Non-aligned Emerging Forces'. Moreover, the Vatican was among the early proponents of 'development aid', beginning with Pius XII's Christmas message of 1954 where he urged what would now be called the 'developed' nations to give economic aid to the underdeveloped ones.[249] He reiterated this plea on 13 June 1957 to members of the Council of Europe when he told them that European states must use their influence and extend their charitable help to the new states of Africa.[250] But the strong Communist elements in Indonesia, whose president, Sukarno, was a contender for the leadership of the NEFOS (Newly Emerging Forces), and the growing involvement of Marshall Tito of Yugoslavia, who would eventually host the founding conference of the non-aligned movement in Belgrade in 1961, prompted a diffident attitude on the part of the Vatican towards the organization.

THE BEGINNINGS OF *OSTPOLITIK* IN THE PONTIFICATE OF PIUS XII?

Following Stalin's death in 1953, the Soviets made some mildly conciliatory gestures towards the Vatican and Pius tentatively sought to reciprocate them. Thus, in November 1954, a Communist Party Central Committee statement dealing with the anti-religious struggle talked about 'Oppressive measures [which] damage the goals of the Communist Party and ultimately result in entrenched prejudices.'[251] A few weeks later, in his Christmas radio message the pope examined the talk of 'cold peace' and of 'coexistence', which had become common in some circles in the West since Stalin's death. He expressed the hope that a bridge between East and West could be built, but that coexistence could only be sustained by truth, in other words that there should be no compromises on principles.[252] A much more tangible gesture of goodwill came from the Soviets when Adenauer made his famous trip to Moscow in September 1955, for, just as he was doing so, two bishops

[249] *Pio XII Discorsi*, VII, 1944–1945, Ecce Ego Declinabo, 24 dicembre 1944, 292–293.

[250] *Pio XII Discorsi*, XIX, 1957–8, Per l'Unità d'Europa, 13 giugno 1957, 267.

[251] As quoted in Stehle, *Eastern Politics*, 286.

[252] *Pio XII Discorsi*, XVI, 1954–1955, L'Augurio e il Messaggio el Sommo Pontificio per le Solennità del Natale ai popoli di tutto il mondo, 24 dicembre 1954, 333–334.

were consecrated in Vilnius, capital of Lithuania—the first since Soviet reoccupation in 1945.[253] Such was the impact of this gesture in the Vatican that the Secretariat of State gave its unofficial blessing to a 'non-committal fact-finding' visit made by theology professor Fr Marcel Reding of the University of Graz in December 1955.[254] But Reding came back with little that was either hopeful or definite.[255]

All this must have seemed *déjà vu* to Papa Pacelli who, as nuncio in Berlin, had been involved in behind-the-scenes negotiations with the Bolshevik regime back in the early and mid-twenties (see Chapter 5). Nevertheless, when, in August 1956, an official of the Soviet embassy to the Quirinale contacted the nuncio to Italy, Mgr Fietta, to deliver Moscow's various new proposals for nuclear disarmament, he was not rebuffed.[256] Pius XII's response, in an address to the September *Katholikentag* in Cologne, was to set out the clear terms on which any sort of agreement with the Communist states might be reached:

> it [the Church] does demand for itself the freedom to live in the land according to its own constitution and laws, to care for its believers and to be able to openly proclaim the message of Jesus Christ. This of course is the unalterable basis for any honourable coexistence.[257]

The year 1956 was, of course, one of major upheavals in the Communist East, with the bloody uprising in Poznań, Poland, in June, and the uprising in Hungary in October, followed by its bloody suppression by Soviet troops the next month. These events and the intransigent opposition of elements of the *partito romano* to having any truck with Moscow meant that there could not be a very enthusiastic response to the Soviets' admittedly muted overtures. Pius was clear-cut in his public statements on developments in the two countries. In *Laetamur Admodum*, November 1956, he called for prayers for peace in Poland, Hungary, and the Middle East, and expressed his joy at the fact that Mindszenty and Wyszynski had been released.[258] *Datis Nuperrime*, of November 1956, was inevitably very different given the changed situation in Hungary. In consequence, the pope bewailed the fact that 'A blood-drenched people have been reduced once more to slavery by the armed might of foreigners.'[259]

Pius has been rightly criticized for his policies towards Communism by more than one author,[260] and there is little evidence that, in the last few

[253] Stehle, *Eastern Politics*, 288. [254] Stehle, *Eastern Politics*, 288.
[255] Stehle, *Eastern Politics*, 290. [256] Stehle, *Eastern Politics*, 292–293.
[257] As quoted in Stehle, *Eastern Politics*, 293.
[258] Carlen, *Papal Encyclicals*, IV, 316. [259] Carlen, *Papal Encyclicals*, IV, 319.
[260] For instance Stehle, *The Eastern Politics*, 300; Luxmoore and Babuich, *The Vatican*, 106–107; and Jean Chélini, *L'Église de Pie XII: La Tourmente (1939–1945)*, Paris, 1985, 452–455.

years of his reign, he did much that would have prepared the ground for his successor's 'Opening to the East'. Frank Coppa is perhaps overstating the case a little when he asserts that, 'By 1958 and the end of Pius XII's pontificate, the Vatican was moving to reach some sort of accommodation with the Soviet system. . . .'[261]

[261] F. Coppa, 'Pope Pius XII and the Cold War: The Post-war Confrontation between Catholicism and Communism', in Kirby (ed.), *Religion and the Cold War*, 63.

11

'Angelic Pastor'? Pius XII and the Worldwide Church

THE ECCLESIOLOGY OF PAPA PACELLI

The ecclesiology of Pius XII was as 'high church' as that of his predecessor, but he took it a stage further by formally exercising the power of infallibility in the definition of the dogma of the Bodily Assumption of the Blessed Virgin Mary into Heaven in Holy Year, 1950. Again, like, Pius XI, he repeatedly stressed the importance of what might nowadays be called 'virtual infallibility', that is, that *all* papal pronouncements shared in the authority of the infallible *magisterium*. Thus, in his encyclical *Humani Generis* of 1950 he declared:

> Nor must it be thought that what is propounded in Encyclical Letters does not of itself demand consent, since in writing such Letters the popes do not exercise the supreme power of their Teaching Authority . . . if the Supreme Pontiffs in their official documents purposely pass judgment on a matter up to that time under dispute, it is obvious that the matter, according to the mind and will of the same pontiff, cannot any longer be discussed among theologians.[1]

The encyclical *Mystici Corporis Christi* of 1943 is a great restatement of the nature of the Church as the 'Mystical Body of Christ', the visible form and agency of the continuing work of Christ's redemption of humankind.[2] It is, in a rather different form, an affirmation of Pius XI's belief in the Roman Catholic Church as 'the Kingdom of Heaven on earth' (see Chapter 5). The concept of the Church as the Mystical Body of Christ had been elaborated into a *schema* for the First Council of the Vatican in 1870, but because the Council was prorogued due to the Italian attack on Rome, it was never discussed.[3] According to McDonnell, 'Vatican I was the first in the historic sequence of

[1] Carlen, *Papal Encyclicals*, IV, 178.
[2] For the text, see Carlen, *Papal Encyclicals*, IV, 31–61.
[3] J. Powell, *The Mystery of the Church*, Milwaukee, 1967, 4.

Councils . . . in which the nature of the Church was addressed.'[4] The encyclical, while it is indeed a disquisition on the nature of the Church, an exposition of Pius XII's thinking on the subject, is also very specific in responding to the dangers and evils, as he perceived them, which the war-torn world posed to Catholicism. Thus, in the opening sections he declared that it was motivated 'also by the circumstances of the present times'.[5] The particular circumstances were the strains and potentially divisive effects which a world-wide, total war imposed on the universal Church—by June 1943 when the encyclical was published there was fighting going in every continent except the Americas and Catholics were involved on both sides. Thus he talks about the Church's role in seeking to unite under the authority of the Vicar of Jesus Christ men who were otherwise engaged in fighting each other.[6]

The encyclical's exposition of the Mystical Body of Christ was meant to be a salutary antidote to those dangers. A further grave peril was that this war involved powers with demonical ideologies and objectives—the 'return to ancient paganism' of the German Nazis and the violent godlessness of the Soviet Union.[7]

But Pius believed that the Church was facing other perils. Schisms, 'false rationalism', 'popular naturalism', a 'false mysticism', and 'grave errors about this doctrine [the Mystical Body of Christ] are being spread outside the true Church and that, among the faithful, also, inaccurate or thoroughly false ideas are being disseminated. . . .'[8] The encyclical is clearly directed against non-Catholics and even non-Catholic churches in its insistent statements that Christ's Church is not merely a 'pneumatological' (spiritual) entity, but visible and institutional and that the Roman Catholic Church is the sole, unique form which it takes.[9] The pope clearly feared that the ecumenical activity being encouraged by the horrors of the war might, in some way, diminish Catholicism's claims to be the 'one, true church'.

Finally, there is an extremely significant passage in which he confronts the issue of forced conversions, a practice that had become extremely common in Croatia where Orthodox Serbs were converting *en masse* in order to avoid being massacred by the Ustasha (see Chapter 8). So Pius declared that ' whenever it happens, despite the constant teaching of this Apostolic See, that anyone is compelled to embrace the Catholic faith against his will, Our sense of duty demands that we condemn the act'.[10]

There can be no other explanation of Pius XII's decision to publish this encyclical in 1943, an encyclical which is more or less a complete defence

[4] John J. McDonnell, *The World Council of Churches and the Catholic Church*, London and New York, 1985, 108.

[5] Carlen, *Papal Encyclicals*, IV, 37.

[6] Carlen, *Papal Encyclicals*, IV, 38.

[7] Carlen, *Papal Encyclicals*, IV, 37.

[8] Carlen, *Papal Encyclicals*, IV, 39.

[9] Carlen, *Papal Encyclicals*, IV, 40.

[10] Carlen, *Papal Encyclicals*, IV, 58.

of the theological beliefs and position of the Roman Catholic Church, than that he believed that he was possibly living in 'the end times', that he was facing a potentially apocalyptic situation which, in the short term, threatened to destroy the unity and character of the Church, and the purity of its doctrine.

PIUS XII AND MARY

Pius XII's pontificate is remarkable for the attention which was paid Mary. Not since the pontificate of Pius IX had a pope focused so much attention on the Mother of God. In 1942 the pope consecrated the world to the Immaculate Heart of Mary and two years later he established an eponymous feast for the universal Church to be observed in August. The proclamation of the dogma of the Bodily Assumption of the Blessed Virgin Mary into Heaven in 1950 was, of course, the most spectacular example of Pius XII's devotion to the Mother of God, made all the more solemn and significant by his use of *ex cathedra* authority. In 1953 he published the encyclical *Fulgens Corona*, which prepared for the first centenary of the definition of the Immaculate Conception by Pius IX in 1854, proclaiming that 1954 would be a 'Marian' year, the first in the history of the Church. The Marian year was marked by celebrations throughout the Catholic world and though they were not on the scale of Holy Year, those in Rome were impressive, with Pius going first to crown the statue of the Immaculate Conception in Piazza di Spagna and then to the basilica of Santa Maria Maggiore on the feast of the Immaculate Conception, 8 December 1954. In the same year, Pius published his encyclical *Ad Caeli Reginam*. While this did not quite extend to the definition of Mary as co-saviour with Christ, in the process of proclaiming Mary as Queen of Heaven, it came very close to it. The encyclical speaks of Mary not only, as was usual, as 'The New Eve', but also of 'Her Cooperation in the Redemption' and even of the 'all but divine dignity of the Mother of God'.[11] It goes on to declare that, after Christ himself, Mary was the most perfect being and consequently he used her in the great work of bringing redemption to humankind.[12]

This is strange language for an infallible pope to use, almost as if he were straining to go beyond the accepted, established lines of Marian theology but not quite brave enough to do so. This tendency did not go unnoticed among non-Catholics, many of whom saw it as 'Mariolatry', and as therefore presenting yet another barrier towards ecumenical objectives. There was not only opposition outside the Church to this further elevation of Mary; there were

[11] Carlen, *Papal Encyclicals*, IV, 274–276.

[12] Carlen, *Papal Encyclicals*, IV, 276.

also dissenters inside, including Cardinal Angelo Roncalli, Patriarch of Venice and future Pope John XXIII, who presciently warned that such moves would 'alienate many . . . however well-disposed towards the Catholic Church'.[13] The encyclical *Haurietis Aquas* reinforced the impression of Mariolatry by declaring, 'By the will of God, the most Blessed Virgin Mary was inseparably joined with Christ in accomplishing the work of man's redemption. . . .'[14]

DOCTRINAL ORTHODOXY

Throughout his pontificate, Pius clearly felt assailed by false doctrines arising both outside and inside the Church. The encyclical *Humani Generis* of 1950 is an example of an attempt to confute just such doctrines. In particular, even though it does not name names, it was targeted at the French *nouvelle théologie* the work of such men as the Jesuits Henri de Lubac (regarded as their 'leader'), Jean Daniélou and Pierre Teilhard de Chardin, and the Dominicans Marie-Dominique Chenu and Yves-Marie Congar.[15] As a sort of mini 'syllabus of errors', *Humani Generis* condemns what it describes as 'historicism', 'immanentism', 'idealism', and 'dogmatic relativism',[16] which confirms that the encyclical was very much the work of Ottaviani at the Holy Office. De Lubac was a formidable intellect, both an historian and exegete, and, according to the *Oxford Dictionary of the Christian Church*, he 'was one of the thinkers who created the intellectual climate that made possible the Second Vatican Council'.[17]

De Lubac, and his colleagues Henri Bouillard and Henri Rondet, were punished (forbidden to teach) because of their research on the patristic sources of Catholic teaching. As in the encyclicals of Pius X which attacked 'modernism', the encyclical condemned them for something of which they weren't really guilty, claiming that 'Others destroy the truly gratuitous supernatural order by suggesting that God cannot create rational beings without ordaining them to the beatific vision and calling them to it.'[18]

The French Dominicans were another target of the encyclical. Georges-Yves Congar, the author of *Vraie et Fausse réforme dans l'Église* (True and False Reform in the Church) was the target of the condemnation of 'false irenicism'

[13] As quoted in Hebblethwaite, *John XXIII*, 249.

[14] Carlen, *Papal Encyclicals*, IV, 310–311.

[15] For a brief discussion of the effects of *Humani Generis* on these men and Catholic scholarship in France more generally, see Hebblethwaite, *John XXII*, 228–229.

[16] Carlen, *Papal Encyclicals*, IV, 175–176.

[17] ODCC, 1001.

[18] Carlen, *Papal Encyclicals*, IV, 179.

in the encyclical, because of his sympathy with and closeness to Anglicans and other Protestants.[19]

Congar was banished first to the École Biblique in Jerusalem and then to Cambridge(!), forbidden to teach in 1954, but in 1955 he was allowed to return to France, to live in Strasbourg.[20] Like other protagonists of the *théologie nouvelle* he was rehabilitated under Pope John XXIII and played a crucial role at the Second Vatican Council. It is testimony to the immense contribution which Congar and De Lubac made to twentieth-century Catholic scholarship that they were both made cardinals in 1983.[21]

The Vatican's 'purge' of dangerous theologians went beyond high-profile figures. In 1953, Pizzardo, Secretary of the Holy Office, charged the Master General of the Dominicans, Emanuel Suarez, with 'rooting out excessive spirit of insubordination and indiscipline' prevalent among French Dominicans, and so Suarez sacked three French provincials of his order.[22]

Again and again *Humani Generis*, as the very title implies, inveighs against theories concerning the origins of the human race, in other words, evolution. Indeed, the encyclical points the finger at the theory of evolution as the origin of so many false ideas, above all, existentialism. Declaring that evolution 'has not been fully proved even in the domain of the natural sciences', it associates the theory with Communism.[23] This ensured that the 'existentialist' writings of Pierre Teilhard de Chardin, which sought to 'Christianize' evolution, by claiming that it was now a continuation of the Incarnation, were particularly attacked.[24] More seriously, the encyclical attacked those who held to the theory of 'Polygenism', evolution under another name, because it destroyed the basis of the doctrine of original sin, that is, if the human race did not all descend from Adam, then he could not have transmitted that defect to it.[25] This marked a break with the more open, ambiguous position which the Holy Office had exhibited towards Darwin in the previous pontificate (see Chapter 5).

The Holy Office seems to have decided that the stick in the papal hand could be used to beat other dangerous heretics. It came down particularly hard on those whom it accused of rejecting the divine authorship of Holy Scripture and seeking to create a sort of 'symbolical or spiritual exegesis'.[26] On the same plane, it warned of the danger of 'dogmatic relativism', an attempt to interpret Catholic doctrine 'symbolically'; thus, for example, warning against a tendency to reduce the doctrine of the Real Presence (of Christ in the Eucharist) to a purely symbolical matter.[27]

19 Carlen, *Papal Encyclicals*, IV, 177.
20 ODCC, 396.
21 Hebblethwaite, *John XXIII*, 228.
22 Hebblethwaite, *John XXIII*, 251–252.
23 Carlen, *Papal Encyclicals*, IV, 176.
24 Carlen, *Papal Encyclicals*, IV, 170.
25 Carlen, *Papal Encyclicals*, IV, 182.
26 Carlen, *Papal Encyclicals*, IV, 179.
27 Carlen, *Papal Encyclicals*, IV, 179.

Humani Generis reads like a re-run of Pius X's condemnation of 'modernism', it is often emotional and even hysterical. It betrays the strong feeling of alarm in the Vatican for the grave dangers which, it was believed, contemporary currents of thought posed for the Church in the middle of the twentieth century, most of which seemed to emanate from France and were consequently regarded with even greater suspicion and horror in the Vatican. It is therefore fitting that, in 1954, Pius should have canonized Pius X, who had lead the witch hunt against 'modernism' nearly fifty years earlier.

BIBLICAL SCHOLARSHIP

The year 1943 was marked by the publication of another major encyclical, *Divino Afflante Spiritu*, ostensibly to commemorate the fiftieth anniversary of Leo XIII's encyclical *Providentissimus Deus*.[28] It is not easy to interpret, but it has been seen by some as opening the way towards the 'liberalization' of biblical studies in the Roman Catholic Church.[29] While it enjoins the need to follow the literal meaning of the Scriptures wherever possible, by allowing the study of literary forms, it 'opened the way for a more liberal approach to biblical criticism by Catholic scholars'.[30] The encyclical particularly stresses 'The Importance of Textual Criticism' as a means of 'purifying text from the corruptions due to the carelessness of the copyists'.[31] Throughout the encyclical, there is clear evidence of the emergence of a dichotomy, even conflict, between the 'literal sense' and the 'spiritual sense' of scripture.[32] But the loosening up of biblical studies after the straitjacket imposed upon them by Leo XIII and Pius X is most clearly evident in the reference to the difficulty in explaining the 'first chapters of Genesis . . .'.[33]

But as well as the encyclical, 'the party line' on exegesis was laid down in a letter sent by Pontifical Commission on Biblical Studies, in January 1946, which reasserted the basic historical reality of the first eleven chapters of the Old Testament and declared that the interpolations were not myths.[34] 'Polygenism' was again condemned in the letter, which suggests that the Holy Office was now firmly under the control of Ottaviani and the anti-modernists.[35]

[28] For the text, see Carlen, *Papal Encyclicals*, IV, 64–79. [29] ODCC, 1997, 1296.
[30] ODCC, 1997, 1296. [31] Carlen, *Papal Encyclicals*, IV, 69.
[32] See for, example, Carlen, *Papal Encyclicals*, IV, 71.
[33] Carlen, *Papal Encyclicals*, IV, 72.
[34] AAS, XL, II, XV, Comissio Pontificio de Re Biblica, 16 January, 45–48.
[35] See P. Fothergill, 'Towards an Interpretation of Evolution, the Teaching of *Humani Generis*', *The Tablet*, 4 April 1955.

CHRISTIAN MORALITY

Pius XII not only used the medium of great encyclicals to state the Church's teaching on moral issues, he also increasingly used, for this purpose, addresses to specialist groups who had audiences with him, knowing that they would be widely reported in the Catholic press throughout the world. Thus, on 29 October 1951, he made a major statement on 'Marriage and Childbirth' to an audience of the Italian Catholic Union of Midwives.[36] In it, he reiterated the Catholic teaching on 'the sole great law of *generatio et educatio prolis*', that the first and fundamental purpose of marriage was the procreation and education of children.[37] Furthermore, he adopted an almost puritanical approach to the question of sex, 'Banish from your minds the cult of pleasure, and do your best to stop the diffusion of literature that thinks it a duty to describe in full the intimacy of conjugal life under the pretext of instructing, directing and reassuring.'[38]

In this address, he also dealt with the questions of abortion and contraception. In regard to the first, he declared that, 'Every human being, even the infant in the maternal womb, has the right to life *immediately* from God.' In response perhaps to the latest medical developments, he went on to say, ' to save the life of the mother is a most noble end, but the direct killing of the child as a means to this end is not licit'.[39] In so doing, Pius was imposing on many mothers and doctors a terrible moral dilemma which became a major public issue in many countries in the 1950s.

Another major public issue which Pius XII addressed was that of contraception. In this, he was largely restating Pius XI's pronouncement in *Casti Connubii*, twenty-one years earlier, 'Every attempt on the part of the married couple during the conjugal act or during the development of its natural consequences to . . . hinder the procreation of new life is immoral.'[40] This also meant repeating the condemnations of sterilization, which, because of its increasing use, especially as part of the racial policies of Nazi Germany, the Holy Office had felt obliged to declare immoral in February 1940 (see Chapter 9). As artificial contraception and the practice of family planning became even more widespread and routine in the northern hemisphere after the war, Pius turned his attention to it, giving the most specific and detailed instructions to his audience of midwives. In particular, he addressed the question of what advice they should give to their patients when pregnancy was ruled out for medical reasons and the 'safe period' could not be relied upon: he told them

[36] See *The Tablet*, 24 November 1951, 'On Marriage and Childbirth'.

[37] *The Tablet*, 24 November 1951, 383.

[38] *The Tablet*, 24 November 1951.

[39] *The Tablet*, 24 November 1951, 342.

[40] Carlen, *Papal Encyclicals*, IV, 399–400; see Uta Ranke-Heinemann, *Enuchs for Heaven: The Catholic Church and Sexuality*, trans. John Bownjohn, London, 1988, 222–225.

that 'there is but one way open, that of complete abstinence from every complete [*sic*] exercise of the natural faculty'.[41] In all of these counsels to the midwives, he claimed to be seeking to elevate their work, their profession to the glory of an apostolate—'Your apostolate is carried out in the first place by yourselves'[42]—a striking example of the tendency of the papacy, since the late nineteenth century, to increasingly entrust the laity with a share in the enforcement of the moral and social teaching of the Church.

DEVOTIONS AND LITURGICAL REFORM

In the field of devotions, both for the clergy and the laity, Pius XII introduced no great innovations. Rather, he strongly encouraged existing ones, like the rosary in *Ingruentium Malorum*, 1951,[43] the Stations of the Cross, and the cults of the sacred hearts of Jesus and Mary. Indeed, he devoted a quite lengthy (5,000-word) encyclical to the cult of the Sacred Heart of Jesus, *Haurietis Aquas*, in 1956, vigorously defending it against those who saw the devotion as 'purely optional', 'useless or irrational', or 'too passive', and linked it to the cult of the Immaculate Heart of Mary.[44] In *Mediator Dei*, an encyclical essentially dealing with liturgy, on three separate occasions he reiterated his support for personal devotions, not just the solemn liturgy, dedicating a whole section to the 'Necessity of personal piety, meditation, devotions and the Spiritual Exercises.'[45] His pontificate was arguably the last period in the history of the Roman Catholic Church when devotions—the use of the rosary, prayers to the sacred hearts of Jesus and Mary, and para-liturgical Eucharistic devotions like Benediction and Exposition of the Blessed Sacrament and so on—were in full flower. After the Second Vatican Council they would largely pass out of fashion.[46]

On the other hand, in the field of liturgy Pius XII was, later in his reign, quite innovative, and, had he lived, it seems likely that he would have inaugurated a more general reform of the prevailing liturgical arrangements, which had effectively been established at the Council of Trent.[47] The impetus for liturgical change in the Latin rite had been building up since before the First World War. Beginning with Dom Prosper Guéranger of the abbey of Solesmes in France, the torch had passed to Belgium, which became the focus of the

[41] *The Tablet*, 17 November 1951.
[42] *The Tablet*, 10 November 1951, 342.
[43] Carlen, *Papal Encyclicals*, IV, 214.
[44] Carlen, *Papal Encyclicals*, IV, 292.
[45] Carlen, *Papal Encyclicals*, IV, 124, 137, and 147–148.
[46] For an account of the 'collapse' of these devotions in the American Church, see James M. O'Toole (ed.), *Habits of Devotion: Catholic Religious Practice in Twentieth Century America*, Ithaca, NY, and London, 2004.
[47] O'Toole, *Habits of Devotion*, 179–180.

Catholic liturgical movement with figures like Dom Beaudouin of the abbey of Mont César, and then Germany with Dom Ildefons Herwegen of the abbey of Maria Laach.[48] As early as 1942, Fr Pio Alfonz, O.S.B., another Benedictine and a consultor of the Sacred Congregation of Rites, had drawn up 'general norms' for a reform of the liturgy, though these were not taken any further.[49] A new Latin version of the Psalms published in 1945 by the Pontifical Biblical Institute, of which Fr Augustin Bea, the pope's weekly confessor, was rector, was very important inasmuch as it ' helped to ripen in the pope's mind a reform of the entire liturgy'.[50] On 10 May 1946 Pius told Mgr Alfonso Carinci, Secretary of Rites, 'that a special commission of experts should reflect on the general reform of the liturgy and offer concrete proposals'.[51]

But in his encyclical *Mediator Dei* of 1947, Pius seemed to hesitate when faced by the Liturgical Movement rather than, as Bugnini suggests, 'putting the seal of his supreme authority on this movement'.[52] Bugnini, who has quite rightly been described as 'the chief architect of the Roman liturgical reform',[53] was probably giving Pius XII more than his due. While there was praise for the movement in *Mediator Dei*, there was also a clear expression of the pope's concerns about aberrations or novelties,[54] and the encyclical exhibited a particular concern about the tendency to indiscriminately revive ancient, presumably local or regional, liturgies.[55] There was also concern about the increasing demand for the use of the vernacular in the Church's worship. *Mediator Dei* came out firmly against its use in the Mass, but encouraged it for other ceremonies:

> The use of the Latin language, customary in a considerable portion of the Church, is a manifest and beautiful sign of unity . . . In spite of this, the use of the mother tongue in connection with several of the rites may be of much advantage to the people.[56]

With this statement, Pius had taken a crucial step towards liturgical change. The vernacular would come to be used for all the other sacraments given to laypeople: the next step would be its use in the Mass itself.

In *Musica Sacrae*, 1955, which, as its title suggests, was dedicated to the encouragement of the right kind of music in church, Pius repeated the injunction that, 'The law by which it is forbidden to sing the liturgical words themselves in the language of the people remains in force . . .' though the encyclical

[48] ODCC, 987–988.

[49] A. Bugnini, C.M., *The Reform of the Liturgy, 1948–1975*, Collegeville, MN, 1990, 7.

[50] Bugnini, *The Reform of the Liturgy*, 7.

[51] Bugnini, *The Reform of the Liturgy*, 7, fn. 5.

[52] Bugnini, *The Reform of the Liturgy*, 6.

[53] *NCE*, 2nd edn, 2, Bugnini, Annibale, 276.

[54] Carlen, *Papal Encyclicals*, IV, 120.

[55] Carlen, *Papal Encyclicals*, IV, 130.

[56] Carlen, *Papal Encyclicals*, IV, 130.

did give much more encouragement to the singing of hymns by the congregation at the Eucharistic liturgy, so long as it was not a Solemn High Mass.[57]

Given that, a year after the encyclical's publication, Pius XII established a commission for liturgical reform, to meet the 'movement of the Holy Spirit in the Church',[58] it seems likely that there had been a struggle inside the Roman curia, between the innovators in the Sacred Congregation of Rites, and the Holy Office, where the rather more conservative Mgr Alfredo Ottaviani reigned supreme as *Assessore*. The Liturgical Movement was, after all, a 'grass-roots' movement, whose centres were located outside not only the Vatican, but outside of Italy as well. Rites won out in the end and the commission was led by Cardinal Clemente Micara, prefect of Rites, plus Fathers Bugnini, Albareda, and Bea, with Bugnini as secretary.[59] In 1952, Enrico Dante, the papal master of ceremonies from 1940, became a member: in 1953, Micara was replaced by Gaetano Cicognani, now prefect of Rites. This was a powerful grouping of major figures in the Roman curia, well able to take on Ottaviani at the Holy Office.

The work of the 'Pian' Commission (1948–60) was intense. Indeed, as early as October 1946, Fr Joseph Lòw had begun drafting a *Positio Memoria sulla riforma liturgica* on behalf of the Commission, and finished it two years later, with addenda: in 1956–7 the document was used in a consultation exercise among over 400 bishops.[60] Lòw always worked in complete secrecy, so much so that his brainchild, the *Ordo Sabbati Sancti instaurati*, caught even officials of the Sacred Congregation of Rites by surprise. Bea, as Pius XII's confessor, kept the pope abreast of developments.[61] The concrete outcome of Lòw's work was the revised liturgical order of Holy Week, and most significantly the restoration of the Easter (Saturday) Vigil Mass in 1952. In 1957, the whole of the revised Holy Week liturgy was published.

The next major stepping stone was the Assisi International Congress of Pastoral Liturgy of 1956, at which all sorts of issues were raised, including the use of the vernacular and reform of the Divine Office.[62] In his blessing on the congress, Pius declared that: 'The liturgical movement is a . . . sign of the providential dispositions of God for the present time [and] of the movement of the Holy Spirit in the Church.'[63]

Under Pius XII, Rites also relaxed the pre-Mass fasting rules which forbade eating or drinking for twenty-four hours before receiving Holy

[57] Carlen, *Papal Encyclicals*, IV, 284.
[58] A. Bugnini, C.M and C. Braga, CM, *Cerimoniale della Settimina Santa*, Rome, 1957.
[59] Bugnini, *The Reform of the Liturgy*, 8–9.
[60] Bugnini, *The Reform of the Liturgy*, 342.
[61] Bugnini, *The Reform of the Liturgy*, 9.
[62] Bugnini, *The Reform of the Liturgy*, 11–12.
[63] As quoted in Bugnini, *The Reform of the Liturgy*, 12.

Communion: in the decree *Christus Dominus*, issued in 1953, Pius permitted those receiving Communion to drink ordinary (not mineral) water without breaking the fast, with the result that, in America at least, there was a remarkable increase in the numbers communicating.[64] In 1957, the *motu proprio Sacram Communionem* was much more radical, reducing the fast from twenty-four to three hours for solid food and to one hour for liquids other than water, with results that were as dramatic as those before.[65] In that same year, further recognition of the inexorable demands of urban, industrial society was evidenced by Pius XII's institution of the 'vigil Mass', that is, permitting those who had difficulty observing the precept of Sunday as a holy day of obligation to go to Mass, to attend a Mass on Saturday evening. Evening Mass was also permitted on Sundays for the same reasons.

The liturgical changes of Pius XII paved the way for the more radical ones, like the introduction of the vernacular into the Mass, the priest celebrating Mass facing the people, and so on, by the Second Vatican Council after 1965. Without all of the preparatory work of the Commission, Lòw, Bugnini, and others, it would have been impossible either to have pushed the decision to embark on liturgical reform through the Council or to have brought the project of liturgical reform to fruition so soon afterwards.

CLERGY AND RELIGIOUS: *SACRA VIRGINITATIS*, 1954

Pius XII's only major public statement on the priesthood, and on the life of male and female religious, the encyclical *Sacra Virginitatis* of 1954, was a reaffirmation of the necessity and desirability of celibacy against what he perceived to be the 'sexualized' spirit of the age. He was especially concerned about what he perceived to be a 'Protestant' trend of thought in the Church:

> However, since there are some who, straying from the right path in this matter, so exalt marriage as to rank it ahead of virginity and thus deprecate chastity consecrated to God and clerical celibacy, Our apostolic duty demands that We now in a particular manner declare and uphold the sublime state of virginity, and so defend Catholic truth against these errors.[66]

He evoked great saints like St John Bosco, St Francis Xavier, and St Vincent de Paul as examples of what could only be achieved by a celibate priesthood, and then offered a final, clinching argument for it:

[64] McGuiness, 'Let Us Go to the Altar', 213–214.
[65] McGuiness, 'Let Us Go to the Altar', 214–217.
[66] Carlen, *Papal Encyclicals*, IV, 240.

> Consider again that sacred ministers do not renounce marriage solely on account of apostolic ministry, but also by reason of their service at the altar . . . is it not much more fitting that the ministers of Jesus Christ, who offer every day the Eucharistic Sacrifice, possess perfect chastity?[67]

Once again, he had firmly distinguished the Roman Catholic Church from other churches, including the Orthodox, but perhaps inadvertently had delivered a slight to all those *married* clergy in Oriental rite churches who were in communion with Rome.

PIUS XII AND THE MISSIONS

Pius XII's first encyclical on the missions, *Evangelii praecones* of 1951, came at a critical point in the process of decolonization, when the papacy had already established diplomatic links with some of the major new independent nations—Egypt, India, and Indonesia. The encyclical is a sort of celebration of the success of Catholic missionary outreach of the previous twenty-five years:

> In 1926 the number of Catholic missions amounted to 400, but today it is almost 600. At that date the number of Catholics in the missions did not exceed 15,000,000 while today it is almost 20,800,000. At that time the number of native [sic] and foreign priests . . . was about 14,800; today their number is more than 26,800. Then all the Bishops in the missions were foreigners; during the past 25 years 88 missions have been entrusted to native clergy.[68]

It was an impressive achievement, though problems remained. As usual, the number of labourers in the vineyard was not sufficient for the work in hand.

The encyclical was innovative in two particular ways. In the first place, it stressed the need for social reforms, demanding that 'Missionaries Should Promote the Social Apostolate'.[69] It was not only the religious truths of Catholicism that should be taught to the newly converted but also those of 'Social Catholicism', 'not only charity but justice'.[70] In the Cold War era, the Vatican was even more acutely conscious than ever of the worldwide threat which Communism posed and it believed that it could only be countered though the promotion of Catholic social teaching and the mobilization of the lay social apostolate—Catholic Action—in mission lands, in other words in the emerging Third World. A second innovation was the admonition that 'Pagan philosophies and culture could be perfected' with the integration of the best with Catholic, Christian civilization: 'Christian Principles

[67] Carlen, *Papal Encyclicals*, IV, 242.
[68] Carlen, *Papal Encyclicals*, IV, 190.
[69] Carlen, *Papal Encyclicals*, IV, 198.
[70] Carlen, *Papal Encyclicals*, IV, 197.

Fit into Any Culture.'[71] Here we see most clearly the influence of Mgr Celso Costantini, secretary of Propaganda, who almost certainly had the guiding hand in the writing of the encyclical. Costantini had shown great perception about the future of Catholic missionary efforts in his handling of the situation in China when he was apostolic delegate there in the 1920s (see Chapter 5). He anticipated many of the problems which decolonization would bring to missionary Catholicism, especially in Asia, and he pressed for the Church to adopt a more respectful attitude towards local cultural traditions, many of which, of course, were much older than those of Christian Europe.

Pius's second missionary encyclical, *Fidei Donum*, of April 1957, came on the eve of the British granting independence to black Africa's first new state, Ghana (formerly the Gold Coast). Decolonization in the 'Dark Continent' proceeded rapidly thereafter, especially in the territories of the former French Empire in west and central Africa. *Fidei Donum* treated Africa as the Roman Catholic Church's chief mission field, but also expressed concern about the 'boundless spaces of South America', and referred to the 'Catholics of Oceania, and to the missions in Asia', including mention of persecution there.[72] It even talked of 'those regions of Europe where the faith has been cast off' and, more broadly, of 'the lamentable state of innumerable souls, especially of those young people who because of the atheistic propaganda of our times are growing up in the wretched condition of complete ignorance of religions, and in some cases of active hatred of God'.[73] This was a curious echo of the concerns in the French hierarchy that France was now a 'mission territory' (see Chapter 9) and the first public admission that the Church in Europe, East and West, was facing serious problems.

Pius rejoiced for the large numbers of African priests elevated to the Episcopate, a development that would be recognized by his successor, John XXIII, when he made Bishop Laurean Rugambwa of Rutabo, Tanzania, Africa's first cardinal in 1958. Pius was very aware of the great changes in Africa: 'The Church . . . cannot help turning her attention to those nations that are now on the point of obtaining the rights of civil liberty.' But he also admitted that the Church in Africa faced serious problems, notably a lack of clergy, indigenous and European:

> In one district some forty priests are working very hard among a million natives of whom only 25,000 profess the Catholic faith. In another locality, fifty priests are stationed in the midst of a population of 2,000,000 persons, where the care of 60,000 Catholics in the area alone requires almost full-time service.[74]

Worse, '85,000,000 people still sit in the darkness of idolatry'.[75]

[71] Carlen, *Papal Encyclicals*, IV, 199.
[72] Carlen, *Papal Encyclicals*, IV, 324.
[73] Carlen, *Papal Encyclicals*, IV, 324.
[74] Carlen, *Papal Encyclicals*, IV, 324.
[75] Carlen, *Papal Encyclicals*, IV, 324.

Consequently, much of the encyclical was a litany of exhortations to the episcopate, clergy, and laity of non-mission territories to assist in increasing the number of priests by encouraging and helping to finance missionary vocations and the training of indigenous clergy, through the Clergy Missionary Union and other societies in Europe and North America.[76] As has been seen, in his last consistory for the creation of cardinals, he included one for Africa, even if the cardinal created there was in fact a Portuguese citizen, the archbishop of Lourenço Marques in Mozambique, a Portuguese colonial possession.

It is appropriate to give the last word on the state of Catholic missionary outreach at the end of Pius XII's reign to Celso Costantini, the man who had dedicated his life's work to the missions and had a major hand in the writing of *Fidei Donum*. His verdict on the fruits of the Church's endeavours in this field was not a positive one. In the very last letter of his life, to Cardinal Masella, Camerlengo of the Holy Roman Church, excusing himself from the General Congregations preceding the Conclave of 1958 because of illness, he wrote:

> Another very important fact. The Church is fundamentally missionary, but after nearly 2000 years it has only brought together roughly 500 million Catholics. The Catholic Church, venerable brother Cardinals, represents a minority. When 5 babies are born, four see the light of day outside of the Catholic Church. We must fully take up the missionary mandate of Christ . . . Despite the immense and meritorious work of missionaries, in Asia we can count only 10–13 million Catholic in comparison with a total of nearly one billion pagans. The *tabula rasa* method was used especially in South America. We have tried to spread a foreign religious colonialism, not the Church with its natural native hierarchy . . . Conclusion. All this suggests, I believe, that the only candidate (for the papacy) who can respond to the needs of our time which cannot be postponed is cardinal Pietro XV Agagianian.[77]

Agagianian was indeed one of the main contenders in the battle for the succession to Pius XII.[78]

THE EASTERN CHURCHES

In keeping with the policy first established by Leo XIII, Pius XII devoted much attention to the Oriental churches, both those in communion with Rome and those 'in schism', such as the Orthodox churches. He used his encyclical

[76] Carlen, *Papal Encyclicals*, IV, 325.

[77] As cited in Bruno Fabio Pighin, *Il Ritratto Segreto del Cardinale Celso Costantini in 10,000 lettere dal 1892 al 1958*, Venice, 2012, 638–639, letter to Cardinal A. B. Masella, 12 October 1958.

[78] Hebblethwaite, *John XXIII*, 282.

Orientalis Ecclesiae of April 1944 to put forward St Cyril of Alexandria (died 444) as the shining model of a leader of the Eastern churches who steadfastly uphold the primacy of the Holy See.[79] Cyril was indeed that, he was also a great theologian, but he was belligerent and ruthless in his defence of the faith, most particularly the doctrine of the two natures of Christ, human and divine.[80] That belligerence was rather glossed over in the encyclical. Only half was really a commemoration of the great patriarch, the other was essentially an appeal to 'The Separated Eastern Churches' to return to the Roman fold. Pius promised 'Respect for their Ancient Traditions' and lauded 'Variety in Unity'.[81] He also established a 'Day of the East' for prayers for reunion, and made a particular 'Appeal to the Monophysites', that is, those churches, like the Egyptian and Ethiopian Copts, who refused to accept the Council of Chalcedon's declaration on two natures of Christ, to return to the true faith.[82] These churches were not only schismatic, they were also heretical given their beliefs about Christ.

The appeals to the schismatic churches to return to Rome was repeated in *Orientales Omnes Ecclesias*, of December 1945, where he urged that 'the orientals should have no fear at all of their being compelled to abandon their lawful rites and customs if the unity of faith and government is restored',[83] and in *Sempiternus Rex Christus*, September 1951, on the Council of Chalcedon, which had reaffirmed the oneness of the person of Christ, as two natures united in hypostatic union, where he rather proudly declared that, referring to Pietro Agagianian, 'We have bestowed the Roman purple on the patriarch of the Armenians.'[84]

Pius XII's insistence upon pursuing the dream of reunion with the Orthodox churches never wavered. Even in *Orientales Ecclesias*, of December 1952, the encyclical on the 'Persecuted Eastern Church', in which he drew attention to the Communist persecution of the both Latin and Oriental churches in Bulgaria, Romania, and the Ukraine, there is a call for the return of the 'separated churches'.[85] But there was strong Orthodox antipathy to what were seen as Roman claims and pretensions: there was particular hostility in predominantly Orthodox countries towards so-called 'Uniate' Catholics, that is, those belonging to churches of the Oriental or Byzantine rite, reconciled with Rome;[86] consequently, as in previous pontificates, there was absolutely no sign that the Orthodox reciprocated Rome's advances. They had long memories of slights and offences suffered at the hands of Rome. Professor Nicholas Glubokovsky, in a paper read at the Stockholm Ecumenical Conference of

[79] Carlen, *Papal Encyclicals*, IV, 81–88.
[80] ODCC, 442–443.
[81] Carlen, *Papal Encyclicals*, IV, 85.
[82] Carlen, *Papal Encyclicals*, IV, 87.
[83] Carlen, *Papal Encyclicals*, IV, 91.
[84] Carlen, *Papal Encyclicals*, IV, 210.
[85] Carlen, *Papal Encyclicals*, IV, 218–219.
[86] See Hebblethwaite, *John XXIII*, 120–122, on the treatment of 'Uniates' in Bulgaria and 150–151 on their treatment in Greece.

1925, made a number of accusations against the Roman Catholic Church such as 'aggressive proselytism', especially in overwhelmingly Orthodox Bulgaria, claiming Santa Sophia at the Paris Peace Conference of 1919, and even demolishing Orthodox cathedrals in Lublin and Warsaw, which would all have found an echo among his fellow Orthodox.[87]

THE PAPACY AND THE RISE OF THE WORLD ECUMENICAL MOVEMENT

The role played by the Orthodox churches in the ecumenical movement was a matter of great concern to the Holy See in the pontificates of both Pius XI and Pius XII. In 1920, the Ecumenical Patriarch in Istanbul issued an appeal to 'all the Churches of Christ' for 'closer intercourse and mutual cooperation'.[88] Orthodox representatives were present at meetings of the 'Faith and Order' and 'Life and Work' organizations. And when the World Council of Churches was founded in 1948, the Ecumenical Patriarch of Constantinople sent a delegate, though the Orthodox churches behind the Iron Curtain did not join (the Moscow patriarch delayed his adhesion until 1961). But even these limited signs of the emergence of an 'alliance' between the Orthodox churches of the East and the Protestant ones in the West was deeply troubling to the Vatican.

As has been seen (Chapter 5) the greatest impetus for the ecumenical movement came from Anglicans and Protestants, in particular Archbishop William Temple of York and the Rev. Willem Visser 't Hooft, who organized the founding conference of the World Council of Churches in Amsterdam in 1948. The Vatican remained firmly aloof from this development. Its position was clearly expressed by the Jesuit journal shortly after the Amsterdam meeting:

> The attitude of the Catholic Church towards the Protestant ecumenical movement, and in particular the WCC, can be summarised as follows—a) sympathy towards the efforts for unity, as well as indicating the most suitable means to achieve it and b) determination not to take part.[89]

For the Vatican, 'the most suitable means' to achieve unity was, of course, submission to the Holy See. Equally, as soon became apparent, there was considerable opposition among many non-Catholic churches to Roman

[87] N. Glubokovsky, 'Christian Fellowship in Life and Work', in C. G. Patelos (ed.), *The Orthodox Church in the Ecumenical Movement: Documents and Statements, 1902–1975*, Geneva, 1978, 144–146.

[88] As quoted in the ODCC, 528.

[89] LaCC, anno 9, vol. IV, 20 November 1948, no. 2362, 442–444, 'Intorno al Congresso Protestante di Amsterdam'.

Catholicism, not only for historical and theological reasons, but also because of ongoing persecution of Protestants in such countries as Colombia, Italy, and Spain.[90]

On the other hand, in various countries, especially France, Germany, and the Netherlands, the common experience of war, suffering, concentration and POW camps, and participation in resistance movements had, at least temporarily, brought many Roman Catholics and Protestants together. In the Netherlands, Roman Catholic bishops and leaders of the Reformed Churches jointly signed public statements protesting the Nazi occupation, and in Germany the experience of Nazism and the war actually led to the creation of an effectively 'ecumenical' political party—the CDU/CSU (see Chapter 10).

More significantly, these experiences heightened interest in the ecumenical movement inside the Church itself, especially in Belgium, France, and Germany.[91] The Vatican response to the announcement of the meeting of the Amsterdam Assembly was to issue instructions, in a decree *Cum Copertum* of the Holy Office of June 1948, refusing official permission for Roman Catholics to attend, which did nothing to dampen this interest.[92] The gulf between the centre and the periphery persisted: the Dutch bishops issued a pastoral about the Amsterdam Assembly which exhorted their flocks to pray for the success of the enterprise, and the interest among Roman Catholic theologians and other writers increased.[93] Whatever Rome's attitude, by the 1950s, theologians like Yves Congar and Dom Bede Winslow, and publications like *Irénikon, Vers l'Unité Chrétienne*, and *Études* had firmly taken ecumenism onto their agendas.[94]

Jan Willebrands, later a cardinal and archbishop of Utrecht, when president of a Catholic college in the Netherlands was deeply interested in the ecumenical project and was in correspondence with Visser 't Hooft in 1953 and 1954 over the Ecumenical assembly at Evanston, USA. Willebrands, Secretary of the 'Catholic Conference for Ecumenical Questions' in the Netherlands, wrote to Visser 't Hooft on 1 December 1953 requesting a meeting in Geneva, which took place in January 1954.[95] In a further letter, Willebrands explained that: 'During the meeting of the World Council of Churches I have not been able to do anything but pray for God's blessing for this meeting . . . may I congratulate you upon the results achieved.'[96] Meanwhile, Willebrands awaited

[90] See AWCC, General Correspondence, 2 July 1947, Gustave Hentsch to Mgr Tardini, protesting about persecution of Protestants in Cardinal Segura's diocese of Seville and the press cutting of 26 January 1956 regarding persecution of Protestants in Colombia.

[91] Tompkins, 'The Roman Catholic Church', 688.

[92] AAS XXXX, II, 5 June 1948, 257, Monitum.

[93] Tompkins, 'The Roman Catholic Church', 689.

[94] Tompkins, 'The Roman Catholic Church', 692–693.

[95] AWCC, Cd'A, 994.1.13/2, Willebrands to Vissers't Hooft, 1 December 1953.

[96] AWCC, Cd'A, 994.1.13/2, Willebrands to Vissers't Hooft, 1 December 1953.

the return of a certain Fr Dumont who had been able to attend the meeting. Willebrands would become the secretary of the Pontifical Council for the Unity of Christians in 1962.

Inside the Roman curia itself, a powerful official in the Secretariat of State, Mgr Montini, showed a keen interest in the ecumenical movement. His sympathy towards ecumenism stretched to meeting Canon Bernard Pawley, a key member of the Archbishop of Canterbury's ecumenical team, and his wife Margaret.[97] These sympathies were out of place in the Vatican of Pius XII, Ottaviani, and Pizzardo, and may have contributed to the decision to send Montini to Milan, where he continued his ecumenical efforts.[98]

An even more important role was played by Fr Augustin Bea, rector of the Pontifical Biblical Institute and consultor of the Holy Office and other congregations, in the last years of Pius XII's reign, in creating a network of relationships with ecumenical centres.[99] The most important of these were with of Mgr J. Hoefer, ecclesiastical counsellor of the German Embassy to the Holy See, who helped put Bea in contact with the Catholic ecumenical group centred around Mgr Jaeger, archbishop of Paderborn.[100] Bea also had contact with Willebrands' group in the Netherlands. Schmidt claims that the contacts Bea built up with other ecumenical centres convinced him of the need for the Holy See to create its own 'ecumenical commission'.[101] Bea also appears to have had a decisive role in helping to prepare the note of the Holy Office of 1950 that replaced *monitum* of 1948.[102] While increasingly sympathetic towards the World Council of Churches, Bea was afraid that proposed merger of the WCC and World Missionary Council would help promote Protestant proselytism in Latin America and that the WCC would become an international 'super-church' under the direction of Visser 't Hooft.[103] Despite these reservations, Bea actively assisted the ecumenical cause before the death of Pius XII by ensuring that a Roman Catholic delegation would be permitted to attend the Christology Conference in Oxford in 1952 and also supported collaboration between Catholics and non-Catholics in the field of social action.

The course of events which led to John XXIII making Bea a cardinal and choosing him to be head of the new Secretariat for the Unity of Christians is still not entirely clear but without his years of 'preparation' prior to 1958 Bea would not have been able to make the impact which he did at the Second Vatican Council, and ensure the establishment of the Secretariat for Christian Unity.

[97] Hebblethwaite, *Paul VI*. [98] Hebblethwaite, *John XXIII*, 267–271.

[99] Stjepan Schmidt, S.J., 'Il Cardinale Bea: Sua Preparazione alla Missione Ecumenica (nel decimo anniversario della Morte)', *AHP*, 16 (1978), 313–336.

[100] Schmidt, 'Il Cardinale Bea', 317. [101] Schmidt, 'Il Cardinale Bea', 318.

[102] AAS XXXXII, II, XVII (1950), 142–147, Istructio Ad Lororum Ordinarios: 'De Motione Oecumenica'.

[103] Schmidt, 'Il Cardinale Bea', 322.

Another Vatican 'casualty' of ecumenism was a very distinguished and prominent Spanish Jesuit, Carrillo de Albornoz, who went to work in the Vatican in 1947 as international head of the Marian Congregations, pious confraternities of Catholic males. After only two years, Albornoz lost patience with Rome's hostility to the ecumenical movement. Claiming that he ' could not stand the lack of spiritual freedom in the Vatican', he jumped ship in 1949, ending up as one of Visser 't Hooft's advisers at the World Council of Churches in Geneva.[104] Albornoz brought with him much 'insider knowledge' of the mentality and *modus operandi* of the men in the Vatican, thus, in a memorandum of 1951, he warned that:

> There is only one kind of [Christian] unity possible and it is certainly not that between churches . . . the Roman Church does not have sisters . . . no one is allowed to negotiate with her children . . . on an equal footing.[105]

This summed up perfectly the principles which officially guided the Vatican in its policy towards the ecumenical movement throughout the reigns of Benedict XV, Pius XI, and Pius XII.

The official Roman 'recognition' of both the inauguration of the World Council of Churches at Amsterdam and the ferment of debate which the ecumenical movement had already provoked inside the Roman Catholic Church came with the Holy Office decree *Ecclesia Catholica* of December 1949. The decree sought to control and regulate ecumenical encounters between the faithful and non-Catholics, laying down the absolute necessity for permission to be granted in advance by the local ordinary, or, in the case of inter-diocesan or international gatherings, by the Holy See itself. While 'all participation in sacred rites' was forbidden, such gatherings could open or close with the Lord's Prayer, which was at least a step forward.[106] And that remained the policy until early in the pontificate of Pope Paul VI (1963–78). The WCC assembly in Evanston, Illinois, was a big event attracting more reporters than virtually any other major event in 1954, and the fact that President Eisenhower opened the session must have caused some alarm in Vatican circles.

It would thus be unwise to imagine that the ecumenical trends which emerged inside the Roman Catholic Church during the pontificate of Pius XII moved in a smooth, linear progression towards the much more open attitude regarding the world ecumenical movement exhibited by Pope John XXIII after his election in 1958 and by the Second Vatican Council of 1962–5. Less than a year after *Ecclesia Catholica*, the definition of the dogma of the Assumption of the Blessed Virgin Mary into heaven and the publication of

[104] AWCC, CdA, Correspondence, 94.1.13/2, memorandum of September 1950.

[105] AWCC, CdA, Correspondence, 4 226.100, 1951–2, Carrillo de Albornoz, 22 February, 1951, 'Quelques Notes sur l'attitude du Vatican à l'égard du Conseil Œcuménique et de l'union des églises'.

[106] AAS XXXXI, Ecclesia Catholica.

the encyclical *Humani Generis* suggested that though some individuals and groups of Catholics may have entertained a lively interest in and sympathy for the ecumenical movement outside the Church, Rome saw it as nothing less than a grave threat be countered by the assertion, in the most uncompromising and intransigent terms, of the uniqueness and superiority of the Roman Catholic Church. Indeed, by the mid-1950s, the Vatican was clearly rattled by the success of the World Council of Churches, by the emergence of a rival non-Catholic international religious organization in Geneva under the energetic leadership of Visser 't Hooft and, above all, by the undesirable effects of the growing influence of ecumenism on Catholic theologians, clergy, and lay intellectuals. There was a real fear of the 'contamination' of clergy and laity as a result of ecumenical contacts, and of a consequent growth of indifferentism, heresy, and so on within the ranks of the faithful.

THE HOLY YEAR, 1950

(The Year of the Great Return and the Great Pardon).

The grandiose celebrations in Rome of the Year of Jubilee, 1950, were meant to be the ultimate reply to the assembly in Amsterdam and, to the ecumenical and liberal movements inside the Church, an unashamedly triumphalist reassertion of Roman Catholic orthodoxy. The 1950 Holy Year was, in consequence, undoubtedly the culmination of Pius XII's pontificate and, indeed, the high point of 'traditional', pre-Vatican II Catholicism. It was the occasion when for the first, and so far only, time in the history of the Roman Catholic Church, a pope *formally* exercised the power of papal infallibility, that is, defining a dogmatic truth *ex cathedra*: the belief that the Blessed Virgin Mary had been bodily assumed into heaven. Moreover, Pius XII chose the Holy Year to announce the discovery of the tomb of St Peter in the Vatican grottoes, a pointed reassertion of the claim to the primacy of the papacy among Christians.[107]

Huge numbers of pilgrims came to Rome for the event: according to the film commissioned by the Vatican, *Anno santo 1950*, 5 million people from all over the world, including humble workers, students, and politicians.[108] During the course of the year, eight new saints were proclaimed, four of them Italians. The most important of the latter was Maria Goretti, the teenager who had been raped and murdered and whose murderer was present at the canonization.[109] This was an important response to Hollywood and other 'modernizing' influences which downplayed the virtue of purity. More generally, the

[107] John Walsh, *The Bones of St Peter*, London, 1982, 73–75.
[108] *Anno santo 1950*, 1951, Filmoteca del Vaticano.
[109] Walsh, *Saints*, 393.

emphasis on Italian saints was also part of the campaign to strengthen Italian Catholicism against the ongoing threat from Communism.

By 1950, the Via Della Conciliazione and the Piazza Pio XII, the 'antechambers' so to speak of Piazza San Pietro, had been completed, thus making it possible for literally millions of people to fill the now unified space between the Tiber and the Basilica. As a result, the Holy Year celebrations culminated in a procession of 1 million people from the Campidoglio, the Roman Capitol, to St Peter's, far eclipsing any of Mussolini's 'oceanic gatherings' ten years earlier. The ceremony ended with representatives of the Sacred College, the episcopate, the religious orders and congregations, and finally of the secular clergy, making obeisance and paying homage to the pope himself. Pius XII had truly become 'the Emperor of Rome'.

For the non-Catholic churches, Pius XII's rigid doctrinal orthodoxy, his emphasis upon the role of Mary in salvation history through the definition of the dogma of the Assumption and the encouragement of Marian devotions, and his unbending adherence to a strict interpretation of the traditional moral law in relation to sexuality and procreation were all distinctively unfriendly and unwelcome. Like his predecessors, and perhaps even more so, he seemed to mark out the Roman Catholic Church from the other Christian churches as 'the one, true, church'. The ecumenical activities among other churches, which culminated in the establishment of the World Council of Churches, with its headquarters in Geneva, was firmly ignored by the Vatican, even when the Orthodox churches, including that of Russia, did seek membership. At the end of Pius's pontificate in 1958, Catholics and other Christians seemed as far away from each other as never before. Nothing which Pius did or encouraged Catholics to do during his reign contributed towards the flurry of contacts and activities with the non-Catholic churches which ensued in the ten years following his death.

PIUS XII AND THE SCIENCES

Pius XII continued the attempts by his two predecessors to place the Roman Catholic Church firmly in the scientific mainstream. The Pontifical Academy of Sciences continued to grow in prestige, with the names of such Nobel prize winners as Sir Alexander Fleming, bacteriologist (1946), Sir Edward Appleton, Physics (1948), Otto Hahn, Physics (1955), and Werner Heisenberg, Chemistry (1955) being added to the list of the world's leading scientists in the Academy. Fleming was already a scientist of great international stature when he joined the body of papal laureates. When Fleming visited the Vatican in September 1945, as part of a sort of 'lap of honour' round the European capitals, ' despite his Presbyterian upbringing, he bowed and kissed the papal ring . . .' and he remarked that 'he found the pope "very cordial" and knowledgeable about penicillin'.[110] He was right, because Pius XII always did his homework, 'mugging up' on the profession, expertise, knowledge, or skill represented in the next day's round of audiences. But the audience with Fleming must have been the only occasion on which the pope was presented with, literally, a 'scientific specimen'—in this case a culture of the mould of penicillin![111]

Pius XII's pontificate was notable for other important 'encounters' between Catholicism and science, the first being Fr Gemelli's posthumous 'rehabilitation' of Galileo, starting in 1941. At the annual inaugural meeting of the Pontifical Academy of Science, attended by Pius XII, on 30 November 1941, Gemelli announced that the historian who was the rector of the Lateran University, Mgr Pio Paschini, had been commissioned by the Academy to write a new biography of Galileo.[112] Paschini's book would not appear until 1964, but in the meantime at his own university, the Cattolica in Milan, in 1942, at a tricentennial commemoration of Galileo, Gemelli had publicly acknowledged that:

> Catholics are not afraid to sincerely recognise that the trial against him [Galileo] was an error. This error does not refute either the infallibility of the pope or the authority of the Church; nor was it contrary to the norms of charity observed by the Church in legal proceedings. It was an error of theologians which 'has become a constant warning', as Pastor stated.[113]

In the rest of his lecture, Gemelli was able to present an entirely novel interpretation of Galileo's trial and of his state of mind afterwards. According to Finnochiaro:

> 'the suspected heretic' had become the embodiment of the harmony between science and religion, and this Galilean lesson was all the more instructive insofar as Galileo had not only preached such harmony, but also practiced it; and what is more, he had continued to uphold it after his condemnation.[114]

This whole operation was such an extraordinary climbdown, that it must be concluded Gemelli had agreed his various statements in advance with Pius XII, but it was also a very successful one. Gemelli had managed to square the proverbial circle, turning Galileo from a victim into a 'victor', and using him to provide unimpeachable historical backing for the very essence of the project which the Pontifical Academy of Sciences represented: a confirmation that science and the Catholic faith were not at all incompatible.

[110] Kevin Brown, *'The Penicillin Man': Alexander Fleming and the Antibiotic Revolution*, London, 2004, 167–168.

[111] Brown, *'The Penicillin Man'*, 168.

[112] M.A. Finnochiaro, *Re-trying Galileo, 1632–1992*, Oakland, CA, 2005, ch. 14.

[113] As quoted in Finnochiaro, *Re-trying Galileo*, 177.

[114] Finnochiaro, *Re-trying Galileo*, 280.

The second encounter was that between the Church and psychoanalysis. Though the Holy Office had never pronounced on the psychoanalytic theories of Sigmund Freud, and the attitudes of French Catholic intellectuals were ambivalent, Italian Catholic attitudes to Freud remained fairly hostile.[115] There were some obvious reasons why the Roman Catholic Church should have been hostile to psychoanalysis. There was, first, Freud's focus on sex and sexuality as lying at the heart of the human psyche, which seemed to reject such fundamental features of Catholicism as the doctrine of Original Sin, the Ten Commandments, and the elaborate codes of ethics which moral theologians had derived from them. Worse, it could be argued that Freud's process of psychoanalysis constituted a competitor with the Catholic sacrament of Confession (Penance) if it didn't render it entirely redundant.

Whereas Gemelli had been quite open-minded about Freud in the 1920s and 1930s (see Chapter 5), he seems to have become more critical of Freudian psychoanalysis after the Second World War. In 1950 he published an article 'Psychoanalysis and Catholicism', which urged Catholics not to subject themselves to psychoanalysis on the grounds that, in analysis, the patient surrenders his will and responsibility to the analyst. In this he was at one with American Catholic broadcaster Fulton J. Sheen.[116] But this did not stop Pius XII from stating to the First International Conference of Histopathology and Neurology in Rome in 1952 that 'psychoanalysis if rightly applied, is not contrary to Christian morals'.[117] Gemelli later claimed, in his 1955 book, which was itself backtracking on his own, earlier ideas on the subject, that, 'However . . . the Holy Father not only made certain reservations but has pointed out the limits to be observed in employing psychoanalysis.'[118] Pius XII's address did not immediately lead to a greater acceptance of psychoanalysis in Italy, and Colombo argues that the change did not occur until after the election of a new pope, John XXIII: 'Beginning in the early 1960s, various congresses and meetings convened in which psychology and psychoanalysis were engaged with by theologians.'[119]

The irony of Gemelli's involvement in the debates over Freudian psychoanalysis was that, having helped break down some of the hostility towards it in the 1930s and 1940s, as Colombo says, 'Gemelli took a rather definitive anti-psychological stance only in the 1950s, at the very moment that interest was finally flourishing in Italy.'[120] But what mattered was that Gemelli had

[115] Colombo, 'Psychoanalysis and the Catholic Church', 333–348.

[116] Colombo, 'Psychoanalysis and the Catholic Church', 344.

[117] H. Msiak and V. M. Staudt, *Catholics in Psychology: A Historical Survey*, New York, Toronto, and London, 1954, 29.

[118] As cited in Colombo, 'Psychoanalysis and the Catholic Church', 345.

[119] Colombo, 'Psychoanalysis and the Catholic Church', 335.

[120] Colombo, 'Psychoanalysis and the Catholic Church', 334.

not taken up a stance against psychoanalysis *earlier*, and given his powerfully influential roles as both a consultor to the Holy Office and as president of the Pontifical Academy of Sciences, he had probably prevented an official Catholic condemnation of Freud, whose death in 1939 was even commemorated in the Vatican newspaper.[121] The obituary in *L'Osservatore Romano* was balanced but ambivalent, 'The psychological work is applauded. His [Freud's] philosophical digressions were, on the other hand, the object of severe criticisms. [Freud's work] . . . is the most audacious adventure in the thought of the contemporary epoch.'[122]

By far the most important scientific issue which Pius sought to address during the course of his reign was that of the origins of the universe and, in particular, the theory of the 'big bang'. The issue came to his attention precisely because Fr Georges Lemaître, S.J., a professor at the University of Leuven/Louvain and member of the Pontifical Academy of Sciences, was, in fact, one of the originators of this scientific idea. Though in some sense an acolyte of Einstein's, Lemaître differed from him on some key issues. Lemaître published his theory, *Hypothèse de l'atome primitif* in 1927, unaware that the Russian mathematician, Alexander Friedmann, had already reached more or less the same conclusion. Lemaître's publication received little attention until the 1940s.[123]

However, Pius XI made the theory his own in November 1951, in an address to the Pontifical Academy of Sciences called 'The Proofs for the Existence of God in the Light of Modern Natural Science':

> In fact, it would seem that present-day science, with one sweeping step back across millions of centuries, has succeeded in bearing witness to the primordial *Fiat lux* uttered at the moment when, along with matter, there burst forth from nothing a sea of light and radiation, while the particles of the chemical elements split and formed into millions of galaxies . . . Therefore, there is a Creator. Therefore God exists![124]

His declaration made headline news and stirred great controversy in scientific circles throughout the world.[125] It also prompted the alarm of Lemaître who, as a good priest and a good scientist, believed that Pius was in grave danger of saddling the Roman Catholic Church with a scientific theory that could so easily and so quickly be superseded by another, a sort of reverse of its disastrous decision regarding Galileo:

> As far as I can see, such a theory remains entirely outside any metaphysical or religious question. It leaves the materialist free to deny any transcendental

[121] L'OR, 23 September 1939.
[122] G.La., 'Sigmund Freud e l'opera sua: al di là del bene e del male', L'OR, 1 October 1939.
[123] S. Singh, *The Big Bang*, London and New York, 2004, 156–161.
[124] As quoted in Singh, *The Big Bang*, 360.
[125] Singh, *The Big Bang*, 361.

> Being ... For the believer, it removes any attempt at familiarity with God ... It is consonant with Isaiah speaking of the hidden God, hidden even in the beginning of the universe.[126]

Recent developments in the field of cosmology have proved his intuition correct. Working in conjunction with Fr Daniel O'Connell, S.J., the director of the Vatican Observatory, Lemaître succeeded in persuading Pius to desist from any further public pronouncements on cosmology.[127] Lemaître would succeed Gemelli as president of the Pontifical Academy of Sciences in 1960.

PIUS XII AS THE GREAT COMMUNICATOR

Pius XII was much more of an all-round communicator than either Benedict XV or Pius XI. He grasped the vital importance of all the media to the Church's mission, thus, in 1953, under the prompting of Mgr Montini, the Vatican established its first press office (Sala Stampa) to brief journalists from all over the world.[128] Pius also made far greater and more regular use of the radio than his predecessor, making literally dozens of broadcasts during his nineteen-year reign, and it was during his pontificate that Vatican Radio opened a new and bigger transmitter at Santa Maria della Galleria, 27 kilometres from Rome, in 1956. According to *L'Osservatore Romano*, the pope went in a solemn motorcade from the Vatican along a route lined by crowds and papal guards, and when he arrived at the transmitter he blessed it with holy water: it must be assumed that it did not actually fall on the electrical equipment![129]

He also appeared, arguably 'starred', in three films—*Congresso Eucaristico di Budapest*, which commemorated his role as papal legate at that Eucharistic congress in 1938, *Pastor Angelicus*, and *Anno santo, 1950*[130]—and he was the first occupant of the Throne of St Peter to use television, when his blessing *Urbi et Orbi* ('to the City and the World') was broadcast to eight countries via the newly established Eurovision link in 1954.[131]

He was, nevertheless, wary of the new dangers which the communications media of his day presented to Catholic faith and morals. In 1954 he set up the Pontifical Commission for Motion Pictures, Radio and Television to monitor the effects of the electronic media, give directives for Catholic use of them,

[126] As quoted in Singh, *The Big Bang*, 343. [127] Singh, *The Big Bang*, 342.

[128] C. Zizola, 'L'ufficio stampa del Vaticano', *Cristianesimo nella storia*, 25(3) (2004), 997–1013.

[129] Bea, *Qui Radio vaticana*, 189–192.

[130] *Congresso Eucaristico di Budapest*, titolo 34, *Pastor Angelicus* 1943, and *Anno Santo, 1950*, 1951, all in the Filmoteca Vaticana, Vatican City.

[131] *The Tablet*, 11 October 1958.

and train priests, religious, and laypeople in their use.[132] Two years later, in an audience which he granted in October 1955 to representatives of the international associations of cinema owners and managers and distributors of films, he made detailed observations on the use of the motion picture in modern society.[133] As usual, he had carefully prepared his 'script' in advance, being advised by experts in his Pontifical Commission, whose head, not by chance, was an American, Mgr Martin O'Connor.[134]

The pope's most detailed pronouncement on the media came in the encyclical *Miranda Prorsus*, of September 1957, in which he renewed his warnings about the abuses of motion pictures, radio, and television, and provided a set of detailed guidelines about their use by Catholics.[135] He saw film as 'neutral' or 'secular', hence dangerous ground for Catholics, and was concerned about the representation of evil in films, by making it the object of 'entertainment and recreation'.[136] He was especially worried about the misuse of the media for political or economic purposes, in other words, propaganda and advertising, and he insisted that the public authorities had a right to enforce 'Public Morals' in relation to the censorship of films.[137] Following on from his predecessor's encyclical, *Vigilanti Cura*, which had lauded the initiatives of Catholics, other Christians, and Jews in watching over the American cinema industry (see Chapter 5), he urged Catholics to continue to press for a proper 'Rating of Motion Pictures' and for Catholics to assume the role of film critics in their own communities.[138] He also encouraged the development of networks of Catholic cinemas, as had already happened in Italy and other Continental countries, and Catholic radio stations, singling out the Dutch experience for especial praise.[139]

He was also already aware of what he described as 'The Special Power of Television', or rather its dangers: a prophetic stand indeed.[140] In 1950, French Catholics donated a television transmitter to the pope, but the lack of viewers in Italy, and technical and financial problems, dissuaded the Vatican authorities from inaugurating a television service.[141] In *Miranda Prorsus*, Pius showed himself to be well informed and up to date about the pace of technological developments, combining that knowledge with what he believed to be a healthy wariness of their potentially harmful effects. Anxious that Catholics should use the new media to spread the faith, but not

[132] AAS, XXXXVI, II, XXI (1954), 783–784, Secretaria Status.
[133] *Pio XII Discorsi*, XVI, 1955–1956, 341–357.
[134] *Pio XII Discorsi*, XVI, 1955–1956, 342.
[135] Carlen, *Papal Encyclicals*, IV, 347–364.
[136] Carlen, *Papal Encyclicals*, IV, 348–350.
[137] Carlen, *Papal Encyclicals*, IV, 350–351.
[138] Carlen, *Papal Encyclicals*, IV, 354–355.
[139] Carlen, *Papal Encyclicals*, IV, 356–360.
[140] Carlen, *Papal Encyclicals*, IV, 361.
[141] Bea, *Qui Radio vaticana*, 173.

a little fearful that they could also seriously undermine it, in the concordat with Spain the Vatican hence inserted a clause guaranteeing access to the State's media (Chapter 10).[142]

If Pius was a good 'performer' in the electronic means of communication, he was also adept in his use of the more traditional ones, in particular, the face-to-face encounters with large numbers of people in papal audiences—in 1957 alone he received a staggering 800,000 in public audiences.[143] In both his general (i.e. large-scale) as well as private audiences he succeeded in projecting himself as a world 'celebrity'. Indeed, for Pius XII, the general audience was, above all, a teaching medium on a par with encyclicals and other major papal pronouncements. Through them, he could reach an audience of the great and good, the elites of the world of medicine, economics, business, the professions, the media, and so on. Like popes before him, he gave thousands of audiences during the course of his reign but the difference between him and, for example, Benedict XV or Pius XI, was that he received increasingly large numbers of *non-Catholics* and also specialist groups of all kinds, from all over the world, thanks, in the latter case, to the increasing ease of air travel. In 1953–4 alone, Pius XII gave audiences to national (usually Italian) and international gatherings of small farmers, psychotherapists and psychologists, producers of tobacco, Italian state and para-state employees, ophthalmologists, representatives of food-processing industries, surgeons, the International Statistical Institute, the International Microbiological Institute, the Wine and Vine Congress, the International Maritime Agency, psychiatric nurses, the International Congress of Criminal Lawyers, family doctors, representatives of the steel, silk, and felt industries, urologists, engineers, accountants and financial consultants, military doctors, the American Association of Travel Agents and Tourist Operators, watchmakers, representatives of social housing organizations, Catholic lawyers, a delegation from the UN Food and Agriculture Organization (whose headquarters had recently been established in Rome), and Italian secondary school teachers.[144] In August 1958 he even received the Harlem Globetrotters baseball team in audience. And for most of these gatherings he prepared speeches, sometimes lengthy ones, which clearly demonstrate that he had done considerable, detailed homework beforehand. What is particularly striking is the geographical and religious diversity of the groups received: in April 1958, for example, he received a parliamentary delegation from Iceland, where there were 2,000 Catholics out of a total population of just over 100,000.[145] The diversity of those specialist groups, and their largely international character,

[142] Cipriotti and Talamanca, *I Concordati*, 65.

[143] UK NA/PRO, Kew, FCO, Vatican, Rv1011/1, Annual Political Report of the British Minister for 1957.

[144] See *Pio XII Discorsi*, XV, 1953–1954.

[145] *Pio XII Discorsi*, XX, discorso ad un gruppo di parliamentari dell'Islanda, 3 April 1958.

testify to the fact that, by the end of his reign, Pius XII was truly one of the world's most famous celebrities.

TOWARDS VATICAN II?

If the liturgical reforms which followed the Second Council of the Vatican were greatly facilitated by the work embarked upon in Pius XII's reign, and positively encouraged by him, then arguably the same applies to the Council itself. Vatican II emphatically was not John XXIII's idea: Ottaviani and Ruffini had already suggested it to Pius XII in March 1948.[146] But they, like Pius XI who had also thought of reconvening the First Vatican Council, conceived it in a conservative key. They intended to use it to consolidate and entrench the authority of the Church, to reaffirm doctrinal orthodoxy, and to mobilize Catholics against Communism.[147] Pius told Ottaviani that he wanted to 'consider' the question of a council.[148] The result was the establishment of another commission, which never had the opportunity to seriously discuss the arrangements for agenda for the council before the death of Pius XII supervened.

THE END

The last years of Pius XII's reign were characterized by an increasingly personal rule: just as no replacement had been made for Maglione as Secretary of State in 1944, so no one was found of the stature of Montini to replace him when he was sent off to Milan ten years later. In these circumstances, Tardini was still the number one in the Secretariat of State but he was overshadowed by the dominant influence of the 'pentagon' cardinals. Papa Pacelli seems to have had a veritable phobia about making staff appointments in the last years of his life. Thus, he failed to appoint a *Camarlengo* to act as caretaker of the Church in the event of his death, so the cardinals in the first General Congregation in October 1958 had to elect one of their own number, Aloisi Masella, to the post.[149] Similarly, Pius made no new cardinals after 1954, despite the fact that, in the period 1956–8, nine cardinals had died,[150] with the result that the 1958 conclave was seventeen short on the usual maximum of

[146] Hebblethwaite, *John XXIII*, 310–312.
[147] *Cultura e Libri*, n. 166/7 (gennaio–giugno 2009), Rome, 82.
[148] ASV, Conc. Vat II, 682 Relazione 1948.
[149] Hebblethwaite, *John XXIII*, 271.
[150] UK NA/PRO, FCO, Rv1011/1, 1958, Annual Political Report of the British Minister, 1957.

seventy cardinals, quite apart from the fact that the occupants of several 'cardinalatial' residential sees lacked their red hat.[151] There were signs of 'drift' in other decision-making areas, particularly in relation to the Italian Church.[152] There have even been suggestions of nepotism and corruption during Pius XII's last years.[153]

The most unsavoury developments seem to have been related to the pope's declining health: Pius had recurrent bouts of serious illness in 1953, 1954, 1956, and then his final illness in the autumn of 1958. During the 1953 illness, the pope developed double pneumonia but was successfully treated with penicillin.[154] When Pius took ill in 1954, he suspended his audiences 'on account of an indisposition arising from overwork', the official medical bulletin speaking of 'slight fever, symptoms of gastritis, preceded by persistent hiccoughs'.[155] The illness, whatever its cause, was serious. It was not until March that Pius resumed his walks in the Vatican gardens and it was June before he resumed his audiences. The pope's physician or *archiatra* was Riccardo Galeazzi-Lisi, an oculist and half-brother of Pius's friend Count Enrico Galeazzi. It is not clear whether he came on Galeazzi's recommendation but he seems to have had the support of Sister Pascalina.[156] A tussle developed between the ever-protective Sister Pascalina and the doctors on the one hand, and the men in the Secretariat of State on the other. She was anxious to reduce the number of papal audiences so that the pope might conserve his strength, they were frustrated because lack of access to him hindered the despatch of business during the periods when the pope was indisposed. Unlike the situation in the late 1930s, there was no 'vice-pope', that is, a cardinal Secretary of State, to hold the fort during the pope's illnesses.

If there was not already a sufficient air of 'quackery' around Galeazzi-Lisi, the situation was worsened by the arrival of a doctor with a 'miracle cure', the Swiss Protestant pastor, Paul Niehans.[157] Niehans, following the pioneering work of Voronoff, claimed to cure illness and to slow or stop cellular degeneration by means of 'therapy with living cells', from the foetuses of sheep or monkeys, usually the brain, which were injected into the patient.[158] The more common name given to this therapy, 'monkey glands treatment' aroused salacious gossip in the press in several countries. But it seemed to work and the fact that Niehans was also able to cure what was to become a recurrent medical problem for Pius XII, hiccoughs that lasted days and weeks, by the simple method of applying doses of iced water to ease little stomach ulcers, confirmed

[151] Hebblethwaite, *John XXIII*, 271–272.
[152] See Pollard, *Catholicism*, 127.
[153] Hebblethwaite, *John XXIII*, 271.
[154] Shad, *Signora del Sacro Palazzo*, 187–188.
[155] *L'Osservatore Romano*, 31 January 1954.
[156] Schad, *Signora del Sacro Palazzo*, 185.
[157] Schad, *Signora del Sacro Palazzo*, 185.
[158] Schad, *Signora del Sacro Palazzo*, 185.

his new standing in the papal entourage.[159] Conversely, Galeazzi-Lisi fell into disfavour, and in 1956 was banned from the papal apartments, his place as *archiatra* being taken officially by Dr Antonio Gasbarrini: presumably because, however good a physician he was, as a Protestant pastor Niehans could not possibly serve in a senior position in the papal court. On the other hand, Niehans did become a member of the Pontifical Academy of Sciences in 1956.[160] To add to the fevered press speculation of the last years, in December 1954 Pius announced to his entourage that he had seen a 'vision' of Christ in his bedroom.[161] Despite his plea for secrecy, the story quickly got out, as Cardinal Spellman discovered when he was summoned to Rome.[162] Pius claimed to have had other visions, like the 'spinning sun' in the Vatican gardens, which was remarkably similar to the alleged experience of the children at Fatima.

The circumstances of the pope's final illness, death, and funeral were not entirely edifying. He took ill at the beginning of October 1958, while he was at Castel Gandolfo. He suffered yet another prolonged bout of hiccoughs and a *lavanda gastrica* (gastric wash) was administered. Somehow, Galeazzi-Lisi managed to regain access to the papal apartment and it was even alleged that he took photographs of the dying pope.[163] Was it Sister Pascalina who let him in, desperate to find anyone who could help Pius? Tardini said Mass *pro infermo* for the pope, as he had done for his predecessor and this was broadcast by Vatican Radio. One of the pope's secretaries, Fr. Wilhelm Herbert, administered Extreme Unction on 6 October and Pius died at 3.25am on the 9th.[164] Galeazzi-Lisi now proceeded to embalm the corpse using his 'special system'. Unfortunately, it did not work and his failure to remove the entrails resulted in decomposition and discoloration which was plain for all to hear, see, and smell during the funeral procession and the lying-in-state.[165] Once again banned from the Vatican, Galeazzi-Lisi nevertheless made a lot of money out of press conferences and the publication of his memoirs.[166]

There are a number of reasons which would help explain the 'drift' and 'decay' that appeared to surround the papacy during Pius XII's last years. One was his obstinate insistence on 'personal government', which was vitiated by his failing health. There was his poor judgement in the choice of assistants, like Galeazzi-Lisi and Niehans. He was also a truly Roman pope, the first for many years. His close geographical proximity to his family gave rise to strong suspicions of nepotism. Then there was the changing nature of Rome in the wake of the economic 'miracle' which began in the mid-1950s, and also the

159 Schad, *Signora del Sacro Palazzo*, 185.
160 *Annuario Pontificio*, 1957, 675.
161 Schad, *Signora del Sacro Palazzo*, 192.
162 Schad, *Signora del Sacro Palazzo*, 192.
163 Schad, *Signora del Sacro Palazzo*, 186, fn. 27.
164 Schad, *Signora del Sacro Palazzo*, 194.
165 Hebblethwaite, *John XXIII*, 270.
166 Schad, *Signora del Sacro Palazzo*, 186, fn. 27.

'Americanization' of Italian society which also began at the same time. In consequence, the Eternal City in the 1950s increasingly became a location of the Italian *demi monde*, the heart of the *dolce vita*, and the setting for the sexual scandals of film stars, nouveau riches bourgeoisie, and Roman aristocracy, like Prince Orsini, an attendant at the papal throne who attempted suicide in 1954 because of his affair with actress Belinda Lee.[167] The latter affair could hardly be blamed on the pope or the Vatican, but the scandal inevitably rubbed off on both. The 'media age' may have brought benefits to the papacy, but in opening it up to closer press scrutiny it laid bare to the world its less salubrious aspects.

Whatever the explanation, change was in the air in the Vatican after the death of Pius XII, though most of the curial cardinals would not have welcomed it.[168] When Cardinal Bacci gave his peroration *De eligendo pontifice* on 25 October, before the cardinals assembled in Conclave, it was, as Hebblethwaite says, 'a point by point description of what Pius XII was not'.[169] According to Bacci's papal 'job description':

> Rather than someone who has explored and experienced the subtle principles belonging to the art and discipline of diplomacy, we need a pope who is above all holy, so that he may receive from God what lies beyond natural gifts . . . .[170]

As always in a conclave, the ultimate conflict was between the supporters of the previous pontiff and his critics, but unlike in 1939 there was no obvious candidate to succeed Pius XII in 1958. Yet, in the end, the cardinals elected someone who was arguably the antithesis of Pius XII and a man who corresponded in so many respects to Bacci's 'job description': Cardinal Angelo Roncalli, by now Patriarch of Venice, who would become 'the pope of the Council' and inaugurate a very different chapter in the history of the papacy.

CONCLUSION: 'THE LAST REAL POPE'?

Pius XII was a man of remarkable contrasts. On the one hand he was notoriously hesitant and timid in his handling of external events, most especially the Holocaust, over which he clearly agonized for years. On the other hand, he could show extraordinary courage and resolution, as in his agreement to act as a conduit between plotting German generals and the British government during the 'phoney war'. Again, he presented the appearance not only of someone who was distant, aloof, and conscious of his elevated status and

[167] Hebblethwaite, *Paul VI*, 258.
[168] Hebblethwaite, *Paul VI*, 271–272.
[169] Hebblethwaite, *Paul VI*, 281.
[170] As cited in Hebblethwaite, *Paul VI*, 281.

position, but hieratic, being different from the rest of common humanity, as befitted the 'Vicar of Christ' on earth. On the other hand, he clearly had a close, personal relationship with Mother Pascalina and he showed great affection for his canary.

His rigid doctrinal orthodoxy, and the Vatican's aloofness from the emerging ecumenical movement, also contrasts with the fact that he permitted and even encouraged tendencies towards reform during the course of his pontificate, especially in the liturgical sphere. But, whatever his limitations and contradictions, as Andrea Riccardi has pointed out, Pius XII followed an original and successful strategy as pope within the context of the reality of the Church in a mass society:

> his teaching, his rapport with crowds, his image as a great world leader during the crisis of the war and (post-war) reconstruction and his confidence in the efficacy of the word show that he met the challenge posed by mass society to the Church, establishing an immediate relationship between pastor and faithful, between the Church and the world.[171]

For most of those Catholics, and many non-Catholics, who are now over 60 he remains the 'model pope', 'the ideal-type' of pope, an iconic figure who personified a papacy, and a kind of Catholicism which has long gone. It is this sort of Catholicism, at least in the form of the Tridentine Latin Mass, which many inside the Church still revere. It is also revered and practised by Catholic traditionalists, like the French-based St Pius X Society, the followers of Mgr Marcel Lefebvre, who broke allegiance to Rome because he believed that the Second Vatican Council had been hijacked by 'Freemasons, Jews and modernists', and perhaps the Devil himself. Lefebvre founded what is in effect a schismatic, traditionalist Church which still has a small but devoted band of faithful in many countries.[172] Then there are the even more extreme traditionalist Catholics, the *Sede Vacantisti*, those who believe that the papal throne has been vacant (*sede vacante*) since the death of Pius XII.[173] To all these people, Pius XII was, to paraphrase Antonio Spinosa, 'the last real pope'.[174]

[171] Riccardi, '*Il Partito Romano*', 44.

[172] G. Miccoli, *La Chiesa dell'anti-concilio. I tradizionalisti alla conquista di Roma*, Bari and Rome, 2011.

[173] R. Scott Appleby, *Being Right: Conservative Catholics in America*, Indianapolis, IN, 1995, 257.

[174] A. Spinosa, *L'ultimo papa*, Milan, 1992, 153.

12

The Papacy in the Age of Totalitarianism

THE 1914–58 PERIOD IN PERSPECTIVE

The death of Pius X and the election of Benedict XV as his successor in 1914 marked a major watershed in the history of the papacy. Papa Sarto's foreign policy, low profile, non-interventionist, but intransigent towards anti-clerical states like France and Portugal, was replaced by the much more active, interventionist policy of Benedict XV, who also adopted a more conciliatory stance towards France and Portugal. Similarly, the anti-modernist hysteria of Pius X's pontificate was replaced by a much more cautious, albeit still suspicious, attitude towards innovation in the fields of theology, exegesis, and ecclesiastical history, while, most importantly, the purges of offending 'modernists' that had characterized the previous pontificate were abandoned. These policy changes were also accompanied by changes in key personnel, the marginalization of Merry del Val, De Lai, and Benigni, a 'changing of the guard' that was not repeated on the deaths of either Benedict XV or Pius XI. There were some important carryovers from Pius X's pontificate into that of his successor, like his reform of the Roman curia, the inauguration of the process of codifying Canon Law, and the first, tentative steps towards liturgical change, such that it can argued that the Liturgical Movement began under St Pius X. All of these had profound implications for the development of the papacy over the next 100 years.

COMMON THEMES, COMMON CHALLENGE, COMMON POLICIES

Nevertheless, there is a unity in the nature and thrust of the policies pushed forward under Benedict, Pius XI, and Pius XII that distinguishes their pontificates so clearly from that of Pius X on the one hand, and, to a lesser extent, from that of John XXIII on the other. This unity was ultimately derived from a return to a 'Leonine' vision of the papacy and the Roman Catholic Church. After Benedict's election, the Holy See resumed a more active, high-profile diplomatic role, perforce because of the outbreak of the First World War. Thereafter it would take upon itself a more specifically peace-making role in time of war and threat of war, and in peacetime it would seek to influence governments on a wide range of issues, which was very typical of Leo XIII's pontificate.[1] This is hardly surprising given that Benedict XV, Cardinal Pietro Gasparri, and Pius XII had all served in papal diplomacy under Leo XIII and his formidable Secretary of State, Cardinal Rampolla del Tindaro, early in their careers. Pius XI had not, but he had worked in the papal diplomatic corps under Benedict, and his appointment of, first, Gasparri and then Pacelli as his secretaries of state ensured that the Leonine diplomatic model would persist throughout his pontificate. Further abiding themes of all three pontificates were also of Leonine derivation: the concern about the Oriental churches in communion with Rome, a burning desire to achieve reunification with the schismatic, Orthodox, churches, and a commitment to the renewal of the Roman Catholic Church's missionary outreach.[2] Finally, the *leitmotif* of the public utterances of the three pontiffs in this period is that of the Christian 'restoration' of society, which was also the watchword of Leo XIII, though it can be said to have emerged as a key trope under Pius IX, or even Gregory XVI, in reaction against the rise of the secularist agenda pursued by liberal, anti-clerical movements in early nineteenth-century Europe and Latin America. The desire to bring about a re-Christianization has remained a major preoccupation of the papacy down to the present day in the face of the accelerating secularization of European society and its legislation during the last few decades.

All three pontiffs also faced the challenge of the emerging ecumenical movement among the Anglican and Protestant churches, with, later, some support from the Orthodox. In the end, these popes would ultimately turn their backs upon the ecumenical movement. Reunion with the Orthodox churches was a slightly more practical proposition if only because they were essentially schismatic, rather than thoroughly heretical, as the Protestant and Anglican churches were perceived to be in the Vatican. But experience in all three pontificates showed that it was difficult, very difficult, to achieve results, despite all the Vatican's efforts in the direction of conversion of or reunion with the Orthodox, especially the Russian Orthodox. Nevertheless, it remained an absolute obsession with successive popes. The Polish foreign minister, Joseph Beck, hit the nail on the head when he exclaimed in 1938,

[1] Jean-Marc Ticchi, *Aux Frontières de la Paix: Bons Offices, Médiations, Arbitrages du Saint-Siège 1878–1922*, Rome, 2002, 1–265.

[2] See Leo's encyclical in Carlen, *Papal Encyclicals*, II, 241–261.

'the lure of [Orthodox] Russia possessed an age-old power to entrance and befuddle the Vatican'.[3]

Human continuities played a big part in giving unity to this phase in the history of the papacy. Certain key figures played powerful roles in the Vatican in this period, and in some cases beyond it. Apart from Popes Benedict XV and Pius XI themselves, Pietro Gasparri determined the main lines of Vatican foreign policy between his appointment as Secretary of State in 1914 and his replacement by Eugenio Pacelli in1930. Indeed, his reappointment by newly elected Pius XI in 1922 was quite exceptional in the history of the modern papacy. Even allowing for the strong control exerted on the formation of policy by Benedict XV and Pius XI, who both had experience in papal diplomacy, Gasparri must be counted as one of the most important and influential secretaries of state in the history of the modern papacy, on a par with Consalvi, Antonelli, Rampolla del Tindaro, and, in our own time, Agostino Casaroli. His great achievements—the Codification of Canon Law and the Lateran Pacts of 1929 and some other concordats—have stood the test of time. What influence he continued to exercise after his retirement in 1930 is much more difficult to assess. Eugenio Pacelli, in his turn, wielded considerable influence in his role as Secretary of State between 1930 and 1939 and then as Camerlengo during the *sede vacante* after Pius XI's death. And, of course, he then succeeded Papa Ratti in March of that year.

The figure who has truly emerged from the papers now available in the Vatican Archives as the *éminence grise* of Pius XI's pontificate is Fr Wlodomir Ledóchowski, the head of the Jesuits. His essentially behind-the-scenes, and sometimes malevolent, influence on so many major decisions and major papal public utterances can now be fully documented, as is obvious from Chapters 5, 6, and 7. Given the lack of access to the papers of Pius XII, it is impossible at this stage to evaluate the influence of Ledóchowski's successor as 'black pope', Fr J. Janssens. Another Jesuit of absolutely crucial importance in the pontificates of both Pius XI and Pius XII was Fr Tacchi-Venturi. Indeed, even though his role in the negotiations for the Lateran Pacts of 1929 and the 'September Accords' of 1931 has long been documented, his work as *the* channel of communication between the Vatican and the Fascist Regime, between Pius XI, and to a very much lesser extent Pius XII, and Mussolini, is only now being fully recognized. The Jesuits, then, probably reached the peak of their influence in the Vatican in this period.

Padre Gemelli was undoubtedly another important influence on the making and execution of policy by Pius XI, and even Pius XII. His rectorship of the Catholic University in Milan gave him a major place in the intellectual life of Catholic Italy, and a controversial, pro-Fascist, role in Italian politics.

3 As quoted in Pease, *Rome's Most Faithful Daughter*, 171.

Gemelli was also a key player in decision-making in both the Holy Office and Pontifical Academy of Sciences. It would be no exaggeration to say that, in the latter role, he was largely instrumental in carrying forward the process of re-engaging the Catholic Church with modern science during the pontificates of Pius XI and Pius XII.

Though Cardinal Van Rossum clearly deserves recognition as one of the most important non-Italian senior members of the curia in the pontificates of Benedict XV and Pius XI, the evidence suggests that his subordinate, Celso Costantini, probably eclipsed him in determining the shape of the encyclicals on the Church's missionary strategy as put forward by both Pius XI and Pius XII. The Chinese experiences of Costantini, and Fr Lebbe, were crucial in encouraging those popes towards the indigenization of clergy and episcopacy in the mission fields, and the way in which the Vatican handled the processes of decolonization after 1945 for which those policies were a preparation.

Five other major players in Vatican politics in this period deserve mention, Canali, Pizzardo, Ottaviani, Montini, and Tardini, for strangely different reasons. Canali was the great survivor: the spiritual heir of Merry del Val, who went down with his patron upon the election of Benedict XV, but managed to crawl back to a position of influence in the later years of Pius XI. By the beginning of the Second World War he was the effective ruler of the State of the Vatican City, a position of enormous material power, and the head of Vatican finances, save the IOR and the ASSS. He would continue to exercise much influence in a conservative direction during the rest of Pius XII's reign. Pizzardo owed his rise to obsequious self-serving, and an absolute dedication to the charge entrusted to him by Pius XI of 'exporting' the Italian model of Catholic Action to the rest of the Catholic world. He was truly *mediocritas homo*, a fact which, along with the choices of Edmund Walsh and Michel D'Herbigny to head missions to Russia, raises serious doubts about Pius XI as a judge of men. Pizzardo sailed on to become a major influence in Pius XII's reign as part of the Vatican 'pentagon'.

Alfredo Ottaviani was another rising star in the reign of Pius XI, though more slowly than Pizzardo. His specialization in questions of heresy during Pius XI's reign eventually led to the top job in the Holy Office, as secretary, because the pope was prefect, in the reign of his successor. In this position he became the scourge of new types of 'modernism', theological and political. Pizzardo and Ottaviani would lead the conservative, curial opposition during the Second Vatican Council.[4] For both Pizzardo and Ottaviani, Montini, the powerful joint pro-Secretary of State with Tardini in 1950, was *the* dangerous enemy of the Church, hence his banishment from the Vatican in 1954.[5] Given

[4] See Hebblethwaite, *Paul VI*, ch. 19.

[5] Hebblethwaite, *Paul VI*, 255.

that Ottaviani was in part responsible for that ouster, there is an exquisite irony in the fact that, as first cardinal deacon, he would be called upon to crown Montini pope nine years later.

Finally, Domenico Tardini, though a relatively late arrival to a senior position in the Vatican—he did not become Under-Secretary of the Congregation for Extraordinary Ecclesiastical Affairs until 1929 and *Sostituto* to the Secretary of State in 1937—nevertheless worked at the heart of Vatican diplomacy for forty-one years and was also involved in making key decisions in the Holy Office. This 'romano dei romani'—Roman born and bred—had an acute, shrewd understanding of the Vatican's relations with states, despite having had no actual experience of a foreign posting.[6] His growing influence on Vatican foreign policy in reign of Pius XI was surpassed only by that which he exercised in the reign of Pius XII, especially after the death of Maglione in 1944. After Montini's departure to Milan in 1954, he was in effect, though not in name, Secretary of State. His official appointment to that post after the election of John XXIII in 1958 was natural, though not inevitable, considering the circumstances. Roncalli had been away from Rome since 1923 and did not return to Italy until 1954 so there was need for the proverbial 'safe pair of hands' in the Vatican when he became pope. Tardini would thus act as an element of continuity between Pius XI/Pius XII and John XXIII.

THE CHALLENGE OF TOTAL WAR

It could be said that the papacy's first experience of 'total war' or at least ideologically inspired conflict came with French Revolutionary and Napoleonic Wars at the end of the eighteenth and beginning of the nineteenth centuries. The French armies, and the radical economic, social, political, and ecclesiastical reforms which came in their wake, brought the papacy to its knees, with two popes, Pius VI and Pius VII, in captivity and the incorporation of the Papal States into Napoleon's new European and Italian state systems.[7] Pius IX also saw the dangers of war and nationalism in 1848 when, in his April allocution, he argued that he could not declare war on Austria on behalf of Italians seeking to liberate themselves from its domination of the peninsula because he represented 'Him who is the author of peace and lover of concord and who seeks after and embraces all races, peoples and nations with an equal devotion of paternal love.'[8] While it

[6] According to Casula, *Domenico Tardini*, photograph between pp. 388 and 389, his only foreign 'posting' was to accompany Cardinal Pacelli as pontifical legate to Lisieux in 1937.

[7] Hales, *Revolution and the Papacy*, chs 6, 7, and 12.

[8] As quoted in Hales, *Pio Nono*, 77.

is true that Pio Nono also had the specific aim of seeking to preserve the Papal States against the rising tide of Italian nationalism, he was setting forth, for the first time, the modern papacy's views on the dangers of nationalism, and first making the claim, continued by all his successors, to be the Vicar of 'the Prince of Peace'. His worst fears were confirmed when the clash between Napoleon III and Bismarck in the Franco-Prussian War of 1870–1 indirectly led to the occupation of Rome by Italian troops and his own self-proclaimed 'exile' as 'the prisoner of the Vatican'. This was a far cry indeed from the 'warrior' popes—like Julius II—of the late medieval and Renaissance periods.

The clash of nationalisms, the ideological nature of the First and Second World Wars, and the horrors of modern technological warfare created enormous problems for the papacy. A further problem was that the seat of the papacy was geographically located inside one of the belligerents, Italy, in both world wars, on the Entente side in the first and the Axis side in the second. And, last but not least, like all the other European powers, the papacy itself had 'war aims'. In these circumstances, it could only seek to maintain a neutral and impartial stance during the two conflicts, but while it was just about possible to maintain formal diplomatic neutrality, maintaining the plausibility of its impartial stance proved much, much more difficult.

In both world wars, millions of Catholics found themselves fighting on opposing sides. National feelings, brought to fever pitch by the exigencies and horrors of war, left little room for papal peace appeals. Catholics on each side *expected* the moral support of their Holy Father and both were disappointed when they did not get it, so Benedict XV ended up as both the *pape boche* and *Der französische Papst*. The anti-German activities of an outstandingly patriotic churchman like Cardinal Mercier of Belgium created enormous problems for the wartime diplomacy of Benedict and Gasparri. Pius XII had a similar experience, being strongly criticized by many Polish Catholics for not condemning German aggression and war crimes. And undoubtedly one of the reasons why he was unwilling to publicly condemn German war crimes, including the Holocaust, was fear of straining the allegiance of German Catholics. Many had already abandoned the Church under Nazi pressure in peacetime so that a constant fear of further defections, and perhaps even schism, hung over Pius XII. If the popes were successful in avoiding the dangers of schism during the two wars it is due to the fact that neither of them put Catholic loyalties to the test by publicly condemning various governments for the crimes they had committed.

Thanks to Hitler, the Second World War was a highly ideologically charged conflict—after June 1941 the Nazis were fighting *two* ideological enemies, the Western Democracies on the one side and Soviet

Communism—or 'Judeo-Bolshevism', as they liked to call it—on the other. For Hitler it was, above all, a war of racial extermination and survival. There was even an undercurrent of racial Darwinism in the First World War, between Teuton and Slave, which was felt strongly, but not exclusively, on the German side.[9] It was particularly discernible in the attitude of Germans towards Belgium and the general staff's demand for *Lebensraum* in the East. Benedict sensed the racial undertones of the struggle taking place between 1914 and 1918 and denounced them in his encyclical *Ad Beatissimi* of November 1914 when he wrote 'Race hatred has reached its climax.'[10] But it was Pius XII who had to face the full horror of racial war with its programmes of genocide, although he was not prepared to denounce racialism and its horrifying consequences publicly, for all the reasons set out in Chapter 9. Had he done so, he would also have had to condemn the war crimes of the Soviets, this time committed in the name of class rather than race.

Total war is usually defined as the total mobilization of resources—cultural, psychological, economic and demographic, and technological—by the warring powers. In the First World War this approach increasingly involved civilians, either being starved because of the Allied blockade of Germany and the other Central Powers or being bombed from the air while they were in their own homes. These horrors were magnified a hundredfold in the Second World War, indeed the Germans sought to starve whole populations as a form of warfare and the Allies to carpet-bomb cities in order to destroy morale. Benedict had been quick to publicly denounce the new methods of modern warfare, especially aerial bombardment and the shelling of cities, and submarine warfare against civilian passenger ships and merchantmen.[11] Pius repeatedly denounced the horrors of modern warfare between 1939 and 1945, but to no avail.

Total war created serious, practical problems for the functioning of the papacy as the headquarters of a worldwide religion. The Vatican's capacity to communicate with the various parts of the Church, especially in Europe, and especially in those countries under German occupation, and especially during the Second World War, was seriously obstructed. A similar problem presented itself in areas of South-East Asia overrun by the Japanese in 1942 and 1943, which induced the Vatican to establish diplomatic relations with the Empire of the Rising Sun, much to the fury of the Americans

[9] Holger H. Herwig, 'Germany', in Richard F. Hamilton and Holger H. Herwig (eds), *The Origins of World War I*, Cambridge, 2003, 163–164.

[10] Carlen, *Papal Encyclicals*, III, 144–145.

[11] See ACS, MdI, DGPS, b. 33, letter from the Commissario del Borgo to the Capo della Polizia, 6 July 1915, where he says that the pope instructed the nuncios in Munich and Vienna to request the governments there 'not to use those terrible forms of destruction and warfare not permitted by existing conventions and international law, and whose existence for warlike extermination people of Christian faith have with such horror'.

(see Chapter 9). And as David Alvarez has also demonstrated so clearly, the cracking by Italian intelligence of the Vatican's rather primitive codes meant such communication as the Vatican had with its nunciatures and foreign governments was far from secure.[12] But when Italy entered the Second World War in June 1940, the Holy See now operated from a base inside a sovereign, independent state ruled by the pope himself. Thus the First World War experience of having to communicate with German and Austro-Hungarian embassies banished to Switzerland was not repeated in the Second. Similarly, by 1940 the finances of the Vatican were very much stronger than in 1914 and were thus less dependent on Peter's Pence contributions from Catholics in the belligerent states. Even if there were times when, during the German occupation of Rome between September 1943 and June 1944, the independence and inviolability of the Vatican seemed very fragile, it afforded Pius XII and his collaborators a rather more secure base from which to conduct their humanitarian efforts and peace diplomacy than that available to Benedict XV.

While the relief of human suffering and the brokering of peace were undoubtedly the major objectives of papal policy during the two world wars, the Vatican had important aims of its own. The preservation or restoration of the *status quo ante bellum*, in particular the preservation of the balance of power in Europe among the Western democracies, Germany, and Russia, was a key aim. Benedict also hoped that inter-power rivalry and conflict might provide an opening for a satisfactory resolution of the Roman Question. Erzberger's attempts to use the Roman Question against Italy, and achieve greater independence for the Holy See, encouraged such hopes (see Chapter 2). But Salandra's diplomacy trumped these hopes. If Papa Pacelli, in the grim years of German military success between 1940 and 1942, had any aim beyond that of the restoration of the status quo of March 1938, that is, before *Anschluss*, then it was, quite simply, survival.

Russia was the invariable factor in this equation. Orthodox Tsardom's harassment of the Catholic Church in Russian Poland and the Baltic States had been repeatedly protested by popes from Pius IX to Pius X. Part of the Entente with Protestant Britain (and later the USA) and anti-clerical France, its military success during the First World War threatened to upset the balance of power, especially in the Balkans, and thus precipitate a resurgence of Orthodoxy, the Catholic Church's great rival (Chapter 2). The revolutions of 1917 and the Brest-Litovsk Treaty of 1918 temporarily banished this nightmare, but it reappeared in a new guise with the consolidation of Bolshevik power during the civil war, the persecution of the churches in Russia, and the Red Army's short-lived thrust towards Central

[12] Alvarez, *Spies in the Vatican*, chs 3 and 5.

Europe in 1920. After the development of the Vatican's anti-Communist crusade during the 1930s, the nightmare returned, first in the Molotov–Ribbentrop Pact of 1939, the ultimate 'axis of evil', to use a more contemporary expression, and then in the form of the Grand Alliance, in other words the resurrection of the old Entente. The Hobson's choice of either a Nazi or a Soviet victory was thus the great agonizing dilemma facing Pius after June 1941, and one that would affect his peace diplomacy and his attitude towards war crimes.

In this context, therefore, Gasparri's entreaties to the Central Powers to block the Russian armies approaching Constantinople in 1916 (see Chapter 2), and Pius XII's willingness to act as a conduit between disaffected German generals plotting to overthrow Hitler and the British government (Chapter 2) must be seen as clamorous breaches of both neutrality and impartiality.

The First and Second World Wars imposed tremendous strains upon the spiritual and institutional unity of Catholicism and the loyalty of Catholics to the pope. Considering the huge problems that the wars posed for the Holy See, it came out of both conflagrations in some ways stronger than before. Its humanitarian activities and peace-making efforts bolstered the moral and political influence of the papacy: witness the growth in the number of states establishing or re-establishing diplomatic relations with it during or immediately after 1918, and the initial reluctance of some newly installed Communist regimes to break relations with the papacy after 1945. Indeed, as John Lukas has stated, 'the Vatican's influence during the Second World War was very great, far greater than during the First World War; greater indeed than at any time in the modern history of Europe'.[13] Of course, at the time of writing he could not have anticipated the role which John Paul II would play during the later stages of the Cold War.

THE CHALLENGE OF THE COLD WAR

'Hot' wars were not the only ones that posed grave problems for the Holy See and its diplomacy. The Cold War presented Pius XII with a major dilemma. The expansion of Communism was clearly a much more serious ideological and material threat to the Catholic Church after 1945, both in Europe and Asia, than previously. Consequently, though 'the West', especially the United States, was the Church's natural ideological ally in such a conflict, the Vatican was, understandably, equally anxious to preserve its traditional neutrality—in

[13] John Lukacs, *The Last European War*, London, 1976, 367.

this case, impartiality was not an option. Hence, the worries about being seen as the 'chaplain of NATO'. It could be said that Pius never resolved this dilemma, despite his attempts to get close to the Non-Aligned Movement. Only his successor John XXIII, in his theoretical distinction between an ideology (Marxism–Leninism) and the practical application of that ideology, as set forth in the encyclical *Pacem in Terris*,[14] in his peace-making efforts during the Cuban Missile Crisis of 1961, and his policy of an 'opening to the East', would find a way out.

NATIONALISM AND THE PAPACY

Nationalism had its positive aspects for the Vatican, particularly the application of the Wilsonian doctrine of 'national self-determination' after the First World War. The break-up of the European empires—Habsburg, Hohenzollern, and Romanov—and the Ottoman Empire brought into being the 'successor states', whose sovereignty and territorial confines were settled by international agreements between 1919 and 1925. Vatican diplomatic recognition of these new states became an almost obligatory milestone along the road to an assured international status and often a key element in the process of nation-building. Though, as has been seen, these new states would pose serious problems for the Holy See over the years, particularly over the treatment of minorities, initially at least there was a fine balance of interests between them and the papacy. On the one hand, the Vatican was anxious to obtain the maximum guarantees for the life of the Church within the new political and constitutional frameworks emerging in these countries. On the other hand, binding, international legal agreements with the Holy See were a key source of legitimacy for new states, especially in the eyes of their populations: Mussolini and Hitler both learned this lesson, and some Communist regimes in Eastern Europe were slow to dispense with their diplomatic relationship with the Vatican during the early stages of their revolutions for precisely the same reason.

Equally importantly, the aligning of ecclesiastical boundaries with national ones and the exclusion of foreigners, especially from the ranks of the higher clergy, were often key weapons in the battle to secure boundaries against neighbouring states in the aftermath of Versailles. So the concordatory policy of Benedict XV, Pius XI, and Gasparri was both necessary and, largely, successful. Early diplomatic recognition of countries emerging from decolonization in Asia and Africa was one lesson learnt from the experience of dealing

[14] Carlen, *Papal Encyclicals*, V, 167–189.

with the successor states, but the very different ethno-religious complexions of the former colonies excluded the possibility of applying a concordatory policy to them. In any case, the pursuit of concordats in the 1920s and 1930s by Della Chiesa, Ratti, Gasparri, and Pacelli, as the ultimate guarantee of the Church's rights and interests, had not been entirely successful even with parliamentary democratic regimes.

Overall, the balance sheet of the experience of war and nationalism was a positive one for Vatican diplomacy. Apart from anything else, it was obliged to grow—between 1914 and 1939 the number of states with some form of diplomatic relations with the Holy See nearly trebled, from fourteen to forty-one.[15] These included all the great European powers except the USSR and most of the non-European states. Austrian *Anschluss* and the Nazi and Soviet invasions and occupations of Eastern Europe during the war reduced this figure, as did the Sovietization of Eastern Europe after 1945, but decolonization brought some compensation: diplomatic relations with nine Third World countries (see Chapter 10) by the end of Pius XII's reign.

Yet this growth did not lead to much diversification or internationalization of the papal diplomatic corps: as both the Brazilian ambassador and the British minister complained at the height of the Second World War (see Chapter 9), the overwhelmingly *Italian* character of the corps was a source of considerable difficulty for the neutral and impartial Vatican in wartime. But a greater mix of nationalities might have made things even more awkward for the Secretariat of State. On the other hand, the entry of American prelates into the Secretariat of State and even the ranks of its envoys is a noticeable feature of this period. This trend became even more marked after 1945 and the development of the Cold War (see Chapter 10). This matched the massively increased American Catholic influence in the Vatican in the 1940s.

It is probably correct to say that the papal diplomatic corps became a more *professional* body with a common training at the Academy of Noble Ecclesiastics and a stint in both the Vatican and in the field. But, as Morozzo della Rocca has pointed out, this did not prevent 'amateurs' being plucked from their thoroughly non-diplomatic careers and sent off as apostolic delegates or nuncios, like Ratti (Poland), Hinsley (East Africa), O'Hara (Romania), and Muench (Germany).[16] On the other hand, those papal diplomats who had filled important postings—like Tedeschini in Madrid, Pacelli in Berlin, Maglione in Paris, Fumasoni-Biondi and Gaetano Cicognani in Washington, and so on, continued to end up as cardinals, holding major posts in the

[15] Compare *Annuario Pontificio*, 1914 and 1958.

[16] R. Morozzo della Rocca, 'Le nunziature in Europa fra le due guerre', in De Rosa and Cracco (eds), *Il Papato e l'Europa*, 408.

Vatican. Thus papal diplomacy remained one of the chief training grounds for high office in the Roman curia.

VATICAN DIPLOMATIC DISASTERS

The history of papal diplomacy in this period is far from being one of unalloyed success. Indeed, there were several situations in which the Vatican came off very badly from its diplomatic dealings, sometimes even with Catholic states. Probably the most clamorous was Pacelli's peace mission to Germany, which was supposed to provide some solid ground from which Benedict XV would launch his 'Peace Note' of August 1917. Pacelli and the Vatican misread the German domestic situation, just as they were hopelessly optimistic about the prospects for a positive response from the Entente Powers. Another disastrous initiative in the short term was the Luzio mission to Ireland in 1923 (see Chapter 6). Neither the mission of Walsh to Russia nor the grand plan for the 'conversion' of that country spearheaded by D'Herbigny's cloak-and-dagger activities (see Chapter 6) proved successful. Mildly anti-clerical regimes closer to home, like that of Masaryk and Benes in Czechoslovakia, caused huge problems for Vatican diplomacy (see Chapter 6), and conflicting territorial interests between friendly 'Catholic' states, like Lithuania and Poland, were a serious headache for the Vatican (see Chapter 6), as was the similar conflict between Yugoslavia and Fascist Italy. The grievances of the Slovenian and Croatian minorities which ended up under Italian rule after Versailles caused tensions in the Vatican's relations with Fascism. Sometimes, it was the choice of papal envoy that was the problem: Orsenigo in Berlin was incredibly weak, not to say passive, in the face of the Nazi regime during the Second World War. Here the blame can be attributed to Pius XI, who apparently chose him for such a vital posting because he was a long-term friend.[17]

In its handling of the post-1945 Communist regimes in Eastern Europe, Vatican diplomacy was also sometimes less than sure-footed, the most obvious example being its relations with Poland. Pius XII's obstinate refusal to recognize the Lublin, Communist government, rather the London one, provided Poland's new Communist rulers with a perfect excuse to ignore the Vatican and its representative. Furthermore, the decision to appoint German prelates to administer Polish sees during the wartime German occupation, thus breaching the terms of the 1925 concordat, provided grounds for the Communists to unilaterally abrogate that agreement.

[17] David I. Kertzer, *The Pope and Mussolini: The Secret History of Pius XI and the Rise of Fascism in Europe*, New York, 2014, 202–204.

THE THREAT FROM TOTALITARIANISM

Since the outbreak of the French Revolution, Catholicism in Europe, and later Latin America, had faced the secularizing agendas of parliamentary politicians, and even bloody persecution. These mainly legislative attacks on the Church were aimed at reducing the Church's wealth, stripping it of legal privileges and even status by separating Church and State, and eliminating its influence in such matters as marriage, divorce, and education. They were usually instigated by politicians of liberal and Masonic inclinations, political liberalism and Freemasonry frequently going together in Continental Europe. On the other hand, the Prussian-German *Kulturkampf* in the 1870s and 1880s was led by an old-fashioned conservative, Bismarck, which demonstrates that the power and influence of the Church was under attack from all sides. The 'culture wars' of the nineteenth century continued into the twentieth, in France after 1904, Portugal after 1910, Mexico and Russia from 1917 onwards, and Spain under the Second Republic.[18] And hostility to the Church was to be found elsewhere, as the Holy See's difficult relations with countries such as Lithuania and Czechoslovakia demonstrate. In these cases, a more specifically Socialist, even Marxist, element played an increasingly important role in the attacks on the Church, though the men in the Vatican undoubtedly exaggerated Communist influence in the Mexican Revolution.

But Communist anti-clericalism represented a more dangerous, even mortal threat because, like National Socialism, and potentially Italian Fascism, it offered an alternative *Weltanschauung*, in this case a comprehensive philosophy and way of life that explicitly proclaimed atheistic materialism, hence the Catholic crusade against it that developed from the 1930s onwards. As the 'Godless' campaigns in Russia had demonstrated, there could be no compromise between Soviet Communism and Catholicism, or any other religion for that matter: in effect, Communism *was* a religion. Similarly, National Socialism, with its Social Darwinian, Nietzschean, and pagan racial elements, represented the anti-thesis of Christianity, especially its Catholic variant, and there can be no doubt that, like the Bolsheviks, the Nazi leadership planned the elimination of all Christian churches in the longer term: the experiments in the Warthegau prove that conclusively (see Chapter 8). Hitler had to bide his time during the Second World War when a full-scale attack on the Catholic Church, or any other churches, would have endangered the morale of German civilians.

[18] C. M. Clark and W. Kaiser (eds), *Culture Wars: Secular–Catholic Conflict in Nineteenth Century Europe*, Cambridge, 2003.

PERSECUTION AND MARTYRDOM

The consequences for the Church of this clash between Catholicism and competing ideologies were very serious. This was a period when the papacy was forced to become a helpless bystander of much persecution and martyrdom for the Catholic clergy especially, though martyrs were not lacking among the laity. Then there were thousands of persecuted Catholics who were not, strictly speaking, martyrs, because they did not die for their faith, but were 'confessors', that is, bore witness to their faith under imprisonment, torture, and other forms of repression. This period of the persecution and martyrdom of Catholics must be ranked alongside those under the Roman emperors, during the Reformation and wars of religion in the sixteenth century, and in the years following the French Revolution of 1789.

In Russia, of course, the chief victim of the 'Godless' campaigns was the Russian Orthodox Church. Hundreds of thousands of Orthodox clergy, faithful, and religious were arrested and imprisoned, and most were shot.[19] The numbers of Catholic victims of the 'Godless' campaigns is less easy to calculate, but the Catholic minority was also hit by Soviet policy. Even when Stalin relaxed his repression of Orthodoxy for opportunistic reasons during the Great Patriotic War, 'this was not reflected in the policy towards Catholicism in the USSR'.[20] While the logic behind the persecution of Catholicism in the USSR was much the same as that against other Christians who were imprisoned, tortured, and murdered, there was the added element that Catholicism was identified with Poland and a 'foreign power', the Vatican. When the Red Army invaded eastern Poland in 1920 groups of ethnically Polish Catholics were summarily shot by the Bolsheviks, and the persecution was repeated when the Soviets annexed eastern Poland and the Baltic States in 1939 and 1940, and again when they reconquered them from the Nazis between 1944 and 1945. Because Catholicism was the majority religion in Lithuania, the Catholic Church was subject to particular repression as a symbol of national resistance to Sovietization: hundreds of priests were imprisoned or deported to Siberia and the episcopal hierarchy effectively eliminated.[21] Further Catholic minorities were subjected to Communist anti-religious policy so that in the former Polish Ukraine, for example, the Greek Catholics suffered badly on the basis of allegations that they had 'collaborated' with the Poles.[22] This was a brutal irony considering that the Greek Catholic Church had long been regarded with much suspicion by the Polish authorities because of its alleged links with the anti-Polish terrorist organization, OUN (see Chapter 7).

[19] A. Riccardi, *Il Secolo del Martirio. I Cristiani nel Novecento*, Milan, 2000.

[20] A. Riccardi, *Il Secolo del Martirio. I Cristiani nel Novecento*, Milan, 2000, 29.

[21] Chadwick, *The Christian Church*, 106–108.

[22] Chadwick, *The Christian Church*, 55.

The Church was eventually liquidated by the new Communist rulers of the Ukraine in 1946 (see Chapter 10). Its leader, the metropolitan of Lvov, Mgr Josif Slipji, remained in prison as a symbol of its martyrdom until the Vatican secured his release in 1963.

The impact of Sovietization on the 'Church of Silence' in Eastern Europe has already been recorded in Chapter 10. This process also produced Catholic martyrs, and not just the trials and imprisonment of *causes célèbres* like Stepinac, Mindszenty, Beran, and Wyszyński. But it is significant that none of these leading churchmen was actually executed. In fact, real martyrs, that is, those who *died* for their faith, were few in the 'Church of Silence' after 1945, though imprisonments of bishops and clergy were legion.[23] Robert Royal has argued that the rulers of the new Communist states in Eastern Europe relied less on brute force than their Soviet masters did in the territories they acquired after 1945, often using more subtle methods of repression of the churches instead.[24] But, in Albania and Romania, brutality and murder on a large scale were used, for different reasons in each state. In the case of Albania, as has been suggested before (see Chapter 10), Catholicism was identified as 'anti-national', an agency of the Italian Fascists who had invaded the country on Good Friday 1939, and occupied it for the next four years. In addition, the Communist rulers of post-war Albania, and in particular their leader Enver Hoxha, were committed to an especially fanatical anti-religious policy such that, by the end of the 1950s, they boasted that theirs was the first 'atheistic state on the planet'. In Romania both Greek and Latin Catholics were regarded with particular suspicion by the Romanian Communists because they were largely drawn from ethnic minorities, the Germans and the Hungarians respectively, who inhabited Transylvania, the border region which was only acquired from Hungary in the Versailles Peace Settlement.[25] In consequence, members of the two churches were brutally persecuted and produced dozens of martyrs for their faith.[26] In the case of both Albania and Romania the Communists denounced Vatican 'treachery', and attempted to persuade Catholic bishops to abjure Rome and either join the Orthodox Church or establish schismatic churches.[27] The dangers of schism among national churches was the fear that haunted the Vatican throughout this period and, in the great tradition of the Church, Pius XII undoubtedly preferred Catholic martyrs to schismatics.

Persecution of Catholicism by Communist revolutionaries in Asia was more intense and brutal than anything in Eastern Europe. The Catholic

[23] Robert Royal, *The Catholic Martyrs of the Twentieth Century: A World History*, n.p., n.d., ch. 9.
[24] Royal, *The Catholic Martyrs*, 222–223.
[25] Royal, *The Catholic Martyrs*, 222–223.
[26] Royal, *The Catholic Martyrs*, 260–266.
[27] Royal, *The Catholic Martyrs*, 235 and 263.

Church in all three Asian Communist states was suspect because of its largely missionary status, and was thus associated with the colonialist, imperialist Western powers, because of the links to the Vatican and its anti-Communist propaganda, and in the case of Vietnam because Catholics were among the strongest elements of resistance to Ho Chi Minh and the Communist Party. The Communist revolutions in China, Korea, and Vietnam in the 1940s and 1950s, gave Pius XII martyrs aplenty. According to Valentina Ciciliot, Pope John Paul canonized 120 Chinese, 118 Vietnamese, and 103 Koreans, though not all were martyrs and some of these came from earlier periods.[28]

National Socialist rule also gave rise to many martyrs, both inside the Reich and in the territories the Nazis invaded and occupied from March 1938 onwards, that is, Austria and the western half of Czechoslovakia. It could be said that the first Catholic martyrs were those leaders of Catholic Action murdered during the 'Night of the Long Knives' in the summer of 1934.[29] With thousands of priests in concentration camps, especially Dachau (see Chapter 7), some were bound to die there because of ill-treatment, overwork, malnutrition, or lack of medical care. Ciciliot lists four martyrs of Nazism who were beatified by John Paul II: the priests Nikolaus Gross, Karl Leisner, and Rupert Mayer, plus the former Jew Edith Stein, who was eventually raised to the altars in 1994.[30] Stein remains a controversial figure because she is 'claimed' by many Jews as a victim of the Holocaust.[31] A further 130 martyrs of Nazism, clergy and laypeople, were beatified by John Paul II.[32] But these probably represent only a fraction of those German Catholics who suffered under National Socialist rule.[33] In addition, there were further victims of Nazism in occupied territories like Poland. The most famous of these martyrs, Fr Maximilian Kolbe, who was raised to the altars by John Paul II in 1982, like Stein has been the focus of controversy.[34] In Poland, Catholic clergy were persecuted, sent to concentration camps, and sometimes murdered as much because they were part of one of those intellectual elites which the Nazis were intent on eliminating in their attempt to destroy the Polish nation.[35] It is significant in this regard that the Nazis also targeted the clergy of the tiny, minority schismatic Mariavite Church, whose leader, Archbishop Joseph Kowalski, died in a concentration camp.[36] The fact that nearly 3 million Polish Catholics died during the Second World War on the battlefields, in air raids, and in concentration camps, almost as many as the Polish Jews

[28] Ciciliot, 'La Politica delle Canonizzazioni', 227.
[29] Riccardi, *Il Secolo del Martirio*, 70.
[30] Riccardi, *Il Secolo del Martirio*, 70.
[31] Marchione, *Pope Pius XII*, 28.
[32] Ciciliot,' La Politica delle Canonizzazioni', 235
[33] See Riccardi, *Il Secolo del Martirio*, and Royal, *The Catholic Martyrs*, ch. 6.
[34] Royal, *The Catholic Martyrs*, 208.
[35] Ciciliot, 'La Politica delle Canonizzazioni', 125, makes exactly this point.
[36] J. Peterkiewicz, *The Third Adam*, London, 1975, 179–183.

who were exterminated, led the 'Polish Pope', John Paul II, to dub his homeland 'the martyr nation'. Catholics were also among the thousands of Belgian, Dutch, French, and Italian people who died resisting the Nazis, some because they gave shelter to Jews.[37] Whether they can all be described as martyrs for the faith, rather than because they stuck fast to the path of humane and Christian conduct dictated by their consciences, is open to question.

It is worth reiterating that *the papacy* itself was one of the causes in all these cases of persecution. Governments, whether Marxist or National Socialist, were suspicious of, and would ultimately not tolerate, the links between local Catholic churches and a 'foreign power', in other words, the papacy. Thus martyrdom was sometimes the price which had to be paid for loyalty to the Holy See. Generally speaking, those Catholics in schismatic bodies—like the Catholic People's Association in China—fared better under Communist rule.

The persecutions of the Church in Mexico, and Spain under the Second Republic, present elements which do not fit exactly with the paradigms of Communist or fascist anti-Catholicism. In both cases, they suggest a continuation of the 'culture wars' of the previous century, more akin to the experiences of France and Portugal were it not for the extreme violence which accompanied them. In both cases, again like France and Portugal, they began with largely legislative measures against the Church but then they degenerated into vandalism and violence. One of the factors which radicalized the Mexican situation was the guerrilla warfare conducted by some Catholics, the *Cristeros* against the federal government in the late 1920s. As a result, during the pontificate of John Paul II there were twenty-seven beatifications and twenty-five canonizations of Catholics martyred during the Mexican Revolution.[38] In Spain, the violence was often spontaneous, an explosion of pent-up anger against the Church on the part of sections of the industrial and agrarian proletariat. After the outbreak of the actual civil war in 1936, much such violence was organized by anarchist or Marxist-controlled militias.[39] The results for the Spanish Church were horrendous. The Spanish 'holocaust', as the massacres perpetrated by sides in the civil war have been dubbed by some historians,[40] resulted in the deaths of over 6,800 bishops, clergy, and religious, male and female, and some laypeople.[41] As Vicente Cárcel Ortí has stated, 'The Church was the great victim of the persecution unleashed in the Republican zone, the greatest known in the history of Spain, maybe in the history of the Catholic Church.'[42]

[37] Riccardi, *Il Secolo del Martirio*, 99–116.

[38] Ciciliot, 'La Politica delle Canonizzazioni', 130–131.

[39] Cárcel Ortí, 'Notas sobre la mission pontificia', 53.

[40] P. Preston, *The Spanish Holocaust*, London, 2012; and Royal, *The Catholic Martyrs*, 107—the latter uses this description as the title of chapter 5.

[41] V. Cárcel Ortí, *Buio sull'altare. La persecuzione della Chiesa in Spagna*, Rome, 2001, 111–118, and Ciciliot, 'La Politica Delle Canonizzazioni', 126–130.

[42] Cárcel Ortí, 'Notas sobre la misiòn pontificia', 53.

The anti-clerical campaigns of the Liberals and the anarchist–Marxist left against Church in this period could be regarded as being a part, albeit a violent one, of a continuing process of 'modernization'. It is noticeable that, in Eastern Europe, Spain, and also parts of Latin America, land reform was a key issue between the Church and its opponents, both before the Second World War, as in Czechoslovakia, Hungary, Mexico, Poland, and Spain, and afterwards in virtually all of the Sovietized states. In places like Hungary, where the Catholic Primate also had a legal claim to be regent of the kingdom, and in Spain, the Church was closely associated with the establishment, the feudal vestiges of the *ancien régime*, both in the minds of anti-clericals and in reality. The papacy, and in particular Pietro Gasparri as Secretary of State, did not always accommodate itself to these reforms. It was apt to dig its heels in over traditional ecclesiastical privileges, whether in Europe or in Latin America, and to seek to entrench them through concordats. In these circumstances, the Church as a major institution in civil society was perceived by liberal, Socialist, anarchist, and Marxist revolutionaries as constituting a serious obstacle to their programmes of modernization, reformation, or revolution.

THE POWER OF ROME: THE INSTITUTIONAL DEVELOPMENT OF THE PAPACY, 1914–58

All three popes in this period built on the tradition established by their predecessors during the previous seventy years of exercising a quasi-infallible magisterium by means of encyclicals and apostolic letters, solemn pronouncements usually addressed to the whole Church or sometimes to the hierarchy and faithful of specific countries. Benedict XV did so with his encyclicals on war and peace, *Ad Beatissimi* of November 1914 and *Pacem Dei Munus* of June 1920, in his apostolic letter on the missions, *Maximum Illud* of November 1919, and on the Eastern churches, *Petrus Princeps Apostolorum* of October 1920. All constituted definitive statements of the papal position on these matters.

Pius XI's various encyclicals on marriage (*Casti Connubii*, 1930), the economic and social order (*Quadragesimo Anno*, 1931), Communism (*Divini Redemptoris*, 1937), National Socialism (*Mit brennender Sorge*, 1937), and so on, further entrenched the teaching authority of the papacy. Pius XII's invoking of Infallibility in 1950 to proclaim the dogma of the Assumption reinforced this exercise of the *magisterium* and made absolute obedience to it by all Catholics routine. Hence, all the teaching in encyclicals thus became in this period 'virtually' infallible.

St Pius X's reform of the Roman curia in 1907 finally recognized the loss of the temporal power and consequently cleared the way for the concentration of all the Holy See's material, and especially monetary, resources on the difficult task of governing the Universal Church. After 1917 the reformed and expanding bureaucracy of the Roman curia was underpinned by a unified system of Church law, the completion of Papa Sarto's great project of codifying Canon Law. Vatican bureaucrats were now immensely assisted in their government of the Church by detailed rules and regulations in all ecclesiastical matters, from hierarchical organization and the discipline of clerics of all ranks, to sacramental discipline, to the law of marriage and annulments and to the administration of the property of the Church at every level. Above all, the 1917 Code of Canon Law encouraged *uniformity*, the abandonment of local traditions and practices in favour of Vatican-imposed and enforced norms.

One of the most important engines of uniformity in the 1917 Code was Canon 329, which reserved the right of appointment of bishops to the papacy.[43] Canon 329 was, in reality, simply the institutionalization of a practice whereby the papacy had, *de facto*, come to enjoy unlimited control over appointments to bishoprics formerly ruled by Propaganda Fide in Canada and the United States of America, those parts of Western Europe where episcopal hierarchy was restored in the nineteenth century—England and Wales, Scotland, and the Netherlands—and other 'mission' territories. Apart from the curious Swiss anomaly, whereby the 'election' of Catholic bishops had to receive the sanction of some cantonal governments,[44] now all episcopal appointments would lie within the purview of the Holy See, a powerful tool in 'Romanizing' the Church throughout the world. And this would be enforced by the many concordats concluded by Pius XI and Pius XII, even if some national governments retained the right to what was, in effect, a kind of 'preventive' veto. As battles over episcopal appointments in the British Empire in the 1920s and 1930s (see Chapter 6) and the territories occupied by Nazi Germany in the 1940s (see Chapter 8) demonstrate, the Vatican was prepared to fight to the bitter end to retain control over nominations to the episcopacy.

Another example of the trend towards establishing and imposing uniformity is to be found in the insistence of Pius XI and Pius XII that the statutes of religious orders and congregations be reviewed and brought into line with the dictates of Canon Law, notably Canon 489.[45] In their reigns, the statutes of almost all existing bodies of religious were revised.[46] Furthermore, Benedict XV's creation of the Congregation of the Oriental Churches while, on the

[43] Peters, *The 1917 Code of Canon Law*, 132.
[44] J. Steinberg, *Why Switzerland?*, Cambridge, 1985, 274–278.
[45] Peters, *The 1917 Code of Canon Law*, 190.
[46] Jedin, Repgen, and Dolan, *The Church in the Modern Age*, X, 352–371.

one hand, granting greater attention and recognition to those churches of the Middle East in communion with the Holy See, on the other was intended to bind them more closely to Rome. And here also the ideal of uniformity was pursued with the launching of a project to establish a code of canon law for the Oriental churches in parallel with that for the Latin Church.

'Romanization', the thorough assimilation of local churches to the ecclesiastical culture and praxis of Rome, had already been the policy of both Pius IX and Leo XIII, hence their establishment of nine national institutions for the training of priests in Rome—including the French, German, North American, Polish, Armenian, Canadian, Czech, Portuguese, and Spanish colleges. Under Pius X and Benedict XV a further three were established. Pius XI created six more, including two for the training of indigenous clergy, the Ethiopian College in the Vatican and the college of Propaganda Fide on the Janiculum. Pius XII set up three, including the Lithuanian and the Hungarian colleges. In addition, in Pius XI's reign, major religious orders, whatever their national origins, were encouraged to set up specialist colleges for their members.[47] In the early 1930s, Pius gave pontifical university status to a number of ecclesiastical institutions of higher education, like the Lateran, the Anselmo (for Benedictines), and the Angelicum (Dominican), and gave the most prestigious Roman *ateneo* of them all, the Jesuit Gregorian University, a new headquarters in Piazza della Pilotta. The aim was to ensure that more and more Catholic clergy from all over the world experienced Rome and some of the elements of a Roman ecclesiastical education, graduating with Italian-style doctorates in theology and canon law and perhaps even a spell in the Roman curia. In this way, many eventually became bishops, or religious superiors, in the 'younger' churches such as those in Canada, the USA, Australia and New Zealand, Oceania, Asia, and even Africa.

One of the most serious attempts to impose Roman uniformity upon Catholics worldwide was the project to 'export' the Italian model of Catholic Action to the rest of the Catholic Church as the normal means of mobilizing lay activism in defence of the Church's interests, especially against Communism, as carried on by Pius XI and Pizzardo in the 1920s and 1930s. A 'congregation' for Catholic Action, L'Ufficio Centrale dell'Azione Cattolica, was even established in the Roman curia (see Chapter 6). This project was, ultimately, unsuccessful, but it testifies to Pius XI's conviction that the fruits of Italian experience were universally applicable and his determination to induce local churches to adopt them.

It is no accident that this period witnessed the substantial expansion of the network of papal envoys, apostolic nuncios, and delegates, whose purpose was to act as a transmission belt between centre and periphery, Rome

[47] *Annuario Pontificio*, 1948, 892.

and the individual 'national' churches. Between 1914 and 1958, the number of apostolic delegates doubled.[48] Delegates, unlike nuncios, were supposed to restrict their activities to liaise with and supervision of churches in national or colonial territories: in practice, however, they often carried out quasi-diplomatic functions as well. This tightening of Rome's control over the worldwide Church met some resistance in the periphery. In the Irish Free State and Britain in the 1930s there were strong episcopal objections to the very idea of appointing a papal envoy, and in the USA and Canada Pizzardo's attempts to impose the Italian model of Catholic Action were largely ignored. In the 1920s and 1930s, some Mexican Catholics, bishops, clergy, and laity, found the papacy's attitude towards the religious persecution in their country too moderate and pacific: they would have preferred definite papal approval of armed struggle against anti-clerical governments. In Spain the Primate Cardinal Segura, obstructed Nuncio Tedeschini's patient, conciliatory policy towards the Second Republic. In Lithuania, clergy and laity joined in a nationalist revolt against the Vatican's pursuit of a concordat with Poland, and in the latter country the hierarchy successfully resisted the Vatican's attempts to impose a policy of total intransigence towards the new Communist rulers after 1945. In all these incidents the underlying feeling was that the local Catholic hierarchy, and not the Vatican, knew best. The Lebanese Maronites and Melkites were touchy about their autonomy and consequently unhappy about the decision to create a code of canon law for the Oriental churches. And the growth of dissent with the Holy Office among French, German, and American theologians (see Chapter 11) in the 1940s and 1950s began to seriously rattle Ottaviani and would result in the overturning of his policies at the Second Vatican Council.

THE PAPAL 'CULT OF THE PERSONALITY'

The power of Rome over the rest of the Church in this period was also reinforced by the development of a papal 'personality cult'. That cult had a long previous history: Pius IX had been its first embodiment. His role as the 'victim pope', that is, the victim of Italian aggression during the unification of Italy, and early photography had combined to make him a charismatic figure.[49] The 'victim' remained central to the cult throughout the following century when the papacy, or the Church, was the target of persecution. The cult had continued to be developed quite deliberately around Leo XIII and St Pius X (the latter a very handsome man).[50] But Benedict XV's unprepossessing

[48] *Annuario Pontificio*, 1948, 797–800.

[49] Logan, 'Pius XII', 238.

[50] Logan, 'Pius XII', 209.

appearance did not lend itself to a personality cult. Photographs were bad enough but he would have been a public relations disaster in the cinema or on television. With Pius XI, the projection of papal charisma was resumed and he became the first pope to make frequent, if irregular, radio broadcasts. Pius XII exploited the full array of the electronic media, radio, cinema, and television, and his massive general audiences to project his charisma (see Chapter 11). A key stage in this development was the film *Angelic Pastor* (See Chapter 9), which laid the basis for his emergence as virtually 'a living saint'.[51] But the personality he projected was a multifaceted one: according to Logan, like Pius X and Pius XI, he was 'il dolce Cristo sulla terra', 'sweet Christ on earth'.[52] On the other hand, he was 'the Pope of the Madonna'.[53] The papal personality cult was particularly efficacious in binding Catholics together throughout the world during the Second World War and the Cold War. By 1958 the papacy itself had become a charismatic institution, rather like the modern British monarchy.

THE PAPACY AND ITALY

Part and parcel of the evolution of the papacy into a much stronger institution at the end of this period was the transformation of its relationship with Italy, its geographical 'home' and hinterland. At the end of the pontificate of St Pius X, the relationship was uncertain, uneasy, and prone to minor squalls so long as radical and republican elements were represented in Italy's parliaments. The 'balance of power' with Italy shifted against the papacy with Salandra's insertion of the clause into the Treaty of London in 1915 excluding the pope from any peace conference, since this represented further diplomatic isolation. Consequently, the Vatican's precarious position during the course of the First World War was largely dependent upon Italy's goodwill. The Italian defeat at Caporetto in 1917 provided only a temporary strengthening of the papacy's position vis-à-vis the Italian state.

With the advent of the *Conciliazione* in 1929, Fascist Italy and the papacy entered into a much more balanced diplomatic relationship, a 'marriage of convenience' akin to the Church's relationship with various counter-revolutionary forces and authoritarian regimes in other parts of Europe during the 1920s and 1930s. The Italo-Ethiopian War of 1935–6 was the first major test of the independence from Italy which Pius XI believed he had obtained in the Lateran Pacts. However, as Lucia Ceci has pointed out, the Vatican's uncertain and sometimes contradictory response to the Ethiopian war suggested

[51] Logan, 'Pius XII', 243.
[52] Logan, 'Pius XII', 239.
[53] Logan, 'Pius XII', 244.

that there were limits to its independence from the policies of its big neighbour in the areas of colonialism and the missions, Catholic universalism and nationalism, and that it might prove very difficult to maintain the credibility of a neutral and impartial stance during any war in which Italy became involved.[54] Certainly, in the later 1930s there was a dangerous tendency on the part of Vatican officials, from Pacelli down, to seek to appease Mussolini: this became particularly pronounced during the rows over the Racial Laws in 1938–9.

War again altered the balance of power between 1940 and 1943. In the wake of the Axis defeats in North Africa and growing Italian popular desire to leave the war, Pius XII's close relationship with Roosevelt offered a way out. But in May 1943 Mussolini turned down a very serious offer from the Vatican to broker a peace deal with the USA.[55] After the overthrow of Fascism and the armistice with the Allies, the Italian state effectively collapsed. Papal diplomacy operated as the direct interlocutor with Washington in defence of Italian interests, including the terms of the Peace Treaty of 1947. After the final defeat of Fascism, and the abolition of the monarchy in 1946, the Church emerged as the sole surviving national institution of any importance in Italy, a situation which Chabod very aptly compared to the role played by the papacy after the collapse of the Roman Empire.[56] In the first ten to twenty years after the end of the war Italy was effectively 'the Papal State of the Twentieth Century' such was the power and influence of the Vatican over the entire peninsula.[57] By the time Pius XII died it had achieved a hegemonic influence in Italian politics and society through Catholic Action and the church-sponsored political party, the Christian Democrats. Italy thus became a sort of ideal Catholic state, apparently a model for the application of papal teaching to public morality, to impress the millions of Catholic pilgrims who came to Rome from all over the world.

A TRULY UNIVERSAL CHURCH?

A striking feature of this period is the way in which all three popes, but especially Benedict XV and Pius XI, built upon earlier initiatives to renew the missionary outreach of the Church. As early as 1839 Gregory XVI had endorsed the abolition of slavery and the slave trade 1839, and urged the ordination of indigenous clergy and even the consecration of indigenous bishops, a move that was well ahead of its time.[58] Pius IX and Leo XIII subsequently

[54] Ceci, *Il Papa non deve parlare*, 24. [55] Morgan, *The Fall of Mussolini*, 24.
[56] F. Chabod, *L'Italia Contemporanea (1918–1948)*, Turin, 1961, 140.
[57] Webster, *The Cross and the Fasces*, 214.
[58] F. Coppa, *The Modern Papacy since 1789*, London, 1998, 79.

responded to the imperialistic expansion of the European powers in the mid and late nineteenth century by expanding the Church's presence, creating hundreds of missionary jurisdictions—apostolic vicariates or prefectures—in Asia, Africa, and Oceania.[59] The three popes of our period, by their rejuvenation of the missionary arm of the Roman curia, Propaganda Fide, their successive encyclicals and apostolic letters on the Church's missionary strategy, and their insistence upon the progressive 'indigenization' of the local churches, transformed the Church's presence in what rapidly became the Third World during the process of decolonization after 1945.

The popes also devoted much attention to the Latin American Church and its problems and by the end of Pius XII's pontificate, the Vatican's relations with the states of Latin America were better than they had been in 1914, and even in the 1930s. The electronic media, especially radio, were used to reach out to the faithful throughout the world, in particular to the Americas. It could be said that, by 1958, the Catholic Church really had become, geographically speaking, what it had always claimed to be, a universal Church. Yet, there were still limitations to this achievement, the *centre*, Rome, was far from being international in personnel and outlook because of the failure to internationalize the Roman curia and the papal diplomatic service.

CATHOLIC TOTALITARIANISM? THE DEVELOPMENT OF THE DOCTRINE OF THE CHURCH

Under Popes Pius XI and Pius XII, the Catholic Church's understanding of itself in the form of the 'Doctrine of the Church' went through a significant process of development. Building on the premises of Infallibility and the concept of the Church as a 'perfect society', Pius XI developed a 'high church' ecclesiology which conceived of the Church as 'The Kingdom of God on Earth' (see Chapter 5). In his unpublished encyclical *De Ecclesia Christi* Papa Ratti also referred to the concept of the Church as the Mystical Body of Christ:

> Behold, therefore, the mystical body of Christ, which is the Church, a supernatural and indeed true mystery of faith, but one which is at the same time visible to its members, its structures, its service. Behold the mystical body whose innermost life is so absorbed into and joined to its outer that one has to say that

[59] Mazzonis, 'Pio IX, il tramonto del potere temporale', 266.

> the Church in itself expresses the mystery of the Incarnate Word in a most faithful reflection.[60]

Pius XI's successor fully developed this idea in his encyclical *Mystici Corporis Christi*, on the 'Mystical Body of Christ', which effectively reasserted the traditional belief that 'there is no salvation outside the Roman Church'. It thus implicitly reaffirmed 'supersessionism', the doctrine according to which the Jews had been superseded as the Chosen People by Christians, and ruled out any Catholic truck with ecumenical initiatives, any compromises over Catholic teaching and tradition. The coupling of the foregoing concepts with Pius XI's idea of 'The Social Kingship of Christ', as expounded in his encyclicals *Ubi Arcano Dei* (1922) and *Quas Primas* (1925) also laid the basis for a sort of 'Catholic totalitarianism', as several historians have observed.[61] Chappin, in particular, makes the point that:

> The implications of this new term were that Christ is not only king of each individual person, but also of human society as such. It did not limit itself to a spiritual or religious dimension, but also included the social dimension: politics, culture, society etc. In other words, the term seeks to set the framework for the establishment of a theocracy, which should be implemented by the Catholic Church.[62]

At the heart and summit of this theocracy was, of course, the pope. The words of the service during which the popes were crowned had, since the Middle Ages, suggested the absolute, totalitarian power which the Roman pontiff, on behalf of the whole Church, should exercise over all humanity:

> I crown you with a crown of glory and righteousness . . . Receive the tiara adorned with three crowns, and know that thou art the father of princes and kings, ruler of the earth here below, the vicar of our Saviour Jesus Christ, to whom is honour and glory through all the ages.[63]

To some extent, Pius XI's increasingly 'totalitarian' view of the nature of the Church and its relationship with the world was a response to the rise of the totalitarian regimes in Europe, and he openly admitted this. For example, Mussolini alleged that, during his meeting with Pius XI in the 1932, the latter declared that 'This totalitarianism is in the circle of the State but, besides material interests, there are also spiritual ones and it is here

[60] Walsh, translation of *De Ecclesia Christi*, 9.

[61] See, for example, D. Menozzi, 'Regalità di Cristo e secolarizzazione. Alle origini di "Quas primas"', *Cristianesimo nella Storia*, 16 (1995), 79–113; and Chappin, 'Cardinal van Rossum', 97–98.

[62] Chappin, 'Cardinal van Rossum', 97–98.

[63] From the papal coronation service as described in F. P. Henry, *The Primacy of the Papacy Vindicated*, Baltimore, London, and Pittsburgh, 1857, 252.

that Catholic totalitarianism enters.'[64] As far as Pius XI was concerned, there was 'nothing contrary to Catholic belief' in Fascism's emphasis on the virtues of 'order, authority and discipline'.[65] Of course not, they were exactly the same things the Church now required of the faithful. But it is significant that Pius XI clearly believed that only *the Church* could approve them and give them legitimacy. The idea of Catholicism as 'totalitarianism', of the Catholic Church as a totalitarian 'regime' is not as fantastic as it might initially sound: by now Catholicism was a *Weltanschauung*, just like the other *Weltanschauungen* of Soviet Communism, German National Socialism, and Italian Fascism. And, by the end of the 1930s, Catholicism had acquired all the tools necessary to successfully compete with its rivals, a highly centralized, rigid, governing bureaucracy located in the Roman curia, a system of laws, a charismatic leader, and an underlying ecclesiological philosophy that required the absolute obedience of Catholics to the pope. All it lacked was the apparatus of violence which totalitarian states used to enforce their rule. But even though the Holy Inquisition had fallen into disuse, the Catholic Church did not need such an apparatus, it had other, equally efficacious means of imposing its will upon its spiritual subjects.

THE PAPACY AND THE JEWS

It is impossible to understand the papacy's relationship with the Jews of Europe in this period except within the broader context of Christian anti-Semitism. Anti-Semitism of theological origin, based on the Jews' rejection of Christ and his new covenant, and, worse on their alleged role as the 'deicide people', had been prevalent in Christian Europe for hundreds of years. The history of Christian persecution, discrimination, and intolerance of the Jews was something rather more lethal than the 'anti-Judaism' or 'religious anti-Semitism', presumably not very different from anti-Protestant prejudice, which Margherita Marchione and others have presented as the prevailing sentiment among Catholics in the first half of the twentieth century.[66] The worst anti-Semitic excesses of the late nineteenth century and the early years of the twentieth took place in the overwhelmingly Orthodox Tsarist Empire.[67] Then there were the

[64] As quoted in Kent, *The Pope and the Duce*, 193.

[65] As quoted in R.J.B. Bosworth, *Mussolini's Italy: Life under the Dictatorship, 1915–1945*, London, 2005, 259.

[66] See the analysis of the terms in Marchione, *Pope Pius XII*, 38–42.

[67] Roberto Finzi, *Anti-Semitism: From its European Roots to the Holocaust*, Moreton in Marsh, 1999, 54–56.

devoutly Orthodox supporters of Codreanu's Iron Guard/Legion of the Archangel Michael in Romania who were fanatical anti-Semites,[68] and German Protestants, largely the *Deutsche Christen*, who gave enthusiastic support to the various phases of the Nazi persecution of the Jews leading up to *Kristallnacht*.[69] Catholics could also be fanatically anti-Semitic in equal measure, like Ledóchowski and the Jesuit fortnightly *La Civiltà Cattolica*, and the Croatian Ustasha, to give just two examples. And anti-Semitism among Catholic Poles was endemic: even the Holocaust did not prevent some Poles from carrying out pogroms against a few of its survivors in 1946, events which elicited a very ambivalent response from the ecclesiastical authorities.[70]

The official papal attitude was complex, ambivalent, even confusing in this period. On the one hand, *La Civiltà Cattolica* raged against the Jews throughout most of this period, unrestrained by any censorship on the part of the Secretariat of State. On the other hand, during the First World War, Benedict XV gave a not unsympathetic reception to Deloncle's plea to help in the establishment of a Jewish 'homeland' in Poland, though he was rather less supportive when a homeland did materialize, this time in Palestine after the war.[71] Mgr Angelo Roncalli, who behaved as a 'righteous Gentile' while apostolic delegate in the Levant, helping to save many Jews, was nevertheless hostile to Jewish settlement in Palestine which, at the time, was probably the only viable alternative to death in the Holocaust for many of Europe's Jews.[72]

Pius XI was probably the most ambivalent, even conflicted, of Vatican leaders in this period in his attitude towards the Jews. There is evidence from the period he spent in Milan and Poland of his sympathy for Jews there,[73] and in 1931 he ordered the nuncio in Warsaw to protest against anti-Semitic violence.[74] In 1926 he missed an opportunity to move away from the traditional Catholic theology on the Jews when he endorsed the Holy Office's rejection of a plea for a change in the Good Friday liturgy, yet he inserted into the same

[68] C. Iordachi, *Charisma, Politics and Violence: The Legion of the Archangel Michael in Interwar Romania*, Trondheim, 2004, 50–51.

[69] See the essays by Doris Bergen,' Storm Troopers of Christ: The German Christian Movement and the Ecclesiastical Final Solution', and Susanna Heschel, 'When Jesus was an Aryan: The Protestant Church and Anti-Semitic Propaganda', in Robert P. Ericksen and Susanna Heschel (eds), *Betrayal: German Churches and the Holocaust*, Minneapolis, MN, 1999, chs 3 and 4.

[70] Robert Blobaum (ed.), *Anti-Semitism and its Opponents in Modern Poland*, Ithaca, NY, 2005, 269–275.

[71] Pollard, *The Unknown Pope*, 148–151.

[72] ADSS, 9, Doc. 324, Le délégué apostolique à Istanbul Roncalli au Cardinal Maglione, 4 septembre 1943.

[73] Pease, *Rome's Most Faithful Daughter*, 152.

[74] AES, Stati Ecclesiastici, Quarto Periodo, 430 (1930–1938), 348, 1931, 'Taccuini di S. Emo. Cardinale Pacelli, Segretario di Stato di Sua Sanita', 341, 14 December 1931.

Holy Office decree a condemnation of anti-Semitism (see Chapter 5). Another lost opportunity came when he issued the encyclical *Mit brennender Sorge*, for this condemnation of most of the ideological apparatus of the Nazis failed to mention their anti-Semitism. Hubert Wolf is not far wrong when he concludes that 'Pius XI wasted his big chance. It took decades and more than six million murdered Jews for the Church to summon the courage to cleanse its relationship with the Jews of anti-Semitism, even in the liturgy.'[75]

Similarly, there was virtually no Catholic condemnation of the introduction of discriminatory laws against the Jews in Germany, Hungary, Italy, Poland, or Romania in the late 1930s, even after *Kristallnacht*. Catholic opinion welcomed restrictions on a minority who were seen to be achieving success at the expense of Christians. It would be much the same story when two Nazi client states, Slovakia and Vichy, introduced similar laws in 1940. Pius XI's biggest failure was not standing up to Mussolini when he introduced the Racial Laws in 1938. By then, the pope had become distressed and ashamed by the apparently Europe-wide upsurge of anti-Semitism but allowed his originally strident protests to be muted by his subordinates in the Vatican as he moved into his final illness.[76]

The papacy could be said to have at least partially redeemed its reputation by its enormous efforts to rescue Jews all over Europe during the Holocaust. But Catholics were not alone in this work of mercy. Orthodox bishops and clergy helped save Jews in Bulgaria, Romania, and the Ukraine.[77] Similarly, Protestants in Denmark, France, and Germany endeavoured to save Jews from the Nazi murder machine.[78] That still leaves the problem of Pius XII's refusal to carry out what many perceive to be his absolutely essential moral duty as the self-proclaimed Vicar of Christ on Earth: to condemn publicly and specifically the Holocaust, which remains one of the greatest, if not the greatest crime, of the twentieth century.

It took another twenty years until the papacy finally divested itself of the last trace of anti-Semitism. In 1961 John XXIII excised the prayer for the 'perfidious Jews' from the Good Friday liturgy, and in *Nostra Aetate* of October 1963 Paul VI formally proclaimed the 'Declaration on the Jews' which had been agreed overwhelmingly in the second session of the Second Vatican

[75] Wolf, *Pope and Devil*, 121.

[76] Fattorini, *Hitler, Mussolini and the Vatican*, ch. 7.

[77] See, for example, Leah Cohen, *You Believe: 8 Glances at the Holocaust*, trans. Tanya Ryan, Sofia, 2012, 42–49, where she examines the attempts by Bishops Stefan and Cyril to prevent Bulgarian Jews being deported.

[78] Richard Petrow, *The Bitter Years: The Invasion and Occupation of Denmark and Norway, April 1940–May 1945*, London, 1974, ch. 15; for the efforts of the Protestant churches in France, see Paul Webster, *Pétain's Crime: The Full Story of French Collaboration in the Holocaust*, London, 1992, 141–142; and Jackson, *France: The Dark Years*, 377–378.

Council, though not without some last-ditch, behind-the-scenes manoeuvring by traditionalists like Cardinal Ruffini, archbishop of Palermo.[79]

THE PAPACY IN 1958: THE LEGACY OF THE AGE OF TOTALITARIANISM

Throughout the 1920s and 1930s, there was an increasing tendency for both Pius XI and Pius XII to have recourse to a concept of 'human rights', as derived from Catholic natural law, as a weapon against persecution by totalitarian and other regimes, and in condemnation of war crimes. In *Mit brennender Sorge* and *Humani Generis Unitas* Pius XI, in his assertion of the fundamental unity of the human race to refute Nazi racialist doctrines, implied the existence of equal and universal human rights. Similarly, Pius XII in *Summi Pontificatus* reiterated his predecessor's rejection of both racialism and a totalitarian concept of the State as in conflict with the natural law, though more on the basis of the Catholic doctrine of 'solidarity' and the rights of the family.[80] In his various broadcasts during the war deploring war crimes and atrocities he would appeal as much to notions of charity as justice. As Menozzi points out, in both cases there was an assumption that only the Church could define what was and was not the 'natural law', and therefore what these human rights were.[81] Furthermore, as has been seen, the Church accepted and supported discriminatory legislation against Protestants and Jews in this period. Faced with the Western Allies' Atlantic Charter and then the Allied victory, the papacy was obliged to accommodate itself to the new human rights doctrine that was gaining ground, hence, in his Christmas message of 1944, Pius XII spoke of the 'true liberties' of men and 'possible declarations of the rights of man'.[82] According to Menozzi, after 1945:

> Thus began a process on the part of Rome to manipulate history which served not only to absolve it for its previous behaviour, but also in order to be able to continue to present itself as the source of political and social truth in a post-war scenario in which human rights were becoming the hope of a better form of civil coexistence.[83]

When the United Nations promulgated the Universal Declaration of Human Rights in 1948, Pius XII was silent. Nevertheless, as John Nurser acknowledges,

[79] John Connelly, *From Enemy to Brother: The Revolution in Catholic Teaching on the Jews, 1933–1965*, Cambridge, MA, 2012, 250 and 270.

[80] Carlen, *Papal Encyclicals*, IV, 11–13.

[81] D. Menozzi, *Chiesa e diritti umani*, Bologna, 2010, 129 and 132.

[82] *Pio XII Discorsi*, 1944, 248–249.

[83] Menozzi, *Chiesa e diritti umani*, 143.

the representatives of the non-Catholic churches on the Committee to Study the Bases of a Just and Enduring Peace, noted the significance for the human rights cause of the pope's Christmas radio messages.[84] Until the end of Pius XII's reign, the Vatican remained uncomfortable with and suspicious of human rights: they smacked too much of nineteenth-century liberalism.

The human 'right' which really troubled the papacy was, of course, in relation to religion. Whereas the Church expected and demanded religious liberty for itself and its followers in those countries where Catholics were in a minority, in 'Catholic states' like Spain, several Latin American countries, and even Italy, Protestants were actively either persecuted or discriminated against. Ecumenism was still effectively anathema at the end of Pius XII's pontificate. All this was based on a long-held and long-practised conviction that 'error has no rights'.

So, at the death of Pius XII in 1958 the papacy had still not accepted the principle of freedom of religion. While, on the one hand, in the periphery of the Church, Catholic theologians, philosophers, and lay politicians were enthusiastically pursuing a human rights agenda,[85] in the Vatican a rearguard action was being fought against any suggestion of relaxing the centuries-old Catholic rejection of freedom of religion.[86] Thus, the American Jesuit theologian, John Courtney Murray, who advocated religious liberty, was silenced by Ottaviani's Holy Office.[87]

It is also clear that the papacy had still not fully reconciled itself to liberal democracy. Its experience of democracy in Europe between the wars, especially in the successor states, had not been a happy one: it had clearly been more comfortable with semi-authoritarian states like Primo de Rivera's Spanish Directory, Dollfuss's Austria, and Horthy's Hungary, and after the war it continued to see Portugal and Spain as 'ideal' Catholic states. As far as the papacy's attitude to the totalitarian regimes is concerned, Chenaux is right when he says, 'the simultaneous, one might even say, symmetrical condemnation of the totalitarianisms . . . should not be interpreted as an acceptance of liberal democratic values'.[88] Some writers, and Chenaux is one of them, regard Pius XII's Christmas message of 1944 as a sort of papal 'baptism' of democracy.[89] Yet the papacy also refused to allow the Catholic leaders of the Democrazia Cristiana in Italy freedom to make their own political choices. Democracy was still regarded with deep suspicion in many

[84] John S. Nurser, *For All Peoples and Nations: The Ecumenical Church and Human Rights*, Washington, DC, 2005, 59.

[85] Menozzi, *La Chiesa e diritti umani*, 156–163.

[86] Menozzi, *La Chiesa e diritti umani*, 171.

[87] Hebblethwaite, *Paul VI*, 247.

[88] P. Chenaux, 'LÉglise catholicque et la démocratie chrétienne en Europe 1925–1965', in Michael Gehler, Wolfram Kaiser, and Helmut Wohnout (eds), *Christdemokratie in Europa im 20. Jahrhundert/Christian Democracy in 20th Century Europe*, Vienna, 2001, 607.

[89] Chenaux, 'L'Église catholique', 608.

quarters of the Vatican precisely because it was associated with liberalism, secularism, anti-clericalism,[90] and the influence of the Jews, Freemasonry, and Protestantism. And those things in their turn were associated with the Anglo-Saxons and the French.

The papacy still had an ambiguous relationship with America and American Catholicism, for precisely these reasons. On the one hand, America had been the salvation of Europe, militarily saving it from Nazism and economically from Communism. In this process *the papacy* had probably also been saved by America, and saved financially thanks to American Catholic contributions to Peter's Pence. The European Great Powers, having been rescued by the USA and the USSR, had been forced to embark upon painful processes of decolonization so this was beginning of the end, geopolitically, for Europe. Now the future lay in the Americas, including the future of Catholicism, which admittedly would not become completely obvious until the election of Francis I in 2013. On the other hand, in the 1950s, the European relationship with America involved democracy, modernization of European economies through Marshall Aid, and 'modernization' of manners and lifestyles through the influence of cinema and radio, and television as well. These forces were at work all over Western Europe after 1945, and nowhere more so than in Italy. Ultimately, they represented the greatest challenge to the Church, eroding traditional Catholic values and lifestyles. They reached their culmination in the 1970s.[91]

Moreover, the papacy had not fully reconciled itself with *capitalism*, the ultimate driving force of modernization, either. Its investment managers might have very successfully come to terms with the market, especially financial markets, but not so some of the ecclesiastical leaders in the Vatican. A part of the problem was that, despite the Church's underlying universal mission and raison d'être, and despite some attempts to bring fresh foreign blood into the Roman curia and papal diplomatic corps, the papacy was still not truly *international*: in reality, it was still an overwhelmingly *Italian* institution in terms of its culture and personnel.

All this would begin to change after the election of Pope John XXIII in October 1958. In the short term, there were no immediate radical and abrupt changes in papal policy or style after 1958, certainly fewer than in 1914. The appointment of Tardini as Secretary of State by the new pope is the clearest evidence of the strong elements of continuity between the pontificates of Pius XII and John XXIII: all of the other major office-holders remained in place too, including Ottaviani and Pizzardo. The big policy changes, *Ostpolitik*, the attempt to disengage the Church from Italian politics, and *aggiornamento*

[90] Chenaux, 'L'Église catholique', 608, where he says that Pius XII publicly repudiated Ottaviani's depiction of Franco's Spain as the ideal Christian state.

[91] For the Italian experience, see Pollard, *Catholicism*, 135–137.

('updating'), would take years to develop: the biggest, the launching of Second Vatican Council, which was really the culmination of *aggiornamento*, would take nearly four.

The Council was the great 'Pandora's box', an event process that would bring into play, openly and for the first time, all those peripheral, and not so peripheral, forces for change which had been forced to abide in silence during the pontificate of Pius XII. Much of what was achieved in the Council—the Declaration on Religious Liberty and therefore the ecumenical opening to non-Christian churches, the Declaration on the Jews, the constitution on the Church (*Lumen Gentium)* with its definition of the Church as 'the people of God' so different from the 'high church' ecclesiology prevalent during the pontificates of Pius XI and XII—was the result of battles royal between conservative curial elements led by Ottaviani and Pizzardo and more liberal, non-Roman elements led by Montini of Milan, Lercaro of Bologna, Suenens of Brussels, Meyer of Chicago, and others.[92] This was truly the legacy of the papacy in the age of totalitarianism. The deep divisions on many issues between conservatives at the centre and liberals on the periphery, which had been largely hidden for several decades, had now broken the surface. Of course, the picture was never as simple as that. Cardinal Bea and Mgr Willebrands, the advocates of ecumenism, were both *inside* the Curia. Cardinals Siri of Genoa and Ruffini of Palermo, who were outside, were far from being liberals, and many 'backwoods' bishops, especially in Europe and Latin America, were only interested in a further definition of Mary's role in salvation history and another condemnation of Communism.

Yet the reign of Pius XII was, at least, in a very real sense a sort of prelude or 'antechamber' to the Council. Liturgical reform, which resulted in the vernacular Mass, had, in some way or another, been on the papal agenda for much of the period between St Pius X's reforms of 1907 and those of Pius XII nearly fifty years later. By then, liturgical change had gathered a huge head of steam. The very idea of a Council, or at least a reconvening of the First Council of the Vatican, had first appeared on the papal agenda in the 1920s (see Chapter 5) and began once more to be taken seriously in the later years of Pius XII (see Chapter 11). Indeed, without the preliminary studies ordered by Pius it seems unlikely that the actual Council between 1962 and 1965, which changed the Roman Catholic Church radically and forever, would have been such a success. This is the ultimate irony, that the forces which would sweep away so many of the characteristic features of Catholicism in the period 1914–58 were actually generated in that period itself and, in large part by, the very pope, Pius XII, who most especially symbolized that kind of Catholicism.

[92] For accounts of the battles in the Council, see Hebblethwaite, *John XXIII*, chs 20, 21, and 22; and *Paul VI*, 19, 21, 22, and 26.

Glossary

ABSS. Amministrazione per I Beni della Santa Sede (Administration of the Assets of the Holy See). Main agency responsible for administering Vatican palaces and gardens (prior to 1929), other property in Rome, and the capital assets accumulated as a result of the investment of the surplus from Peter's Pence.

Ad Limina Visit. The visit which all Catholic bishops are obliged to make to the pope to report on the administration of their diocese.

Agréement. Acceptance by one state of the person nominated by another to be ambassador.

Americanism. A 'heresy' condemned in Leo XIII's apostolic letter, *Testem Benevolentia* of 1899. It allegedly consisted of such ideas as the rejection of external spiritual direction, the elevation of natural virtues over supernatural ones, and a preference for 'active' virtues to 'passive' ones. At bottom, the concern in Rome and France was about the liberal democratic climate in which the Catholic Church existed in America.

Amministrazione per le Opere di Religione/Pias Causa. Created by Leo XIII to secretly administer and invest cash funds and stocks and bonds of Italian religious orders and occasionally diocese.

Apostolic Letter. Papal document of lesser importance than an encyclical (q.v.).

Arbitrage. Simultaneous purchase and sale, normally in different places, of currencies, sometimes for delivery at different times, with no price risk.

ASSS. Amministrazione Speciale della Santa Sede (Special Administration of the Holy See). Vatican agency created by Pius XI in 1929 to administer and invest funds received from the Italian government as laid down in the Financial Convention of that year, whose management was entrusted to Bernardino Nogara.

Beatification. A process carried out by officials of the Roman curia (q.v.) by means of which a dead person is judged to have led an especially holy life in conformity with the Church's teaching, and may even have been responsible for a miraculous cure. The person is then given the title of 'venerable' or 'blessed'.

Benefice, ecclesiastical. An ecclesiastical office—e.g. that of bishop or parish priest—whose income was originally derived from an endowment.

Camarlengo, Cardinal. The cardinal responsible for the administration of the affairs of the Holy See, including finance, during a *sede vacante* (q.v.). He is also responsible for the smooth running of the funeral of the deceased pope and the conclave.

Canon. An ecclesiastical regulation, part of Code of Canon Law (q.v.).

Canon Law, Code of. The manual of laws which regulates all aspects of the life of the Roman Catholic Church. The first Code was promulgated in 1917 and a revised version in 1983. There is also a separate Code for the Eastern rite (q.v.) and Uniate (q.v.) churches.

Canon of the Mass. The part containing the consecration and communion of the bread and wine.

Canonization. The process, carried out in the same way as for Beatification (q.v.), whereby a dead person is declared to have led an especially holy life in conformity with the Church's teaching, to have demonstrated signs of 'heroic virtues', and to have performed miracles, and is therefore given the title of 'saint', judged to be worthy of veneration by the faithful.

Casa Generalizia. The Rome headquarters of a religious order, or alternatively the residence in the city of a religious order whose base is outside of Italy.

Catechism. A comprehensive manual of Catholic religious belief which, in a simplified form, is used for the religious instruction of children.

Caudillo. 'Chief', Franco's title as head of the Nationalist forces in Spain.

Chirograph. A papal administrative decree of limited circulation within the Roman curia.

Clerico-moderates. Italian laymen with a more conciliatory attitude towards the Italian state than their intransigent (q.v.) fellow Catholics. Many were businessmen, financiers, and large farmers, and some became members of the Italian Parliament after the *Non expedit* (q.v.) was relaxed from 1904 onwards.

Concordat. A treaty between the Holy See and the government of a secular state which regulates relations between the Church and the government of that state, and guarantees certain rights to the Church in the free exercise of its ministry.

Delegate, Apostolic. A representative of the Holy See to the ecclesiastical hierarchy of a given country or countries. He does not have diplomatic standing but has, in the past, nevertheless, frequently performed a secret diplomatic role in relationship to governments.

Dicastery or Congregation. Department of the Roman curia (q.v.).

Drang nach Osten. Tendency to the eastward expansion of German states, especially Prussia, through the eleventh to twentieth centuries.

Eastern Rite Churches. Those churches, like the Catholic Copts, Maronites, and Melkites, who have different liturgies and discipline (married priests, etc.) from the 'Latin' rite Catholics of the West.

Élysée. The place of the French president in Paris; hence a seat of power.

Encyclical. The most important of all the public communications of the pope, usually addressed to the hierarchy of the whole Church, the hierarchy of a given country, or to both hierarchy and faithful together.

Ex cathedra. Literally 'from the seat'. Only papal pronouncements made solemnly on the basis of the teaching authority of the apostolic see ('seat') are to be regarded as infallible.

Exegesis. The scholarly study of the Bible, with the purpose of interpreting its content in the light of the times.

Falange. The name of the Spanish fascist party founded and led by José Antonio Primo de Rivera.

Fondo per il Culto. The department of the Italian Ministry of Justice which distributed the revenues of the expropriated properties of the Italian Church to holders of ecclesiastical benefices—like parish priests, cathedral canons, and bishops—throughout the peninsula from the 1860s onwards. In 1929, it was transferred to the Ministry of the Interior.

Glagolithic, or Old Slavonic. Alphabet used in the (Canon of the) Mass in Dalmatia.

Holy See. The bishopric of Rome, claimed to have been founded by St Peter, who was its first bishop. Because of this connection with the 'Prince of the Apostles', his successors in the see, the popes, claim spiritual primacy and authority over the whole Christian Church. It is also known as the papacy and often referred to, as in this book, as 'the Vatican'.

Indulgences. A device whereby the temporal punishment due for sin in purgatory is remitted by authority of the papacy.

Intransigents. Catholics who maintained an uncompromising attitude of hostility towards the Italian state after the capture of Rome in 1870.

IOR. Istituto per le Opere di Religione. Literally 'Institute for the Works of Religion'. The name given to the Amministrazione per le Opere di Religione, which had originally been established by Leo XIII to administer the funds of certain religious orders and Italian diocese, when Pius XII reorganized it in 1942. Nowadays, it is commonly known as the 'Vatican Bank'.

Lateran Pacts. The agreements signed by Mussolini for the Italian state and Cardinal Gasparri for the Holy See, on 11 February 1929, in the palace of the Lateran, Rome. They consisted of the Treaty which brought the Roman Question to an end and created the sovereign and independent State of the Vatican City, the Concordat which regulated Church–State relations in Italy down to 1984 and the Financial Convention which resolved outstanding financial questions between the two signatories.

Law of Papal Guarantees. Passed by the Italian Parliament in 1871 to 'regularize' the status and role of the pope in Italy following the occupation of the last remnant of the Papal States, its annexation to Italy, and the proclamation of Rome as capital city.

Letter, Apostolic. A papal communication having lesser authority than an encyclical and usually addressed to individual or small groups of bishops.

Metropolitan. Usually the ordinary (q.v.) of an archbishopric, with a limited supervisory jurisdiction over the (suffragan) bishops in his province.

Minor and Major Seminary. The first was a 'preparatory' school for adolescent boys proposing to train for the priesthood: the latter was the seminary proper taking men from 18.

Minutante. A junior official in the Secretariat of State and other 'dicasteries' of the Roman curia.

Modernism. 'The synthesis of all heresies'. A set of ideas condemned by the Holy Office in *Lamentabili* of 1907 and in Pius X's encyclical *Pascendi* of the same year. Essentially, what was attacked were the ideas of various French and British Catholic scholars that, among other things, the Bible should be subject to historical–critical study, that religious dogma develops within history, and that sociological concepts can play a useful role in the study of the history of the Church. Most of these ideas have been generally accepted since the Second Council of the Vatican in the 1960s.

Modus vivendi. An agreement between the Holy See and the government of a state for the same purposes as a concordat (q.v.) but less binding.

Motu Proprio. A decree issued on the authority of the pope to regulate the administration of a given part of the Roman curia.

Non expedit. A papal decree prohibiting Italian Catholics from voting and standing as candidates in the parliamentary elections of the Kingdom of Italy. It was finally abolished in 1919.

Nuncio, Apostolic. The diplomatic representative of the Holy See to the government of a state.

Oblate. Literally, 'offering' or 'sacrifice'. It usually refers to a junior member of a religious order or congregation.

Obolo. Italian name for the collections of Peter's Pence. Sometimes used to refer to all offerings received by the Pope.

Opera dei Congressi. The umbrella organization of the various organizations of the Catholic movement—youth and adult groups, newspapers, credit and cooperative institutions, and so on—until it was dissolved by Pius X in 1904.

Opus Dei (the work of God). The Spanish-based religious institute of clergy and lay people founded by Josemaría Escrivá de Balaguer y Alba.

Ordinary. The bishop of a diocese who has 'ordinary' spiritual jurisdiction over the clergy and faithful in that area.

Peter's Pence. The name used to describe the major form of monetary contributions of the Catholic faithful throughout the world to the support of the Holy See. It originated in Anglo-Saxon England and was revived in the mid-nineteenth century.

POWs. Prisoners of war.

Prefettura dei Sacri Palazzi Apostolici. (Prefecture of the Sacred Apostolic Palaces). The administration of the papal palaces in Rome, including, before 1870, the Quirinale palace.

Primate. The leading metropolitan within a given country or region. The pope, as bishop of Rome, is the primate of Italy. The Archbishop of Baltimore has an 'honorary' primacy or precedence over all other bishops in the United States of America by virtue of being the occupant of the oldest bishopric in the country.

Propaganda. The Congregation of De Propaganda Fide, which is responsible for the Church's missionary activities and which has a budget independent of the rest of the Roman curia.

Quai d'Orsay. The seat of the French Ministry of Foreign Affairs, hence colloquially, the institution itself

Quirinale. Palace in Rome, formerly of the popes, later of the kings and presidents of Italy. Ambassadors to Italy are accredited to the Quirinale, as opposed to he Holy See.

Regio Placet et Exequatur. The power claimed by Italian rulers to give permission to newly appointed ecclesiastics to enter into their benefices (q.v.). The Law of Papal Guarantees (q.v.) promised to abolish this permission, but did not follow through until 1929.

Religious. Men and women, monks, nuns, friars, and so on, who have taken solemn vows.

Roman Curia. Central government of the Roman Catholic Church situated in the Vatican and in other parts of Rome, consisting of the Secretariat of State and the other various congregations, offices, and tribunals.

Roman Question. The dispute between the papacy and the Italian state following the latter's occupation and annexation of Rome in 1870 and consequent destruction of the last remnant of the temporal power (q.v.).

Secular Clergy. Those clergy who have not taken solemn vows.

Sede Vacante. The interregnum between the death of one pope and the election of his successor.

Sedia Gestatoria. The portable throne on which the popes were carried into St Peter's Basilica. It was abolished by Pope Paul VI.

Sostituto. The substitute or deputy to the Cardinal Secretary of State.

Sudeten Lands. Border areas of western part of Czechoslovakia, that is, Bohemia and Moravia, largely inhabited by German speakers.

Temporal Power. The pope's political sovereignty over the former Papal States of central Italy. Revived in the form of the miniscule State of the Vatican City in 1929.

Third Order. An association of either secular clergy or laity who take limited vows and share externally in the spiritual religious congregations and orders, for example, Franciscans.

Uniat. A Church of the Eastern rite, for example the Ukrainian, which was reunited with Rome after previously being a part of the Orthodox Church.

Usury. The lending of money at excessive rates of interest. Until the nineteenth century, *all* moneylending at interest was regarded as being, potentially, usury.

Visitor, Apostolic. A special, temporary representative of the Holy See to the hierarchy of a country. The term is also used about papal 'inspectors' during the reign of Pius X (1903–14), who visited dioceses or their seminaries looking for signs of the 'modernist' heresy.

Sources

Printed Primary Sources

ADSS: *Actes et Documents du Saint-Siége relatifs á la Seconde Guerre Mondiale*, 11 vols, ed. P. Blet, SJ, R. Graham, SJ, A. Martini, SJ, and B. Schneider, SJ (Vatican City, 1965–81).

1. *Le Saint Siége et la Guerre Mondiale*, Mars 1939–Aout 1940.
2. *Lettres du Pape aux Eveques Allemands.*
3. *Le Saint Siége et la Situation Religieuse en Pologne et dans les Pays Baltes, 1939–1945; 1939–1941.*
4. *Le Saint Siége et la Situation Religieuse en Pologne et dans les Pays Baltes, 1941–1945.*
5. *Le Saint Siége et la Guerre Mondiale, Juin 1940—Juin 1941.*
6. *Le Saint Siége et la Guerre Mondiale, Juillet 1941—Octobre 1942.*
7. *Le Saint Siége et al Guerre Mondiale, Novembre 1942–Décembre 1943.*
8. *Le Saint Siége et les Victimes de la Guerre, Janvier 1941—Décembre 1942.*
9. *Le Saint Siége et les Victimes de la Guerre, Janvier–Décembre 1943.*
10. *Le Saint Siége et les Victimes de la Guerre, Juin 1944–Juillet 1945.*
11. *Le Saint Siege et la Guerre Mondiale, Janvier 1944–Mai 1945.*

Allocuzioni e radiomessaggi di S.S. Pio XII, con commento degli scrittori della Civiltà cattolica (Rome, 1943).

Atti Parlamentari del Regno d'Italia. Camera dei Deputati. Discussioni, vol. 1 (Rome, 1929); vol. III (1903–39).

Constitución Política de los Estados Unidos Mexicanos (Mexico City, 1917).

Discorsi di Pio XI, 2 vols, ed. U. Bellocchi (Turin, 1960).

Documents on British Foreign Policy, 1919–1939 (London, 1954–86).

Documents on German Foreign Policy, 1918–1945 (London, 1949–57).

FRUS: *Foreign Relations of the United States: Diplomatic Papers* (Washington, DC, Vols. 15a and 15b, 1984), Vol. 16 (1981).

Hachey, E. (ed.) (1972), *Anglo-Vatican Relations* (Boston, MA).

I Documenti Diplomatici Italiani, Ministero degli affari esteri, 1939–1943 and 1918–1922 (Rome) published 1954.

Index Librorum Prohibitorum (SSMI. D.N. PII PPXI) (Vatican, 1938).

The New Testament of Our Lord and Saviour Jesus Christ according to the Rheims Version Revised by Bishop Challoner (London, n.d.).

Opera Omnia di Benito Mussolini (1883–1945), 44 vols, ed. Edoardo and Duilio Susmel (Florence, 1951–89).

Ordo Hebdomadae Sanctae Instauratus (Vatican City, 1956).

The Papal Encyclicals, 6 vols, ed. C. Carlen, I.H.M. (Raleigh, NC, 1981).

II. 1878–1903, III. 1903–39, IV. 1939–58, V. 1958–82.

Pio XII Discorsi e radiomessaggi, 20 vols (Milan, 1940–59).

Records and Documents of the Holy See Relating to the Second World War; the Holy See and the War in Europe, March 1939–August 1940, ed. Pierre Blet, Angelo Martini, and Burkhart Schneider (English edition by Gerard Noel) (Dublin, 1968).

The Small Roman Missal (Leeds, 1944).
Tutte le Encicliche e Documenti Pontifici, VIII: *Benedetto XV (1914–22)*, IX: *Pio XI (1922–30)*, X: *Pio XI (1930–39)*, XI: *Pio XII (1939–58)*, ed. U. Bellocchi (Vatican City, 2000–03).

Diaries and Memoirs

Charles-Roux, F. (1947), *Huit ans au Vatican, 1932–1940* (Paris).
Charles-Roux, F. (*c*.1961), *Souvenirs diplomatiques. Une grande ambassade à Rome, 1919–1925* (Paris).
Ciano, G. (1947), *Ciano's Diary, 1939–1943*, ed. with intro. M. Muggeridge (London).
Ciano, G. (1952), *Ciano's Diary, 1937–1938*, trans. with notes A. Mayor, with intro. M. Muggeridge (London).
Diaries of Angelo Roncalli—Pope John XXIII, Fondazione per le Scienze Religiose (Bologna).
Edizione nazionale dei diari di Giuseppe Roncalli—Giovanni III/Angelo Giuseppe Roncalli (Bologna, 1994).
Engel-Janosi, F. (1973), *Il Vaticano tra nazionalismo e fascismo* (Florence).
Pacelli, F. (1959), *Diario della Conciliazione*, ed. M. Maccarone (Vatican City).
Pirelli, A. (1984), *Taccuini, 1922–1943*, ed. D. Barbone with intro. E. Ortona (Bologna).
Poincaré, R. (1928), *Au Service de la France*, vol. V (Paris).
Pompei, Gian Franco (1994), *Un Ambasciatore in Vaticano. Diario 1969–1977*, ed. Pietro Scoppola, with notes by Roberto Morozzo della Rocco (Bologna).
Scottà, A. (ed.) (1997), *La Conciliazione ufficiosa. Diario del barone Carlo Monti 'incaricato d'affari' del governo italiano presso la Santa Sede (1914–1922)*, 2 vols (Vatican City).
Tittman, H.H., Jr (2004), *Il Vaticano di Pio XII. Uno sguardo dall'interno*, trans. Marco Sartori (Milan).

Official and Periodical Publications

Archivum Historiae Pontificiae (Rome).
Annuario Pontificio (Vatican City).
Bollettino della Diocesi di Bologna.
Byzantine and Modern Greek Studies.
Church and State.
Catholic Historical Review (Washington, DC).
Civitas (Milan).
Corriere della Sera (Milan).
The Court Historian.
Cristianesimo nella Storia (Bologna).
Cultura e libri (Rome).
English Historical Journal (Oxford).
European History Quarterly (London).
Il Giornale d'Italia.
História.

Historical Journal (Cambridge).
Intelligence and National Security.
Journal of Contemporary History (Cambridge).
Journal of Ecclesistical History (Cambridge).
Journal of the Behavioural Sciences.
La Civiltà Cattolica (Rome).
L'Osservatore Romano (Rome; Vatican City after 1932).
Mid-America.
Modern Italy: Journal of the Association for the Study of Modern Italy.
The Month.
National Geographic Magazine.
Nuova Antologia (Rome).
Revue des Deux Mondes.
Revue d'histoire diplomatique.
Revue d'Histoire Moderne et Contemporaine (Paris).
La Revue Nouvelle.
Rivista Storica Svizzera.
Rivista di Storia della Chiesa in Italia (Milan).
The Statesman's Yearbook, 1930 (London, 1930).
Storia Contelporanea.
Studi Storici.
The Tablet (London).
The Times (London).
The Yearbook of American Religion (New York, 1941).
Totalitarian Movements and Political Religions (Abingdon, England).

Secondary Sources

Aarons, Mark and Loftus, John (1991), *Ratlines: How the Vatican's Nazi Networks Betrayed Western Intelligence to the Soviets* (London).

Absalom, R.N.L. (1991), *L'Alleanza inattesa: Mondo contadino e prigionieri alleati in fuga in Italia (1943–1945) [A Strange Alliance: Aspects of Escape and Survival in Italy, 1943–1945]* (Florence).

Abse, T. (1992), 'Italy', in J. Noakes (ed.), *The Civilian in War: The Home Front in Europe, Japan and the USA in World War II* (Leicester).

Adams, C. (2007), 'Leap of Faith: Futurism, Fascism and the "Manifesto of Futurist Sacred Art"', *Piety and Pragmatism: Spiritualism in Futurist Art*, catalogue of the Exhibition at the Estorick Gallery (London).

Adams, J. (1965), *Peace and Bread in Time of War* (New York).

Adler, Jacques (2004) '"The Sin of Omission"? Radio Vatican and the Anti-Nazi Struggle, 1940–1942', *Australian Journal of History and Politics*, 50(3), 402.

Alexander, S. (1979), *Church and State in Yugoslavia since 1945* (Cambridge).

Alix, C. (1967), 'Le Vatican et la décolonisation', in M. Merle (ed.), *Les Eglise chrétiennes et la decolonisation* (Paris).

Alvarez, David J. (1996), 'A German at the Vatican: The Gerlach Affair', *Intelligence and National Security*, 2(2) (April), 443–453.

Alvarez, David J. (2002), *Spies in the Vatican: Espionage and Intrigue from Napoleon to the Holocaust* (Lawrence, KS).

Alvarez, David J. and Graham, Robert A. (1997), *Nothing Sacred: Nazi Espionage against the Vatican, 1939–1945* (London).

Andeweg, Rudy D. and Irwin, Galen A. (1993), *Dutch Government and Politics* (Basingstoke).

Anon (1916), 'Il Papa e il congresso di Pace', *Nuova Antologia*, 1 March.

Applebaum, Anne (2012), *Iron Curtain: The Crushing of Eastern Europe, 1944–1956* (London).

Aquarone, A. (1965), *L'Organizzazione dello Stato Totalitario* (Turin).

Atti del Convegno Pio XII, la Chiesa e la societá civile (1939–1958) (Bari, 1982).

Aubert, R. (1994), 'Le Cardinal Mercier et la Question Romaine en 1918–1919', in Jean-Pierre Hendrickx, Jean Pirotte, and Luc Courtois (eds), *Le Cardinal Mercier (1851–1926), Un prélat d'avant-garde/Publications du professeur Roger Aubert rassemblées à l'occasion de ses 80 ans* (Louvain-la-Neuve).

Azzolini, G. (2003), *Gaetano De Lai, 'L'uomo forte'. Cultura e fede nel Novecento nell'esperienza del cardinale vicentino* (Vicenza).

Bakvis, Herman (1981), *Catholic Power in the Netherlands* (Kingston and Montreal).

Barany, Zoltan (2002), *The East European Gypsies: Regime Change, Marginality and Ethno-politics* (Cambridge).

Barry, Colman J., OSB (1969), *American Nuncio: Cardinal Aloisius Muench* (Collegeville, MN).

Bastianini, G. (1959), *Uomini, cose* (Milan).

Baxa, P. (2010), *Roads and Ruins: The Symbolic Landscape of Fascist Rome* (Toronto).

Bays, D. (2008) 'From Mission to Chinese Church', *Church History and Biography, 98* (Spring), 9–10.

Bea, F. (1981), *Qui Radio vaticana. Mezzo secolo della radio del Papa* (Vatican City).

Benedictus PP. XV (1914), 'Ad Universos Orbis Catholicos', LaCC, 1542, 19 September, i–iv.

Bergen, Doris (1999), 'Storm Troopers of Christ: The German Christian Movement and the Ecclesiastical Final Solution', Ericksen and Heschel (eds), *Betrayal: German Churches and the Holocaust*.

Bernstein, Carl and Politi, Marco (1996), *His Holiness: John Paul II and the Hidden History of our Time* (London and New York).

Binchy, D.A. (1970), *Church and State in Fascist Italy* (Oxford).

Black, G. (1997), *The Catholic Crusade against the Movies: 1940–1975* (Cambridge).

Blet, P., SJ (1999), *Pius XII and the Second World War: According to the Archives of the Vatican*, trans. L.J. Johnson (Herefordshire).

Blobaum, Robert (2005) (ed.), *Anti-Semitism and its Opponents in Modern Poland* (Ithaca, NY).

Bodó, Béla (2008), '"Do Not Lead us into (Fascist) Temptation": The Catholic Church in Inter-war Hungary', in M. Feldmann and M. Turda (eds), *Clerical Fascism in Inter-war Europe* (Abingdon, Oxford).

Bosworth, R.J.B. (2010), 'L'Anno Santo (Holy Year) in Fascist Italy 1933–34', *European History Quarterly*, 40, 404–439.

Bosworth, R.J.B. (2005), *Mussolini's Italy: Life under the Dictatorship, 1915–1945* (London).

Bosworth, R.J.B. (2005), *Whispering City: Rome and its Histories* (Yale, CT).
Bouthillon, F. (2001), *La naissance de la mardite. Une théologie politique totalitaire. Pie XI (1922–1939)* (Strasbourg).
Boyea, E. (1987), *The National Catholic Welfare Conference: An Experience in Episcopal Leadership, 1935–1945* (Washington, DC).
Brandmüller, W. (2004), *L'Olocausto nella Slovacchia e La Chiesa Cattolica* (Vatican City).
Brown, Kevin (2004), *'The Penicillin Man': Alexander Fleming and the Antibiotic Revolution* (London).
Brown-Fleming, S. (2006), *The Holocaust and the Catholic Conscience: Cardinal Aloisius Muench and the Guilt Question in Germany* (Notre Dame, IN).
Browning, Christopher R. (2004), *The Origins of the Final Solution: September 1939 to March 1942, with Contributions by Matthaus Juergen* (London).
Brunori di Siervo, M. T. (1981), '"L'Istituto Cattolico di attivita" Sociale dalla nascita all seconda Guerra mondiale', *Storia Contemporanea*, 12(4–5) (October), 737–791.
Bruti Liberati, L. (1963), 'La Santa Sede e gli Stati Uniti negli anni della Grande Guerra', in Rumi (ed.), *Benedetto XV*.
Buchanan, Tom (1996), 'Great Britain', in Buchanan and Conway (eds), *Political Catholicism in Europe*.
Buchanan, Tom and Conway, Martin (1996) (eds), *Political Catholicism in Europe, 1918–1965* (Oxford).
Bugnini, A., CM (1990), *The Reform of the Liturgy, 1948–1975* (Collegeville, MN).
Bugnini, A., CM and Braga, C., CM (1957), *Cerimoniale della Settimana Santa* (Rome).
Buonaiuti, E. (1946), *Pio XII* (Rome).
Caprile, G., SJ (1966), 'Pio XI e la ripresa del Concilio Vaticano', LaCC, 117(3), 37–39.
Cárcel Ortí, V. (2001), *Buio sull'altare. La persecuzione della Chiesa in Spagna* (Rome).
Cárcel Ortí, V. (2004), 'Notas sobre la misíon pontificia de Mons. Antoniutti en Espana nacional durante la Guerra civil (1937–1938)', *AHP*, 42, 51–85.
Cárcel Ortí, V. (2008) 'La Nunciatura de Madrid Durante la Guerra Civil (1936–1939)', *AHP*, 46, 163–356.
Cárcel Ortí, V. (2008), *Pío XI entre la republica y Franco. Angustia del Papa ante la tragedia española* (Madrid).
Caroleo, A. (1976), *Le Banche cattoliche* (Milan).
Carr, R. (1980), *Modern Spain 1875–1980* (Oxford).
Carvalho, Rita (1997), 'Concordata com la Santa Sè', *História*, 31, 4–15.
Casella, A. (1992), *Azione Cattolica nell'Italia contemporanea (1919–1969)* (Rome).
Castagna, Luca (2011), *Un ponte oltre l'oceano. Assettti politici e strategicie diplomatiche tra Stati Unit e santa Sede nella prima metà del novecento (1915–1940)* (Bologna).
Casula, C.-F. (1998), *Domenico Tardini (1888–1961) e l'Azione della Sede nella crisi fra le due guerre* (Rome).
Casula, C.-F. (2003), 'Santa Sede e Guerra d'Etiopia. A proposito di un discorso di Pio XI', *Studi Storici*, 46(2), 512–525.
Casula, C.-F. (2001), 'Le segreterie di stato tra le due guerre', in De Rosa and Cracco (eds), *Il Papato e L'Europa*.
Ceci, Lucia (2012), 'The First Steps in "Parallel Diplomacy": The Vatican and the U.S. in the Italo-Ethiopian War, 1935–6', in Gallagher, Kertzer, and Melloni (eds), *Pius XI and America*.

Ceci, Lucia (2010), *Il Papa non deve parlare. Chiesa, fascismo e guerra d'Etiopia* (Rome and Bari).

Ceci, Lucia (2010), 'Santa Sede e impero fascista. Contrasti, silenzi e fiancheggiamenti', in Guasco and Perin (eds), *Pius XI: Keywords.*

Chabod, F. (1961), *L'Italia Contemporanea (1918–1948)* (Turin).

Chadwick, O. (1986), *Britain and the Vatican during the Second World War* (Cambridge).

Chadwick, O. (1992), *The Christian Church in the Cold War* (Harmondsworth).

Chadwick, O. (1998), *A History of the Popes, 1830–1914* (Oxford).

Chappin, M. (2010–11), 'Cardinal van Rossum and the international Eucharistic congresses,' in Poels et al. (eds), *Life with a Mission.*

Cheetham, Nicholas (1971), *Mexico: A Short History* (New York).

Chenaux, Philippe (1990), *Une Europe vaticane? Entre le plan Marshall et les traités de Rome* (Brussels).

Chenaux, Philippe (2009), 'Pie XI et le Communisme (1930–1939). D'auprès les Archives du Vatican', in Delville and Jacov (eds), *La Papauté Contemporaine.*

Chélini, Jean (1985), *L'Église de Pie XII. La Tourmente (1939–1945)* (Paris).

Chiron, Y. (2004), *Pio XI. Il papa dei Patti Lateranensi e dell'opposizione ai totalitarismi* (Milan).

Ciampani, A. (2000), *Cattolici e Liberali durante la trasformazione dei partiti. La 'questione romana' e la politica nazionale e progetti vaticani (1870–1883)* (Rome).

Cipriotti, P. and Talamanca, A. (eds) (1976), *I Concordati di Pio XII* (Milan).

Civardi, L. (1934), *Manuale di azione cattolica*, 17th edn (Rome).

Clark, C. (2006), *The Iron Kingdom: The Rise and Downfall of Prussia, 1600–1947* (London).

Clark, C.M. (2013), *The Sleepwalkers: How Europe Went to War in 1914* (London).

Clark, C.M., and Kaiser, W. (eds) (2003), *Culture Wars: Secular–Catholic Conflict in Nineteenth Century Europe* (Cambridge).

Clark, M. (1996), *Modern Italy: 1870–1995* (London).

Cobban, A. (1962), *A History of Modern France*, vol. 3: *1871–1962* (London).

Coco, G. (2006), *Santa Sede e Manciuko (1932–1945). Con Appendice di documenti* (Vatican City).

Cohen, Leah (2012), *You Believe: 8 Glances at the Holocaust*, trans. Tanya Ryan (Sofia).

Coleman, J. (1986), 'Development of Catholic Social Teaching', in Charles E. Curran and Robert McCormick (eds), *Readings in Moral Theology No. 5* (New York).

Colombo, D. (2003), 'Psychoanalysis and the Catholic Church in Italy: The Role of Father Agostino Gemelli, 1925–1953', *Journal of the History of the Behavioural Sciences*, 39(4) (Fall), 333–348.

Comacini, G. (1985), *Gemelli* (Milan).

Confalonieri, C. (1993), *Pio XI visto da vicino. Nuova edizione con l'aggiunta di due appendici a cura di Giuseppe Frasso* (Milan).

Connelly, John (2012), *From Enemy to Brother: The Revolution in Catholic Teaching on the Jews, 1933–1965* (Cambridge, MA).

Conway, J. (1968), *The Nazi Persecution of the Churches, 1933–1945* (London).

Cooney, J. (1983), *The American Pope* (New York).

Cooney, J. (2000), *John Charles McQuaid, Ruler of Catholic Ireland* (Syracuse, NY).

Coppa, F.J. (1999), *Controversial Concordat: The Vatican's Relations with Napoleon, Mussolini and Hitler* (Washington, DC).
Coppa, F.J. (ed.) (1999), *Encyclopedia of the Vatican and the Papacy* (Westport, CT).
Coppa, F.J. (1998), *The Modern Papacy since 1789* (London).
Coppa, F.J. (2011), *The Policies and Politics of Pope Pius XII: Between Diplomacy and Morality* (New York and Oxford).
Cornwall, M. (ed.) (1990), *The Last Years of Austria-Hungary* (Exeter).
Cornwell, J. (1999), *Hitler's Pope: The Secret History of Pius XII* (London).
Corsetti, A. (1969), 'Dalla preconciliazione ai Patti del Laterano. Note e Documenti', in *Annuario 1968 della Biblioteca Civica di Massa* (Lucca).
Costa Pinto, A., and Inácia Rezola, M. (2007), 'Political Catholicism, Crisis of Democracy and Salazar's New State', *Totalitarian Movements and Political Religions*, 8(2) (June), 353–368.
Croce, Giuseppe M. (2010–11), 'Regards sur la Curie romaine de 1895 à 1932', in Poels et al. (eds), *Life with a Mission* (London).
Cronin, M. (2007), 'Catholicising Fascism, Fascistising Catholicism? The Blueshirts and the Jesuits in Ireland', *TMPR*, 8(2) (June), 189–200.
D'Agostino, P.R. (2004), *Rome in America: Transnational Catholic Ideology from the Risorgimento to Fascism* (Chapel Hill, NC, and London).
D'Alessio, Giulia (2012), 'The United States and the Vatican (1936–1939)', in C. Gallagher, David I. Kertzer, and A. Melloni (eds), *Pius XI and America*.
Dalla Torre, G. (1965), *Memorie* (Milan).
De Felice, R. (2001), *The Jews in Fascist Italy: A History* (New York).
De Felice, R. (1974), *Mussolini il Duce*, vol. I: *Gli anni del consenso, 1929–1936* (Turin).
De Felice, R. (1968), *Mussolini il Fascista. L'organizzazione dello stato totalitario, 1925–1929* (Turin).
De Felice, R. (1974), 'La Santa Sede e il conflitto Italo-Etiopico nel diario di Bernardino Nogara', *Storia Contemporanea*, 8(4), 823–834.
De Giorgi, F. (1994), 'Forme spirituali, forme simboliche, forme politiche. La devozione al Sacro Cuore', *Rivista di Storia della Chiesa in Italia*, 48(2) (July–December), 365–459.
Delville, J.-P., and Jacov, M. (eds) (2009), *La Papauté Contemporaine/Il papato contemporaneo* (Leuven and Louvain-la-Neuve).
Delzell, C. (ed.) (1971), *Mediterranean Fascism, 1919–1945* (New York).
De Rosa, G. (1977), *Luigi Sturzo* (Turin).
De Rosa, G. (1954), *Storia politica dell'Azione Cattolica in Italia*, vol. 2 (Bari).
De Rosa, G. and G. Cracco (eds) (2001), *Il Papato e l'Europa* (Soveria Mannelli).
De Vecchi di Val Cismon, C.M. (1960), *Memorie*, *Il Tempo*, 17, January–March.
De Wilde, M. (1984), *L'Ordre Nouveau* (Paris).
Dicks, J.A. (1989), *The Malines Conversations Re-visited* (Leuven).
Duffy, E. (1997), *Saints and Sinners: A History of the Popes* (New Haven, CT).
Dunnage, J. (2002), *Twentieth Century Italy: A Social History* (London).
Duquesne, Jacques (1966) *Les Catholiques français sous l'Occupation* (Paris).
Durand, J.-D. (2001), 'Lo stile di governo di Pio XI', in G. De Rosa and G. Cracco (eds), *Il Papato e l'Europa*.
Dussel, D. (1981), *The History of the Church in Latin America: Colonialism to Liberalism*, trans. and rev. A. Neeley (Grand Rapids, MI).

Dwyer, Judith A., I.H.M. (ed.) (1994), *The New Dictionary of Catholic Social Thought* (Collegeville, MN).

Eizenstat, S.E. and Slany, W.Z. (1998), *Supplement to the Preliminary Study on US and Allied Efforts to Recover Gold and Other Assets Stolen during World War II* (Washington, DC).

Ellwood, D.W. (1985), *Italy 1943–45* (Leicester).

Epstein, K. (1959), *Matthias Erzberger and the Dilemma of German Democracy* (Princeton, NJ).

Ericksen, Robert P. and Heschel, Susanna (eds) (1999), *Betrayal: German Churches and the Holocaust* (Minneapolis, MN).

Evans, R. (2005), *The Third Reich in Power* (London).

Fairbanks, J. K. and Liu, K.-C. (eds) (1976), *The Cambridge History of China: 1800–1911*, vol. 11 (Cambridge).

Falconi, C. (1960), *Chiesa e organizzazioni cattoliche in Europa* (Milan).

Falconi, C. (1967), *The Popes in the Twentieth Century*, trans. M. Grindrod (London).

Fattorini, E. (2011), *Hitler, Mussolini and the Vatican: Pope Pius XI and the Speech that was Never Made* (Cambridge).

Felice, G. (n.d.), *Il Cardinale Pietro Gasparri* (Milan).

Finnochiaro, M.A. (2005), *Re-trying Galileo, 1632–1992* (Oakland, CA).

Finzi, Roberto (1999), *Anti-Semitism: From its European Roots to the Holocaust* (Moreton in Marsh).

Fisichella, R. (ed.) (1993), *Catechismo della Chiesa Cattolica. Testo integrale e commento teologico, Direzione e coordinamento del Commento teologico* (Vatican City and Casale Monferrato).

Fitzgerald, S. (1994), *The Russian Revolution*, 2nd edn (Oxford).

Fitzmaurice, John (1983), *The Politics of Belgium: Crisis and Compromise in a Plural Society* (London).

Fogarty, G. (2012), 'The Case of Charles Coughlin', in Gallagher, Kertzer, and Melloni (eds), *Pius XI and America*.

Fogarty, G. (1982), *The Vatican and the American Hierarchy from 1870 to 1965* (Collegeville, MN).

Foot, J. (1997), '"White Bolsheviks"? The Catholic Left and the Socialists in Italy, 1919–1920', *Historical Journal*, 40(2), 415–433.

Fothergill, P. (1955), 'Towards an Interpretation of Evolution, the Teaching of *Humani Generis*', *The Tablet*, 4 April.

Fouilloux, E. (2011), *Eugène, cardinal Tisserant (1884–1972). Une biographie* (Paris).

Friedlander, S. (1996), *Pius XII and the Third Reich: A Documentation* (London).

Galeazzi-Lisi, A. (1960), *Dans l'ombre et la lumière de Pie XII* (Paris).

Gallagher, Charles R., SJ (2008), *Vatican Secret Diplomacy: Joseph P. Hurley and Pope Pius XII* (New Haven, CT).

Gallagher, Charles R., Kertzer, David I., and Melloni, A. (eds) (2012), *Pius XI and America: Proceedings of the Brown University Conference (Providence, October 2010)* (Zurich and Berlin).

Gallo, M. (1973), *Spain under Franco: A History* (London).

Gannon, R., SJ (1963), *The Cardinal Spellman Story* (New York).

Garzia, I. (1988), *Pio XII e l'Italia nella seconda Guerra mondiale* (Brescia).

Garzia, I. (1981), *La Questione Romana durante la I guerra mondiale* (Naples).

Gatz, Erwin (1981), 'Charity and Ecclesiastical Works of Assistance', in Jedin, Repgen, and Dolan (eds), *History of the Church*, vol. X.

Gehler, Michael, Kaiser, Wolfram, and Wohnout, Helmut (eds) (2001), *Christdemokratie in Europa im 20. Jahrhundert/Christian Democracy in 20th Century Europe* (Vienna).

Gentile, E. (2000), 'The Sacralisation of Politics: Definitions, Interpretations and Reflections on the Question of Secular Religion and Totalitarianism', *Totalitarian Movements and Political Religions*, 1(1), 18–55.

Gentiloni Silveri, U. and Carli, M. (2007), *Bombardare Roma. Gli Alleati e la 'citta aperta' (1940–1944)* (Bologna).

Gildea, R. (2002), *Marianne in Chains: In Search of the German Occupation, 1940–1945* (Basingstoke and London).

Gillette, Aaron (2002), *Racial Theories in Fascist Italy* (London and New York).

Ginsborg, P. (1990), *Contemporary Italy: Society and Politics, 1943–1988* (London).

Giovagnoli, A. (1978), 'La Pontificia Commissione di Assistenza e gli aiuti americani 1945–48', *Storia Contemporanea*, 5–6, 1081–1111.

Giovagnoli, A. (ed.) (1999), *Roma e Pechino. La svolta extra-europea di Benedetto XV* (Rome).

Giovanelli, A. (2000), *La Santa Sede e la Palestina. La custodia della Terra Santa fra la fine dell'impero ottoman e la Guerra dei sei giorni* (Rome).

Glubokovsky, N. (1979), 'Christian Fellowship in Life and Work', in Patelos (ed.), *The Orthodox Church in the Ecumenical Movement.*

Godin, A. and Daniel, Y. (1950), *France. Pays de mission?* (Paris).

Goebbels' Diaries, 1939–1941, trans. and ed. Fred Taylor (London, 1983).

Goldhagen, D. J. (2003), *A Moral Reckoning: The Role of the Catholic Church in the Holocaust and its Unfulfilled Duty of Repair* (New York).

Goldstein, E. (1991), 'Holy Wisdom and British Foreign Policy 1918–1922: The St Sophia Redemption', *Byzantine and Modern Greek Studies*, 15, 36–65.

Goni, Uki (2002), *The Real Odessa: How Peron Brought the War Criminals to Argentina* (London).

Graziano, M. (2010), *Il secolo cattolico. La strategia geopolitica della Chiesa*, preface by Lucio Caracciolo (Rome and Bari).

Gregory, J.D. (n.d.), *On the Edge of Diplomacy: Rambles and Reflections, 1902–1928* (London).

Grenville, J. A. S. (n.d.), *The Major International Treaties, 1914–1945: A History and Guide with Texts* (London).

Griech-Polelle, Beth A. (2012), *Bishop Von Galen: German Catholicism and National Socialism* (New Haven, CT, and London).

Groth, Alexander J. (2011), *Accomplices: Churchill, Roosevelt and the Holocaust* (New York).

Guasco, A. (2013), *Cattolici e Fascisti. La Santa Sede e la Politica Italiana All'Alba del Regime (1919–1925)* (Bologna).

Guasco, A. and Perin, Rafaella (eds) (2010), *Pius XI: Keywords. International Conference, Milan 2009* (Berlin and Vienna).

Guasco, M. (2001), 'La formazione del clero al tempo di Pio XI', in De Rosa and Carcco (eds), *Il Papato e l'Europa.*

Guida dell'Archivio della Sacra Congregazione per la Dottrina della Fede (Rome, 1998).

Gundle, S. (2011), *Death and La Dolce Vita: The Dark Side of Rome in the 1950s* (London).

Guspini, U. (1973), *L'Orecchio del Regime* (Milan).

Hagerty, J. (2008), *Cardinal Hinsley: Priest and Patriot* (Oxford).

Hales, E.E.Y. (1956), *Pio Nono: A Study in European Politics and Religion in the Nineteenth Century* (London).

Hales, E.E.Y. (1969), *Revolution and the Papacy, 1769–1846* (London).

Hammond, P. (ed.) (1962), *Towards a Church Architecture* (London).

A Handbook of Korea (Seoul, 1998).

Hanebrink, Paul A. (2006), *In Defense of Christian Hungary: Religion, Nationalism and Anti-Semitism, 1890–1944* (Ithaca, NY, and London).

Hansom, Eric O. (1990), *The Catholic Church in World Politics* (Princeton, NJ).

Hardach, H. (1977), *The First World War, 1914–1918* (London).

Hebblethwaite, P. (1984), *John XXIII: Pope of the Council* (London).

Hebblethwaite, P. (1993), *Paul VI: The First Modern Pope* (London).

Hebblethwaite, P. (1995), 'Pope Pius XII: Chaplain of the Atlantic Alliance?', in C. Duggan and C. Wagstaff (eds), *Italy in the Cold War: Politics, Society and Culture* (Oxford and New York).

Hendrickx, J-P., Pirotte, J., and Courtois, L. (eds) (1994), *Le Cardinal Mercier (1851–1926), Un prélat d'avant-garde/Publications du professeur Roger Aubert rassemblées à l'occasion de ses 80 ans* (Louvain-la-Neuve).

Hennessy, James (1974), 'American Jesuit in Rome: The Diary of Vincent McCormick 1942–1945', *Mid-America*, 56(1).

Henry, F.P. (1857), *The Primacy of the Papacy Vindicated* (Baltimore, London, and Pittsburgh).

Herwig, Holger H. (2003), 'Germany', in Richard H. Hamilton and Holger H. Herwig (eds) (2003), *The Origins of World War I* (Cambridge).

Heschel, Susanna (1999), 'When Jesus was an Aryan: The Protestant Church and Anti-Semitic Propaganda', Ericksen and Heschel (eds), *Betrayal: German Churches and the Holocaust.*

Hochhuth, R. (1997), *The Deputy*, trans. R. and C. Winston, preface Dr A. Schweitzer (Baltimore, MD).

Holmes, J. D. (1981), *The Papacy in the Modern World* (London and New York).

Housden, Martyn (1997) *Resistance and Conformity in the Third Reich* (London).

Ickx, J. (2008), 'Gli omissis di Emma Fattorini', *Archivum Historiae Pontificae*, 46, 425–439.

Innes, A. (2001), *Czechoslovakia: The Short Goodbye* (London and New Haven, CT).

Iordachi, C. (2004), *Charisma, Politics and Violence: The Legion of the Archangel Michael in Interwar Romania* (Trondheim).

Jackson, J. (2001), *France: The Dark Years, 1940–1944* (Oxford).

Jankowiak, F. (2007), *La Curie romaine de Pie IX à Pie XI. Le gouvernement centrale de l'église et la fin des états pontificaux, 1846–1914* (Rome).

Jedin, H. (ed.) (1981), *History of the Church*, vol. IX: *The Church in the Industrial Age*, trans. M. Resch (London).

Jedin, H., Repgen, K., and Dolan, J. (eds) (1981), *History of the Church*, vol. X: *The Church in the Modern Age* (London).

Jemolo, A. C. (1960), *Church and State in Italy, 1850–1950* (Oxford).
Kaiser, W. (2007), *Christian Democracy and the Origins of the European Union* (Cambridge).
Kennedy, P. (1987), *The Rise and Fall of the Great Powers: Economic Change and Military Conflict from 1500 to 2000* (London).
Katz, R. (1967), *Death in Rome* (London).
Katz, R. (2003), *Fatal Silence: The Pope, the Resistance and the German Occupation of Rome* (London).
Kent, Peter C. (2002), *The Lonely Cold War of Pius XII: The Roman Catholic Church and the Division of Europe, 1943–1950* (Montreal and London).
Kent, Peter C. (1981), *The Pope and the Duce: The International Impact of the Lateran Agreements* (London and Basingstoke).
Kent, Peter C. and Pollard, John F. (1994), *Papal Diplomacy in the Modern Age* (Westport, CN, and London).
Keogh, I. (1994), 'Ireland and the Vatican, 1921–1949', in Kent and Pollard (eds), *Papal Diplomacy in the Modern Age.*
Keogh, I. (1986), *The Vatican, the Bishops and Irish Politics* (Cambridge).
Kershaw, I. (1998), *Hitler, 1889–1936: Hubris* (London).
Kertzer, David I. (2014), *The Pope and Mussolini: The Secret History of Pius XI and the Rise of Fascism in Europe* (New York).
Kertzer, David I. (2001), *The Popes against the Jews: The Vatican's Role in the Rise of Modern Anti-Semitism* (New York).
Kevorkian, R. H. (2011), *The Armenian Genocide: A Complete History* (London).
Kirby, D. (2003), 'Harry Truman's Religious Legacy: The Holy Alliance, Containment and the Cold War', in D. Kirby (ed.), *Religion and the Cold War* (London).
Kissane, Bill (2007), 'Éamon de Valéra and the Survival of Democracy in Inter-War Ireland', *JCH*, 42(2) (April), 213–226.
Kogan, N. (1983), *A Political History of Italy: The Post-War Years* (New York).
Korbel, J. (1977), *Twentieth Century Czechoslovakia: The Meanings of its History* (New York).
Korzec, P. (1970), 'Les relations entre le Vatican et les organisations juives pendant la première guerre mondiale. La mission Deloncle-Perquel (1915–1916)', *Revue d'Histoire Moderne et Contemporaine*, 29, 301–333.
Kreutz, Andrej (1994), 'The Vatican and the Palestinians: A Historical Overview', in Kent and Pollard (eds), *Papal Diplomacy in the Modern Age.*
La Bella, F. (1996), *La Questione irlandese e il vaticano* (Turin).
Ladous, R. (1994), *Des Nobels du Vatican. La fondation de l'académie pontificale des sciences* (Paris).
Lai, B. (1979), *Finanze e finanzieri del Vaticano tra l'Ottocento e il Novecento da Pio IX a Benedetto XV* (Milan).
Lannon, F. (1987), *Privilege, Persecution and Prophecy: The Catholic Church in Spain, 1875–1975* (Oxford).
Lapide, P. (1967), *Three Popes and the Jews* (New York).
Larkin, M. (1974), *Church and State after the Dreyfus Affair: The Separation Issue in France* (London and Basingstoke).

Larkin, M. (2004), *L'Église et L'État en France, 1905. La crise de la Séparation* (Toulouse).
Larkin, M. (1995), *Religion, Politics and Preferment in France since 1890* (Cambridge).
Larousse Dictionary of Scientists (London, 1994).
La Vie Politique au Grand-Duché de Luxembourg (Luxemburg, 1995).
Lazzarini, L. (1937), *Pio XI* (Milan).
Lehnert, P. (1984), *Pio XII. Il privilegio di servirlo* (Milan).
Leslie, S. (1953), *Cardinal Gasquet: A Memoir* (London).
Leung, S. (1992), *Sino-Vatican Relations: Problems in Conflicting Authority, 1976–1986* (Cambridge).
Levillain, P. (ed.) (1997), *Dictionnaire de la papauté* (Paris).
Levillain, P. (ed.) (1998), *Encyclopedia of the Papacy*, vol. II (London).
Lewy, Gunter (1964), *The Catholic Church and Nazi Germany* (London).
Liebman, M. (1963), 'Journal secret d'un conclave', *La Revue Nouvelle*, 19(38), 32–52.
Livingstone, E.A. (ed.) (1997), *Oxford Dictionary of the Christian Church*, 3rd edn (Oxford).
Logan, O. (1998), 'Pius XII. Romanità, prophesy and charisma', *Modern Italy: Journal of the Association for the Study of Modern Italy*, 3(2) (November), 237–249.
Loiseau, C. (1966), 'Ma mission auprès du Vatican (1914–1918)', *Revue d'histoire diplomatique*, 64, 100–115.
Loiseau, C. (1956), 'Une mission près le Saint-Siège, 1914–1919', *Revue des Deux Mondes* (May), 54–60.
Lukacs, John (1976), *The Last European War* (London).
Luxmoore, J. and Babuich, J. (2000), *The Vatican and the Red Flag: The Struggle for the Soul of Eastern Europe* (London).
Luzzatto, S. (2007), *Padre Pio. Miracoli e politica nell'Italia del novecento* (Turin).
Lyttelton, A. (1987), *The Seizure of Power: Fascism in Italy, 1919–1929* (London).
McDannell, Colleen (2009), 'The United States during the Inter-war Years,' in Hugh McLeod (ed.), *The Cambridge History of Christianity*, vol. 9 (Cambridge).
McDonnell, John J. (1985), *The World Council of Churches and the Catholic Church* (London and New York).
McGoldrick, P.M. (2012), 'New Perspectives on Pius XII and Vatican Financial Transactions during the Second World War', *Historical Journal*, 55(4) (December), 1029–1048.
McGuiness, M.M. (2004), 'Let Us Go to the Altar', in J. O'Toole (ed.), *Catholic Religious Practice in Twentieth Century America* (Ithaca, NY, and London).
McMillan, J.F. (1996), 'France', in T. Buchanan and M. Conway (eds), *Political Catholicism*.
McNutt, F.A. (1936), *A Papal Chamberlain* (London).
Maderthaner, Wolfgang (2002) '12 February 1934: Social Democracy and the Civil War', in Rolf Steininger, Gunter Bischof, and Michael Gehler (eds), *Austria in the Twentieth Century* (New Brunswick, NJ, and London), 54–56.
Majoloni, A. (1925), *Il Giornale D'Italia*, 19 June.
Mamara, R. (2012), *Verso le relazioni diplomatiche tra la Santa Sede e la Turchia. Secondo I documenti dell'Archivio Segreto Vaticano* (Istanbul).
Manhattan, Avro (1947), *The Catholic Church against the Twentieth Century* (London).
Mann, M. (2004), *Fascists* (Cambridge).

Marchese, S. (1969), *Francia e problema dei suoi rapporti con la Santa Sede (1914–1924)* (Naples).
Marchione, M. (2000), *Pope Pius XII: Architect of Peace* (Mahwah, NJ).
Margiotta-Broglio, F. (1966), *L'Italia e Santa Sede dalla prima Guerra Mondiale alla Conciliazione. Aspetti politici e giuridici* (Bari).
Marks, S. (1976), *The Illusion of Peace: International Relations in Europe, 1918–1933* (London and Basingstoke, 1976).
Martin, Malachi (1987), *The Jesuits and the Betrayal of the Roman Catholic Church* (Linden, NJ).
Maryks, R.A. (2012), *'Pouring Jewish Water into Fascist Wine': Untold Stories of (Catholic) Jews from the Archives of Mussolini's Jesuit Father Pietro Tacchi Venturi* (Leiden and Boston, MA).
Mazzonis, F. (1981), 'Pio IX, il tramonto del potere temporale e la riorganizzazione della chiesa', in B. Angloni et al. (eds), *Storia della Societá Italiana*, vol. XVIII: *Lo stato unitario e il suo difficile debutto* (Milan).
Meda, F. (1928), *I cattolici e la Guerra* (Milan).
Menozzi, D. (2010), *Chiesa e diritti umani* (Bologna).
Menozzi, D. (1995), 'Regalità di Cristo e secolarizzazione. Alle origini di "Quas primas"', *Cristianesimo nella Storia*, 16 (1995), 79–113.
Meyer, J. (2005), *La Cristiada. I. La Guerra de los cristeros* (Mexico City).
Miccoli, G. (2011), *La Chiesa dell'anti-concilio: i tradizionalisti alla conquista di Roma* (Bari and Rome).
Miccoli, G. (2000), *I dilemma e I silenzi di Pio XII* (Milan).
Miccoli, G. (1997), 'Santa Sede, questione ebraica e antisemitismo fra Otto e Novecento', in C. Viviani (ed.), *Storia d'Italia; annali 11: gli ebrei in Italia* (Turin).
Minerbi, S. (1986), *The Vatican, the Holy Land and Zionism, 1895–1925* (Oxford).
Misner, P. (1991), *Social Catholicism in Europe: From the Onset of Industrialisation to the First World War* (New York).
Mizzi, P. (1979), *L'Unione Europea nei documenti pontifici* (Malta).
Molinari, F. (1966), 'Il carteggio di Benedetto XV con Mons. Ersilio Menzani', *Rivista di Storia della Chiesa in Italia*, 20(2) (July–December), 410–450.
Moloney, T. (1985), *Westminster, Whitehall and the Vatican: The Role of Cardinal Hinsely, 1935–43* (London).
Molony, J. N. (1977), *The Emergence of Political Catholicism in Italy: Partito Popolare, 1919–1926* (London).
Montero, F. (2010), 'La Iglesia y el catolicismo español durante el pontificado de Pio XI: la historiografia español y la investigación actual', in Guasco and Perin (eds), *Pius XI: Keynotes*.
Monticone, A. (1961), *Nitti e la Grande Guerra, 1914–1918* (Milan).
Montini, G.-B. (1963), 'Pius XII and the Jews', *The Tablet*, June.
Moretti, V. (ed.) (1981), *Le Auto dei Papi: Settant'anni di Automobilismo Vaticano* (Rome).
Morgan, P. (2007), *The Fall of Mussolini* (Oxford).
Morley, John F. (2002), 'The Holocaust in Hungary', in Carol Rittner and John K. Roth (eds), *Pope Pius XII and the Holocaust* (Leicester).

Morozzo Della Rocca, R. (1993), 'Benedetto XV e Costantinopoli: fu vera neutralità?' *Cristianesimo nella Storia*, 14, 375–384.

Morozzo Della Rocca, R. (1996), 'Benedetto XV e nazionalismo', *Cristianesimo nella Storia*, 17, 542–566.

Morozzo Della Rocca, R. (2001), 'Le nunziature in Europa fra le due guerre', in De Rosa and Cracco (eds), *Il Papato e l'Europa*.

Mosse, G.L. (1975), *The Nationalisation of the Masses: Political Symbolism and Mass Movements in Germany from the Napoleonic Wars through the Third Reich* (Ithaca, NY, and London).

Msiak, H. and Staudt, V. M. (1954), *Catholics in Psychology: A Historical Survey* (New York, Toronto, and London).

Murphy, P. (1983), *La Popessa* (New York).

New Catholic Encyclopedia, 2nd edn, vols I, III, IV (Washington, DC, 2003).

Noel, G. (2008), *The Hound of Hitler* (London).

Nolte, E. (1965), *Three Faces of Fascism: Action Française, Italian Fascism, National Socialism*, trans. Leila Vennewitz (London).

Norton, N. (1995), 'Benedict XV and the Save the Children Fund', *The Month*, 28 July.

Nurser, John S. (2005), *For All Peoples and Nations: The Ecumenical Church and Human Rights* (Washington, DC).

O'Brien, A.C. (1971), 'L'Osservatore Romano and Fascism: The Beginning of a New Era', *Church and State*, 13(3) (Autumn), 445–463.

Okey, R. (2001), *The Habsburg Monarchy c. 1765–1918* (Basingstoke).

O'Neill, H.C. (1920), *A History of the War* (London and Edinburgh).

Onofri, N.S. (1966), *La Grande Guerra nella città rossa. Socialismo e reazione a Bologna dal 1914–1918* (Milan).

O'Toole, James M. (ed.) (2004), *Habits of Devotion: Catholic Religious Practice in Twentieth-Century America* (Ithaca, NY, and London).

Padellaro, N. (1956), *Portrait of Pius XII*, trans. M. Derrick (London).

Pagano, S., Chappin, M., and Coco, G. (2010), *I 'Fogli di Udienza' Del Cardinale Eugenio Pacelli, Segretario Di Stato*, vol. I: *1930* (Vatican City).

Pallenberg, C. (1961), *Inside the Vatican* (London).

Pallenberg, C. (1973), *Vatican Finances* (Harmondsworth).

Panzera, F. (1993), 'Benedetto XV e la Svizzera negli anni della Grande Guerra', *Rivista Storica Svizzera*, 43, 321–340.

Paris, Edmond (1959), *Le Vatican contre l'Europe* (Paris).

Paris, Edmond (1960), *The Vatican against Europe* (London).

Passalecq, G. and Suchecky, B. (1997), *The Hidden Encyclical of Pius XI*, with intro. G. Willis (New York, San Diego, CA, and London).

Patelos, C. G. (ed.) (1978), *The Orthodox Church in the Ecumenical Movement: Documents and Statements, 1902–1975* (Geneva).

Pawley, B. and M. (1981), *Rome and Canterbury through Four Centuries* (London and Oxford).

Pease, N. (2009), *Rome's Most Faithful Daughter: The Catholic Church and Independent Poland, 1914–1939* (Athens, OH).

Pellicani, A. (1964), *Il Papa di Tutti. La Chiesa cattolica, il Fascismo e il Razzismo* (Milan).

Penco, G. (1977), *Storia della Chiesa in Italia*, vol. II (Milan).

Perna, V. (2010), *Relazioni tra Santa Sede e Repubbliche Baltiche (1918–1940): Monsignor Zecchini Diplomatico* (Udine).

Peterkiewicz, J. (1975), *The Third Adam* (London).

Peters, E. N. (ed.) (2001), *The 1917 or Pio-Benedictine Code of Canon Law in English Translation* (San Francisco, CA).

Peters, W. H. (1959), *The Life of Benedict XV* (Milwaukee).

Petracchi, G. (2004), 'I Gesuiti e il Communismo tra le due Guerre', in Vincenzo Ferrone (ed.), *La Chiesa Cattolica e il Totalitarismo. Atti del Convegno di Torino, 25–26 ottobre 2001* (Florence).

Petrow, Richard (1974), *The Bitter Years: The Invasion and Occupation of Denmark and Norway, April 1940–May 1945* (London).

Phayer, M. (2000), *The Catholic Church and the Holocaust, 1930–1965* (Bloomington, IN).

Phayer, M. (2008), *Pius XII, the Holocaust and the Cold War* (Bloomington and Indianapolis, IN).

Piekarski, A. (1978), *The Church in Poland* (Warsaw).

Pighin, B. F. (2010), *Chiesa e Stato in Cina: Dalle Imprese di Costantini alle Svolte attuali* (Venice).

Pighin, B. F. (2012), *Il Ritratto Segreto del Cardinale Celso Costantini in 10,000 lettere dal 1892 al 1958* (Venice).

Pirotta, G. A. (2006), *Malta's Parliament: An Official History* (Malta).

Pisanò, G. and P. (1992), *Il Triangolo della Morte: La Politica della Strage in Emilia durante e dopo la Guerra Civile* (Milan).

Plans pour cercles d'études d'action catholique, La Royauté de Christ dans la Société Humaine (Bruges, 1927).

Poels, V., Salemink, T., and de Valk, H. (eds) (2010–11), *Life with a Mission: Cardinal Willem Marinus van Rossum (1854–1932)* (Nijmegen).

Poggi, G. (1972), 'The Church in Italian Politics', in S. J. Woolf (ed.), *The Rebirth of Italy, 1943–1950* (London).

Pollard, John F. (2010), 'Catholicism and Fascism', in R.J.B. Bosworth (ed.), *The Oxford Handbook of Fascism* (Oxford).

Pollard, John F. (2008), *Catholicism in Modern Italy: Religion, Society and Politics since 1861* (London).

Pollard, John F. (1990), 'Conservative Catholics and Italian Fascism: The Clerico-Fascists', in M. Blinkhorn (ed.), *Fascists and Conservatives: The Radical Right and the Establishment in Twentieth Century Europe* (London).

Pollard, John F. (2007), 'A Court in Exile: The Vatican, 1870–1929', *The Court Historian*, 12(1) (June 2007), 35–47.

Pollard, John F. (2010), 'Electronic Pastors: Radio, Cinema and Television from Pius XI to John XXIII', in J. Corkery and T. Worcester (eds), *The Papacy since 1500: From Italian Prince to Universal Pastor* (Cambridge).

Pollard, John F. (1998), *The Experience of Fascism in Italy* (London).

Pollard, John F. (2011), 'Fascism and Religion', in A. Costa Pinto (ed.), *Re-thinking the Nature of Fascism: Comparative Approaches* (London and Basingstoke).

Pollard, John F. (2005), 'Leo XIII and the United States of America, 1898–1903', in Viaene (ed.), *The Papacy and the New World Order.*

Pollard, John F. (2012), 'Pius XI's Promotion of the Italian Model of Catholic Action in the World-Wide Church', *Journal of Ecclesiastical History*, 64(4) (October), 758–784.

Pollard, John F. (2005), *Money and the Rise of the Modern Papacy: Financing the Vatican, 1850–1950* (Cambridge).

Pollard, John F. (1999), *The Unknown Pope: Benedict XV and the Pursuit of Peace, 1914–1922* (London).

Pollard, John F. (1985), *The Vatican and Italian Fascism 1929–1932: A Study in Conflict* (Cambridge).

Pollard, John F. (1991), 'Il Vaticano e la politica estera Italiana', in Richard J.B. Bosworth and Sergio Romano (eds), *La politica estera italiana, 1860–1985* (Bologna).

Pontifica Accademia Ecclesiastica. Terzo centenario (1701–2001) (Rome, 2003).

Poulat, E. (1977), *Catholicisme démocratique et socialisme. Le movement catholique et Mgr Benigni e la naissance du socialisme a la victoire du fascisme* (Paris).

Poulat, E. (2007), *Les Diocésains. République française, Église catholique: Loi de 1905 et associations cultuelles, le dossier d'un litige et de sa solution (1903–2003)* (Paris).

Powell, J. (1967), *The Mystery of the Church* (Milwaukee).

Preston, Paul (1997), *Concise History of the Spanish Civil War* (London).

Preston, Paul (2012), *The Spanish Holocaust* (London).

Procacci, G. (1993), *Soldati e prigionieri italiani nella Grande Guerra* (Rome).

Protestant Truth Society (1989), *New Holy Roman Empire* (London).

Pyrah, R. (2007), 'Cultural Politics and "Clerical Fascism" in Austria, 1933–1938', *TMPR*, 8(2) (June), 369–382.

Randall, R. (1956), *Vatican Assignment* (London).

Ranke-Heinemann, Uta (1988), *Eunuchs for Heaven: The Catholic Church and Sexuality*, trans. John Bownjohn (London).

Rees, T.J., SJ (1996), *Inside the Vatican* (Cambridge, MA).

Rhodes, Anthony (1983), *The Power of Rome in the Twentieth Century: The Vatican in the Age of the Liberal Democracies* (London).

Rhodes, Anthony (1992), *The Vatican in the Age of the Cold War, 1945–1980* (Norwich).

Rhodes, Anthony (1973), *The Vatican in the Age of the Dictators, 1922–1945* (London).

Riccardi, A. (1990), 'Benedetto XV e la crisi della convivenza multireligiosa nell'Impero Turco', in Rumi (ed.), *Benedetto XV*.

Riccardi, A. (2008), *L'inverno piú lungo 1943–44. Pio XII, gli Ebrei e I Nazisti a Roma* (Rome and Bari).

Riccardi, A. (1983), *'Il Partito Romano' nel secondo dopoguerra (1945–1954)* (Brescia).

Riccardi, A. (2000), *Il Secolo del Martirio. I Cristiani nel Novecento* (Milan).

Richards, M. (1998), *Vicars of Christ: Popes, Power and Politics in the Modern World* (New York).

Rivelli, Marco Aurelio (1998), *L'Arcivescovo del genocidio. Monsignor Stepinac, il Vaticano e la dittatura ustacia in Croazia, 1941–1945* (Milan).

Rodogno, D. (2006), *Fascism's European Empire: Italian Occupation during the Second World War* (Cambridge).

Romano, S. and Bosworth, R.J.B. (eds) (1991), *La politica estera italiana, 1860–1985* (Bologna).

Rouse, R. and Neil, S.C. (1954) (eds), *A History of the Ecumenical Movement* (London).

Royal, Robert (n.d.), *The Catholic Martyrs of the Twentieth Century: A World History* (n.p.).

Rubinstein, R. (2002), 'Pius XII and the Shoah', in Carol Rittner and John K. Roth (eds), *Pope Pius XII and the Holocaust* (London and New York).

Rubinstein, William D. (1997), *The Myth of Rescue: Why the Democracies Could Not Have Saved More Jews from the Nazis* (London and New York).

Rumi, G. (1975) 'La Santa Sede e la Politica di Potenza', in E. Di Nolfo, R. H. Rainero, and B. Vigezzi (eds), *L'Italia e la politica di Potenza, 1938–1940*, Settimo Milanese, 17.

Rumi, G. (1990) (ed.), *Benedetto XV e la Pace—1918* (Brescia).

Rumi, G. (1991), 'Un epistolario inedito', *Civitas*, XXXX, 105–117.

Rychlak, R. J. (2000), *Hitler, the War and the Pope* (Huntington, IN).

Sale, G., SJ (2009), *Le Leggi Razziali in Italia e il Vaticano* (Milan).

Salter, J. A. (1921), *Allied Shipping Control: An Experiment in International Administration* (Oxford).

Salvatorelli, L. (1937), *La Politica della Santa Sede dopo la guerra* (Milan).

Sanchez, José M. (2002), *Pius XII and the Holocaust: Understanding the Controversy* (Washington, DC).

Sanchez, José M. (1987), *The Spanish Civil War as a Religious Tragedy* (Notre Dame, IN).

Schad, Martha (2008), *La Signora del Sacro Palazzo. Suor Pascalina e Pio XII*, Cinisello Balsamo (Milan).

Schmidlin, J. (1953), *Papstgeschichte der neuesten Zeit*, vol. III (Munich).

Schmidt, Stjepan, SJ (1978), 'Il Cardinale Bea. Sua Preparazione alla Missione Ecumenica (nel decimo anniversario della Morte)', *AHP*, 16, 313–336.

Scoppola, P. (1963), 'Cattolici neutralist ed interventisti all vigilia del conflitto', in G. Rossini (ed.), *Benedetto XV, i cattolici e la prima Guerra Mondiale. Atti del convegno di studio tenuto a Spoleto nei giorni 7–8–9 settembre 1962* (Rome).

Scoppola, P. (1971), *La Chiesa e il fascismo. Documenti e interpretazioni* (Bari).

Scott Appleby, R. (1995) *Being Right: Conservative Catholics in America* (Indianapolis, IN).

Seldes, G. (1934), *The Vatican: Yesterday, Today, Tomorrow* (New York).

Serra, E. (1990), 'La Nota del primo Agosto 1917 e il Governo Italiano. Qualche Osservazione', in Rumi (ed.), *Benedetto XV*.

Seton-Watson, C. (1967), *Italy from Liberalism to Fascism, 1870–1925* (London).

Sforza, C. (1944), *Contemporary Italy* (New York).

Shekhovtsov, A. (2007), 'By Cross and Sword: "Clerical Fascism" in Interwar Western Ukraine', *Totalitarian Movements and Political Religions*, 8(2) (June), 271–285.

Sicari, Giuseppe (2002), *Cenni biografici su tutti I Cardinali (1198–2001)* (Rome).

Singh, S. (2004) *The Big Bang* (London and New York).

Slawson, D. J. (1992), *The Foundation and the First Decade of the National Catholic Welfare Conference* (Washington, DC).

Snyder, Timothy (2010), *Bloodlands: Europe between Hitler and Stalin* (New York).

Spadolini, G. (ed.) (1972), *Il cardinale Gasparri e la Questione Romana. Con brani di documenti* (Florence).

Spadolini, G. (1977), *Giolitti e I cattolici* (Florence).

Spinosa, A. (1992), *L'ultimo papa* (Milan).

Stehle, H. (1981), *Eastern Politics of the Vatican: 1917–1979*, trans. Sandra Smith (Athens, OH, and London).

Stehlin, Stewart A. (1994), 'The Emergence of a New Vatican Diplomacy during the Great War and its Aftermath', in Kent and Pollard (eds), *Papal Diplomacy in the Modern Age*.

Stehlin, Stewart A. (1974), 'Germany and a Proposed Vatican State, 1915–1917', *The Catholic Historical Review*, 60(3) (October), 402–426.

Stehlin, Stewart A. (1983), *Weimar and the Vatican, 1919–1933: German–Vatican Relations in the Interwar Years* (Princeton, NJ).

Steinacher, Gerald (2012), *Nazis on the Run: How Hitler's Henchmen Fled Justice* (Oxford).

Steinberg, J. (1985), *Why Switzerland?* (Cambridge).

Stephenson, J. (2006), *Hitler's Home Front: Wurttemberg under the Nazis* (London).

Taylor, A. J. P. (1970), *English History, 1914–1945* (London).

Taylor, A. J. P. (1966), *From Sarajevo to Potsdam* (London).

Taylor, Frederick (2011), *Exorcising Hitler: The Occupation and De-Nazification of Germany* (London).

Ticchi, Jean-Marc (2002), *Aux Frontiéres de la Paix. Bons Offices, Médiations, Arbitrages du Saint-Siege 1878–1922* (Rome).

Tompkins, Oliver (1954), 'The Roman Catholic Church', in Rouse and Neill, *A History of the Ecumenical Movement*.

Vadan, Mariuca (2001), *Le Relazioni Diplomatiche tra la Santa Sede e la Romania (1920–1948)* (Vatican City).

Valente, M. (2010), *Diplomazia Pontificia e Kulturkampf. La Santa Sede e la Prussia tra Pio IX e Bismarck, 1862–1878* (Rome).

Valvo, Paolo (2013), 'La Santa Sede e la Cristiada (1926–1929), *Revue d'histoire ecclésiastique*, 108(3.4), 840–875.

Valvo, Paolo (2013), '"Una Turlupinatura stile messicano". La Santa Sede e la Sopensione del Culto Pubblico in Messico (Luglio 1926)', *Quaderni di storia*, 78 (July–December), 198–199.

Veneruso, D. (1982), 'Benedetto XV', in F. Traniello and G. Campanini (eds), *Dizionario Storico del Movimento Cattolico in Italia, II, I Protagonisti* (Casale Monferrato).

Ventresca, R. A. (2012), *Soldier of Christ: The Life of Pope Pius XII* (Cambridge, MA, and London).

Vercesi, E. (1925), *Il Vaticano, l'Italia e la guerra* (Rome).

Viaene, V. (ed.) (2005), *The Papacy and the New World Order: Vatican Diplomacy, Catholic Opinion and International Politics at the Time of Leo XIII, 1878–1903/ La papauté et le nouvel ordre mondial. Diplomatie vaticane, opinion Catholique et politique internationale au temps de Léon XIII* (Leuven).

Vinen, R. (2000), *A History in Fragments: Europe in the Twentieth Century* (London).

Vistalli, F. (1929), *Benedetto XV* (Rome).

Von Nell-Breuning, O. (1986), 'The Drafting of *Quadragesimo Anno*', in Charles E. Curran and Robert McCormick (eds), *Readings in Moral Theology No. 5* (New York).

Walsh, John (1982), *The Bones of St Peter* (London).

Walsh, M. (2007), *A New Dictionary of Saints East and West* (London).

Weber, E. (1964), *L'Action française* (Paris).

Webster, Paul (1992), *Pétain's Crime: The Full Story of French Collaboration in the Holocaust* (London).

Webster, Richard A. (1961), *Christian Democracy and Fascism in Italy, 1860–1960* (London).

Webster, Richard A. (1960), *The Cross and the Fasces: Christian Democracy and Fascism in Italy* (Stanford, CA).

Weinberg, G. (1994), *A World at Arms* (Cambridge).
Weiss, O. (2010–11), 'Glaubenswechter van Rossum', in Poels et al. (eds), *Life with a Mission*.
Wolf, H. (2010), *Pope and Devil: The Vatican's Archives and the Third Reich*, trans. K. Kronenberg (Cambridge, MA, and London).
Woodhouse, C.M. (1986), *Modern Greece: A Short History* (London and Boston, MA).
Zangheri, R. (1986), *Storia delle città. Bologna* (Bari).
Zivojinovic, D.R. (1978), *The United States and the Vatican Policies, 1914–1918* (Boulder, CO).
Zizola, C. (2004), 'L'ufficio stampa del Vaticano', *Cristianesimo nella storia*, 25(3), 997–1013.
Zizola, G. (1993), *Il Conclave: storia e segreti. L'elezione papale da San Pietro a Giovanni Paolo II* (Rome).
Zuccotti, S. (2000), *Under His Very Windows: The Vatican and the Holocaust in Italy* (New Haven, CT).

Court Case

Alperin v. Vatican Bank, 2006, US District LEXIS 42902 (N.D. Cal. June 15 2006).

Unpublished Dissertations and Theses

Ciciliot, V. (2008), 'La Politica delle Canonizzazioni di Giovanni Paolo II', dissertation, Universitá degli Studi di Padova, Facoltá di Lettere e Filosofia.
Di Stefano, Andrea (2008), 'Stati Uniti-Vaticano. Relazioni Politiche e Aspetti Diplomatici, 1952–1984', doctoral thesis, University of Teramo.
Faltin, F. (2004), 'Czechoslovakian–Vatican Relations between 1945 and 1948 with Particular Reference to the Beginning of the Cold War', MPhil thesis, Anglia Ruskin University.

Index

Note: In cases where there are several headings relating to the same country or event, these are arranged in chronological order.

Made in the USA
Monee, IL
25 August 2024